PATRONS, BROKERS, AND CLIENTS IN SEVENTEENTH-CENTURY FRANCE

Patrons, Brokers, and Clients in Seventeenth-Century France

SHARON KETTERING

New York *Oxford*
OXFORD UNIVERSITY PRESS
1986

Oxford University Press

Oxford New York Toronto
Delhi Bombay Calcutta Madras Karachi
Petaling Jaya Singapore Hong Kong Tokyo
Nairobi Dar es Salaam Cape Town
Melbourne Auckland

and associated companies in
Beirut Berlin Ibadan Nicosia

Published by Oxford University Press, Inc.,
200 Madison Avenue, New York, New York 10016

Library of Congress Cataloging in Publication Data
Kettering, Sharon, 1942–
Patrons, brokers, and clients in seventeenth-century France.
Bibliography: p.
Includes index.
1. France—Politics and government—17th century.
2. Patron and client—France—History—17th century.
3. Patronage, Political—France—History—17th century.
4. Decentralization in government—France—History—17th century
I. Title.
JN2341.K47 1986 944'.03 85–13820
ISBN 0–19–503673–5

Printing (last digit): 9 8 7 6 5 4 3 2 1

Printed in the United States of America
on acid-free paper

For Aunt Byrd and Thomas,
IN MEMORY

Acknowledgments

I have incurred a number of debts of gratitude in writing this book. I would like to thank Orest Ranum and Alex Sedgwick for their encouragement and kindness over the years, and for their help in reading and commenting. Chuck Tilly offered advice on revision and encouragement at a critical moment. Richard Bonney helped to focus the manuscript and corrected numerous errors of fact. Gary McCollim, John Salmon, and Joe Klaits made insightful observations and suggestions for improvement. Any problems or errors that remain are my own.

This book owes its inception to the comments of Jack Reece, Marty Wolf, and Jim Davis during a history faculty workshop at the University of Pennsylvania in the autumn of 1977. It was finished because my department chairmen, Paul Van Der Slice and Ruth Dinbergs, scheduled me time to write and because the staffs of the Library of Congress and the Folger Library in Washington, D.C. provided me with assistance. I would especially like to thank Kay Blair of the Interlibrary Loan Division of the Library of Congress for her help over the years. I would also like to thank Frank Biancheri, archivist of the Palace Archives of Monaco, for his prompt assistance with microfilm. Research and writing were made possible by an American Council of Learned Societies fellowship in 1982–83, a Mellon grant in the Humanities at the University of Pennsylvania in 1977–78, and summer grants from the National Endowment of the Humanities and the American Philosophical Society. Special thanks are due to Philip Dawson who introduced me to the study of Old Regime France many years ago at Stanford. Finally, I would like to thank my mother for her support and devotion over the years and my husband for patiently listening to endless "book ideas". His knowledge of Washington politics helped to shape this book.

Bethesda, Maryland S.K.
July 1985

Contents

PATRONS, BROKERS, AND CLIENTS IN SEVENTEENTH-CENTURY FRANCE

The fame of great men ought always to be estimated by the means they used to acquire it.

François, duc de La Rochefoucauld (1613–1680)
Réflexions ou sentences et maximes morales.

INTRODUCTION

Power and Patronage

Patronage studies concern the realities of power—who gets it, who keeps it, and what they do with it. Power is control over the behavior of others, and it may be derived from physical force, political authority, control over scarce economic resources, social prestige, personal relationships, or a combination of these. It may be expressed directly as coercion or constituted authority, indirectly as manipulation or influence.[1] Patronage is an indirect form of power: a patron influences the behavior of his clients because he can grant or withdraw benefits, thereby rewarding compliance or punishing disobedience. He can manipulate his clients because of their indebtedness for past favors and fear of future reprisals: his control over their behavior gives him power. Patronage is the art of obligation, of manipulation through rewards and punishment. Politics is the art of persuasion, of inducing men to cooperate and do what is demanded voluntarily. The political process has failed when it is necessary to use force. Patronage will probably always have a place in politics, whatever the system, because it encourages cooperation and is effective in moving people to action.

A patron assists and protects his clients, providing them with offices, arranging profitable marriages, finding places for their children, helping them with lawsuits or tax problems. He gives them economic aid and opportunities for career advancement and offers protection from the demands of others. Patronage also refers to material rewards: a patron has the power to distribute goods and resources, especially political offices and favors. It may mean no more than recommending someone for an office or a promotion, but it shades imperceptibly into building a political clientele, a network of officeholding dependents. For this reason, the term patronage may also be used to describe a mode of recruitment to officeholding. A clientele is a network of clients headed by a patron, and a political clientele is a client network used to influence or control a society's decision-making positions.[2]

Clientage is the loyalty and service a client owes a patron in exchange for advancement and protection. A client acts as a reliable, obedient subordinate in what is often a political jungle, helping a patron to perform the duties of office, providing information, offering advice, lending money, securing places for other dependents, fighting for him, even following him into exile. The term clientage describes the nature of the patron-client relationship, which is unequal, personal, and reciprocal. A patron is expected to give material benefits because he can do so, while a client offers in exchange more intangible assets of loyalty and service. Clientelism is the term used to describe a system of patron-broker-client ties and networks.[3]

A patron-client relationship is a personal, direct exchange, a two-party, usually face-to-face transaction, and a patron uses resources he himself owns or controls. A patron-broker-client relationship, on the other hand, is a three-party, indirect, more impersonal exchange in which a broker mediates between parties separated by distance, using resources he does not always directly control. A broker's resources are the people he knows who can provide access to power and place.[4] A broker acts as a middleman to arrange an exchange of resources between parties who are separated by physical or personal distance. He is a mediator in an indirect exchange—he does not always control what is transferred, but he influences the quality of the exchange in negotiating the transfer. A broker is more than a go-between because he has resources of his own which he can add to the exchange, and he does more than transmit the negotiations: he also influences them, doing his own manipulating and lobbying.

Brokerage is an essential aspect of patronage. Brokers introduce men with power to men seeking its use who are willing to give favors in return for it, then they arrange an exchange. They bring people and opportunities together, allowing them to trade resources and, in conducting the negotiations, they facilitate the use of power and the distribution of resources. Brokers are usually important individuals in their own right with independent resources and large clienteles. This is why they became brokers, and their new role adds to their status. Brokerage is a role that can be played by someone who is a patron, a broker, and a client: he can play two roles at the same time as patron-broker or broker-client, or one role at a time.[5] The duality of their role as patron-brokers or broker-clients, however, sets brokers apart from ordinary patrons and clients, who have direct, personal relationships and operate within one milieu: they do not cut across physical, social, or political distances.

The society and government of early modern France was organized loosely in layers of clienteles reaching vertically to the king at court. One man's patron was another man's client, and brokers bridged the distances between patrons. When clienteles pyramided as they did when expanding horizontally and vertically, brokers handled the exchanges between levels of patrons and clients separated by distance, place, and rank. The pyramiding of clienteles produced, besides layers and layers of patrons and clients, the need for a third but not necessarily distinct role, that of a broker who linked the layers.

Clienteles were necessary to exercise political power in early modern France: clients were used to promote the career goals of their patrons and to provide essential political services. Clienteles were patron-created, patron-centered, and patron-led, and clients were vertically linked to a common patron, not horizontally linked to each other. An ambitious man used all his resources—reputation, family, rank, office, wealth, and patrons—to build a large clientele, giving him political power. The power of a patron depended upon his ability to mobilize his clients in coordinated political activity. When a man acquired a reputation for generously rewarding those who served him, he could exercise power because he had the potential to reward compliance and could motivate behavior. Clienteles waxed and waned with the fortunes of their patrons, and when a patron's fortunes dwindled so did the number of his clients.[6]

Government by patron-client ties was characteristic of an incompletely centralized state such as France in the sixteenth and seventeenth centuries.[7] The crown used royal officials to govern, but institutional procedures alone were insufficient because royal authority in the provinces was still too uncertain and its enforcement too weak. The French provinces were only partially under royal control for most of this period.[8] So the crown had to supplement its authority with patron-broker-client ties that functioned inside and outside the institutional framework: they were used to manipulate political institutions from within, to operate across institutions, and to act in place of institutions. They were interstitial, supplementary, and parallel structures.[9]

Brokers mediated between the provincial power structure and the national government in Paris, performing the critical function of linkage in a state with a weak central government.[10] Local notables acted as brokers in negotiating an exchange of services and goods between a highly placed patron in the national government in Paris, perhaps a royal minister, and his supporters among the provincial ruling elite including their own clients; in fact, they used their influence and clients to mobilize support for him and his projects. Although they did not control the flow of royal patronage from the national capital, brokers appeared to do so in provincial eyes, and they played the functionally equivalent role of patrons in distributing royal patronage from which they took a commission for brokering, sometimes diverting the flow of royal patronage for their own use. Brokers in early modern France did not see themselves as brokers, however; we have the advantage of hindsight in that. They did see themselves as loyal clients helping their patron, a royal minister, to govern the province. Brokers tried to achieve a monopoly in brokering, but they were not always successful: they had too many rivals.[11] Brokers helped the king and his ministers to govern and were an important way of getting things done in a weakly centralized state. Broker-clients were recruited and used by the Paris royal ministers to integrate the peripheral provinces of France and to create a strong central government.

The centralization and bureaucratization of the French state was a long, difficult, and far from inevitable process.[12] The critical years were 1624 to 1683, when Richelieu, Mazarin, and Colbert worked to create the early modern French state. The creation of a strong national government is usually described as a lengthy, external process of extending royal control over provincial institutions. The Paris monarchy sent intendants into the provinces to supplant existing authorities, while simultaneously suppressing the power of regional institutions and intimidating their uncooperative members. The intendants had developed enough bureaucratic characteristics by the late seventeenth century to identify them as a newly emerging species of political animal, the early modern bureaucrat.[13] This book suggests that the Paris ministers also extended their control over the provinces, especially those on the frontiers, by another method that was just as effective, distributing royal patronage to secure provincial loyalty and support. The Paris ministers used broker-clients in the provinces to distribute royal patronage to their own and other noble clients in exchange for their loyalty and support. The monarchy's success in governing was due as much to its ability to buy—in different kinds of coin—the loyalty and support of the provincial nobility as it was to the surveillance and coercion of the intendants.

Clientelism has been widely studied within the last two decades by anthropologists, political scientists, and sociologists.[14] When anthropologists move from the study of primitive to complex societies, they tend to be interested in societies with traditional characteristics, the so-called peasant societies, preindustrial, agrarian, and elitist, and they tend to investigate the effects of patronage upon rural village life. They view patronage as a form of interpersonal relationship, focusing on the links between patrons and clients, particularly between local leaders and their followers and between landlords and tenants. Patronage in this context is usually not considered within a formal system of government.[15]

Political scientists, on the other hand, consider patronage a characteristic of government, and usually study it within the context of a formal political system. They have been interested in its political functions, especially party patronage, the way in which political parties distribute public jobs and favors in exchange for electoral support in modern societies. They have also been interested in how patron-client ties act as political linkage, and have done much of the work on brokerage, a subject that has been studied only within the last decade or so.[16] Sociologists, in contrast, have seen patronage as an example of the exchange theory of interpersonal relationships.[17] All proponents of clientelism, however, consider it a useful concept in understanding social organization, as useful as social classes and perhaps more so in traditional societies.

Historians have done surprisingly little work on patronage, although patron-client systems flourished in early modern Europe and dominated its politics. English historians have done more work on this subject than French historians—in recent years a group of historians known as the revisionists have emphasized the role of patronage in early Stuart politics and in the causation of the English civil war—but their inquiries have tended to describe the operation and uses of patronage without much concern for theorization or formal structures.[18] Their work does not help observers trying to understand the role of patronage in early modern French politics because there were significant differences between the two systems. England had a parliamentary, nonvenal political system with nascent political parties after 1700, and studies of English political patronage have tended to focus on elections to seats in parliament. A national representative assembly sitting periodically, parliament was an institution of political linkage and integration that France did not have. France was a mélange of different regions speaking different dialects added to the throne at different times, and the government of early modern France was formally venal, authoritarian, nonparliamentary, without political parties. The centralizing French monarchy sought to bind independent regional institutions, hereditary royal officials, and local notables to the national government at Paris. A successful method was the brokerage of royal patronage in the provinces to secure the loyalty and support of the nobility and the cooperation of officials in formal political institutions.

Recent studies by early modern French historians have demonstrated the need to understand the political impact of patron-client ties, but there have been few studies of client networks within the Paris government and even fewer of provincial networks.[19] The work of French historians so far has been largely descriptive, mostly exposés of client networks and inquiries into contemporary values and terminology. French historians have shown little interest in how patron-broker-client ties actually affected the functioning of the political system, and the theorization they have developed is eccentric when compared to that proposed by English-speaking anthropologists, political scientists, and sociologists.[20] In general, scholars have tended to work independently on patronage without being aware of each other's conclusions.[21] A goal of this book is to introduce French historians to the interdisciplinary literature on clientelism.

Patronage studies are often case studies of regions—for instance, Mediterranean societies in which patron-client ties have appeared as the dominant mode of organization—and case studies of individual patrons, specifically, incidents in their careers when they exercised patronage.[22] This book uses case studies to explore brokerage, a form of political clientelism. It describes a new type of statebuilder in seventeenth-century France, a provincial broker. He was not a great noble or a provincial governor as he had usually been in the sixteenth century. He was a regional notable, a member of the lesser nobility who rose socially and economically by collaborating politically with the expanding Paris government in return for royal patronage, for example, by helping the new intendants to perform their administrative duties. He was the client of a highly placed Paris official, usually a royal minister, and a member of a Paris-based administrative clientele stretching into the provinces. Royal ministers such as Richelieu, Mazarin, and Colbert distributed royal patronage to reliable broker-clients to achieve the political integration of such peripheral provinces as Provence, Languedoc, Guyenne, Burgundy, Alsace, and the Franche-Comté.

Provence, Languedoc, and Guyenne were provinces in the Midi, in southeastern, south-central, and southwestern France on the frontier with Spain and Spanish-dominated Italy, while Burgundy, Alsace, and the Franche-Comté lay on the eastern frontier with Habsburg-dominated Germany. Alsace and the Franche-Comté were newly conquered provinces in the seventeenth century. Burgundy, in fact, ceased to be a frontier province only after the Franche-Comté was permanently annexed in 1678. These provinces endured heavy troop movements during the Habsburg wars, extensive military damage and destruction, and high taxes to pay the cost of the wars. In addition, Burgundy, Guyenne, Languedoc, and Provence were *pays d'Etats*, provinces with traditional tax-granting assemblies, customary privileges or liberties, and parlements or provincial high courts. The pays d'Etats were the scenes of widespread popular protest against the royal government during the Habsburg wars. All of these provinces had strong regional identities. Their peripheral characteristics meant that patron-broker-client ties and networks stretching to Paris, inside and outside the formal institutional framework of government, were important in attaching these regions to the central administration.

The operation of patronage is difficult to observe because patrons often veiled their activities, an obscurity that is intensified by a distance of several hundred years and a reliance upon written documents. It is not always easy to find evidence of patronage activities, and patterns emerge only after intensive archival study; in fact, the evidence for this book appeared during the course of another study on Provence.[23] Seventeenth-century Provence was a good choice for a regional study of brokerage as a technique of statebuilding because of its distance from the central government at Paris. One of the most remote and unruly of the French provinces during the Old Regime with a strong tradition of regionalism and a long history of political independence, Provence is a model for other peripheral provinces and their relations with the central government.[24] The archival evidence on brokers and brokering in this book is largely Provençal in origin. The primary evidence on Provençal brokers is supported by secondary evidence on brokers from five other peripheral provinces, Languedoc, Guyenne, Burgundy, Alsace, and the Franche-Comté. Published evidence from these other provinces reinforces the Provençal archival examples and suggests that brokerage as a method of regional-national integration was widely used in the peripheral provinces of seventeenth-century France.

The political careers of thirty provincial brokers are described. The Provençal brokers include Henri de Forbin-Maynier d'Oppède; Charles de Grimaldi-Régusse; Barthélemy, Cosme, and Antoine de Valbelle; Toussaint de Janson-Forbin; Fortia de Pilles; the bailli de Forbin; the chevalier Paul; archbishop Grignan of Arles; and the comte de Grignan. Brokers from the other provinces include archbishops Claude de Rébé and Pierre de Marca, Cardinal Pierre de Bonzi, Jean de Bertier, and the comte de Mérinville from Languedoc; Antoine d'Aguesseau and Joseph Dubernet, archbishops Henri d'Escoubleau de Sourdis and Henry de Béthune from Guyenne; parlementaires Claude and Gabriel Boisot and Jean-Ferdinand Jobelot from the Franche-Comté; Charles Guntzer, Ulrich Obrecht, Jean-Baptiste Klinglin,

Jean Dietremann, and Jean Dietrich from Alsace; and Claude Bouchu and Nicolas Brûlart from Burgundy. Brief career sketches of these brokers demonstrate that they were clients of highly placed patrons in the Paris government, who offered royal patronage to them and their dependents in exchange for their brokering services, and these career sketches describe their services and the resources that made them possible.

Because brokerage is an aspect of patronage and both are forms of clientelism, this is also a book on the structure and operation of political clientelism, a system that produced the early modern state of Louis XIV and the first bureaucracy in Europe. The first three chapters present the basic identifying characteristics of patron-broker-client ties and networks, laying the groundwork for an analysis in the last three chapters of their use in early modern French statebuilding. The thesis on brokers and brokerage ties the book together. And because the system of clientelism dominated the nobility of France, this book is also a study of the nobility's role in early modern French statebuilding.

How did patron-broker-client ties and networks contribute to the development of the early modern French state? Provincial brokers acted as political middlemen in attaching nobles and institutions in the peripheral provinces to the French throne. Royal ministers such as Richelieu, Mazarin, and Colbert used the distribution of royal patronage in the provinces by networks of their own broker-clients to secure the loyalty and support of independent provincial nobles and institutions. In so doing they bypassed the provincial governors who had enjoyed a near-monopoly on the brokerage of royal patronage in the provinces in the sixteenth century. Royal ministers in the seventeenth century created new provincial administrative clienteles directed from Paris. These ministerial clienteles enabled the Bourbon monarchy to survive the civil war of the Fronde at mid-century and combat the resistance of the nobility to the growth of royal absolutism. Less positively, the conflict and corruption generated by patron-broker-client ties and networks were disruptive enough to force the monarchy to seek a more professional, businesslike basis for its administrative relationships. The result was the emergence of a quasi-public corps of officials, an early modern bureaucracy, during the seventeenth century. Clientelism did not disappear as the new royal bureaucracy developed but adapted to it, coexisting comfortably inside and outside the new political system.

There are some inherent difficulties in doing patronage studies. The first problem is finding archival information on patrons, brokers, and clients and their activities. The second is the amount of detail necessary to establish the political connections between men and explain their significance: a forest of factual detail soon springs up. The third is the lack of a natural narrative or story line: patronage studies sometimes appear to be a bewildering heap of examples, one piled upon the other. It is hoped that by studying the power structure of one province in detail, Provence, and by studying the careers of a small group of exemplary Provençal brokers, familiar faces in a crowd, these differences may be lessened and a sense of continuity achieved.

Four types of archival evidence have been used: administrative and personal correspondence; diaries and memoirs; family papers; and statements by contemporary political observers including biographies and local histories. Letters between Paris ministers and their provincial clients allow a rare glimpse into the workings of relationships because provincials usually visited the national capital only once a year, and for this reason much was committed to paper that would otherwise have been conducted in private conversations at Paris. Personal diaries and memoirs in which men look back on their political careers, discussing who helped or hindered their advancement, are another valuable source on patron-broker-client relationships. Family papers often provide information on client ties, for example, the names of godparents, witnesses to marriage contracts, and beneficiaries in wills. Descriptions by observers of the contemporary political scene often indicate significant relationships.

Patron-broker-client relationships are always hard to document, however, and sources can be deceptive. Three basic types of evidence have been accepted as indicating that an individual was, indeed, the client of a specific patron: their correspondence, that is, letters containing client language, patronage requests or recommendations, promises of rewards, and expressions of gratitude for favors granted; personal statements in memoirs and diaries; and remarks by contemporary political observers. Letters, however, can be misleading: prospective clients soliciting patronage often used effusive client language without achieving the status. Family papers, too, can be misleading: individuals who acted as witnesses or beneficiaries were not always clients, while family members were not necessarily clients because of kinship ties. For this reason sources have been carefully scrutinized, and more than one source has been used wherever possible. Brokers have been identified from descriptive evidence of their brokering.

Political power in early modern France was exercised by an elite, and a study of early modern French politics and government is also a study of elites. There is a current debate on the role of the nobility in the early modern state. It has become apparent that a knowledge of patron-broker-client ties, which dominated noble relationships on a regional basis, is central to this debate, but little is known about them. Did the nobility, the traditional ruling elite, successfully adapt to the changes of the postfeudal world, exercise political power, and help the French monarchy govern a fragmented, unintegrated state? In an older interpretation, nobles experienced serious economic and social difficulties, making them ever more dependent upon a centralizing monarchy that finally refused to tolerate their unruliness any longer and brought them to heel.[25] This book argues that the monarchy used the nobility of France, great and small, sword and robe, in governing; in fact, the nobility was indispensable in governing until the late seventeenth century. The natural leaders of the nobility, whether great court nobles or provincial governors, were linked to the lesser nobility by patron-broker-client and kinship ties, as well as by landholding, remnants of vassalage, and regional interests, and in this way were able to motivate the provincial nobility to political action. This book suggests that the basic characteristics of patron-broker-client ties binding the nobility together and motivating it to action are central to understanding its role in the early modern French state. It also suggests that the Bourbon monarchy had a broad underlying base of support among the French political elite, both sword and robe nobles, whose antagonism to the crown has been exaggerated.

This book does not explore the infrastructure of noble clienteles, where they extended horizontally or vertically or how they connected regionally or nationally, and it does not explore their operation at Paris. Noble clienteles need diagramming internally and externally to perceive their overall structure, which appears to have been loosely hierarchical. This book does, however, offer a theoretical understanding of noble ties and networks drawn from the social sciences, and a new perspective from which to view politics and power in early modern France. It was written because the answers to many of the questions it poses on the political influence of patron-broker-client ties and networks could not be found in other studies. A knowledge of these ties and networks affords a clearer understanding of what constituted political power in early modern France and how the upper ranks of that society were organized. This book suggests that patron-broker-client ties as underlying structures were an important determinant of the political interests, motives, and actions of the French nobility in the early modern period, and were flexible enough to allow choice and voluntarism in French political life. This book proposes clientelism as a form of political association that explains both individual and institutional political behavior, and also as an organizing social principle within the elite. In fact, once we know more about how these ties stretched across the gulf to the masses below and affected their actions, we may find them a valuable social concept for explaining early modern French behavior and organization, more valuable perhaps than horizontal class alliances or hierarchical corporate orders.[26]

CHAPTER ONE

Patrons and Clients

The traditional knocks on the stage are heard, and the red velvet curtains of the Comédie Française open on a production of Molière's *Le Misanthrope*, first presented in 1666. The main character, a young nobleman named Alceste, is sitting alone, disturbed and restless, when his friend Philinte enters the room, stops in surprise, and asks what is bothering him. Alceste answers that he no longer wants to belong to society. Philinte asks why, and Alceste answers that he can no longer endure the insincerity and hyprocrisy that civility requires. Alceste asks, "What good can come from a man who flatters you, swears his friendship, loyalty, zeal, esteem, and affection for you, praises you extravagantly, then does the same for the first scoundrel he meets?"[1] He complains that in Louis XIV's Paris with its mannered social rhetoric he cannot tell friend from foe. Philinte replies that a member of polite society must observe its customs and manners. Alceste protests that honesty and truthfulness are more civil forms of behavior which he intends to adopt. Molière's comedy depicts with bittersweet humor the difficulties resulting from his vow.

The words friendship, loyalty, zeal, esteem, and affection are repeated over and over in the correspondence of sixteenth- and seventeenth-century France, for instance, in the letters between patrons in the royal government at Paris and their clients in the provinces. Formal courtesy phrases using these words open and close letters, adorning their text with rhetorical flourishes and sweeps reflecting a world of patron-client relationships that has long since disappeared. The language of clientage cloaked a network of reciprocal personal relationships stretching from the top of the Paris government into the distant provinces of the Midi. We need to pierce the cloak of language veiling clientage in order to understand it.

A patron assured a client of his friendship and esteem, his protection and gratitude for services rendered. For instance, Cardinal Mazarin assured his client, Henri de Forbin-Maynier, baron d'Oppède, of his friendship which led him "joyfully to seize occasions to serve you."[2] The Cardinal assured another client, Charles de Grimaldi, marquis de Régusse, a president in the Parlement of Aix, that "I shall seek every day to show you the growing esteem and friendship which makes me affectionately inclined to render you service."[3] A client in turn expressed his loyalty and affection for his patron, promised zealous and faithful service, and swore humility and obedience: Toussaint de Janson-Forbin, bishop of Marseille, wrote Colbert that "as You are my patron, I have recourse in all my needs to the honor of Your protection."[4] Louis d'Oppède, bishop of Toulon, thanking Colbert for the honor of his protection, swore "an inviolable attachment to Your service," and requested "the opportunity to render You useful service."[5]

What type of relationship was masked by these formal courtesy phrases? Did they describe sincere emotion, or were they hypocritical flattery as Alceste charged? What obligations lay behind the declarations of friendship and loyalty? As historian Roland Mousnier has noted, "These relationships are little studied and badly understood for our period. There existed a world of beliefs and ideas which are completely strange, it seems, to Frenchmen of the nineteenth and twentieth centuries, requiring an attempt to recreate and understand it."[6]

General Characteristics of Patron-Client Relationships

Observers have agreed on several common characteristics of patron-client relationships. Such relationships are dyadic (two-person), personal, and emotional. Participants are unequal in status: there is a superior (a patron), and an inferior (a client) in a voluntary, vertical alliance. The patron-client bond is a reciprocal exchange relationship in which patrons provide material benefits and protection, and clients in return provide loyalty and service. There is a wide range of possible interactions, or services and benefits exchanged. The relationship is continuous, more than a single, isolated exchange.[7] These traits distinguish patron-client relationships from others in early modern French society.

Patron-client relationships were a personal, emotional bond between two persons.[8] For example, François de Bassompierre, born in Lorraine, owed allegiance by birth to the dukes of Lorraine whom his family had traditionally served, and to the Holy Roman Emperor whom the dukes of Lorraine had served. But when he was twenty Bassompierre swore allegiance to the French king, Henri IV, after a visit to his court. Bassompierre, as he later wrote, told the king that "He had charmed me so much that without going farther to look for a master, if He wanted my service, I would devote myself to Him until death. Then He embraced me and assured me that I could not find a better master than He, who would be more affectionate to me or would contribute more to my good fortune and advancement. That was Tuesday, March 12, 1599. I have considered myself French since them."[9]

Charles de Lorraine, duc de Guise, was named governor of Provence by Henri IV in the autumn of 1594 in order to secure his political support.[10] Guise sullenly and unenthusiastically met the new king for the first time on January 15, 1595.[11] Henri IV's charm and bonhomie, however, struck a responsive chord in him as it had in Bassompierre, and the two men became friends.[12] In fact, Guise and Bassompierre became drinking and gambling cronies of Henri IV, competing with him in tournaments of love for the favors of court ladies.[13] Bassompierre reported Guise's last conversation with Henri IV on the morning of May 14, 1610, a few hours before the king was stabbed to death by an assassin.[14] Guise laughingly told him, "You are, in my opinion, one of the finest men in the world, and our destiny meant for us to be friends because even if You were an ordinary man, I would have been in Your service at whatever price, but since God made You a great king, it could not be otherwise than I am Your man."[15] Guise cried openly at the news of his death.[16] Bassompierre and Guise had warm, personal, and emotional relationships with their patron.

The terms friends and friendship were often used by patrons and clients to indicate the personal, affectionate nature of their relationships. Cardinal Mazarin described the newly appointed first president of the Parlement of Aix, his client Oppède, as "a particular friend."[17] At the same time in a letter of condolence on a client's death, Mazarin wrote that the deceased, Antoine de Valbelle, had been "one of my good friends."[18] Charles de Grimaldi, marquis de Régusse, declared in a letter to his patron, Cardinal Mazarin, that "I am counting on your previous assurances of friendship."[19] The terms friend and friendship, however, were also used to indicate the political loyalty and support of clients. For instance, Mazarin wrote angrily to the marquis de Gordes, lieutenant general of Provence, "Your best friends have fomented the recent trouble at Aix, which was against the King's service. It is not enough that your intentions are good. It is necessary that those who are attached to you by friendship and interest end the disturbances, and demonstrate their zeal and fidelity for the King's service."[20] At the same time, Mazarin thanked first president Oppède for "the service to the King which you and your friends render in your company."[21] Governor Mercoeur complained in a letter to Mazarin that president Régusse was silent during controversial discussions in the Parlement, but he was allowing his friends to argue.[22]

Genuine friendship could and did exist within clientage, but such friendships had usually been forged before the patron-client bond. Friends were bound together by mutual respect and affection in a relationship that was enjoyable and useful but not absolutely necessary to them both. It was a free, horizontal alliance of equality in what was exchanged. But this balanced reciprocity changed as one or the other moved up the political ladder—as one friend advanced in the world, he took the other with him. The imbalance grew, and they became patron and client.[23] Patron-client relationships were vertical, unequal alliances characterized by dependence and by dominance and submission, by a superior who acted as a patron and an inferior who acted as a client.[24] A client needed the protection and material benefits that were provided by his patron, he gave loyalty and service in exchange for them. Friendship was transformed into a patron-client relationship when one friend became dependent on the other for advancement. The boundaries between friendship and clientage were never clearly marked, however. Client loyalties were expressed in terms of friendship, masking inequalities and conflicts of interest. Technically, clientage was a bond between men of unequal rank, usually a less affectionate relationship in which a client needed what he received from a patron. But the metaphors of friendship were used in clientage, and the two were easily confused.[25]

The formal rhetoric of clientage was the language of master and servant. For instance, the comte de Mérinville, lieutenant general of Provence, wrote to Colbert, his patron, "I am a very devoted servant who is concerned about all Your interests."[26] Henri de Forbin-Maynier d'Oppède, first president or chief justice of the Parlement of Aix, declared to his patron, Cardinal Mazarin, that "I would be infinitely unhappy if Your Eminence were to doubt the fidelity and sincerity of my feelings. I must add that You are my sole master, and that it is blindly I must execute all the wishes and orders of Your Eminence."[27] The duc de Mercoeur wrote Mazarin, his patron, from Barcelona and signed himself, "Your most humble, fond servant," while the chevalier Paul wrote his patron, Colbert, "I beg You very humbly to be persuaded that I have no wishes other than those of His Majesty and Your own, and I await the honor of Your orders, which I will always obey with great submission and respect."[28] Antoine de Valbelle described himself as "an old and faithful servant of Your Eminence" in writing Cardinal Mazarin, his patron.[29] The rhetoric of clientage was studded with expressions such as "I am your servant," "to render" or "to give service," and "I am entirely yours," while the standard closing of letters was "your very obedient and faithful servant," sometimes varied with "very humble and affectionate servant." The language of clientage became the language of courtesy.[30] Joseph Dubernet, who was first president of the Parlement of Aix in the 1630s, described himself as "the servant of the archbishop of Bordeaux," his patron, in writing to Cardinal Richelieu. When Du Bourg delivered the Bastille to Henri IV in 1594, he was asked to recognize the new king as "a good prince." He answered that he did not doubt it, but that "he was the servant of the duc de Mayenne."[31]

The terms used to describe the favors bestowed by a patron upon a client indicate the inequality of the relationship. These terms included *grâces*, or favors; *bonté*, goodness or kindness; *bons offices*, or good offices; and *bienfaits*, or benefits. Such terms implied the gracious, voluntary bestowal of a gift by a superior upon an inferior. First president Dubernet of the Parlement of Aix assured Cardinal Richelieu ingratiatingly that "I have found prompt obedience in our company and great gratitude for the favors we have received from the King through the protection of Your Eminence."[32] A client was obsequiously grateful for a patron's generosity. First president Séguiran of the Aix Cour des Comptes swore to Cardinal Richelieu that "the obligations I have from Your goodness are infinite. I am so aware of Your benefits that I will do anything to support Your interests."[33] Governor Alais wrote with deference to the secretary of state for Provence a decade later, urging him to use his "good offices" at court on the governor's behalf.[34]

The notion of receiving favor from a patron contained within it the potential of falling from grace and losing favor—"broken friendships" were an integral part of clientage.[35] The terms used to indicate a failed relationship included falling into a patron's bad graces, his *mauvaises grâces*, and being disgraced; losing his protection and friendship; suffering his bad offices, his *mauvais offices*. Antoine de Valbelle, formerly a Marseille bigwig, wrote Secretary of State Brienne on February 21, 1645, that he was at Aix, "where I am trying to get back into the good graces of governor Alais."[36] Valbelle had lost control over the municipal government of Marseille a few years earlier because of Alais's opposition. Alais had written to his friend at court, the comte de Chavigny, "It may be true that lieutenant Valbelle of the Marseille admiralty court has testified in your presence to wanting to regain my favor, but his perfidy and deceit are without equal."[37] Régusse wrote to Mazarin in 1659, from the north where he had been sent in exile a year earlier, "I am a faithful servant languishing in the bad graces of my master. I ask to be restored to the goodness of Your Eminence."[38]

A third characteristic of early modern French client relationships was the reciprocity of the exchange. A patron who controlled essential, scarce resources was expected to give material assistance in exchange for the loyalty and service of a client who provided more intangible benefits. For example, Colbert wrote to his client Oppède, "I know you have asked the King for the abbey vacated by the death of the abbé de Foix. You can count on it, without flattery or having to write to me, and I shall provide it with great pleasure, knowing the services you have rendered."[39] Antoine de Villeneuve-Mons, member of an old Provençal noble family, had married Louise d'Albert de Luynes, sister of Louis XIII's favorite. Through his brother-in-law's influence, Villeneuve found a place in the household of the king's brother, Gaston d'Orléans, whom he served well. As a reward he was named first master of the duke's household, marshal of royal camps and armies, governor of the Provençal fortress of Les Baux, and governor of the port of Honfleur, the city of Pont L'Evêque, and the region of the Auge in Normandy.[40]

The reciprocity of the patron-client exchange is demonstrated by Cardinal Richelieu's relationship with Louis XIII. He was the king's chief minister, and his position and power depended upon his personal relationship with the king, his patron. In addressing expressions of affection to the king, Richelieu often referred to himself as Louis XIII's *créature*, thereby recognizing the source of his power and prestige. The word créature was commonly used in seventeenth-century France as a term of politeness, appearing frequently in thank-you letters and formal closings of administrative correspondence. Richelieu served the king well and enjoyed extensive royal patronage as a result. He used it to build his own party within the royal government and to surround himself with créatures.[41]

Historian Orest Ranum has studied the administrative créatures of Richelieu, and found that they merited the term "created," which they used to describe themselves: they owned their political power and office to Richelieu as he owned his to the king. Although they had considerable experience and ability in their own right, it was not for these qualities that Richelieu favored them. Their "obsequious fidelity" in thought and deed, even to the point of risking their own lives, explains Richelieu's decision to share political power with them: they were his eyes and ears in the royal government, and they helped him to govern.[42] One of these créatures was Claude de Bullion, surintendant of finance.

Claude de Bullion had a special place among Richelieu's créatures because of his greater age and experience. He was probably about seventy when he died in 1640, and he had been serving the king in his councils since 1619: he had more years in the royal service than any of Richelieu's other clients, and was not inclined to let them or the Cardinal forget it. From a rich and influential family, Bullion became chancellor to the Queen Mother, and through her gained access to the royal council. He joined Richelieu's party sometime before 1630, informing the Cardinal of a court intrigue developing against him two months in advance and even lending him money.[43] Bullion held the crown's ramshackle financial structure together and found money for the Habsburg War under the most difficult conditions; he served Richelieu well.[44] He was the most influential of the Cardinal's créatures, whom the others were careful not to alienate.[45] Generously rewarded for his loyalty and service, he amassed a huge fortune.[46] One son became a president in the Parlement of Paris, while another son replaced his brother in the Parlement of Metz when he became abbot of Saint Fanon de Meaux, and Richelieu arranged the marriage of at least one of Bullion's sons. Bullion was highly successful at placing his numerous relatives in office.[47]

A wide variety of benefits and services were exchanged by patrons and clients. For example, Léon le Bouthillier, comte de Chavigny, another of Richelieu's créatures, was treated like a son by the Cardinal and became secretary of state for foreign affairs at a young age, serving as the personal liaison between Richelieu, Louis XIII, and Gaston d'Orléans. The king was accustomed to receive the political advice of his chief minister through Chavigny, who then reported his success or failure in managing the king back to the Cardinal: Chavigny's reports on the king's disposition and attitudes helped Richelieu to decide how to behave when they met.[48] After 1635, Chavigny became the friend and chancellor of the duc d'Orléans, although this position did not interfere with his loyalty to Richelieu: he headed a party of *Cardinalistes*, clients and agents of Richelieu within the duke's household. They included the duke's personal secretary, almoner, doctor, apothecary, chamberlain, guard captain, and several nobles in his entourage. All served two masters without apparent ill effects.[49] In return for his loyalty and service to Richelieu, Chavigny received the titles of royal councillor, secretary of state, royal secretary, notary, and he inherited his father's office of treasurer of the king's orders. He was named governor of the royal châteaux of Vincennes and Antibes, received substantial royal pensions, made frequent land purchases, constructed his own château at Chavigny, and enjoyed considerable revenues, although he was always heavily in debt.[50]

As another example, Melchior de Chevières, marquis de Saint Chamond, began his career in the army where his exploits attracted Richelieu's attention. Securing the Cardinal's patronage, he embarked upon a successful diplomatic career, serving as envoy to the Queen Mother at Compiègne in 1631 after she fled France.[51] For this delicate mission, he was rewarded with appointments as governor of the citadel of Sisteron and lieutenant general of Provence. In a letter of gratitude to Richelieu on May 30, 1632, Saint Chamond wrote that "I have such a feeling of obligation for the honor it has pleased You to do me in employing me that I beg You very humbly, Monseigneur, that You henceforth recognize me as Your Créature."[52] He became ambassador to Germany and negotiated with Count Oxenstierna, chancellor to the Swedish king, and with the king of Denmark.[53] A list of services rendered and favors received can be as long and varied as a list of clients.

Early modern French patron-client relationships had another characteristic: they were continuous or enduring, that is, interactions were repeated over a number of months or years.[54] This was true for the patron-client relationships of Henri IV and Bassompierre; Henri IV and Guise; Villeneuve and Gaston d'Orléans; Richelieu and Louis XIII; Richelieu and Bullion, Chavigny, and Saint Chamond, all of which endured for years. Patron-client relationships were characterized by reciprocal exchanges in which a patron gave material benefits, advancement, and protection in return for a client's loyalty and service, demonstrations of respect and esteem, information and advice.

Fidelity Relationships

Early modern European historians have done comparatively little work on the nature of patron-client relationships. Roland Mousnier is among the few French historians who have worked on this subject. But differences exist between the definition of patron-client relationships he proposes and the one presented in this chapter. Mousnier has developed the concept of *fidélité*, or fidelity, to describe bonds of personal loyalty in early modern France, which he sees as a postfeudal society of corporate social orders linked by vertical ties of loyalty, man-to-man personal ties of fidelity. The client vowed total allegiance and absolute devotion to his patron, offering support and obedience, and in exchange the patron placed confidence and trust in his client, offering advancement and protection. Mousnier emphasizes that while reciprocal benefits and services were one source of fidelity relationships, the emotional bond was basic. A reciprocal exchange of services should be understood in emotional, effective terms as producing gratitude and gratefulness, which cemented the bond of loyalty.[55] This bond was not feudal, although it was a feudal legacy.[56] Mousnier writes that "fidelity was an emotional tie, founded on mutual affection, uniting two men totally, by free choice, independent of duty toward the nation, the king, law, and society....

[fidelity was] not a question of a simple service relationship, a simple exchange of service and compensation, but a total devotion, a gift of self on one side and affection on the other. The tie which united master and fidèle was an affective bond."[57]

Mousnier describes two basic types of fidelity relationships, master-fidèle and protector-créature. Master-fidèle relationships existed among nobles and gentlemen, while protector-créature relationships existed among members of the royal government. A master who was a great noble advanced his faithful gentlemen servant at court, arranged a good marriage, and acted as a patron to the children of the marriage. A protector named his créature to office, assuring his administrative career and advancement in exchange for his loyalty and service.[58]

Developing Orest Ranum's observations on créatures, Mousnier continues that "the king can only have his orders obeyed through his fidèles acting as intermediaries. These are the king's men who in turn have their own faithful servants, their own créatures."[59] Denis Richet graphically describes a government composed of tiers of créatures when he writes: "The man whom the king puts in an important post is himself surrounded by fidèle relatives or protégés whom he in turn puts in command positions. Thus is established a cascade of fidelities permitting the regime to survive ... a sequential caricature of the old feudal pyramid."[60] Mousnier notes that "in the fidelity relationships defined as master-fidèle and protector-créature, regional variations do not appear important."[61] Mousnier's theory of fidelity has received wide support.[62]

Mousnier's use of the term fidelity to describe personal bonds of loyalty in early modern France is misleading, however, because intense emotional loyalty was not the determining characteristic of most relationships, albeit of some. These relationships were more varied than Mousnier has recognized. All were characterized by loyalty, a minimal level of which was implicit in effective service, but the degree of loyalty varied with the relationship. Some were fidelity relationships as Mousnier has described them, permanent, exclusive, and intensely emotional, and some were not. Many relationships were characterized by self-interest and by short-term, serial loyalties in which a dependent changed protectors for reasons of self-interest; multiple loyalties were not uncommon. Mousnier's definition of fidelity has also been criticized.[63]

In an attempt to clarify his theory of fidelity, Mousnier has introduced the concept of a clientele relationship, that is, the bond between patron and client as a separate relationship from that of fidelity. Mousnier has written that "the patron gives protection and assistance; the client honor, obedience, and political service ... a clientèle relationship is distinct from that of fidelity, which is a reciprocal gift of self, having an element of affection evocative of love, at least warm friendship, without anything ambiguous or doubtful. It [a clientèle relationship] is also distinct because changing clientèles is legitimate ... it is illegitimate, scandalous, dishonorable to break a fidelity relationship, to change masters, although there were numerous cases of this ... the fidelity relationship, master-fidèle, protector-créature, is distinct from that of clientèle and feudalism and more important."[64]

This attempt to clarify the original definition does not solve its problems, however. It muddies the water even more—it is confusing—and raises more questions than it answers. Mousnier has created a separate category, a clientele relationship, for all those relationships that do not fit his definition of a fidelity relationship. Clientele relationships were easily severed, and were not characterized by a strong bond of affection. However, loyalty was characterisic of clientele relationships, too—was not loyalty implicit in the service of all clients? It may not have been affectionate loyalty of the intensity or durability of that in fidelity relationships, but it was personal loyalty. The patron-client relationship has been defined in this book as a dyadic, personal, vertical, unequal, reciprocal, exchange relationship in which there was some degree of loyalty binding the participants together, although the degree of loyalty varied with the relationship. A fidelity relationship was a *type* of patron-client relationship in which the bond of loyalty was intensely affectionate and durable rather than an entirely different relationship.

Mousnier has overemphasized the importance of loyalty as the determining characteristic of patron-client relationships. It was only one of several determining characteristics: these relationships were complex. For example, was depth of emotion enough to distinguish fidelity as a separate relationship from other patron-client relationships? Did the scandalousness and unpleasantness of a break indicate deep emotion and thus a fidelity relationship? Were rancorous partings only characteristic of fidelity relationships? If it was illegitimate to break a fidelity relationship, although this occurred often, did such a relationship exhibit fidelity as Mousnier has described it? Would not such a relationship be infrequently or never broken? Did fidèles and créatures belong to clienteles, that is, how different were Richelieu's fidèles and créatures from his other clients? Did they belong to his clientele?

Mousnier has stated that fidelity relationships were reciprocal exchanges based on loyalty and service, with loyalty as the fundamental tie. He emphasizes the strength and nature of the emotional bond as the differentiating characteristic of fidelity relationships. But what determined the strength of this bond? What determined the degree of loyalty and affection in fidelity relationships? Was it always the same? How was the balance between loyalty and service determined? Was the mix always the same? How was reciprocity measured, and how important was it?

There are other problems with Mousnier's definition. For instance, he persists in attaching his view of the nature of personal bonds of loyalty, whether client or fidelity, to his notion of a society of orders, which has not received wide acceptance among French historians.[65] These concepts are separate, and should be discussed separately. And Mousnier has used the term *fidélité* to describe other relationships besides those that are patron-client, for instance, the relationship of the king to the church and the kingdom of France, of his subjects to the king, of Christians to God and the church, among men-at-arms and peers inside an order, corporation, territorial community, pressure group or secret society, and among members of a profession such as judges or university professors. What were the differences between these fidelity relationships and those that were dyadic, personal, vertical, unequal, reciprocal exchange relationships? Did not the exchange of advancement and protection for loyalty and service distinguish patron-client relationships from other relationships characterized by emotional loyalty?[66]

Mousnier has overlooked elements of materialism and self-interest in fidelity relationships. Differences in rank, position, and power could impede the formation of an "affectionate friendship," or distort its nature when it did develop. Differences in rank tended to give patron-client relationships an artificial, sycophantic air, and unequal relationships characterized by dependency had built-in tendencies toward deceit and hypocrisy, reflected in the exaggerated rhetoric of their language. Unequal relationships based on gratitude and dependence did not always produce a genuine emotional bond, particularly when rewards were much-needed. A superior's ability to distribute necessary material benefits to an inferior influenced the nature of the relationship: a créature's effusive gratitude and his eager desire for favors often had an air of obsequious self-interest that belied declarations of eternal devotion and self-sacrificing loyalty. The devotion of most dependents was not absolute until death regardless of their claims: there were too many broken relationships and too much clientele-hopping for that. In fact, the common practice of changing clienteles has an air of opportunism that clashes with the fervent declarations of undying loyalty. Clients not infrequently changed patrons when it was to their material advantage to do so. The intensity of emotional loyalty varied with the relationship and was tempered by material interests.

Michel Harsgor, in describing French personal relationships in the fifteenth century, has noted what he calls "double fidelities": a client served two masters at once, or a client asked his patron to secure him a position with a more important patron so that he could serve both their interests at once.[67] Harsgor gives several examples of the first category, for instance, Réginer Pot, who served the duke of Burgundy and the king of France at the same time, and his brother, Guyot Pot, who did the same; Odet d'Aydie, who served the duke of Brittany, the king of France, and the king's brother at the same time, while soliciting the patronage of the duke of Burgundy. Harsgor finds double fidelities a peculiarity of fifteenth-century politics: the collapse of feudalism and the resulting political and military confusion created a need for rapid mobility and change, for "personal zig-zags as the human and social expression of political dilemmas." It was sometimes necessary for a man to change masters to continue his political career or even to preserve his property and freedom.[68]

However, a study of French bonds of personal loyalty in the seventeenth century indicates that switching patrons was a common practice in clientage not limited to its infancy or to an unusually stressful period. The practice of subpatronage or subclientage—a client, with his patron's consent, became the client of his patron's patron, a sort of patron-leapfrogging as it were—was widespread in the seventeenth century, and examples can be seen in the careers of Jean Hérauld de Gourville and Henri de Forbin-Maynier d'Oppède.[69] The ideal may have been a fidelity relationship of lifelong devotion to one patron, but the political reality was messier. Multiple allegiances were common, and clients could belong to two networks at once, although this sometimes caused problems. Clients, even those who were fidèles and créatures, switched allegiances when the political situation demanded it, for instance, when the political fortunes of their patron declined, while regional and material interests and other personal loyalties influenced these relationships. Fidelity relationships as described by Roland Mousnier certainly existed in seventeenth-century France, but they were not the most prevalent type of patron-client relationship. The ordinary garden variety was less durable and more materialistic.

Modern observers should not be misled by the language of clientage nor should they confuse the political reality of these relationships with the effusive rhetoric in which they were expressed. Observers have too often relied for their understanding of patron-client relationships on the rhetorical declarations of participants and on theoretical treatises rather than on actual behavior.[70] They have too often confused images of the ideal with political reality, and have accepted at face-value fervent declarations of loyalty and abstract definitions without investigating the actual conditions and subterranean realities of relationships. Social scientists have warned that there are strong elements of myth and hyperbole in patronage, and that "relationships must be analyzed quite apart from the meanings attributed to them."[71] And historians have warned about the pitfalls of trusting literary evidence too much.[72] Patron-client relationships in practice were not always characterized by the blind devotion which clients ritualistically swore to their patrons. If we study the actual conditions of patron-client relationships, a discrepancy often appears between what was said and done. The formal rhetoric of clientage conceals the cold, hard reality of men and their ambitions meshing into place. The professed goals in relationships were not always the real goals. We need more studies of actual practice in these relationships. Bonds of personal loyalty in early modern France were generally more varied, multiple, material, and fragile than we have recognized.

Variability among Patrons and Clients

There has been wide disagreement among social scientists on what clientelism is, on its important and unimportant elements and how they mix.[73] In fact, some social scientists believe there has been such a proliferation of variations that so-called general characteristics have become meaningless descriptive labels. Most observers, however, accept the notion of a common corps of characteristics differentiating patron-client relationships from other relationships in a society.[74] For example, a reciprocal exchange of loyalty and service characterized patron-client relationships in early modern France, but the degree of loyalty varied with the relationship and so did the type of services exchanged. Patron-client relationships were always personal and emotional, but the degree of personalism and emotion varied with the relationship, that is, some were warmer, closer, and more affectionate than others. There were varying degrees of intensity, dependency, reciprocity and durability, and there were different types of exchanges in patron-client relationships depending on the participants and their circumstances. The balance between the instrumental and the effective varied in relationships, too, that is, the balance between the pragmatic, self-interested exchange of service and emotional loyalty.[75] For example, Cardinal Mazarin named Henri de Forbin-Maynier d'Oppède, a former *Frondeur*, first president of the Aix Parlement because Oppède had convincingly demonstrated his willingness to use his considerable power and prestige in Provence on the Cardinal's behalf.[76] Pragmatic considerations determined this relationship.

Emotional considerations, on the other hand, shaped the patron-client relationship of Colbert and Pierre Arnoul. Pierre's father, Nicolas Arnoul, had served Colbert as intendant of the royal galleys at Marseille, and had become the friend of Louis XIV's minister. A client who had served long and well, as Arnoul had, often developed a close personal relationship with his patron—length of service was important and tended to produce close bonds. At his father's death, Colbert appointed Pierre Arnoul to serve as naval intendant at Toulon because of the regard he had for Nicolas, and because of Pierre's friendship with his own son, the marquis de Seignelay: Pierre Arnoul had been at school with Colbert's son, and they had made a trip to Italy together.[77]

Pierre's performance as naval intendant left much to be desired, however, as Colbert repeatedly warned him. On July 17, 1678, the minister wrote: "It is necessary that the friendship I had for your deceased father to be great for me to overlook all that I see of your conduct," and Colbert warned Pierre that if he continued in his behavior, "the King will take away your office."[78] On February 22, Colbert had written sarcastically that "I have always heard Toulon is more Mediterranean than Paris in climate, and the weather better. Nonetheless, every time you have four ships to arm, God opens the heavens for a flood, and sends every rainstorm to Toulon in order to delay the execution of the King's orders."[79] On April 10, 1677, Colbert wrote Pierre that "in your letters, you often criticize the advice and opinions of commander Du Quesne. Be assured that when you've studied twenty years under Du Quesne, you won't be as smart as you now think yourself to be . . . you cannot do more for yourself, or the royal service, than to apply yourself with great care to learn all you can, and do as well as you can . . . if your father were alive, he would tell you that."[80]

Unfortunately, Pierre Arnoul did not learn all he could, and Colbert was forced to recall him for his incompetence. Pierre's career was not ruined, however. His friendship with the marquis de Seignelay saved him: Seignelay sent him as naval intendant to Le Havre and then to Rochefort. Pierre eventually became a good administrator and returned to Marseille to serve as intendant of the galleys like his father.[81] Colbert had tolerated the blundering incompetence of Pierre Arnoul far longer than usual out of regard for his father. When Colbert's patience finally snapped, Arnoul was saved by his friendship with Colbert's son. In these relationships, personal and emotional elements were dominant.

Most patron-client relationships, however, were a mix of personal and pragmatic elements, for example, Richelieu's relationship with his nephew, Pont de Courlay. The twenty-four-year-old Pont de Courlay, or Monsieur Du Pont as he was contemptuously called in Paris government circles, arrived at Toulon in 1636 to take up his post as general of the royal galleys. He was ignorant, extravagant, presumptuous, and vain, and his difficulties were immediate and enduring.[82] He was a spendthrift, running up huge personal and professional debts.[83] The Cardinal wrote his nephew tartly in one letter, "If you cannot live on 50,000 livres a year at Marseille, the whole world would not be enough."[84] By the time Pont de Courlay left office, his silver plate was pledged at Avignon, and he had "borrowed" from the galleys' treasury to pay his debts, which totaled 400,000 livres.[85]

His extravagance and stubborn ignorance created problems in the galleys' administration, and the galley captains soon complained to Richelieu about his ineptitude.[86] Pont de Courlay, although young and inexperienced, refused to take advice, and quarreled openly with the bailli de Forbin, a Knight of Malta who had been chosen by Richelieu to teach him how to command; in fact, he chased Forbin with drawn sword from his house at Toulon. Their quarrel paralyzed the galleys as a fighting force.[87]

Richelieu was furious because of the dangerous military situation in Provence: the Spanish had seized two islands off Cannes, and their fleet patrolled the Mediterranean coast. The Cardinal wrote Pont de Courlay on August 26, 1636: "I am so ashamed of your conduct that, asking you never to think you belong to me, I promise to forget forever what you are to me . . . I would never have believed that you had so little judgment nor so much impudence to flout the orders of the King. . . . If you have done this, be assured that I shall never forget, and that it will be impossible for me to express all the resentment I'll feel because of your bad conduct."[88] At the same time, Richelieu wrote Forbin and the galley captains to apologize for his nephew's conduct.[89] When Forbin asked to resign, Richelieu told him that his services were too valuable to lose.[90] Finally, the Cardinal recalled his nephew in disgust in 1639, and Forbin became acting general of the galleys, a post he held until Richelieu's death.[91]

The amazing aspect of this whole episode was its duration. By the end of 1636, Pont de Courlay was heavily in debt, had alienated Forbin and the galley captains, and had crippled the galleys as a fighting force. Yet Richelieu, who was known for his angry impatience with blundering subordinates, did not recall Pont de Courlay for three more years: he would have sent anyone else to the Bastille for insubordination. Richelieu had sent the governor of Provence, the maréchal de Vitry, there in 1637 for conduct no worse than that of his nephew.[92] Richelieu tolerated more disobedience and inefficiency from his client-relatives than from anyone else. But when their ineptitude seriously threatened royal government, he recalled them. Emotional and personal elements dominated patron-client relationships between kin. But when these relationships were also political, instrumental or pragmatic values usually triumphed in the end: a patron's need for useful political service proved stronger in the long run than his emotional loyalty to client-relatives.

The degree of client dependence varied in relationships, too. A client's personal resources—his reputation, wealth, rank, family, offices, clients, and other patrons—determined how dependent he was. As a rule the fewer his own resources, the more dependent a client, the greater the difference in rank between himself and his patron. And the extent of asymmetry in a relationship determined its degree of coercion or voluntarism.[93] For example, Louis de Vendôme duc de Mercoeur, had married Mazarin's niece, Laura Mancini, during the Cardinal's exile in Germany, despite the opposition of his father and brother who considered the match a mésalliance. Mercoeur's father was César de Bourbon, duc de Vendôme, the legitimized son of Henri IV. Mercoeur, who became governor of Provence in 1652, made the marriage because he had political ambitions—the government of Provence may have been part of the marriage settlement. His voluntary political relationship with the Cardinal had been cemented by a marriage alliance, a not uncommon occurrence. His father was also named governor of Burgundy in 1650.[94] Mercoeur wrote Mazarin a long créature letter from Barcelona in May 1650, declaring that "I do not know how to receive these new proofs of friendship without expressing my intense gratitude.... My intendant writes me that you work continually in my interests, and are not niggardly when it is a question of considering my interests. Your good offices obligate me that much more because you give them to someone far away from court."[95] And his large personal fortune was politically useful.[96] Mercoeur's name, rank, and wealth made him a valuable ally for the king's chief minister, who offered him the opportunity to acquire power.

Charles de La Porte, marquis de La Meilleraye, owed his appointment as lieutenant general of Brittany to the patronage of his first cousin, Cardinal Richelieu, the absentee governor of the province.[97] La Meilleraye acted as governor in his cousin's place, and received substantial rewards from Richelieu and the Estates of Brittany. For example, the Cardinal made him a grand master of the artillery, a sinecure that offered ample opportunity for peculation, and the Estates made him large cash gifts, for instance, 36,000 livres in 1636, with an extra 6,100 livres for his officers.[98] La Meilleraye received an army command from Richelieu and the title of maréchal; eventually he became a duke.[99] He would probably have remained an obscure, impoverished nobleman if his cousin had not become the king's chief minister and promoted him. In this sense, La Meilleraye's service had been materially secured—in addition, he was Richelieu's kinsman—and he was more dependent on the Cardinal than Mercoeur was. La Meilleraye's loyalty and cooperation for these reasons was less voluntary than that of Mercoeur, although in no way less sincere or reliable. The extent of asymmetry in a relationship determined the degree of voluntarism in the relationship, and also its exclusivity—relationships between near-equals were less likely to be exclusive.

In an asymmetrical relationship, a client sometimes found that his obligations to a patron conflicted with his own honor and dignity. Parades de L'Estang, a contemporary observer of the Provençal political scene, wrote ruefully in his memoirs that

> it is necessary to cultivate the acquaintance of the great and the powerful without whose support you cannot maintain a party. To this end, it is necessary to pay them court.... But that is ruinous to the party, and its chief, because, whatever their intentions, the grands, and those in authority in a province, admit no one to their affections except dependents. And dependence sometimes has a high cost, being detrimental to conscience, honor, and your own interests. But if you resist what they want, you bring upon yourself their indignation.[100]

Parades de L'Estang did not need to add that losing the favor of the powerful could mean political ruin.

Clients were especially vulnerable as the inferior parties in unequal relationships because they had to do most of the adjusting. There was a loss of self-respect in having to curry favor and in the demonstrations of esteem and self-abasement that a client was required to perform, a public ritual of dominance and submission in an age that placed great emphasis on the outward symbols of rank and power. For this reason, a client's obligation to a patron and his own interests and dignity were not always compatible. For example, Abraham Du Quesne, a Huguenot who was Colbert's client, learned through a conversation of the minister with his wife that Louis XIV was displeased with his religion, which he stubbornly refused to change. Du Quesne promptly offered to resign. An exasperated Colbert suppressed his letter of resignation and chided him for writing it: Colbert wrote that although Du Quesne had been upset at the time, he should have known that the king read all naval correspondence and would immediately take him up on his foolish offer. Du Quesne sheepishly withdrew his resignation in a letter to Colbert's son, Seignelay, in March 1677. Colbert and Seignelay put more pressure on Du Quesne to change his religion for the king when he was at court in the winter of 1679–80, but he steadfastly refused. The death of his protector, Colbert, and the continued pressure of the king to convert caused Du Quesne to resign in 1684. He was old and tired, and not on good terms with Colbert's successor, Seignelay.[101] Du Quesne's personal interests and honor had clashed with those of the king, the patron of his patron, Colbert. The king's wishes became more pressing at Colbert's death, and Du Quesne was eventually forced to resign because he would not convert.

The duc de Navailles had much the same experience. Philippe II de Montault-Benac, duc de Navailles, was a client of Richelieu, then of

Mazarin, and rose high at court under Louis XIV. But he was disgraced in 1662 when he refused to obey the king's wishes. His wife, the duchesse de Navailles, was a lady-in-waiting to the queen, Marie-Thérèse. She became upset at the attention the king was paying to another lady-in-waiting, Anne-Lucie de La Mothe Houdancourt, so she made certain that all the doors to their apartments at Saint-Germain-en-Laye were tightly shut at night. The king complained to the duc de Navailles, who sided with his wife. They had to leave court as a result, and Navailles was forced to give up his guard company of light horse and the government of Le Havre, which he had received from the king a few years earlier in gratitude for his military service.[102] Le Havre during the Fronde was considered the most important fortress in France. Navailles's personal honor had clashed with the interests of his patron, and he was punished when he refused to obey, although he would have suffered personally if he had. Dependence was the emotional reality of clientage. It sometimes meant the loss of personal honor and dignity and the neglect of personal interests. The alternative was the loss of a patron's favor and protection.

The extent of reciprocity varied in patron-client relationships. In most relationships, patrons gave more. They gave more material benefits, at least: they were expected to give more because they had the resources to do so. Equivalence in a relationship was often difficult to determine: the bond between two men was an ongoing affair that did not balance on a day-to-day basis, and there was the additional difficulty of trying to weigh a patron's tangible benefits against a client's intangible services.[103] Reciprocity in a relationship was a subject of dispute and a common source of broken relationships.

The understanding between patron and client was individual, informal, and unwritten, reached through an ongoing process of negotiation and bargaining in which the contributions of one participant were periodically weighed against those of the other. The process was ambiguous and indirect enough to allow for misunderstandings and false expectations, opening the door to disillusionment, charges of betrayal, cries of ingratitude, and broken relationships. The disappointment of Henri de Séguiran, sieur de Bouc and first president of the Cour des Comptes at Aix, is an example. Richelieu made him a naval lieutenant general in 1632, and sent him on an inspection tour of the Provençal ports and coastal fortifications. Séguiran became a regular correspondent of the Cardinal, and his letters were full of client language. In February 1633, he wrote to ask that "You always continue in the same protection and goodness which is has pleased You to promise me, and which I will try to merit by my loyalty and attention to duty."[104] On August 2, Séguiran wrote that "I have no greater ambition in the world than to be Your créature."[105] In 1635, he asked that his son and brother be made galley captains—they were—and recommended captain Montmeyan for the royal service.[106] Richelieu made Séguiran a royal councillor, named him an honorary galley captain, and gave him a pension.[107] However, Séguiran's letters to the Cardinal stopped abruptly in 1636. One of the last in December thanked Richelieu for a letter which his brother had brought back from a recent trip to court.[108]

Why did Séguiran stop writing? Apparently, he had hoped to be named first president of the Parlement of Aix, but his hopes were dashed. His disappointment at losing the office may have been too great for him to continue in a client relationship with the Cardinal. Evidently he considered Richelieu's failure to reward his services a betrayal. Séguiran's hopes were destroyed in the autumn of 1635 when his friend, the bailli de Forbin, returned from one of his trips to court to tell Séguiran that he was not being considered for the appointment because it was said that his unpopularity would impair his efficiency: Séguiran protested in a letter to Richelieu that he was not unpopular in Provence; most Provençaux had expressed respect and esteem for him, and the Parlement supported his candidacy. Séguiran declared that he was well liked, with many friends and much influence in the province, and that he could be useful to the crown politically. He concluded by writing that "whoever represented me in this way to Your Eminence did not have much experience in this province."[109] He was referring to the newly appointed naval commander-in-chief for Provence, Henri d'Escoubleau de Sourdis, archbishop of Bordeaux, who was then at court, and whose client, Joseph Dubernet, received the appointment a few months later. Sourdis, a créature of Richelieu, had undoubtedly been whispering into the Cardinal's ear.[110]

Clients such as Séguiran ended relationships when they thought their interests had been neglected: the extent of reciprocity in a relationship helped to determine the degree of loyalty. Most relationships were not fidelity relationships as Roland Mousnier has defined them. Clients often changed allegiances when a more promising patron appeared. Even in stable relationships of long standing, clients kept an eye open for a more promising patron who could offer faster promotion and sometimes switched when one appeared. However, the switch from patron to patron and from clientele to clientele was usually blurred, not neat and clean: semblances of old relationships were maintained while new ones were being formed, and clients often found themselves beginning one relationship before they had ended another. The secret was to change patrons at the right moment; otherwise an angry, vindictive ex-patron could be left behind, hurling accusations of betrayal and treachery. It was not uncommon for a client to have multiple patrons and multiple loyalties. Combinations of loyalties were acceptable as long as they did not conflict; then a choice had to be made. Clients changed allegiances more frequently than did patrons, who hesitated to lose clients because their loss implied a loss of power and prestige—patrons were ever mindful of their reputations which helped them to attract clients. Even the most cautious patron, however, could not indefinitely tolerate an openly disloyal client without damaging his own reputation.

For example, Daniel de Cosnac, who became archbishop of Aix, switched patrons after the Fronde because it appeared that his interests would be better advanced by Cardinal Mazarin than by his former patron, the prince de Conti, a Frondeur chief whose star had dimmed. As first gentleman of the prince de Conti's bedchamber, Cosnac had followed the prince to Bordeaux in 1651, and even offered to follow him into exile in Spain a few years later when the prince found himself on the losing side in the Fronde. Conti decided not to go to Spain, and as a reward for his loyalty the prince secured for Cosnac the bishopric of Valence. Cosnac resigned his post as first gentleman of the bechamber, but he continued in the prince's service at Paris, watching his interests while he was away in the south commanding the army in Catalonia and acting as royal representative at the Estates of Languedoc. In the autumn of 1656, however, Cosnac was seduced away from Conti's service by Cardinal Mazarin, who appeared as the more promising patron. An angry Conti charged Cosnac with betrayal for his switch in allegiance.[111]

Cosnac is understandably vague about the exact sequence of events in his memoirs. He wrote that "what the Cardinal proposed did not appear to me against my honor nor the interests of my master, and I was not so eager to please His Eminence that I did whatever he desired."[112] Cosnac did not clarify what the Cardinal proposed, and the passage has a defensive tone. Conti's other clients and friends at Paris carried tales south, and Conti protested to Cosnac that "you get along too well with the Cardinal."[113] Conti became cold and withdrew his friendship.[114] An open break occurred when Cosnac lost 1,000 livres gambling at cards with the duchesse de Mercoeur, Mazarin's niece, and collected a debt owed him by the princesse de Conti in order to pay: Conti was outraged and accused Cosnac of treachery.[115] Cosnac openly attached himself to the duchesse de Mercoeur. She died in 1657, but the patronage of Mazarin and the Queen Mother secured for him the office of first almoner in the household of the king's brother.[116]

The durability or continuity of patron-client relationships, that is, how long-lived they were, how stable or fragile, varied greatly. Some relationships were impermanent and ephemeral; others were durable and long term; and some were in-between.[117] Many were multiple relationships, in which a client had more than one patron. For example, Claude de La Châtre, governor of Berry in 1557, abandoned his patron, Anne de Montmorency, the Old Constable, in whose household he had been raised, to become a client of his enemy, the Guises. In the 1570s and 1580s, Claude combined this tie with loyalty to the ducs de Nevers and d'Anjou. Nicolas Hennequin, seigneur Du Fay, was a financial secretary in the household of François duc d'Anjou, in the 1570s and 1580s. At the same time he and his family were well-known clients of Henri, duc de Guise, Anjou's greatest enemy at court, and were among the keenest supporters of the League after Anjou's death. The royal ambassador, Françcois de Noailles, bishop of Dax, was a créature of Coligny and secretary of state Villeroy simultaneously.[118] Several of Mazarin's clients and financial agents had dual loyalties, for instance, Claude des Boislève, who was Mazarin's nominee for the post of financial intendant. As far as Mazarin was concerned, Boislève was his client operating in an official position. As far as François Jacquier, an important *munitionnaire* or munitioneer, a war contractor, was concerned, Boislève was using his confidential position in Mazarin's clientele as a cover to arrange things for Jacquier.[119] Chavigny had dual loyalties to Cardinal Richelieu and the duc d'Orléans.

It was not unusual for a successful politician to have had several patrons during his career. Michel Particelli d'Hémery owed his early career to membership in the clientele of the financier Nicolas I Le Camus, whose daughter he had married in 1616, but his career developed rapidly only after he secured Richelieu's favor to become the Cardinal's créature.[120] Denis Marin, another financier, was a member of five successive clienteles. He began as the client of Arnoul de Nouveau, postal surintendant general; he became a client of the financier Claude Cornuel, whose death allowed him to enter Mazarin's service; and finally, he joined Colbert's service after Mazarin's death.[121]

Relationships with a marked degree of personalism and emotional loyalty, for instance, between relatives or reinforced by marriage ties, tended to last longer because of the additional cement. The degree of dependency also affected durability. The nearer a client was to his patron in rank and power, the less likely the relationship was to be durable, a common problem of great court nobles. The extent of reciprocity and self-interest affected durability. Clients who felt their interests were not protected, as in the case of Séguiran, or who had found a more promising patron, as in the case of Cosnac, often switched patrons. Clientele-hopping for personal advancement was a common reason for terminating relationships.

Clients who advanced politically by moving from one clientele to another played a dangerous game by leaving behind a string of rancorous, deserted patrons. Cosnac escaped unharmed, but this was not always the case. Patrons betrayed by clients could be as angry and vindictive as neglected or abandoned clients. In fact, the frequency with which relationships were dissolved and the conflict caused by broken relationships, which was severe enough at times to disrupt government, were the classic problems of clientelism. Early modern French politics was a maze of overlapping, serial client relationships whose dissolution generated strife. Political interaction often had a tense and distrustful air for this reason; sometimes it became frenetic, shrill, and bitter.[122]

Conflicts of interest were a common reason for the dissolution of patron-client relationships. The term *intérêt*, or interest, appears often in the documents. For example, Mazain assured his client and nephew-by-marriage, the duc de Mercoeur, governor of Provence, "You must not doubt that your interests are as dear to me as my own."[123] Séguiran wrote Cardinal Richelieu that "all the interests of Your Eminence are of particular interest to me," while the comte d'Harcourt swore to Richelieu, his patron, that "I have never had any interests but those of Your Eminence and the King . . . I have never had any particular interests."[124] Governor Alais, writing on behalf of his client, the baron de Marignane, declared that "he is so loyal a friend to me that I make his interests mine."[125]

Private or particular interests could interfere with a client's duties and obligations to his patron and threaten their relationship. A client sought an unequal, dependent relationship to achieve personal material goals, and his self-interest sometimes conflicted with his loyalty and obligations to a patron. A client who was demonstrably *intéressé* or self-interested was not trusted by a patron. For instance, Oppède seems to have been answering charges of private interest when on October 5, 1660, he wrote Mazarin:

> For myself, Monseigneur, I would be infinitely unhappy if Your Eminence were to doubt the fidelity and sincerity of my feelings. I must add that You are my sole master, and that it is blindly I must execute all the wishes and orders of Your Eminence. No other consideration will make me fail in this duty, and I shall never do it for anyone else. I am filled with sadness if I can persuade myself that Your Eminence, who is just, can doubt the truth of these words. Please remember that You cannot accuse me of being *intéressé*. I can say that if I eat better in the royal service, and am agreeably occupied, I also have obligations, which I have never refused. I have never found anything too rude or difficult in the service of the King, and I have never considered my family, nor friends, nor relatives, in His Service. I have made many enemies in serving the King, and because I have blindly obeyed, I have not made out of it what I might a hundred times over. Whatever Your Eminence orders me to do to please Him, as my duty I will do, and I shall have the honor of warning Your Eminence if I do the least thing against His wishes. If Your Eminence has the goodness to add to my words, I shall profit from it. I take on these duties only to please Your Eminence.[126]

The vehemence of Oppède's disclaimers of personal interest, and his fervent declarations of blind obedience, make it likely that he had been accused of pursuing his own interests at the expense of those of his patron and the state.

This supposition is reinforced by Oppède's letter to Mazarin a month later, on November 16, in which he wrote that "as a very submissive créature of Your Eminence, I must account to You for all my actions, and basing my fortune and my house on the honor of Your protection, I cannot take any step in my family without submitting it to the scrutiny of Your Eminence."[127] Oppède then recounted his financial plans for the marriage of his daughter, which he had never done before in writing to the Cardinal, and which he never did again. In another letter to Mazarin, Oppède assured his patron that "where it is a question of the service of the King, I shall never consider old friendships or relatives, and I would break with my father, if I had one [living] on this issue."[128] In a letter to Colbert, Oppède swore that "particular interest will never influence me when it is a question of pleasing You or the King; be assured that for me Your orders will always be law."[129]

However, Monsieur Poncet, a royal commissioner visiting the Midi in 1662, wrote a memoir for the royal council on Oppède and Fortia de Pilles, the deputies chosen to investigate royal rights in the Comtat Venaissin, because "as we know, provincials often think more of their own interests than those of the King." He described them both as reliable, but he felt they should be watched because Fortia de Pilles owned much property in the Comtat Venaissin, while Oppède was "likely to consider the interests of his many friends."[130] President Régusse of the Parlement of Aix warned Colbert that "the first president [Oppède] has neglected the interests of our company for his own interests, which do not serve to enhance his reputation."[131] But Mazarin sharply reprimanded Régusse for the same fault when he wrote that "you have been following your particular interests to the extent of making the King's interests suffer."[132]

The charges of particular interest had some foundation. For instance, Oppède did not persuade the parlement to register a royal edict in 1656 proclaiming that new purchasers of royal domaine lands had to pay the crown a tax equal to one year's revenue. The edict had been issued a year earlier, presented to the Cour des Comptes at Aix for registration and refused despite four royal decrees ordering its registration, then presented to the parlement and refused despite two royal decrees ordering its registration. It was only reluctantly registered by the parlement after Mazarin threatened to send the tax to the Trésoriers Généraux of Aix for collection without registration. From his letters and the parlement's deliberations, it appears that Oppède did not work for the edict's registration for good reason: he was one of eleven parlementaires who had recently purchased domaine lands, and he did not want to pay the tax.[133] In this case, Oppède's self-interest outweighed his obligations to Mazarin and the crown.

The intendant of Languedoc, writing a memorandum for Colbert on the abilities of the parlementaires of Toulouse, noted that Cambon was "a man bold and clever enough, who looks for his own interest everywhere and is dangerous." He remarked that Caulet-Roque was 'too attached to his own interest," and that Fermat, Madron, and Torreille were self-interested (*intéressé*), and so was Papus, "who never sees ill in his friends," and Aimable-Castelan, "who is a friend of the first president because of the sack" (in which the first president put legal cases for distribution to the judges). The intendant in Normandy, writing the same type of memorandum for Colbert, described president Alexandre Bigot de Monville as "a very capable man and very powerful in his company, having there a large, strong party; he is very honest in matters in which neither he nor his friends have interests; but when it is a question of his interests or those of his friends, he does not know what justice is. He is the most powerful robe noble in the parlement and the province because of the strong support he gives his friends."[134]

Interest was recognized as a political problem by contemporaries because it caused errors in judgment. For example, the duc de Rohan, leader of the Huguenot resistance, wrote a book entitled, *De l'Intérêt des Princes et des Etats de la Chrétienté*. Rohan's theme was that the private interest of a prince, regent, royal minister, or favorite could become an obstacle to the realization of state interest, and he gave seven examples of international crises in which the miscalculation or distortion of reason, through private interest, had prevented rulers and statesmen from acting in the best interest of the state.[135] Rohan himself, in every stage of his career, had exploited the self-interested aims of his political opponents with cynical realism.[136] The manipulation of private interest was an important source of political power in early modern France.

There was a wide variety of possible patron-client exchanges. As examples of client services, Antoine de Villeneuve managed the household of Gaston d'Orléans; Bullion ran the crown's financial machinery for Richelieu; Saint Chamond conducted diplomatic negotiations for Richelieu; Chavigny served as Richelieu's political go-between with the king; Régusse led the Provençal party of Mazarin's supporters during the Fronde; and Arnoul administered the royal galleys at Marseille for Colbert. Richelieu, Mazarin, and Colbert were enthusiastic patrons of writers, especially historiographers, for their use in political propaganda.[137] The royal ministers Mazarin and Fouquet depended on their clients to lend them money when they needed it.[138] As patronage rewards for their services, Villeneuve and Saint Chamond received political and military appointments; Bullion and Richelieu accumulated large fortunes and obtained places for the numerous members of their families; and Richelieu arranged a marriage for one of Bullion's sons.

The nature of the patron-client exchange was affected by the resources of the participants. Clients who had independent resources, for example, the first president of a parlement, were able to offer patrons a greater variety of more valuable services than clients with fewer resources such as household servants. Clients who had utility because of their independent resources and high status were eagerly sought, and may have had greater influence on a patron and higher rank in a clientele than clients with fewer resources and less status. Clients brought different resources with them to relationships, and their resources helped to determine their ranking within a clientele.

The concept of variability within a corps of general characteristics helps to explain some of the differences between clients. The range of personalism and dependency within client relationships, for example, makes it possible to distinguish different types of clients: family and friends, household members, créatures, neighbors, professional colleagues, allies, and brokers. Family and friends, domestic servants, and créatures had more personal, dependent relationships with their patrons, while neighbors, professional colleagues, allies, and brokers usually had more impersonal, independent relationships. Family, friends, and domestic servants were often fidèles.[139] These categories of clients could overlap. Not all family, friends, or domestic servants of a patron, of course, became his clients.

Kinship is an involuntary relationship based on birth, which imposes obligations. Kinsmen are persons related by blood and by marriage, too. The exchange need not be reciprocal, and kinsmen are often equal in status. Clientage, on the other hand, is a voluntary relationship based on a reciprocal exchange between participants who are unequal in status.[140] Kinsmen became clients as friends did when they became dependent on their kin for advancement. Patron-client relationships between family and friends were usually warmer, more affectionate and personal, and often longer-lasting. Fidèles were usually found among those in close proximity to a patron and were at the heart of his clientele. They often ranked higher in his affections and had more influence with him than did some of his other clients.

Both Richelieu and Mazarin promoted unexceptional clients who were their brothers. Alphonse-Louis Du Plessis-Besançon, for example, was always in precarious health: he was sickly and nervous from childhood, clumsy, with a stumbling walk, facial tic, and weak voice. Timid and withdrawn, he was happiest retired from the world in the strict, contemplative order of the Carthusians. But his life as a monk ended in 1624 when his brother was admitted to the royal council. The king, at Richelieu's request, named Alphonse bishop of Aix in 1625, and he left the Carthusian monastery at Lyon forever to accept secular office. Richelieu secured his appointment as archbishop of Lyon and then obtained a cardinal's hat for him.[141] Alphonse would probably never have left the Carthusian monastery at Lyon if his brother had not become the king's chief minister. His leaving and secular career were the result of his brother's ambitions, and his advancement stopped at his brother's death, probably to his own relief.

Michel de Mazarin had been a Dominican for ten years when his older brother left for France. Through his brother's influence, he became in quick succession General of the Dominican order, Archbishop of Aix, Cardinal Sainte-Cécile, and Viceroy of Catalonia. A blunt, outspoken Italian with little respect for those around him, Michel de Mazarin was frequently absent from Aix on diplomatic and military missions for his brother. His handwriting is irregular, badly formed, and difficult to read, suggestive of his restless, impulsive nature. The abbé Arnauld described him as having "a fiery and turbulent nature, violent and uncontrolled," while a client, Grimaldi-Régusse, whom we have already met, noted that he was "quick-tempered, impatient, ambitious, and energetic." His older brother was devoted to him, but constantly reproached him for his angry impatience because it created political problems. Michel de Mazarin died unexpectedly in 1648, while extraordinary ambassador at Rome.[142]

Cardinal Mazarin accepted a number of friends into his service as clients, and rewarded them with clerical offices in Provence. Hyacinthe Serroni, a Dominican friar from Rome who had been the Cardinal's confessor, was named bishop of Orange in 1647, and died as archbishop of Albi.[143] A papal diplomat when he met Mazarin at Rome, Joseph Zongo Ondedei came to Paris as the Cardinal's secretary, received the bishopric of Fréjus, and was at Mazarin's bedside when he died.[144] Alessandro Bichi, cardinal-bishop of Carpentras, met Mazarin while serving as papal nuncio at Paris, and helped to obtain the archbishopric of Aix for his brother Michel.[145] Another Italian, Jerôme de Grimaldi, also met Mazarin while serving as papal nuncio in France. Through Mazarin's influence he became a cardinal and archbishop of Aix.[146] Several of these men belonged for a time to Mazarin's household.

The size of a man's household indicated his rank and wealth. In order to keep his status and prestige and to display the wealth that promised generosity to his clients, thereby increasing his power, a great noble needed to maintain a large household. *Grands* or great nobles could easily have 100 salaried individuals on their staff, the majority stationed at one or perhaps two provincial châteaux. The governor of Champagne had 113 household members on his account books in 1542.[147] Léonard-Philibert, vicomte de Pompadour and lieutenant general in the Limousin from 1621 to 1634, maintained a household of about 100 at his château of Pompadour.[148] The princes de Condé had 75 at Chantilly in 1660 and 1676, and 83 in 1692.[149] The duc de Gramont had a household of 106 from 1650 to 1675; the Pontchartrain kept a household of 113; the duc de Nevers had a household of 146.[150]

Households had two basic groups of members, administrators and domestic servants. The administrative staff of the princes de Condé included an intendant of the household with overall responsibility for its smooth running; the intendant supervised secretaries, bookkeepers, accountants, recordkeepers and file clerks, lawyers and legal agents, estate administrators and managers. Also in this group were noble and gentlemen household officials and servants, pages, confessors, chaplains, almoners, doctors, apothecaries, musicians, the steward or *maître d'hôtel* in charge of the domestic staff, and craftsmen who did fine repair work. The domestic staff, headed by the maître d'hôtel, was at the bottom of the household hierarchy, and included the kitchen and household staff and stable personnel.[151] A contemporary observer noted that a grand seigneur needed to have a household of at least 31 servants, and preferably 36 to 38, not including those of his wife, who needed another 16 servants—22 or 23 if there were children—for a bare minimum of 53 servants to staff a great noble household in the seventeenth century.[152]

Households were an important source of noble clients.[153] The households of great nobles with entrée to court were usually the largest, with a greater number and variety of household officials and domestic servants, some of whom were clients (only some servants became clients because of the distance between them and their masters). But these households declined in size during Louis XIV's reign.[154] Grands in high office also maintained entourages until the last decades of the seventeenth century. These included armed retainers—provincial governors, for instance, maintained guard and gendarmes companies composed at least partly of nobles—and grands were surrounded in addition by members of the local elite who were their clients, courted their favor, or were in their debt. Entering the Paris town hall in 1551, the governor of the Ile-de-France was accompanied by an entourage of 20 to 40, and five years later his successor was followed by 200 noblemen.[155] Charles du Cambout, baron de Pontchâteau, a client of Cardinal Richelieu, arrived at Nantes in December 1636, for a meeting of the Estates of Brittany, accompanied by 80 gentlemen loyal to him.[156] Jean de Pontevès, comte de Carcès and lieutenant general of Provence, attended an assembly of the provincial nobility at Marseille in April 1649, accompanied by 300 of his noble clients and supporters.[157] In addition to a household of 180 persons, Cardinal Richelieu maintained one guard company of 150 footguards with muskets and one guard company of 100 horseguards, to whom 20 to 50 mounted gentlemen were added on special occasions.[158] Great noble entourages were meant to impress, and they swelled with the occasion since they reflected the wealth and status of their patron.

Great noble households included an additional category of clients, créatures, who were usually secretaries or intendants. Many famous créatures began their political careers in the household of a master who later became their patron. Jean Hérauld de Gourville, for instance, began as a valet in the household of the duc de la Rochefoucauld, worked his way into the duke's confidence, became his secretary and créature, and then attracted the favor of the duke's patron, the prince de Condé.[159] The Condés maintained a large entourage of créatures, among whom the most famous were Gourville, Pierre Lenet, and Jean Perrault. Of 24 créatures who began their careers under Henri II, prince de Condé, 14 finished under his son Louis; and of 37 who began under Louis, 23 finished under his son Henri-Jules.[160] Many créatures were not household members. Isaac Laffemas, Richelieu's créature; Louis Berryer, Mazarin's créature; and Denis Marin, who owed his loyalty to Colbert, were not household members;[161] nor were Richelieu's créatures Bullion, Chavigny, and Saint Chamond.

Household members and créatures had personal relationships with their patron, whom they saw frequently. This was not true of clients who were neighbors, professional colleagues, allies, and brokers. They were less dependent, with more impersonal relationships. Neighbors and professional colleagues based their relationship on a regional or occupational tie. They met because they lived in the same neighborhood, belonged to the same institution, frequented the same artistic or intellectual circles. The degree to which these relationship became personal and dependent was determined by the personalities involved, their resources, and what was exchanged. These relationship tended to be more impersonal than those of family, friends, household members, or créatures.[162]

For example, Alessandro Bichi, cardinal-bishop of Carpentras, was one of Mazarin's oldest friends. For years he was permanently resident at Carpentras in the Comtat Venaissin, a small papal principality that lay between Provence and the Dauphiné. Provençaux seeking the assistance of someone with influence at court usually approached Bichi. The barony of Oppède was located near Carpentras, and when Oppède sought Bichi's help in 1645, the cardinal obligingly recommended him to Mazarin as the purchaser of an office of parlement president. Oppède visited Bichi several times before the outbreak of the Fronde.[163] Jean de Pontevès, comte de Carcès and lieutenant general of Provence (an office equivalent to a modern lieutenant governor), was a kinsman of Oppède. He also had lands in the Comtat Venaissin near Carpentras.[164] As he wrote Mazarin on June 2, he joined the Aix parlementaires in their 1649 revolt against the crown because of kinship and client ties.[165] His ties with Oppède, a rebel leader, were among the most important of these. Carcès appeared with 300 of his clients and supporters at the General Assembly of Provençal Nobility at Marseille in April 1649, and these men fought under his command in June when he led the parlementaire forces against the governor's troops in the first battle of the Provençal Fronde.[166] Afterward Cardinal Mazarin called Carcès to Paris to explain his participation.[167] Carcès first made a trip to Carpentras to ask Bichi to intervene with Mazarin on his behalf.[168] Oppède wrote Carcès at Paris in November 1650, asking him to recommend him to Mazarin.[169] Forced into political retirement on his estates in the Comtat Venaissin, Carcès died in Oppède's arms in

August 1656.[170] Carcès and Oppède were friends, kinsmen, and allies as well as neighbors, and each sought the protection and assistance of Cardinal Bichi, based upon their proximity as neighbors in the Comtat Venaissin. Neighbors could also be cousins, friends, and political allies.

Patron-client ties developed between men who were professional colleagues. For example, Guillaume Du Vair, first president of the Parlement of Aix in 1600, became the friend and patron of Nicolas-Claude de Fabri, sieur de Peiresc, councillor in the same court, probably about 1605. Both men were bachelors who were well-known humanists. They were drawn together by their professional and intellectual interests, and they established a celebrated humanist circle at Aix. When Du Vair became Keeper of the Seals in 1616, he took Peiresc with him to Paris as his secretary. Peiresc negotiated for Du Vair to obtain the bishopric of Lisieux, and as a reward was named abbé de Guitres. Through Du Vair, Peiresc met a number of leading Paris intellectuals and politicians.[171] The professional acquaintance of Du Vair and Peiresc had developed into a patron-client relationship.

Political allies were different from other clients because they had substantial independent resources. They were power figures in their own right, nearly equal in status to their patrons. In fact, their relationship was patron-client only because an ally was dependent upon his patron in some way. The relationship was easily transformed into a political friendship when this was no longer true. Allies ceased to be clients and became friends when they did not absolutely need what they received from a patron. A political alliance was more horizontal for mutual gain than vertical: patrons and allies cooperated in a reciprocal exchange that was useful to them both; the more necessary it became, the more it was a client relationship.[172] Brokers were similar to allies in having independent resources and impersonal relationships with their patrons, but they had a brokering function in addition (see chapter 2).

The comte de Chavigny was a friend and patron of Louis de Valois, comte d'Alais. They wrote frequently after Alais went to Provence as its governor. Alais asked Chavigny to provide introductions and places at court for his Provençal clients and reciprocated by finding places for Chavigny's clients in Provence: Alais's secretary, Villeronde, and one of his intendants, Vautorte, were Chavigny's clients. Chavigny had great influence at court as Richelieu's créature, and his services were important to Alais. For example, Alais wrote Chavigny in 1642 that he was sending his secretary, Villeronde, to court, and that "I have ordered him to see you and submit entirely to your guidance all my interests. . . . You are the principal author of my good fortune. . . . I have the obligation and inclination to honor you all my life."[173] There was no great distance between them, however, because Alais as a Valois had a higher rank, more illustrious family name, and other patrons at court. Chavigny's protection was useful, but Alais had significant resources of his own; their alliance was similar to that of Mazarin and Mercoeur. A conflict of interest cooled their relationship in 1645, and it was never resumed. Allies and brokers belonged to an outer circle of clients loosely bound to their patrons, in contrast to an inner circle of family, friends, fidèles, servants, and créatures who had more personal, dependent relationships.

A client might secure the attention and favor of a patron in several ways. He could be a family member, the case with Richelieu's brother and nephew, or a friend, as were the Italian clerics promoted by Mazarin. He might be recommended by kinsmen or clients of a patron: Pierre Arnoul was recommended to Colbert by his father, and Séguiran was recommended to Richelieu by his Uncle Gaspard, Louis XIII's confessor.[174] A client might attract the attention of a patron through his exploits. The marquis de Saint Chamond's reputation for valor, earned while fighting with the army in Italy, attracted Richelieu's attention. Nobles often attracted favor in high places by their military exploits. Séguiran attracted Richelieu's attention after writing a book about his participation as a galley captain in the famous naval battle off La Rochelle in 1622. When Richelieu appointed Séguiran naval lieutenant general a decade later, he asked him to write a report on the commerce, ports, and coastal fortifications of Provence. The report, written after a tour of inspection, was excellent and must have impressed Richelieu.[175] The career of Abraham Du Quesne, vice admiral of the sailing fleet at Toulon, was undistinguished under Richelieu and Mazarin, but it took off when he wrote a memoir on naval armament at Brest which Colbert read. The minister made him a squadron commander under Admiral Beaufort at Toulon, promoted him to vice admiral, and protected him against a steady stream of complaints about his irascibility.[176]

The variety of clients indicates the complexity of patron-client relationships, which were not rigid or fixed: they were fluid, varying human relationships. All client relationships, however, shared five general characteristics: they were dyadic, personal, and emotional; they were unequal; they were reciprocal; they had multiple types of exchanges; and they were continuous. How did contemporaries regard patron-client relationships? Seventeenth-century political observers took a functional approach. They asked why a relationship had been established, for what purpose. What bond united two men? What interests did they share, and what did each receive from the relationship? What was the balance of power in a relationship? This emphasis upon interest should be kept in mind by modern observers. Patron-client relationships facilitated an exchange of resources, and material interests were important for that reason.

Client relationships were a variable mix of loyalty and service, and loyalty was characterized by varying degrees of intensity and durability. The ideal was a fidelity relationship of lifelong devotion to one patron, and such relationships did exist. However, most relationships were more fragile and material, and multiple loyalties were not uncommon. Kinship ties and marriage alliances reinforced the patron-client bond. An informal, ongoing process of bargaining and negotiation characterized most patron-client relationships in which the interests, resources, and contributions of one participant were weighed against those of the other for the duration of the relationship. It was a loose, inexact system of accounting, and what satisfied one client did not always satisfy another; the degree of reciprocity varied. Relationships were severed when an imbalance in reciprocity became too great. Government by patron-client ties is better understood as the utilization of changing interests and resources, motivating men to political action, than as tiers of fixed, immutable client loyalties.

CHAPTER TWO

Brokers

Oppède-le-Vieux is a late-medieval village of stone houses perched on one of the rocky spurs of the Lubéron mountains east of Avignon. Clinging to the very tip of the spur, a ruined fifteenth-century château can be glimpsed through a gate in the village walls. The château of Oppède should be seen on a rainy day when rolling clouds of mist shroud the Cavalon valley and the Vaucluse plateau. Veiled by rain, tumbling down the steep incline in great limestone blocks overgrown with weeds, the château would inspire a romantic poet: it needs only a dungeon, a tolling bell, and a ghost. The château of Oppède was the ancestral home of Henri de Forbin-Maynier, baron d'Oppède, first president of the Parlement of Aix from 1655 to 1671, acting intendant of Provence, sometimes acting governor, and a client of both Mazarin and Colbert. He was a leading figure in Provençal politics for decades. Historian Pierre Clément noted long ago that Oppède was worthy of study in his own right as an important provincial administrator.[1]

In contrast to the château d'Oppède perched on its hillside, the Provençal coastal village of La Ciotat fans out along a wide bay sweeping around the coast from Marseille to Toulon. When Henri de Séguiran visited La Ciotat on a tour of inspection for Cardinal Richelieu in 1633, he reported that the village had 900 houses and a population of 8,000 to 9,000, of whom 2,500 were employed in fishing and trading. The round harbor with its two quais contained over sixty ships, mostly square-sailed *polacres* and the small fishing boats known as *barques*. Offshore, there were five long-legged fishing engines called *madragues*, and there was a municipal sentry posted on the rocks at the harbor entrance.[2] In the hills behind La Ciotat lay the family lands of Charles de Grimaldi, marquis de Régusse, president in the Parlement of Aix and stubborn political rival of Oppède. The careers of Oppède and Régusse, two political *gros bonnets* (bigwigs) of seventeenth-century Provence, tell us much about the roles and resources of provincial brokers.

General Characteristics of Brokers

Oppède and Régusse were presidents or presiding judges in the *Parlement* of Aix, the provincial court of final appeal in civil and criminal cases. The other sovereign judicial court sitting at Aix-en-Provence, the provincial capital, was the *Cour des Comptes*, the court of final appeal in royal financial cases. Both courts had to register royal legislation before it could be enforced in Provence, and both sat in the palace of justice at Aix which they shared with the tax collection bureau and court of the *Trésoriers Généraux de France*, who administered the assessment of royal taxes, verified the records, and transferred the money to Paris. The governor's official residence was also in the palace of justice.

The archbishop of Aix served with three elected consuls and one assessor of the Aix municipal government as the *procureurs du pays*, the interim executive authority of the Estates of Provence, the traditional tax-granting assembly that assessed and levied the royal tax on land or taille. The last Estates sat at Aix in 1639; they were not called again to sit by the crown until the Revolution. They were replaced by the Third Estate sitting separately as a General Assembly of Provençal Communities, a meeting of deputies from 37 represented communities in the province. The consulate form of municipal government was widespread in Provence, and consuls served as deputies to the General Assemblies. These assemblies included two *procureurs* or representatives of the clergy and two of the nobility, and met annually at the town of Lambesc near Aix after 1664.[3]

Henri de Forbin-Maynier, baron d'Oppède, a local notable with independent resources, put his influence and clients at the disposal of Cardinal Mazarin, his Paris patron, to use in achieving political goals in Provence in exchange for royal patronage. Oppède, for example, used his influence and clients among the deputies attending the General Assembly of Provençal Communities at Orange in the spring of 1655 to persuade them to approve the crown's tax demands. Oppède's maternal uncle, Jean-Baptiste de Castellane, seigneur de La Verdière, who had recently been elected first consul of Aix, was able to influence the other procureurs du pays in favor of granting the crown's tax requests. Implicit in Oppède's help was the expectation of Mazarin's reciprocity at some future date in rewarding him with royal patronage, and in fact, Oppède was named first president of the Parlement of Aix in the autumn of 1655, as we shall see.

Cardinal Mazarin wrote to La Verdière after his election, "I have received with pleasure your assurances of friendship, and all that president d'Oppède has told me about you."[4] A year later Mazarin wrote La Verdière expressing satisfaction with his conduct at the recent General Assembly: La Verdière had helped governor Mercoeur to obtain passage of the crown's tax requests, "confirming what I ordered you to do and what I understood about you from a long chat with president d'Oppède." Mazarin added that "you would also oblige me by facilitating through your *crédit* [influence] the things which Monsieur Colbert will ask you to do for me."[5] Oppède wrote to Mazarin to confirm that his uncle was working for the Cardinal at the General Assembly.[6] Cardinal Mazarin wrote governor Mercoeur that he was well satisfied with the conduct of Monsieur de La Verdière, and added that "I would be greatly mistaken if you have servants in Provence who are more committed to your interests than president d'Oppède and Monsieur de La

Verdière."[7] In a letter a week later to the governor, Mazarin expressed surprise that the General Assembly was not yet finished, "with the assistance of all your friends and those of Monsieur d'Oppède."[8] A few months later Mazarin wrote Mercoeur and royal commissioner Serroni, "You will both admit that the friends of president d'Oppède worked wonders there" (at the assembly).[9]

Oppède had acted as a client in helping Mazarin, but he had also acted as a broker because he had arranged an exchange of resources between men who were physically and personally distant, separated by the hundreds of miles between Paris and Aix and by the differences in rank and power between a royal minister and a provincial noble. Oppède had arranged for La Verdière and his other clients in the General Assembly to use their influence on behalf of Mazarin in the expectation of receiving a reward, acting as a power broker because he had arranged an exchange of political influence. A broker was more than an intermediary or a go-between because he had resources of his own which he could add to the exchange—in Oppède's case his own influence, wealth, and patronage—and for this reason he did more than transmit the negotiations: he influenced them by doing his own manipulating and lobbying. He was a mediator or middleman in an indirect exchange. He did not directly control what was transferred, for example, La Verdière's influence or Mazarin's patronage, but he influenced the quality of the exchange by negotiating it. A broker acted as a patron in promising rewards to his clients, and he acted as a client in securing their loyalty and service for his patron: a broker's clients became the subclients of his patron, and sometimes his clients.[10]

A broker's services were selective, however, and often intermittent: Oppède's refusal to broker for a Provençal delegation at court is an example. His refusal was described by Jacques de Parades de L'Estang, a member of the Arles municipal government sent to court in 1662 to protest royal taxation of that city. The deputies visited secretary of state Brienne and royal ministers Colbert and Le Tellier. Brienne promised them an interview with the king, which was postponed when Oppède arrived at court a month later to join his ally, the governor of Provence.[11] Suddenly the deputies found that interviews with Brienne and Colbert were harder to obtain, and shorter and nastier when they did occur. Parades de L'Estang commented that "threats, rudeness, and bad treatment were natural to Colbert."[12]

An interview with Colbert could be an unnerving experience, as Madame de Sévigné wrote her daughter on November 18, 1676, after she had spoken to him about the renewal of her son-in-law's pension. She had been warned in advance of the cold reception she would receive, and the warning proved accurate: Colbert answered her with one sentence, "Madame, I will think about it," and showed her the door.[13] Colbert usually maintained strict silence and his features remained immobile during these interviews. He had heavy eyebrows, deep-set eyes with heavy lids, and a cold stare that made his response unnerving.[14] It was an effective tactic for discouraging place-seekers and cutting short unwelcome interviews.

In his memoirs Parades de L'Estang quoted a highly placed friend at court as having said, "This rascal, president d'Oppède, has made your projects fail and spoiled my attempts to intervene on your behalf."[15] Parades de L'Estang wrote that as a result of "the manipulations, ruses, and bad will of Monsieur d'Oppède," the Arles deputies were rebuffed when they finally saw the king.[16] He wrote that "Oppède destroyed all our efforts and ruined our audience with the King . . . the intrigues of these two gentlemen [Oppède and governor Mercoeur] with the royal minister [Colbert] worked against the success of our deputation."[17]

Why did Oppède defeat the efforts of the Arles delegation? He refused to smooth their path—in fact, he blocked it—because he was acting intendant in Provence, and Arles was a *terre adjacente*. The cities of Marseille and Arles, traditionally classified as adjacent areas, were taxed separately and came directly under the financial jurisdiction of the provincial intendant. The refusal of Arles to pay royal taxes and its deputies' complaints reflected badly on Oppède and on his patron, Colbert, who as finance minister was directly responsible to Louis XIV for provincial taxation. To protect their own interests and reputations, Oppède and Colbert worked together to silence the Arles deputies.

In order to act as a broker, an individual needed *crédit* at home and at Paris. The word crédit appears frequently in the administrative documents of the period. Its primary meaning was the belief or trust inspired by someone, and its secondary meaning was the influence or power enjoyed by inspiring trust.[18] For instance, Cardinal Bichi, who was sent by Mazarin to negotiate a settlement with the rebel parlementaires of Aix, wrote in February that governor Alais had lost his crédit as a result of his imprisonment by the rebels, and a *mazarinade* (a political propaganda pamphlet) warned the governor that he was surrounded by untrustworthy advisers who lacked crédit and authority in Provence. Régusse reported in his memoirs that Alais retreated to Marseille in March after his release to arm himself with friends, crédit, and authority because his party controlled the municipal government.[19] Commenting upon the prospective appointment of the marquis d'Aiguebonne as acting governor to replace the discredited Alais, Jerôme de Grimaldi wrote that "he [Aiguebonne] does not have an eminent enough rank to govern a province . . . to pacify the [Provençal] nobility, you need someone of crédit, power, and character above the rank of the [rebel] comte de Carcès, someone who can make peace with the marquis de Trans and other members of the high nobility detached from Carcès."[20]

Crédit was derived from personal reputation, rank, title and family name, wealth, officeholding, clients, and patrons. Oppède, for instance, had influence in Provence because he enjoyed the trust of Cardinal Mazarin, the king's chief minister, and because he had a good personal reputation, noble rank and well-known family name, wealth, parlement office, and an extensive clientele, resources that made him politically valuable to Mazarin and gave him crédit at Paris. President Forbin de La Roque of the Parlement of Aix recommended his brother-in-law, the marquis d'Oraison, for the vacant office of Provençal lieutenant general by noting that "his house has enough wealth, kin, and friends in the province to sustain the weight of this office and to make it valuable for the royal service."[21] The bishop of Nantes wrote to his patron, Cardinal Richelieu, from Cannes where he was on a temporary mission that "the bishop of Fréjus has a great aversion to the service of the King. . . . It is very important to order his nephew and coadjutant to make a trip to court to learn the attitudes and obligations he must have for the royal service. . . . his uncle has so little influence and so few alliances in this province that his example will not have much effect."[22]

In a secret memorandum for Colbert in 1663, Claude Bazin, sieur de Bezons, intendant in Languedoc, assessed the value of individual Toulouse parlementaires for the royal service, noting their wealth, family alliances, and reputations. The intendant noted which parlementaires were wealthy (incomes ranging from 20,000 to 40,000 livres a year) and which were not. He noted that Papus "had been poor but has enriched himself through his office." He noted that Caulet was a brother of the bishop of Pamiers; Marmiesse was a brother of the bishop of Conserans; Cambon was a cousin of the king's confessor; Dumay was a friend of the duc de Roquelaure; and Berthier de Saint Génie was a brother of the bishop of Montauban. He also noted that Laterrasse had crédit in the company; Chastanet had courage and many friends, although little ability; and Torreille's ability was mediocre, but he had crédit and was esteemed by the company.[23] Crédit was frequently used in the documents with the word authority, the legitimate right as a representative of constituted government to command others. Authority was the formal exercise of structured power. Crédit was influence outside the formal exercise of structured power which, nonetheless, determined its operation.

A broker who had provincial crédit did not owe everything to a Paris patron: he had not been "created" by him, although he may have been elevated, and he did not belong to him "body and soul."[24] He was not a fidèle or a créature. In fact, his provincial influence and clients, which made him independent, had probably secured him patronage in the first place and enabled him to act as a broker. The broker-client used his provincial power and prestige on behalf of his Paris patron, helping him to govern in exchange for patronage, increasing his own provincial power. A broker and a royal minister became partners in a political marriage of convenience, a practical governing alliance in which material considerations were important: how much help a broker could offer his patron and how much advancement a patron could offer him in return. Broker-clients with crédit had outside sources of power and prestige before they chose to serve a Paris patron, and in normal circumstances had them after the relationship ended. They remained local notables.

An illustration is provided by the political rivalry between two ambitious Provençal power brokers, Oppéde and Régusse. They sought the patronage of the king's chief minister and offered him in return their brokerage services in Provence. Cardinal Mazarin preferred Oppède, whose services he found more useful, and secured for him the office of first president or chief justice of the Parlement of Aix-en-Provence. However, Régusse remained a president or presiding judge in the parlement and a power figure in Provence for years, although he had lost the Cardinal's patronage and could no longer act as a provincial broker. The rivalry between Oppède and Régusse illustrates the general characteristics of brokers and their individual variability.

The new governor, the duc de Mercoeur, Mazarin's nephew by marriage, had been warned when he came to Provence in the spring of 1652 that Oppède through his influence and wealth was a dangerous leader of the Provençal party of a princes, the *Sabreurs*, who had opposed Mazarin's government during the Fronde. In fact, a year or so earlier Oppède had sought the patronage of the prince de Condé in the hope of becoming the first president of the parlement.[25] Oppède now abandoned the Sabreurs as a lost cause. In one of the most spectacular switches in Provençal politics, he allowed himself to be recruited by governor Mercoeur to the support of Mazarin in the summer of 1652, starting a stampede among provincial notables to join the winning side and ending the Fronde in Provence.[26] In September Mercoeur captured Toulon, the headquarters of the Sabreurs, because Oppède had convinced the officers of the garrisoning regiment to surrender by promising them amnesty and payment of back wages.[27] This success assured Mercoeur's permanent appointment as governor, and Oppède was named first president of the parlement.

Charles de Grimaldi, marquis de Régusse, had a greater claim to appointment, however, and he was an ambitious man who deeply wanted to become first president. François Bosquet, intendant in Languedoc, wrote to Chancellor Séguier that it was said the first president of the parlement had agreed to sell his office to Régusse, a president.[28] This proved to be rumor rather than fact, but it showed the direction of Régusse's ambitions. Needing the protection of a court patron to advance, Régusse saw his chance when Mazarin's brother was named archbishop of Aix in 1645. He entered the archbishop's service, writing in his memoirs that "I entered not only in his friendship, but also in his confidence, and as his generosity brought him to secure many favors for his friends, it was certain that he would always help me."[29]

The sudden death of Michel de Mazarin could have been a political catastrophe for Régusse, left without a patron. But he seized the opportunity to approach Cardinal Mazarin as his brother's friend. On October 7, 1648, a month after the archbishop's death, Mazarin wrote Régusse that his brother's "very special esteem" for him prompted similar feelings.[30] Régusse bombarded the Cardinal with letters full of client language and unsolicited advice, declaring that "of all Your créatures, there will never be one more submissive or attached than I."[31] Mazarin granted him the titles of marquis de Régusse and baron de Roumoules, probably in recognition of his attempt to reconcile the rebel parlementaires and the governor. Their feud was rapidly escalating into the Provençal Fronde.[32] Régusse was soon recognized as the Cardinal's client and a leader of the Provençal party supporting his government, the *Mazarinistes*, a minority party in Provençal politics. Régusse wrote to Mazarin that "since You have so generously rewarded so many of Your créatures, please do not forget my services." Mazarin replied that "I shall seek every day an occasion to show you the growing esteem and friendship which makes me affectionately inclined to render you service."[33]

Régusse performed an invaluable political service for Mazarin by holding the Parlement and the provincial capital of Aix-en-Provence loyal to him in 1651, the nadir of the Cardinal's political fortunes: Régusse had considerable influence within the high court and the capital. When Mercoeur arrived in Provence, he immediately sent his secretary to ask Régusse's help. The new governor was able to take the city of Toulon, the last redoubt of the Sabreurs, because Régusse introduced him to a naval commander temporarily anchored off La Ciotat and en route to Barcelona with ten ships. Together they convinced him to use his ships to blockade the harbor of Toulon from the sea, while on land Mercoeur closed the surrounding roads. The plan worked because the grape harvest was imminent, and the Toulonnais feared for their vines; they threw open the city gates to Mercoeur, and a general peace was declared in October. Upon Régusse's advice a General Assembly of Provençal Communities was called at Aubagne to request Mercoeur's permanent appointment as governor, which Mazarin happily granted. In September 1653, five days after the Cardinal had bought the office of governor for 400,000 livres from its previous holder, the comte d'Alais, he sold it to Mercoeur for 600,000 livres.[34] Mazarin's feelings of kinship and gratitude had not interfered with his making a tidy profit. They did not interfere with his political interests either: he named Oppède first president of the parlement two years later, although everyone had expected the office to go to Régusse.

It was widely known that the first president, Jean de Mesgrigny, wanted to resign, and Régusse expect to receive the office as a reward for his services to Mazarin during the Fronde. The office went on the market in 1653 for 60,000 écus (180,000 livres).[35] President Oppède offered the full price, although his father had bought the office for 105,000 livres in 1621 and sold it for 100,000 livres ten years later.[36] President Régusse submitted a counteroffer of 55,000 écus (165,000 livres). As a good businessman Régusse had offered 10 percent less than the asking price, which still left Mesgrigny a handsome profit. Régusse explained the lower offer in his memoirs by saying that he was short of cash.[37] But he was just being careful with his money, and he obviously expected to be appointed first president, anyway.

To everyone's surprise, however, Mesgrigny signed a bill of sale for the full price with Oppède, who promptly went to court to solicit Mazarin's approval for the appointment. As Régusse wrote later, Mercoeur promised him the full support of his crédit at court but did not keep his promise.[38] Régusse went to Paris at the same time, ostensibly to secure repayment of the 60,000 livres he had lent his patron, Michel de Mazarin, before his death. Colbert repaid the money, and Régusse returned to Provence a month later to serve as the crown's representative at the General Assembly of Communities sitting at Manosque in August 1653.[39] Oppède remained at court. Mazarin postponed making a decision on the parlement appointment until he saw how Régusse performed at Manosque and could assess for himself Oppède's character and ability.

Although Régusse had boasted in 1649 to intendant Sève of his influence within the parlement and his connections with the nobility of Aix, Sève was dubious: he thought Régusse was exaggerating his crédit.[40] The Aix municipal elections of 1650–1651 proved his assessment correct because Oppède's candidates defeated those of Régusse.[41] Although Rascas Du Canet, a friend and client of Régusse, was elected first consul of Aix in 1652, he betrayed his friend by leading the opposition to the tax demands that Régusse presented as the royal representative at the Manosque General Assembly. He did so because he was feuding with the governor.[42] But his friend had the uncomfortable task of explaining in a letter to Mazarin why the crown's demands had not been met: Régusse wrote that he was a victim of the "intrigues and cabals of my enemies," and begged the Cardinal to be satisfied with the sum granted.[43] Mazarin was not satisfied. To make matters worse Hyacinthe Serroni, bishop of Orange, obtained the same demands in January 1654 from the new General Assembly sitting at Brignoles.[44] As a result, Régusse appeared easily intimidated, weak, and without influence in Provence, and this cost him the office of first president.

Oppède at court profited from his rival's failure by convincing Mazarin that he had the influence and the clients to assist him in governing Provence: Oppède insisted that his clients could help in controlling the General Assemblies and procureurs du pays. As proof his party dominated the municipal elections at Aix in October 1653, ousting Régusse's men and naming his own clients as consuls and assessor. The new first consul, nominated by outgoing consul Rascas Du Canet, was André d'Oraison, marquis d'Oraison, the Sabreur brother-in-law of president Forbin de la Roque, who was Oppède's cousin and client. The other consuls were Sabreurs, too.[45] At least fifteen of Oppède's relatives served as consuls of Aix during his years in power, often as first consuls who were traditionally sword nobles.[46] Oppède's election victory convinced Mazarin that he could do as he promised, although his willingness to do so over time was still in question.

Oppède again demonstrated his loyalty during the General Assembly at Orange in the spring of 1655 when his uncle, first consul La Verdière, and his other clients convinced the assembly to cooperate with the crown. Contemporary political observer Parades de L'Estang wrote that "when the court saw Oppède was so well-considered in the province, it wanted to acquire him, and by the time he was named first president, he was one of the most faithful créatures of Cardinal Mazarin."[47] Oppéde wrote to Mazarin from Paris on April 22, 1655, immediately after the close of the assembly, asking for the appointment as first president; he received it on September 19.[48]

Régusse had lost the appointment because he appeared to have less provincial crédit and less political utility than Oppède, and because he had spent less time and money than Oppède in soliciting it. Oppède was willing to spend two years at court with the attendant expense and aggravation to secure the appointment, although he had written Mazarin on April 22 that nineteen months away from home had seriously interfered with his domestic affairs.[49] Régusse had spent forty days at Paris in 1653, and did not return. He expected Mercoeur to lobby for him, and he depended upon the strength of Mazarin's gratitude for the services he had rendered during the Fronde. But he was disappointed on both counts, unwisely leaving Oppède alone in Paris to make whatever impression he could on Mazarin and Mercoeur, who had recently gone to court.

Oppède visited the court regularly throughout his political career, although trips to Paris were time-consuming and expensive.[50] He was there in 1641, 1646, 1648, and from the summer of 1653 through the autumn of 1655. He saw Mazarin in November 1658 when the court stopped briefly at Lyon on its way to Paris, and Mazarin stayed at Oppède's townhouse when the court visited Aix in January and February 1660.[51] Oppède went to Paris in April 1661 to see Colbert, his new patron, and he was there again with Mercoeur in 1662, 1665, and 1666.[52] He was at court in December 1670, returning home in time to entertain Colbert's son, the marquis de Seignelay, when he visited Marseille in January and February 1671. Colbert thanked Oppède in a letter of February 27 for this gesture, which he considered "a sign of friendship," and indicated that he "intended to reciprocate."[53] Regular trips to Paris to see patrons were a political necessity for distant clients.

Oppède was willing to use his wealth for political purposes. He paid 15,000 livres more than Régusse had offered for the office of first president in 1653, and 75,000 livres more than his father had paid for it. He had overpaid to obtain his office of parlement president in 1645—because there were no offices available, Oppède had persuaded Armand Monier to exchange his recently inherited office of president for his own office of councillor by paying 144,000 livres for it at a time when these offices usually sold for 75,000 to 78,000 livres.[54] Oppède also spent money freely on "gifts" to get what he wanted. Régusse wrote in his memoirs that Oppède had secured the office of first president by "offering many generous presents."[55] Oppède was rumored to have offered Joseph Zongo Ondedei, bishop of Fréjus and one of Mazarin's secretaries, 30,000 livres for his help in obtaining the appointment.[56] And Oppède indirectly purchased the support of Mercoeur and his wife. When the governor's father, César, duc de Vendôme, visited Aix in 1655, he attempted unsuccessfully to borrow money from Régusse, who had already lent Mercoeur considerable sums that had never been repaid. Régusse refused, but Oppède obligingly offered the duc de Vendôme 30,000 livres. Oppède later allowed the duchesse de Mercoeur, Mazarin's niece, to win large sums from him playing cards at court. And it was reported that Oppède helped Mercoeur, who was viceroy of Catalonia, to obtain loans at Aix for his expensive military campaigns. Not surprisingly, the Mercoeurs switched their support to Oppède, strengthening his suit at court.[57]

Oppède was also obliging in lending money to Mazarin. Willingness to lend money increased a client's usefulness and a patron's favor. Oppède lent the Cardinal 6,000 livres in September 1656.[58] Mazarin wrote Oppède two years later that he would be back in Paris in a few days, and would then reimburse him for the monies he had lent for tax deficits and expenditures of the royal galleys at Marseille.[59] Oppède wrote to Mazarin in the same year that he could not advance more money for the support of the galleys because he was running low on cash, Colbert not yet having reimbursed him for the sums he had previously advanced.[60] In a letter in 1659, Oppède noted that his expenses in office had exceeded his means, and asked Mazarin to see that his pension and loans were promptly paid.[61] Oppède wrote to Colbert in 1664 to ask that his pension be paid for the previous two years, adding that "I can say all the extraordinary services I render are from my own pocket, although I do them willingly and with much zeal."[62]

Oppède may have gone into debt because of his political expenses—it was easy to do. His debts amounted to 220,000 livres in 1649. He reduced them to around 75,000 or 80,000 livres over the next four years.[63] But when he began his 1653 campaign for the office of first president, he was still in debt, and the office itself cost him at least 225,000 livres, perhaps as much as 275,000 livres. This put him 300,000 livres in debt by 1655. He probably sold some land to pay these debts, but it is doubtful that he amortized them completely. It was rumored that Oppède was 600,000 livres in debt when he died. This sum is undoubtedly exaggerated, but he may well have been in debt because he spent heavily in entertaining deputies at the General Assemblies, providing lavish banquets to influence their voting: he was known for his "magnificent table."[64] Oppède kept an "open table," as many contemporary politicians did, and this was expensive. For instance, in January 1649 during the parlementaire revolt, Oppède brought a large number of men into Aix from his estates, and gave a large banquet for them in the courtyard of his town mansion, which had been provisioned for siege with a large quantity of fresh meat, easily spoiled.[65]

Régusse, in contrast, did not go often to court, and he was not as generous as Oppède in making loans or gifts. According to his memoirs he only went to court five times during his lifetime, and three of these visits were in the 1640s before he attracted Mazarin's attention.[66] Régusse made the mistake of not being in Paris during the decisive years of 1654 and 1655, and he did not keep an agent at court as did many provincials. When he was sent into exile at Issoudun in 1658, and again to Abbeville in 1663, his son became his agent seeking his reestablishment. Oppède had a low opinion of the son's ability, calling him incompetent, *trop peu habile homme*.[67] Régusse did not like lending money to great nobles because they were poor financial risks—their repayment rate was low. He wrote in his memoirs that "I could not avoid" lending 60,000 livres to Michel de Mazarin, a sum which was not repaid until five years after the archbishop's death. Mercoeur never repaid the sums he had borrowed from Régusse, who noted sourly in his memoirs that "closeness to grands brings with it the necessity of never refusing a service, especially that of interest."[68]

Régusse's fortune was as large as that of Oppède, so his frugality was not the result of need. Régusse's income was variable but averaged at least 50,000 livres a year, perhaps as much as 60,000 livres, and his total fortune was at least 1,000,000 livres.[69] Régusse noted in his memoirs that his wealth came from investments in maritime commerce, community debts, and tax collection.[70] He regularly invested in the Levant and Italian trade at Marseille in spices, textiles, and hides.[71] His account book shows that he collected over 16,000 livres in interest on loans to communities and individuals in 1640, and that he had nearly 100,000 livres invested in these loans.[72] Oppède contemptuously observed that much of Régusse's wealth came from tax farming, a statement confirmed by his memoirs and account book.[73]

In his memoirs Régusse lamented every penny lost on various tax treaties, giving the impression of being careful with his money: he was still basically a merchant and financier, new to the robe nobility. He had not yet assumed the pose of disdain for making money, and he did not have the security of a largely landed income as Oppède did. So he was more frugal with his money, less willing to leave his business affairs at Marseille for long periods of time or to make loans and gifts for political purposes. His frugality proved to be a political liability because money was power, and generosity was a political asset vital to the maintenance of large client networks.

Régusse came from a wealthy merchant family of La Ciotat and had recently joined the robe nobility through his mother's family.[74] The château and fief of Régusse had been purchased by his father in 1613.[75] As the heir as well of a grandfather and a childless maternal uncle, Régusse was a wealthy man, and he married the daughter of a wealthy Corsican merchant at Marseille. The amount of her dowry is unknown, but she inherited much property at her father's death. Régusse used his wife's inheritance to purchase an office of councillor in the Parlement of Aix in 1633 from his maternal uncle, and he later purchased an office of president.[76]

A substantial landowner Régusse was the owner or co-owner of fourteen fiefs, most of which were purchased to legitimize wealth from other sources.[77] In 1635, he bought land for a townhouse at Aix, two doors down the street from Oppède, and in the next few years constructed an impressive mansion that Louis XIV occupied during his visit to the city.[78] Régusse furnished the mansion with furniture from Paris, which only wealthy Provençaux could afford to do, and collected an extensive library. He kept six or seven servants.[79] Régusse was aware of the lifestyle he was expected to maintain as a parlement judge. After he bought his office of councillor he wrote in his memoirs: "I bought a house at Aix because this was the honorable and expected consequence of officeholding, and I adopted the lifestyle and furnishings which the pride and pomp of the city required of its judges."[80]

Oppède was a wealthy man, too, According to his *livre de raison*, or account book, his income was at least 30,000 livres a year in 1649, most of it from land in the Comtat Venaissin and Basse-Provence.[81] His fortune at the time of his death has been conservatively estimated at 600,000 livres, but was probably closer to 1,000,000, and his annual income has been estimated at 45,000 livres, although it may have been as high as 60,000.[82] Oppède wrote Mazarin that his maternal uncle, Jean-Baptiste de Castellane de la Verdière, who was childless, intended to leave him 25,000 livres a year in revenue from land. His fortune eventually went to Oppède's eldest son, Jean-Baptiste, who was named for him.[83] Oppède lent money to fellow judges, to neighboring communities, and to the parlement; these were his major financial investments.[84] But he was not a tax farmer. In 1637, for the substantial dowry of 100,000 livres, he had married Marie-Thérèse de Pontevès, who came from a cadet branch of a large family of the Provençal sword nobility.[85] Oppède's annual income as first president was about 2,500 livres, but he noted that other sources of judicial income (fees and gifts) brought the total to about 15,000 livres a year. Royal pensions and gifts made this total even higher; he received about 11,000 livres in royal pensions and gifts in 1671, the year of his death.[86]

Oppède, one of four feudal baronies in the Comtat Venaissin, had been in the family's possession since 1500. The Mayniers d'Oppède had been first presidents of the Parlement of Aix since 1500, too. The Forbins, the paternal side of the family, were fourteenth-century Marseille merchants who had prospered to become one of the most illustrious noble families in Provence. Prolific, they had intermarried with most of the Provençal sword nobility to establish numerous family branches.[87] The Forbins-Maynier d'Oppède were not members of the old sword nobility: the Mayniers did not belong because of their parlement service, the Forbins because of their mercantile origins. But if they were not members of the feudal nobility, they had old and well-known noble names. They moved among the highest circles of the Provençal robe nobility and intermarried with the sword. Henri de Forbin-Maynier, baron d'Oppède, had a higher rank than Charles de Grimaldi, marquis de Régusse, and his family connections made it easier for him to attract the support of the Provençal nobility.

Oppède lived in a late fifteenth-century mansion at Aix, acquired at the same time as the barony in the Comtat. His mansion had been extensively renovated and was one of the finest in the city. He had a library valued at 4,500 livres, and forty six paintings valued at 2,329 livres, as well as eight carriage horses, two saddle horses, and ample silverware. The total value of Oppède's furnishings in 1671 was about 19,000 livres. No value was set on his townhouse.[88] The *capitation* of Aix, a population census for tax purposes in 1695, showed that nineteen servants were employed in the household of Oppède's son, while seven were employed in the neighboring household of Régusse's son. The two households were among the most luxurious in Aix. Only eight families in the provincial capital employed more than ten servants, while the average number of servants employed in the households of other judges in the sovereign courts was five.[89]

Oppède had personal charm and a reputation for courage and generosity. A chubby face and large, candid brown eyes gaze directly at the viewer from his portrait.[90] Historian Pierre-Joseph de Haitze wrote that "first president d'Oppède was of medium height, well-proportioned, with a round face and laughing air, an agreeable appearance, engaging and generous manners, always ready to please, always a warm friend."[91] Parades de L'Estang noted his "happy and agreeable nature."[92] Régusse, after mentioning his rival's "boundless ambition and artful dissimulation," praised his "pleasing manner, flexibility, and political skill."[93] Oppède's charm attracted clients.

His reputation for military courage attracted the support of the provincial nobility, and he was a leader of the 1649 parlementaire revolt at Aix.[94] The next year he became a chief of the Sabreurs and showed considerable bravery when he pushed through an anti-Sabreur mob in the streets of Aix on October 3, 1651, to attend a session of the Parlement.[95] Eight years later he showed courage again when angry protesters stormed the palace of justice demanding his death: Oppède refused to take refuge, declaring that "I prefer to die on the fleurs de lys [the covering of the first president's chair] in serving the King and fulfilling the functions of my office than in cowardly saving my life." His attitude did, in fact, save his life because men were waiting to kill him in the back passage leading from the courtroom.[96] Oppède multiplied his crédit by his generosity and willingness to do favors for his Paris patrons. Favors and gifts were expensive, time-consuming, and a nuisance, but they helped a provincial client to establish a close relationship with a Paris patron. For example, in 1662, Oppède's client, Toussaint de Janson-Forbin, convinced the abbé of Grasse to relinquish his priory on behalf of a member of Colbert's family, at the minister's request, in exchange for its monetary equivalent during his lifetime.[97]

Régusse, in contrast, had a well-earned reputation as a jurist, but he had less personal charm than did Oppède and lacked a reputation for generosity. Régusse had earned a doctorate in law at the University of Avignon, and his judicial learning was widely respected in the parlement.[98] Oppède described him as "knowledgeable in judicial affairs" in a secret memorandum written for Colbert.[99] But Régusse's judicial learning was not likely to attract the support of the Provençal nobility, and he does not seem to have been a particularly charming man. The daughter of Madame de Sévigné described Régusse in 1680, a few years before his death, as "a dribbler with a dirty beard" (*une barbe sale et un vieux fleuve*).[100] His memoirs have a dry, bookish quality about them. Oppède, on the other hand, had received a good education but was not known for his legal learning; he was known for his fighting ability. Oppède had been tutored as a child by Abraham Remy, a young poet who later became a professor of rhetoric at the Collège de France.[101] He may have attended the Collège de Navarre in Paris, and he received a doctorate in law from the University of Aix. But the university did not have a first-class reputation, and Oppède had only one law book in his library at his death.[102] His contemporaries never mentioned his ability as a jurist.

Régusse had many friends and supporters within the Parlement and city of Aix. Both intendant Sève and Governor Mercoeur attested to this.[103] So did President Coriolis.[104] Régusse himself mentioned it in his memoirs.[105] Well-liked and respected among the robe nobility at Aix, Régusse had fewer clients and less influence outside the city walls. His sister, Jeanne, had married Jean-Antoine de Glandèves, vicomte de Pourrières, from an old noble family of

Marseille, and Régusse considered it a social coup when he married his oldest daughter, Françoise, into the family of Grimaldi-Antibes in 1645.[106] Although his family name was originally Grimaud, Régusse used the name of Grimaldi and claimed, falsely, to be a collateral branch of the old feudal family of Grimaldi-Monaco; he was delighted when the prince of Monaco stayed with him on a visit to Marseille.[107] His oldest son, Gaspard, had married Charlotte de Castillon from an old noble family of Arles, a good marriage but not as illustrious as that of his oldest daughter.[108] Sextius d'Escalis de Sabran, baron de Bras, several times first consul of Aix and a member of an old feudal family of the Comtat Venaissin, was Régusse's friend.[109] But this seems to have been the extent of his connections with the Provençal sword nobility. In general, Régusse did not have the rank or family to attract the kind of support that Oppède enjoyed among the provincial nobility through his kinship with the Forbins. Régusse's clientele was smaller than Oppède's and confined to the Parlement and city of Aix-en-Provence.

The Forbin family was the heart of Oppède's clientele in Basse-Provence. During the Fronde Oppède was described as a chief of the Sabreurs, "who included Forbin de La Roque, Forbin de La Barben, and almost all the Forbins in Provence."[110] Kinship with the prolific Forbins gave Oppède an extensive, ready-made noble clientele in Provence, while the Mayniers d'Oppède, who had held office in the parlement for over a century, allied him to the major robe families at Aix and to noble families in the Comtat Venaissin where their barony was located. When Oppède became first president of the parlement and acting intendant, his power attracted a large administrative clientele.

In the final analysis, political power is the ability to compel obedience to commands or decisions.[111] The key idea in this definition is the ability to use physical force if necessary to obtain compliance. Oppède had political power in Provence because he could command local military support. His extensive lands provided him with fighting men on a number of occasions. For instance, he levied troops in the Comtat Venaissin in 1648 to aid the rebel parlementaires.[112] He brought armed clients into Aix during the revolt of January 1649 and recruited fighting men again in the spring and summer of the same year.[113] In the autumn of 1651, he brought men to join the Sabreurs from his estates at La Fare and Vitrolles near Aix.[114] When Governor Mercoeur called upon the provincial militia to rescue Oppède from imprisonment by the rebels at Aix in February 1659, his clients responded enthusiastically. The towns where his family had lands—Janson, Oppède, Cavaillon, and Apt—sent militia, while cavalry contingents were recruited and led by his uncle, the seigneur de La Verdière, his brother-in-law, the baron de Bormes, and his cousin, the marquis de Janson.[115]

Oppède also had ties to other clients of Mazarin in Provence who acted as subpatrons in helping him obtain the Cardinal's favor. For example, through his maternal uncle, Castellane de La Verdière, Oppède was a kinsman of Jean de Pontevès, comte de Carcès and lieutenant general of Provence, a neighbor in the Comtat Venaissin and a good friend.[116] Both La Verdière and Carcès were older, childless men with whom Oppède seems to have had a father-son relationship. Carcès was also a neighbor of Cardinal Bichi, whose bishopric of Carpentras was near Oppède's barony in the Comtat Venaissin, and Oppède was friendly with Bichi, Mazarin's old friend.[117] The bailli de Forbin, commander of the royal galleys, was Oppède's cousin and Mazarin's client. The bailli praised Oppède in his letters to Mazarin.[118] In a letter to the Cardinal on October 10, 1656, Oppède noted that the archbishop of Arles, another of Mazarin's clients, was "a close relative and a good friend." The archbishop was also a kinsman and friend of Carcès.[119] Oppède had kinship and friendship ties with several members of the small circle of Mazarin's clients in Provence, and they acted as subpatrons for him in soliciting the Cardinal's favor.

Oppède had extensive crédit in Provence because he had a good personal reputation, old nobility and title, alliances with the Provençal sword nobility, a family tradition of parlement officeholding as first president, and old landed wealth. Régusse had less crédit because he had wealth with a commercial and financial taint, newly purchased fiefs, new noble rank and title, alliances with Marseille merchant families, recent parlement officeholding, and a judicial clientele. His influence was limited to the provincial capital and its sovereign courts, and he did not have Oppède's noble ties or his influence in the General Assemblies. Régusse's resources, however, made him a regional power figure, if not one of the same stature as Oppède.

Brokers such as Oppède and Régusse eagerly sought royal patronage as a reward for their services: they were motivated by private interest, which they were frank in avowing, and they were unabashedly self-interested, in contrast to other clients who often veiled their motives behind a cloud of rhetoric.[120] For example, Régusse's younger son, Sauveur, received a priory in Normandy from Mazarin, later exchanged for a priory in the Dauphiné; he eventually joined the Aix cathedral chapter.[121] Oppède secured the appointment of his younger brother, Louis, as bishop of Toulon in 1663.[122] He had previously secured a priory and an abbey for him.[123] Régusse's oldest son, Gaspard, became a lieutenant in the senechal court at Brignoles in 1651, and two years later was provided to his father's office of president in the parlement, although he did not obtain its exercise for another thirty years.[124] Oppède bought his oldest son, Jean-Baptiste, an office of president in the parlement and obtained for him letters of dispensation for age.[125] His two brothers received commissions to levy cavalry companies in 1657 and 1659.[126] Forbin de La Roque's son also received a commission to levy a cavalry company as a reward for his father's support of Oppède.[127] Régusse's younger son, Pierre, later baron de Moissac, became captain of an infantry regiment in 1652 and captain of a light horse company in 1657.[128] Oppède secured the appointment of his cousin's brother, the chevalier de Janson, as a galley captain in 1666.[129] One of Oppède's brothers, a Knight of Malta, was made a galley captain at the same time.[130]

Brokers became conduits or channels for distributing royal patronage in the provinces. Although brokers did not control the flow of patronage, they appeared to do so in the province, and they played the functionally equivalent role of a patron in its distribution.[131] They took their commissions for brokering from this flow—they diverted it for their own use. Oppède and Régusse as broker-clients of Mazarin received royal patronage for their services, which they distributed as patron-brokers among their family, friends, and clients: they acted as clients of patrons who rewarded their services with patronage, and as patrons to clients among whom they distributed patronage.[132]

Brokers not only secured material benefits for their clients, they also connected them to the outside world and interceded for them when regular channels proved inadequate. For example, Oppède in 1661 wrote to Chancellor Séguier asking him to intervene on behalf of his first cousin, Thomasin d'Ainac, who was involved in a lawsuit.[133] He later asked for a conciliar decree in favor of another cousin who was engaged in a lawsuit against a Provençal community.[134] Oppède asked Colbert to see that Forbin de La Roque's pension was paid in 1663, since it was badly in arrears.[135] He made the same request two years later for his friend and client, Reynaud de Séguiran.[136] He also asked that his clients Guidy and Laurens be rewarded "for their faithful service to the King."[137] Mazarin arranged to have the venue of a client's trial changed.[138] Governor Alais asked a friend at court for introductions for several of his Provençal clients in the 1640s.[139] Oppède asked the same favor of chancellor Séguier in the 1660s.[140]

Oppède saved the political career of his client, Jacques de Laurens, sieur de Vaugrenier, who had fought as a Sabreur under his leadership during the Fronde and who was the brother of Pierre de Laurens, a councillor in the Parlement of Aix and a client of Oppède.[141] Laurens de Vaugrenier had built an extensive clientele at Draguignan to control the municipal government. In June 1659, he survived a popular protest against his regime with Oppède's help. Governor Mercoeur sent 200 troops to his rescue, while Oppède dispatched an investigatory committee of the parlement headed by a client, Forbin de La Roque, accompanied by the prévôt des maréchaux, Antoine de Laurens. The prévôt was head of the provincial mounted police and Vaugrenier's nephew; Oppède later praised his "loyal service" in a letter to chancellor Séguier.[142] The committee indicted those rebels who had not fled at the news of the troops' coming, and Vaugrenier remained in control of Draguignan. (He was mysteriously murdered in September 1659, and his killer was never found.)[143] Oppède defended Vaugrenier and his regime to Mazarin in a letter on October 28, 1659.[144] As a provincial broker, Oppède had provided his client Laurens de Vaugrenier with timely military assistance to keep him in power.

Brokers interceded for clients and mustered influence and resources on their behalf. They opened doors for them, secured offices for them, and provided patronage allowing them to build their own clienteles—creating a large client network was the first step in obtaining political power. Membership in a clientele was necessary for political advancement, and clientele hopping was essential to political preferment.[145] For example, Dominique Guidy, a trésorier général, was Oppède's client.[146] In 1670, he obtained an office of councillor in the Parlement of Aix, undoubtedly with Oppède's help.[147] However, Oppède refused to help those who were not his clients or friends and even obstructed their paths. For instance, he advised Colbert to deny the request of the abbé Du Chaine for an office of clerical councillor in the parlement.[148] The abbé was vicar general of the archbishop of Aix, who was Oppède's political enemy, and Oppède insisted that "a well-earned refusal such as this would serve as an important example."[149] Du Chaine did not receive the office. Oppède also defeated the enemies of his cousin, Laurent de Forbin, marquis de Janson.

The marquis de Janson was governor of Antibes.[150] He claimed in addition the government of Grasse, a claim he was able to support because of his ties to Oppède. When he announced his intention to make a formal entry into the city in December 1662 as its new governor, the consuls of Grasse refused to recognize him and appealed for help to the presiding judge of the seneschal court, Lombard de Gourdon, whose family was influential in the Draguignan-Grasse area.[151] A riot occurred when the marquis rode into the city, and shouts of "Down with Janson," "Long live Gourdon," could be heard on all sides. Janson was accompanied by a large entourage of family and friends from prominent Provençal noble families—he had the military power to enforce his claim. The outcome was inevitable. Despite their hostility, the consuls and citizens of Grasse were forced to accept the marquis as their new governor.[152] They had nowhere to turn for help to expel him. Oppède controlled the parlement, and he refused to send an investigatory committee to Grasse. Nor would he intercede for them at court where the marquis de Janson had influence.[153] Governor Mercoeur, Oppède's old friend and ally, refused to send troops to aid the consuls of Grasse or to intervene on their behalf. Regular channels of help were closed to them, and they did not have access to a broker who had the influence to counter Oppède. They were forced to accept his client as their governor.

It might be useful at this point to distinguish between go-betweens and brokers. Go-betweens performed functions similar to, if not exactly the same as, those of brokers. The essential difference between go-betweens and brokers is that brokers had independent resources of their own which they could add to the negotiations, affecting their outcome, while go-betweens did not—they acted as envoys or liaisons.[154] For instance, in January 1650, Mazarin summoned Ours-François Miron to an audience. Miron had been a councillor in the Parlement of Rouen since 1646, but he had lived permanently in Paris for two years. In the spring of 1649, he had acted as the representative of the Rouen court to the Parlement of Paris and as the liaison or go-between for the two courts in signing the Treaty of Rueil with the crown. This was probably why Mazarin thought of him. Mazarin asked Miron to write the court at Rouen to assure them that the arrest of the princes would in no way affect royal declarations of the previous two years suppressing the Semester at Rouen. Miron acted as an envoy, carrying letters back and forth from Paris to Rouen, but he did not himself act as a participant in the negotiations.[155] Another example is Jean-Henri de Grimaldi, seigneur of Corbons and Cagnes, who acted as an intermediary between the prince de Monaco (Morgues in the seventeenth century), Honoré II de Grimaldi, to whom he was distantly related, and Cardinal Richelieu in negotiating the terms of a proposed alliance between Monaco and France. Corbons shuttled back and forth between Monaco, Cagnes, and Paris, but he personally contributed nothing substantive to the negotiations: he was an intermediary or go-between, not a broker.[156]

The essential difference between brokers and lobbyists was that lobbyists tried to influence decision making from the outside, to argue and persuade in order to have decisions made in favor of their own interests. They were not mediating or negotiating an exchange as brokers were. President Alexandre Bigot de Monville of the Parlement of Rouen noted in his memoirs that he and a colleague, kinsman, and friend, president Bretel de Grémonville, made a number of trips to Paris in the years from 1640 to 1643. These trips were lobbying missions: they were members of parlement delegations requesting the revocation of the new Semester doubling the court's membership and the return to office of the interdicted parlementaires who had protested the Semester. They had one hundred interviews on these trips. They saw the comte de Guiche, governor of Rouen, twenty two times, asking him to intervene for them and arrange an interview with Richelieu. They saw the duc de Longueville, governor of Normandy, twenty five times for the same purpose. They saw chancellor Séguier twenty three times, the prince de Condé four times, the duc d'Orléans four times, Richelieu twice, Mazarin three times, the secretaries of state and surintendents of finance Sublet de Noyers, La Vrillière Bouthillier, Bouthillier de Chavigny, Bailleul, Potier de Novion twenty one times, and assorted masters of requests and intendants six times.[157]

The rudeness of highly placed officials during lobbying interviews was notorious, an expression of the patron-client ritual of dominance and submission. For instance, when the Rouen parlementaires went to see Chancellor Séguier, they had just begun their presentation when he replied loudly that he could tell them nothing other than what he had already told them: they should ask favors from the king. Séguier said that he had heard nothing more about their affairs and walked out and down the staircase with the delegation trailing along behind. He never looked back. They went back to their lodgings.[158] When they went to see Secretary of State Sublet de Noyers, they did not even have the opportunity to speak. Noyers said, "Messieurs, seeing you here I understand well what you want without you telling me. I am your servant, as I am to all men, and will do what I can for your happiness." With that, he walked through the room, out the door, and down the staircase. Following him, they found themselves in the street.[159]

In mid-November 1640, the comte de Guiche arranged an audience for them with Richelieu after mass. They were apprehensive because Richelieu had a reputation for rudeness. A delegation of three presidents and five councillors followed Guiche into the Cardinal's bedroom past armed guards. Richelieu was standing beside the bed and Bouthillier, surintendent of finance, the bishop of Chartres, and several others were in the room. Richelieu said to Guiche when they entered, "And why, Monsieur, did you tell me to see two or three judges from the Parlement of Rouen when you have brought the whole court, which is late?" Guiche made some excuse, and Richelieu said to the parlementaires, "You should not have come in such numbers. I intended to say something good, and you have obliged me to say something bad." First President Faucon de Ris explained that their number was the result of a chance meeting in the street, and Richelieu sarcastically replied that chance was also responsible for his anger. And when he began to speak, Richelieu interrupted him impatiently to say, "Messieurs, I can only hear from you a few particulars. I cannot receive you because you are in the King's bad graces for what you have done. At present I believe that patience is the best course. I will speak to the King on your behalf, and do what I can for your satisfaction." With that Richelieu walked toward the door to indicate the interview had ended. Guiche introduced the members of the delegation one by one, and they left. Guiche considered it a successful interview.[160] Evidently Richelieu was capable of far worse.

Presidents Criqueville and Bigot de Monville, deputies from the Parlement of Rouen, were admitted to see Cardinal Mazarin at about seven o'clock on the morning of May 7, 1643. Mazarin took the initiative, announcing that their affairs were going badly and that they had misused their time in harassing the new Semester judges. President de Criqueville replied that their cause was just, and requested the support of the Cardinal's authority. Mazarin replied that he would do what he could for them but that he was of the opinion they owed the new judges full recognition, as he had told them the preceding week. These words concluded the interview.[161] Mazarin was more polite than some of his colleagues.

The process of lobbying was fraught with pitfalls. There was the distance between the national capital and the provinces, making it necessary to take lodgings in Paris, sometimes for months on end, especially when the personages they wanted to see had left Paris for a while. There were long waits in antechambers—lobbying was particularly difficult for those whose inferior status made it hard for them to gain entrance to the proper drawing rooms. There was the public humiliation of the interviews themselves, the rudeness of high officials, the care with which precedence and protocol had to be observed, the strain of making a presentation to a bored and indifferent audience. In general, provincial brokers had more influence, prestige, and political clout than either lobbyists or go-betweens. Provincial brokers had power in their own right, while lobbyists and go-betweens were the agents of others.[162]

To increase their access to privilege and power, brokers sometimes acquired more than one patron, but multiple patrons meant multiple loyalties that could create conflict. This did not happen in the case of Oppède, who was simultaneously the client of Mercoeur and Mazarin, because Mercoeur was also the client of Mazarin. Oppède became the Cardinal's subclient until he established his own relationship; in fact, Mercoeur helped him to secure the Cardinal's patronage. Oppède had similar relationships with Cardinal Bichi, the bailli de Forbin, and the comte de Carces.[163] Multiple loyalties did create conflict, however, in other cases—for instance, that of the comte de Mérinville, Mazarin's créature, who hurriedly sought a new court patron at the Cardinal's death. Mérinville wrote Colbert that "Le Tellier has honored me with his protection . . . and I hope that You will continue with Yours."[164] Colbert obligingly accepted Mérinville into his service, and Mérinville assured the minister that "You can count on me as a person You have absolutely acquired."[165] However, Parades de L'Estang noted that Mérinville's strongest supporter at court remained Le Tellier, probably the result of his long army career.[166] Colbert and Le Tellier had drawn apart by 1663, and their relationship fluctuated hot and cold for six years until it became permanently hostile. Colbert became the bitter enemy of Le Tellier's son, the marquis de Louvois, who followed his father as secretary of war.[167] Mérinville's dual allegiance to Le Tellier and Colbert had created a political conflict for him by 1665. This was probably why he did not receive more royal patronage after being named governor of Narbonne the previous year—his career came to a sudden halt at this point.[168] Neither Colbert nor Le Tellier would advance him because of his ties to the other, and he was left effectively without a court patron. The chevalier Louis-Nicolas de Clerville, Knight of Malta, fortifications expert and army engineer who had served Mazarin in the navy at Toulon, had ties to Le Tellier which had been acquired before he attached himself to Colbert at Mazarin's death. His career faltered in the mid-1660s, too.[169] The growing enmity between Colbert and Le Tellier may have caused a conflict in allegiance among their mutual clients.

Multiple patrons increased a broker's access to privilege and power, thereby increasing his ability to broker and to attract clients who needed his intercession. Clients served two patrons simultaneously to obtain more benefits, for political insurance in shaky relationships, and as part of the process of switching patrons. A problem arose only when their patrons' interests clashed and they had to choose which one to support, potentially a difficult decision. But until this happened they could discreetly maintain ties to both. Brokers did it all the time. The single-patron model, with permanent fidelity and little mobility, was not the prevalent form of patron-client relationship in early modern France. The multiple-patron model with rapid mobility, in which clients shifted from patron to patron in a search for benefits and advancement, was more common, especially for brokers.[170]

Brokers occasionally tried to secure a monopoly on the brokerage services they offered to Paris patrons, as both Oppède and Régusse did. Régusse was acting first president of the parlement in 1650, but he was forced in the next year to alternate in this position on a weekly basis with a younger colleague, Oppède, an arrangement he did not like.[171] He solved the problem by driving Oppède and his brothers from Aix in October 1651, as Sabreurs.[172] The next month he resisted an attempt by the acting governor, the marquis d'Aiguebonne, to enter Aix.[173] Régusse intended to be the only broker for the parlement and city of Aix. He controlled the city until the autumn of 1653, when Oppède's party won the municipal elections, and the parlement until the autumn of 1655, when Oppède won permanent appointment as first president and successfully challenged Régusse's monopoly. Oppède then tried to establish his own monopoly, but his efforts to discredit Régusse and expel him from Aix were unsuccessful, as we shall see.

Variability among Brokers

What happened when Oppède finally obtained the office of first president? Did victory end his rivalry with Régusse? Oppède had extensive influence in Provence because of his family connections and wealth; this was why he had been named first president of the parlement. He appeared invincible, but Régusse did not accept defeat philosophically. Expecting to be rewarded with the office of first president for his loyalty to Mazarin during the Fronde, he felt cheated and betrayed. He severed his relationship with Governor Mercoeur, and if Mazarin had not been the king's chief minister and the major source of royal patronage in Provence, he probably would have ended that relationship, too. As it was the relationship never recovered: Régusse indicated in his memoirs that several effusive letters of gratitude and offices for his sons were inadequate compensation for his services to the Cardinal during the Fronde.[174]

Régusse cast around for another patron with influence at court and approached the new archbishop of Aix, Jerôme de Grimaldi, a friend and client of Mazarin.[175] Régusse and the archbishop may have been drawn together by a mutual dislike of Oppède, who as first president had recently triumphed over the archbishop in an administrative dispute.[176] Régusse told Governor Mercoeur that Oppède did not have the influence in Provence he claimed to have, and decided to prove his statement, hoping that if he could discredit Oppède and cause his dismissal he might get the office he had wanted for so long.[177] As a result Régusse and Grimaldi encouraged Provençal opposition to a military tax that Oppède was trying to levy as acting intendant in the winter of 1658.[178]

Oppède had conducted a slander campaign against Régusse for several years, making certain that his rival's obstructionism, suitably exaggerated and distorted, reached Mazarin's ears at Paris. In weekly letters Oppède complained about his rival's uncooperative behavior. For instance, in a letter to Mazarin in August 1656, he wrote that Régusse had encouraged political protest at Draguignan, where he had gone as the presiding judge of a parlement investigatory tribunal.[179] The target of the riot had been Oppède's client, Laurens de Vaugrenier.[180] In a letter on August 15, Oppède criticized his rival's conduct of a criminal case and denounced him for encouraging intrigue within the court.[181] In January 1658, Oppède accused Régusse of contributing to the parlement's internal strife, while Mercoeur complained that he was conspiring with their political enemies inside and outside the court.[182] The political unreliability of Régusse was a constant theme of their letters.

A popular protest against the new military tax exploded at Aix on February 25, 1658.[183] Oppède and Mercoeur blamed Régusse for helping to provoke this protest. In a letter two days later Mercoeur accused Régusse of helping to incite the riot, and asked for a *lettre de cachet* exiling him from the city.[184] In a letter on March 12, Oppède accused Régusse of complicity in the riot and asked for a lettre de cachet exiling him from Aix on March 19, as "the soul of all these cabals and the advice which guides them."[185] In the memoir and *procès-verbal* which the parlement sent on the riot, Régusse was condemned for not appearing at the palace of justice with the other presidents until the crowds had dispersed, implying that he had been elsewhere in the city inciting the rioters.[186] But no evidence of this was ever sent to Paris. Nonetheless, Régusse received two lettres de cachet and was sent into internal exile at Issoudun in Berry for a year at Oppède's request.[187] Mazarin wrote Régusse that "I am astonished you express surprise at the order you have received sending you to Issoudun, since not only did the King have reasons to send you there, but I can truthfully say that He has shown too much patience with your conduct. You have been pursuing your particular interests to the extent of making the King's interests suffer."[188] Archbishop Grimaldi was threatened with a lettre de cachet, and told not to be in Aix when Mazarin visited in 1660. Grimaldi was sent to Rome as an extraordinary ambassador and did not return to Aix until after Mazarin's death.[189]

After a year in Berry, Régusse began his homeward journey.[190] As soon as Oppède heard the news, he asked Mazarin to send him back into exile as a troublemaker.[191] Régusse went straight home to La Ciotat and did not return to Aix for months. However, before the parlement had even convened for its autumn session, Oppède was again writing Mazarin that Régusse was causing trouble.[192] After the court's opening session, Mercoeur wrote Mazarin that Régusse was refusing to help control the parlement—he had removed himself from controversial discussions but was allowing his friends and supporters to argue.[193] Oppède wrote that Régusse should be forced to sell his office to his son, who was too incompetent to cause further trouble in the parlement.[194] Oppède was still fulminating against Régusse four years later, when he wrote Colbert that he had done everything possible to encourage Régusse's loyalty and cooperation, without success.[195] In fact, Régusse seems to have kept a low profile after he returned from exile. He may have been quietly uncooperative, but a year in exile had made him too cautious to be openly hostile.

Régusse had written to Mazarin from Issoudun on February 20, 1659, "I am a faithful servant languishing in the bad graces of my master. I ask to be restored to the favor of Your Eminence."[196] His request was ignored. Although Mazarin felt enough gratitude for Régusse's services during the

Fronde to allow him to continue in his office of parlement president, Régusse did not receive more patronage. Through rotation he became second president of the parlement in 1664, and acting first president for nearly three years after Oppède's death in 1671, but he was never permanently appointed to the office that had been the ruling ambition of his life.[197] However, Régusse's crédit within the parlement and city of Aix was not destroyed by the loss of Mazarin's favor, as the events of 1661 demonstrate.

It was well known in Provence that Oppède was not a client of Colbert, and it was presumed that his influence would end with Mazarin's death.[198] The Cardinal died on March 9, 1661, three days after a General Assembly of Provençal Communities had convened at Lambesc, where Oppède as the royal representative was asking for 600,000 livres to support royal troops in Provence. Taking advantage of the confusion created by the news of the Cardinal's death, the deputies voted a derisory 50,000 livres, which they later reluctantly increased to 150,000 livres. They called for a meeting of the defunct Provençal Estates.[199] Oppède knew that to survive politically he had to prove to Colbert that he could control the General Assemblies, so he hurried to Paris as soon as the disastrous Lambesc assembly had closed. He managed to convince Colbert that he was not responsible for their failure to cooperate, blaming their actions on the effect produced by the news of Mazarin's death.[200] He was given another chance when a second assembly was convened at Saint Rémy in August.

Two months before the assembly was to meet, army intendant Louis Machault arrived at Saint Rémy with four companies of infantry and three of cavalry, which were billeted on the town as a warning of the penalty for disobedience. In addition, Oppède saw each of the deputies in private conferences before the assembly met, and it is not surprising that the deputies voted what he wanted when the assembly finally convened.[201] The Saint Rémy assembly was a personal victory for Oppède, confirming his skill as a broker, and he was accepted into Colbert's service as a reward. The first president retained his reputation for managing difficult provincial assemblies until his death: Colbert wrote to Oppède on September 25, 1671, that "His Majesty strongly desires that you persuade the assembly of communities to finish all its business in a month."[202] Oppède died in November at the age of fifty one, while representing the crown at the General Assembly at Lambesc.

Régusse, on the other hand, saw Mazarin's death as an opportunity to demonstrate his own influence within the parlement. He intended to impress Colbert and cast doubt upon Oppède's crédit. Régusse was acting first president while Oppède was away at Lambesc.[203] Under his leadership, the parlement attacked one of Oppède's clients, President Coriolis, who had recently brawled inside the palace of justice with Councillor Du Périer to the scandal of the other judges—violence was prohibited in the courts, and no one was even allowed to wear a sword. Through Oppède's influence, Du Périer was blamed for the incident and summoned to Paris. But Régusse assembled the parlement to discuss the incident, and the court voted to suspend Coriolis instead, sent a remonstrance to Paris on Du Périer's citation, and ordered Du Périer to exercise his office until the issue was settled.[204] The court's decision contradicted a royal order and challenged Oppède's power. It also indicated that Régusse had considerable influence in the parlement, even in 1661.

Since Oppède was already in Paris to explain the failure of the Lambesc assembly, Régusse hurried north to explain the parlement's actions. He wrote in his memoirs that he saw Colbert, Le Tellier, and the comte de Brienne, secretary of state for Provence, as well as Hyacinthe Serroni, Mazarin's old friend.[205] But he was unsuccessful in obtaining a new court patron: Oppéde retained Colbert's favor because he had already discredited Régusse, who was sent into internal exile at Abbeville in Picardy as punishment for disobeying a royal order. Both Coriolis and Du Périer were suspended from office.[206]

Oppède recognized the importance of reputation in a society dominated by patron-client ties, and for this reason he was able to outmaneuver and defeat Régusse. A man's reputation preceded him from clientele to clientele and from province to court, and a man with a reputation for untrustworthiness had difficulty attracting patrons or clients. Rumors or allegations tarnishing a broker's image and diminishing his crédit were a serious political threat because reputation was an all-important resource that could be destroyed by slander. Régusse lost Mazarin's patronage because his reputation had been destroyed by Oppède's innuendos and allegations, and this ended his career as a provincial broker. He retained his crédit at Aix, however, as well as his office in the parlement, and outlived Oppède by some fourteen years: Régusse was always there in the background as second president, and after Oppède's death he served as acting first president for nearly four years. Oppède was not successful in establishing a monopoly on brokering—brokers usually sought exclusivity unsuccessfully because they had too many rivals. The loss of crédit either at home or at Paris meant the end of a career as a provincial broker, but the loss of crédit at Paris did not necessarily destroy a local reputation or cause the end of a provincial political career, as the case of Régusse demonstrates.

Oppède and Régusse provided their Paris patrons with a wide variety of brokerage services.[207] For example, Oppède obtained the parlement's registration of royal letters naming Mazarin abbot of Saint Victor at Marseille in 1656, and a year later he wrote Mazarin that he had handled an administrative matter concerning the tax farm of Saint Victor, suggesting ways to increase its revenues.[208] On Mazarin's orders, Oppède mediated a quarrel between the sieurs Gravier and de Ternes, naval intendants at Toulon. He investigated charges that Gravier was guilty of graft and used his position illegally to make money, and reprimanded Ternes for a violent temper.[209] Régusse, on the other hand, tried to negotiate a peace settlement between the rebel parlementaires of Aix and the angry governor in 1649, and served as Mazarin's representative at the General Assembly at Manosque in 1653.[210]

The nature of a broker's commission varied, too. For instance, Mazarin permitted Oppède to build twenty shops in the courtyard of the palace of justice in Aix and to lease them for his own profit.[211] Oppède wrote to Colbert in December 1666, asking for a decree of the royal council to straighten out the tax classification of his estate at La Fare, an exemption worth 200,000 livres to him.[212] In March 1668, Oppède thanked Colbert for exchanging his salt marsh at Berre for a fief with a château and house at Peyrolles.[213] Oppède requested, but did not receive, a lucrative monopoly on the production of soap in Provence.[214] He also unsuccessfully requested that he become the Spanish consul at Marseille, a post that would have brought him 1,500 to 1,800 livres annually.[215] In contrast, Régusse was never offered personal financial opportunities by Mazarin as a reward for his services. Oppède and Régusse showed marked differences in the nature of their crédit, the scope of their brokering services, the extent of their influence at Paris, the extent of their monopoly over brokering, and the nature of their commissions. Their differences demonstrate the variability among brokers, which was as great as that among clients.[216]

Oppède and Régusse were motivated partly by self-interest in their relationship with Mazarin, but they also acted from political conviction. It is clear from their letters that they sincerely tried to defend traditional provincial privileges, and to serve the king and his ministers loyally as the national government of France, although these were potentially conflicting aims. Their defence of traditional privilege, however, was distorted by their self-interest, which often coincided with the crown's interests. For example, Oppède and Régusse had been identified as leaders of the 1649 parlementaire revolt at Aix. The rebels' goals included the monarchy's recognition of traditional privileges. Régusse needed to reconcile his support for the revolt with his client loyalty to the archbishop of Aix, Mazarin's brother, and his desire to obtain Mazarin's patronage. He did so by attacking the governor and the intendant, especially the governor who had joined the party of Mazarin's enemies at court. Régusse and the rebel parlementaires made these two men political scapegoats and demanded their recall—their primary responsibility for the royal attack on traditional privilege was a polite fiction, of course, and a face-saving device that gave Mazarin and the king an opportunity to mend their ways, while simultaneously allowing Régusse to reconcile his political principles and his self-interest. Régusse also used his role as an adviser to Mazarin on Provençal affairs to reconcile his defense of traditional privilege with his oath as a royal judge to serve the king and his ambition to secure the chief minister's patronage—he told himself that he could simultaneously defend traditional privilege, serve the king, and promote his own interests by wisely advising Mazarin in his letters to Paris.[217]

In explaining his switch to Mazarin's support during the Fronde, Oppède declared that he was following a century-old family tradition of royal service in seeking to become first president of the parlement (he told Mazarin this) and that in loyally serving Mazarin and the king, he could gain crédit at court which he would then use on behalf of the province, as he told the General Assemblies of Provençal Communities on several occasions.[218] Oppède had the same problem as Régusse of having to reconcile his earlier support for the rebel parlementaires, and in Oppède's case the Sabreurs, too, with his solicitation of Mazarin's patronage. Both Oppède and Régusse identified provincial interests with their own interests in order to satisfy the chief minister and secure his patronage, for example, by demanding the approval of the General Assemblies for royal tax requests so that the institution would not be suppressed, or the end of resistance to Mazarin's government during the Fronde so that peace would be restored to Provence. In this way their patronage loyalties and interests became compatible with their political convictions.

Brokers such as Oppède and Régusse, who were separated from their patrons in the Paris government by hundreds of miles, discovered that distance created special problems. It made attracting a Paris patron difficult, and it made maintaining the attachment even more difficult: infrequent visits diminished the emotional intensity of long-distance relationships. Lacking daily contact with a patron and natural opportunities to cultivate "an affectionate friendship," provincial brokers found their relationships were less emotional and personal, more pragmatic and utilitarian. Service became all-important in long-distance relationships: service was loyalty made concrete, the long-distance expression of devotion, and distance increased the importance of performance as the concrete evidence of allegiance. What counted was a client's performance on paper—a provincial broker had to project an image of useful political service in his letters to Paris and in the letters of his contemporaries. A successful broker was skilled at masking his defects and presenting an image of competence and reliability on paper, whatever the reality of his performance. He embellished his exploits, solicited testimonials from his friends, distorted the truth if necessary, and destroyed or silenced his enemies. Regular trips to Paris, generosity in lending money, flattery, willingness to do personal favors, gift-giving, and political entertaining were important to long-distance brokers because they helped to create a warmer, more affectionate relationship with an understanding patron.

Oppède realized this. He was more generous with his money and his time than Régusse, and he went to Paris more often. He was adept at creating a good image of himself in letters: Oppède wrote Mazarin and Colbert long, articulate letters on Provençal affairs in a graceful, flowing script once a week until 1664, when his secretary began writing for him. His letters have a regularity, a clarity, and a concern for detail sadly lacking in the disordered, chaotic, and badly written letters of his predecessors.[219] Oppède was lavish with self-praise. He wrote Mazarin in 1658, that Provence had been well rid of the Estates for twenty years and added, "I dare to say without vanity that the Estates would be my forte and that I would dispose of all sentiment in regulating the power of the assemblies."[220] And he solicited favorable testimonials from friends. Mercoeur in a letter to Colbert requested the bishopric of Toulon for Oppède's brother, noting that "the service of the one and the virtue of the other merit this consideration . . . no other family has as much honor in this province."[221] Intendant Arnoul frequently praised Oppède's performance in his letters to Colbert, beginning a letter in 1667 with the remark that "anything the first president begins is a thing done."[222]

Oppède sometimes deliberately misinformed Mazarin to further his own interests. On June 4, 1658, he wrote that he had overcome all obstacles in the way of enforcing a May 30th ordinance as acting governor. In fact, the ordinance was never enforced because it had been prohibited by the sovereign courts on May 31 and June 1 as Oppède well knew: he was trying to maintain his image of administrative efficiency. Mazarin annulled this ordinance two days after the outbreak of the 1659 revolt at Aix.[223] Oppède wrote Mazarin on March 5, 1659, that the governor had assembled three thousand infantry and five hundred cavalry to march on Aix to rescue him from the rebels, although Mercoeur himself had written on February 27 that he had assembled half that number, one thousand infantry and two hundred cavalry.[224] Oppède was probably trying to protect his reputation by inflating the numbers of Provençaux willing to come to his rescue. He was even willing to prevaricate a little to save his reputation. On August 12, 1648, he assured Mazarin that reports of his recruiting troops in the Comtat Venaissin to aid the rebellious parlementaires at Aix were untrue, based on rumors and false testimony, despite the fact that intendant Sève had sent nine eyewitness reports to Paris.[225]

Régusse wrote regularly to Mazarin from 1650 through 1655, and his letters are well written, articulate, and informative. But he seldom wrote after 1655, and he did not try to counter Oppède's influence. He did not use his letters to discredit his rivals, and he was not as adept at marketing himself as Oppède was; for example, he did not solicit testimonials from friends or embellish his exploits.[226]

The royal visit to Provence in the winter of 1660 underlined the fact that Oppède had more crédit at court than did his rival. The king, his mother, and Cardinal Mazarin arrived at Aix in January and stayed several weeks, a rare visit—there were only three such official visits in the seventeenth century. The Queen Mother took up residence in the archbishop's palace where royal troops exercised every morning in the courtyard. A wooden gallery was built across the street to the hôtels on the other side where Louis XIV and his entourage lodged in Régusse's mansion and adjacent houses, and Cardinal Mazarin stayed a few doors up the street at the hôtel Oppède. The parlement greeted the king and his mother in full judicial regalia a few days after they arrived, and Oppède insisted that the entire company also visit the Cardinal as a mark of honor: Mazarin received the parlementaires in bed, in his nightclothes, with the surprised comment, "There certainly are a lot of you." Evidently he had been expecting a deputation, which had been the original plan.[227]

Régusse tried repeatedly to obtain an interview with Mazarin alone during his visit to Aix. He went to the Cardinal's hôtel several days in a row but was able to see only his secretary, Monsieur Rose. Finally, after the Cardinal returned from a brief visit to Toulon, Régusse was admitted to see him at four o'clock in the afternoon and spent two agreeable hours in conversation according to his memoirs. Régusse complained about the conduct of his rival, Oppède, in whose house he was sitting, and the Cardinal was conciliatory but noncommittal.[228] A few days later Régusse had to sit two seats down from Oppède in the choir of the cathedral of Saint Sauveur for the *Te Deum* mass to celebrate the announcement of the Spanish peace, a public admission that he had lost to a younger rival the office he had coveted for so long. Living two doors apart intensified their hostility, and their wives quarreled in public, the sure sign of an irreparable breach.[229] Régusse had lost to a younger rival who had more influence in Provence, a larger clientele he was willing to use in the Cardinal's service, and better brokerage skills.

CHAPTER THREE

Clienteles

An excellent natural harbor, long and narrow, stretches into the heart of the port of Marseille, its entrance guarded by the island fortress-prison of the Château d'If. Visitors Thomas Platter in 1596, Jean-Jacques Bouchard in 1630, and Charles de Brosses in 1739 found the harbor fascinating with its multitude of ships at anchor: lateen-rigged royal galleys with twenty-five oars on a side; Italian feluccas and Spanish tartanes, long-oared and lateen-rigged for coastal trading; double-masted brigantines with great, square sails; caïques, oared Mediterranean fishing boats without sails; lateen-rigged, single-sail boats; and a flock of nondescript merchant vessels. Exotic goods were sold directly from the ships—coral, pearls, African animals, Arabian horses, spices, silks, drugs, and tropical fruit. The streets of Marseille teemed with men of many nationalities.[1]

When Henri de Séguiran inspected the ports, commerce, and fortifications along the Provençal coast for Cardinal Richelieu, he reported that Marseille traded with the coastal cities of Italy and Spain, the Barbary coast cities of North Africa, and the Levant cities of Alexandria, Acre, and Constantinople. The warehouses were filled with bolts of woolen, linen, and cotton cloth, Cordovan and Moroccan leather, rugs, spices, dyes, and tobacco. The quais of earthen bricks, with ships under construction in dry docks on the sides, were busy at all times.[2] The old city to the west of the port was ugly and smelly. But the sun shone every day, and on the far horizon islands shimmered in a white haze on a blue sea—they were the island fortresses of Ratonneau and Pomègue, defending the roads and the approach to the harbor. This view in the distance compensated for the immediate reality: dirt, noise, and jostling crowds.

Nicolas Arnoul, the new intendant of the royal galleys, took up residence in the city in 1665 and fell in love with Marseille. He wrote to Colbert, "It is a beautiful sight to see the port of Marseille at the moment, filled with 28 galleys; it has been a long time since it has been that busy and made strangers open their eyes."[3] On another occasion he wrote, "You know that I do not overly like the Marseillais, but I love Marseille, a royal city, which merits being indulged and pampered as the one city in France capable of achieving a truly grand appearance."[4] Arnoul himself did much to improve the appearance of Marseille, adding a large new district of wealthy mansions to the east of the port, dredging and enlarging its harbor, widening the streets, and renovating the public buildings.[5] It was a labor of love.

The largest city in Provence, Marseille was the commercial and manufacturing center of the region. It was also the largest port in France and soon became the second largest city. The economic importance of Marseille made its politics significant, and much has been written on this subject.[6] The government for much of the seventeenth century was dominated by a dynasty of big-city political magnates, the Valbelles, who used a family clientele as a political machine to dominate municipal politics. The maneuverings and intrigues of the Valbelle network tell us much about how clienteles were used as political machines within, across, and outside formal political institutions to influence behavior and decision making.

There are important differences between political machines and clienteles. A machine is a way of mobilizing votes in a modern electoral system characterized by mass adult suffrage and political parties. A machine secures and holds political office for its boss by getting out the vote. It distributes rewards to those who run it, work for it, and vote for it. A machine depends on individual material rewards to maintain and extend its political control. It is held together by patronage, by what it promises to do for its supporters, and by what it actually does. It is not held together by ideology, discipline, coercion, or the charisma of its leader, although these qualities may be present. A machine is not a disciplined, ideological party, although it may operate inside or outside such a party. It is a reward network composed of reciprocal relationships that are pragmatic, opportunistic, and flexible, and its members often come from a wide variety of backgrounds.[7] A classic example is the political machines that have flourished in the big cities of the United States.[8]

Clienteles are also reward networks, but they are not used to mobilize mass electoral support. They usually operate in nonelectoral political systems lacking mass suffrage and are especially characteristic of traditional, premodern societies, although they may also be present within political parties. Their function is to achieve the career goals of their patrons, whatever these might be, not to mobilize voters. A patron's personal and political goals become the collective goals of his clientele. A machine boss is by definition the most powerful man in his political arena. The patron of a clientele is not: he can be one of many actors in his political arena. Patron-client relationships in early modern France employed the effusive rhetoric of personal affection, and were less pragmatic and utilitarian than modern machine relationships, although they became more performance-oriented as the early modern state developed. They also tended to be more solid and longer-lasting than machine relationships. A boss may have personal charm and popularity, but his relationship with machine members is pragmatic: the reality of the exchange is what counts. His power is derived from the inducements and sanctions at his disposal, not from affection, rank, or status. In contrast, emotional and social qualities played a greater role in the relationship of early modern French patrons and their clients, although the inducements and sanctions at their disposal were important, too.[9]

When a clientele was used to mobilize provincial support for a royal project or policy, it has been described here as a political machine because of the way it functioned in mobilizing support. But technically it was not a machine because it was not used to get out the vote, that is, to mobilize mass electoral support. The political clienteles of early modern France helped royal officials to govern in an age when political authority was more apparent than real. The king and his government in faraway Paris had less authority in the provinces than did provincial officials, who used their clienteles as political machines in governing. Cardinal Richelieu's network of clients in Brittany demonstrates the administrative use of clienteles as political machines.

Richelieu's interest in Brittany dated from his 1626 scheme for naval reorganization and expansion, which met provincial resistance.[10] He overcame Breton resistance by assuming the governorship himself in 1630, having decided that the best way to get his maritime proposals accepted and funded was to work through the traditional provincial institutions of the Estates and sovereign judicial courts. He used the governorship to build a clientele among provincial officials, nobles, and clergy attending the Estates, officiers of the Estates, and judges in the sovereign courts. His clients endeavoured to mobilize support for his proposals and guide them through their respective institutions, in this way acting as a political machine to help him in governing Brittany and building the royal navy; occasionally they served as royal commissioners, too. Their efforts were successful: Richelieu's ability to influence the actions of the Estates of Brittany was considerable after 1632, and he accomplished his scheme for naval reorganization.

The Cardinal entrusted the acting governorship of Brittany to a thirty-year-old cousin, Charles de La Porte, marquis de La Meilleraye, whom he named lieutenant general of the province and who served as the royal representative at the Estates. La Meilleraye's correspondence with Richelieu and Chavigny is one of the best sources of information on the assemblies; on at least one occasion he drew up a memorandum naming Bretons most disposed to serve the king and thus worthy of honors and pensions. La Meilleraye appointed his cousin governor of Nantes and replaced the city's garrison with men loyal to himself. The other lieutenant general in the province, François de Cossé, duc de Brissac, occasionally attended the Estates and La Meilleraye worked hard at influencing and controlling him. He was more inept and less reliable than La Meilleraye, but was occasionally employed by Richelieu. Henri, duc de La Trémoille, a great Breton noble, also served the Cardinal and usually sat in the Estates where he had considerable influence because of his house and name. Three other Breton nobles in the Estates whose support was important to Richelieu were the duc de Retz, governor of Belleisle and Machecoul; the comte de Vertus, governor of Rennes; and Vertus's son.

The Cardinal's clients in Brittany included another cousin, Charles du Cambout, baron de Pontchâteau, who had clients and influence among the nobility in the Estates which he used on behalf of Richelieu. The baron presided over his order in the Estates and was governor of the important port and naval base of Brest. Another cousin, the abbot of Geneston, who was Richelieu's procureur for the administration of his Breton benefices, also sat in the Estates. Richelieu's créatures in Brittany included Achille de Harlay, baron de Sancy, who became bishop of Saint Malo in 1632. He served as president of his order in the Estates, and thus as presiding officer of the assemblies on many occasions, and as their deputy to court on several occasions. Richelieu's clients among the Breton clergy included the bishops of Nantes, Rennes, and Léon, who worked with Harlay to convince the Estates to support their patron's proposals. Richelieu's clients among the officers of the Estates included the syndic, La Grée de Bruc, and his successor, Vincent de Brenugat; the herald Jean Melot; and the treasurer Michel Poullain and his son. The Cardinal's clients in the Breton sovereign courts included President Claude de Marbeuf and his son François, a councillor in the Parlement of Rennes, and First President Louis d'Harouis, sieur de La Seilleraye, of the Cour des Comptes of Nantes, who worked to secure their courts' support for the projects of their patron.

Richelieu could generously reward his Breton clients with money, offices, and pensions because he controlled the Estates' pension list, and the Estates customarily spent large sums of money in pursuing political favor. For example, the 1632 Estates granted 16,000 livres to La Meilleraye in pensions or gifts, 4,000 livres to Pontchâteau, 4,000 livres to Brissac, 2,000 livres to the comte de Vertus, 8,000 livres to Bouthillier, 2,000 livres to Richelieu's secretary, 12,000 livres to his guards, and 100,000 livres to the Cardinal himself. In 1634, the efforts of La Meilleraye, Harlay, and Marbeuf were responsible for the deputies to the Estates voting a *don gratuit* (a "voluntary" gift of tax money in addition to the taille) of 1.2 million livres. In 1636, after a long struggle, La Grée de Bruc was replaced as syndic by Brenugat; an alternate candidate was the brother of Louis d'Harouis; all were clients of the Cardinal. Brenugat's candidacy was supported by La Meilleraye, La Trémoille, the bishops of Saint Malo and Rennes, and their clients. The Estates compensated La Grée de Bruc with a gift of 12,000 livres.

Attendance of nobles at the 1636 Estates was exceptionally large because of the dispute over the choice of syndic, and La Meilleraye had more difficulty than usual in manipulating the assembly. The crown asked for a don gratuit of 3 million livres. The nobility offered 1.8 million livres, but the clergy was inclined to give only 1.2 million livres. Eventually the nobles convinced the clergy to contribute more, and they offered the crown 2 million livres, which was less than demanded. Attendance fell off at the 1638 Estates; only two of Richelieu's important clients, La Meilleraye and Brenugat, attended. The crown asked for a don gratuit of 2.5 million livres, and was voted 2 million livres without difficulty. All of Richelieu's clients attended the 1640 Estates because La Meilleraye was to present the Cardinal's request to establish seven new admiralty courts in Brittany, opposed by the Parlement of Rennes as an infringement of its jurisdiction. The Estates finally approved the courts' establishment and the Cardinal, with the help of his clients in the parlement, managed to secure registration of the appropriate legislation in the following year.[11]

In these examples, Richelieu's clients in the Estates of Brittany and the sovereign judicial courts acted together under his leadership to mobilize provincial support for his projects and goals, for example, the approval of large dons gratuits to be spent on naval improvements and the establishment of new admiralty courts. The Cardinal's clients functioned as a political machine in helping him to manipulate provincial institutions and to govern. The Cardinal's clients in Brittany were a disparate body of people whose common link was their client relationship to him as their patron. They included provincial lieutenants general, nobles, town governors, bishops, abbots, officers of the Estates, judges in the sovereign courts, and their clients. Several were his cousins; some were his créatures. Besides his Breton clients, Richelieu's clientele included numerous family members,[12] domestic servants (especially those he had placed in the households of important court personages such as Gaston d'Orléans), men from his family estates in the west,[13] créatures in the royal government at Paris,[14] and clients in other provinces, as we shall see. These clients did not necessarily know each other, and they acted together only when asked to do so by their patron. A client often introduced family members into a clientele. For example, Nicolas Hennequin, seigneur Du Fay, one of two principal financial secretaries in the household of François de Valois, duc d'Anjou, in the 1570s, obtained places in the household for seven members of his family. Noble clients of the duc de La Trémoille introduced numerous family members into his clientele.[15] Clienteles were heterogeneous in composition and linked people of varying rank, status, and resources. Clienteles were composed of dependents, close family members down to obscure cousins, household members and domestic servants, entourages of nobles and gentlemen, companies of guards and gendarmes, estate administrators, lawyers, financial agents, tenant farmers and vassals, members of the local elite eager for favors or in debt for them, and many others.[16]

Clienteles and Provincial Institutions

Contemporary observers of early modern French government identified the politics of a man by asking who his protector was, that is, what patronage he enjoyed. This information is almost always mentioned in memoirs, letters, diaries, and political accounts of the period.[17] It seems odd, therefore, that historians have ignored the clientele affiliations of early modern power figures in writing about them, since these ties were comparable in political importance to modern party affiliations. Patron-broker-client ties and networks were a way of organizing and regulating power relationships in a society where the distribution of power was not completely institutionalized. These ties and networks were both intra- and extra-institutional and operated inside, across, and outside formal political institutions.[18] Modern observers need to understand the role played by these ties and networks in old Regime government in order to understand how its institutional functioned and what its structures were.

Patron-broker-client ties and networks were informal structures operating within the existing formal framework of provincial, municipal, and community institutions. For example, they influenced the internal politics of provincial high courts. A small circle of prestigious older judges within the Parlement of Aix headed clienteles composed of younger colleagues attached to them by ties of clientage, kinship, marriage, friendship, and shared political opinion. Client politics helped to determine the role of the Parlement of Aix in the revolts of 1630, 1649, and 1659.[19] Thirty-nine judges within the Parlement of Toulouse held the ten most important offices in that court from 1600 to 1683. Twenty-six of these judges were linked by family ties, fifteen in one network, three in a second, and eight in a third. One of the most important networks was that of first president Bertier de Montrave, who used his clients to keep the Parlement of Toulouse loyal to Mazarin during the Fronde.[20]

Kinship ties often lay at the heart of clienteles for functional reasons. The first group of potential patrons and clients to whom a man had access was his own family and, if he was a great noble, the household in which he was reared; after his marriage, these ties included his in-laws. Kin were willing to aid him for reasons of affection, family honor, and duty—they had known him since he was a child, and his reputation and prestige reflected on them. Since family relationships were among a man's oldest ties, they tended to be the core of any clientele he later built. Client ties often began as kinship ties, while client ties based on kinship offered the additional cement of family affection and loyalty. The role of kin in clienteles, particularly the importance of marriage alliances, and the changing role of the family in seventeenth–century politics are subjects that need investigation.

Jacques de Parades de L'Estang noted in his memoirs that the archbishop of Arles, François d'Adhémar de Monteil de Grignan, who came from an old Provençal noble family, dominated the Arles municipal government through a noble clientele based on his family connections. Arles had the highest percentage of resident sword nobles of any city in Provence. The archbishop's clients controlled municipal elections in 1649, 1650, and 1651, and his influence over the municipal government continued for three decades.[21] Parades de L'Estang noted that the archbishop kept a good table to attract clients, and that his *présence*, or personal charisma, rank, and family name, attracted the support of the nobility of Arles. He also noted that "the archbishop had much crédit and was skilled at political intrigue."[22] Grignan used his clients and influence to keep Arles loyal to Mazarin during the Fronde.[23]

Jean-Louis de La Valette, duc d'Epernon, governor of Guyenne, used his clients to dominate the municipal government of Bordeaux. The city was divided into six districts, or *jurades*, from which one *jurat* each was elected. These six jurats were composed of two nobles, two lawyers, and two bourgeois, and one from each category was elected annually in August for a term of two years; they rarely served a second term. The jurats selected twenty four electors and voted with them to elect the three new jurats each year. Occasionally the governor would suspend elections and name the jurats himself by royal letters, as in 1627 and 1630, and there is documentary evidence that he influenced the municipal elections of 1625 and 1626 to put his own clients into office. We can infer that he manipulated elections in other years, too, probably by influencing the jurats' selection of electors. Once his clients were in office, it was easier to put other clients in office. The jurats of Bordeaux were regarded by the rest of the city and the province as Epernon's men, and they were dismissed in 1633, when he was temporarily disgraced, and in 1638, when he was permanently disgraced, because they were considered too closely attached to him.[24]

Patron-broker-client ties and networks also functioned within community or local institutions. For example, Charles de Lombard, seigneur de Gourdon, a councillor in the Parlement of Aix, claimed ownership of the château and fief of Montauroux, a small town in the mountains between Draguignan and Grasse. In 1649, he halted the municipal elections of Montauroux to put his own clients in office, hoping in this way to substantiate his claim to the fief and to revive certain lapsed fiscal rights of the bishop of Fréjus, from whom he had recently acquired the fief. His action provoked a riot, and the town appealed to Governor Alais for help. The governor was only too happy to help because he had quarreled with the parlementaires. For his part, Lombard de Gourdon turned to his colleagues in the parlement for help, and the result was the first armed clash of the Provençal Fronde in June.[25] Patron-broker-client ties and networks operating within the formal framework of provincial, municipal, and community institutions influenced the functioning of these institutions.

Patron-broker-client ties and networks also operated across institutions within the larger political arena to influence behavior. For example, provincial governors influenced local politics by filling municipal governments with their clients, as the duc d'Epernon had done.[26] The maréchal de L'Hôpital, who was governor of Provence from 1631 to 1637, regularly suspended municipal elections and used royal letters to name his own clients to office, a practice that was much resented. The Parlement of Aix sent a remonstrance to Paris in 1635 for his behavior. The parlement often quarreled with the governor because the court had traditionally influenced the government of Aix through consuls and councillors who were parlementaire clients, and it resented his interference. For example, when the third consul of Aix quarreled with the second consul in April 1633, the third consul sought the parlement's help. The parlement arrested the second consul, who immediately turned to his patron, Governor Vitry, for help. The governor rode into town to free his client, toured Aix with him and a trumpeter, then had the prévôt des maréchaux, commander of the mounted provincial police force based at Aix, arrest the third consul in front of the parlement's deputies. The second consul attended mass that Sunday in the cathedral of Saint Sauveur, sitting in his accustomed seat in the choir with forty of the governor's guards at his back. The parlement, outraged, complained to Paris.[27]

The municipal government of Arles is another example. By unwritten tradition the old nobility of Arles held the office of first consul: the old nobility had incontestable authenticity of rank in contrast to the recent, more dubious rank of the new nobility who held the office of second consul. The old nobles refused to hold the office of second consul or share their monopoly on the office of first consul, much to the chagrin of the new nobles who were eager for social and political recognition. A series of incidents during municipal elections culminated in street disturbances during Mardi Gras in February 1644.

The new nobility had been lobbying the governor to reform the municipal constitution to eliminate differences between the first and second consul—governor Alais was glad to oblige because the quarrel offered him the opportunity to put his own clients into municipal office. The old nobility turned to the parlementaires for help. Despite their protests the governor reformed the municipal constitution of Arles on February 24 and changed the electoral procedure to eliminate the old nobility's monopoly on the office of first consul. He also dismissed twelve municipal councillors who were old nobles and filled their offices with new nobles who were his clients.[28] In both of these cases, patron-client ties stretching across institutions from the municipal governments of Aix and Arles to the parlement and the governor influenced their political behavior.

Patron-broker-client ties and networks formed separate, parallel structures outside and apart from formal political institutions. They were used to perform extra-institutional functions for which there was no institution. They were used to replace indecisive or uncooperative institutions and sometimes operated at cross-purposes to existing institutions. For example, Oppède used his clients in the Parlement of Aix to conduct the trial of the Marseille rebels in 1660. Cardinal Mazarin was determined that the rebels be tried for treason, but he did not want the trial conducted by a full parlement sympathetic to their plight. So, the rebels were tried by a *Grands Jours* Chamber of the parlement, a specifically constituted traveling court of twelve parlementaires sitting at Marseille in January 1660.[29] Eight of the twelve parlementaires, a voting quorum, were clients of Oppède and included Forbin de La Roque, Coriolis, Laurens, Maurel, Villeneuve, Saint Marc, Antelmi, and Foresta de La Roquette. Seven of the eight had been among the sixteen parlementaires who had left their rebellious colleagues at Aix in February the previous year and had ridden to Lambesc to establish a second court loyal to Oppède.[30] The trial of the Marseille rebels proceeded as Mazarin wished, with stiff penalties for the guilty. Oppède's clients had been used to perform an extra-institutional function and to act in place of a recalcitrant, uncooperative institution.

Great noble clienteles could act as cross-purposes or in direct opposition to provincial institutions, as they did during the Provençal Fronde. The governor of Provence, the comte d'Alais, had an extensive clientele among the sword nobility. He was the second son of Charles de Valois, duc d'Angoulême, whose support of Richelieu at court was responsible for his son's appointment as governor. Alais used client language in writing to Richelieu and cultivated the Cardinal's créatures, Chavigny and Sublet de Noyers. The last Valois, Alais was the grandson of a king, Charles IX, by Marie Touchet, and his mother was Charlotte de Montmorency. Through her he was the nephew of Henri II de Bourbon, prince de Condé, and first cousin of his son, Louis II, the Grand Condé. His name, rank, office, and connections at court brought him the support of the Provençal sword nobility. When his long and bitter quarrel with the parlementaires of Aix flared into violence in 1649, the nobility flocked to fight beneath his banner of the fleurs de lys. They were also attracted by his promises of royal commissions as camp masters and marshals. In a pitched battle on June 14, 1649, eight hours from Aix on the plain of Val near Brignoles, the clients and supporters of the governor defeated those of the parlementaires, who had a force twice as large, because the parlementaires' troops were inexperienced and ran in panic when the cavalry charged.[31] The noble clientele of Governor Alais had opposed the Parlement of Aix in what became the first pitched battle of the Provençal Fronde.

Association and conflict are the two basic forms of political behavior. Association, the art of getting men to cooperate and voluntarily do what is demanded, plays the more important role in politics. The use of physical force to obtain compliance or halt conflict is a last resort, a public admission that the political process has failed. Patron-broker-client ties and networks, operating inside, across, and outside the political institutions of early modern France, influenced institutional behavior to produce both cooperation and conflict.[32] This is illustrated by the activities of the Valbelle clientele in Marseille during the Fronde.

The Valbelles claimed to be descended from a tenth-century vicomte of Marseille, but in fact they were a family of merchants who had prospered in the eastern trade in medicines and spices to become wealthy, buy fiefs, acquire municipal and judicial offices, serve as galley captains, fight in the army, make good marriages, and enter the nobility toward the end of the sixteenth century. Cosme I de Valbelle had fought in the army in Italy and enjoyed favor at the Valois courts. One of his sons was raised in the entourage of the duc d'Alençon, the brother of Henri III.[33] Another son, Barthélemy de Valbelle, sieur de Cadarche, became admiralty lieutenant of Marseille in 1586 by purchasing a newly created maritime judicial office. Barthélemy founded the family's political fortunes when he obtained the patronage of the first president of the Parlement of Aix, and through him the patronage and protection of the governor of Provence. With the governor's help, Barthélemy built a large clientele which he used to control municipal elections and pack the city council of Marseille from 1610 to 1618, when he stepped aside in favor of his nephew, Cosme de Valbelle.[34]

Cosme II de Valbelle, seigneur de Baumelles, the son of Barthélemy's brother, Léon, had begun his political career as a captain in the Marseille city guard. His succession to the leadership of the Valbelle clientele was recognized in 1618 when he was elected first consul of Marseille at the age of 42. Although he was elected to this office only once more, in 1631, Cosme de Valbelle controlled the municipal elections and government of Marseille for twenty years with the assistance of his first cousin, Antoine de Valbelle, Barthélemy's second son, who had inherited his father's office of admiralty lieutenant; he had also inherited the family mansion at Marseille, one of the largest in the city.[35]

The Valbelles were angered when the governor, the duc de Guise, created new admiralty courts at Arles, Martigues, Toulon, and Fréjus. Guise's motives were fiscal. He received the crown's share of all fees collected, a goodly sum increased by more courts, but his action decreased the authority and income of the Valbelles' original admiralty jurisdiction at Marseille.[36] When the governor's star began to fall, Cosme and Antoine de Valbelle switched their support from Guise and sought the protection of his enemy, Cardinal Richelieu, as the more promising patron. In the autumn of 1630, Cosme de Valbelle and his Uncle Léon, sieur de La Tour-Saint Symphorien, first consul of Marseille, used their influence and clientele to keep the city loyal to Richelieu during the Cascaveoux Revolt at Aix, despite Guise's sympathy for the rebels and his open hostility to Richelieu.[37]

Richelieu ignored protests about the Valbelles because they were useful and difficult to dislodge, and kept them in power. He ignored an anonymous memoir in 1632, protesting that Cosme de Valbelle had come to power through the favor of the duc de Guise, and that "he has since maintained himself through intrigues and monopolies so that no one can become a member of the municipal government without his consent." The memoir complained that Valbelle's "particular interests" were "harmful to the service of the King," that his party had provided "bad government," and that "he was filling the city with confusion and disorder." The memoir asked that new consuls be named by royal letters and that Cosme de Valbelle be banished from the city.[38] Instead, Richelieu wrote a letter of gratitude to the first consul, sieur d'Aiglun, who was Valbelle's client, for his political service, and had the king do the same.[39] For his own part, Cosme de Valbelle assured Richelieu that "neither in affection for me, nor for the rest of my family, will the city of Marseille find glory or satisfaction comparable to that we are receiving from the present opportunity to prove our humble obedience. . . . I will spare no care in all that touches Your Eminence."[40]

Cosme de Valbelle died heroically on September 1, 1638, sword in hand, defending his galley, *La Valbelle*, against five Spanish ships in a battle off the Genoa coast. Aged sixty-five and wounded twelve times, he had himself tied to the mast to give his last orders. Three of his nephews were killed in the same battle, and his young son was seriously wounded.[41] Cosme's heroism increased the prestige of his successor, his cousin Antoine.

Antoine de Valbelle's control over the government of Marseille was immediately challenged by Henri de Cauvet, baron de Marignane, whose patron was the new governor of Provence, the comte d'Alais. Valbelle turned to Cardinal Richelieu for support. But the Cardinal preferred the abbé François de Valbelle, sacristan of the abbey of Saint Victor at Marseille and brother of Cosme de Valbelle. The abbé enjoyed the patronage of Richelieu's brother, Alphonse, cardinal-bishop of Lyon and abbot of Saint Victor, who had chosen him as his vicar general. But the abbé had no taste for politics and suggested instead his cousin, Léon de Valbelle de La Tour-Saint Symphorien, to head the family clientele. Léon, too, had no taste for municipal politics, so he supported Antoine's claim, and spoke to his good friend at court, Cardinal de La Rochefoucauld, who spoke to Richelieu: Antoine thus became the chief minister's choice to inherit the family political machine. Richelieu's support enabled Valbelle to defeat his rival, Cauvet de Marignane, for the office of first consul, and Valbelle controlled the city government of Marseille, unopposed, until Richelieu's death five years later. His son was baptized by the Cardinal in 1640, and named Alphonse for his brother.[42]

Patron-broker-client ties and networks were used to promote harmony and cooperation within the provincial government, to breach barriers, to heal wounds, and to reconcile hostile factions, and they could be used to calm unruly institutions and keep them loyal to the crown. However, the opposite was also true. Patron-broker-client ties and networks could be used to heighten the hostility between competing factions or authorities and to increase the likelihood of conflict within the larger political arena. Antoine de Valbelle's political career after 1643 illustrates the dual potential of these ties.

After Richelieu's death, Governor Alais used his influence at Paris through the prince de Condé to secure royal letters naming his own clients to municipal office at Marseille.[43] He did this for seven years, from 1643 to 1650, in this way destroying the hold of the Valbelle political machine over the Marseille government. Writing to the comte de Chavigny, his friend at court, Alais noted that Antoine de Valbelle had controlled the government of Marseille for years through an extensive family clientele, and still "had enough influence to move the Marseillais to action."[44] Alais announced to Chavigny his intention of destroying what he called "Valbelle's absolute and tyranical power" over the government of Marseille.[45] Alais also charged that Valbelle was only concerned with his own power and interests, not about serving the king.[46] Valbelle countered in a letter to Secretary of State Brienne, declaring that Alais was envious of the rank and wealth of his many relatives and friends who belonged to the nobility of Marseille. He insisted that Alais and his client, the baron de Marignane, had filled municipal offices with low-born dependents, domestic servants, and poor people because they did not have the support of the city's elite: Valbelle wrote that "it is not in the service of the King to fill the municipal council with persons of this sort, who have neither influence nor authority, and who are involved in all sorts of shady deals."[47] Valbelle's clientele included some of the best families in Marseille (see Table 1).

Antoine de Valbelle was intelligent, ambitious, and capable, implacable toward his enemies and loyal to his friends, even at some personal risk, with a reputation for generously rewarding his clients.[48] Maintaining an "open table" for his many friends and clients at Marseille, he also had extensive connections at court, and traveled to Paris to maintain them whenever necessary. For decades he entertained everyone of importance passing through Marseille, including Richelieu's brother, who lodged with him, and the comte de Chavigny, who dined with him. Careless remarks about Richelieu and Louis XIII made at Valbelle's table by Henri d'Escoubleau de Sourdis, archbishop of Bordeaux, and duly reported to Paris, resulted in the archbishop's disgrace.[49]

Marseille was a uniquely independent city in the seventeenth century and jealously guarded its privileges.[50] Under Valbelle's government, the city maintained its independence, angrily fighting off royal attacks on its right to self-government and never contributing fully to royal taxation of the province.[51] Valbelle defended the traditional municipal liberties and privileges of Marseille to safeguard his own power and to protect the interests of its elite who were his clients. If he was unpopular among some segments of the population, such as the poor people of the city who paid taxes, he was popular among many others, including the most influential.[52]

The enmity between Valbelle and Alais flared into street violence in 1644.[53] Valbelle hurried to court immediately afterward to defend himself against possible charges of misconduct by Alais. He was able to befriend the new secretary of state for Provence, the comte de Brienne, to whom he wrote on August 18, 1648: "Since I have put myself in the shelter of your protection for so long, I hope yet to enjoy the good fortune that you will never condemn me without first hearing from me, and that you will do me the favor of believing in me more and more."[54] Valbelle wrote in his memoirs that Brienne had "reliable and powerful enough friends at court to protect me from oppression."[55] Valbelle also made the acquaintance of Alais's old friend, the comte de Chavigny, and he was able to convince Chavigny that he was a victim of Alais's machinations and that his tax exactions had not been excessive. Chavigny had become estranged from Alais and was thus receptive to Valbelle's blandishments.[56]

Valbelle first met Mazarin during his 1644 trip to court, and saw the Cardinal repeatedly during trips to Paris in the next four years. He had met Mazarin through the good offices of an old school friend, Abel de Servien, who was secretary of state for Provence from 1630 to 1636. Antoine de Valbelle had attended the Collège de Tournon in Paris and had become a good friend of one of his classmates there, Abel de Servien, marquis de Sablé, despite their differences in rank, probably because they shared the handicap of having only one eye, an occasion for laughter in the seventeenth century. Their friendship endured after they left school. It was through Servien, whom he described in his memoirs as "the closest and most powerful of my friends on the royal council," that Antoine de Valbelle met Servien's nephew, Hugues de Lionne, secretary to the Queen Mother and later secretary of state for Provence, and it was through Lionne that he met Mazarin.[57] Valbelle

Table 1. The Valbelle clientele

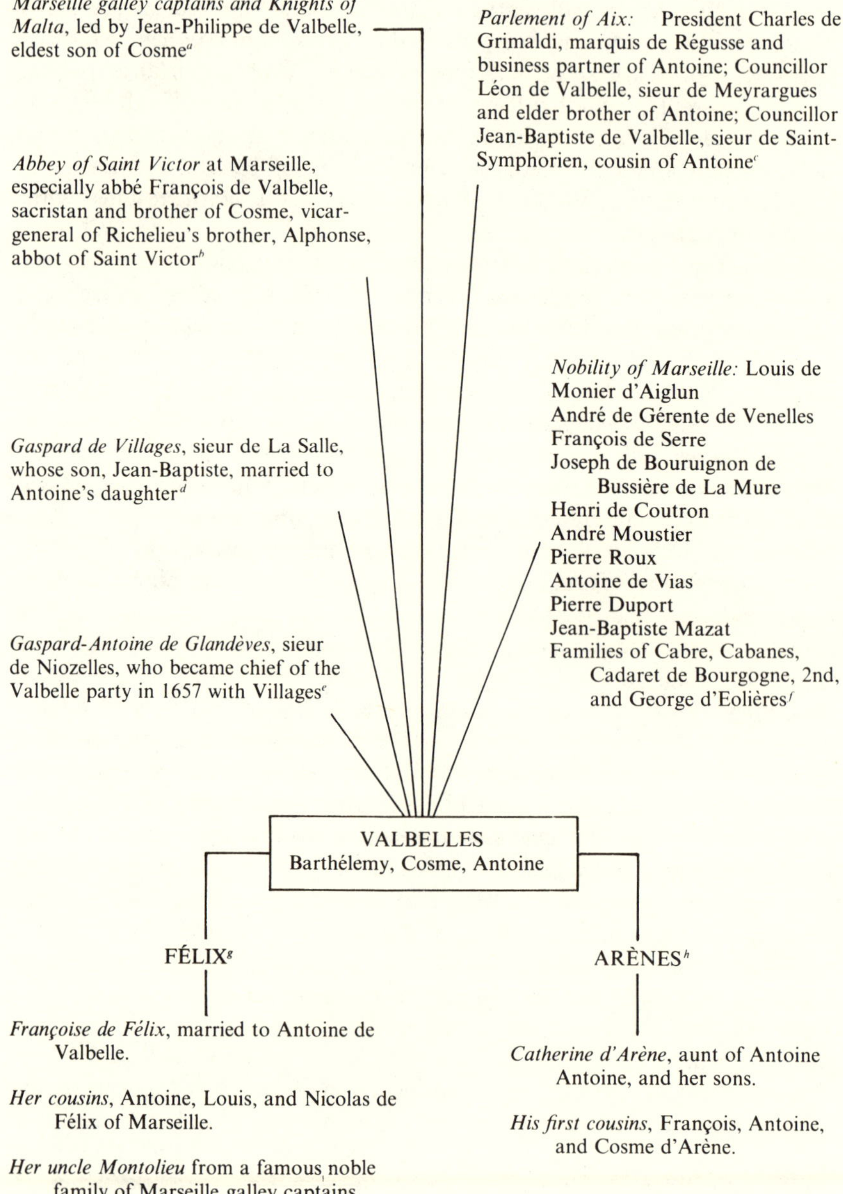

[a] There was a Valbelle party among the Marseille galley captains and officers, especially among those who were Knights of Malta, led by the chevalier Jean-Philippe de Valbelle, the oldest son of Cosme. Charles de La Roncière, *Valbelle, Le Tigre, marin de Louis XIV* (Paris, 1935), pp. 11–12; René Pillorget, *Les Mouvements insurrectionnels de Provence entre 1596 et 1715* (Paris, 1975), pp. 545–47, 551 n. 357; EDB, IV-2, 481.

wrote Mazarin on June 15, 1646, that "from my last trip to court, and all the times I have seen you, you must know of my desire for a reconciliation with governor Alais. I am trying to obey your command."[58] In Provence, Valbelle cultivated the acquaintance of the new archbishop of Aix, Michel de Mazarin, the Cardinal's brother. Charles de Grimaldi, marquis de Régusse and Valbelle's old business partner, had already become the archbishop's client.[59]

Cardinal Mazarin was receptive to Valbelle's solicitation of his patronage because he distrusted their mutual political enemy, the governor. The comte d'Alais had enjoyed close ties with Richelieu, but at the Cardinal's death he had joined the party of Mazarin's enemies at court led by his maternal cousin Condé, and he broke with Mazarin in 1646 when the Cardinal gave the governorship of Toulon, which he wanted, to one of his own clients, the chevalier de Garnier.[60] Mazarin attempted to regain Alais's loyalty in 1647 by proposing the marriage of his nephew to the governor's only daughter, but his plans were blocked by Condé; instead she married Louis de Lorraine, duc de Joyeuse, two years later.[61] The hostility between Alais and Mazarin intensified after this episode.[62] Mazarin was eager to recruit new clients in Provence to counter the governor's influence and was thus glad to accept Valbelle and his network into his service.

Cardinal Mazarin accepted Antoine de Valbelle as a client sometime after 1646, chiefly to undermine Alais's position at Marseille, an example of how clientelism could intensify political tensions and increase the likelihood of conflict. As Mazarin's client Valbelle received a royal pension of 600 livres in 1646, increased to 1,000 livres in 1647 and to 2,000 livres in 1650.[63] Legal proceedings against him for the Marseille incidents were transferred to another jurisdiction in a neighboring province, then quietly dropped.[64] On November 26, 1648, Valbelle wrote Mazarin, "I am obliged to you, and I thank you for your recent services. Please continue your favors to me and protect me from Alais's ill-will."[65] They had become regular correspondents by 1648: Mazarin wrote to Valbelle on February 7, mentioning two letters in January, and wrote again in March and April. In his letter on April 7, Mazarin made a flattering reference to Valbelle's political influence at Marseille, and noted that he had followed his recommendation in naming a

[b] Several Valbelles held benefices in the abbey of Saint Victor in which the abbé François de Valbelle was sacristan. Pillorget, *Les Mouvements*, p. 263; Adolphe Crémieux, *Marseille et la royauté pendant la minorité de Louis XIV*, 2 vols. (Paris and Marseille, 1917), vol. 1, p. 179, n. 1.

[c] EDB, IV-2, 481; Sharon Kettering, *Judicial Politics and Urban Revolt in Seventeenth-Century France: The Parlement of Aix, 1629–1659* (Princeton, 1978), pp. 240–43.

[d] A quarrel with the baron de Marignane brought a traditional foe, Gaspard de Villages, sieur de La Salle, into Valbelle's camp in 1647, and his son, Jean-Baptiste, married Valbelle's daughter. EDB, IV-2, 496–97; Pillorget, *Les Mouvements*, pp. 552, 838–40.

[e] Pillorget, *Les Mouvements*, pp. 767–72, 776–83, 812–18, 839–41.

[f] *Ibid.*, pp. 543, 551–52.

[g] Augustin Fabre, *Notice historique sur les anciennes rues de Marseille* (Marseille, 1862), p. 48; EDB, IV-2, 200–1; Crémieux, *Marseille et la royauté, vol. 1, 179 n. 3;* Pillorget, *Les Mouvements*, pp. 364–66, 369 n. 306, 371–73, 543 n. 309, 551 n. 336, 552 n. 363, 553 n. 364.

[h] Pillorget, *Les Mouvements*, p. 552; EDB, IV-2, 31.

galley lieutenant.[66] In a letter to the intendant on April 3, Mazarin praised Valbelle's performance of his duties.[67] On October 9 and November 27, Mazarin expressed satisfaction at Valbelle's seizure of illegal shipments of merchandise in coastal ports.[68] This was a normal function of the admiralty lieutenant and did not customarily merit the praise of the chief minister, but Valbelle was a new, eagerly sought political ally and client who had a record of dealing in contraband. Mazarin was careful to encourage his cooperation.

On January 28, 1649, a week after the parlementaire revolt had exploded at Aix, Mazarin asked Valbelle to use his political influence to keep Marseille calm and to aid the royal mediator, Cardinal Bichi, in negotiating a settlement.[69] Although Valbelle's sympathies lay with the Aix rebels, who included his older brother Léon—he had lent money to the rebels to recruit troops a few months earlier—Valbelle honored Mazarin's request.[70] Régusse attributed the city's calm to Valbelle's influence in a letter to Mazarin on March 23; so did the bailli de Forbin in a letter a month later; and Valbelle received letters of gratitude for his loyalty from the king and from Mazarin.[71]

When Mazarin arrested the princes at Paris in January 1650, Alais lost his protector at court, and Valbelle seized this opportunity to reassert his control over Marseille. He wrote Mazarin on February 15 that he was "forming a party to take over the city government so that the King can be assured of the fidelity of Marseille."[72] In March, Valbelle's supporters surrounded the town hall, expelled the governor's appointees, held elections, substituted Valbelle's clients in municipal office, and refused to admit Alais to the city.[73] On March 29, Valbelle informed Mazarin that "this city is calm and well-intentioned for the service of the King."[74] He had not sought the Cardinal's permission for his coup, acting on his own and informing Mazarin after the fact. However, he received royal letters in May acknowledging his takeover, and on June 15 he wrote to Mazarin "to swear my obedience and loyalty to the service of Your Eminence. I ask for Your continued protection and good will."[75] Valbelle kept Marseille loyal to Mazarin during the Fronde, and the Cardinal sent letters of gratitude to him and to his client, Louis de Monier d'Aiglun, first consul of Marseille, for their support during these years.[76] On June 4, 1652, Valbelle thanked Mazarin "for the perfect and generous friendship with which You have chosen to honor me."[77] The Valbelle clientele had thus been used to promote harmony as well as to cause conflict within the city of Marseille during the Fronde. Valbelle remained the Cardinal's client until his death of a stroke in 1655 at the age of forty five. Their relationship was a delicate balance of power: Valbelle got a free hand in Marseille politics and the largest port in France remained loyal to the crown.

Barthélemy, Cosme, and Antoine de Valbelle were municipal brokers with enormous crédit at Marseille. They headed a family clientele used to control the municipal government of Marseille for a half-century. They had noble rank, a well-known family name, and an inherited maritime judicial office. As a younger son, Antoine de Valbelle did not have a personal fortune, but he was able to acquire one through officeholding although his methods caused some protest.[78] He earned a reputation for generosity and loyalty toward his clients. The Valbelles were able to obtain patronage at the highest level in the national government because they controlled the politics of the largest port in France. Their patrons included Cardinal Richelieu; Richelieu's oldest brother, Alphonse, archbishop of Aix and later abbot of Saint Victor at Marseille; Cardinal de La Rochefoucauld; the comte de Brienne; Abel de Servien; Hugues de Lionne; Cardinal Mazarin; and Mazarin's younger brother, Michel, who was archbishop of Aix.

The Valbelles did not tolerate much interference in the day-to-day running of the municipal government. René Pillorget has noted that Antoine de Valbelle was

> a man representative of a certain style of relations between Marseille and the central government. For the King, Valbelle was an ally or a fidèle, but—despite his role as a royal official—he was hardly a subject. On the one hand, he freely chose to remain faithful to the King and to Mazarin, and despite all solicitations he scrupulously kept to this line of conduct. But, on the other hand, he would not permit any intrusion whatsoever by the central government into the internal life of Marseille. In particular, he would not permit the city to make the least fiscal concession to the King. On the eve of his death, he refused to pressure the municipal consuls to make them grant a modest *don gratuit* (a royal tax). For him as for the Marseillais jealously attached to their privileges—what they called their "agreements with France"—Marseille must in no way become an integral part of the kingdom. The King must be content knowing that he was attached to him [Antoine de Valbelle] by a single tie, that of political and military fidelity—a tie at once very solid as to the essentials and very loose as to the details, fiscal questions for the Marseillais evidently being among the latter.[79]

The nature of this relationship, always a delicate balance of power, is illustrated by Valbelle's reform of the municipal constitution at the end of the Fronde.

Valbelle reformed the municipal constitution of Marseille to give his clients control in perpetuity. Cardinal Mazarin allowed these reforms in gratitude for his loyalty during the Fronde but probably regretted his generosity later. Valbelle had received royal letters in October 1652, authorizing his proposed changes in the municipal election procedure. These reforms, known as the *Règlement du Sort*, created a permanent election council of three hundred members to name candidates for office. Municipal officials were to be elected by lot from a list of three candidates for each office, and a rotating panel chosen by lot from the election council would name the three candidates. Valbelle stressed the "freedom" of these elections because the choice was by lot. But he had already used royal letters to pack the election council with his clients, and the council was self-perpetuating—it filled its own vacancies, which only occurred through death, resignation, or expulsion. The election council, therefore, would always be filled with Valbelle clients and so would municipal offices because the council named the candidates chosen by lot. For this reason, the Valbelle clientele was able to continue its control over the municipal government after Valbelle's death.[80]

Oppède and Mercoeur convinced Mazarin, their mutual patron, that Marseille should pay a larger share of provincial taxes, and consequently, they encouraged the creation of an anti-Valbelle party at Marseille to challenge the family's political power. These were years of confusion in which no Valbelle stepped forward to assume leadership of the family political machine. Antoine's oldest son, Léon, who had inherited the office of admiralty lieutenant and used the title of marquis de Montfuron, had married the daughter of Auge de Pontevès, marquis de Buous, an old family of the Provençal sword nobility. He was not interested in municipal politics and remained aloof from what followed. Léon's cousin, Jean-Baptiste de Valbelle, the younger son of Cosme de Valbelle and a famous galley captain, was out of favor at court because he had supported the princes during the Fronde and thus was not a serious candidate. Cosme's oldest son, Jean-Philippe, had died of war wounds a decade earlier.[81] The leadership of the family clientele thus passed to other hands, to the Valbelle clients Gaspard de Villages, sieur de La Salle, and Gaspard-Antoine de Glandèves, sieur de Niozelles.

Oppède advised Cardinal Mazarin to revoke the Règlement du Sort as a threat to royal authority in Marseille and advocated a direct attack upon the party's control over the municipal government. Reestablishing the old electoral method—direct nomination by the outgoing municipal officials—Oppède made certain that opponents of the Valbelle party were elected to office in 1656, and he secured royal letters suspending municipal elections and reappointing the enemies of the Valbelle faction to office in 1657. The Valbelle party reacted violently, inciting a popular protest in July 1658, reestablishing the use of the Règlement du Sort, and electing their own men to office in 1658 and 1659.[82]

The angry response of Mazarin at Paris was to declare the city in revolt, threaten the use of troops, and order the leaders of the Valbelle faction to leave the city. Fearing royal reprisals the moderates, led by Fortia de Pilles, took control and drove the Valbelle chiefs from the city, ending their protest. The king and his court paid a state visit to Provence in the winter of 1660, to emphasize the weight of royal authority, and when Louis XIV visited Marseille in March he reformed the municipal government.[83] He abolished the election council of three hundred, reduced the number of municipal councillors to sixty, and changed the consulate to three échevins. He decreed that no nobles were to serve as échevins and abolished the tradition of reserving the first office for the sword nobility. Since the échevins were to name candidates for vacancies on the municipal council, this decree effectively excluded nobles from the council, too.[84] These reforms were designed to remove the Valbelle clientele from the municipal government of Marseille: Antoine de Valbelle himself had described his clientele as drawn from the city's nobility. The Valbelle clientele had become too independent so Mazarin destroyed it.

To summarize, patron-broker-client ties and networks helped to determine individual and institutional political behavior in seventeenth-century France. They were interstitial, supplementary, and parallel to existing political institutions. They were used to reconcile internal factions, or to intensify them and increase factionalism and, because they were cross-institutional, they could be used to promote cooperation or conflict within the larger political arena. In addition, they existed outside institutions as separate, parallel structures that could be used in place of formal institutions as a remedy for institutional weakness, or even at cross-purposes to institutions. The monarchy needed to harness the resources of important clienteles in order to increase its control over the provincial power structure, and it used client ties and the material rewards of royal patronage to do this, as we shall see in the next chapter.

Great Noble and Administrative Clienteles

There were two basic types of political clienteles in early modern France, great noble and administrative. Great noble clienteles were headed by members of the great old families of the feudal nobility and were heavily sword noble in composition, their members attracted by a patron's rank and family and by his ability to reward their loyalty and service. In the sixteenth century the function and composition of great noble clienteles were largely military. But in the seventeenth century great noble clienteles became increasingly political in use, with more royal and provincial officials among their members. In contrast, administrative clienteles served their patrons as political machines in helping them to exercise power and to govern. They were composed of robe and sword nobles attracted by the power and influence of their patron to whom they looked for political advancement. Robe nobles in administrative clienteles were usually royal or provincial officials. Historians Julian Dent and Roland Mousnier have recognized two basic types of political clients, those clustered around great sword nobles and those surrounding men of power.[85]

Provincial administrative clienteles can be subdivided into two groups, those that were institutional, that is, in which the membership was drawn primarily from one political institution, and those that were geographic, that is, in which the membership was drawn from more than one political institution in a geographic area that might be provincewide, regional, or municipal. Municipal clienteles were a variant on administrative clienteles, that is, they were mixed noble in composition and were used administratively as political machines in governing. But they operated in a city that elected at least some members of its government, and some of their members were elected officials. Municipal clienteles were used to mobilize electoral support, although not in a system of mass suffrage. In contrast, the majority of officials in great noble and administrative clienteles were venal, not elected. Clienteles of political importance at the provincial level usually had twenty five to one hundred members, and often more on the national level.

The Valbelle clientele of Marseille is an example of a municipal clientele. Archbishop Grignan of Arles headed a municipal clientele that was also a great noble clientele because of the rank of its patron and most of its members. The clienteles of Oppède and Régusse were administrative clienteles: Oppède's clientele was provincial, with a heavy composition of sword nobles, and Régusse's clientele was institutional within the Parlement of Aix. Great noble clienteles discussed in this chapter include the networks of the comte d'Alais, the princes de Condé, the ducs d'Epernon, and the duc de Longueville. Provincial governors who were great nobles usually had the most extensive noble clienteles in a province, although provincial grands also maintained clienteles of this type.

Henri de Forbin-Maynier d'Oppède used his clientele to manipulate the Parlement of Aix for his patrons, Mazarin and Colbert. Parades de L'Estang noted that Oppède had "numerous friends and much crédit within the parlement," and that "his political gifts were so skilled and authoritative that he governed both the province and the parlement."[86] Cardinal Bichi wrote Mazarin that Oppède has "one of the best heads in this parlement . . . and by his intelligence and birth has acquired much crédit among the others."[87] Mazarin thanked Oppède profusely for persuading the parlement to register his provision letters as the new governor of Antibes.[88] In a letter to Oppède a month later Mazarin protested the court's refusal to register a conciliar decree giving Madame de Venel a monopoly on the construction of icehouses in Provence.[89] There was a new craze for Italian ices, and the privilege promised to be lucrative, bringing 20,000 livres a year in revenue; in fact, the monopoly was sold back to the province in 1692 for 200,000 livres.[90] Royal letters granting Madame de Venel this privilege were issued on December 29, 1656, but they were not registered. A year later Mazarin asked Oppède to use his crédit and that of his friends in the parlement to have these letters registered, which he did.[91]

The Forbin, Maynier, Castellane, Oraison, Laurens, Maurel, Puget, Pontevès, and Séguiran families were among Oppède's most important clients and allies in Provence (see Table 2). As chief of the Sabreurs, Oppède enjoyed wide support among the provincial nobility. He had many clients in the high courts of the province, for instance, councillors Laurens, Gallifet, and Saint Marc in the Parlement, and councillor Jean-Louis Antoine and first president Reynaud de Séguiran in the Cour des Comptes.[92] Gaspard de Cauvet, baron de Bormes, and Vincent de Boyer d'Eguilles, councillors in the Parlement of Aix, were Oppède's brothers-in-law.[93] Dominique Guidy, a trésorier général at Aix, was also his client; Mercoeur wrote Colbert on October 9, 1666, that a scurrilous poster had appeared anonymously at Aix linking the names of Oppède and Guidy.[94] Oppède's client network stretched from the parlement into the other judicial courts at Aix.

Oppède also had clients in the municipal governments of Marseille, Aix, Toulon, Draguignan, Carpentras, and Oppède and Kinsmen in the municipal government of Arles.[95] His clientele included the procureurs du pays (the consuls of Aix), the procureurs of the nobility and clergy, and the deputies (usually the first and second consuls) in the General Assemblies of Provençal Communities.[96] He had the support of the governor, the duc de Mercoeur, and the provincial lieutenant general, Jean de Pontevès, comte de Carcès. He also had extensive support among the Provençal sword nobility in the Comtat Venaissin and Basse-Provence, where he owned land. Oppède's clientele extended throughout the province after he became acting intendant, but it was concentrated in the institutions and cities of Basse-Provence. It is an example of a geographic administrative clientele: provincewide, cross-institutional, mixed noble in composition, attracted by the political power of its patron, and used as a political machine in helping him to govern.

Charles de Grimaldi, marquis de Régusse, also had an extensive judicial clientele at Aix, although it was concentrated within one institution, the Parlement. It was mixed noble in composition, although robe nobles predominated. They had been attracted by the power of their patron and were used as a political machine in helping him to influence parlement decision making. Régusse had many clients and friends within the Parlement and city of Aix, as intendant Sève and Governor Mercoeur attested.[97] President Coriolis wrote to Mazarin that Régusse could easily have convinced his fellow judges to issue a remonstrance (requiring a majority vote) on his summons to court in 1658, but he chose not to do so.[98] Governor Mercoeur wrote to Mazarin that, on his return to Aix a year later, Régusse had removed himself from controversial discussions in the parlement but was allowing his many friends and supporters to argue.[99] Régusse's kinship ties with the Leidets, a large, influential robe family, were at the heart of his judicial clientele.[100] He had a tightly knit clientele within the Parlement of Aix rivaling Oppède's in influence (see Table 3).

Great noble clienteles had three basic components—military, domestic, and political—illustrated by the clientele of Louis-Emmanuel de Valois, comte d'Alais, later duc d'Angouleme, and governor of Provence from 1638 to 1653. Alais was a great court noble who flew the banner of the fleurs de lys and had powerful protectors at court. He is another type of provincial power broker, a governor who was also a great court noble. This type was more prevalent in the sixteenth century, as we shall see in Chapter 5. As governor of Provence, Alais exercised extensive military patronage and expanded the number of provincial troops under his command. After 1641 he increased the provincial infantry regiment, sometimes known as the governor's regiment, from twenty to thirty companies of approximately 1,200 men and added a new provincial cavalry regiment of six companies and 150 men known as the Colonel's regiment for its commanding officer, Colonel Marcin.[101] In addition, Alais kept a company of horse and foot guards commanded by sieur Mathan, an ordinance company of gendarmes, and two provincial companies of gendarmes with fifty to one hundred men each.[102] Alais also commanded the garrisons of nineteen royal fortresses along the coast and of the viguiers or governors of the larger Provençal towns.[103] Alais used his military patronage to build a sizable clientele among the Provençal sword nobility (see Table 4).

Table 2. The Oppède clientele

HENRI DE FORBIN-MAYNIER, BARON D'OPPÈDE, FIRST PRESIDENT OF THE PARLEMENT OF AIX

LAURENS[c]

Henri de Laurens, councillor in the Parlement of Aix, and his son, Pierre-Joseph, seigneur (later marquis) de Saint Martin de Pallières, husband of Oppède's daughter, Aimare

Antoine de Laurens, prévôt de la maréchaussée d'Aix, brother of Henri

Jacques de Laurens, sieur de Vaugrenier, boss of Drauignan municipal government, uncle of Henri

Dominique de Benault de Lubières, councillor in the Parlement of Aix and maternal uncle of Pierre-Joseph

MAURELS[e]

Suzanne de Laurens, sister of Henri, married to Pierre Maurel, provincial treasurer, who had two sons and a nephew, councillors in the Parlement of Aix

SÉGUIRANS

Reynaud de Séguiran, sieur de Bouc, first president of the Cour des Comptes, former Sabreur, father-in-law of Laurens de Vaugrenier and brother-in-law of André de Forbin de La Fare

ORAISONS[g]

Aqua d'Oraison, wife of Melchior de Forbin de La Roque

Her brother, André d'Oraison, marquis d'Oraison, former Sabreur and first consul of Aix

Their mother, Louise de Castellane, marquise d'Oraison, godmother of Oppède's younger brother, Louis, bishop of Toulon, and a maternal relative

MAYNIERS[i]

Ties to the nobility of the Comtat Venaissin

PONTÈVES[b]

Jean de Pontèves, third comte de Carcès and lieutenant general of Provence, distant cousin of Oppède's wife, Marie

PUGETS[a]

Jean-Henri de Puget, baron de Saint Marc, co-chief of the Sabreurs, and his brother Jean-Baptiste, seigneur de Barbentane

FORBINS[f]

Forbin de La Roque: uncle Jean-Baptiste, president in the Parlement of Aix, and his son Melchior, also a president, and Melchior's brother-in-law, Pierre de Coriolis-Villeneuve, also a president

Forbin de Janson: cousins Laurent de Forbin, marquis de Janson, and his brother, Toussaint de Janson-Forbin, bishop of Marseille

Forbin de La Barben: cousin Jacques de Forbin de La Barben, noble syndic and consul of Aix

Forbin de Lambesc: cadet branch of La Barben, cousin Paul-Albert de Forbin-Lambesc, bailli in the Order of Malta and Grand Prior of Saint Gilles near Arles

Forbin de La Fare: first cousin François-Anne de Forbin de La Fare-Saint Croix, councillor in the Cour des Comptes of Aix, and his son, André, councillor in the same court

Forbin de Solliès: cousin Louis de Forbin, marquis de Solliès, consul of Aix

CASTELLANES[h]

Jean-Baptiste de Castellane, sieur de La Verdière and consul of Aix, Oppède's maternal uncle, who made Oppède's son, Jean-Baptiste, his heir

Alais's promises of royal military commissions as camp masters and camp marshals brought nobles in droves from the Rhône valley and the neighbouring provinces of Languedoc and Dauphiné to join his forces in 1649.[104] Jacques de Cambis, baron d'Alès, and the marquis de Montpezat from Languedoc levied three hundred horsemen for Alais in that province and brought them, with the Perrault infantry regiment and one hundred riflemen, to the châteaux of Tarascon and Orgon.[105] As a lieutenant colonel in the light cavalry, Alais diverted the cavalry regiments Saint André Montbrun and Saint Auney from Dauphiné to the citadel of Sisteron, and placed these troops under the command of his brother-in-law, Villefranche; they lived off the countryside. The baron d'Hughes levied troops for Alais in Haute-Provence and in Dauphiné.[106] The governor issued commissions to levy

---

[a] The baron de Saint Marc and the seigneur de Barbentane helped Oppède to put his clients into municipal office at Aix in 1650–1651; cf. Charles de Grimaldi and Jacques Gaufridy, *Mémoires pour servir à l'histoire de la Fronde* (Aix, 1870), pp. 42–43; René Pillorget, *Les Mouvements insurrectionnels de Provence entre 1596 et 1715* (Paris, 1975), pp. 666–70, 758, 760; EDB, IV-2, 393; Pierre-Joseph de Haitze, *Histoire de la ville d'Aix*, 6 vols. (Aix, 1880–92), vol. 5, pp. 195–98; Sharon Kettering, *Judicial Politics and Urban Revolt in Seventeenth-Century France: The Parlement of Aix, 1629–1659* (Princeton, 1978), p. 286.

[b] See chap. 1.

[c] Oppède enjoyed the support of three generations of the Laurens. Pierre-Joseph, seigneur de Saint Martin de Pallières, married Oppède's daughter, Aimare, in 1665. As a mark of honor, the duc de Mercoeur attended the wedding. Also present was Reynaud de Séguiran; the groom's uncle, Antoine de Laurens, head of the provincial police force based at Aix; and Parlement councillor Dominique de Benault de Lubières, the groom's maternal uncle. All were clients of Oppède; cf. Scipion Du Roure, baron, *Les Anciennes familles de Provence: Généalogie de la maison de Forbin* (Paris, 1960), p. 51; idem *Généalogie de la maison de Benault de Lubières* (Paris, 1906), p. 13. Oppède recommended Antoine de Laurens to chancellor Séguier in a letter on January 21, 1664; cf. B.N., Ms. fr. 17404, fol. 13. The brother of Pierre de Laurens was Jacques de Laurens, sieur de Vaugrenier, whose clientele controlled the government of Draguignan for a decade. Oppède wrote to Mazarin in his defense on October 28, 1659; cf. A.A.E., 1725, fol. 149.

[d] The Laurens family brought Oppède the support of the Maurels; cf. marquis de Boisgelin, *Maurel de Villeneuve de Mons* (Digne, 1904), p. 29; Kettering, *Judicial Politics*, pp. 244–45; Emile Pierrer, *L'Hôtel et le château d'un financier aixois: Pierre Maurel de Pontevès* (Valence, 1902). Oppède recommended Maurel de Chateauneuf for a Parlement office in 1667; cf. B.N., Ms. fr. 17409, June 28, 1667, to chancellor Séguier. The comte de Grignan praised Pierre de Maurel, the provincial treasurer, to Colbert in a letter on January 24, 1672, declaring that "His Majesty has few servants in this province who are more loyal and useful; he has great crédit among the communities"; cf. B.N., M.C. 158, fols. 156–57.

[e] Reynaud de Séguiran, sieur de Bouc, became a councillor in the Cour des Comptes and eventually succeeded his father as first president. Séguiran was a Sabreur during the Fronde. His sister married Oppède's cousin André de Forbin de La Fare-Sainte Croix, a councillor in the Cour des Comptes, and Séguiran's son-in-law Laurens de Vaugrenier, was Oppède's client; cf. EDB, IV-2, 450–51; Haitze, *Histoire*, vol. 4 pp. 114–15, vol. 5 p. 212; Baltasar de Clapiers-Collongues, *Chronologie des cours souveraines* (Aix, 1909–12), pp. 196–97, 231, 235, 239; A.A.E., 1703, fol. 99, March 22, 1635; Jean-Scholastique Pitton, *Histoire de la ville d'Aix* (Aix, 1666), p. 574. Séguiran was known to both Mazarin and Colbert; cf. A.A.E., 1726, fol. 90, October 13, 1660; B.N., M.C. 131, fols. 65–66, August 1665; 137 bis, fol. 498, May 1666; 142 bis, fol. 490, December 1666; Gaston Rambert, *Nicolas Arnoul: Intendant des galères à Marseille, 1665–1674* (Marseille, 1931), p. 20.

[f] The Oraisons, members of the feudal nobility and chiefs of the Huguenots in Provence during the Wars of Religion, were political allies of Oppède and Sabreurs during the Fronde. Oppède's cousin and client Melchior Forbin de La Roque had married into this family and suggested his brother-in-law, André d'Oraison, marquis d'Oraison, as a possible provincial lieutenant general in 1659; cf. Scipion Du Roure, *Les Anciennes familles de Province: Généalogie de la Maison de Forbin* (Paris, 1906), p. 30; J. H. Albanès, *Gallia Christiana Novissima*, 7 vols. (Valence, 1899–1920), vol. 5 p. 665; A.A.E., 1723, fols. 550–57, June 17, 1659.

[g] See chap. 4.

[h] See chap. 2.

[i] Du Roure, *La Maison de Forbin*, pp. 48–51; Kettering, *Judicial Politics*, p. 286; Clapiers-Collongues, *Chronologie*, pp. 81, 97, 105; A.A.E., 1723, fols. 364–67; 1724, fol. 249; 1725, fols. 220–21; B.N., Ms. fr. 17398, fol. 1; Pierre Daverdi, *Oraison funèbre de Henri de Forbin d'Oppède*, notes by A. J. Rance-Bourrey (Marseille, 1889), pp. 29–70. Also see Roman d'Amat, ed., *Dictionnaire biographie française*, vol. 80 (Paris, 1976); René Borricand, *Nobiliaire de Provence: Armorial général de la Provence, du Comtat Venaissin, de la principauté d'Orange*, vol. 1 (Aix, 1974).

Table 3. The Régusse Clientele

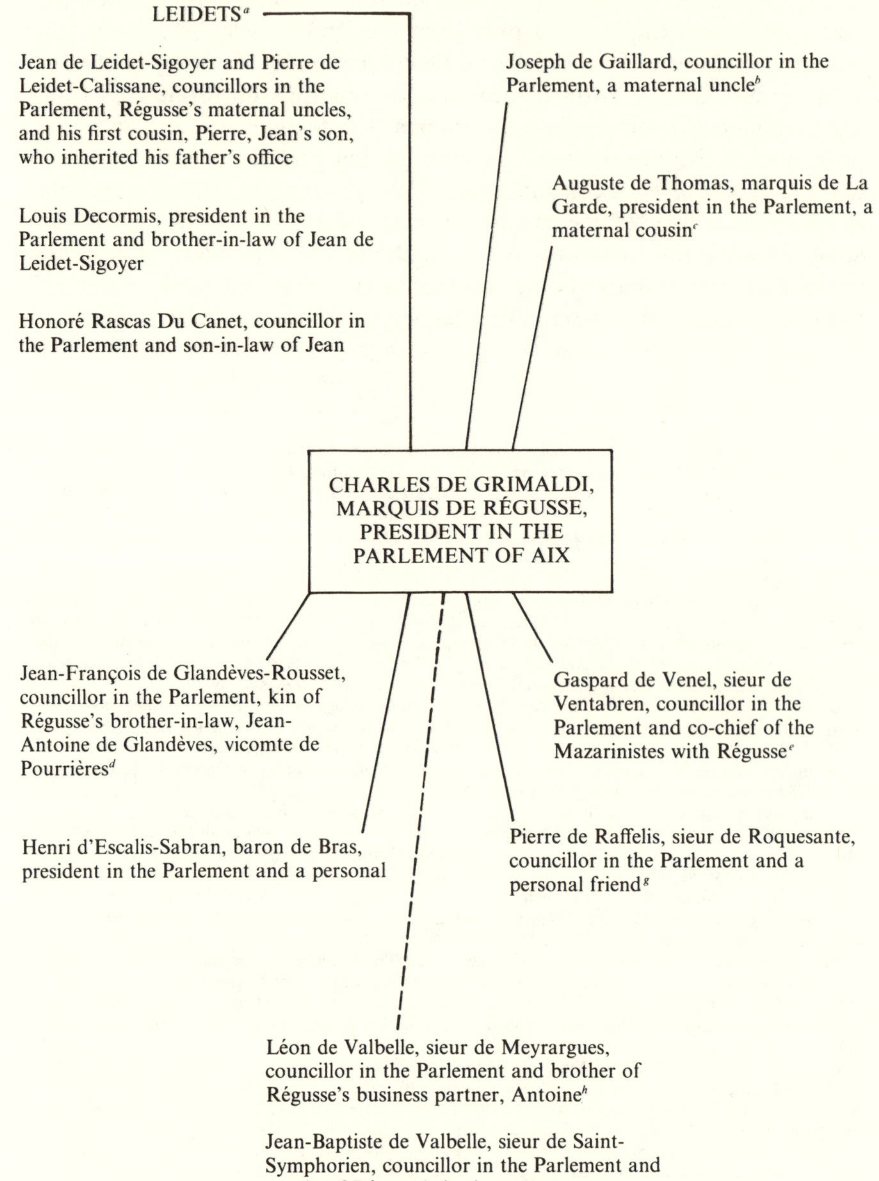

N.B.: Broken line indicates first loyalty to Antoine de Valbelle of Marseille; the Valbelles were also cousins of Oppède.

[a] Régusse's mother was Louise de Leidet, who came from a parlementaire family, and his uncles were parlement councillors Jean de Leidet-Sigoyer and Pierre de Leidet-Calissane. His clients included Parlement president Louis Decormis, who had married Jean's sister, and councillor Honoré de Rascas Du Canet, who had married his daughter; cf. Sharon Kettering, *Judicial Politics and Urban Revolt in Seventeeth-Century*

troops in Basse-Provence to the chevalier de Vins and commander Montmeyan.[107] A number of nobles left Alais's service, however, when he was unable to fulfill his promises of royal military commissions.[108]

Most sixteenth- and seventeenth-century provincial governors used their military patronage to create large clienteles among the provincial nobility and, with their access to royal patronage, became important provincial power brokers.[109] The crown in the seventeenth century weakened great noble clienteles in the provinces by diverting the flow of royal patronage nourishing them to its own administrative networks of ministerial clients while enticing away their members, and thus seriously undermined the power of the great nobles as we shall see in later chapters. The princes de Condé, for example, were governors of Burgundy, cousins of the king, and royal ministers. Louis II de Condé, at his own expense in 1651, maintained both cavalry and infantry regiments as well as companies, and as governor of the province commanded a company of guards, an ordinance company of gendarmes, and the regiment of Burgundy. These troops offered places to Burgundian nobles as colonels, captains, lieutenants, ensigns, camp masters, and marshals.[110] Condé also secured the governorships of fortified towns and royal fortresses in Burgundy for his noble clients.[111] There were additional places for nobles in his entourage, which during the Fronde included the duc de La Rochefoucauld (lover of Condé's sister), Jean de Rieux, comte de Chateauneuf, the duc de Bouillon and vicomte de Turenne, who were brothers, Gaspard, comte de Chavagnac, and Jacques-Henri de Durfort, marquis de Duras.[112]

His father, Henri II de Bourbon, prince de Condé, governor of Burgundy from 1631 to 1646, had created an extensive provincial clientele to control the Parlement of Dijon, the Burgundian Estates, and the municipal governments. His clients included Jean Bouchu, who was first president of the

---

France: The Parlement of Aix, 1629–1659 (Princeton, 1978), pp. 214, 298–99, 304; G. Lavergne, *Inventaire des archives de la famille Grimaldi-Régusse* (Monaco and Paris, 1911), p. 29; A.P., Fonds 48, p. 8; A.P. Fonds 5.

[b] Régusse's aunt had married parlement councillor Joseph de Gaillard. He and his wife stood as godparents to several of Régusse's children. Gaillard bought Régusse's household furnishings for him in Paris and sold him his own parlement office in 1633; Charles de Grimaldi and Jacques Gaudfridy, *Mémoires pour servir à l'histoire de La Fronde* (Aix, 1870), pp. 3, 19; A.P., 43–4, fols. 1, 2, 18, 26v.

[c] One of his mother's sisters had married seigneur de Thomas, baron de La Garde, later marquis, who became a parlement president in 1662, and she stood as godmother to Régusses's son, Michel, in 1639; cf. A.P., 43–4; Baltasar de Clapiers-Collongues, *Chronologie des cours souveraines* (Aix, 1909–12), p. 22; Grimaldi and Gaufridy, *Memoires*, p. 3.

[d] Régusse's brother-in-law was Jean-Antoine de Glandèves, vicomte de Pourrières, godfather to Régusse's daughter Marguerite in 1638, and he brought him the support of parlement councillor Jean-François de Glandèves-Rousset; cf. Kettering, *Judicial Politics*, pp. 235, 304–5; Grimaldi and Gaufridy, *Mémoires*, p. 3; A.F., 43–4.

[e] Kettering, *Judicial Politics*, pp. 208, 215, 286, 290; Grimaldi and Gaufridy, *Memoires*, pp. 24–25, 43–44, 52.

[f] Régusse's friendship with Sextius d'Escalis, baron de Bras, first consul of Aix, brought the support of his son, Henri, president in the Parlement of Aix. Henri was the brother-in-law of Glandèves-Rousset; cf. Kettering, *Judicial Politics*, pp. 239–40, 255, 281–82, 297, 303–4, 314, 322; Clapiers- Collongues, *Chronologie*, p. 22.

[g] Pierre de Raffelis, sieur de Roquesante and parlement councillor, was an old friend who stood as godfather to Régusse's son, Joseph, in 1652; Paul de Faucher, *Un des juges de Fouquet: Roquesante (1619–1707)* (Aix, 1891).

[h] Kettering, *Judicial Politics*, pp. 240–42, 282, 314–15, 319–20.

Table 4. The Alais Clientele

PROVENÇAL SWORD NOBILITY[a]

Members of the families of:

Villeneuve	Valavoire
Grasse	Pontevès
Forbin	Sade
Castellane	Villages
Vintimille	Grimaldi-Antibes
Glandèves	Agoult-Simiane

HIGHER CLERGY[b]

Modeste de Villeneuve, bishop of Apt
Antoine de Godeau, bishop of Grasse
Raphaël de Bologne, bishop of Digne
Dori d'Attichy, bishop of Riez
Le Clerc, bishop of Glandèves
Magdelon de Vintimille, Oratorian
Abbess of Saint Césaire at Arles, a member of the Grille-Robiac family

ROYAL FORTRESS GOVERNORS[c]

Marquis de Valavoire, Sisteron
Pontevès de Buous, Tour d'Agay
Campel, Antibes
Guitaud, Sainte Marguerite
Cauvet de Marignane, Tour de Bouc
Villeneuve, Saint Paul
Chevalier de Mesgrigny, Toulon

REGIMENTAL OFFICERS[d]

Colonel Marcin, cavalry regiment of Provence
Marquis de Janson and marquis de Valavoire, captains of provincial gendarmes companies
Chevalier de Vins, lieutenant colonel of Angoulême infantry regiment
Antoine Grasse Du Bar and chevalier Thomas de Villages, captains of companies in the Angoulême regiment
Baron d'Hugues, marquis de Marignane, baron d'Alès, marquis de Montpezat, captains of light cavalry companies
Colonel Villefranche, cavalry regiments of Saint André Montbrun and Saint Auney

LOUIS DE VALOIS, COMTE D'ALAIS (LATER DUC D'ANGOULÊME), GOVERNOR OF PROVENCE, 1638–1653

MUNICIPAL CONSULS AND VIGUIERS[f]

Villeneuve, baron de Flayosc, viguier of Marseille
Glandèves, comte de Pourrières, viguier and consul of Marseille
Vintimille, comte Du Luc, viguier of Marseille
Families of Vento, Cipriani, and Albertas, consuls of Marseille
Consuls and viguiers of Aix, Toulon, Draguignan, Arles, and Grasse

NAVAL[e]

Armand-Jean de Vignerod Du Plessis, duc de Richelieu, general of royal galleys
Chevalier Philandre de Vincheguerre, lieutenant general of galleys
Galley captains and officers

PROVINCIAL INTENDANT[h]

François Bochart, sieur de Saron-Champigny, 1637–1640 and 1643–1647, terms in Provence

HIGH COURT MAGISTRATES[g]

Jean-Augustine de Foresta de La Roquette, president in the Parlement of Aix
Gaspard de Cauvet, baron de Bormes, councillor in the Parlement
Jean-François de Glandèves de Rousset, councillor in the Parlement
Joseph Gaufridy, president in the Semester Parlement
Councillors in the Chambre des Requêtes and Semester Parlement
Claude Rolland de Réauville, president in the Cour des Comptes of Aix
Antoine de Bausset, lieutenant general, Marseille seneschal court

[a] The list of the governor's clients and supporters in 1649 included most of the great names of the Provençal sword nobility: ten Villeneuves, four Grasses, six Castellanes, six Forbins, four Vintimilles, four Glandèves, three Valavoires, and several each from the families of Agoult-Simiane, Grimaldi, Pontevès, Sade, and Villages. Twelve of the thirty great feudal families in Provence supported Alais in 1649 as well as a host of lesser nobles and gentlemen; cf. A.A.E., 1715, fols. 99–103; B.N., Ms. fr. 18977, fols. 322–326; B.M., Harleian 4575, fols. 115–115v; René Pillorget, *Les Mouvements insurrectionnels de Provence entre 1596 et 1715* (Paris, 1975), p. 622.

[b] Alais's connections with the great old families of the Provençal sword nobility brought him the support of bishops, abbots, and priors from these families, for instance, Modeste de Villeneuve, bishop of Apt, who was the brother of Alais's client, Antoine de Villeneuve, marquis de Trans. Antoine de Godeau, bishop of Grasse, was a personal friend of Alais, which may explain why he later became the political enemy of Oppède. The abbess of the Saint Césaire monastery at Arles was the sister of Pierre de Grille-Robiac, one of the governor's supporters. Other clients included the bishops of Glandèves, Digne, and Riez and the Oratorian Magdelon de Vintimille; cf. Pillorget, *Les Mouvements*, pp. 623–24.

[c] Alais's clients included the marquis de Janson and the marquis de Valavoire, who were captains of his gendarmes companies; Valavoire also became governor of the royal citadel at Sisteron; cf. A.A.E., 1707, fol. 4v, January 1640; 1715, fol. 87, February 1649. Another Provençal sword noble, Pontevès de Buous, was named governor of the Tour d'Agay, near Fréjus, at Alais's request; cf. B.N., Clairambault 398, fol. 215, February 21, 1645; fol. 267, March 1645. Sieurs Campel and Guitaud, governors of the royal fortresses of Antibes and Sainte Marguerite on the islands of Lérins, became clients of Alais; cf. B.M., Harleian 4575, "Semestre de Provence par M. de Sève," fols. 127v–131v; A.A.E., 1711, fol. 286, December 7, 1646; 1712, fol. 207, May 14, 1647; 1713, fol. 236, August 18, 1648. Henri de Cauvet, baron de Marignane and chief of Alais's party at Marseille, was named governor of the royal fortress of the Tour de Bouc. His brother Gaspard, baron de Bormes and parlement councillor, became the leader of this party at the baron's death in 1647. Two years later Gaspard gave his nephew, the new marquis de Marignane, whose title had been upgraded at Alais's insistence, the money to raise a company of light cavalry for the governor's defense; A.A.E., 1709, fol. 25, February 1644; B.N., Clairambault 409, fol. 286, April 23, 1647; 390, fol. 234, December 22, 1643; B.M., Harleian 4575, fol. 126v. Alais secured a pension for Grimaldi, marquis de Courbons. He secured royal favors for other Provençal clients, Villeneuve, governor of the Saint Paul fortress; Villeneuve, baron de Flayosc and viguier of Marseille; the comte and the chevalier Grasse Du Bar; the baron de Beaudinard; and Antoine de Villeneuve, marquis de Trans; cf. A.A.E., 1707, fol. 133, November 1641; 1708, fol. 119, November 15, 1642; 1715, fols. 99–103; B.N., Clairambault 390, fol. 279, November 22, 1643; 395, fol. 320, October 27, 1644; B.M., Harleian 4575, fols. 115–115v; B.N., Ms. fr. 18977, fols. 322–26.

[d] The chevalier Thomas de Villages, a Knight of Malta from an old noble family of Marseille, became captain of a company in the governor's infantry regiment, and the chevalier de Vins, a Provençal sword noble and former galley captain, was named lieutenant colonel of the Angoulême infantry regiment in 1651; A.A.E., 1710, fol. 268, November 6, 1645; 1711, fol. 261, October 29, 1646; 1715, fol. 88, February 1649; Pillorget, *Les Mouvements*, pp. 547, 622, 639, 677, 679. Antoine Grasse Du Bar, seigneur de La Malle, captain of the government's regiment, was killed in his defense during the 1649 revolt at Aix; cf. comte de Grasse, "Documents inédits concernant l'histoire du Semestre en Provence," *Bulletin de la société d'études scientifiques archéologiques de Draguigan* 32 (1918–19); 6–8. The marquis de Janson and the marquis de Valavoire were captains of the governor's gendarmes companies; A.A.E., 1707, fol. 4v, January 1640; 1715, fol. 87, February 1649.

[e] The general and lieutenant general of the royal galleys were also Alais's clients. The general, Armand-Jean de Vignerod Du Plessis, duc de Richelieu and the son of Pont de Courlay, had been appointed to this office by his great-uncle on his deathbed. His loyalty to Mazarin was questionable, and the Cardinal asked that he be watched in a letter on November 2, 1650; cf. A.A.E., 1715, fol. 333. Mazarin had wanted to marry his niece to the duc de Richelieu, but Condé had prevented it; cf. Célestin Moreau, ed., *Mémoires de Jacques de Saulx, comte de Tavannes* (Paris, 1858), p. 13. The duc de Richelieu resisted the government of Oppède and Mercoeur after the Fronde, and they forced his resignation; cf. EDB, IV-2, 418; III, 662–63; Kettering, *Judicial Politics*, pp. 260–61; Pillorget, *Les Mouvements*, pp. 583, 595, 768–83. The lieutenant general of the royal galleys, the chevalier Philandre de Vincheguerre, was a Knight of Malta and a galley captain. As a client of Alais, he commanded the governor's troops at Toulon during the Fronde; cf. A.A.E., 1708, fol. 219, November 15, 1643; fol. 318, June 21, 1644; Pillorget, *Les Mouvements*, pp. 652, 678, 680; Paul Cousot, "Paul-Albert de Forbin, lieutenant général des galères, 1580–1661, "*Provence historique* 19 (1969): 112. With the help of Richelieu and Vincheguerre, Alais secured the loyalty of a number of galley captains and officers.

[f] Alais's clients in 1649 included the first consul of Marseille, Glandèves, comte de Pourrières, and the viguier or governor of the city, Vintimille, comte Du Luc; they were both sword nobles. Important Marseille families who were his clients included the Ventos, Ciprianis, Albertas, and Baussets; cf. A.A.E., 1714, fol. 245, March 29, 1649; Pillorget, *Les Mouvements*, p. 551. Alais placed clients as consuls and viguiers in the municipal governments of Marseille, Aix, Toulon, Draguignan, Arles, and Grasse; cf. Pillorget, *Les Mouvements*, pp. 607, 611; Kettering, *Judicial Politics*, p. 131, nn. 109, 110.

[g] Alais's political clients in the provence included royal judges who were members of the new Chambre des Requêtes in the Parlement of Aix and the new Semester Parlement and their relatives; cf. Kettering, *Judicial Politics*, pp. 209–10, 247, 340. Tressemanes de Chasteuil was a councillor in the Requêtes; his brother, the chevalier, was recommended by Alais for appointment as a royal fortress governor and his brother-in-law, Suffren, became a councillor in the Semester; cf. B.N., Clairambault 399, fol. 236, May 23, 1645. Alais's other clients included parlement councillors Glandèves-Rousset and Cauvet de Bormes, parlement president Foresta de La Roquette, and Cour des Comptes president Rolland de Réauville. The latter two both hoped to be named first president; cf. A.A.E., 1709, fol. 92, May 13, 1644; 1710, fol. 125, May 16, 1645; B. N., Clairambault 389, fols. 190–91, October 1643; fol. 236, May 23, 1645; Kettering, *Judicial Politics*, p. 262.

[h] François de Bochart, seigneur de Saron-Champigny, served his second term as intendant in Province from 1643 to 1647 at the request of Alais; cf. A.A.E., 1708, fols. 169, 171–72v, 193, April and May 1643.

parlement: Condé had forced the resignation of Pierre Le Goux de La Berchère in 1638 in order to have Bouchu named to this office.[113] The Bouchus were a wealthy old Burgundian family who had been ennobled through royal officeholding in the late sixteenth century.[114] Through Condé's patronage, Jean Bouchu was able to name a brother abbé of Cîteaux; another brother doyen of Autun cathedral; a son abbé of Sept-Fonds; two sons captains in the regiments of Champagne and Picardy; and to obtain several pensions for himself, one as large as 10,000 livres. A political enemy denounced him before the parlement in these words: "The opinion of Bouchu should not be counted because he is a créature of the prince [de Condé] through the favors he has received, having been elevated from a mediocre rank to a much greater place."[115] Bouchu, an able man, enjoyed much influence within the parlement and created an extensive clientele which he put at the disposal of the Condés.[116] Other Condé clients in the Parlement of Dijon included Pierre Lenet, procureur general, and his successor, Guillon; councillor Arviset, Bouchu's uncle, who was doyen; and councillor De Thesul-Lens, intendant of the princes' provincial affairs.[117]

The princes de Condé confirmed nominations to most municipal offices in Burgundy including the mayoralty of Dijon and many provincial offices. A contemporary observer noted that "no one obtained an office, whether in the parlement or in other jurisdictions, other than through the mediation of Monsieur the son or Monsieur the father. No one received a clerical office other than by their nomination. The military service of nobles was only in their regiments, and all municipal officials, whether mayors, échevins, captains, lieutenants, or ensigns, received these coveted honors only through them. In short, Messieurs the princes, father and son, exercised all authority in governing Burgundy for more than twenty years."[118] Control over municipal offices meant that Condé clients were sent as deputies to the Burgundian Estates. This, in fact, was the advantage of controlling municipal elections and appointments in provinces with Estates and explains why provincial governors were eager to do so. The Saulx-Tavannes, who had been provincial lieutenants general and governors of the fortified château of Dijon for several generations, were clients of the Condés and served as household officials and as captains of their gendarmes company. The intendants in Burgundy from 1635 to 1638 and from 1644 to 1650, the brothers Charles and Louis Machault, were also clients of the Condés.[119]

The comte d'Alais did not have family ties in Provence, but such ties could be an important source of noble clients as demonstrated by the clientele of Henri II d'Orléans, duc de Longueville, governor of Normandy from 1619 to 1663. Longueville had numerous clients among the Norman sword nobility, noted by Louis XIII and Le Tellier, and extensive support among the parlementaires of Rouen, noted by first president Faucon de Ris and Cardinal Mazarin.[120] His large provincial clientele was the product of family ties with some of the leading noble families of Normandy and of military patronage from his long tenure as governor. For example, François, comte de Matignon, lieutenant general of Basse-Normandie and governor of

Cherbourg, was a cousin of the duke through his grandmother and was probably Longueville's most important client in Normandy. The duke also enjoyed the loyalty of Matignon's brother, Leónor de Matignon, bishop of Coutances, later of Lisieux, and of François d'Harcourt, marquis de Beuvron, lieutenant general of Haute-Normandie and governor of Rouen, who was first cousin to the Matignons. René Charbonnel de Canisy, governor of Avranches, another client, was closely related to the Matignons. Charles-Léon, comte de Fiesque, also a client, was a relative of Harcourt-Beuvron through his mother, Gillone d'Harcourt. The judicial family of Le Roux became attached through Charbonnel de Canisy, and the financial family of Le Tellier de Tourneville through the Harcourts-Beuvron.

Antoine de Montenay, the captain of Rouen who engineered Longueville's admittance to the city in 1649, was related to the governor through a grandmother, and his grandfather had served as lieutenant in a Longueville gendarmes company. An important parlementaire client, Romé de Fresquienne, had a son who was captain of the governor's guards and a son who had married into the Le Tellier de Tournevilles to become a brother-in-law of Harcourt-Beuvron. Philippe de Montigny had served as a page in the household of the duc de Longueville, then as lieutenant of his guards, before becoming governor of Dieppe upon the death of his father. Another important parlementaire client, Pierre de Rosnyvinen, sieur de Chambois, had served as lieutenant of a cavalry company under Longueville's command and was named governor of Pont-de-l'Arche. Anne Le Blanc de La Croisette had been a gentleman member of Longueville's Paris household. A web of family ties was at the center of Longueville's clientele among the Norman nobility. He also owned much land in the province.[121]

The comte d'Alais did not own land in Provence. Extensive provincial landholdings, however, could provide a patron with important clients. For example, Jean-Louis de La Valette, duc d'Epernon, governor of Guyenne from 1622 to 1638, received homage from forty eight men who owned property within his fiefs in Guyenne, and they included one councillor in a presidial court, three councillors or presidents in the Parlement of Bordeaux, one trésorier de France, and several Bordeaux municipal officials.[122] Epernon's estates in Guyenne were large enough to raise 2,000 to 4,000 men for his military campaigns. Much of his land was concentrated in the Bordeaux area on the seacoast or the banks of the Garonne River and was extensive enough to bring him 64,000 livres a year in revenue. His other lands in Guyenne brought him 75,000 livres a year, a total of 139,000 livres, which was 47 percent of his income in the 1620s and 1630s. The income from Epernon's lands at Bordeaux and in Guyenne rose to 150,600 livres in 1654, an increase of 12 percent, but dropped to 45 percent of his total income.[123] The princes de Condé also owned extensive lands in Burgundy, mostly inherited, and their estates were an important source of clients; the base of their power in Burgundy was the ability to muster a large army of provincial nobles.[124]

The duc d'Epernon and his second son, Bernard, who was governor from

1643 to 1651, named garrison and regimental commanders in Guyenne and kept a guard company of forty men, at least half of whom were noble. Jean's garrison commanders included clients such as Joseph Magnas de Saint Géry, commander of Nérac, and Jean-Louis de La Valette, an illegitimate son, commander of Bergerac. The duc d'Epernon was able to muster at least 600 nobles from Guyenne for his military campaigns, and his entourage included noble clients from the region such as Guy-Aldonce de Durfort, marquis de Duras, and the seigneur Duplessis-Bansonnière.[125] Epernon's household numbered more than sixty servants and cost him 60,000 livres in 1639. He employed four secretaries. Bernard's household numbered seventy-three in 1660, and included five secretaries.[126] There is no detailed information on Alais's household, although he was described as maintaining an extensive entourage of nobles and a large household. Alais employed three secretaries in the 1640s, Messieurs de Villeronde, de Berville, and de Musnier, while sieur Mathan was captain of his company of horse and foot guards.[127] The domestic component of great noble clienteles, therefore, included family and household members as well as vassals and tenants from their provincial estates.

The political clients of a great noble included members of the local elite who owned him their offices, pensions, and titles or who hoped to acquire these with his patronage, as we have seen in the case of the Condés in Burgundy. Sixteenth- and seventeenth-century provincial governors regularly filled municipal governments with their clients and recruited others who were provincial officials, royal judges, tax farmers, financial officials, city governors, and captains.[128] Governor Alais had a large number of clients who were municipal officials (see Table 4), and he placed clients as consuls and viguiers in the municipal governments of Marseille, Aix, Toulon, Draguignan, Arles, and Grasse.[129] The municipal government of Bordeaux was filled with Epernon's appointees in the 1620s and 1630s, and he also filled the governments of other towns in Guyenne such as Agen.[130] Alais recruited magistrates in the royal courts of Provence as his clients (see Table 4). The duc de Longueville and the duc d'Epernon had several parlementaires and royal judges among their clients.

Provincial intendants were often clients of the governor. The duc d'Epernon chose Pierre Séguier, sieur d'Autry, to help him as intendant in Guyenne in 1622, and he selected François de Verthamon, baron de Béarn, to serve as intendant nine years later.[131] Governor Guise chose Dreux d'Aubray, sieur d'Offremont, and acting governor Condé chose Charles Le Roy de La Potherie as intendants in Provence in 1630–1631.[132] Le Tonnelier de Breteuil, intendant in Languedoc in the 1640s, was a client of the governor, the duc d'Orléans.[133] François Bochart, seigneur de Saron-Champigny, intendant in Provence from 1643 to 1647, was the client of Governor Alais. It was upon Champigny's recommendation that Jean de Mesgrigny was appointed first president of the Parlement of Aix in 1644. At the same time Mesgrigny's brother, the chevalier François de Mesgrigny, was named governor of the Tour de Toulon at Alais's request.[134] Most governors were able to name their own clients as provincial lieutenants general, too, for example in Brittany, Languedoc, and Normandy, but this was not the case in Provence in the seventeenth century.[135]

This chapter has presented a scheme for classifying political clienteles according to their composition and function. But clienteles could also be classified according to their patron's arena of political activity, whether national, provincial, or local, since most patrons distributed favors, recruited clients, and acted politically within one milieu. National patrons were active at court and in the royal government at Paris. They included the royal family, great court nobles, royal ministers, and other high officials in the royal government, for instance, secretaries of state, surintendents of finance, and controllers general, and their clients. They operated within the national political arena in Paris and were members of the national ruling elite. Provincial patrons, on the other hand, operated at the provincial, regional, or municipal level and included court nobles permanently resident in the provinces, members of great old families of the provincial nobility, sword nobles, robe nobles, gentlemen, and "new men" who had recently been ennobled. They operated on the province-to-Paris level and within the provincial arena and were members of the provincial ruling elite. Local or community patrons operated in small towns, villages, and the countryside. They lacked the crédit to attract a Paris patron or to influence national decision making. Local patrons might be non-noble, and they usually had greater variability in their social backgrounds. In addition to being great noble or administrative, therefore, political clienteles can also be classified as national, provincial, or local depending on their patron's arena of political activity. Most political clienteles, whether national or provincial, great noble or administrative, provincewide, institutional, or municipal, were used by their patrons as political machines in helping them to exercise power and to govern.

CHAPTER FOUR

Brokers and Political Integration

Louis XIV paid a state visit to Marseille in the winter of 1660. A great crowd gathered at the recently cut breach in the city walls, which became the new royal gate, to cheer loudly as he descended from his carriage, and Paul de Fortia, seigneur de Pilles, stepped forward to present him with a set of golden keys to the city. Louis XIV returned them with the gracious compliment, "Keep them, Pilles, and guard them well. I give them to you."[1] On the previous day, March 6, 1660, he had named Pilles governor of Marseille for life.[2] Louis XIV's gesture of returning the keys to the city was a calculated expression of royal policy: he was publicly honoring a man who had used his clients and his crédit to hold Marseille for the crown during the recent revolt incited by the Valbelle party.

Newly ennobled of merchant origins, Fortia de Pilles had inherited his offices of governor of the Château d'If and viguier of Marseille from his father.[3] He had supported Mazarin during the Fronde.[4] In the summer of 1658, he used his influence with the moderates and negotiated with the Valbelle chiefs to restore peace, and most observers credited him with holding the city for the crown.[5] Cardinal Mazarin in gratitude wrote Pilles that he was "well satisfied with the great zeal you have demonstrated for the King's service during the recent troubles."[6] In a letter Oppède described Fortia de Pilles and the bishop of Marseille, Etienne de Puget, as "men of every merit, strongly attached to the royal service, with characters worthy of special admiration."[7] As governor of the city, Fortia de Pilles replaced Antoine de Valbelle as the most powerful man in Marseille, although he was never as independent.

Fortia de Pilles had first attracted Mazarin's attention through the good offices of the duc de Mercoeur, who sent him to Paris to consult with the Cardinal on "the most important of my affairs" in the spring of 1650.[8] Mercoeur had met Pilles the previous year while outfitting a military expedition to Barcelona.[9] Pilles wrote regularly to Mazarin after his trip to Paris and was soon accepted as the Cardinal's client. On December 4, 1656,

Mazarin assured him that "I promise to tell the financial officials concerned to investigate on behalf of your interests. I've been thinking of giving you something substantial for you or your children. Tell me what you need or would like."[10] A short while later Mazarin wrote that "you have no better friend than I, and I hope that I'll have a chance to prove it."[11] Fortia de Pilles signed himself, "one of the most respectful créatures of Your Eminence," in a letter to Mazarin three years later.[12] He became a provincial broker, one of a small but powerful group dominating provincial politics in the sixteenth and seventeenth centuries.

What services did provincial brokers offer highly placed patrons in the Paris government in exchange for royal patronage? How did they help to extend the central government's control over the frontier provinces of France? This chapter describes seventeenth-century brokers and their role in early modern French statebuilding through a series of portraits of brokers from six peripheral provinces, Provence, Languedoc, Guyenne, Alsace, Burgundy, and the Franche-Comté. Career sketches demonstrate that patrons in the royal government at Paris provided provincial brokers with patronage in exchange for their brokerage services and describe these services, the resources that made them possible, and their contribution to the political integration of France.

Brokers used their influence and client networks to convince independent local institutions to cooperate with the goals and projects of their Paris patrons. For example, brokers secured the approval of provincial Estates for royal tax demands and the cooperation of provincial parlements in registering royal legislation, and they acted unofficially as administrative troubleshooters to resolve difficult problems. They offered their Paris patrons a way to get things done beyond regular institutional channels, for example, acting as mediators, providing information and advice on local politics and personalities, intimidating and silencing opponents of the crown, and securing extraordinary assistance of all kinds—fighting men, money, clients, personal favors. They also assisted the intendants, the new agents of the central government in the provinces, for example, by securing the cooperation of the Estates and parlements. And brokers influenced political decision making on the national level through letters offering information and advice on local politics as well as by lobbying for their own interests and views.

Brokers and Institutions

Brokers used their local influence to convince independent institutions such as the Estates, parlements, and municipal governments to support the policies of their patrons in the Paris government. For example, Oppède and Mercoeur, Janson-Forbin and Grignan, and the comte de Mérinville helped Mazarin and Colbert to influence the decision making of the General Assemblies of Provençal Communities. In Languedoc, archbishops Rébé and Marca helped Richelieu and Mazarin to control the Estates, and intendant Claude Bouchu helped Colbert to control the Burgundian Estates. As we have already seen, Oppède and Régusse helped their patrons to control the Parlement of Aix, while Nicolas Brûlart in the Parlement of Dijon and Claude and Gabriel Boisot and Jean-Ferdinand Jobelot in the Parlement of Besançon performed the same service for their Paris patrons. The Valbelles kept the city of Marseille loyal to the crown.

Oppède and his protégé, Toussaint de Janson-Forbin, used their influence to persuade the General Assemblies of Provençal Communities to grant the taxes demanded by the chief minister. On February 27, 1664, Oppède wrote Colbert that "I am leaving tomorrow with the governor [Mercoeur] for the assembly . . . as I see it composed of a quantity of honest men among whom I count many friends, I can for this reason assure you that it will do as you want."[13] Oppède was not exaggerating. The General Assembly meeting at Lambesc in March, April, and May 1664 was, indeed, composed of his friends as he claimed, and it granted the taxes the crown demanded.[14]

Oppède's friends were the procureurs du pays. At least fifteen of his kinsmen and clients were elected consuls and assessors of the Aix municipal government during his years in power, many as first consul, the office traditionally reserved for the sword nobility: the first consul acted as spokesman for the procureurs du pays. The consuls included his cousins, the Forbins de La Barben and Forbins de Solliès; his uncle, Castellane de La Verdière, and his oldest son, Jean-Baptiste. Another client, Laurens de Vardier, marquis de Saint Andiol, was first consul in 1665.[15]

The traditional Estates of Provence were replaced as the provincial tax-granting body by the Third Estate sitting alone as a General Assembly of Communities, and the procureurs du pays were empowered to act for the assemblies when they were not in session. The First and Second Estates met infrequently as General Assemblies of the Provençal Clergy and Nobility. The Assembly of the Nobility elected three syndics to serve as its interim executive authority. Oppède's maternal uncle, Jean-Baptiste de Castellane de La Verdière, was second syndic from 1632 to 1639, and his cousin, Jacques de Forbin de La Barben, was first syndic in 1656 and from 1661 to 1667.[16] Childless, La Verdière left his fortune to Oppède's oldest son, besides occasionally subsidizing his nephew's political activities. He was one of Oppède's most important allies.

The nobility of Provence was represented in the General Assemblies of Communities by two noble procureurs elected in 1642, one of whom was Oppède's client. The first procureur, the sieur de Boyer-Bandol, left Provence the next year, never to return, so his office remained vacant until 1664, when François de Vintimille, comte Du Luc, was named to it; he died two years later. He was replaced by Antoine de Porcellet, marquis de Maillane, a client of Oppède, who assured Colbert of his fidelity in serving the crown.[17] The other procureur of the nobility was Jean de Sabran, baron de Beaudinard, who had served since 1642. He was an old man by this time. His name never appears in the deliberations, and age may well have limited his participation.

The clergy of Provence were represented in the General Assembly of Communities by two procureurs who were also Oppède's clients. He had secured the appointment of his younger brother, Louis, as bishop of Toulon in 1664, and two years later Louis was named a procureur of the clergy in the General Assembly. The vote to name him was unanimous, indicating Oppède's influence in the assembly.[18] The other procureur of the clergy was his cousin and client, François-Toussaint de Janson-Forbin, bishop of Digne and then of Marseille, whose nomination he had secured in 1658.[19] The bishop of Marseille became senior procureur of the clergy nine years later. The senior procureur of the clergy was politically important because the first procureur du pays, the archbishop of Aix, was an old enemy of Oppède who discouraged his presence at the assemblies, and Janson-Forbin acted in his place to preside over the assemblies.[20]

Janson-Forbin chaired the debates of the deputies on royal tax demands. By tradition the king's representatives were not allowed to be present at these debates. But the procureurs visited the royal representatives each evening to report on the day's debates and, when the deputies reached an agreement, the royal representatives returned to hear the results of their deliberations—Oppède usually appeared alone because the governor or lieutenant general only came to the opening and closing sessions. Oppède immediately relayed the results to the king and his ministers and, after receiving their reply, he accepted or rejected the deputies' offer. If the offer was rejected, he presented the king's tax demands again, and the deputies debated once more, a process that could go on for weeks, even months.[21] Oppède's control over the provincial procureurs was important in allowing him to influence the deputies' debates and negotiations.

Oppède did not limit his efforts at influencing the assemblies to naming his clients and kinsmen as procureurs of the clergy, nobility, and pays. Cardinal Mazarin wrote Oppède in 1656, "I am pleased that the dispensation for age you obtained for the son of sieur Meyronnet [the assembly's secretary] will be advantageous for the service of the King in future provincial assemblies because of the crédit he has among the deputies."[22] As we have seen, Oppède lavishly entertained the deputies to the assembly. In the 1664 assembly, Oppède's clients included provincial treasurer Pierre Maurel and deputies Leydet, first consul of Sisteron, Aymar, first consul of Forcalquier, Boyer, first consul of Apt, and Revest-Maynier, first consul of Draguignan, who belonged to parlementaire families allied to Oppède; so did the syndic or deputy of the unrepresented Provençal communities, sieur Decormis, whom Oppède had described in a letter to Colbert the previous year as "well-intentioned and full of zeal for Your Majesty's service."[23] Oppède was not boasting when he declared that the 1664 assembly was full of his friends.

Oppède was successful in handling the General Assemblies because of his clients and his skill in negotiating, which reflected an understanding of Provençal chauvinism. He emphasized Provençal interests, for example, at the February 1671 assembly when he convinced the deputies to approve a tax of 600,000 livres to support royal troops in Provence, 100,000 livres more than usual. He pointed out that part of the money would be spent in the province on the construction of new galleys, which would use local workmen and materials. These galleys were meant to rid the Mediterranean of pirates and would aid Provençal commerce. Oppède concluded his speech by noting that he had used whatever he could of his talents, authority, and influence to provincial advantage as "a zealous and loyal compatriot"; now the province had to reciprocate.[24]

Oppède died in November at the next General Assembly, and assessor Julianis pronounced his eulogy to the deputies, declaring Oppède to be "one of the great geniuses and protectors of our province." He noted that Oppède had always used his royal authority in such a way that "by his wisdom and manner he sweetened the bitterness of angry [royal] orders, and avoided fatal ones which would have increased provincial miseries." Julianis concluded that "as we often heard him say, he was a royal commissioner, so he had to protect the interests and service of the King, but he was also our compatriot, who had love and tenderness for our province, desiring to protect it and do his best for it."[25] Oppède was a provincial broker. He acted as a mediator between the Provençal power structure and the royal government in Paris.

His successor as provincial intendant, Jean-Baptiste de Rouillé, comte de Meslay, was not a Provençal, and he was not as effective in handling the General Assemblies because he did not emphasize Provençal interests. The speeches he made to the assemblies are printed in their entirety in the deliberations. Rouillé spoke exclusively about what the king needed and what the province owed the king. There were no references to helping the province or protecting its interests.[26] The approach Oppède used was more likely to succeed in a fiercely chauvinistic region such as Provence than was a panegyric of the king.

When Oppède died, his cousin Janson-Forbin, bishop of Marseille, replaced him as head of the Forbin clientele. The bishop wrote Colbert as senior procureur of the clergy that he was presiding over the debates of the deputies in the General Assembly, and added that "as I have the honor of being at their head, and of having acquired influence among them, I shall try to influence their opinions."[27] The procureurs du pays were all Forbin clients. The first consul of Aix in 1670, Louis de Forbin, marquis de Solliès, was a cousin whom Madame de Sévigné had identified as "the bishop's man."[28] Villeneuve, baron de Vence, was first consul in 1671, and François de Julianis was assessor.[29] Janson-Forbin and Grignan had praised the loyalty of both men in letters to Colbert.[30] In 1672, the first consul of Aix was Forbin de La Barben, the bishop's cousin: Janson-Forbin had happily announced his election to Colbert with assurances of his "fidelity and zeal for the royal service, which he will soon demonstrate."[31] He praised his cousin's service in glowing terms in a letter on December 23, 1672, and suggested that he be named to the vacant office of procureur of the nobility a year later.[32]

The procureurs of the nobility were also Forbin clients: they were the marquis de Maillane and the young baron de Beaudinard, who had replaced his father in office as the nephew of the marquis de Valavoire. Grignan reported to Colbert that Maillane was a great help to them in the General Assemblies and praised the zeal of the young Beaudinard.[33] Madame de Sévigné wrote her daughter that it was rumored the baron de Beaudinard was entirely in the interests of Janson-Forbin.[34] She described Maillane as a cousin and friend of the bishop.[35] Both procureurs of the nobility were attached to Janson-Forbin, although Madame de Sévigné gamely tried to entice them away to the support of her son-in-law, the comte de Grignan. She wrote her daughter that she had recently dined with the marquis de Valavoire and his wife, who were most cordial, and that she had enjoyed a pleasant interview with the marquis de Maillane at Versailles.[36]

François-Toussaint de Janson-Forbin had begun his ecclesiastical career as coadjutor to the bishop of Digne in 1653 and became bishop himself two years later. He had obtained the appointment as coadjutor through the good offices of his older brother, Laurent de Forbin, marquis de Janson, who had visited the court that year as a deputy from the General Assembly of Communities.[37] The marquis had been a Sabreur during the Fronde. Through him, Janson-Forbin obtained the patronage of their mutual cousin, Oppède, who had secured his appointment as procureur of the clergy in the General Assemblies. When the bishop of Vence was successfully pressured to resign and Oppède's brother replaced him, Janson-Forbin became senior procureur of the clergy. In this capacity, he headed the Provençal deputations to court, often simultaneously attending the General Assemblies of the French Clergy at Paris.[38] He was named bishop of Marseille in 1668.[39] His regular trips to court and Oppède's praise brought him to Colbert's attention.[40]

Janson-Forbin was widely respected in Provence, where he had much crédit and many clients as a bishop and a member of the Forbin family: Parades de L'Estang noted that he came from "a numerous, rich, and powerful family, and had many friends and dependents in the province, particularly in the parlement."[41] Even Madame de Sévigné, who disliked him as a political rival of her son-in-law, admitted that he had influence in Provence, recognizing his intelligence and his skill at polite dissembling and courteous deceit—what she called *la perfidie douceureuse*.[42] When Oppède died, the political star of Janson-Forbin, long in his shadow, shot into the sky, and he was openly recognized as Colbert's client and an influential broker. In a letter about this time, Janson-Forbin thanked the minister for giving his nephew a galley command, writing that "I count on Your favor and protection. I can only respond to it in words, but I'll keep all my life an unbreakable attachment to You."[43]

Janson-Forbin was sent to Florence and Rome as extraordinary ambassador in the spring and summer of 1673. In the spring of 1674 he was in Warsaw serving as ambassador; he remained there three years. He proved to be a skillful diplomat, and for this reason earned the favor of Louis XIV. Named bishop of Beauvais and a cardinal, he left Provence permanently for the court to embark upon a successful diplomatic career.[44] Louis XIV thought so well of Janson-Forbin that in 1700 he told his ambassador in

Rome, the prince de Monaco (who was soon to die) that he could tell the bishop anything he wished.[45] Janson-Forbin replaced the prince as ambassador in Rome and served until 1706. When he returned, old and ill, the king praised him at a *coucher* (a ceremony when the king retired at night), declaring that "he spent seven years at Rome without causing me any worry, and was delighted when he was recalled; that is how everyone should conduct a foreign assignment."[46] As a reward the king gave him a gift of 50,000 livres and made his nephew archbishop of Arles. He was named Grand Almoner of France and died in Paris in 1713 at the age of eighty three.[47] The duc de Saint Simon, a personal friend, praised his abilities.

> Cardinal Janson was a tall man, well-made, with a face that was not shocking, but not attractive, with something pensive about it. He was full of honor and virtue, with a great love of duty and piety, and a wise and excellent mind. He was always in control of himself, and self-possessed, the reason he was so successful in negotiating. He better served as the King at Rome than any of his other ambassadors.[48]

Janson-Forbin's patrons at court included his cousin, Louis de Forbin, who had pursued a successful army career to become a lieutenant general. He was liked by the king who had called him "one of the bravest and wisest gentlemen in France."[49] Louis de Forbin was a good friend of the king's first valet, Alexandre Bontemps, who became a good friend of Janson-Forbin, too: Saint Simon noted that Bontemps served the bishop well with the king.[50] Janson-Forbin was also helped by his older brother, the marquis de Janson, who had introduced him to Oppède and protected his interests at court. The bishop wrote Colbert in 1662 that he was greatly pleased by the minister's kind words about his brother.[51] Ten years later Janson-Forbin wrote Colbert that he was sending a courier to his brother at court with special information for the minister.[52] Both brothers vainly hoped that the marquis de Janson would be appointed Provençal lieutenant general and acting governor after Mercoeur's death.[53] Janson-Forbin's most important patron, of course, was the king himself: Mazarin on his deathbed had advised Louis XIV to award royal patronage himself so that everyone would look to him for favors, a policy that would strengthen the monarchy, and Louis took his advice.[54]

Grignans and Forbins

François de Castellane d'Adhémar de Monteil, comte de Grignan, was the king's choice in 1669 as lieutenant general and acting governor in Provence. He was the successful political rival of Janson-Forbin whom he replaced in managing the General Assemblies. Grignan came from one of the oldest, most illustrious noble families in Provence. His family claimed to be descended from Charlemagne and went back at least to the first crusade.[55] He had served as first gentleman of the duc d'Orléans's bedchamber and enjoyed a distinguished military career. After serving as colonel of the regiment of

Champagne, captain of the Queen's light horse, and army lieutenant general in Languedoc, he was appointed lieutenant general of Provence. He became acting governor two years later, served for decades, and fought in several major campaigns at the head of a contingent of Provençal nobles. Colbert congratulated him in 1673 for taking the château of Orange, which he retook twice more, forcing mass abjurations and emigrations of Huguenots each time. He annexed the Comtat Venaissin to the crown in 1688 and became its governor.[56] In 1707, at the age of 76, he helped to stop the advance along the Provençal coast of the army of prince Eugène and the duc de Savoie, receiving a personal letter of thanks from Louis XIV in November for helping to lift the siege of Toulon.[57]

His massive, imposing château of Grignan south of Montélimar had a magnificent view of the Rhône valley from its terrace and an Italian facade of 365 windows. It was staffed by eighty servants and Madame de Sévigné, a frequent visitor, wrote that the château was always bustling: her son-in-law lived extremely well and saw a great deal of company. The château lodged about a hundred visitors and their servants. Traveling groups of actors stopped frequently, and musicians were permanently in residence.[58] For decades Grignan entertained everyone of importance passing through Provence, including the dukes of Burgundy and Berry, the king and queen of Spain, the queens of Spain and Poland, and a host of princes, bishops, cardinals, and ambassadors on their way to and from Italy.[59] He held open court for the Provençal nobility during the season: Madame de Sévigné lectured her daughter about maintaining four or five "open tables." She wrote that the château was becoming a famous inn, and they would soon ruin themselves. In addition, Grignan and his wife gambled for large sums of money.[60] Grignan melted his plate in 1706 to contribute toward the king's military expenses, not the only time he lent the crown money.[61] The duc de Saint Simon had this to say about him:

> Grignan was a tall, well-built man, with the appearance and manners of a grand seigneur, which he was, extremely polished, a good and honest man, much esteemed, with many friends, whom the King treated well, with a sensitive but mediocre intelligence, highly respected in Provence, of which he was master, and as much loved there as his wife was not. They ruined themselves living grandly. [His death] was generally regretted.[62]

Parades de L'Estang concurred in this judgment, writing that Grignan kept "a magnificent table," and was "an extremely pleasant seigneur with beautiful manners who they say loved his pleasures, and had little inclination or application to the affairs of government."[63] Grignan's lavish hospitality increased his influence in Provence: Colbert noted in 1671 the crédit that Grignan had among the deputies to the General Assembly of Communities.[64] Colbert wrote in 1673 to congratulate Grignan on the speedy termination of the General Assembly, noting that "His Majesty attributes this success principally to the crédit which you have with the deputies."[65]

Replacing the governing team of Oppède and Mercoeur, Janson-Forbin and Grignan successfully used the same strategy to manipulate the General Assemblies: an example of their teamwork is the General Assembly at Lambesc in the autumn of 1671. Grignan opened the session on September 30 as acting governor, and Oppède appeared a week later as royal commissioner and acting intendant, seated in an armchair to Grignan's right. To their left was a bench for the procureurs of the Provençal clergy, Janson-Forbin and Louis d'Oppède, and to their right was a bench for the procureurs of the Provençal nobility, the marquis de Maillane and the baron de Beaudinard. Behind them was a table covered with a tapestry used by the secretary, sieur Meyronnet, who was recording the proceedings, and by the provincial treasurer, Pierre Maurel, who sat in an armchair. To one side was an armchair for sieur Decormis, syndic of the unrepresented communities, and a bench for the procureurs du pays. All these men belonged to the Forbin clientele.

Across the room sitting in rows on hard, backless benches were sixty-four deputies, two each from thirty-seven communities with some absences. They stood respectfully when the king's representatives entered, and mass was heard at a curtained, portable altar behind the dais on which Grignan sat in an armchair covered with a tapestry. Afterward Grignan presented the royal tax demands, and Janson-Forbin as senior procureur of the clergy answered for the province.[66] Janson-Forbin was newly returned from court where he had seen Colbert and discussed the assembly.[67]

Colbert had told Oppède in September that the assembly must finish within a month as the king had ordered, because the Estates of Brittany had finished in three weeks and those of Burgundy in less time.[68] A month later Colbert urged Oppède to push the assembly into cooperating with the king's tax demands as fast as possible.[69] Louis XIV and Colbert were insisting on shorter meetings of the provincial tax-granting assemblies to force compliance. The Estates and General Assemblies under Richelieu had usually sat for several months.[70] But this had changed: Madame de Sévigné noted in a letter to her daughter, the comtesse de Grignan, that "your [Provençal] assemblies last no longer than two weeks, and our Estates [of Brittany] only three weeks; they will become even shorter."[71] The time limit put additional pressure on the king's representatives.

The king's tax demands were presented, and the deputies began the negotiations by offering the crown 200,000 of 600,000 livres requested to supplement the taille. Janson-Forbin warned Colbert that it would be difficult to get the sum much above 400,000 livres.[72] The deputies had agreed to 300,000 livres by October 25, when the assembly recessed to allow the procureurs of the clergy to spend All Saints' Day (November 1) in their dioceses. Oppède fell ill with a lingering fever, and his absence retarded the negotiations. Colbert wrote sternly to Grignan on October 30 that Oppède's illness must not be permitted to cause delay because "the King orders me to tell you that it is absolutely necessary to finish promptly."[73] Grignan wrote to Colbert on November 2 that the deputies had reassembled, but he advised waiting for Oppède's recovery before continuing because the deputies were uncooperative—they were delaying, awaiting the outcome of Oppède's illness, and hoping to gain the advantage in the negotiations if he did not recover.

Oppède died on November 13, and the deputies used the confusion of the occasion to approve a lower tax subsidy: Janson-Forbin wrote Colbert on November 18 that the deputies had approved 350,000 livres, increased to 400,000 livres after much haggling, but still much less than the king had demanded. Janson-Forbin hesitantly inquired if the king would accept 450,000 livres. Colbert answered no: the king insisted on 500,000 livres and not a penny less.[74] Janson-Forbin had already stepped into Oppède's place in helping the crown's representatives to manage the General Assemblies.

Grignan noted in a letter to Colbert on December 13 that it was difficult to get the deputies to go above 400,000 livres. Learning that the king was displeased by the assembly's length and lack of cooperation, Grignan wrote that he and the bishop of Marseille were doing the best they could.[75] Grignan was visibly flustered by Colbert's insistence on speed. By December 31 the deputies had granted 450,000 livres, but Colbert still declared the sum unsatisfactory.[76] The deputies finally granted 500,000 livres in January,and Grignan adjourned the meeting with a sigh of relief on January 24.[77] The General Assembly had taken four months to grant 100,000 livres less than the king demanded.

The assembly cooperated because Grignan had threatened to use force. On December 13, he wrote Colbert that he had read aloud the king's letter expressing dissatisfaction at the assembly's stubbornness. Grignan advised sending royal orders to disperse the deputies and "several lettres de cachet to punish the most seditious, who have started the rumor that I want to gain favor at their expense, and who say that I lie about the letters you send in order to frighten them.... The bishop of Marseille and I are working hard to win them back, and to convince them by sweetness or fear to do their duty."[78] Grignan wrote to Colbert on December 20, that "I beg you, in case I discover those who from particular interest belong to this cabal, to give me the authority to punish them, because the threats I am obliged to make are insufficient to force them to do their duty."[79] Grignan received by return mail ten lettres de cachet to exile the most "ill-intentioned" deputies to Brittany and Normandy. These letters were sent blank as he had requested so he could fill in the names.[80] Grignan reported on January 9 that after he had read the royal letters dispersing the assembly and exiling the deputies, the assembly had reluctantly voted what the king wanted.[81]

Grignan also read aloud a letter from his uncle at court, the bishop of Uzès, who had recently talked with Colbert and the king: Uzès reported that the king was threatening to suspend provincial privileges and to billet royal troops on Provence as punishment; he feared there might be worse to come.[82] Colbert had written Janson-Forbin on December 31 that the king had threatened never to permit another General Assembly to convene in Provence.[83] Intimidated, the deputies acquiesced and granted what the king demanded.

Janson-Forbin supplied the "sweetness' and Grignan the "fear" in manipulating the deputies of the General Assemblies. Janson-Forbin followed Oppède's model in persuading the deputies to cooperate by stressing his concern for their interests. He depicted himself as a native-born Provençal who was fortunate in having influence at court which he could use on their behalf. For instance, on January 9, 1672, he worried aloud in a letter to Colbert that he could lose his crédit at court because he had been asked by the General Assembly after Oppède's death to head a provincial deputation, which the king had refused to receive. But he also worried that if he refused to head this deputation, he would lose his crédit in Provence. Caught on the horns of a dilemma, he expressed great relief in a letter on January 26 when the king changed his mind and decided to receive the Provençal deputation.[84] Grignan, on the other hand, was acting governor and commanded troops in Provence. He coerced the deputies into cooperating by using a threat of reprisals for disobedience. In the name of Colbert and the king, he threatened revocation of provincial privileges, arrest of recalcitrant deputies, and billeting of troops on Provence if the deputies refused to cooperate. Janson-Forbin and Grignan made an effective team, alternating in their use of "sweetness" and "fear" to manipulate the deputies and secure their approval for royal tax demands.

Grignan is chiefly remembered for his third wife, Marguerite-Françoise de Sévigné, the adored, spoiled daughter of Madame de Sévigné who dispelled her daughter's provincial boredom with witty letters from court. Grignan had married Marguerite-Françoise in 1669 when he was forty and she was twenty three. Her mother was delighted with the match because she had been left with considerable debts at her husband's death. Madame de Sévigné had half the income of Grignan, who enjoyed 50,000 to 60,000 livres a year; his total fortune was around 1,700,000 livres.[85] Her less enchanted daughter wrote that Grignan "had abused the freedom given men to be ugly". He had a big nose and was nicknamed the tomcat because his hair stuck up in tufts all over his head.[86]

Grignan's mother-in-law watched over his interests at court and used her friendship with Simon Arnauld, marquis de Pomponne, on his behalf, occasionally even acting as a broker. Replacing Hugues de Lionne as secretary of state for Provence and foreign affairs, Pomponne served in this post from 1671 to 1679 and defended Grignan's interests with the king.[87] In a letter to her daughter on December 9, 1676, Madame de Sévigné reported a conversation between Pomponne and the king in which the marquis had requested and secured the king's approval for renewal of Grignan's pension of 5,000 livres. The king said laughingly, "You tell me every year it will be the last time," and Pomponne replied, "Sire, it is all spent in Your Service." When the king was told that the marquis de Saint Andiol, Grignan's brother-in-law, had been named first consul of Aix, he smiled knowingly, and Pomponne stressed that the nomination had passed unanimously "without contestation or cabal."[88] Another useful friend of Madame de Sévigné was her first cousin's wife, Madame de Coulanges, who was a niece of Le Tellier and first cousin of Louvois.[89]

One of Grignan's uncles was François de Castellane d'Adhémar de Monteil de Grignan, archbishop of Arles for a half-century. He was Mazarin's client and patron himself of a client network that acted as a political machine to control the municipal government of Arles. His nephew may have been named for him. Another uncle was Jacques de Castellane d'Adhémar de Monteil de Grignan, bishop of Uzès in Languedoc from 1660 until his death in 1674. These two clerics were the patriarchs of the family. Uzès was frequently at court as a client of Colbert, and he wrote regularly to the minister when in the Midi. Uzès wrote to Colbert in 1665 to declare "the profound respect that I have for You and the great desire I shall always have to merit a place in Your memory and Your esteem ... I have never had for anyone the respect and veneration which I have for You."[90]

One of Grignan's brothers, Jean-Baptiste, became coadjutor of the archbishop of Arles, exercising the office for his blind uncle until he succeeded to it himself in 1689. Another brother, Louis, abbé de Grignan, became bishop of Evreux in the Eure, and then bishop of Carcassone in Languedoc. A third brother, Joseph, became captain of a light horse company and then colonel of the Grignan regiment. A fourth brother, who was a Knight of Malta, died young. Grignan was related to most of the great noble families in Provence: the signees of his third marriage contract read like a guide to the nobility of Provence in the seventeenth century.[91] Grignan was a provincial grand seigneur who was patron of a great noble clientele.

The cooperative relationship of Janson-Forbin and Grignan soured almost immediately with potentially dangerous consequences: they began to compete for Colbert's favor and Oppède's power. Their rivalry flared openly after the death of the marquis de Maillane. Janson-Forbin wanted a kinsman, Forbin de La Barben, to replace Maillane as procureur of the nobility. But Grignan proposed his own cousin, Pontevès, marquis de Buous, to the General Assembly at Lambesc. The bishops of Marseille and Toulon, Janson-Forbin and Louis d'Oppède, protested that the nomination was against traditional privilege: a General Assembly of the Nobility, or at least its noble syndics, were supposed to nominate the noble procureurs. The bishops also opposed giving Grignan his annual pension, a salary supplement of 5,000 livres granted in previous years by the province to pay for a guard company. Grignan argued that since he acted as governor, he needed a provincial guard company; it was the standard privilege of governors. Colbert told the intendant to mediate and noted that "there is nothing so harmful to the royal service as the division of a province between its principal personnages." Colbert and the king promptly wrote Grignan and the bishops telling them to reach an agreement.[92] Parades de L'Estang observed that the government of Provence was divided between Grignan and Forbin, each advancing his own particular interest under the pretext of the public good.[93]

The bishops of Marseille and Toulon conceded defeat when they received letters from the king and secretary of state ordering the appointment of Buous.[94] Secretary Pomponne, the old friend of Madame de Sévigné, had convinced the king to support Grignan, and Madame de Sévigné declared herself well pleased with her son-in-law's victory in a letter on December 24, 1673.[95] Janson-Forbin had written Colbert on December 17 that the marquis de Buous was named procureur of the nobility only because he and Louis d'Oppède had used their friends in the assembly to secure his nomination.[96] Five months later Janson-Forbin was writing to Colbert from Warsaw where he was serving as ambassador. He did not return to Provence for another three years.[97] In a letter on New Year's Day 1675, Madame de Sévigné announced triumphantly that "the ghost of Monsieur de Marseille has been laid to rest, and the crédit of his party in Provence has vanished."[98] His absence undoubtedly had a good deal to do with this.

Grignan replaced Janson-Forbin as the provincial broker who controlled the General Assemblies. Grignan's brother, coadjutor to the archbishop of Arles, became senior procureur of the clergy in the bishop's absence, and when the other procureur of the clergy in the General Assemblies, Louis d'Oppède, died in 1674, he was replaced by Grignan's client. Forbin control over the consulate of Aix and the procureurs du pays was successfully challenged by the Grignan party in the elections of 1675—there had been much talk at Aix in the previous year of "the tyranny of the Forbins and [their clients] the Sèguirans."[99] Grignan, therefore, came to control the procureurs du pays and the procureurs of the nobility and clergy as Oppède had done, and he took Janson-Forbin's place in the General Assemblies with the tacit approval of Colbert and Louis XIV.

Ambitious for her son-in-law, Madame de Sévigné defended his interests at court, using her wit to the discomfort of Janson-Forbin: he may have reversed the order of his name because of a bon mot of Madame de Sévigné about his *fourberies*, or double dealing, which she called *fourbineries*.[100] She merrily wrote her daughter that she had attended a funeral at Versailles and had not seen the bishop. Her companion had laughed aloud when she whispered, "If the guest of honor had been living, he wouldn't have missed it."[101] She wrote her daughter later, with tongue in cheek, "You will see by the enclosed letter from the bishop that we are 'fast' friends; it seems to me I've received this same letter ten times already. Continue your 'sincere' friendship, and don't let your mask slip."[102] Madame de Sévigné delighted in portraying Janson-Forbin as a pious hypocrite of the type satirized by Molière in his comedy *Tartuffe*. She wrote her daughter that the bishop "testifies to a friendship of which dissimulation is the attachment and his own interest the basis."[103] Janson-Forbin was not the only Provençal to suffer from the sharp wit of Madame de Sévigné. She wrote that she had seen Séguiran de Bouc, first president of the Aix Cour des Comptes and a Forbin client, but "I do not believe it was he who invented gunpowder and printing."[104] Evidently Séguiran boasted.

Madame de Sévigné angrily reported a conversation between the king, the marquis de Janson, and the bishop of Uzès in which derogatory remarks had been made about Grignan. The bishop was her source, of course. The marquis had laughingly remarked that his brother's political rival was well known for his laziness. There was probably some truth to this remark because Madame de Sévigné herself mentioned her son-in-law's laziness in a letter a few years later.[105] Parades de L'Estang noted that Grignan's inattention to his administrative duties was well known.[106] The comte de Grignan had military ambitions, and he wanted to become a duke. But politically he was satisfied with being Provençal lieutenant general and acting governor, much to the chagrin of Madame de Sévigné. Her loyalty to old friends who had been disgraced (including the Cardinal de Retz, Fouquet, and Pomponne) caused her to lose the king's favor in 1680 and she could no longer help Grignan, but she retained the friendship of Madame de Maintenon, Madame de Coulanges, and Madame de La Fayette, all of whom were in favor at court.[107]

Janson-Forbin, on the other hand, was politically ambitious. A contemporary historian, Pierre-Joseph de Haitze, described the bishop as having a natural genius for intrigue and a desire to become the guiding hand in Provençal politics.[108] Madame de Sévigné criticized his political ambitions to Pomponne, reporting complacently to her daughter that Pomponne "did not seem pleased that a man of the Church should take on the governorship of Provence."[109] Parades de L'Estang remarked that Grignan was less ambitious than Janson-Forbin and less intelligent than Oppède.[110] This difference in their ambitions and intelligence was probably the reason Grignan remained in Provence to manage the General Assemblies with the assistance of the intendants, while Janson-Forbin began a diplomatic career outside Provence: Grignan was easier for Colbert to control. For decades Grignan managed the General Assemblies and the procureurs du pays for the crown, with the help of the provincial intendants. He died on the road to Marseille in December 1714, at the age of eighty five, returning home from representing the king at the annual General Assembly at Lambesc. He had been attending these meetings regularly for thirty four years.[111] Grignan Janson-Forbin, and Oppède were provincial brokers who used their influence and clients to persuade the General Assemblies of Provençal Communities to grant royal tax requests.

Brokers and Institutions in Other Provinces

Brokers in the other remote frontier provinces of Languedoc, Burgundy, and the Franche-Comté helped their patrons in the royal government at Paris to influence the conduct of the provincial Estates, high courts, and municipal governments, in this way contributing to national statebuilding. In neighboring Languedoc, for example, archbishops Rébé and Marca and the comte de Mérinville earned reputations at Paris for their success in managing the Estates. Claude de Rébé, archbishop of Narbonne, presided over the Languedoc Estates for three decades and usually secured their acceptance of royal tax demands. A forceful, eloquent speaker on the crown's behalf, he was recruited as a client by Richelieu during the Montmorency revolt—the rebellious governor of Languedoc, the duc de Montmorency, had put him under house arrest in the summer of 1631 to prevent him from reversing the deliberations of the Pézenas Estates, which had declared for Montmorency against Richelieu—and he was rewarded for his loyalty after the revolt with a royal pension.[112] At Richelieu's death, Rébé became a client of Mazarin, and attacked the politics of the absentee governor of Languedoc, the duc d'Orléans, who was a Frondeur. As a result, Rébé was unable to leave Narbonne for fear of arrest.[113] At the end of the Fronde, he used his influence with Mazarin to demand the punishment of the marquis de Rabat for brutalizing the gardener of the bishop of Rieux.[114]

Pierre de Marca, archbishop of Toulouse, assisted Rébé in managing the Estates of Languedoc. Marca had been a president in the Parlement of Pau when he was appointed intendant in Béarn in 1631. He served in this post for seven years and was named bishop of Conserans in Languedoc in 1642, although he was not immediately received in office. Instead, he served as intendant in Catalonia where his performance secured for him the patronage of Le Tellier, Mazarin, and Louis XIV.[115]

Conserans had annual revenues of only 10,000 livres, and Marca's expenses in Catalonia were heavy so he was soon requesting financial assistance. On June 27, 1646, he solicited the Benedictine abbey of Saint-Jean-de-Luc in the diocese of Oloron from Le Tellier, and the small abbey of Notre Dame de Sauvelade in the diocese of Lescar, for his protégé, first cousin, and vicar general, Paul de Faget. On March 25, 1648, he asked Le Tellier for the bishopric of Rodez, and in September and November for the bishopric of Mans or the archbishopric of Aix. In October and November 1649, he requested the bishopric of Montpellier from Le Tellier and Mazarin, three years before the death of its elderly incumbent, Pierre de Fenouillet, and at the same time he asked the king for the first bishopric or archbishopric with large revenues that came vacant in Guyenne, Languedoc, or near Paris. In 1650, he wrote several letters to Le Tellier and Mazarin asking for the bishoprics of Chartres or Beauvais. His persistence was finally rewarded at the death of the archbishop of Toulouse in September 1651. After attending the funeral, Marca hurriedly went north to the court at Fontainebleau to see the king, and then followed the court to Poitiers, Saumur, Tours, Blois, and Saint-Germain-en-Laye before the king finally named him archbishop of Toulouse in May 1652. Mazarin had given his support in a letter from Bonn where he was in exile. Marca was not received in office for another two years, however, because he refused to pay the tax of the papal annates. He was never resident at Toulouse, and his vicar general, Paul de Faget, acted for him.[116]

Marca attended the Languedoc Estates at Montpellier in December 1654 as archbishop of Toulouse, and he presided over the Languedoc Estates in 1655, assisting intendant Bazin de Bezons. The crown's difficulties in controlling the Béziers Estates the next year were due to the absence of both Rébé and Marca—the intendant had to rely upon the less influential bishop of Lavaur. Marca wrote to Mazarin that "the secret of succeeding in the Estates is to unite the bishops and the barons in the same opinion," and this became the crown's strategy in Languedoc. Rébé, old and tired, reluctantly ceded the presidency of the Estates to Marca in 1656. Marca saw the king at Lyon in October 1658, but was sent posthaste back to Languedoc in November to preside over the Estates because Rébé had been taken ill; he soon died. As a reward for his service, Marca was named a minister of state, and his cousin Faget was elected general agent of the French clergy. Named archbishop of Paris by the king in 1662, Marca died before he could assume office.[117]

The Languedoc Estates were dominated by twenty-two bishops who led the resistance to the crown's attacks on traditional liberties.[118] The royal ministers diluted their influence by appointing their own clients as bishops, for instance, as the bishops of Agde, Lavaur, Albi, Montpellier, Béziers, Saint Papoul, and Saint Pons—this was why the loyalty of the presiding archbishops of Narbonne and Toulouse was so important. Gaspard Daillon Du Lude, bishop of Albi, was besieged by a mob in his episcopal palace during the Fronde for his loyalty to Mazarin. The Fouquets, François, bishop of Agde and then archbishop of Narbonne, and his brother, Louis, who succeeded him as bishop of Agde, were brothers of Mazarin's minister of finance, Nicolas Fouquet, while Michel Tubeuf, bishop of Saint Pons, was the brother of a financial intendant. The treasurer of the Languedoc Estates was also a ministerial client.[119]

The comte de Mérinville, a client of Mazarin and Colbert, was sent to Provence to help in controlling the General Assemblies. François de Moustiers, comte de Mérinville, was a Norman by birth. He had married a rich Languedoc heiress, Marguerite de La Jugie, comtesse de Rieux, in the 1630s, and emigrated to Languedoc to live on his wife's estates.[120] Mérinville pursued a military career, and as an army lieutenant general he commanded troops in Catalonia under the prince de Conti, securing the protection of Le Tellier.[121] His political connections in Languedoc included Governor Schomberg, Richelieu's client, and Daillon Du Lude, bishop of Albi, Schomberg's cousin and Mazarin's client. During the Fronde Mérinville became Mazarin's client, too, probably through the intercession of Daillon Du Lude.[122] At Mazarin's death, Mérinville switched his loyalty to Colbert.[123]

In October 1659, Mérinville was sent to Provence by Mazarin to command in the absence of the governor and was named provincial lieutenant general by royal letters a year later.[124] He regularly represented the crown at the General Assemblies of Communities, reported to Paris on their proceedings, encouraged their cooperation with royal tax demands, and threatened them with the use of force if they balked.[125] He also promoted his own interests and those of his friends. In 1662, Mérinville asked Colbert for confirmation of the succession of Fortia de Pilles's son as governor of Marseille and the Château d'If because "as You know, he is a person of merit attached to your interests and those of His Majesty." Mérinville thanked Colbert in 1666 for a conciliar decree in his favor, noting that "You oblige Your servants with such good grace." Later he wrote Colbert from his estate at Mérinville on behalf of the archdeacon of Narbonne cathedral, "Knowing how much I am in Your interests and that I honor You, I beg You very humbly to grant him Your protection with the King."[126] In 1664, Mérinville was appointed governor of the city of Narbonne where he served until his death, although he seems to have hoped for another provincial appointment from Colbert.[127] His name does not appear in the Provençal documents after this date, and he probably resided permanently in Languedoc.

Brokers Claude Bouchu and Nicolas Brûlart secured for their Paris patrons the cooperation of the Burgundian Estates and the Parlement of Dijon. The governors of Burgundy during this period—until the Revolution, in fact—were the princes de Condé.[128] One of their clients was Jean Bouchu, first president of the Dijon Parlement. He had created an extensive clientele of his own that survived the departure of Condé as governor in 1651 and his own death in 1653.[129] Bouchu's third son, Claude, baron de Loisy, a native-born Burgundian, was named intendant in 1656 to utilize his father's clientele in governing the province for Mazarin and Colbert and served the royal ministers for twenty-eight years. Bouchu became Condé's client, too, after he returned as governor in 1660.[130]

Bouchu intervened in municipal elections all over Burgundy, for example, at Dijon, Semur, Montbard, Beaune, Avallon, and Auxerre, to name his own clients to office. He cultivated men who had recently been elected to municipal office. He used his authority to liquidate community debts to influence the échevins who were community creditors, and his authority to verify the authenticity of noble rank to pressure those whose nobility was under investigation. Having selected, he thus domesticated the Third Estate.[131] His two uncles in the chamber of clergy helped, as did an extensive network of subdelegates who were his clients.[132] Bouchu wrote to Mazarin on May 16, 1656, "I am using with all imaginable care my crédit and that of my friends and relatives in this assembly [the Estates of Burgundy] in order to make the King's intentions succeed." A month later Bouchu wrote, "I would dare to assure Your Eminence that without the influence that I have among them [the deputies], the patience with which I have used it, it would be impossible to bring them [the Estates] near this sum." Three years later, on April 3, 1659, he wrote Mazarin that "I have travelled throughout Burgundy, and seen all my relatives and friends in all [three] orders, and I have persuaded them to attend the Estates at Noyers to satisfy the King." Bouchu and Condé were able to reduce royal taxation of Burgundy by interceding with Colbert and the king.[133]

Bouchu did very well for himself financially as intendant. He received an annual salary of 13,500 livres from the crown and an annual pension of 4,000 livres from the Burgundian Estates.[134] He took advantage of his financial opportunities to add another 20,000 livres a year in investments and obtained a number of clerical offices for his dependents, for instance, a brother who became abbé de La Ferté-sur-Grosne and a sister who became abbess of Fontaine-Guérard.[135] His son, Etienne-Jean, was named intendant in the Dauphiné in 1686, at the age of thirty without prior experience and having only been a master of requests (*maître des requêtes*) for a few months, through ministerial protection and his father's influence.[136]

Nicolas Brûlart, marquis de La Borde, was born at Dijon into the famous family of the Brûlart de Sillery, who produced a chancellor of France, several royal ministers and ambassadors. His father and grandfather had been first presidents of the Parlement of Dijon, and he was named to this office in 1657 at the age of thirty, where he remained until his death thirty-five years later.[137] Brûlart and Bouchu were rivals for political power in Burgundy and personal enemies as the result of a family feud. The expressions in their portraits are similar, energetic and intelligent, haughty, authoritarian, and demanding.[138] Bouchu was an indefatigable worker who slept only four hours a night, and Brûlart had a reputation for quarreling with colleagues, family, and servants alike.[139]

Brûlart requested that Colbert replace Bouchu in 1660, with someone "wise and moderate," complaining that the intendant was "hated and despised ... in his hands the simplest things become difficult to do." Brûlart accused the intendant of corruption and enriching himself through office-holding, and waged a long battle over authority and jurisdiction. Vainly seeking the governor's patronage enjoyed by Bouchu, Brûlart complained to Condé about him in 1663, and to the king about him in 1670 and 1671. He repeatedly complained to Colbert. But Colbert supported Bouchu and wrote some rather severe letters to Brûlart about his inability to get along with the intendant.[140]

Brûlart and ten councillors from the Parlement of Dijon were sent into exile at Perpignan in 1659 because they resisted registering a royal edict creating a host of new judicial offices in Burgundy; two more councillors were sent to the prisons of the château of Dijon. They were not reinstated for a year.[141] This incident and his quarrel with Bouchu hindered Brûlart's efforts to obtain the patronage of Colbert and the king: he had acquired the reputation of being too independent. Nonetheless, Brûlart established a working relationship with Condé, Colbert, and Louis XIV. He regularly wrote flattering letters to them, to other royal ministers, and to the secretaries of state, although he never obtained their patronage.[142] He acted as a mediator between the Paris government and the Parlement of Dijon, where he had great influence, and functioned as a broker when his assistance was required and he felt inclined to give it, although he did not function regularly in this capacity after Mazarin's death. For example, Brûlart intervened on several occasions on behalf of his first cousin, the comte de Tavannes, whom he recommended for the governorship of Auxonne, and on behalf of a friend, the comte d'Harcourt. He requested a benefice for one of his brothers and thanked the Grand Master of Malta for making another brother a commander in the order. He defended the authority, rights, and privileges of the parlement—the majority of his letters are on this subject—but he also reported to Paris on the conduct of individual parlementaires who had incurred royal displeasure.[143] Claude Bouchu and Nicolas Brûlart were provincial brokers who influenced decision making in the Estates of Burgundy and the Parlement of Dijon. Provincial crédit and clients were inherited with a family name, and dynasties of provincial brokers were established such as the Forbin and Grignan in Provence and the Bouchu and Brûlart in Burgundy. The Boisots in the Franche-Comté were another such dynasty.

Claude and Gabriel Boisot were brokers in the newly conquered frontier province of the Franche-Comté. They helped their Paris patrons to control the Parlement of Besançon. Claude Boisot founded a family dynasty of brokers and created an institutional clientele in the Parlement similar to those of Bouchu and Régusse. He used his clientele on behalf of Louvois and Louis XIV. Claude Boisot was a "new man," recently ennobled by his office of clerk in the Parlement of Dôle (which became the Parlement of Besançon in 1676). He had been a banker, financial entrepreneur, and owner of mines and forges. Originally from Burgundy, his family had settled in Besançon during the late fifteenth century and had become wealthy through commerce. He served as governor of Besançon for the first time in 1664, and was serving as co-governor at the time of the first French conquest four years later. Boisot was known for his pro-French sympathies. He worked on the city's fortifications for the French, personally met Louis XIV, and acted as the agent of the marquis de Listenois, the chief French ally, a grand seigneur of the house of Bauffremont and the bailli of Aval. Boisot was briefly imprisoned in March 1674 for his French sympathies, and his house was sacked during a popular protest in May, preceding the second French conquest. In June, Boisot met Louis XIV at his camp outside the city and presented him with a suggested list of reliable new members of the parlement, including himself as head clerk. He became a master of requests in the Parlement of Besançon in 1676 and a president two years later when the French permanently annexed the Franche-Comté. He enjoyed the patronage of Louvois and Louis XIV, and founded a dynasty of magistrates who served in the Parlement of Besançon for decades.[144]

Seven new judges were named to the parlement at Boisot's suggestion, and six were non-noble in origin or newly ennobled like Boisot himself: the king filled the parlement with new men, probably because they were more cooperative. They included his brother, Jean-Antoine Boisot, lieutenant general in the bailliage court, who had married into a parlementaire family; Antoine-Désiré Linglois, Claude's personal friend; Jean-Baptiste Pouhat, an ex-Jesuit; Charles Bouvot and Guillaume Loriot, lawyers; and Jean Favière, the household intendant of the marquis de Listenois. They were from merchant families. The only one of Boisot's appointees and clients to have connections with the preconquest robe nobility was Antoine Mairot de Mutigny, the son and great-nephew of councillors in the parlement, who had married into a parlementaire family. Mairot de Mutigny was related to Boisot.[145] Bouvot's brother-in-law, Claude Marin, also became a councillor in the parlement.[146]

Claude Boisot's other clients in the parlement included his son-in-law, Pierre-François Jolyot, a clerk ennobled by officeholding; his half-brother, Gabriel Boisot, a former mayor of Besançon who became procureur general in the parlement, president, and then first president; and Claude's son, Jean-

Jacques, who became a councillor by dispensation in 1679 at the tender age of twenty three; he later became president.[147] A third brother of Claude, Jean-Baptiste, became abbot of the rich Benedictine abbey of Saint Vincent at Besançon; erudite, the friend and correspondent of Pellisson and Mademoiselle de Scudéry, he wrote a biography of Louis XIV, and his library became the nucleus of the municipal library of Besançon.[148] A brother-in-law, Nicolas-Louis Boudret, became the *subdélégué* or agent of the intendant.[149]

Gabriel Boisot had fourteen living children, and he besieged the secretary of state and the controller general at Paris with demands for favors. Gabriel's son, Jean-Antoine, became a councillor in the parlement and succeeded his father as first president in 1714. He had acquired a fortune of 384,000 livres at the time of his death.[150] Gabriel's son-in-law, Pierre-Joseph Mouret de Châtillon, became a councillor in the parlement at the same time as his brother-in-law, Jean-Baptiste Petit. Another brother-in-law of Mouret, Jean-Joseph Petit, also became a councillor. Mouret's maternal uncle, Pierre Vigoureux Bondieu, bought an office of councillor, and so did his nephew.[151] Gabriel proposed Mouret de Châtillon as first president of the Chambre des Comptes, but he became a president instead. Mouret's father was a newly ennobled forge owner who had bought the fief of Châtillon in 1673. When Mouret married Marie-Claude Boisot, he had a fortune of 60,000 livres, and when he died in 1729, he had amassed a fortune of 377,000 livres.[152] Gabriel Boisot asked for the abbey of Saint Vincent de Besançon for one son; the priory of Chaux for another son; and the bishopric of Meaux for a third son, who received the abbey of Lieucroissant and a canonate at Besançon instead.[153] Gabriel's grandson, Jean-Jacques-Antoine, served as advocate general in the parlement for ten years and in 1747 took holy orders. He did not marry and was the last of the Boisots to serve in the Parlement of Besançon. He became abbot of the Augustinian canons of Saint Paul and canon at Besançon in the office of his uncle.[154] Claude Boisot had created an extensive clientele of relatives and friends in the Parlement of Besançon, a reward for his brokerage services at the time of the French conquest of the Franche-Comté.

Another French sympathizer, an ally of Claude Boisot and a power broker in the Franche-Comté, was Jean-Ferdinand Jobelot, who served as first president of the parlement for twenty-seven years, from 1675 until his death; he was followed in this office by Gabriel and Jean-Antoine Boisot. Non-noble in origin and the son of a lawyer, Jobelot had begun his parlement career as an advocate general, becoming a councillor in 1660. He served as emissary to the French in 1667–68 and was instrumental in securing the surrender of Dôle. His house was sacked, and he was physically threatened when the French withdrew after the first conquest. He faced a Flemish inquiry into his conduct. But he was reinstated in the parlement by the French in 1674 and made its first president. He undertook the task of reconciling the traditional law of Burgundy with French law, and published a commentary in French on Burgundian customary law. He was not as eager as the Boisots to please his new masters: Jobelot defended provincial and parlement privileges whenever he could, and he did not ask for rewards as the Boisots did; he lived spartanly and did not amass a large fortune. He was a devout Catholic opposed to the reformed religion, which had many adherents in the Franche-Comté.[155]

Provençal brokers such as Oppède and Mercoeur, Janson-Forbin and Grignan, and the comte de Mérinville who helped their minister-patrons to influence the General Assemblies were not unique in seventeenth-century France. Brokers in other frontier provinces, Languedoc in the south, Burgundy and the Franche-Comté in the east, provided similar services for minister-patrons in the royal government at Paris. In fact, as we shall see, these brokers and their clients belonged to extensive ministerial networks in the frontier provinces of France in the seventeenth century. The members of these networks came from all ranks of the provincial nobility. Some were great nobles such as Mercoeur and Grignan. Others were sword nobles such as Janson-Forbin and Grignan, while others were robe nobles such as Oppède and Régusse, or Nicolas Brûlart in the Parlement of Dijon and Claude Bouchu in the Estates of Burgundy. Some, such as the Boisots and Jobelot in the Parlement of Besançon, were "new men" who had been recently ennobled. As we shall see, brokers of royal patronage in the provinces of sixteenth-century France tended to be governors and lieutenants general who were great nobles known personally to the king at court. But increasingly in the seventeenth century, brokers of royal patronage in the provinces were robe nobles, minor sword nobles, and "new men," who were clients of the statebuilding royal ministers Richelieu, Mazarin, and Colbert.

Brokers as Troubleshooters

Provincial brokers were able to help their patrons in the royal government at Paris in other ways, too. They provided administrative assistance outside the formal institutional framework of government, and for this reason proved invaluable when regular channels became inoperative, acting unofficially as troubleshooters to help their Paris patrons solve difficult administrative problems. They helped beleaguered royal officials in the provinces to enforce unpopular policies of the Paris government and were able to rescue other clients of their patron when they got into trouble. Cosme de Valbelle, for example, helped a royal commissioner sent by Richelieu to raise the salt tax at Marseille. The bailli de Forbin instructed the incompetent nephew of Richelieu in the command of the royal galleys. Archbishop Sourdis sought to obtain the levy of an unpopular tax to garrison the Provençal coast for Richelieu.

Brokers also served as mediators between feuding officials and rebellious officials and the crown. For example, archbishop Béthune mediated during the Fronde between the governor and the parlementaires of Bordeaux, keeping Mazarin informed on events in the city. Archbishop Grignan of Arles mediated between the rebellious parlementaires of Aix and Governor

Alais during the Provençal Fronde. Joseph Dubernet, first president of the Parlement of Bordeaux, mediated between his rebellious colleagues and Governor Epernon, who was Mazarin's client, until he was forced to leave the city. Brokers sought to intimidate and silence political opposition to the policies of their patron and to the crown. For example, First President Aguesseau of the Parlement of Bordeaux kept his court loyal to Richelieu during the Croquants' Revolt in the 1630s. First President Bertier de Montrave of the Parlement of Toulouse crushed opposition within his court to the policies of Richelieu and Mazarin, while the chevalier Paul helped Mazarin to destroy the Valbelle party at Marseille. Finally, brokers provided information and advice on local affairs, lent their patron money, entertained his political allies, and recruited new clients and fighting men for him. Their information and advice on local affairs, which sometimes became lobbying, could influence decision making at the national level.

Brokers sometimes rescued royal officials. Cosme de Valbelle, for example, proved an invaluable aid to the royal commissioner charged with the unpleasant task of increasing the salt tax at Marseille in October 1634.[156] There had already been four increases in the salt tax in Provence since the turn of the century, and the price had more than doubled.[157] The crown now tripled the tax and attempted to reduce the measure.[158] Not surprisingly, there was a near-riot when the salt tax commissioner, Jacques Talon, tried to post the higher price on the door of the Marseille warehouse on the morning of October 10. The municipal government, packed with Valbelle's clients, supported the tax increase, but his political opponents decided to use the intense popular hostility, particularly among the fishermen of Marseille who used large quantities of salt to preserve their catch, to attack Valbelle's control over the city government. They disrupted municipal elections on October 28 and demanded the "free" election of men who would oppose the tax increase. Valbelle and his client, first consul Spinacy, hurried to Paris to ask Richelieu for royal letters appointing the new consuls and councillors of Marseille. While they were gone, there was another popular protest, and the crowd attacked the house of another client, second consul Savornin.[159] Valbelle returned from Paris on January 11 with royal letters naming the new consuls and councillors, and they assumed office three days later. The marquis de Saint Chamond, Richelieu's client who was provincial lieutenant general, wrote on January 16 that he had recently installed the new government of Marseille composed "entirely of Valbelle's relatives and friends."[160] The increase in the salt tax was levied without further difficulty, and the crown dropped its demands for a change in measure.[161]

As another example, Paul-Albert de Forbin-Lambesc, a bailli in the Order of Malta, used his influence and prestige in the royal galleys on behalf of his patron's nephew. He came from a well-known family of the Provençal sword nobility. He had joined the Knights of Malta, become a galley captain and then a bailli sometime around 1622, when he entered the service of the French king. His courage attracted attention in high places.[162] He was named lieutenant general of the galleys and second-in-command in 1626, a post he held for seventeen years. His appointment undoubtedly had Richelieu's approval because in the next year he wrote a memoir at the Cardinal's request on conditions in the Mediterranean fleet.[163] He commanded the galley escorting Richelieu's brother to Italy as ambassador in December 1634 and served as acting general of the galleys for several years. When the Cardinal's nephew, Pont de Courlay, whom we already met in the first chapter of this book, was appointed general of the galleys in 1636, Forbin was asked to tutor the inexperienced young man in his new naval command. Forbin agreed in order to serve Richelieu, but he was unsuccessful: Pont de Courlay was arrogant, stubborn, inept, and unpopular among the galley captains, and the two men were at sword's point within the year.[164]

Forbin remained Richelieu's client, however. In 1634, he had requested a naval office of his nephew, writing that "the enthusiasm with which I have given my humble service to Your Eminence might merit the honor of seeing one of mine in Your Émploy."[165] Three years later at his nephew's death, Forbin successfully requested that the office remain in his family.[166] He wrote regularly to Richelieu.[167] And he also corresponded with the Cardinal's créatures, for instance, asking père Joseph to discuss something with Richelieu.[168] He wrote regularly to Servien, who was secretary of state of Provence, and on one of his frequent trips to court he sought a rapprochement with Sublet de Noyers, who replaced Servien in this post.[169] He was also friendly with several of Richelieu's clients in Provence.[170]

Forbin retired voluntarily as lieutenant general of the galleys after Richelieu's death. The reasons are unknown, but he was probably tired of too little money, too few galleys, and too much bickering. He also may not have relished losing command to Pont de Courlay's son, the duc de Richelieu, a youngster of fifteen who had recently been appointed general of the galleys.[171] In 1644, Forbin became second-in-command of the Provençal nation within the Order of Malta and Grand Prior of Saint Gilles, the order's oldest western house whose annual revenues he increased from 30,000 to 77,000 livres.[172]

Three years later Forbin was approached by Mazarin's brother, Michel, the new archbishop of Aix, about entering the Cardinal's service. Mazarin was looking for Provençal supporters, particularly within the galleys at Toulon, and he thought of Forbin. Writing to Mazarin on October 22, 1647, Forbin declared himself pleased that his advice had been sought and recalled his forty years of faithful service in the galleys.[173] He became Mazarin's client and corresponded regularly throughout the Fronde.[174] Forbin acted as a provincial mediator during these years. Attempting to mediate unsuccessfully between Alais and the rebel parlementaires at Aix in May 1649, he spent the month of June at Arles with archbishop Grignan planning a similar mission to Marseille to mediate between Alais and Valbelle, also unsuccessful. And he mediated between the Sabreurs and the Mazarinistes at Aix in 1651.[175] On all these occasions, Forbin negotiated between feuding officials because his patron, Cardinal Mazarin, had requested his help. Named commander of the royal galleys in 1652, he aided the new governor, the duc de Mercoeur, to occupy the city of Toulon that summer, bringing an end to the Provençal Fronde. Cardinal Mazarin paid a special visit to Forbin when he came to Provence in 1660. Forbin was still active politically at the time of his death in 1661 at the age of eighty one.[176]

Henri d'Escoubleau de Sourdis was a prelate who served his patron, Cardinal Richelieu, as a naval commander and a provincial broker. He had succeeded his uncle as bishop of Maillezais (a seat later transferred to La Rochelle) in 1623, and four years later he became coadjutor to his older brother, the archbishop of Bordeaux, succeeding him in this office at his death in 1628. Maillezais and Bordeaux had been in the Escoubleau family since the early sixteenth century, and Sourdis inherited prestige, influence, and a ready-made clientele in Guyenne with his offices. Richelieu probably appointed Sourdis archbishop of Bordeaux to counter the influence of an unreliable governor, Jean-Louis de La Valette, duc d'Epernon.[177]

Sourdis had begun his career in Richelieu's household. Assigned in 1627 by the Cardinal to the defense of Oléron, an island in the harbor of La Rochelle, he was made an army lieutenant general and sent to Bordeaux to gather ships and supplies for the royal army besieging La Rochelle. He took part in the naval operations against La Rochelle, accompanying Richelieu during his campaign, and went with him and the king on the military expedition to Italy. He also spent several years at Le Havre and La Rochelle, assisting in the construction of the French navy.[178] Sourdis's portrait shows a handsome, aquiline face with the high forehead, intelligent eyes, trim mustaches, pointed beard, and arrogant expression of a seventeenth-century duelist.[179] Sourdis was a warrior-cleric who pursued a successful naval career to become an admiral.

Sourdis's favor with Richelieu increased after he defeated and humiliated the governor of Guyenne, Epernon, an old enemy of the Cardinal.[180] He soon became widely known as the Cardinal's créature.[181] From 1633 to 1637, Sourdis filled the municipal government of Bordeaux with his own clients, replacing those of Epernon.[182] Councillor Jean de Briet of the Parlement of Bordeaux supervised the installation of Sourdis's clients and kept his new patron, who was frequently absent from Bordeaux, and Cardinal Richelieu informed on events in the city.[183] The archbishop's brother, the marquis de Sourdis, was named lieutenant general of Guyenne around this time.[184]

Appointed "chief of the royal council in the naval army of the Levant," commander-in-chief of the French naval forces gathered to drive the Spanish from the Provençal coastal islands, Sourdis sailed for Marseille in 1636.[185] The coastal islands were successfully retaken by the French in May 1637, and Sourdis was sent that winter to Languedoc to lift the Spanish siege of the fortress of Salses on the Mediterranean coast. Once again successful, he was named commander of the Atlantic fleet and led a daring raid on the Spanish coast. However, he lost Richelieu's favor when the French siege of Tarragona had to be abandoned in 1641, and was sent into exile at Avignon until Richelieu's death; he then returned to Bordeaux. Sourdis died at Paris in 1645, at the age of fifty one, while attending the annual General Assembly of French Clergy.[186]

Sourdis put Bordelais clients into office in Provence. For example, Joseph

Dubernet, a native of Bordeaux and a president in its Parlement, was named first president of the Parlement of Aix through Sourdis's patronage.[187] Eustache and Jean-Baptiste Gault, priests of the Oratory of Jesus, were named bishops of Marseille. Eustache had been Sourdis's vicar general and was succeeded at his death by his brother, Jean-Baptiste, who had been curé of Sainte Eulalie at Bordeaux.[188] Sourdis also recruited and promoted Provençal clients. He brought Philippe Des Gouttes, a Knight of Malta and sailing captain who had served under his command, to Richelieu's attention, and Des Gouttes was named to tutor Richelieu's other nephew, the duc de Maillé-Brézé, when he assumed command of the Atlantic fleet in 1640.[189] Sourdis probably also promoted the naval career of the chevalier Paul who fought under his command and whom we shall meet later in this chapter. Sourdis created a provincial clientele and acted as a broker both at Bordeaux and at Aix.

Troop withdrawals began immediately after the coastal islands were recaptured in 1637, much to the relief of the province since troop maintenance was expensive. The withdrawals, however, were halted abruptly when Sourdis as commander-in-chief ordered garrisoning of the recaptured islands. The consuls of Aix, acting as the procureurs du pays, borrowed 36,000 livres to support temporary garrisons.[190] But they balked when the archbishop presented a royal order on August 13, making the garrisons permanent. Fearing this was the first step in having to garrison the entire coast, the procureurs du pays refused to authorize the necessary tax and called for a meeting of the Provençal Estates, declaring that they did not have the authority to grant such a tax and threatening to resign if pressured. They submitted, reluctantly, a month later when the royal council issued a decree ordering payment.[191]

Sourdis tried to repeat an earlier success: he had already provoked an attack upon his person by the choleric governor of Provence, who had been sent to the Bastille for his foolhardiness in striking the archbishop with his malacca cane.[192] Now Sourdis persuaded Richelieu to call the consuls of Aix to Paris for explanations by lettres de cachet, and they rode north at the end of September.[193] He suspended scheduled municipal elections by conciliar decree and filled the offices with his own clients. They included the young Paul de Fortia, seigneur de Pilles, governor of the Château d'If, who became first consul, and two old men in their eighties, Louis de Pena and Esprit d'Audifredi, who were named second and third consuls. With their aproval, Sourdis ordered the trésoriers généraux to collect the garrison tax. He also advised Richelieu that in the interests of efficiency the procuration should be lifted from the city of Aix, which had traditionally enjoyed this privilege, and suppressed or granted to another city; a royal order to this effect was issued on September 29.[194] Sourdis declared that the consuls of Aix were unworthy of this privilege because "they have no respect for themselves or for those who serve the King."[195]

Sourdis undoubtedly hoped to be named the new governor of Provence, having demonstrated his skill at handling uncooperative provincial officials and securing the garrison tax that Richelieu wanted. But his scheme backfired. To everyone's surprise and Sourdis's chagrin, the comte d'Alais was named governor of Provence, probably to reward his father for his support of Richelieu at court.[196] On November 21, the consuls of Aix were allowed to return home, and all charges against them were dropped.[197] Troop withdrawals continued; the procuration was restored to Aix; new municipal elections were held in December despite Sourdis's protests; and his clients were removed from office.[198] Sourdis went to Paris in January 1638 and did not return.[199]

What had happened? We can only guess, but apparently Sourdis had gone too far. In pursuit of his own ambitions he had advised Richelieu badly, and this had cost him the governorship of Provence. The Provençaux had responded generously with money and men to meet the Spanish invasion.[200] The coastal islands had been retaken, but the Spanish had not yet been defeated; their fleet was still in the Mediterranean. The military situation was too delicate to permit a loss of Provençal confidence in the Paris government: their support might be needed again in the near future. Richelieu could not risk alienating the province, so the royal council reversed itself. The Cardinal may also have realized that in appointing Sourdis he would be dealing with someone who was not only ambitious, intelligent, and strong-willed, but who would now have an independent provincial power base.

The royal ministers often recruited bishops and archbishops as clients in distant provinces because they were well equipped to broker if they were so inclined. It was natural for the cardinal-ministers to look for clients among the higher clergy, who made effective mediators because they were perceived as comparatively disinterested. They also regularly attended the annual General Assemblies of the Clergy at Paris, allowing them to renew their ties in the national capital, and they were often recruited at these meetings. Cardinal Mazarin manipulated the annual assemblies of the clergy by distributing favors, influencing the choice of clerics who attended and the election of the presiding prelate. To encourage cooperation among those attending the 1645 assembly, Mazarin wrote in his notebook that he would delay awarding benefices and abbeys during the assembly to keep alive the hope in each participant that he would receive one.[201]

Nobles occupied a majority of French bishoprics, and a significant minority were recently ennobled; bishoprics were often held by provincial nobles allied to great noble families. The bishops' local ties and the prestige of their office made them influential and useful to the royal ministers. Episcopal dynasties developed; Sourdis, for example, successively held two seats that his family had held for over a century. Episcopal recruitment under Louis XIV was random as it had always been, but it favored men from the Midi, Provençaux, Languedociens, and Dauphinois.[202] Toussaint de Janson-Forbin, Claude de Rébé, Pierre de Marca, and Henri d'Escoubleau de Sourdis were prelates from the Midi who were broker-clients of royal ministers, as were archbishops Béthune of Bordeaux and Grignan of Arles, who served Cardinal Mazarin as mediators during the Fronde.

Prelates and First Presidents

Henry de Béthune came from the family of the duc de Sully, the famous finance minister. His father, Philippe, comte de Selles, had pursued a successful diplomatic career, and his influence with the king and the pope in Rome, where he was serving as French ambassador, secured for Henry, his fourth child, the bishopric of Bayonne in 1628 and of Maillezais in 1629 (where he succeeded Sourdis).[203] Resident in his diocese, Béthune earned a reputation for piety, good works, and excellent administration, and attracted the patronage of Saint Vincent de Paul, who recommended him for the archbishopric of Bordeaux at Sourdis's death. Mazarin nominated him to this seat in 1646, and he entered the city two years later preceded by his reputation.[204]

Béthune was loyal to Mazarin during the Fronde when many of the bishops and clergy in Guyenne were not. He supported governor Epernon, Mazarin's client, against the parlementaires, and mediated between them to restore peace. Royal commissioner Argenson wrote to Mazarin on June 6, 1649, that "the archbishop of Bordeaux has contributed (to the peace) as a good prelate very devoted to the service of the King, and merits a compliment from his Majesty and Your Eminence." Béthune wrote to Mazarin the same day that "God has ordered that I might serve as a mediator to extinguish the disorders [in this province] which have been growing greater." On December 2, the maréchal Du Plessis-Praslin wrote to Mazarin that "I think you should write a note to the archbishop of Bordeaux telling him how beneficial his services have been on this occasion, and I am certainly obliged to testify that he has acted with all the devotion that he could." Not surprisingly, Béthune became Mazarin's client. He wrote regularly to the Cardinal during the Fronde, keeping him informed of events at Bordeaux until he left the city in 1651 after Condé's arrival at governor. He retired to Paris and did not return until the end of the Fronde.[205]

Béthune had several protégés whose careers he was able to promote through his office of archbishop and his client relationship with Mazarin. His young nephew, Armand de Béthune, entered the Jesuit college at Bordeaux in 1649, at the age of fourteen, and the Jesuit order in the next year. In 1652, he was named abbé of Notre Dame de La Vernusse in the diocese of Bourges, and the next year a canon in the chapter of Saint André of the cathedral of Bordeaux, later becoming a deacon. He was sent as a representative from Bordeaux to the General Assembly of French Clergy at Paris in 1660 and the next year was named bishop of Puy by the king. He was consecrated bishop by his uncle, who was attended by another nephew, César d'Estrées, bishop of Laon. Béthune also promoted the careers of Mathurin Sauvestre and Pierre Dussaussay, his business agents. He named Sauvestre his procureur general and intendant for temporal affairs, a canon in the cathedral of Bordeaux, and a canon and treasurer in the church of Saint Seurin at Bordeaux. Sauvestre resigned the first canonate in favor of a nephew when Béthune made him archdeacon of Fronsac. He resigned the second canonate in favor of Béthune's vicar general Henri D'Arche. Pierre Dussaussay also received several benefices in the archdiocese of Bordeaux. He received a prebend in the chapter of Saint Emilion at Bordeaux and became curé of Saint Vincent de Moulon, which he resigned to become curé of Notre Dame de Créon.[206]

François d'Adhémar de Monteil de Grignan, archbishop of Arles and uncle of the comte de Grignan, was another clerical broker who used his provincial influence to mediate between feuding officials. He used his clientele to control the Arles municipal government for decades, and his nephew succeeded him in office. Grignan became archbishop of Arles in May 1645 and attended a General Assembly of French Clergy at Paris the next month.[207] There he made the acquaintance of Mazarin, who asked him to mediate in the quarrel between Valbelle and Governor Alais.[208] The Cardinal soon recruited him as a client. In a letter on September 29, 1648, Grignan wrote, "I am attached by so many reasons to the service and interests of Your Eminence that You will believe me when I express my deep sorrow at the death of Your brother."[209] In a letter on December 1, Grignan described himself as "a very submissive and faithful créature of Your Eminence."[210] Mazarin asked Grignan to mediate between the governor and the parlementaires in the autumn of 1648, and Grignan wrote on November 17 from Aix that "Your Eminence will always have in me a true créature who would rather die than live without submission and respect."[211] In spite of his efforts, however, the enmity between the governor and the parlementaires flared into violence in January, and Grignan spent twenty four hours without food or sleep trying to negotiate a compromise and arrange a temporary truce. He also transmitted the rebellious parlementaires' demands to Mazarin, although Cardinal Bichi did the actual negotiating.[212] Six months later the archbishop was at Marseille with the bailli de Forbin, trying to reconcile Alais and Valbelle.[213]

Joseph Dubernet, a client of Sourdis, followed in his patron's footsteps by soliciting Richelieu's patronage and trying to become a provincial broker. As the archbishop's client, he assured Richelieu that he was also the Cardinal's client, and referred to himself as Richelieu's créature, "who hopes for Your protection."[214] Although Dubernet sought Richelieu's patronage energetically, he probably never obtained it.

Dubernet came from an old sword noble family of Guyenne. A wealthy baron who owned a number of fiefs, he became a councillor in the Parlement, earned a reputation as an orator to become a president and a Catholic presiding judge in the *Chambre de l'Edit* (the Huguenot court) at Agen.[215] He was named first president of the Parlement of Aix in 1636 through Sourdis's patronage: it was reported that Sourdis had appointed him "in order to use his influence and authority in pursuing his own projects." He received the office over a Provençal candidate, Henri de Séguiran, and for this reason his appointment was unpopular.[216] Dubernet was soon disliked in Provence. He halted rambling speakers in the parlement, although he permitted long trials. As a parlement deputy to Paris in the summer of 1639 he was sent to protest a royal edict creating new presidial courts in Provence. He secured the edict's revocation by agreeing to the establishment of new offices in the lower judicial courts, and then invested himself secretly in their sale, or so it was rumored. Dubernet had solved an administrative problem for Richelieu—the palement's refusal to register a royal edict—but at the cost of his own popularity in the court and the province. The Parlement of Aix protested to the king about him, and a faction against him developed, intensifying its activities when he quarreled with the governor, the comte d'Alais, late in 1640.[217]

Governor Alais did not like Dubernet.[218] The governor had disliked his patron, conspired in his disgrace, and probably preferred to have his own client as first president of the parlement.[219] Dubernet complained to Richelieu that Alais was encouraging a faction against him in the parlement which was threatening to develop into a provincial party. As a result Richelieu told Alais's father at court that he was displeased with his son's behavior, and Alais in a fury, believing that he had lost Richelieu's favor, broke with Dubernet completely; their wives quarreled in public.[220] Alais set about to obtain the dismissal of Dubernet.

Alais reported in a letter to Richelieu that Dubernet's unpopularity had factionalized the parlement. Alais also accused Dubernet of trying to usurp his authority as governor, exerting undue influence over the provincial intendant, and misrepresenting provincial conditions in his letters to Paris.[221] He accused Dubernet of being a self-interested servant of Sourdis, not of Richelieu or of the king.[222] He demanded that Dubernet be dismissed when he saw the king at Perpignan and the Cardinal at Tarascon.[223]

Dubernet defended himself to Richelieu, protesting that he was being defamed and falsely accused by an enemy of his patron. He wrote that "it is impossible for me to live if my loyalty is doubted. I am the servant of the archbishop of Bordeaux, but I have never been self-interested (*intéressé*), not for my relatives or friends, wife or children, while in the royal service, which is why the archbishop proposed me for the office of first president."[224] Sourdis had accused Alais of encouraging a "cabal" against Dubernet in the parlement in a letter to Richelieu a year earlier.[225] Dubernet saw Richelieu in a personal interview at Tarascon in 1642 to plead his case, but the effort was futile. He was sent to Bourges by lettre de cachet in June, and he resigned his office shortly thereafter. Alais jubilantly thanked Secretary of State Brienne for the removal of Dubernet.[226]

Dubernet's portrait shows a strong brow and a determined chin, and he was described by contemporaries as a capable but stubborn magistrate. Like his patron Sourdis, he was honest, intelligent, and loyal, but too arrogant, quick to anger, and stubborn; he lacked tact and the ability to compromise. Dubernet suffered the additional handicap of being a Bordelais without Provençal ties, although he was resident in the province. Worse, he was the client of Sourdis, a non-Provençal sent to Languedoc because of his high-handedness at Aix. Dubernet's judicial office made him a local notable. But he was unable to secure the patronage of the new governor, and he appeared too sympathetic to the crown's money-making schemes. By 1640, it was apparent that he could not be useful as a provincial broker, and this probably destroyed whatever hope he had of receiving Richelieu's patronage. Dubernet was an aspiring broker-client who had failed the test of utility.

However, Dubernet's career was not ruined. Nine months after the death of Richelieu he was appointed first president of the Parlement of Bordeaux, an office for which he paid 150,000 livres.[227] The archbishop of Bordeaux was once more at court, and he or his brother may have intervened on Dubernet's behalf. In addition, Mazarin had no liking for Governor Alais, and he may have decided that an enemy of Alais was a friend of his. In any event, Mazarin appointed Dubernet first president of the Parlement of Bordeaux, where he had kinship and client ties, and accepted him as a client. Dubernet served Mazarin as a mediator during the Fronde.

The judges of Bordeaux considered Dubernet "too attached to the royal council ... he has more crédit at court than the parlement itself."[228] He was soon as unpopular at Bordeaux as he had been at Aix. He had frequent, acrimonious exchanges with the younger parlementaires, who made references to his problems at Aix, and he intensified the antagonism between the city's merchant community and the parlement.[229] He was steadfastly loyal to Mazarin, however, and supported the Cardinal's client, Governor Epernon, attempting to mediate between him and the parlementaires. This made him more unpopular than ever: Dubernet was expelled from the parlement in July 1649 for having visited the governor on the previous day. Dubernet's brother, son-in-law, and a councillor whose son was fighting with the governor were expelled at the same time. Dubernet was readmitted to the court in December 1650, then expelled again in April with the others. When the new governor, the prince de Condé, arrived at Bordeaux that summer, he lodged a formal complaint with the parlement against Dubernet, whom he accused of intriguing against him. The real problem, of course, was that Dubernet was Mazarin's client. He was expelled from the court for the third and last time, and sent from the city; he retired to Limoges, where he died a few years later.[230]

Dubernet had received a letter from Mazarin on April 22, 1650, praising him as a good servant of the King and a good friend of the Cardinal, and Mazarin noted that he had already arranged a pension for Dubernet's grandson. He wrote that the Queen Mother was overcommitted at the moment, but he promised to obtain something for Dubernet in the near future.[231] After his record at Aix, Dubernet was probably a bad choice as first president of the Parlement of Bordeaux, but his indisputable loyalty to Mazarin and the crown may have been the deciding factor in his selection.

Dubernet's predecessor as first president at Bordeaux had been Antoine d'Aguesseau, sieur de Puiseux, whose son became a famous intendant and whose grandson became a chancellor of France. Brokers tried to intimidate the political opponents of their patrons, and Aguesseau sought to silence critics of Richelieu's policies within the Parlement of Bordeaux. The Aguesseau family originally came from Saintonge where they possessed fiefs including one on the island of Oléron; they had been recently ennobled by royal letters.[232] Antoine had left Saint-Jean d'Angély to go to Paris to pursue a judicial career. In quick succession he became a criminal lieutenant in the Châtelet court, a president in the Grand Conseil court, a councillor of state, and then intendant at Grenoble. A few years later he was named first president of the Parlement of Bordeaux through Richelieu's patronage.[233] Aguesseau wrote to the Cardinal from Bordeaux on Christmas Day 1632:

> If, however, Your Eminence does not find this satisfactory, I assure You, Monseigneur, that our company will obey in the way that it pleases You to order it, and that in any way You may do me the favor of honoring me with Your commands, I shall receive them with the respect and reverence that I owe You, and I will use in all thereto pertaining the authority that You have given me to see that they are executed. I pray God that He will keep Your Eminence in perfect health for a long and happy life, and that He will give me the opportunity of making known the constant gratitude that I have for Your goodness.[234]

Aguesseau's toughness in handling the parlement during the Croquants' Revolt in the 1630s guaranteed that the Cardinal would continue to protect him.[235]

The office of first president at Bordeaux had fallen vacant in September 1628. The holder at this time, Marc-Antoine de Gourgues, had lost his self-control during an interview with the king at La Rochelle to present a remonstrance, and blurted out, "Sire, it is certainly strange and without precedent that, on two occasions, the deputies of Your Parlement have presented themselves to make remonstrances and have not been heard." Louis XIII rose in a fury, took Gourges by the arm, and said, "On your knees, little man, before your master." Gourges had a stroke the next day and died. The office had remained vacant ever since, the object of endless intrigues, and Richelieu wanted to make certain that it was filled by someone reliable and cooperative.[236] He gave the office to Aguesseau, who held it until Richelieu's death then voluntarily resigned it and retired to Paris, where he died in 1645.[237] He may not have wanted to face the obstinacy and endless bickering of the parlement without a protector at court.

Antoine d'Aguesseau and Joseph Dubernet were first presidents of provincial parlements. Their ability to broker secured for them the patronage of royal ministers in the Paris government. First presidents were named to office by the crown, so their offices were revocable, not hereditary, and many had been former intendants.[238] Some had roots in the provinces in which they served, others were strangers, but all became permanent residents after appointment and their judicial offices made them provincial notables. Oppède, Régusse, Brûlart, Boisot, Jobelot, Dubernet, and Aguesseau were parlement first presidents who became broker-clients of royal ministers. Another was Jean de Bertier who sought to crush opposition to ministerial policies within his provincial high court.

Jean de Bertier, baron de Montrave, was named first president of the Parlement of Toulouse in 1631 at Richelieu's recommendation. He came from an old noble family of Languedoc, with branches serving in the parlement and the church, and he had numerous relatives in both institutions. His brothers were bishops of Rieux and Montauban, while he was patron of an important family clientele within the parlement. Bertier had begun his career as a councillor and inherited his father's office of president in 1610 at the age of thirty-three.[239] His firm leadership as first president halted a public protest in 1633 against a conciliar decree annulling a parlement order and suspending several judges.[240] Bertier complained regularly to Paris about the behavior of the more radical judges in his court.[241] When the Croquants' Revolt exploded in neighbouring Guyenne, causing waves of sympathy in Languedoc, he advocated a hard line in dealing with the rebels and repression by force if necessary: he spoke of exemplary punishment to halt the rioting. He assured Chancellor Séguier that the Parlement of Toulouse was ready "to arrest and chase those crazy rebels."[242] He went to Paris the next year as a parlement deputy and was sent posthaste back to Toulouse by Richelieu to convince the parlementaires to comply with an agreement negotiated by their deputies.[243] Bertier wrote Chancellor Séguier on December 12, 1643, that he had stopped a meeting of the full court to prevent the issuance of a decree contrary to royal interests, having told the parlementaires that he would not sign their decree.[244] He wrote to Secretary of State La Vrillière on March 9, 1646, asking for a letter from the king forbidding private meetings of the opposition at the house of President Donneville; he had been excluded from these meetings.[245] Learning that several magistrates had written letters to Paris criticizing him, he asked Séguier on March 28 to prohibit those involved from exercising their offices.[246] He wrote again on May 12, noting that he was doing the best he could to execute the royal council's decrees in the face of the parlement's hostility, and warned the chancellor to ignore the "lies" being told about him.[247]

An energetic, loyal supporter of Mazarin's government, Bertier's firm leadership and extensive clientele helped to hold the parlement for the crown during the Fronde until the defection of the governor, the duc d'Orléans, to the rebels in January 1652. Orléans also had an extensive clientele, and Bertier was unable to counter his influence in the parlement, which became more active in protesting Mazarin's government. The parlementaires levied troops, fortified Toulouse, collected weapons, and borrowed 30,000 livres to purchase powder and muskets, but their preparations ended when Orléans was reconciled with Mazarin in October.[248] After Bertier's death Mazarin wrote his brother, the bishop of Rieux, that "the King has lost a good servant in his person."[249] He was replaced as first president of the parlement by another distinguished royalist.[250] It is difficult to be certain of the motives of men such as Dubernet, Aguesseau, and Bertier in soliciting ministerial patronage and coercing their high courts to obey, or the motives of prelates such as Sourdis, Béthune, and Grignan. Ambition and self-interest undoubtedly lay behind their actions, but so did a genuine desire to serve the king. The letters of these men ring with sincerity in their desire for law and order and their commitment to the king, and their actions must also have reflected their political convictions.

The chevalier Paul is a last example of a provincial broker who acted as a troubleshooter to help defeat the Valbelle party at Marseille. He was born in 1598, the illegitimate son of a washerwoman at the Château d'If. His godfather, possibly his real father, was Paul de Fortia, seigneur de Pilles and baron de Baumes, governor of the fortress. The child was known as Jean-Paul Saumur. Joining a merchant ship as a cabin boy at an early age, he became a soldier in the Order of Malta. Despite his humble birth he was admitted into the Provençal nation of the order for his courage and was known thereafter as the chevalier Paul. He became a galley captain, joined the service of the king of France, and distinguished himself fighting under Sourdis. He remained loyal to the archbishop in his disgrace, writing several letters in his defense. He was probably the archbishop's client.[251]

The chevalier Paul fought bravely as a galley captain under the command of Richelieu's nephew and cousin, but he never gained Richelieu's patronage. He was ennobled by Mazarin, however, in November 1649 as part of the Cardinal's program of recruiting and rewarding loyal provincial clients during the Fronde; he was also promoted to squadron chief at Toulon. The next year he made his first trip to court, where he was a great success: he gained an audience with the king and his mother, a great honor for a commoner of illegitimate birth, and he returned to court frequently for the rest of his life. He remained loyal to Mazarin during the Fronde, and in 1652 he joined the bailli de Forbin and Governor Mercoeur in besieging Toulon, the last redoubt of the Frondeurs. Both he and Forbin had houses at Toulon. He was made a naval lieutenant general and a joint commander of the royal galleys with Forbin when Toulon fell.[252] The chevalier Paul had become Mazarin's client by 1653; in a letter to Mazarin a few years later he signed himself as "one of the most faithful créatures of Your Eminence."[253]

Cardinal Mazarin asked the Grand Master of Malta to make the chevalier Paul a commander of Malta as a reward for his loyalty in the summer of 1658, when as commander of the Toulon squadron, he had responded to Mercoeur's request that he use his galleys to help in blockading the rebellious city of Marseille. Ignoring letters from the Valbelle consuls of Marseille swearing their loyalty and asking him to remain at Toulon, the chevalier sailed to Marseille and menaced the harbor. His show of force helped Fortia de Pilles, possibly his half-brother, to mediate a truce and restore peace to the troubled city.[254]

When Louis XIV visited Toulon in February 1660, he personally greeted the chevalier Paul, who had staged a mock naval battle in the king's honor. He was rewarded with the priory of Saint Gilles at Forbin's death.[255] A few years later he was appointed to the joint command of the royal galleys with Louis-Victor Rochechouart, duc de Vivonne, boyhood friend of Louis XIV and brother of his mistress, Madame de Montespan. The chevalier Paul was expected to tutor Vivonne in the ways of the sea, which he was better able do than the bailli de Forbin. He served Louis XIV and Colbert as joint commander of the royal galleys until his death in 1668.[256]

Brokers and National Decision Making

Brokers sent their Paris patrons information and advice on provincial politics and personalities. Local information was important in an interventionist regime and could affect national decision making when patrons were influential royal ministers. The letters of the bailli de Forbin, Cardinal Bichi, and Archbishop Grignan of Arles, for example, were Mazarin's chief sources of information on Provence during the Fronde.[257] Henri de Béthune was one of the Cardinal's most reliable correspondents at Bordeaux during these years. Régusse wrote regularly to Mazarin on events at Aix from 1650 to 1655.[258] Oppède wrote several times a week to Mazarin and Colbert on Provençal affairs, and Governor Mercoeur wrote regularly when he was in the Midi.[259] Brokers' letters helped to shape royal policy in a province.

Sending information on local affairs was Claude Boisot's most valuable service. After the first French conquest of the Franche-Comté, Boisot wrote weekly letters that were essential in shaping royal policy from the second French conquest in 1674 to permanent annexation in 1678. His letters often resulted in royal instructions being sent to the governor, the duc de Duras, or the intendants, Camus de Beaulieu and Chauvelin.[260] For instance, in a letter to Louvois on July 1, 1674, Boisot advised the king to suspend the tax of 3,000 livres per day established by the Spanish because of recent troop damage to grain stores and livestock. The king took his advice and suspended the levy. Boisot also advised the king that the fortifications of Salins could be restored for 60,000 livres rather than 100,000 livres, as Monsieur d'Aspremont had advised. Because of his practical knowledge of the region, Boisot often saved the crown money.[261]

Historian Maurice Gresset has written that "during the summer and autumn of 1674, Boisot appeared as the inspiration for French politics in the Comté."[262] Boisot advised the duc de Duras on the most effective way to take the two fortresses still resisting the French in July, suggesting that both be razed although only one was.[263] He advised the French on rebuilding the fortifications they had been forced to destroy during the conquest; he visited sites at Salins, Besançon, and Dôle to supervise the work; and he advised the French on how to obtain the best prices. He bought munitions and supplies for the army, careful to get the best quality for the lowest prices.[264] He made a list of Spanish sympathizers for the duc de Duras to use in expelling members of the municipal governments.[265] He recommended the reestablishment of the Parlement of Dôle, which the Spanish had suppressed after the first conquest; he furnished a list of suggested new members; and he supervised the transfer of the court to his native city of Besançon.[266] Claude Boisot's information and advice was invaluable to the French monarchy during a critical period. Maurice Gresset concludes, "What no official appointment could have procured for him, Louis XIV obtained in gaining the loyalty of Claude Boisot ... the ties between the king and the Bisontin banker were among the first threads in the web which the monarchy spun to integrate the province into the kingdom."[267]

Provincial brokers introduced their own clients to their patrons whose service they might join, although not all brokers did so willingly; ambitious clients were potential rivals. For instance, Oppède introduced Toussaint de Janson-Forbin to Colbert, and the bishop became his client. Sourdis introduced Richelieu to Dubernet, who sought the Cardinal's patronage. Mercoeur introduced Fortia de Pilles and the chevalier de La Penne into Mazarin's service, and both became his clients. Charles de Barras, chevalier de La Penne, a Knight of Malta from an old noble Provençal family, was captain of Mercoeur's galley. Mazarin had mentioned in his letters to Mercoeur that he had had a long chat with the chevalier at court and promised to give him an office.[268]

Broker-clients provided their patrons with fighting men. Great nobles were expected to muster client armies. For example, Henri, duc de Montmorency, governor of Languedoc in the early seventeenth century, inherited an extensive noble clientele from his father, the former governor; many of his clients had been raised in his father's household. Although Montmorency owned little land himself in Languedoc—most of his lands were in the Ile-de-France, Normandy, and Brittany—he profited from the prestige and influence of his in-laws, the Ventadours, who were extensive landholders in Languedoc; his sister Marguerite had married Anne de Lévis, duc de Ventadour, lieutenant general of Languedoc. Montmorency also enjoyed the loyalty of the marquis de Mirepoix and the baron de Léran, relatives of the Ventadours, who helped him to control the Vivarais, and he was allied through his mother to the Budos de Portes and to Fay de Peraut, seneschal of Nîmes, who helped him to control the lower Rhône.[269]

In neighbouring Guyenne, the duc d'Epernon was ordered by the king in 1621 to take the field in Béarn against the marquis de La Force. From his château at Cadillac, Epernon wrote to "several men of condition [rank] in Guyenne, Saintonge, and Angoumois," that is, to his clients and supporters, and in response about 1,400 nobles gathered at Cadillac.[270] The old duc de La Rochefoucauld, governor of Poitou, had raised 1,500 Poitevin nobles in four days for the siege of La Rochelle and boasted to the king, "Sire, there is not one who is my relative." His son went out to his government of Poitou in 1650 to raise support for Condé. He summoned the nobility of Poitou and the Limousin to his château at Verteuil, ostensibly to attend his father's funeral. Most came but they refused to follow him in attacking the city of Saumur, whose governor was Mazarin's client. La Rochefoucauld had thought that he could raise an army of 2,000 Poitevin nobles to take Saumur, but he only secured the support of 700 (and possibly as few as 300).[271]

Provincial brokers provided their Paris patrons with extraordinary assistance, for example, loans that were often never repaid: Mazarin and Fouquet regularly borrowed money from their clients, especially in financial emergencies.[272] Oppède lent Mazarin money to use for the sailing fleet at Toulon and the galleys at Marseille, and the bailli de Forbin advanced Richelieu 40,000 écus (120,000 livres) to use for the royal galleys during the Spanish invasion.[273] The comte de Grignan went heavily into debt entertaining deputies to the General Assemblies and notables traveling through Provence; he also lent money to the crown during military emergencies. Forced to use his wife's dowry to pay his gambling debts,[274] he went bankrupt in 1690 and suffered the ignominy of having his salary as lieutenant general garnished for two years; he also caused the bankruptcy of the provincial treasurer who had lent him large sums of money.[275] He received a gift of 200,000 livres from the king to ease his debts, but it was not enough and the château of Grignan had to be sold after his death.[276]

Provincial brokers did personal favors for their patrons. Oppède sent exotic animals, including a male lion and a wild female sheep, at his own expense to the zoo at Vincennes for Mazarin.[277] Régusse sent Richelieu a gift of three barrels of muscat wine, and Chancellor Séguier a cask, from his own vineyard at La Ciotat.[278] Cardinal Mazarin thanked the chevalier Paul for a gift of orange blossoms sent from Provence and Cardinal Bichi for a gift of horses.[279] The marquis de Saint Chamond had written Richelieu that he was sending from Provence chests containing three bunches of orange flowers, thirteen vials of essence of roses, and four vials of jasmine oil.[280] Nicolas Arnoul filled a flood of requests from Colbert, many of which came from the king, who was decorating Versailles: red Moroccan leather and goat skins for book bindings, African animals for the Versailles zoo, Arab horses, flowers, palm leaves from Rome for the king's chapel, rocks, shells, and rare stones from Mediterranean grottos for their replicas at Versailles.[281]

Brokers' services varied in political importance. The information and advice on local politics and personalities they sent to Paris could be as significant as their use of provincial crédit and clients to influence the conduct of institutions such as the Estates, parlements, and municipal governments. The letters of brokers sometimes influenced national decision making; for example, the letters of Oppède, Mercoeur, and Boisot helped to shape royal policy in Provence and the Franche-Comté. However, the letters of brokers could become lobbying efforts for their own viewpoints and interests as in the case of Oppède's letters. However, on serious matters Oppède followed his letters with visits to court. Other brokerage services had less political importance, although they were still useful, for instance, lending money to a patron, entertaining his allies and friends, recruiting new clients and fighting-men for him, and doing personal favors such as providing animals for the zoo or curios for Versailles. Brokerage services occurred inside and outside an institutional framework and provided a way to influence the institutional process or to bypass it.

Brokers and Intendants

What was the relationship between the intendants, the new provincial agents of the central government, and the brokers? Were they allies or enemies?

Cardinal Richelieu had established the intendants as permanent administrators in the provinces of France and made them important centralizing agents of the national government at Paris.[282] Most brokers collaborated with the intendants to help govern the provinces. They used their crédit and clients to help the intendants perform their new administrative duties and served as stalking horses for them, reinforcing their shaky legitimacy and insulating the provincial power structure from the shock of their demands. They assisted the intendants as part of their brokerage services, because they were often members of the same Paris ministerial clienteles.

Arnoul and Oppède, for example, were clients of Colbert in Provence; Camus de Beaulieu and Claude Boisot were clients of Louvois in the Franche-Comté; Jacques de La Grange and Ulrich Obrecht were clients of Louvois in Alsace; Henri d'Aguesseau and Cardinal Pierre de Bonzi were clients of Colbert in Languedoc. They could also be subclients of the same patron. Archbishop Pierre de Marca was a client of Mazarin while intendant Bazin de Bezons was a client of Le Tellier, who was Mazarin's client. The bailli de Forbin was a client of Richelieu, and he sought the patronage of the Cardinal's other clients, for example, Secretary of State Sublet de Noyers. Noyers had sent his own clients, the Du Plessis-Besançon brothers (cousins of the Cardinal), Jean Lequeux, and Nicolas Arnoul as naval intendants to Toulon to work with Forbin.[283] Colbert created an administrative system of provincial intendants indistinguishable from his own network of clients.[284] Ties to mutual Paris patrons fostered cooperation between the intendants and provincial brokers and explain why the latter were often willing to help the intendants in the performance of their administrative duties—they had been asked to do so by a Paris patron or did so voluntarily to curry favor.

A good working relationship existed between Pierre de Marca, archbishop of Toulouse and a former intendant, and Claude Bazin, sieur de Bezons, intendant in Languedoc. As a protégé of Le Tellier, Bezons became Mazarin's client. He served effectively in Languedoc for twenty years. At the Pézenas Estates in 1657, he wrote Mazarin that the assistance of the bishops was essential in achieving the crown's goals.[285] He and Marca helped archbishop Rébé to control the Languedoc Estates. As another example, Louvois ordered intendant Germain-Michel Camus de Beaulieu on several occasions to heed the advice of Claude Boisot because he had access to information that the intendant lacked.[286] Geoffroy Luillier, sieur d'Orgeval, was sent to Provence as intendant in December 1656, the first since the Fronde, but was recalled three months later because his authority had not been accepted by the Provençaux. Oppède was then allowed to exercise the intendant's authority unofficially without letters of commission, a creative solution to an administrative problem; he often received royal letters to act temporarily as governor, too.[287] In this case a provincial broker had become an intendant.

Colbert asked Oppède to work with Louis de Machault, an army intendant sent to Provence in 1661, and with intendant sent to Provence in 1661, and with intendant Bazin de Bezons from Languedoc, who came to Provence in 1664 to help with a new royal tax survey and returned periodically over the next few years.[288] Oppède also regularly assisted Nicolas Arnoul, intendant of the royal galleys at Marseille, as did Janson-Forbin, bishop of Marseille. For instance, Arnoul wrote Colbert on April 2, 1668, "I shall not speak to you again of the port of Marseille; I shall execute what we have decided with the help of the first president and the bishop of Marseille."[289] Arnoul wrote Colbert on April 10 that he was impatiently awaiting the arrival of the bishop of Marseille, "whom I know for a man of intelligence, good conduct, and zeal for the royal service."[290] On November 24, Arnoul wrote that he, Oppède, and Janson-Forbin had acted as mediators in a dispute between the towns of Senary and Ollioules.[291]

Oppède wrote Colbert on August 7 that he was leaving for Marseille to regulate the affairs of the abbey of Saint Victor, accompanied by the bishop of Marseille and the archbishop of Arles. He would see Arnoul while he was there.[292] On December 7, 1666, Arnoul had written that "I am here at Aix for the registration of the royal letters by the parlement permitting the enlargement of Marseille, which was accomplished this morning through the efforts of the first president."[293] Arnoul and Oppède were joined as royal commissioners on this project by other clients of Oppède, first president Reynaud de Séguiran of the Aix Cour des Comptes, and Dominique Guidy, a trésorier général.[294] In 1667, Arnoul wrote that work on the harbor was not proceeding well but would improve when Oppède arrived.[295] The next year Arnoul wrote that he was impatiently awaiting the arrival of the first president, "who is responsible for all the affairs of this province and whose intelligence is everywhere, although his body cannot be."[296] Oppède, a provincial broker, served as mediator between Arnoul and the Marseille government, the Aix Parlement, and various town governments.

Intendant Pellot was able to reduce the size of the Cour des Aides at Montauban because the provincial lieutenant general, François d'Espinay, marquis de Saint Luc, read the royal edict of reduction to the court and warned the judges that the intendant and trésoriers généraux would assume their functions if they resisted.[297] Saint Luc had been a provincial broker for decades, while Claude Pellot, sieur de Portdavid, was a cousin of Colbert. Pellot had been appointed intendant because he had a reputation as a hardliner who favored using troops to collect taxes.[298] Dubernet and his friends in the Parlement of Bordeaux helped Governor Epernon to block the publication of a decree suppressing the intendant's authority.[299]

The careers of five Alsatians demonstrate the nature of the relationship between brokers and intendants. Charles Guntzer, Ulrich Obrecht, Jean-Baptiste Klinglin, Jean Dietremann, and Jean Dietrich, *syndics royaux* and *préteurs royaux* in late seventeenth-century Alsace, were regional notables and brokers who helped the intendants to govern and became their agents or subdélégués. A frontier province in which large numbers of troops were stationed, Alsace had been added to France by military conquest at mid-century, and it took the rest of the century to assimilate the province fully.[300] The French conquest offered those who spoke French and were willing to change their religion an opportunity to advance rapidly, and a group of new men rose meteorically, both socially and economically, by cooperating with the royal government, especially during the intendancies of Claude de La Rond and Le Pelletier de La Houssaye from 1698 to 1715.[301]

Charles Guntzer was named syndic royal in 1681 and held this office for nearly two decades. He had converted to Catholicism sometime before 1685, as did Ulrich Obrecht who was named préteur royal in this year. Both offices were newly created, and their holders acted as the king's representatives in the municipal government of Strasbourg, the provincial capital. They reported directly to the secretary of state for war and assisted the intendants in governing; in fact, Obrecht became the intendant's subdélégué. The office of syndic had been created immediately after the city's conquest in 1681. The syndic attended all muncipal assemblies as the king's representative to make certain that no legislation was passed contrary to royal law. He also made certain that no legislation was passed contrary to the traditional laws of the province. He headed a staff of clerks, supervised procedure, and took minutes of the meetings.[302]

The office of préteur royal was created in 1685, after the Revocation of the Edict of Nantes, to regulate the numerous Lutherans in Alsace. The holder was responsible for implementing the religious policies of the intendants, a task he shared with the syndic royal.[303] Obrecht, a doctor of jurisprudence, a well-known law professor at the University of Strasbourg, a former municipal councillor, and an advocate general of the city, was a Lutheran when he was proposed to Louvois as a subdélégué by intendant La Grande. Louvois vetoed the appointment because of his religion but was countermanded by Louis XIV, who was interested in reliable service. Obrecht had converted by the time of his appointment as préteur royal, possibly because of his long-standing feud with Jean Dietrich.[304]

The préteur royal presided over municipal assemblies. He voted first, spoke first in debates, and had final authority in disputes. He was de facto head of the municipal government and official mediator with the royal government. He held office at royal pleasure—he was appointed, not elected—and enjoyed great influence within the municipal government, increased by his service as director of the municipal hospital, the press, and the university.[305]

Guntzer and Obrecht were the crown's watchdogs over the city of Strasbourg, similar to the prévôts royaux and viguiers in other provinces. But they also defended the city and region of their birth. Guntzer, for instance, emphasized the Lutherans' loyalty, cooperation, and support for the king in his letters whenever he could, and his son later reconverted to Lutheranism. Obrecht promoted regional trade and successfully intervened in 1696–97 on behalf of the merchants of Nancy and the Alsatian towns to have the intendant restore trade regulations and taxation to their 1684 level.[306]

At his death Obrecht was followed in office by his son, but in 1706, Jean-Baptiste Klinglin became préteur royal. Klinglin came from a family of officials who had served the archdukes of Austria when they governed the province, and his older brother was a judge in the royal court at Colmar. The family was Catholic. Klinglin began his career as an interpreter-secretary, became a judge in the provincial high court, then advocate general of the city of Strasbourg, and syndic royal in 1699. Klinglin later remarked that préteurs were chosen for their experience in municipal affairs, their command of the German language and customs, and their knowledge of municipal and customary law.[307] He was replaced as syndic royal of Strasbourg by Georges Hatzel, a judge in the bailliage court of Haguenau. Hatzel had become wealthy as an army supplier and invested his money in land, livestock, and manufacturing farming tools. Strasbourg was not the only Alsatian city to be given preteurs royaux: Haguenau and Colmar also received them.[308] Jean Dietremann was named préteur royal of Colmar in 1701 and permanent subdélégué for Haute-Alsace in 1702. Intendant de La Houssaye had great confidence in Dietremann, who had been a judge in the provincial high court before his appointment; he was still serving the intendant and the crown in these posts decades later.[309]

Jean Dietrich came from a wealthy banking family of Strasbourg that was both German-speaking and Lutheran. Born in 1651, he served in the municipal government for nearly a half-century. Dietrich was useful to the intendants in Alsace because he provided them with large loans, and they were useful to him because they supplied him with mining and manufacturing concessions. For instance, in 1702 Dietrich negotiated a loan of 500,000 livres by a consortium of Strasbourg bankers to the intendant at a rate of 15 percent per annum. He lent the crown 110,000 marcs of silver seven years later, when he was already owed 440,000 livres by the treasury. In return, he successfully obtained mining concessions from Louvois in sulphur, vitriol, quicksilver, and saltpeter in Basse-Alsace, where he already owned iron mines and forges. Dietrich steadfastly refused to convert, went to Paris frequently on business, and died in 1740 at the ripe old age of eighty-nine.[310]

Other "new men" who collaborated with the intendants and the royal government to advance socially and economically included Walter Joseph de Gail, préteur royal of Haguenau; Duvaillé, a lawyer at the bar of the provincial high court who became préteur royal of Colmar; and Jean Noblat, a municipal councillor of Belfort then the city's prévôt and its bailli. His son succeeded him in office to become a subdélégué of the intendant in Haute-Alsace.[311] These men used their provincial influence to help the intendants govern Alsace and were rewarded with offices, social elevation, and opportunities to increase their wealth.

Brokers were often absorbed into the expanding machinery of the royal government, and some became subdélégués or even intendants. For example, Oppède and Claude Bouchu became intendants, and Ulrich Obrecht and Jean Dietremann subdélégués. Claude Boisot was a master of requests in the Parlement of Besançon, although he never actually became an intendant, while his brother-in-law Nicolas-Louis Boudret was the subdélégué of an intendant. Jean-Baptiste d'Oppède, the son of Henri and a president in the Parlement of Aix, became an intendant in Sicily.[312] More brokers probably became subdélégués than intendants, but subdélégués sometimes became intendants, although these were unusual cases: Le Boistel de Chatignonville was the subdélégué of intendant Robert in maritime Flanders, then replaced him when he went with the army into Holland.[313]

Knowledge of Paris-based client ties may help to resolve some of the confusion over the nature of administrative relationships between provincial intendants and governors in the seventeenth century.[314] Some historians see this relationship as strained by conflict.[315] Others see it as cooperative.[316] Its nature, in fact, may have been determined by the participants' ties to Paris. For example, François Bochart, seigneur de Saron-Champigny, intendant in Provence, was a maternal cousin of Richelieu and a cousin and client of the secretary of state for Provence, Sublet de Noyers, who was a client of Richelieu. Governor Alais was also a client of Richelieu and had cultivated the friendship of Sublet de Noyers.[317] Not surprisingly, therefore, Champigny secured Alais's protection and became his client. When Alais broke with Mazarin, Champigny was recalled and sent to the Lyonnais, and Mazarin sent one of his own clients, Alexandre de Sève, to Provence as intendant. Sève did not have a good working relationship with Alais who was not a client of Mazarin.[318] Nor did Alais have a collaborative relationship with François Cazet, seigneur de Vautorte, Champigny's predecessor as intendant in Provence. Vautorte had been appointed because he was the client of Chavigny with whom Alais had ties, but Alais personally disliked him.[319]

Paris-to-province patronage ties helped to determine the nature of provincial administrative relationships. If an intendant was a client of a royal minister, or a provincial secretary of state who might himself be a ministerial client, and if the governor was connected to either man, then their relationship was likely to be collaborative. In fact, the intendant often became the governor's client or came informally under his protection.[320] But when the governor had no ties to the intendant's Paris patron or was hostile to him, their relationship was less likely to be collaborative.

Provincial brokers did not always help the intendants. Sometimes they obstructed their administrative efforts as in the case of Pierre de Bonzi, cardinal-archbishop of Narbonne and president of the Languedoc Estates. The Bonzi family was Florentine and had originally come to France in the entourage of Catherine de Medici; they were distant cousins who were rewarded with the bishopric of Béziers. The son of a Florentine senator, Pierre de Bonzi had gone to the French court in the 1650s, and as an Italian had quickly gained Mazarin's favor. When his uncle, the bishop of Béziers, had died in 1659 Mazarin had named Pierre to this office. He became the sixth generation of Bonzi uncles and nephews to hold it, and he continued to rise at court. He negotiated the marriage of the daughter of Gaston d'Orléans with the Grand Duke of Tuscany, celebrated the marriage at the Louvre, escorted the bride to Florence, and continued to Venice as ambassador. He also served as ambassador to Milan, Madrid, and Poland, and received a cardinal's hat in 1672 upon nomination of the Polish king. He transferred to Colbert's service at the death of Mazarin, and his successful diplomacy earned him Louis XIV's favor. He was rewarded with appointment to the archbishopric of Toulouse in 1669, and four years later to the archbishopric of Narbonne where, as president of the Languedoc Estates, he helped Colbert control these assemblies. Bonzi was popular in Languedoc and had an extensive clientele since his family had been bishops of Béziers for more than a century. He had a good working relationship with Henri d'Aguesseau, who has intendant in Languedoc from 1673 to 1685 and the famous son of the first president, Antoine d'Aguesseau. In fact, they were Colbert's administrative team in Languedoc.[321]

However, Bonzi quarreled bitterly with Aguesseau's successor in Languedoc, intendant Nicolas de Lamoignon, marquis de Basville, who was a client of Louvois, Colbert's political enemy: Bonzi used his authority as president of the Estates to countermand Basville's orders whenever possible. Basville had gained the king's favor by his tough stance toward the Huguenots. While intendant in Poitou, Basville had presided over the first dragonnades and became known for his energetic use of military force to obtain conversions, thereby securing Louvois's patronage. Posted to Languedoc, he submitted long lists of Huguenot conversions to Paris to secure the king's favor and to please Madame de Maintenon and the king's confessor.[322] Basville complained to Louvois about Bonzi's behavior and undermined his relationship with the king.

Bonzi's womanizing was well known in Languedoc—his portrait shows a full, sensual face—and it would have created a worse scandal there if he had not been so popular. His special friend was Madame de Ganges, who had a complaisant husband, as Basville duly informed the king: Louis XIV trod the straight and narrow path in his later years and personally reproached Bonzi for his conduct during one of his visits to court. The king eventually sent Madame de Ganges from the province. Basville also informed the king that Bonzi was using his position as president of the Estates to fill his own pockets, those of Madame de Ganges and her husband, and those of his sister, Madame de Castries, and her son, the marquis de Castries. As a result, the king refused Bonzi's request that his nephew be named mayor of Montpellier, and Basville's candidate, Monsieur de Belleval, president of the Cour des Comptes at Montpellier, was appointed instead. This was a public slap at Bonzi, who never regained the king's favor.[323] It should be remembered that Basville's patron, Louvois, was the enemy of Bonzi's patron, Colbert, who had died in 1683, leaving him without a court protector.

There was a personality clash between Bonzi and Basville as well as a jurisdictional and power struggle, but their Paris ties were critical in determining the nature of their relationship as provincial administrators. The relationships of intendants and provincial brokers were torn by personality clashes and administrative conflicts—what political relationships during the Old Regime were not?—but these differences were often buried in the interests of a mutual Paris patron.

Broker-clients of the royal ministers usually cooperated with the provincial intendants and assisted them in the performance of their duties. Historians have tended to overemphasize the intendants' conflicts with local institutions and officials and the inevitability of their success in overcoming provincial resistance because they have depended too heavily for their analyses on sources preserved in the national collections at Paris: the letters of the intendants themselves, the protest letters of local institutions about them, and the decisions of the royal council.[324] These sources do not tell the whole story, however. Using provincial sources, this book has emphasized the extent of provincial cooperation with the intendants, which has tended to be underestimated.

Brokers were collaborators of the intendants. They helped to achieve the political integration of France by using their influence and clienteles to extend the central government's control over the power structures of distant provinces—over the Estates, parlements, and municipal governments. They sent vital information on local affairs to the Paris government. They encouraged the merger of regional and national elites by themselves becoming clients of Paris patrons, allowing their patrons to use their own provincial resources to achieve national political goals. They helped the Bourbon monarchy and its ministers to survive the civil war of the Fronde and to pacify France after the Fronde, and to secure the money and men to defend the frontiers of France during the Habsburg Wars and Louis XIV's wars. Brokers helped to create the royal navy and to establish the intendants in the provinces, sometimes even becoming intendants or their agents themselves. They were an important resource during emergencies when ordinary avenues of assistance were closed, providing help inside and outside the institutional framework of government.

The careers and services of thirty broker-clients of royal ministers in six frontier provinces have been described in these pages, eleven from Provence, five from Languedoc, four from Guyenne, five from Alsace, two from Burgundy, and three from the Franche-Comté. Most seventeenth-century brokers came from the lesser provincial nobility, but a few came from the great old families, and some were newly ennobled. Most already held positions of authority and power in the provinces, for example, as archbishops, bishops, and first presidents of parlements. Most knew each other because the world of political power was small and self-contained. In the next chapter we shall see how these seventeenth-century brokers differed from their sixteenth-century counterparts, the provincial governors and lieutenants, and what these differences meant in the governments of Richelieu, Mazarin, Colbert and Louis XIV.

CHAPTER FIVE

Brokerage and the Nobility

Early modern France was an elitist society in which an hereditary nobility monopolized political power and decision-making authority. The patrons of important political clienteles were noble. So were many of their clients and most provincial power brokers. France was covered by a loose web of noble clienteles reaching vertically to the king at court—the rural nobility of France was organized regionally by overlapping patron-broker-client and kinship ties.[1] Royal patronage flowed outward from the king at court in an informal system for distributing scarce public resources among the elite of France, and the influence of noble patron-brokers was evaluated by contemporaries in terms of their access to the king as the fount of royal patronage. The recipients of royal patronage in turn brokered benefits and favors downward among their clients in the provinces until the flow became a trickle. A study of early modern French brokers, therefore, is a study of traditional French elites and the distribution or brokerage of royal patronage among them.

Provincial brokers in the sixteenth century were usually provincial governors and lieutenants general who were great nobles. Their authority in the provinces was military, and the extensive great noble clienteles they created among the provincial nobility helped them to keep the peace and to govern. The crown, in fact, was able to govern most of France in the sixteenth century only with the help of the provincial governors and their clienteles. The monarchy distributed royal patronage to secure the loyalty, obedience, and support of the great nobles, especially those who had established themselves as provincial governors, and through them to secure the loyalty, obedience, and support of the provincial nobles who were their clients. The monarchy used the provincial governors and their clients as agents of administration in a fragmented, unintegrated state. Sixteenth-century brokers contributed to national statebuilding by attaching the provincial nobility to the crown through brokering royal patronage to their clients. In this way the monarchs of France allowed the great nobles to dispose of huge blocks of royal offices as patronage with little regard for the long-term effects. In fact, they were creating provincial power blocs outside royal control. As a result, great nobles in the sixteenth century were able to turn royal government into a hotbed of rival influences, creating political conflict and even civil war.[2]

In the seventeenth century Cardinal Richelieu made an administrative change of far-reaching importance when he created a large administrative clientele of his own at Paris, expanded it into the provinces, especially into the peripheral provinces, and used it to extend his control over institutions such as the Estates, sovereign courts, and municipal governments. Richelieu recruited important members of the provincial ruling elite as his own clients without relying upon the provincial governors—he bypassed them, in fact—and used his own clients to increase the crown's control over provincial administrations and to govern directly. Many of his clients were officials whose provincial and municipal institutions were attached more securely to the throne because of their personal loyalty to Richelieu. The Cardinal rewarded them with royal patronage, which they in turn distributed among their own clients, many of whom were also officials.

Provincial governors and lieutenants general continued to act as brokers of royal patronage in the seventeenth century and to attach the provincial nobility to the throne—for example, the ducs de Mercoeur, Epernon, Longueville, the comte d'Alais, and the princes de Condé. But they became less important as brokers of royal patronage as the century went on. They were replaced by a new group of provincial brokers, members of Paris-based ministerial administrative clienteles who were minor sword nobles, robe nobles, officials, gentlemen, and new nobles such as the bailli de Forbin, Oppède, Régusse, the Valbelles, Ulrich Obrecht, Claude Bouchu, the Boisots, and Fortia de Pilles. They headed provincial, institutional, and municipal administrative clienteles of their own, and they brokered royal patronage to their own clients, in this way attaching provincial and municipal institutions to the crown.

Distributing patronage to secure political loyalty is a classic technique of governing: Henri IV had used this technique to pacify France after the Wars of Religion and the League.[3] No royal minister before Richelieu, however, had ever recruited so many provincial administrative clients, especially in frontier provinces, carefully placed them in key institutions to assure provincial control, and retained them over a long period of time. The recruitment and retention of provincial broker-clients by Cardinal Richelieu was a deliberate ministerial policy meant to establish royal control over the peripheral regions of France, and it contributed significantly to the development of the early modern state. The intendants whom Richelieu sent as permanent residents into the provinces were used for this purpose, too, and in many cases they were also his clients. Cardinal Richelieu broke new ground in creating and using ministerial clienteles to govern distant provinces directly, an administrative change that increased the integration and centralization of the early modern French state.

Cardinal Mazarin inherited Richelieu's position as chief minister but allowed his predecessor's client networks in the provinces to lapse as he created his own administrative network in Paris. However, when the Fronde erupted, Mazarin found himself forced to reestablish provincial networks of broker-clients because he could not use the intendants whom the rebels forced him to recall. The civil war of the Fronde (1648–1653) occurred in two stages. The first or judicial Fronde was a rebellion by the sovereign judicial courts of Paris, Aix, Bordeaux, and Rouen. One of their demands was the recall of provincial intendants and Mazarin was forced to comply, although he restored them as soon as he could after the Fronde. The second or noble Fronde was a rebellion by great nobles who were provincial governors and their noble clients. They were able to force Cardinal Mazarin into temporary exile in Germany. Through the distribution of royal patronage and the tactic of divide-and-rule, however, Mazarin was able to return to Paris, reassert control over the great nobles and the royal government, and end the Fronde. His provincial networks of broker-clients, many of whom were inherited from Richelieu, helped him to reestablish control over the French provinces.

Mazarin's client, Colbert, became Louis XIV's finance minister and was responsible for provincial tax collection. Colbert had trouble securing taxes from the *pays d'Etats*, the provinces with traditional tax-granting assemblies and in many cases also frontier provinces. Colbert relied increasingly upon his own intendant-clients in helping him to manage the Estates in these provinces. He created successful administrative teams composed of his intendants, provincial broker-clients inherited from his predecessors, and their clients to help him in managing the Estates. They proved highly effective, combining bribery with intimidation as tactics of control, and functioning as political machines directed from Paris. Constructed ad hoc to meet specific political needs, ministerial administrative clienteles tended to decay in less turbulent times and had to be revived when a crisis occurred. Nonetheless, their construction and maintenance, especially in the peripheral provinces, was a ministerial policy of Richelieu, Mazarin, and Colbert that helped to create the early modern French state.

In creating their own provincial clienteles, the royal ministers challenged the near-monopoly of the governors and great nobles on brokering royal patronage in the provinces by diverting part of the flow to their own ministerial clients. In this way they threatened the size of great noble clienteles and endangered the governors' provincial power bases. Whether the royal ministers actually intended this to happen is difficult to say—probably not—but the destruction of the independent power of the great nobles of France was essential to the development of the early modern state.

Predictably, the great nobles reacted violently. They were angered by their loss of royal patronage and by the royal ministers' diversion of its flow to their own clients for their own use, and their anger became a motive for their participation in the Fronde. They considered the new brokers to be upstarts—they were socially inferior—and resisted what they saw as an attempt to usurp their own provincial brokerage of royal patronage. They resented the creation of ministerial administrative clienteles in the provinces, which they saw as threatening their own clienteles and power. The concept of noble brokerage, therefore, offers a new perspective from which to view the motivation for noble participation in the Fronde, the decline in the power of the great nobility, and the development of the early modern state.

There are several widely recognized trends in the political history of early modern France: the monarchy's selective distribution of royal patronage as a technique of political control; the tendency of this technique to create overmighty subjects; the crown's gradual reduction of the flow of royal patronage to the governors, great nobles, and their clients for this reason; the crown's encroachment upon the authority of the provincial governors for the same reason; and their resentment at royal encroachment, which flared occasionally into violent protest. Brokerage of royal patronage should be added to this list. In the sixteenth century, governors and great nobles acted as provincial brokers of patronage to attach the nobility to the throne. In the seventeenth century, the governors and great nobles were replaced as brokers by lesser nobles and royal officials, ministerial clients who used their crédit and clienteles to attach independent provincial and municipal institutions to the throne. The crown used the French nobility, great and small, sword and robe, through the brokerage of royal patronage in the provinces, to help create the early modern state.

Sixteenth-century Brokers of Royal Patronage

The most important brokers of royal patronage in the provinces of sixteenth-century France were the great nobles who were provincial governors. They shared several traits. All of the 142 major governors from 1515 to 1650 were from old sword noble families. In the seventeenth century, these offices became inaccessible to barons and seigneurs, and the dukes and peers (*ducs-pairs* and *comtes-pairs*) gradually secured a monopoly of these positions. The crown chose high-status governors because their ability to secure obedience in the provinces was roughly in proportion to their status. Provincial lieutenants general and minor governors occasionally came from the robe nobility, and there were some clerics in middle-level governorships in the sixteenth and seventeenth centuries. But the offices of governors at all levels were overwhelmingly monopolized by the sword nobility.[4]

Major governors were independently wealthy. Seven out of eight were the heads of their family lines at the time of their appointment because their fathers were dead—they enjoyed the bulk of the family inheritance—and nearly three-fourths were the eldest surviving sons, which meant they had the lion's share of their family property. In the long run the main financial advantage accruing to the governors from their provincial position was the opportunity to maintain their own clienteles from public funds.[5] There were occasional robe nobles who were provincial brokers in the sixteenth century, and minor sword nobles, too, but the governors were usually the most important brokers of royal patronage in the provinces. They used their influence at court to obtain military, judicial, and financial offices to distribute among their clients in the provinces, and they mediated between their clients and the royal government in Paris. Examples are the duc de Mayenne and the ducs de La Trémoille, governors of sixteenth-century Burgundy and Poitou. While the La Trémoille and their clients were steadfastly loyal to the crown, the duc de Mayenne became chief of the Catholic League after his brother's assassination, waged civil war in opposing the accession of a Hugenot king, Henri IV, and took his clients among the Burgundian nobility with him into revolt.

The Ducs de La Trémoille

In 1527, François, duc de La Trémoille, was named governor of Poitou, where his family held extensive lands, and at his death he was succeeded by his oldest son, Louis III, who held the office until he died in 1577. The La Trémoille were governors of Poitou for nearly a century—they had first received the office in 1492 as a reward for fighting for the crown in Brittany and Italy.[6] The La Trémoille had lived in Poitou since the early thirteenth century, perhaps even earlier, and were members of a great old feudal family. Their lands in Poitou included Thouars, La Trémoille, Mauléon, and Talmond; in nearby Aunis they held Marans, Benon, and the Ile-de-Ré; and they had lands in Saintonge, Anjou, Berry, Orleáns, and Brittany.[7] Historian Lucien Romier has noted that sixteenth-century great nobles such as the La Trémoille used the influence that their service earned them with the king to strengthen their position in their home province where they owned land.[8] The ducs de La Trémoille used the monarchy to strengthen their power and position in western France.[9]

The La Trémoille successfully attracted and held the loyalty of prominent members of the western nobility by employing them as officials in their household.[10] Local officials responsible for managing the La Trémoille estates were supervised by gentlemen officials of the ducal household who provided central direction and coordination in the administration of family lands and revenues. These local officials were family officials and royal officials in the regions where the family had lands; the La Trémoille had probably helped to secure their offices. Local officials were responsible for the day-to-day running of the estates, collection of seigneurial dues, observation of seigneurial rights and privileges, supervision of public works, maintenance of family castles and fortresses, seigneurial justice, and local church affairs. For instance, the staff of the *châtellenie* (estate with a castle) of Thouars, one of many La Trémoille estates in the viscounty of Thouars, had thirty-five administrative officials, slightly more than average. There were five officials at La Trémoille, fifteen officials at the barony of Craon, about twenty officials at Rochefort-sur-Loire; in other words, about seventy-five local officials for these four estates. The total for all their lands must have been in the hundreds, which was why a central administration was needed.[11]

There were twenty-seven men from twenty-four families serving as gentlemen officials in the household of François duc de La Trémoille, in the five years from 1527 to 1532. Most were noble and fifteen were members of the feudal nobility. Most were from the west, the largest number being from Poitou. They were not vassals. Of the approximately six hundred vassals of the house listed as doing homage to François de La Trémoille at the death of his grandfather, only three were officials of his household, although one of these, René d'Appelvoisin, seigneur de Thiois, was one of the most important lords in Poitou. Neither were they kinsmen; only one in twenty-seven definitely had family ties. They all received substantial annual salaries: nine received an average of about 150 livres a year in 1532, and fifteen out of twenty-seven had increases in their salaries ranging from 18 to 26 percent during the five year period. Moreover, the La Trémoille were extremely generous to them with gifts in money and in kind, bed and board, travel expenses, and new clothes.[12] Many, if not most, were clients of the La Trémoille.

There were a number of additional patronage opportunities available to these gentlemen because they served in the ducal household. For example, thirteen of them subsequently served in the governor's gendarmes or ordinance company; provincial nobles often began their service in the governor's household and then moved into his gendarmes company.[13] The La Trémoille owned twenty-six fortified châteaus and fortresses, and gentlemen officials of their household obtained places as commanders of these castles.[14] They also received appointments as governors and lieutenants of royal fortresses and fortified cities in Poitou and the west, and they obtained places in the administration of the family's estates for themselves and for their relatives. A number of family members of these gentlemen officials—sons, brothers, uncles, wives, and daughters—found their way into the service of the La Trémoille.[15] And a number of gentleman officials moved into the royal service, becoming members of the royal administration in order to obtain royal patronage, too.[16] In fact, they would have liked more royal patronage—they were discouraged by how little the La Trémoille had procured for them.[17]

The variety of benefits provided by royal patronage is illustrated by what the La Trémoille themselves received from the crown. They steadily increased their landholdings in the west from the late fourteenth to the early sixteenth centuries with the help of the crown; the viscounty of Thouars, for instance, was made a duchy.[18] Members of the family were governors and lieutenant generals of Burgundy in the fifteenth and early sixteenth centuries.[19] Other members of the family became governors of Poitou at the same time—most of their lands were in the west, and they lived at their château of Thouars on the Thouaret River.[20] Louis II, François, and Louis III became members of the king's order of chivalry, an honorary title, while Louis II served as first chamberlain to kings Louis III and François I. He enjoyed a royal pension of 10,000 livres a year; 4,000 livres a year as governor of Burgundy; and 3,000 and 12,000 livres annually as admiral of Guyenne and Brittany. The ducs de La Trémoille received another 14,000 livres a year from the royal treasury in the west and occasional cash gifts from the crown, for instance, 30,000 livres and 23,500 livres on separate occasions for their military expenditures while fighting the wars in Brittany.[21] In addition, the crown exempted the captains of family châteaux from serving in the provincial militia (*ban-et-arrière-ban*); the family was exempt from royal seigneurial dues; the crown paid 1,200 livres a year for the upkeep of a family ship used along the coast; it paid for troops stationed in family châteaux during the Wars of Religion; it paid the salaries of the family-controlled captains of the cities of Fougères, Nantes, and probably Concarneau; and it interceded in a number of legal suits concerning the La Trémoille.[22] The prospect of such generous royal patronage attracted the nobility, both great and small, into the royal service.

As governor of Poitou, François de La Trémoille made sure that he was not forgotten at court. He sent his son, Louis III, and his nephew, Nicolas d'Anjou, seigneur de Mezières, to court not only for their sake but for his sake as well: they carried letters to the king, played with the royal children, and met as many members of great houses as possible.[23] Undoubtedly, he also kept agents at court. It was common practice for great nobles and provincial political figures to send their children to court where they also kept agents to gather news, carry messages, maintain friendships, and protect their interests. Oppède was represented at court by Governor Mercoeur and Toussaint de Janson-Forbin. The comte de Grignan's interests were protected by the bishop of Uzès, Madame de Sévigné, and her friend Pomponne. Daniel de Cosnac acted as Conti's agent at court from 1654 to 1656 when the prince was in the Midi. Fortia de Pilles, governor of Marseille, kept an agent at court.[24] Joseph Dubernet, first president of the Parlement of Aix, kept a secretary at court.[25] Even the General Assembly of Provençal Communities kept a permanent agent at court to gather news and protect its interests.[26]

Claude Groulard, first president of the Parlement of Rouen, was his own agent at court. A native-born Norman, he had become first president of the parlement in 1585 at the age of thirty-four, although his only previous judicial experience had been as a councillor in the Grand Conseil at Paris, because he enjoyed the patronage of the governor of Normandy, one of Henri III's favorites: Groulard knew the king personally and saw him at least once a year, a relationship that caused him problems after the king's assassination. But Groulard was a Huguenot. After meeting the new king, Henri IV, he became his client and visited him at court at least once a year between 1589 and 1604. He belonged to a network of trusted men who helped Henri IV to govern France, and his relationship with the king made him one of the most powerful men in Normandy.[27] Groulard did not need an agent at court: he acted on his own behalf. Not all provincials, however, were able to do so because of the distance between their home and the national capital

The Duc de Mayenne

Charles de Lorraine, duc de Mayenne was governor of Burgundy for twenty-two years from 1573 to 1595, although he only resided at Dijon only after

1587 and even then was frequently in Paris. His family had been governors of Burgundy since 1543.[28] Between 1578 and 1584, Mayenne created a Burgundian clientele, although he was not resident in the province. Key figures in his clientele were the two provincial lieutenants general, Léonor Chabot, comte de Charny, and his son-in-law, Guillaume de Saulx-Tavannes.[29] Saulx-Tavannes received 3,000 livres a year in salary from the province and support for a fifty-man guard company. He was also governor of the fortresses of Talant and Montsaugeon.[30] His brother, Jean, was governor of Auxonne.[31] Another important client of Mayenne was Jean de Bayault, sieur de Franchesse, a noble originally from the Bourbonnais who had bought land in Burgundy. He was governor of the château of Dijon, for which he received 4,500 livres a year from the province. He obtained a military command for one nephew and an abbey for another, and his lieutenant, Leónard de Marcilly, was named bailli or royal administrator of Bourbon-Lancy in 1592.[32]

Neither Mayenne nor his wife owned land in Burgundy, which was a problem in building a provincial clientele; the type of aristocratic patronage available to the La Trémoille in Poitou was not available to them. As a royal gift, Mayenne had received the revenues from three châtellenies and the governorships of two fortresses in Burgundy, but he did not own land himself in the province.[33] He was not a Burgundian by birth, nor was his family, and he did not build a residence at Dijon. Moreover, he was absent from the province for years on end. For these reasons he was not a popular governor—he seemed too remote and too much of a foreigner.[34] Nonetheless, he did manage to build a large Burgundian clientele by generously distributing royal and provincial patronage when he was resident from 1587 to 1589. Mayenne repeatedly told the Burgundians that he had the good of their province at heart. He received deputies from the Estates affably and listened to their complaints patiently, and he tried not to be personally responsible for disciplining recalcitrant institutions and officials. He confiscated the property of Huguenots and distributed it to his supporters, exploiting the government of Burgundy as if it were a personal resource to fill his political needs.[35]

Mayenne's clients in the sovereign of Burgundy included president Bernard Desbarres of the Parlement of Dijon, councillors Jean Fyot and Perpetuo Berbisey, and advocate general Guillaume Legouz de Vellepeste. Desbarres, Berbisey, and Legouz each received royal pensions and substantial increases in their salaries (*gages*).[36] Mayenne's other judicial clients included first president Bénigne Jacquot and presidents Regnier de Latrecy and Antoine Legrand of the Chambre des Comptes at Dijon. Jacquot received an annual royal pension of 2,100 livres and a cash gift of 2,000 livres. Latrecy received an annual royal pension of 300 livres.[37] Mayenne's client, Pierre Baratier, who negotiated the hiring of Swiss mercenaries for him and served as his envoy to the duc de Lorraine, was rewarded with an office in the Chambre des Comptes at Dijon, then made an usher in the Grand Chancellery of Burgundy and a *général des monnaies*.[38] Mayenne's personal secretary,

Jean Desmarquets, who received a salary of 300 livres a year from the province, was named a president in the Bureau des Finances at Dijon. He was given a hôtel at Paris, confiscated from a supporter of Henri IV, as a reward for a successful mission to Germany on Mayenne's behalf, and he asked to have his office of trésorier général switched from Dijon to Paris. He received in addition a cash gift of the salaries of Burgundian royal officials drawn from the salt warehouse at Auxerre in the autumn of 1592.[39]

Mayenne's Burgundian clients included captains and lieutenants of royal fortresses, garrisons, and fortified cities, and secretaries of important nobles and political figures. They received gifts of money, furniture, land, and pensions.[40] His clients included municipal officials, lawyers, judges in the bailliage courts, financial officials, and officials from the salt warehouses. They received similar rewards.[41] Mayenne was generous in giving cash gifts to his clients. For instance, he gave a gift of 4,500 livres to sieur de Loches in February 1591; 360 livres to sieur de Montmeyan in February 1593; and 3,000 livres to his personal secretary, Prudent Michaut, in 1591.[42] Michaut was a Burgundian who was born at Châtillon and owned land in the bailliage of La Montagne, and he went on numerous provincial missions for Mayenne.[43] The duke also had several printers as clients, for example, Desplanches and Grangier at Dijon, Vatard at Auxerre; this was a common practice for governors.[44]

Mayenne had a number of Burgundians in his personal service as members of his household. They included two gentlemen servants, Jacques Hérard and Mathieu Cathelinet; a lackey, Antoine Dubois; a surgeon, Edme Callon; a silversmith, François Fernier; a pastry cook and wine steward, Martin Maupois; and a bootmaker. The Burgundians among his guards included Jean Travaillot, La Goutte, Foreu, Philibert Oudin, and Nicolas Vincent, and the Burgundians in his gendarmes company included Edme Le Bossu and Benoît de Gonnet.[45] Mayenne's most important Burgundian client was Pierre Jeannin, the son of a tanner from Autun who acted as his chief minister. He secured Jeannin royal letters of ennoblement and an office of councillor in the Parlement of Dijon; later an office of president was created for him.[46] Ducal and royal service were well-trodden paths of social mobility in the sixteenth century, and Mayenne's clientele contained a number of bourgeois and non-nobles, merchants, urban notables, officials, clerks, and royal sergeants.[47]

Mayenne's non-Burgundian clients were given Burgundian property and offices as rewards for their loyalty and service. For instance, Du Gast was made governor of Châlon; Henri de Montpezat, a relative of the duke's wife, received the abbey of Saint Germain d'Auxerre; Antoine-Richard Desportes, Mayenne's personal secretary, received the abbey of Saint Etienne de Dijon; Jean Alix received the abbey of Flavigny; Délage, a noble in the ducal household, received the revenues from the châtellenie of Argilly; Jean Hamilton, the curé of Saint Cosmes in Paris, received 3,000 livres from the Burgundian receiver general.[48] Mayenne's clientele contained many non-Burgundians.

Mayenne was generous to clients among the Burgundian nobility who fought for him during the War of the League. Anne de Pélissier was named governor of Auxonne after several missions to Madrid on the duke's behalf.[49] François de Damas, baron de Thianges, who had much crédit among the Burgundian nobility and was an important provincial client for this reason, raised 400 horsemen and 600 musketmen to fight for Mayenne, and stayed with him until he lost his governorship in 1595. Thianges was made governor of Soissons and commander of Mayenne's ordinance company.[50] Only twenty-three Burgundian nobles and gentlemen remained with Mayenne to the end.[51] Many of his clients changed sides in 1592, when the tide of events began to go against him, and only half of those who supported him then were still with him in 1594.[52] A patron needed a steady supply of patronage and a promising political future to hold the loyalty of his clients. Mayenne's generosity did not secure him permanent political loyalty because he did not have a promising political future after 1592. A nucleus of loyal clients remained with him until his final defeat—the type of client whom Roland Mousnier has called fidèle—but they were few. Most of his clients fell away as his fortunes declined. Emotional affection and loyalty cemented ties forged through the distribution of patronage, but the intensity of the emotional tie varied with the individual and the circumstances. Mayenne's experience indicates that general political conditions and personal material interests were important in determining client loyalties.

The French Monarchy's Use of Royal Patronage

Using patronage to secure cooperative behavior is a time-honored technique of political control. It has long been recognized that the monarchs of early modern Europe used the discriminatory distribution of royal patronage to create strong central governments, for instance, the Tudor monarchs of sixteenth-century England. They successfully used royal patronage to obtain the loyalty and support of the ruling elite, the feudal magnates, and the country gentry.[53] French kings used royal patronage for the same purpose.[54] In the sixteenth century they used royal patronage to secure the loyalty and support of the great nobles and their clients, the provincial nobility, and attach them to the throne. Specifically, they used royal patronage to recruit new supporters, reward loyal supporters, appease enemies, and play off rival factions threatening the authority of the crown.

The crown used royal patronage to reward the loyal service of Gaspard de Saulx, seigneur de Tavannes. Born at Dijon in 1509, he had gone to court as a page, married a cousin of Cardinal Tournon, a royal minister who became his patron, and at the Cardinal's death entered the service of the duc d'Orléans, the king's second son under whose command he had fought. At the duke's death he entered the service of the king's first son, the dauphin, the future Henri II, who made him provincial lieutenant general of Burgundy. Gaspard also owed this appointment to Guise patronage, having gained the favor of the duc de Guise while fighting under his command: Gaspard owed much of his advancement to his military skill. He allowed his older brother, Guillaume, to exercise his provincial office while he remained at court. But Henri II died and the Wars of Religion began. As an ardent Catholic, Gaspard returned to Burgundy in 1559 to hold the province for the crown, and remained for ten years as acting governor. He owned extensive lands in Burgundy and lived at his château, Le Pailly, near Langres, or the new hôtel he built at Dijon.[55]

Saulx-Tavannes created an extensive Burgundian clientele which he used in support of the Queen Mother, Catherine de Medici, and her son, Charles IX. The governors, captains, and lieutenants of royal fortresses and fortified cities in Burgundy were his Catholic clients. His cousins, Alexandre de Torpes and Claude de Saulx, seigneur de Ventoux, for example, were governors of Auxonne and Beaune. The Catholic Burgundian nobility flocked to his service. He established an advisory council of parlementaires to gain the support of that sovereign court and the city of Dijon, which became his headquarters, and he was cofounder of the first Burgundian Catholic League with parlement councillor Jean Bégat. He placed his own clients in municipal office, particularly Bénigne Martin, whom he made mayor at Dijon several times, and with their help was able to influence the provincial Estates. By offering royal commissions, he was able to recruit Burgundian noble companies of cavalry, infantry, gendarmes, muskets, and lances, and appointed his own clients as their captains.[56]

Gaspard de Saulx-Tavannes was rewarded for his loyalty with royal patronage. When the Queen Mother visited Dijon in 1564, she stayed at his hôtel, confirmed the appointment of his clients, and promised to make him a maréchal de France, a distinction he received some years later. He was able to acquire a large fortune while acting as governor of Burgundy. At the death of his brother, he named his cousin, Claude, and at his death, his own son Guillaume, as provincial lieutenant general and acting governor because he had been asked by the Queen Mother to return to court to tutor her second son, the duc d'Anjou. As a reward for his loyal service, he was named governor of Provence and admiral of the Levant a few months before his death.[57] Patron of a large noble clientele, Gaspard de Saulx-Tavannes was a Burgundian power broker from 1559 to 1569. He had a distinguished career in the royal service and was suitably rewarded by the crown.

Royal patronage was used to secure supporters for the crown, for instance, the Provençal clients of Charles de Lorraine, duc de Guise, who was named governor of Provence in 1594 by Henri IV. Guise distributed royal patronage to secure the support of Gaspard de Pontevès, second comte de Carcès and chief of the League in Provence; the marquis d'Oraison, chief of the Huguenot party; and Nicolas de Bausset, Pierre Libertat, and Fortia de Pilles, who delivered to him the important cities of Marseille and Berre. With their support, Guise was able to pacify Provence and end the War of the League in that province.

In 1589 the leadership of the Catholic party and the League in Provence was assumed by Gaspard de Pontevès, comte de Carcès, who had married the daughter of Eléonore de Montpezat, duchesse de Mayenne. The small, opposing Huguenot party was led by the marquis d'Oraison. Gaspard was named governor of the province in 1592 by Mayenne. Two years later, however, he renounced his claim to the governorship against his wife's wishes to recognize Henri IV's candidate, Charles de Lorraine, duc de Guise, who was Mayenne's nephew. Guise invaded Provence at the head of a royal army to restore order. The marquis d'Oraison also recognized Guise as governor. Both Carcès and Oraison hoped to be named provincial lieutenant general.[58]

With the help of Pierre Libertat and Nicolas de Bausset, sieur de Roquefort, Guise was able to take the city of Marseille, which for years had been under the control of the Leaguer Charles de Casaulx. Pierre Libertat was the guard captain of a city gate. The son of a Corsican, he was missing an eye, which he consequently held shut in a squint, but was good-looking in a swarthy way. He was secretly recruited to Guise's cause by Nicolas de Bausset, captain of the royal fortress of the Château d'If, who acted as his envoy to the duke. Libertat offered to assassinate Casaulx and open the city gates to Guise and his men in exchange for a cash gift of 50,000 écus (150,000 livres), the office of viguier of Marseille for himself, and offices for his family, including captain in the city guard for his son. Nicolas Bausset was to be named assessor of the city government; his family became hereditary chief justices of the Marseille seneschal court. Libertat assassinated Casaulx by running a sword through his stomach on February 27, 1596, and then opened the Porte Royale to Guise who was waiting outside with Carcès, Oraison, and a host of Provençal nobles, both Catholic and Huguenot. When Libertat died suddenly, his office of viguier went to his brother, and at his death four years later it went to Paul de Fortia, seigneur de Pilles, who had become governor of Berre by helping Guise to take the last fortified city in Provence to resist his government; Fortia de Pilles later became governor of the Château d'If. Carcès was eventually named provincial lieutenant general.[59] Guise was able to pacify Provence with the help of a few loyal Provençaux whom he rewarded with royal patronage.

Royal patronage was used to appease opponents of the crown—to neutralize their hostility and secure their support. Charles de Lorraine, duc de Guise, was recruited to the support of Henri IV in 1594, when the League cause seemed lost, with an offer of the government of Provence and a cash gift of 380,000 livres.[60] He later became Henri's client. To guarantee his loyalty to the Queen Mother after the king's assassination, Guise received a cash gift of about 200,000 écus (600,000 livres), ostensibly to pay his father's debts, and he received another 300,000 écus (900,000 livres) in January 1613.[61] Henri IV's cash gifts to great nobles had reached the sum of over 5,000,000 livres in 1594. The king placated opponents by rewarding them, spending at least 32,000,000 livres in buying off former League enemies.[62] Many became his clients. As regent his wife continued his policy of generosity to the great nobles—secretary of state Villeroy recommended a policy of satiating the great nobility with large gifts and pensions, and chancellor Bellièvre was in general agreement. In a series of private memos addressed to the Queen Mother, Villeroy wrote that royal liberality would encourage the great aristocrats to "comport themselves with more gratitude and stability," and that the money would trickle down and eventually ameliorate "the misery of those who had mismanaged their houses."[63]

Historian David Parker has observed that "amongst the socially dominant groups in the towns there was always to be found—even in the midst of bitter conflict—a group or faction which could be bought off or incorporated within the clienteles of the ruling groups at Paris."[64] He gives as an example the Rochelais sieur du Coudray, a member of both the Parlement of Paris and the municipal government of La Rochelle, who intervened on behalf of the Queen Mother, Marie de Medici, in the mayoral elections of that city in September 1612: Du Coudray had to flee the city because of the anger of his fellow citizens.[65] The crown bought off the La Rochelle delegation to Paris in 1652 with titles of nobility. One of the Rochelais bitterly condemned by his fellow citizens for his part in this affair was a certain Gobert, who had conducted the negotiations with England in 1627. He was now reviled for accepting an undeserved ennoblement from the crown and for his tax-farming activities.[66] In 1643 a deputation from Toulouse, sent to Paris to see the duc d'Orleáns with instructions to ask for the city's exemption from royal taxation, secured instead their own appointment as members of the municipal government (*capitouls*) in the following year, an act that precipitated a long and bitter feud.[67]

Royal patronage was also used by the crown to play off rival nobles. For instance, Henri II created future trouble by channeling excessive patronage to two noble families, the Guise and the Montmorency, who were rivals—Henri's widow, Catherine de Medici, had to juggle the Guise, the Montmorency, and the Bourbon, who were royal cousins, in order to retain control of France in the late sixteenth century. During the Fronde, Cardinal Mazarin prudently mended his fences with the Huguenots of the Midi to keep them from joining the Frondeurs by carefully rewarding locally prominent Huguenots with offices at Bergerac, Nîmes, and Castres.[68]

Another example of the royal tactic of divide-and-rule is the political career of Henri I de Montmorency-Damville, governor of Languedoc from 1563 to 1614. He inherited his father's provincial office and clientele and soon became a dominant figure in the Midi. His power in Languedoc was based on his control of royal fortresses and fortified cities in the province—he made certain that their captains were his clients—and his control over royal tax collection. He installed clients in key municipal governments, for instance, at Nîmes, Montpellier, Béziers, Castres, Viviers, and Uzès in 1563. His clients included judges in the Cour des Aides at Montpellier and in the Parlement of Toulouse, and he also had clients among the capitouls and leading merchants of Toulouse. His numerous kinsmen and lands in the province, especially in the regions of Pézenas, Béziers, and Frontignan, brought him extensive support among the provincial nobility, both Catholic and Huguenot, and he rewarded his followers with confiscated church property. When Damville met the future Henri IV at Castres in 1585, he brought over 1,000 horsemen with him.[69]

Damville's political enemies included the lieutenant general of Languedoc,

Guillaume, vicomte de Joyeuse, an old client of his father. Guillaume's son, Anne, had gone to court and become a *mignon*, a favorite of Henri III. The king had made him duc de Joyeuse. He ambitiously wanted the government of Languedoc for his father and himself, and he intrigued with the king to obtain it, backed at court by the old enemies of the Montmorency, the Guise and the Catholic League. Together they drove the Catholic Damville into the arms of the Huguenots led by the Bourbon, Henri de Navarre, the future Henri IV, with whom Damville concluded an alliance in 1575. The Huguenot cities of the Gévaudan, the Cévennes, and the coast supported him as a result. Henri III and the Queen Mother, who had already arrested his older brother, François, attempted to have Damville poisoned in 1575, and named the duc de Nevers as governor of Languedoc. But their efforts to dislodge him failed.

So Henri III tried to buy off Damville in the spring of 1577: he promised full amnesty and restoration of the government of Languedoc (which he had never vacated), more men and arms, and extensive fiscal rights in Languedoc (he was given the right to collect the salt tax which the Huguenots opposed). Damville deserted Navarre and returned to the king. But his new alliance was only temporary—the king abandoned him unceremoniously that summer, and he was forced to return to Henri of Navarre and the Huguenots. Henri III later named Joyeuse governor of Languedoc, creating a Catholic League party in the province headquartered at Toulouse. Its strength lay in the city of Toulouse and its parlement, in Carcassone, and in western Languedoc. But Damville played off the Catholic League and the Huguenots in Languedoc to remain in power, helped by the timely death of his rival.[70] As a reward for being Henri IV's most important ally in the Midi, Damville received the confiscated Languedoc estates of Joyeuse, who had been declared a traitor after his death in battle, and was made Constable of France. Damville continued to govern Languedoc, his power unchallenged, until his death in 1614 when his office and clientele went to his son, Henri II, duc de Montmorency. And in his old age, he governed through his son-in-law, the provincial lieutenant general, Anne de Lévis, duc de Ventadour.[71] Unable to control Damville by force, Henri III had tried to buy him off, then to check his power through the ambitious Joyeuse, both without success. The king of France in these examples used the selective distribution of royal patronage to secure the obedience and loyalty of the great nobles and their clients.

Royal Patronage and Noble Fortunes

The crown's generosity played a significant role in the personal fortunes of the great nobles. For example, Louis de Lausignan, seigneur de Lansac, one of Catherine de Medici's favorites and her close adviser in the 1560s, drew 12,800 livres a year from the crown for over four decades, 10,000 livres for his pension and 2,800 livres in salaries for his offices of captain of a company of royal gentlemen and knight of honor to the Queen Mother. The first office he sold to Jean de Laval in 1578 for 20,000 écus (60,000 livres). He also received

3,000 livres a year from the crown after he became a Knight of the Order of Saint Esprit in 1580, and there were major gifts throughout his career. Some of the largest were 48,000 livres' worth of property confiscated from the rebels at Bordeaux that Henri II gave him in 1548; a 30,000 livres' marriage gift from Charles IX in 1565; 20,000 livres from the duc d'Anjou; 20,000 écus (60,000 livres) from Catherine in 1583; and 12,000 livres in her will in 1589.[72]

The family fortunes of the ducs de Nevers are another example of the importance of royal patronage to great noble fortunes. François I de Cleves, duc de Nevers, was appointed governor of Champagne in 1545 at the age of twenty-nine. His total fortune can be conservatively estimated at 2,000,000 livres, and his annual income of 115,085 livres in 1551 was mainly from land. His pension and salaries from the crown came to 10,000 livres, less than 9 percent of his income. In the 1550s, he dissipated much of his fortune on military campaigns, and when he died early in 1562, he left his son, François II, the new governor of Champagne, bankrupt in that the family's income could not meet the interest payments on debts exceeding 540,000 livres. François II died in battle ten months after his father's death, so the job of liquidating the debt fell to the guardian of the new duc de Nevers, Jacques de Cleves, a child. When the child died in 1564 before liquidation had begun, the Cleves male line had ended.

At this point the crown stepped in. Charles IX issued extraordinary royal letters permitting the family property and titles to pass through the female heir, Henriette de Cleves, and a marriage was arranged between her and Louis de Gonzague, who became duc de Nevers. The marriage did not solve the family's financial difficulties, however, and debt remained an excruciating problem: Louis soon began massive sales of family lands. However, the monarchy again came to the rescue: Louis was named governor of Nivernais, and he received powers to name all royal officers in the region. In 1567, he was named governor of Piedmont, and he maintained many Italian clients there at royal expense; in 1568, 9 out of 10 men in his ordinance company were Italians. In 1569, Charles IX assigned to him receipts from the cutting of royal forests in the amount of 184,000 livres. In 1572, the king tried to give him a gift of 42,000 livres, which was blocked by the Chambre des Comptes at Paris. All through the civil wars, Louis received income from his royal pension, salaries, and royal gifts. By his own calculation, he made 513,994 livres in twenty-nine years of royal service from 1549 to 1578. About three-quarters of this was from his annual pension and salaries of 12,000 livres raised to 14,000 livres. The rest was from gifts.[73] The monarchy had rescued his family fortunes at a critical time.

The crown's generosity played an important role in the fortunes of seventeenth-century great nobles as well and was used to attach them to the throne. The duc de Beauvillier received at least 86,000 livres a year from the monarchy, including 30,000 livres as first gentleman of the king's bed-chamber, 20,000 livres as a minister of state, 3,000 livres as a chevalier of the king, and in addition, as chief of the council of state, 95,000 livres a year. In 1611, Sully had evaluated his annual revenues at 202,900 livres; he received

60,000 livres of this sum from his lands and the rest from his offices and royal generosity. In 1664, with total annual revenues of 100,943 livres, the duc de Montausier received 38,950 livres from his lands, 47,493 livres in salaries for his royal offices as governor of Angoulême and Saintonge, captain of the château of Angoulême, and royal lieutenant for upper and lower Alsace, and 14,500 livres from tax farming.[74] The annual revenues of the prince de Conti's children dropped over 400,000 livres after their father's death in 1666, to one-quarter of the total, from the loss in court offices, which may have been as high as 600,000 livres.[75] Nearly half of the annual revenues of the prince de Condé in 1701–1702 came from the monarchy—more than 750,000 livres.[76]

Moreover, the crown was generous in making cash gifts, particularly to great nobles in financial trouble. The crown gave the duc de Vendôme 150,000 livres to pay his debts in 1622.[77] The comte de Grignan received 200,000 livres from Louis XIV to pay his debts.[78] In the six years from 1611 to 1617, ten great nobles received a total of 14,000,000 livres from the crown in gifts and pensions.[79] The crown gave large sums of cash as wedding gifts, especially to members of the royal family.[80] And it bestowed generous royal pensions: the prince de Condé received 150,000 livres a year in the early seventeenth century, and the comte de Soissons 120,000 livres a year, but smaller pensions of 2,000 to 10,000 livres were more common.[81] The crown also granted manufacturing and sales monopolies: the duchesse d'Aiguillon, Richelieu's niece, had a monopoly on the manufacture of coaches, while Madame de Cavaye, the wife of Richelieu's guard captain, received a monopoly on the manufacture of sedan chairs.[82] Great nobles may not have been financially dependent on the crown, but royal patronage played an important part in their family fortunes, especially when they were in financial trouble.

Royal patronage was important to lesser nobles, too. Going to court, attracting the king's attention, gaining his favor or that of a member of the royal family or a royal favorite, could become an avenue to wealth and power for a provincial noble. For example, the comte de Nogaret went to court with an annual income of 800 livres and left with an annual income of 180,000 livres.[83] François de Bonne de Créqui, duc de Lesdiguières and governor of Dauphiné under Henri IV, began his career as an impoverished member of the minor nobility with two small fiefs worth a few hundred livres in rent. By 1610 his annual income was 121,699 livres.[84] As captain of the royal guards, Nicolas de L'Hôpital killed the Italian adventurer Concini with three shots in the courtyard of the Louvre in 1617 for resisting arrest. Louis XIII hated Concini and was glad to be rid of him. As a reward, he gave Nicolas an annual income of 120,000 livres, the title of maréchal de France, and a cash gift of 200,000 livres from Concini's confiscated estates; he erected his fief of Vitry into a marquisat (it became a duchy in 1644), and in 1631, with Richelieu's approval, named him governor of Provence.[85] The captaincy of the royal guards was a stepping-stone for many ducal families.[86]

The lesser nobility also benefited from royal patronage: gifts to great noble patrons filtered down to them indirectly as aristocratic patronage. The career of Blaise de Monluc is an example. In his memoirs, Monluc admitted that his origins were obscure. His grandfather, Amanieu de Lasserau-Massencomme, was a poor gentleman "who sold all his property save for enough to provide 800 to 1,000 livres a year." Blaise was raised in the household of the duc de Lorraine and retained his loyalty to that family for the rest of his life. He built his fortune in the royal service through the mediation of great noble patrons to whom he felt more gratitude than to the king. Monluc observed that "if I could return to my youth, I would never concern myself with depending on the King or Queen, but on those who have crédit with Their Majesties ... Their well-being and honor is to have servants whom They call créatures. If the King only rewards His own, He also clips their nails. But whoever wants to be rewarded and known must give himself to monsieur or madame because the King gives all to them, and only knows others through their relationship [to them]." Elsewhere he noted that "I have not much importuned [Their Majesties] with demands, nor have They much troubled themselves with finding something to give me."[87]

Among his patrons were Lautrec, who secured him a post as an ordinary gentleman in the royal household, and Brissac, who secured him the posts of governor of Alba in Italy and gentleman of the king's bedchamber. Monluc also mentioned Bonnivet as a patron without giving any examples. Saint André, along with the Guises, successfully pressed at court for Monluc's appointment as governor of Siena, and Strozzi and the duc de Ferrara gave him money gifts. Brissac and Saint André were clients of the Guises, and it was the Guises who lay behind Monluc's rise. It was during their hegemony at court that he was appointed lieutenant general in Guyenne, where he served from 1562 to 1577, and greatly increased his personal fortune. He owed his royal pension of 6,000 livres a year to the Cardinal de Lorraine.

Monluc benefited directly from royal patronage at the end of the reign of Henri II when he received a royal pension of 3,000 livres in cash, the revenues the comte of Gauré had lost in the 1559 revocation of domaine alienations, 6,000 livres in cash, two offices of councillor in the Parlement of Toulouse which he could sell, and the revenues of Bregeyrac from which he never received anything because it was already mortgaged.[88] Royal patronage was important, directly or indirectly, to the fortunes of the French nobility of all ranks, great and small, flourishing or declining, in the sixteenth and seventeenth centuries and was used by the crown to secure their cooperation.

Seventeenth-Century Brokers of Royal Patronage

Cardinal Richelieu created a large administrative clientele of his own at Paris which he used to control the royal administration. His clientele was based on his special relationship with the king, who allowed him to channel part of the flow of royal patronage toward his own créatures.[89] The Cardinal recruited many of his clients, including the intendants, from the robe nobility; many were already royal officials or commissioners.[90] They were attracted into his service by his power, his access to royal patronage, and his ability to advance them. A number of the Cardinal's clients were his relatives; his nepotism was well known.[91]

Richelieu's administrative network reached into distant provinces where he constructed clienteles connecting to his original Paris network. The king and his ministers could increase their ability to govern any province, however distant from Paris, by securing the loyalty of patrons of important provincial clienteles, many of whom were also officeholders, and by strategically placing reliable clients within the provincial administration and the economic and demographic centers of the province. The political elite of Provence, for example, was a small cohesive group of nobles known to each other and interconnected by ties of kinship, marriage, friendship, clientage, and office-holding which stretched outside the province to Versailles and the royal government in Paris.

Political power in Provence was concentrated in a cluster of cities at the mouth of the Rhône River in Basse-Provence, the most populated and prosperous region in the province. The three largest cities formed an obtuse triangle at the river's mouth with the apex at Marseille, the long leg at Arles in the west on the Rhône, and the short leg at Aix-en-Provence, the provincial capital, fifteen or twenty miles northeast of Marseille. The distances were not great, and the port and naval base of Toulon, the fourth largest city, was another twenty-five miles along the coast from Marseille. The seats of the two archbishops in Provence were at Aix and Arles, cities with heavy concentrations of resident nobles who dominated their governments. Whoever controlled these four cities and the institutions and officials sheltered within their walls controlled the government of Provence.

Institutions and officials at Aix included the provincial intendant, governor and lieutenant general, archbishop, sovereign judicial courts of the Parlement and Cour des Comptes, Trésoriers Généraux de France, and procureurs du pays. The General Assemblies of Provençal Communities met frequently at Aix. Institutions and officials at Marseille, the largest port in France, included the governor who was often in residence and his entourage of nobles, the municipal government, the royal galleys and their administration. The sailing fleet and naval administration for the Mediterranean fleet were at Toulon. There were the archbishop and municipal government at Arles; the admiralty and seneschal courts at Marseille, Arles, Toulon, and other major towns; and the royal fortresses at Marseille, Arles, Toulon, along the coast, and up the Rhône. This concentration of Provençal institutions within a small geographic region, and the domination of Provençal politics by a small group of interconnected nobles and their clienteles, made it easy for the royal ministers, using the lure of royal patronage, to control the Provençal power structure by securing the loyalty of important noble patrons holding key offices.

Neighboring Languedoc, larger and less compact, sprawling across southern France with a larger nobility, was harder to control through patron-broker-client ties and networks because its power centers were more diffuse.[92]

This was probably true of other French provinces as well, for instance, Brittany or the Dauphiné. Provence may have been unusual in its compactness. The Paris government, however, could increase its ability to govern any province, regardless of its size or diffuseness, by placing reliable clients in the political, economic, and demographic centers and using them to broker royal patronage to secure provincial cooperation and support.

Cardinal Richelieu used the lure of royal patronage to secure the loyalty of important members of the provincial power structures, making them his clients and using them and their resources in governing. Some of his clients acted as brokers to distribute royal patronage among their own clients and widen the web of ministerial influence within the province. Not all members of the Cardinal's client network were brokers, but the most important members were. The Cardinal also used his client networks to undermine, intimidate, and contain hostile or disobedient governors, and whenever possible he suborned great noble clienteles by seducing away their members into his own networks.

Provence is an example: Richelieu created his own Provençal administrative network to encircle two hostile governors, Charles de Lorraine, duc de Guise, and his successor, Vitry.[93] Richelieu named his own brother, Alphonse, archbishop of Aix and abbot of Saint Victor at Marseille.[94] He appointed a créature, the marquis de Saint Chamond, lieutenant general of Provence and made him governor of the citadel at Sisteron.[95] He suborned two important Provençal clients of Governor Guise, Vincent-Anne de Forbin-Maynier d'Oppède, first president of the Parlement of Aix, and Cosme de Valbelle, boss of the Marseille city government. He recruited the bailli de Forbin, a Knight of Malta who was popular in the royal galleys, into his service and made him lieutenant general of the galleys or second-in-command—Richelieu had appointed his own nephew, Pont de Courlay, as general of the galleys. He made Henri de Séguiran, sieur de Bouc and first president of the Cour des Comptes at Aix, a naval lieutenant general. He sent his own créature, Henri d'Escoubleau de Sourdis, archbishop of Bordeaux, to Provence as naval commander-in-chief. Sourdis recruited his own clients who became subclients of the Cardinal, for instance, the Gault brothers, bishops of Marseille; Joseph Dubernet, first president of the Aix Parlement; the young Fortia de Pilles, governor of the Château d'If; and the chevaliers Paul and Des Gouttes, galley captains.[96] Finally, Richelieu sent fifteen provincial, naval, and army intendants to Provence, eight of whom were his own clients.[97] A former intendant, Hélie de Laisné de La Marguerie, was sent to serve briefly as first president of the Aix Parlement.[98] When Richelieu doubted a governor's loyalty, he was more likely to send intendants who were his own clients, which was also true of Mazarin.

Richelieu, therefore, recruited or placed loyal clients in key Provençal offices. They included the provincial lieutenant general, archbishop of Aix, first presidents of the sovereign courts of Aix, city boss and bishop of Marseille, general and lieutenant general of the royal galleys, and he sent a stream of provincial, naval, and army intendants to Provence. They were expected to secure the loyalty of provincial institutions and to check the power of an unfriendly governor.

Richelieu used his clients to govern Provence directly. For example, Cosme de Valbelle helped the intendant to post the new tax at Marseille salt warehouse at Richelieu's request. The bailli de Forbin tried to teach Pont de Courlay how to administer and command the royal galleys. Vincent-Anne de Forbin-Maynier d'Oppède and Henri de Séguiran unsuccessfully tried to help intendant Dreux d'Aubray to secure judicial registration of an unpopular tax edict in 1630.[99] Séguiran conducted a survey of the ports, fortifications, and commerce of the Provençal coast for Richelieu.[100] Sourdis tried to use Fortia de Pilles and other Provençal clients in the consulate of Aix to secure the levy of an unpopular tax for garrisoning the newly captured islands of Lérins. Cosme de Valbelle and Henri de Séguiran paid for the construction, outfitting, and maintenance of their own galleys in the war against Spain.[101] The bailli de Forbin lent money to the crown for naval supplies and to the salaries of personnel in the royal galleys.

Richelieu's clients were able in return to distribute royal patronage to their own clients in the province. For example, Richelieu's clients, Séguiran, the Valbelles, and the bailli de Forbin, used their access to patronage to promote the careers of family members.[102] This was also true of Mazarin's and Colbert's clients: Oppède, for example, profited from the forced sale in 1660 of the parlement offices of his enemies, President Decormis and Advocate General Galaup-Chasteuil, to advise Mazarin on their replacement and supervise the resales.[103] Toussaint de Janson-Forbin recommended his cousin, Forbin de La Roque, to Colbert for appointment as first president in 1671, describing him as "entirely devoted to the royal service ... desintéressé ... and fort accrédité" in the province.[104] He recommended his brother, the marquis de Janson, to Colbert for the office of provincial lieutenant general.[105] The chevalier de La Penne, a client of Mercoeur, recommended three clients of Oppède, the marquis de Janson, d'Oraison, and de Marignane, to Mazarin for the office of provincial lieutenant general; Oppède was both a client and an ally of Mercoeur.[106]

Cardinal Richelieu used the same tactic in extending his control over the neighboring province of Languedoc. He undercut the power and position of an entrenched, unreliable governor, Henri II, duc de Montmorency, by building his own ministerial network in Languedoc. Richelieu began undermining Montmorency's position in the province when he made three key episcopal appointments of his own clients in 1628: Claude de Rébé, archbishop of Narbonne; Silvestre de Crusy de Marcillac, bishop of Mende; and Clément de Bonzi (Pierre's predecessor and uncle), bishop of Béziers. The Cardinal began sending reliable intendants into the province at the same time, such as Robert Miron de Tremblay and Antoine Le Camus d'Hémery, both his clients. In 1633 and 1634, the intendants razed the châteaux of nobles supporting Montmorency, confiscated their property, and redistributed it among supporters of Richelieu and the monarchy. In this way Richelieu attached loyal noble families to the crown and secured their support. After Montmorency's execution for treason in 1632, Richelieu replaced him as governor with his own créature, Charles, duc d'Hallwin, later maréchal de Schomberg, whose secretary at Paris, Jean-Baptiste Baltazar, sieur de Malherbe and intendant in Languedoc from 1643 to 1647, kept in constant touch with Richelieu's secretary, Charpentier. Schomberg began naming his own clients to office in Languedoc, and many of them later became Richelieu's subclients, for example, his cousin Daillon Du Lude, bishop of Albi; the seneschal and governor of Montpellier; and governors of fortresses and towns along the coast. Languedoc nobles approached Schomberg and Daillon Du Lude for recommendations to Richelieu. The Cardinal patronized the parlementaire network of Bertier de Montrave to use against the archbishop of Toulouse, Charles de Montchal, a hostile and embittered ex-client of Montmorency. Rébé, archbishop of Narbonne, was important in countering the influence of Montmorency and Montchal. It would be an exaggeration to say that Cardinal Richelieu created his own administrative clientele in Languedoc to seize control over its government and remove it from the grasp of an independent governor because Schomberg frequently acted as independently as Montmorency had.[107] Nonetheless, by creating an administrative network to increase his control over the provincial government, if not to assume its direction, Richelieu challenged the governor's power, and he followed this strategy in other peripheral provinces.

Richelieu's administrative innovation was continued by his ministerial successors, Mazarin, Colbert, Fouquet, Le Tellier, Louvois, and the Phélypeaux. They all created large administrative clienteles at Paris extending into the provinces.[108] Even great nobles who were royal ministers, such as the prince de Condé and Gaston d'Orléans, recruited administrative clients at Paris and in the provinces outside their governments of Burgundy and Languedoc. Cardinal Mazarin, unfortunately, did not appreciate the political value of the provincial networks he had inherited from Richelieu. He concentrated on building a large administrative clientele at Paris and allowed his predecessor's ministerial networks in the provinces to lapse, for instance, in Guyenne. The gathering storm clouds of the Fronde, however, convinced Mazarin of the need to strengthen his control over the governments of distant provinces, especially those with unreliable governors, and he recruited a number of his predecessor's provincial clients into his service. The strength of the provincial administrative networks built by Richelieu and Mazarin depended upon the political reliability of the provincial governor and the reputation of the province for unruliness.

The Provincial Networks of Cardinal Mazarin

In the case of Provence, Mazarin had to deal with an openly hostile governor, the comte d'Alais. To counter the governor's influence, Mazarin recruited local notables into his service, including several of Richelieu's former clients, and used them to encircle and undermine a hostile governor. They included Antoine de Valbelle, the bailli de Forbin (now Grand Prior of

Saint Gilles), and the chevalier Paul. Forbin and Paul were meant to check the influence of Alais's clients, the galleys' general, the duc de Richelieu, and lieutenant general, Philandre de Vincheguerre. Fortia de Pilles, governor of the Château d'If and a prominent political figure in Marseille, joined the Cardinal's service in 1651 through the good offices of the duc de Mercoeur.

Mazarin sent his younger brother, Michel, to Aix as archbishop in 1645. Michel was frequently at Toulon assisting the new naval intendant, Louis Le Roux d'Infreville, Mazarin's client, in preparing the French fleet to sail. Infreville had arrived in Provence in 1646, the same year that another client of the Cardinal, the chevalier de Garnier, a Knight of Malta, was appointed governor of Toulon.[109] When his brother died suddenly, Mazarin nominated an old Roman friend, Jerôme de Grimaldi, as archbishop of Aix, but he did not take office until 1655.[110] Mazarin sent another client, Alexandre de Sève, to Provence in 1647 as provincial intendant to replace the governor's client, Champigny.[111] Mazarin recruited archbishop Grignan of Arles into his service about this time. Two Aix parlementaires also became his clients at this time, Régusse, a business partner of Antoine de Valbelle and a client of the Cardinal's brother Michel, and Venel, the husband of the governess of Mazarin's nieces. Mazarin later added the services of Henri de Forbin-Maynier d'Oppède, whom he made first president of the Parlement of Aix. Mazarin secured the bishoprics of Fréjus and Orange for old Italian friends.[112] He sent eleven intendants to Provence, six of whom were his clients and three of whom had previously served Richelieu.[113]

Mazarin, therefore, used a total of eleven Provençal brokers, considerably more than his predecessor. He had inherited five from Richelieu: Antoine de Valbelle, Oppède, the chevalier Paul, the bailli de Forbin, and Fortia de Pilles.[114] They were native-born Provençaux who had proven their reliability in Richelieu's service. Mazarin recruited or sent six more clients to Provence who became brokers: Régusse, Venel, Bichi, Grignan of Arles, Mercoeur, and Michel de Mazarin.[115] Five of these eleven provincial brokers and three of Mazarin's six intendant-clients, or roughly 55 percent, had previously served Richelieu. Mazarin recruited or sent a total of fourteen clients into Provence in the five years from 1645 to 1650, excluding Cardinal Bichi who was already in place. They held offices in the key cities of Aix, Arles, Toulon, and Marseille, and in key provincial and municipal institutions—the archbishoprics of Aix and Arles, the Parlement of Aix, the municipal governments of Marseille and Arles, the royal fortresses at Marseille and Toulon, the royal navy at Toulon and Marseille, the provincial and naval intendants, and after 1650 the provincial governorship.[116]

Mazarin's clients in Provence helped him to hold the province during the Fronde—it is unlikely that he could have held the province without this network—and to govern it. Antoine de Valbelle held the city of Marseille for the Cardinal; archbishop Grignan kept the city of Arles loyal; and president Régusse held the Parlement and city of Aix for the Cardinal. Régusse and Venel became co-chiefs of the Mazarinistes, the party of the Cardinal's supporters in Provence, while Forbin, Oppède, and Régusse helped Governor Mercoeur to take the city of Toulon in 1652, the last redoubt of the Frondeurs, and thus to end the Fronde in Provence. Fortia de Pilles and the chevalier Paul helped to hold the city of Marseille loyal to the crown in 1658 during the revolt led by the Valbelle clientele. After the intendants were recalled in 1649, Mazarin's reliable sources of information on Provençal affairs were the letters of Bichi, Forbin, Régusse, Fortia de Pilles, and Mercoeur. The team of Oppède and Mercoeur helped the Cardinal to govern Provence when the Fronde had ended.

Mazarin pursued the same general strategy in Languedoc, although he began recruiting clients later because Languedoc was less turbulent than Provence during the Fronde. Gaston, duc d'Orléans, had been appointed governor of Languedoc for political reasons in early 1644, an office he held until his death in 1660 but, since he had no intention of residing in the province, Schomberg was retained as lieutenant general until his exasperated resignation. Gaston d'Orléans was powerful in the province, even at a distance, because he had inherited the loyalty of Montmorency's clients.[117] He soon obtained the loyalty of most of the provincial sword nobility including the Ventadour, Lévis-Mirepoix, Alais, Saint Bonnet de Toiras, and Budos de Portes, and appointed them as fortress governors.[118]

Montmorency's ex-clients who switched their loyalty to Orléans included Louis de Chadailhac et Lévis, comte de Bioule, seneschal de Castres and seigneur de Gaix, who was named lieutenant general of Bas-Languedoc and had his lands raised to a marquisat. Another was François-Jacques d'Amboise, comte d'Aubijoux and seigneur de Graulhet, who was named lieutenant general of Haut-Languedoc and governor of the citadel of Montpellier. His brother-in-law, Saint Bonnet de Toiras, had been a Montmorency client, and Toiras's son, Louis, now Orléans's client, was named seneschal of Montpellier. Aubijoux and Bioule had family ties; they were friends; and they had fought together at the battle of Castelnaudry for Montmorency. Scipion Grimoard de Beauvoir de Roure, comte du Roure, seigneur de Barjac, was named lieutenant general for the Vivarais and Cevénnes by Orléans; he was first chamberlain of the duke's household. Du Roure had also fought for Montmorency at Castelnaudry, switched his allegiance to Orléans, followed the duke to Paris, and only returned to Languedoc some years later. Rioule, Aubijoux, and Du Roure governed Languedoc for the duc d'Orléans during his absence in the years before the Fronde, enriching themselves and acting as provincial brokers. They assisted several intendants who were also clients of Orléans.[119]

Mazarin had originally relied on the feeble remnants of the Richelieu-Schomberg network in Languedoc, for instance, on Claude de Rébé, archbishop of Narbonne; seigneur d'Argentcour, governor of Narbonne; president Barthélemy de Graumont of the Parlement of Toulouse; and Fenouillet, bishop of Montpellier, all of whom he generously rewarded to ensure their loyalty. But when Orléans joined the Frondeurs and took his clients in Languedoc with him, Mazarin realized that he would have to build his own client network to hold the province, and this he did during the rest of his ministry. He named Pierre de Marca archbishop of Toulouse in 1652; François Fouquet bishop of Agde in 1643 and archbishop of Narbonne in 1659; Louis Fouquet bishop of Agde in 1656; Michel Tubeuf bishop of Saint Pons in 1654; and Pierre de Bonzi bishop of Béziers in 1659. He named Gaspard de Fieubet first president of the Parlement of Toulouse in 1653, and sent a series of intendants to Languedoc who were his own clients. He also recruited new clients and confirmed the loyalty of old clients such as François Bon, first president of the Chambre des Comptes at Montpellier; François de Moustiers, comte de Mérinville, who served as lieutenant general in Provence before becoming governor of Narbonne; and the marquis de Chouppes, who served briefly as an army lieutenant general in Provence.[120] Mazarin constructed a ministerial administrative clientele in Languedoc similar to the one he had constructed in Provence and used it to increase his control over the provincial government.

The events of the Fronde in Guyenne demonstrate that Mazarin made a tactical error in the 1640s when he allowed Richelieu's administrative clientele in that province to deteriorate. Richelieu had constructed a client network in Guyenne to contain a hostile governor, Jean de La Valette, duc d'Epernon, who had been appointed to his post in 1622 through the favor of Louis XIII, after he had served with the king on campaign against the Huguenots in Languedoc the previous year.[121] Epernon had refused to accept Richelieu's dominance at Paris and shadow-boxed with the Cardinal, also quarreling with provincial authorities.[122] Richelieu discovered that in Epernon he had another Guise or Montmorency and dealt with him accordingly: he constructed a network of reliable administrative clients to surround him.

Abel de Servien, a créature of Richelieu, was sent as intendant to Bordeaux in 1627–1628.[123] François de Verthamon, marquis de Manoeuvre, was also sent as intendant to Guyenne at this time, although he was chosen by Epernon, whose client he had become.[124] Henri d'Escoubleau de Sourdis, another créature of Richelieu, was named archbishop of Bordeaux to replace his older brother, an enemy of the governor, and a third brother, the marquis de Sourdis, was named provincial lieutenant general. After leaving the office vacant for several years, Richelieu appointed his own client, Antoine d'Aguesseau, first president of the Parlement of Bordeaux. Etienne Foullé de Pruneau was sent as intendant to suppress the revolt of the Croquants in Périgord and Quercy in 1637 and remained as intendant at Bordeaux until 1641, replacing Verthamon.[125] Foullé was followed by Jean de Lauzon, sieur de Liré, who served until 1648.[126] Richelieu was able to replace Epernon as governor in 1638 with his own supporter, Henri, prince de Condé, whose government of Burgundy was given in his absence to his son Louis. Louis married the Cardinal's great-niece, the daughter of his nephew, Maillé-Brézé, who had been sent to La Rochelle as commander of the Atlantic fleet to replace Sourdis.[127] Richelieu's efforts to build a ministerial clientele in Guyenne slowed after he had secured a reliable governor.

Cardinal Mazarin named Bernard de La Valette, duc d'Epernon, the second son of the old duke, as governor of Guyenne in 1643. Mazarin considered him a loyal client, which he proved to be. But Epernon was arrogant and unintelligent, and he exacerbated the dissatisfaction at Bordeaux with the Cardinal's policies.[128] He was no better a choice than Joseph Dubernet, who was appointed first president of the Parlement of Bordeaux in the same year. Both were loyal clients, and with a reliable intendant at Bordeaux, Jean de Lauzon, and Henry de Béthune as archbishop, Mazarin considered the province to be secure: he did nothing more to recruit or place broker-clients in high administrative posts in Guyenne. Mazarin, however, found himself in difficulty during the Fronde when Lauzon, Epernon, and Dubernet were expelled from the province, and Béthune left because of the new governor whom Mazarin had been forced to appoint, the Frondeur prince de Condé. Mazarin had no administrative network in place to monitor Condé. He was eventually forced to send a royal army under the command of the comte d'Harcourt to deal with Condé and the rebellious city of Bordeaux.[129] Allowing his predecessor's clientele in Guyenne to deteriorate had proved to be a costly error.

Mazarin made the same tactical error in Burgundy with happier results because he was able to recruit reliable client networks on the spot. When the Fronde began at Paris, Mazarin depended upon Louis II, prince de Condé, governor of the province after his father's death, to hold Burgundy for him as his father had held it for Richelieu. In fact Richelieu had depended upon the Burgundian clientele of Henri II, prince de Condé, to the extent that he had not bothered to create his own administrative clientele in the province. It was perhaps inevitable for a clientele to deteriorate, or fail to develop, when a ministerial patron was absent in Paris or when an important client dominated the rest. The young Condé supported Mazarin's government in 1648–1649 and Burgundy remained calm. But in 1650 Condé defected, and with his brother and brother-in-law, he attacked Mazarin's government, hoping to assume the Cardinal's power and position; he was imprisoned as a result. Mazarin's control over Burgundy evaporated for the same reason it had vanished in Guyenne: he had depended upon a "reliable" governor to hold the province for him and the governor had defaulted.

Condé took his Burgundian clientele with him into revolt: Jean Bouchu rallied his network within the Parlement of Dijon to support the princes and become a leader of their party in Burgundy, while Jacques de Saulx, comte de Tavannes, rallied the fortress governors and regimental officers on behalf of the Paris princes; the Burgundian party of princes became known as the "Principions" or "Albions." Bouchu's control over the parlement, however, was challenged by an old enemy, Marc-Antoine Millotet, the court's energetic, intelligent advocate general: Millotet became a leader of the Burgundian supporters of Mazarin's government, who were known as the "Mazarins." Co-chief of this party was Gaspard Quarré d'Aligny, the other advocate general in the parlement and an enemy of the first president. Millotet came from Flavigny to the southwest of Dijon and owned land at Chavignay and Marsannay-la-Côte. He came from a parlementaire family, and was the son of a parlement advocate general whose office he had inherited in 1635 and held until 1680. His brother was a canon of Saint Etienne at Dijon.[130] Quarré d'Aligny was a former captain of the prince de Condé's *carabiniers* (cavalry with guns) who had become an orator and a pamphleteer. He owned land at Ahuy and Fonatine, and his family had roturier origins: they were descended from Jean Quarré, the wine steward of the Burgundian duke, Jean sans Peur.[131]

When Mazarin named César, duc de Vendôme, the legitimized half-brother of Louis XIII and the father of the duc de Mercoeur, as acting governor in Burgundy in 1650, he was supported by Millotet and Aligny. Pierre Lenet, the former procureur general of the parlement and Condé's client, tried to stir the Dijonnais into protesting the arrest of Condé, but his efforts were thwarted by Millotet and Aligny, who secured the acceptance of Vendôme by the parlement, city of Dijon, and most of the province. Vendôme spent a great deal of money recruiting a Burgundian clientele—he became popular in the parlement by making the judges presents of fur-lined ankleboots—and in June 1650, thanks to his efforts, Marc-Antoine Millotet was elected mayor of Dijon; the twenty échevins were named by royal letters. Millotet had a son born at this time, and Vendôme himself held the baby at the baptismal font. Vendôme felt so sure of the province that he returned to Paris in 1651. Mazarin was fortunate in securing the services of Vendôme's clientele and the Millotet-Aligny network to counter Condé's influence in Burgundy.

After Vendôme's departure, Jean Bouchu sponsored a noisy protest at night to celebrate the release of Condé and the other princes, and succeeded in having Millotet's election annulled. Millotet countered by leading a popular protest against grain shortages and encouraging the rioters to burn the mansion of the first president. Mazarin finally stabilized the situation when he replaced the prince de Condé as governor of Burgundy, switching his government with that of Guyenne and naming Bernard de La Valette, duc d'Epernon, as the new governor of Burgundy. Epernon inherited Vendôme's clientele, and his influence returned Millotet to municipal office in June 1652, reelecting him in June 1653.

Condé had left créatures in Burgundy as governors of the royal fortresses of Chalon, Bellegarde (Suerre), and the château of Dijon. The seigneurs d'Uxelle and de La Planchette, governors of Chalon and Dijon, surrendered their fortresses to Epernon, but the hunchbacked comte de Boutteville, who commanded Bellegarde, refused. Epernon took this fortress in five weeks, having been voted a large subsidy by the Burgundian Estates for this purpose, and using 4,000 soldiers and 3,000 prisoners to breach a wall: Louis XIV and the court arrived to watch the final attack, which ended the Fronde in Burgundy.[132] Jean Bouchu died and was replaced as first president of the Parlement of Dijon by a reliable former intendant, Louis de Laisné, sieur de La Marguerie.[133] Condé lost crédit when he fled to Spain, and Epernon remained governor until Condé returned to Burgundy as one of the clauses in the Treaty of the Pyrénées ending the Habsburg War with Spain. Millotet had to leave the province for a while upon his return.[134]

Mazarin named Claude Bouchu intendant in Burgundy in order to use his influence and clientele to help control the Burgundian Estates, a tacit admission of his earlier mistake in not creating his own reliable administrative clientele in the province. Mazarin was more successful in retaining control over Burgundy because he was able to utilize local client networks: Millotet rallied to the Cardinal's support as a result of personal enmity for Jean Bouchu, and Vendôme secured local support by distributing large sums of money. Mazarin depended upon both networks to help him hold Burgundy.

The examples of Burgundy and Guyenne demonstrate that a combination of three factors determined whether or not royal ministers created their own administrative networks in a province: its political reputation, whether or not it had traditional assemblies and privileges and a reputation for political recalcitrance; its military situation, whether or not it was a frontier province subject to heavy troop movements; and the presence or absence of a politically reliable governor. The royal ministers established client networks after 1650 in independent, peripheral provinces with unreliable governors such as Provence, Languedoc, Guyenne, and Burgundy. If Mazarin had been more farsighted in maintaining Richelieu's administrative networks in the provinces, the Fronde might have been less serious.

The Provincial Networks of Colbert

J. Russell Major has suggested that royal control of the Estates took two developmental paths, institutional and personal. The first, proposed by Sully and Marillac, aimed at expanding tax collection by royal officials while undermining the local Estates' negotiating powers. The second, chosen by Richelieu and later by Colbert and Louis XIV, was the more traditional path, leaving tax negotiation to the local Estates and tax collection to local officials, while exercising personal control over the delegates through pensions, bribery, clientage, and intimidation. Major notes that comparatively little is known about the progress toward absolutism under Mazarin.[135] The role of brokers and brokerage in frontier provinces that were pays d'Etats substantiates Major's thesis, and demonstrates that Mazarin passed along Richelieu's tactics to Colbert and Louis XIV.

Although provincial Estates in the center of the kingdom—in the Orléanais, Anjou, Maine, Touraine, Berry, Marche, Limousin, and Périgord, for example—had disappeared by the seventeenth century, traditional tax-granting assemblies still functioned in the outlying provinces of Normandy, Brittany, Guyenne, Béarn, Navarre, Bigorre, Foix, Languedoc, Provence, Dauphiné, and Burgundy. Richelieu had launched a general attack upon the provincial Estates, and his campaign was revived and continued by Colbert and Louis XIV. During the seventeenth century the Estates of Normandy, Guyenne (Agennais, Armagnac, Comminges, Quercy, Rouergue, Lannes, Condomais, Bazadais, and Rivière-Verdun), Auvergne, Dauphiné, Lyonnais, Forez, and Beaujolais were called less and less frequently until they ceased to exist.[136] The Estates of the Franche-Comté were suppressed during the conquest in 1678, and the Estates of Alsace at about the same time.[137] Some Estates were incorporated into others, for example, the Estates of Auxonne were incorporated into those of Burgundy in 1639, as were those of Auxerre in 1668, although the Estates of the Mâconnais resisted absorption.[138] By the end of the seventeenth century, Estates had disappeared in 68 percent of France that had enjoyed them in the early years of the century.[139] Estates continued to exist in the peripheral provinces of Burgundy, Provence, Brittany, and the small Pyrénées provinces of Béarn, Navarre, Bigorre, and Foix.[140]

Colbert used provincial intendants to control the Estates as Richelieu and Mazarin had done. But Colbert and his intendants were more consistently effective in using a combination of persuasion and bribes, intimidation and punishment—what Grignan had called "sweetness and fear" in a letter to Colbert in December 1671—to obtain their cooperation.[141] Colbert created an administrative network of intendant-clients, many of whom were his own relatives, stretching throughout France, and used it to control the Estates; he was as notorious for nepotism as were Richelieu and Mazarin.[142] For example, he sent eleven intendants to Provence, all of whom were his own clients; of his eleven intendants in Provence, six had previously served his ministerial predecessors.[143] Colbert as finance minister was responsible for tax collection in the pays d'Etats, and he depended upon his own intendant-clients to help him secure the cooperation of the provincial Estates. His intendants were aided by local notables, some of whom also became the minister's broker-clients, and they encouraged the deputies attending the Estates to approve royal tax requests.[144] For example, Colbert continued to use Mazarin's administrative team of Oppède and Mercoeur to control the General Assemblies of Provençal Communities, and after Oppède's death he used the administrative teams of Grignan and Janson-Forbin, Grignan and the intendants.[145] He used similar teams in the other pays d'Etats. In Provence, with native-born broker Oppède as acting intendant, and in Burgundy, with Claude Bouchu as a native-born broker-intendant, he combined these roles in one man. Claude Bouchu successfully managed the Burgundian Estates through an inherited clientele, intervening in municipal elections to put clients in office who then became deputies to the provincial Estates. Governor Condé also worked with Bouchu and Colbert to regulate the Estates.[146] Colbert sent Bouchu blank lettres de cachet to intimidate disobedient deputies as he had done in Provence, and ordered the uncooperative bishop of Macôn not to attend the Estates on the intendant's advice.[147] After 1674, the Burgundian Estates regularly voted what Colbert wanted in a single deliberation.[148]

Colbert's administrative team in Languedoc was composed of the archbishop of Narbonne, Cardinal Pierre de Bonzi, who presided over the provincial Estates, and intendant Henri d'Aguesseau, who arrived in Languedoc in 1673, the year Bonzi was named to Narbonne. The governor, the duc de Verneuil, was a political figurehead who had close ties to Aguesseau.[149] Bonzi and Aguesseau maintained a network of reliable client-notables in Languedoc willing to work on Colbert's behalf. For example, the bishops of Béziers, Mende, Viviers, Castres, and Saint Papaoul, the marquis de Castres, the governor, and intendant Bazin de Bezons wrote reports to Colbert in 1662 on the cooperation of the Languedoc Estates in granting the king's tax requests.[150] The bishop of Mende wrote, "I have four votes in my diocese: they will serve me and always be of my opinion. There are some deputies who offer themselves to me, and I am assured that they will serve the King well. I believe that we will finish after two or three more sessions; but in case the business is delayed, You would very much oblige me, Monsieur, if in Your reply, You would put in Your letter some pleasantries for the consuls [deputies] of my diocese, and for those who follow my advice. Ask me to tell You their names so that You can favor them on the occasions which will present themselves, or give some other demonstration of friendship."[151] In this instance the bishop of Mende was acting as a broker.

Colbert arranged for an unfriendly municipal deputy to be excluded from the Languedoc Estates and replaced with a more loyal deputy. He made sure that the starting speakers for the clergy and nobility advocated a generous tax grant; he rallied the governor's clients and encouraged them to influence the deputies of the Third Estate who were dependent upon them.[152] The treasurer of the Estates was ordered to provide money to influence the votes of deputies from the towns selected by the intendant, and 9,000 livres was spent in this manner. Deputies from the other two orders were bribed with pensions. By 1670, it had become customary to give the barons having seats in the Languedoc Estates royal pensions of 2,250 livres a year, and cooperative bishops received similar grants: Colbert put most of the nobles and barons attending the Languedoc Estates on his pension list and distributed substantial sums of money to deputies of the Third Estate.[153] In 1672, 20,000 livres were made available to influence the voting of the deputies, and Cardinal Bonzi distributed part of this money on behalf of intendant Bazin de Bezons.[154] Most of the recipients, of course, did not become clients of Colbert, although a few did. Bribery and clientage should not be confused. In December 1670, Colbert demanded that "the entire sum [tax request] be passed in a single deliberation without any long negotiations and without sending couriers [to court]." In 1671, he complimented Bazin de Bezons for having obtained 14,000,000 livres in royal taxes from the Languedoc Estates in two meetings lasting a total of less than one hour.[155] This demand for speed became part of the crown's tactics.

Colbert used the same tactics in dealing with the Estates in other pays d'Etats. For example, the syndic of the Provençal nobility, Monsieur Baudina, "who has always faithfully done his duty in the assemblies for the service of the King," was rewarded with a pension of 2,000 livres.[156] In 1668, Oppède wrote to Colbert that:

> I avow to You that I have never seen an assembly of the nature of this one. We have absolutely all the leaders here, that is to say, the Church, the nobility, the

> procureurs du pays and the first community [Aix], and those of the deputies who depend on us. Notwithstanding this, we cannot be the masters because the number of unreasonable ruffians and monsters is so great, and so united by the conformity of their tempers that we have carried them to where they are at present only with incredible trouble, and we will assuredly have the greatest difficulty to dispose them for what remains to be done. We forget neither intrigue nor authority, force nor leadership in order to lead them where it is necessary, and we will continue this same application to the end.[157]

To manage the Estates of Brittany, Colbert set aside 60,000 livres as a reward "for the deputies who had served best in the assembly," and sent his own brother to act as the crown's representative in 1663. An uncooperative deputy was excluded from the Estates of Brittany by lettre de cachet in 1667. Colbert relied upon the influential duc de Rohan to use his clients among the Breton nobility to help in controlling the Estates.[158]

What motivated the deputies to cooperate with the royal minister and his provincial clients, or even to become clients themselves? Most deputies and brokers were motivated by political conviction and self-interest: it was the exceptional man who was motivated solely by one or the other.[159] The career of Jacques Gaufridy demonstrates this blend of ideology and self-interest. Assessor of the Aix municipal government and procureur du pays in 1627–28 and 1638–39, Gaufridy had made a name for himself defending provincial interests and privileges. He had made a daring speech at the 1628 Estates at Aix attacking royal taxation, especially the new increase in the salt tax, and ten years later was sent as a provincial deputy to Paris to protest a new royal edict creating more judicial and financial offices.

Sometime in 1639 he became the governor's client, and spent most of 1640 with him at court. When a royal edict was issued in January 1641, creating a new chamber in the Parlement of Aix, Gaufridy bought the office of president, probably with the governor's help. It was rumored that he had personally profited from the negotiations at Paris that resulted in the creation of the new chamber. Later he became first president or chief justice of the new Semester court, which doubled the membership of the parlement. Both courts were extremely unpopular with the existing judges because the flood of new offices threatened their financial investments in officeholding and their social prestige based on officeholding. Gaufridy had switched from defending provincial interests and privileges as a matter of political principle to benefiting personally from the sale of new offices he had formerly attacked. Accused of abandoning provincial interests for personal gain, he became the most unpopular magistrate at Aix. His house was attacked in 1648 during Carnival and sacked in 1649 during the parlementaire revolt.[160]

There are numerous examples of deputies who boldly spoke out in defense of provincial privileges and interests at some risk to themselves, motivated by political principle. For example, Léon de Trimond was given twenty-four hours to leave the city after seeing Richelieu as a deputy from the Provençal Estates in 1630 to protest royal taxation. Another deputy from the General

Assemblies was given twenty-four hours to leave Paris in 1657 for his bluntness. In December 1642, the procureurs du pays were told not to send sieur Blanc "as the one among them who was carried away with himself in the appeal he made to the council in the previous year by speaking with too much heat." Jean and Louis d'Antelmi, deputies from the city and Parlement of Aix in 1631, spent two years in the Bastille for their boldness. The comte de Grignan sent one of the procureurs du pays to the dungeons of the royal château at Tarascon in 1691 for his blunt speech and lack of cooperation.[161]

At the same time it was customary for royal representatives at the Estates, the governor, lieutenant general, intendant, and other royal commissioners to wine and dine the deputies in grand style. Oppède and the comte de Grignan were known for their extravagant entertainment of deputies at the Provençal General Assemblies. The intendant of Brittany hosted a dinner in January 1637 for provincial notables of the Estates, mostly nobles, at which the meat and fruit alone cost 600 livres. During the Estates at Nantes in August 1626, at which the king himself was present, the city of Nantes spent almost 3,900 livres on wine for the Estates and more than 4,000 livres on wine for the royal party. All told, the consumption of wine by the Estates was about 20,000 liters in seventeen days; that of the court was slightly less. It was difficult for deputies to be antagonistic toward hosts at whose table they had dined so well the night before.[162]

The deputies had to weigh gifts of money and other personal favors from royal ministers such as Colbert and from their brokers and clients against being sent home or even imprisoned for bold speech and lack of cooperation. The Estates sought to influence the royal representatives at their meetings—and high government officials, too—through gifts of money or pensions.[163] The deputies to the Estates tried to defend provincial privileges and interests as they saw them, but their defense was inevitably influenced by their own interests. There was no clear dividing line between issues of principle and matters of self-interest in most cases, either for the deputies to the Estates or for provincial brokers. Royal government was most successful when the crown's interests and the private interests of its subjects, particularly the elite, merged as they sometimes did in the Estates after hard bargaining. It was the role of brokers such as Oppède in Provence and Pontchâteau in Brittany to help accomplish this.

Colbert named the intendants in Provence and Brittany as controller general of finance; he also named the intendants in Guyenne, Languedoc, and Burgundy. He named the naval intendants at Toulon, Marseille, La Rochelle, and Brest as secretary of the navy, and his choices were verified by Louis XIV. In the heavily garrisoned, newly conquered frontier provinces of the Franche-Comté, Alsace, Lorraine, Flanders, Artois, and Roussillon, the ministers of war, Le Tellier and his son Louvois, named the intendant and dominated provincial politics.[164]

By these methods Colbert made the Estates docile and cooperative enough to secure the money for Louis XIV's wars. From the initial preparation for an Estates until its conclusion, the royal minister, his intendants, his provincial clients, and their clients operated as a well-run political machine. Few of their tactics were new; Richelieu had used them, and so had Mazarin after a temporary lapse during the Fronde—they went with his clients to Colbert. But Colbert relied more upon his intendant-clients and less upon local notables to control provincial institutions, and in general he used the tactic of "sweetness and fear," a combination of bribery and intimidation, more effectively than his predecessors.[165]

Colbert relied increasingly upon the intendants in governing the pays d'Etats because local notables had the same tendency as provincial governors to become overmighty subjects. The intendants, on the other hand, were easier to control and more reliable.[166] Colbert would not tolerate insubordination or disobedience from provincial clients. Cardinal Mazarin had destroyed the Valbelle clientele at Marseille because it had become disloyal, and sent archbishop Grimaldi into political exile at Rome and Régusse into political exile at Issoudun in Berry for the same reason.[167] Now Colbert destroyed the Forbin clientele in Provence because he doubted its reliability.

The governorship of Provence had been inherited by Mercoeur's son, Louis-Joseph, duc de Vendôme and de Penthièvre, one of Louis XIV's better generals who was always absent on military campaigns or at court—he only visited Provence four times in the forty years he held office.[168] The authority of acting governor was exercised by the provincial lieutenant general, the comte de Grignan. Oppède's son, Jean-Baptiste was not named first president. Instead, Colbert named his own cousin, Pierre Arnould Marin de La Châteigneraye, first president of the Parlement of Aix. Marin was not a Provençal, but his sister had married Oppède's son with a dowry of 220,000 livres: Colbert told Jean-Baptiste to think of this appointment as advantageous to his own interests because it was still in the family, as we learn from a letter Jean-Baptiste wrote to Colbert on January 27, 1675.[169] Colbert made Jean-Baptiste a naval intendant in Sicily, where he served during the expedition to Messina, and then became ambassador to Portugal. His title was upgraded to that of marquis. These appointments had the twin advantages of being a sop to Oppède's pride and removing him from Provence temporarily.[170] Mindful of Mazarin's mistake with Régusse, Colbert compensated those Provençaux whom he deprived of power. The husband of Oppède's sister Aimare, Pierre-Joseph de Laurens, an important Forbin client, was made a marquis.[171] Janson-Forbin was made an ambassador and permanently sent from Provence, and his nephew was made a marquis.[172] In the bishop's absence Grignan's brother, who was coadjutor to the archbishop of Arles, became senior procureur of the clergy and helped Grignan to control the General Assemblies.

Colbert sent Jean-Baptiste de Rouillé, comte de Meslay, a non-Provençal, to Aix as intendant in 1672. The offices of first president and intendant which had both been held by Oppède were split, and Colbert gave them to reliable non-Provençaux. He allowed the office of governor to become absentee. Neither intendant Rouillé, acting governor Grignan, nor first president Marin was as powerful as his predecessor—Rouillé because he was a stranger to the province without a large clientele; Grignan because his authority as acting governor was based on revocable royal letters of commission; and Marin because he was an unpopular first president. For example, Marin quarreled immediately with the other presidents of the parlement over judicial procedure, and prompted a spate of angry letters to Colbert.[173] Madame de Sévigné reported in letters in October and November 1675 that he had beaten his wife with the flat of his sword in a fit of jealousy to the scandal and amusement of Aix.[174] Madame de Sévigné also noted that he spent the winter of 1676–77 in Paris with his father.[175] Not often in Provence, Marin was permanently absent after Colbert's death. When he was at Aix, his lack of self-control made him an ineffectual first president, and his resignation in 1690 was not regretted.

Colbert's destruction of the Forbin clientele was not a unique incident. The minister also made short work of other provincial power figures who had delusions of grandeur, for instance, the chevalier Jean-Baptiste de Valbelle, a Knight of Malta who was the son of Cosme de Valbelle. Jean-Baptiste had contested his cousin Antoine's leadership of the family clientele at Marseille and departed for Paris when he lost. There he became a client of Gaston d'Orléans, which sent him into political oblivion at the end of the Fronde.[176] He recouped his political fortunes, however, during the Valbelle revolt at Marseille by abandoning the family clientele to support Fortia de Pilles, and secured an audience with Cardinal Mazarin and Louis XIV at Lyon in the winter of 1658.[177]

In the spring and summer of 1660, the consuls of Marseille and the governor complained to Mazarin about the piracies of the chevalier de Valbelle. The consuls wrote in April that his attacks on Italian and Spanish shipping were "ruining the commerce of Marseille," while Mercoeur wrote on May 24 that Valbelle's piracies had cast doubt upon "his affection and his fidelity."[178] In a sea battle against the Algerians in February 1660, Valbelle had disobeyed the orders of his commanding officer, the chevalier Paul, to pursue them when they fled. Rumors circulated that he had been engaging in piracy on the side with letters of mark from the duchy of Savoy, and that this was why he chased the ships. In any event the Grand Master of Malta condemned him to death for mutiny, and he became an outlaw. Valbelle hid along the North African coast and around Sicily, preying on corsairs and Barbary pirates. It was these activities that made the merchants of Marseille uneasy.[179]

Anxious to develop the French fleet, Colbert overlooked Valbelle's peccadilloes and accepted him into the royal service. He was given a ship in 1666.[180] He wrote to Colbert from La Rochelle to declare that "I have never been unworthy of Your protestion." The chevalier swore himself "indissolubly tied and attached to Your Service," and offered "best wishes for the glory of Your Ministry."[181] In writing to Colbert in 1675, Valbelle expressed appreciation "for all the kindnesses You have shown me and my family," and swore that he had "a faithful attachment and deep submission."[182] The chevalier and the marquis de Valavoire urged Colbert to send an expeditionary force to Sicily when Messina rebelled against Spanish rule, and the chevalier led a force in 1674.[183] However, Valbelle spent most of his career as a sailing captain in the Atlantic fleet, not as a galley captain at Marseille: Colbert was taking no chances on a resurgence of Valbelle power in that city, and the chevalier probably had the best chance of any family member to reconstitute that power.

Valbelle was disgraced in 1680 for disobedience. He did not arrest some Majorcan pirates who had treated him like "a friend and ally," although he had been ordered to do so by the king because they were Spanish. Valbelle replied that he had received the letters with the king's orders too late to enforce them. His explanation was not accepted, and he was ordered to go to court. He had a glacial interview with Colbert, "who froze the blood in my veins," and a brief interview with the king, who was cold and aloof. Valbelle asked the king about his promotion to naval lieutenant general, which was pending, and the king promised him the promotion in 1683. Valbelle protested that he could be dead by then, and the king answered, "If you die, they'll bury you." That ended the interview. Needless to say, Valbelle did not receive his long-coveted promotion because Colbert blocked it. He retired without it in 1680 and died the next year. The incident with the Majorcan pirates had been too reminiscent of his earlier behavior. Neither Colbert nor Louis XIV would tolerate such independence.[184]

To summarize, Richelieu asserted ministerial control over the distribution of royal patronage in the provinces and used it to create reliable administrative clienteles of his own to help him in governing, particularly in distant frontier provinces with unreliable governors, and to control traditional tax-granting assemblies in the pays d'Etats. Mazarin and Colbert continued these networks, although Mazarin allowed them to lapse until the crisis of the Fronde convinced him of their utility, and Colbert relied increasingly upon his own intendant-clients. Generously rewarding their clients and créatures,[185] the royal ministers shut off the flow of royal patronage to political opponents or disobedient governors as a disciplinary measure: Richelieu, for example, removed twelve governors from office for their lack of cooperation, and he dealt equally harshly with his enemies at court.[186]

It should be noted that Richelieu did not launch a general attack upon the great nobles of France or attempt to undermine the importance of provincial governorships.[187] Neither did he launch a general attack upon great noble clienteles or attempt to destroy them. As Georges Pagès has remarked, "Richelieu did not destroy clienteles; he himself had a client network which grew larger and more obedient until the end of his life, and was used against his enemies. But in obliging the grands to obey, he put their clienteles at the service of the king."[188] Richelieu did not have the resources to destroy the clienteles of the great nobles of France, and the disruptive repercussions of such an assault might have boomeranged back upon his own clientele, which he needed in governing. Richelieu and his successors, Mazarin and Colbert, used administrative clienteles and the brokerage of royal patronage in the provinces to strengthen royal control over provincial power structures and to counter the influence of unreliable governors. The royal ministers did not attempt to destroy the great nobles and their clienteles, which would have been difficult to do, anyway. They encircled, undermined, and co-opted them using the lure of royal patronage to achieve the same effect. Co-optation through patronage is a classic method of forestalling dissent, weakening resistance, and securing cooperation. The tactic of using brokers and brokerage leads us to reassess how the early modern state was created, how it functioned, and how it secured its power. The Bourbon monarchy had a broader base of support among the nobility than we have realized.

Robert Harding has demonstrated the role of provincial governors as brokers of royal patronage in sixteenth-century France.[189] He has argued that a strong central government was achieved by cooperation, not by conflict, which is also a theme of this book, and he has emphasized the importance of patron-client ties, what he has called "social centralization," in creating the early modern French state, although he has focused upon provincial ties between governors and intendants rather than upon Paris-to-province ties.[190] This chapter argues that the brokerage of royal patronage in the French provinces changed in the seventeenth century, a result of the crown's efforts to achieve political integration and centralization. The governors' monopoly on the provincial brokerage of royal patronage was challenged by a new group of brokers who were members of Paris-based ministerial clienteles. Provincial notables entered the service of the royal ministers to advance their careers and to create their own clienteles, and in exchange they helped the ministers to govern the provinces, for example, by assisting the intendants in performing their duties, especially when they were also ministerial clients. This change in the pattern of brokerage helps to explain why the provincial governors and great nobles ceased to be partners with the monarchy in governing France during the seventeenth century.

There was tension between sword and robe nobles at this time because robe nobles often became ministerial brokers, while governors were always sword nobles, but their hostility should not be exaggerated: patron-client ties were a cohesive force criss-crossing and unifying the nobility of France as a social group. Conflict within the nobility was often conflict between rival clienteles, or between patrons and clients, rather than between sword and robe nobles, as we shall see in the next chapter. Members of governors' networks, for example, were pitted against members of ministerial networks rather than sword nobles against robe nobles, who belonged to both types of clienteles. The monarchy used the brokerage of royal patronage in the provinces to secure the loyalty and support of the French nobility, great and small, sword and robe, in order to construct the early modern state.

Noble Power and Brokerage

A steady flow of patronage was necessary to attract and keep clients. A decline in the supply of patronage available to the great nobles for distribution to their clients decreased the size of their clienteles, diminished their provincial power bases, and became a serious threat to their autonomy. For example, the princes de Condé and Conti lost a number of clients at the end of the Fronde because they could no longer distribute patronage. The duc de Bouillon and the vicomte de Turenne, former clients of Condé, switched their loyalty to Mazarin in December 1651 for suitable rewards: Turenne became governor of the Limousin, while he and Bouillon received the duchies of Albret and Château-Thierry, the counties of Auvergne and Evreux, and the titles of sovereign princes. In July 1652, shortly before his death, Bouillon was discussed as a possible finance minister, and in March Turenne had been given command of a royal army.[191] For their switch to the support of Mercoeur and Mazarin in 1652, Oppède became first president of the Parlement of Aix and Saint Marc became captain of Mercoeur's guards. Jacques de Saulx-Tavannes noted in his memoirs that he had gone into political retirement on his estate at Le Pailly in 1652 and ceased to support Condé, because he had not been rewarded for his loyalty as he had expected, perhaps with a fortress governorship, and he had been asked by Condé to share command of his gendarmes company with the prince de Tarente. Saulx-Tavannes noted that Bussy-Rabutin had left Condé's service for the same reason: he had not been suitably rewarded for his loyalty during Condé's imprisonment, and he had been asked to give up his office of lieutenant in the prince's gendarmes company to the young sieur de Guitaut.[192]

The political power of the great nobles, especially those who were provincial governors, was based on the flow of royal patronage through their hands for distribution to their noble clients. This flow declined during the Wars of Religion and the League in the late sixteenth century when the crown nearly went bankrupt. The constriction in the flow of royal patronage caused a crumbling in the governors' provincial regimes, which steadily weakened because they lacked patronage and the financial and political support of the royal government. The governors' military clienteles decayed into regional religious parties, either Catholic or Calvinist, and a series of weak monarchs, the sons of Catherine de Medici, François II, Charles IX, and Henri III, were unable to elicit from the nobility the loyalty and support enjoyed by François I and Henri II. The governors were divided among themselves and increasingly acted on their own authority. France slipped into civil war.[193]

The chaos engendered by the Wars of Religion and the League, however, provided some members of the lesser French nobility with opportunities to enrich themselves. There were notables to be captured and ransomed; confiscations and resales of rebel properties; pillaging of rebel towns; alienations and sales of royal and church lands; cash gifts, pensions, salaries, and forced loans to be extracted from provincial and municipal governments. War was the only means of existence for some nobles who lived as mercenaries.[194] The constant warfare also offered lesser provincial nobles the opportunity to attract favorable attention in high places through their military exploits and to rise rapidly: Gaspard de Saulx-Tavannes and the duc de Lesdiguières are examples. There were fiscal, personal, and patronage opportunities open to the lesser French nobility in wartime which disappeared with the pacification in the 1590s, and were missed.

The reduction in the flow of royal patronage through the hands of the great nobles who were provincial governors, and the resulting decline in their provincial power, continued in the seventeenth century because of the continuing near-bankruptcy of the crown and for several new reasons, specifically, the Edict of the *Paulette*; an increase in the sale of ennobling royal offices by the crown during the Habsburg War; and the expansion of ministerial clienteles under Richelieu, Mazarin, and Colbert.

The crown had a long history of near-bankruptcy. The prodigality of Henri II in dispensing royal patronage to a few court favorites, especially the Guise and the Montmorency, had put the monarchy on the verge of bankruptcy by the time of his death in the mid-sixteenth century. Henri III had liberally dispensed patronage to the mignons, his court favorites, to such an extent than when Henri IV came to the throne in 1589, after four decades of crippling civil war, he was faced with huge debts.[195] This was the reason why Sully, Henri IV's finance minister, had kept careful tabs on the crown's money gifts to the great nobles and was parsimonious in granting royal patronage.[196] Sully's work, however, was undone by the Queen Mother, Marie de Medici, whose Italian favorites, Concini and his wife, Léonora Galigai, not only acquired a personal fortune of 7,300,000 to 8,400,000 livres, but also read and approved the list of royal pensions and gifts, which were not awarded without their consent. The great nobles found the favorites' power disturbing, and there were three noble rebellions in this period. Henri II de Bourbon, prince de Condé, rebelled in 1614, partly because he resented Concini's control over royal patronage, and he and his supporters received 1,500,000 livres from the crown in 1616 to end their rebellion.[197]

French monarchs in general did not exercise restraints in distributing royal patronage, which they tended to give for personal reasons to a few court favorites who made excessive demands. Besides angering the great nobles who were excluded from royal largesse—this was a motive for many noble conspiracies and intrigues—the monarchs' prodigality also created financial shortages. Moreover, when state resources—royal lands and fiscal rights, exemptions from taxation, cash gifts and annual pensions drawn from tax monies—were given to royal favorites, they could not be used for constructive projects such as commercial and industrial development or overseas colonization. The prodigality of the monarchs helped to keep the state on the edge of bankruptcy.

However, the French monarchs' prodigality in dispensing favors to court favorites and in luxury expenditures and building projects was overshadowed by the expenses of their foreign wars, particularly the war against the Austrian and Spanish Habsburgs. By June 1626, most of the revenues for the next year had been anticipated, and the deficit on the current account stood at about 52,000,000 livres. The marquis d'Effiat as finance minister managed to hold the line on expenditures for a while. But military expenditures escalated after 1630, and especially after 1635 when war was declared. There were a series of currency devaluations to raise money. The crown annually borrowed over 5,000,000 after 1634, and 10,000,000 after 1638; two years later the total amount borrowed had reached nearly 38,000,000. There were massive increases in direct and indirect taxes, and the efforts to raise money included creating and selling a flood of new royal judicial and financial offices. There were serious efforts made to reduce court expenditures. But military expenditures continued to rise, and the monarchy found itself one more balanced on the knife-edge of bankruptcy. The crown's fiscal difficulties helped to produce the Fronde and in addition decreased the amount of royal patronage available for distribution to the great nobles.[198]

The royal edict of the Paulette in 1604 worsened the decline in royal patronage. In this edict, the crown renounced its right to resell a royal office whose owner had not made transfer arrangements forty days before his death if he paid an annual royal tax of one-sixtieth the price of the original office. This edict was primarily a fiscal expedient of Henri IV's finance minister, Sully. The Edict of the Paulette guaranteed that with regular payment of the annual tax an office could safely remain in a family for generations without the threat of resale. After three generations of royal officeholding, the noble rank attached to the office, which its holder enjoyed for life, became separate from the office and hereditary in his family whether the family held royal office or not. This explains why investors were willing to pay high prices for ennobling royal offices. Most families holding these offices had achieved hereditary nobility by the late seventeenth century. They became a new social group, the robe nobility, known for the judicial robes they wore as a badge of royal office, and their numbers increased rapidly, especially with the huge increase in the numbers of royal offices for sale during the Habsburg War.[199]

The rapid growth of the robe nobility worsened the patronage problem by increasing the size of the political elite. Noble demand for royal patronge in the seventeenth century outstripped the supply, which did not increase and which may, in fact, have decreased because of the demands of the Habsburg War and the efforts to reduce court expenditures. Moreover, part of the existing sources were rechanneled to the chief ministers and their clients. This caused anger within the nobility, especially among the upper ranks accustomed to receiving royal patronage. Besides reducing their share of royal patronage, an indirect attack upon their wealth and position, the ministerial policy of diverting part of the flow of royal patronage to their own administrative networks in the provinces was a direct challenge to the political power and privileges of the great nobles, who were provincial governors and had traditionally brokered royal patronage in the provinces.

The Edict of the Paulette decreased the patronage power of the great nobles because it removed blocks of royal offices from their control by making them hereditary. The crown could no longer give the right of nomination to the great nobles for distribution to their provincial clients, as it had done in the fifteenth and sixteenth centuries, because these offices had been removed permanently from royal control.[200] In fact, this may have been a secondary motivation for the Paulette—to remove royal offices from the client networks of the great nobles such as the Guises, and to sharply curtail their influence over the royal administration and the robe nobles who held these offices.[201] The Paulette did not decrease the volume of royal patronage available, however, because the crown could always create new royal offices to sell: the crown created so many new offices to raise money for the Habsburg War that it caused a revolt by robe nobles, who feared their investments in royal officeholding would be devalued by the flood of new offices.[202] The Edict of the Paulette had the effect of decreasing the patronage power of the great nobles, whether or not this was its intention.

Richelieu and Mazarin took advantage of their special relationship with the king to direct a steady flow of royal patronage toward themselves and their families, clients, and court supporters. They were the new court favorites. The Cardinal-Ministers became conspicuously wealthy in a few decades and provided lavishly for their dependents. Richelieu, a younger son and obscure bishop, became in turn a cardinal, a duke, and governor of Brittany, and accumulated a fortune of 22,400,000 livres within eighteen years, although he left debts of 6,498,917 livres at his death in 1642. Richelieu's annual income was at least 872,511 livres. His salary as a royal minister and member of the council of state brought him 20,000 livres a year; he received an annual royal pension of 18,000 livres; his estates produced revenues of 175,858 livres a year—he had extensive lands in Normandy, Anjou, Maine, Poitou, and Saintonge; and his twenty-six Church benefices brought him revenues of 342,510 livres a year.[203] He maintained a large household of 180 persons and 140 horses.[204] He turned his Paris hôtel into a Cardinal's palace, bought the château de Limours in the countryside, and built several châteaux; that of Richelieu was comparable in size to Versailles.[205]

Richelieu made his brother a cardinal, archbishop of Lyon, and abbot of Saint Victor at Marseille; his niece, Marie de Vignerod, became the duchesse d'Aiguillon; a cousin, Charles de La Porte, became marquis (later duc) de La Meilleraye, maréchal in the French armies, provincial lieutenant general and acting governor of Brittany; his nephew and great-nephew, Pont de Courlay and the duc de Richelieu, became generals of the royal galleys at Marseille; another nephew, Maillé-Brézé, became a duke, admiral of the Atlantic fleet, and intendant-general of navigation.[206] Numerous lesser members of the Du Plessis-Besançon and La Porte families were provided to royal offices, for instance, as intendants, and a number of Richelieu's créatures, for example, Bullion, the Bouthilliers, and Séguier, did quite well for themselves financially.[207]

Mazarin made himself a cardinal, duke, and governor of Auvergne, and left a considerably larger fortune than did Richelieu, 38,000,000 to 39,000,000 livres and debts of 1,421,000 livres at his death in 1661.[208] In his will, Mazarin expressly forbade an inventory of his property because it was so numerous and hastily acquired.[209] Mazarin heaped royal benefits onto his plate after the Fronde. In Provence, he obtained the abbey of Saint Victor at Marseille at the death of Richelieu's brother in 1653—it brought him 35,900 livres a year and was one of twenty-one abbeys he held. As a result of the purchase of estates such as the duchies of Mayenne and Nivernais, and the outright gift by Louis XIV of 200 parishes in Alsace, Mazarin's holdings in land outside Paris were worth some 7,500,000 livres by 1660. The Palais Mazarin at Paris contained a fine collection of paintings, objets d'art, and jewelry, especially diamonds, and he kept 9,000,000 livres in cash, an extraordinarily large amount.[210] Mazarin's French nephews by marriage included Charles Armand de La Porte, duc de Mazarin and governor of Alsace; Armand de Bourbon, prince de Conti, governor of Guyenne and Languedoc, who was given a cash gift of 600,000 livres at his marriage in 1654; Frédéric-Maurice de La Tour d'Auvergne, duc de Bouillon, who became governor of Auvergne; Louis de Vendôme, duc de Mercoeur, governor of Provence; the duc de Nevers; and the comte de Soissons.[211] They were all rewarded in their marriage contracts. Mazarin inherited a number of Richelieu's créatures, and he created an extensive financial clientele at Paris. Some of these clients, for instance, Nicolas Fouquet and Abel de Servien, did quite well for themselves financially.[212] Mazarin also rewarded a number of his supporters with governorships at the end of the Fronde.[213]

Mazarin lost much of what he had accumulated during the Fronde—his wealth had been one of the grievances of the great nobles—but he hastily recreated his fortune in the decade after the Fronde, not entirely by legal means. Neither he nor his heirs—his nephews by marriage who bore some of the greatest names in France—nor his créatures wanted a royal investigation into his fortune and how it had been obtained: Colbert, for instance, had played a major role in its acquisition as intendant of his household. Colbert's attack on Mazarin's finance minister, Fouquet, shortly after the Cardinal's death was not only to eliminate a rival and put his own clientele in charge of the financial administration, but also to hide an embarrassing past from the king by providing a scapegoat.[214]

If the fortunes of Richelieu and Mazarin—22,400,000 and 38,000,000 or 39,000,000 livres, respectively—are compared with those of the dukes and peers of France at the same time, it becomes clear that they were, in fact, much wealthier than most of the great nobles at court. Great noble fortunes ranged in general from 1 to 10 million livres with most falling on the lower end of the range, from 1 to 3 million livres.[215] Richelieu's fortune was more than twice as large as that of the average great noble, and Mazarin's fortune—a truly enormous one—was more than three times as great, and these fortunes had been put together within a few years. Some of their families and important créatures had amassed fortunes nearly as large.

Not surprisingly, the great nobles resented what appeared to be a reduction in their share of royal patronage because the flow had been rechanneled toward the greedy, outstretched hands of the chief ministers and their dependents, whom they considered *arrivistes*. Richelieu's control over patronage caused a noble conspiracy in 1626–27, and contributed to the revolts of Guise and Montmorency in 1631–32.[216] The Cardinal's patronage policies were so unpopular with the great nobles that after his death the regency government reversed them: Louis XIII on his deathbed pardoned all the governors dismissed by Richelieu except one, and a number of the politically proscribed under Richelieu regained their positions during the first years of Mazarin's ministry. However, Mazarin was forced to reverse the regency policy of reconciliation in the late 1640s, and thereafter he used royal patronage to reward his supporters, deprive his enemies at court, and create an extensive administrative clientele in the provinces, much as Richelieu had done.[217] In addition, the need for political loyalty during the Habsburg War and the Fronde prompted both cardinals to raise high hopes for promotion in the minds of some clients, for instance, Séguiran and Régusse, and not everyone could be satisfied.

The standard accusations against royal favorites—excessive greed in accepting royal pensions and gifts; appropriating royal tax monies; profiteering and engaging in illegal financial transactions; nepotism and favoritism—were all made against Richelieu and Mazarin. In the mazarinades, polemical political tracts published in great numbers in 1649 and 1650, the Cardinals were accused of financial abuses, avarice, and personal corruption. The size of Mazarin's fortune and his concern for family advancement were attacked, and he was called a parvenu and an upstart. The ministers' close personal association was emphasized. Richelieu was called a harpy and a tyrant. Both ministers were accused of excessive ambition and lust for power. Mazarin was denounced as a foreigner, an Italian-born disciple of Machiavelli, and Concini's successor. Both ministers were accused of misgovernment—ignoring the fundamental laws of France and disregarding public welfare.[218] The mazarinades testify dramatically to the unpopularity of Richelieu and Mazarin and to their identification with a long history of rapacious royal favorites.

However, there was an important difference between court favorites and royal ministers: Richelieu, Mazarin, and Colbert were able statesmen who had received royal patronage as a reward for their political and administrative services to the crown, and they in turn rewarded their own clients for their service to the state. The royal ministers did not dispense royal patronage to a few great noble favorites, but to reliable members of their own administrative clienteles who helped them to govern as *bons serviteurs du Roi.*

Not surprisingly, the chief noble Frondeurs made significant patronage demands on Mazarin and the Queen Mother. For instance, the prince de Conti, governor of Champagne, wanted a place on the council of state, a fortress in Champagne, and patronage benefits for his supporters. The duc de Longueville, Conti's brother-in-law and the governor of Normandy, wanted a major royal office, perhaps an admiralty, a fortress in Normandy, and the right of inheritance for his sons. The duc d'Elbeuf, governor of Picardy, wanted the governorship of Montreuil and offices in the army for his two sons. The prince de Condé, governor of Burgundy and Berry, originally supported Mazarin's government, but by January 1650, he was demanding no less than Mazarin's place as chief minister.[219] Condé had wanted the admiralty office of his father-in-law, the duc de Maillé-Brézé, Richelieu's nephew, and was angered when he did not receive it.[220] The comte d'Alais, governor of Provence, was angered when the governorship of Toulon, which he had wanted for one of his clients, went instead to one of Mazarin's clients, the chevalier Garnier; Alais broke with the Cardinal over this.[221] The duc de Beaufort, another Frondeur, wanted the governorship of Brittany for his father, Vendôme; his brother, Mercoeur, had obtained the governorship of Provence by marrying Mazarin's niece, causing a rift in the family for years. The duc de Bouillon, who supported Condé, wanted the governorship of Auvergne, which Mazarin held, and the restitution of his principality of Sedan, which he had been forced to hand over to Richelieu in 1642 for conspiracy, and his younger brother, the vicomte de Turenne, who also fought with Condé, wanted the governorship of Alsace, which went to a supporter of the Cardinal, the comte d'Harcourt.[222] Louis de Foucault, comte Du Daugon and governor of Brouage, a naval base that allowed him to police the waters around La Rochelle, had been a supporter of Condé in 1651, but he bargained with all sides including Mazarin and the English parliament. He abandoned Condé in 1652 for Mazarin, a marshal's baton, and a dukedom.[223]

It is difficult to say how great a real loss in royal patronage the great nobles actually experienced: the sources make such an estimation nearly impossible.[224] They may have perceived themselves as suffering from a far greater loss than they actually endured. The salient factor, however, is that the great nobles at court and in the provinces perceived themselves as suffering a loss in royal patronage which they blamed on the greed and ambition of the royal ministers, whatever the reality of the situation, and their anger became a motive for their participation in the Fronde. Lesser noble clients, who felt the loss indirectly, followed them into revolt. Patronage as a technique of political control and a motive for political action has been insufficiently emphasized by historians of the Fronde and the early modern French state.[225]

If in the short run, the patronage policies of the royal ministers helped to cause the Fronde by alienating the great nobles and their clients, in the long run these policies also helped the Bourbons to survive the Fronde and to create a strong, stable monarchy. The replacement of the governors and great nobles as provincial brokers of royal patronage by more reliable ministerial clients helped to create the early modern French state: Richelieu asserted ministerial control over the distribution of royal patronage to create a reliable administrative clientele of his own in Paris and the provinces, a policy that was continued by Mazarin and Colbert. Provincial clienteles were used as political machines in governing, and the royal ministers brokered royal patronage through their members to secure the support of the provincial nobility, thereby integrating them into the national political scene and broadening the Paris government's base of support in the countryside. The patronage policies of the royal ministers may have alienated the great nobles at court by decreasing their access to royal patronage. But the great nobles were not reliable supporters of the monarchy; they were often disobedient and disloyal. When they brokered royal patronage, they did so to their own clients for their own purposes and they reaped the benefits. Their purposes and goals were not always those of the crown; in fact, they were often contrary. The monarchy was able to survive the rebellion of the great nobles during the Fronde in part because its ministers had created a broad base of support in the provinces independent of the great nobles. The ministerial brokerage of royal patronage in the provinces helped to integrate and centralize the government of France, especially the peripheral provinces not directly under royal control.

The art of politics on both sides of the Channel in the sixteenth and seventeenth centuries lay in reconciling the expanding central government with independent regional power structures. The Tudors across the Channel, especially Elizabeth I, were more adept at managing the distribution of royal patronage for the state's purposes than were their Stuart successors, and the Tudor monarchy was stronger as a result. The Tudors used royal patronage to gain the support of the great magnates and country gentry across England, rather than allowing it to be channeled into the hands of a few court favorites as the Stuarts tended to do. The Tudors established a political partnership with the country gentry, and the strength of their government lay in its close sympathies with the locally influential; loss of local support was a significant factor in the collapse of Stuart government.[226] On the French side of the Channel, royal ministers such as Richelieu, Mazarin, and Colbert were adept administrators who harnessed the distribution of royal patronage for the state's purposes, rather than allowing it to be distributed to a few court favorites as their predecessors had done. As a result, they were able to create the early modern state of Louis XIV, which rested upon a broader base of noble support than is generally recognized.

CHAPTER SIX

Clientelism and the Early Modern State

Long-term political stability, the acceptance by society of its political institutions and the men who control them, has been rare until recent times. J. H. Plumb has written that "stability becomes actual through the actions and decisions of men, as does revolution. Political stability, when it comes, often happens to a society quite quickly, as suddenly as water becomes ice... whatever has brought about sudden political stability merits inquiry."[1] The government of Louis XIV and Colbert was markedly more stable than that of its predecessors, and this book has suggested several reasons why.

Early modern French statebuilding consisted of several major achievements: the attainment of political stability after the religious and popular upheavals of more than a century; the creation of a large, reliable standing army; the development of new patterns of regional-national integration; the growth of political institutions, especially at the center, leading to the emergence of a strong national government in Paris with more control over the provinces; and the growth of a professional body of officials, permanent, paid, and skilled, to staff these institutions.[2] This book has explored the development of new patterns of regional-national integration that strengthened the control of the Paris government over the provinces. It has argued that the royal ministers' creation of their own administrative clienteles to broker royal patronage in the peripheral provinces of seventeenth-century France was a successful new pattern of regional-national integration that contributed to the development of the early modern state.

So far the positive, integrative aspects of political clientelism have been discussed, that is, provincial brokerage of royal patronage as a method of political integration. This chapter explores some of the flaws or weaknesses in clientelism as a system of government. There are two major disadvantages to clientelism as a political system: a high rate of conflict and an inherent tendency toward corruption. The government of France began to undergo the transition to a more modern bureaucratic form in the seventeenth century partly because of these inherent weaknesses in clientelism as a political system.[3]

Critics of clientelism stress its divisiveness, exclusivity, inflexibility, and failure to contribute to positive, long-term political development. They find clientelism a defective system politically because it restricts participation, fails to promote integration, encourages fragmentation, and does not help the state to develop efficiency or legitimacy. They believe that clientelism encourages conservatism and stagnation in a political system and satisfies special interests, using the resources of the state for patronage rather than for growth or development. Critics agree that a bureaucracy exhibiting clientelism is defective or incomplete.[4]

There is uncertainty, however, about the overall effect of clientelism, and it is still unclear whether it contributes to political development or retards it.[5] Advocates of clientelism stress its positive contributions to statebuilding in traditional societies and emphasize its cohesive, unifying, and integrative aspects.[6] They see clientelism as highly adaptable, lending itself easily to change over time, and a useful tool in statebuilding because of its flexibility. They argued that the brokerage functions of local patrons lessen status differences in traditional societies, and accelerate the process of development by maintaining cohesion among ethnically and regionally different groups while permitting accumulation of statebuilding resources at the center.[7]

Clientelism in traditional societies had both strengths and weaknesses as a political system: the advantages and disadvantages of using patron-broker-client ties and networks to govern reflected the paradoxical nature of clientelism, which was both integrative and divisive. Clientelism had both cohesive and divisive features that could produce political stability or instability. Patron-client ties and networks could be used to encourage political cooperation and unity, or they could be used to thrust hostile factions or authorities farther apart and increase fragmentation.[8] This paradoxical duality was a basic characteristic of clientelism.[9]

Clientelism and Conflict

The most serious problem in clientelism as a method of government was the high rate of political conflict that it generated. The personal feuds arising from dissolved patron-client relationships were easily transferred to the political arena and expressed in political and administrative strife that sometimes became so intense it disrupted government, causing political instability and even civil war. In fact, patron-client relationships habitually produced a high rate of political conflict because of the frequency with which they were dissolved—many relationships were fragile and easily severed, especially in times of stress—and there was the problem of ill-will created by acrimonious dissolutions. Clientelism generated a high level of social distrust and a sharply competitive atmosphere, and this atmosphere and the conflict from broken relationships poisoned French politics in general. Political interaction in the sixteenth and seventeenth centuries often had a tense and distrustful air and sometimes became bitter, hateful, even violent, although most conflicts remained at the level of rhetoric.[10]

Clientelism was a reciprocal exchange relationship based on mutual interests. When these interests changed or clashed, or when the exchange ceased to be reciprocal, the relationship collapsed, often amid charges of disloyalty and betrayal. Patrons deserted by clients could be as angry and bitter as clients betrayed by patrons. Client relationships began as a slow, stately dance in which the opening step was a carefully plotted move to attract a patron's attention. They ended in a frenzy of emotion, with cries of disloyalty and ingratitude mingled with charges of betrayal. A patron considered himself betrayed if a client accepted the favors and the patronage he offered and then did not obey him, provide the services he expected, or defend his interests. A client considered himself betrayed if his loyalty and service went unrewarded by a patron, or if his interests were neglected for a long period of time. Both sides charged betrayal when they failed to receive what had been promised or expected. A charge of betrayal was the standard accusation that ended most patron-client relationships. It masked many types of problems and conflicts. "Ingrate" was another frequently heard insult in the sixteenth and seventeenth centuries: a patron or client was accused of ingratitude when he accepted services or favors without reciprocating to the other's satisfaction.

A client agreed to subordinate his own interests to those of his patron, to serve him and to accept an inferior role in the relationship in exchange for the material benefits of patronage. When he felt that he was not being adequately rewarded, or when his personal interests diverged from those of his patron, he could sever the connection. For instance, Régusse broke his relationship with Governor Mercoeur, and jeopardized his relationship with Cardinal Mazarin, because he felt he had not been adequately rewarded for his loyalty and service during the Fronde. Jacques de Saulx-Tavannes and Roger de Bussy-Rabutin broke with the prince de Condé for the same reason. There was no fixed ratio of reciprocity: some clients were content with less patronage than others; in fact, it was difficult to determine reciprocity in an ongoing relationship in which there was no formal contract. The built-in inequality, the lack of formality, the tendency to avoid direct discussion of the terms of the exchange or to obscure it by rhetorical declarations of undying loyalty led to accidental misunderstandings and disappointments in patron-client relationships as well as to deliberate deceit and hypocrisy. Jacques de Forbin de La Barben is an example.

La Barben was a cousin and client of Oppède. He had supported the rebel parlementaires whom his cousin had led in protest against the governor in 1649, and he had fought under Oppède's leadership as a Sabreur during the Fronde.[11] Oppède must have considered him politically reliable because in the autumn of 1657, he intervened in the municipal elections of Aix to have him named first consul.[12] La Barben was expected to help Oppède manage the procureurs du pays: Oppède acted as intendant and exercised his authority unofficially—without letters of commission—for two decades, because the province refused to accept the commission letters of an intendant sent from Paris.[13]

La Barben, however, joined the other procureurs du pays in refusing to approve a new tax demanded by Oppède and Mercoeur.[14] Considering himself betrayed, Oppède severed the relationship and sought the removal and punishment of La Barben, who received a lettre de cachet in February 1658 summoning him to Paris for explanations.[15] He left Aix in mid-April and was arrested at court on June 19, the morning after he had fought in the battle of the Dunes near Dunkerque. He was imprisoned in the citadel of Calais where he remained until the following February when he returned home, his term as first consul having expired.[16] Oppède had named La Barben first consul of Aix so that he could influence the other procureurs du pays in his favor; this was the service he demanded. But La Barben had done exactly the opposite, probably in following the dictates of his conscience. As a result, Oppède severed their relationship and had him removed from office. This was a classic political problem—a patron could place a client in office, but he could not guarantee his behavior once he was there. A client, on the other hand, was faced with the dilemma of doing his duty to a patron at the expense of his own conscience and interests.

Mutual interests could change or disappear over time; they could even be transformed into conflicts of interest. When this happened patron-client relationships collapsed; when the compatibility of interests diminished or disappeared, so did the relationship. An example is the tie between the Valbelles and Governor Guise. By establishing more admiralty courts in Provence to increase his income, the duc de Guise had decreased the income of the Valbelles' original jurisdiction at Marseille, and the Valbelles severed their ties with the governor because their interests had diverged over time. Provincial brokers often had this problem. Their independent resources, which were an important factor in their selection as brokers, created conflicting interests and obligations—their loyalty and service was qualified by whatever was necessary to maintain their provincial influence and clienteles. As a result conflicts of interest occurred, and brokers were accused of having private interests that conflicted with their loyalty and service to a patron. An example is Colbert's program for liquidating community debts.

Colbert launched a national program of liquidating community debts in 1666, and Oppède as acting intendant was put in charge of this program for Provence.[17] However, Oppède was not successful at liquidating community debts because he had to rely on his Provençal clients to accomplish this task, and they were often the creditors of communities whose debts they were supposed to liquidate. Oppède was not as successful as Pierre Cardin Lebret, who became intendant in Provence in 1687 and first president of the parlement a few years later. When Lebret arrived in Provence, community debts stood at 23,000,000 livres. He reduced them to 11,000,000 livres in three years but was not able to eliminate them totally—the demands of Louis XIV's wars increased them once again.[18] Cardin Lebret was more successful because he had previously worked at liquidating community debts as intendant in the Dauphiné and brought to Provence several experienced subdélégués to help him in this task.[19]

Subdélégués came from all walks of life, but the majority were experienced royal officials whom the intendants chose in order to use their local prestige and authority. They were usually judges and financial and municipal officials.[20] In executing the intendant's orders, they exercised a delegated function within their own jurisdictions, that is, they were temporarily given special powers, a written commission or subdelegation of the intendant's authority, to solve a particular administrative problem. Their performance and efficiency were evaluated before another commission was issued, and they could easily be regulated by the withdrawal of their subdelegation. By 1700, subdélégués had become indispensable agents of the intendants, although they were not salaried or permanent until 1704; the office of subdélégué was formally established by the crown and sold by royal edict in April 1704.[21] Because an intendant was a stranger in the province and his professional duties were expanding, he tended to rely more and more on subdélégués to help him—to provide information on local affairs, to execute his orders, and to solve specific problems—and the number of subdélégués increased rapidly during the late seventeenth century.[22] In general, the subdélégués were more deeply embedded in community life than the intendants and acted as spokesmen for local concerns and interests. The intendants chose as subdélégués local officials who often became their clients.[23] Intendants tended to pass along reliable subdélégués to their successors, who were often presented with a ready-made clientele upon arriving in a province.[24] Because he was an unofficial acting intendant without royal letters of commission, Oppède could not subdelegate his authority. He had to use his own provincial clients.[25] They had local interests and were not as easy to regulate.

Because they were Provençaux who had invested in community loans, Oppède and his clients had interests that conflicted with the program for liquidation of community debts. Oppède himself was a creditor of indebted communities, and so were many of his clients. For example, Oppède was a creditor of at least nine communities in 1649, six in the Comtat Venaissin and three in Provence; undoubtedly the communities had changed in twenty years but the pattern of investment had not, because Oppède habitually lent money to communities and fellow judges.[26] Lending to communities was a favorite form of parlementaire investment, and Oppède probably also lent money to colleagues who were community creditors.[27] He himself owed money to community creditors. In 1649, Oppède owed approximately 100,000 livres to seven parlementaires, including community creditors Cauvet de Bormes, Boyer, and Saint Marc.[28] He owed Cauvet de Bormes, his brother-in-law, 21,000 livres on his sister's dowry; Cauvet de Bormes was a heavy investor in community loans.[29] Many of Oppède's relatives, friends, and clients were community creditors. For example, his client Laurens de Vaugrenier, who controlled the municipal government of Draguignan, was the community's biggest creditor.[30] Oppède had extensive support among the provincial nobility, who often invested in community loans. He was not highly motivated to liquidate the debts of communities where he and his clients were creditors. Doing so might have damaged his own financial interests and those of his clients, threatening his provincial crédit and earning him a reputation as a patron who did not protect his clients. In this instance, Oppède was motivated by self-interest. The needs of the royal service, balanced against the needs of maintaining his own influence and clients used in the royal service, undoubtedly posed a delicate problem in judgment, even a dilemma, for Oppède from time to time.

The commissioners selected to liquidate community debts in Provence were Oppède's clients. He had written to Colbert in May 1666 that he was working well with his cousin, Forbin de La Barben, on this project.[31] A year later he requested that the bishops of Toulon and Digne—his brother Louis and his cousin Janson-Forbin—be named commissioners. He also requested that the commissioners include the procureurs du pays, among whom was his son Jean-Baptiste, second consul, and his clients Dominique Guidy, trésorier général at Aix, and sieur Decormis, syndic of the unrepresented communities.[32] These commissioners, specifically, Forbin de La Barben, Decormis, Guidy, and their families, were probably community creditors, too. They were selected because they were Oppède's clients, not because of their experience in settling community debts, which they may not have been motivated to settle. It is not surprising that Cardin Lebret was more successful than Oppède in liquidating community debts. He was less intéressé, with fewer conflicts of interest.

The pressure of external political and economic events changed patron-client interests over time, causing conflict and the collapse of relationships—for example, changes in a patron's politics or in his political fortunes, the ascension of a new king to the throne, the emergence of a new chief minister, the arrival of a new governor. There were wholesale departures of clients from the services of the duc de Mayenne in 1592 and the prince de Condé in 1652, as their political fortunes declined. A better example is the career of Jean Hérauld de Gourville, a political adventurer and opportunist who showed amazing skill at clientele-hopping and an astonishing ability to survive the disgrace of his patrons. Most clients were not that lucky.

Jean Hérauld de Gourville was a commoner by birth. He began his career as a valet in the service of the duc de La Rochefoucauld, advanced to become his secretary and créature, then attached himself to the prince de Condé, who was La Rochefoucauld's patron, through the good offices of the prince's trusted créature Pierre Lenet. Gourville met Cardinal Mazarin while acting as a go-between for the prince. In 1652, as the prince's fortunes declined, Gourville helped Mazarin to negotiate the surrender of the Bordeaux rebels—Condé was governor of Guyenne at the time and never forgave him—and received a pension of 4,000 livres and a cash gift of 2,000 livres as a reward. More important, Gourville entered the Cardinal's service.[33]

But Mazarin had no use for him when the Fronde ended and evidently did not trust him, so Gourville reentered the service of La Rochefoucauld to manage the duke's financial affairs and buy himself an office of supply intendant. In the course of his financial dealings he met Nicolas Fouquet, the minister of finance, entered his service, became deeply involved in his financial affairs, and made himself a fortune of several million livres and a number of enemies including Colbert. Gourville did not survive Fouquet's fall. When Fouquet was arrested in September 1661, Gourville sought refuge with the duc de La Rochefoucauld, but his arrest was ordered a year later and he fled to Spain. He was condemned to death *in absentia* for peculation in April 1663, but the sentence was rescinded five years later. He performed diplomatic missions at the court of Madrid for Louis XIV, and returned to France permanently at Colbert's death.[34]

A clash of interests developed for clients when the political fortunes of a patron declined or when he was disgraced and no longer able to reward and protect them. Clients then had to choose between their own interests and those of their patron, and many clients went in search of a more promising patron, as Gourville and Daniel de Cosnac did.[35] Broken relationships, personal rivalries and feuds, accusations of disloyalty and disobedience as well as conflicts of interest and charges of ingratitude, self-interest, and lack of reciprocity produced conflict that could disrupt government. Patron-client relationships were fragile and often torn by conflict. In a political system dominated by patron-client ties, personal relationships became the basis for political relationships, and when personal relationships broke down, so did the political arrangements based on them. Personal conflicts easily became political conflicts. An example is the feud between Vincent-Anne de Forbin-Maynier d'Oppède and his patron, the duc de Guise, governor of Provence.

The baron d'Oppède [who was the father of Henri] was rumored to have been appointed first president of the Parlement of Aix in 1621, "through the favor and influence of the duc de Guise whom Oppède had put in his interests through his father-in-law [Castellane de La Verdière], the duke's most faithful servant."[36] But Oppède and Guise quarreled in 1625.[37] Oppède sought the protection of Cardinal Richelieu as a more promising patron since Guise was in eclipse at court; in fact, his switch in allegiance was probably why they quarreled.[38] Guise was furious at Oppède's defection and never forgave him, regarding him as ungrateful and disloyal. Guise began a feud with the parlement that lasted six years, usurping the court's authority, insulting its members, and criticizing its conduct in his letters to Richelieu. In 1629 the governor blockaded the city of Aix, ostensibly as a measure to contain an outbreak of plague, but also to harass the parlement and halt its functioning. In the next year Guise refused to aid the parlement in suppressing the Cascaveoux Revolt at Aix. Consequently the revolt became serious, and a royal army had to be sent to Provence to suppress it.[39] Guise had several motives for his refusal, but one was anger at Oppède's defection and a desire for revenge which disrupted the provincial government and contributed to the escalation of a popular revolt at Aix.

The personal feuds of patrons extended to their clienteles. The Fronde can be understood, at least on one level, as the confrontation of feuding noble clienteles. For example, a personal feud between two great nobles, Chaulnes and Elbeuf, developed into a political conflict involving their clienteles and contributed to causing the Fronde in Picardy. Honoré d'Albert, duc de Chaulnes, was lieutenant general of Picardy from 1621 to 1633, and Charles II de Lorraine, duc d'Elbeuf, was governor at the same time, although he was usually absent from the province. When Elbeuf supported the rebel ducs de Montmorency and d'Orléans against Richelieu in 1631, Chaulnes held the province loyal to the Cardinal and was rewarded with the governorship of Picardy. He served as governor for ten years, then lost the office to Elbeuf in the political reshuffling that followed the death of Richelieu, probably through the influence of Gaston d'Orléans with the Queen Mother. Chaulnes's support of Richelieu had made him an opponent of Elbeuf, and they became personal enemies and political rivals. Chaulnes's son was governor of Amiens and became duke in 1649 at his death. Elbeuf supported the princes at court, so Chaulnes supported Mazarin.

Chaulnes's son intervened in the 1649 municipal elections at Amiens, the provincial capital, to place his own clients in office—Charles de Lestocq, a councillor in the bailliage court and a wealthy munitioneer or military supplier, and Gabriel de Sachy, who had administered the confiscated property of the abbey of Corbie. Chaulnes's other clients in the municipal government included Antoine de Lestocq, royal procureur (attorney) in the bailliage court; Antoine Gueudon, clerk in the same court; four municipal councillors; three judges and the chief justice of the presidial court at Amiens. Chaulnes was also backed by a cavalry regiment garrisoned in the province and by intendant Ganun. His purpose was to secure Picardy for Mazarin against Elbeuf, a Frondeur, no doubt hoping to be rewarded in the same manner as his father. Elbeuf, of course, opposed his actions, and sent agents to Picardy to mobilize his clients and supporters. Chaulnes, now duke, intervened again in 1650 in the municipal elections at Amiens. He excluded three would-be members of the government, two merchants and a lawyer, and substituted his own clients. This second intervention provoked a furor—the parlement intervened against Chaulnes and Elbeuf protested strenuously—and began a quarrel that lasted eighteen months. It triggered the Fronde in Picardy, which was essentially a power struggle between the clienteles of two feuding grands, Chaulnes and Elbeuf.[40]

The Valbelle-Alais feud at Marseille and the Oppède-Régusse feud at Aix developed into violent confrontations of their clienteles that soon became engulfed in the Provençal Fronde. Factionalism in the Parlement of Rouen in the 1640s was intensified by a personal feud between president Bretel de Grémonville and first president Faucon de Ris—Grémonville led the opposition party protesting Mazarin's government, many of whose members were his clients, while Faucon de Ris led the royalists.[41] The personal feuds of patrons escalated into confrontations of their clienteles, causing political conflict in the provinces and contributing to the outbreak of the Fronde.[42] Critics of clientelism as a political system have rightly stressed its divisiveness and its tendency to cause factionalism, fragmentation, and political instability. Conflict was a basic problem of clientelism.

Clientelism and Corruption

Did traditional political clientelism have an inherent tendency to produce political corruption? Did it encourage bribery and graft, malversation and peculation, nepotism and favoritism? The answer is yes if modern standards are applied, and no if early modern standards are applied. Critics have tended to exaggerate the abuses in traditional clientelism as a political system because they have applied modern standards in evaluating it.

What is political corruption? The term is difficult to define for the premodern period because it is essentially a modern concept. Social scientists have tended to define certain practices as corrupt regardless of the values of the society in which they are found, for instance, peculation or embezzlement, bribery, extortion, and graft in which officials exchange their services and resources for cash or favors, as well as nepotism and favoritism, the improper or excessive use of influence or pressure. The problem is that in the early modern period these practices were either legitimate or their moral status was confused.[43] What, then, was political corruption in early modern France?

Great care must be taken in applying the concept of corruption backward in time—nearly all early modern officials were corrupt by twentieth-century standards. The modern definition of corruption is the abuse of public office for private gain, that is, the misuse of public responsibility and trust for personal interest. A corrupt official allows personal interests to interfere with his public duties to the extent of subverting the public interest.[44] The early modern patronage system was inherently corrupt by modern standards because it confused public and private interests and systematically served special interest groups: it was a political network of personal relationships based on the reciprocal exchange of public patronage. Patrons provided their clients with public or royal patronage—for instance, offices—as part of personal relationships, and personal services were rewarded with public funds—for instance, client networks were maintained with royal pensions. By modern standards, seventeenth-century officials were corrupted by patron-client demands and by low salaries, ill-defined duties, a confusion of public and private funds, and an absence of inspections, systematic bookkeeping, and regular accounts.[45] But they were not considered corrupt by their contemporaries who understood corruption differently. The concept of corruption did exist in seventeenth-century France. Public perception of the corruption of the governments of Richelieu and Mazarin, for instance, helped to provoke the Fronde, and royal officials were prosecuted for corruption, even condemned to death: Gourville, for instance, was condemned to death for peculation in April 1663. What did corruption mean in seventeenth-century France? Why were some officials indicted for corruption and others were not? Which profits of office were legitimate and which were not?

There are no simple answers to these questions. Whether or not an individual was judged guilty of corruption depended on his family connections and rank, his competence or incompetence, that is, his success or failure at his job, the frequency and extent of his illicit activities, and the political situation at the time—the difficulties the government faced, the government's reputation, and how the corrupt act affected the government.[46] Public interest in seventeenth-century France was equated with the interests of the king and the monarchy or French state.[47] Corrupt activities were those that damaged the interests of the crown, and their definition varied over time. The development of the concept of corruption accompanied the growth of the early modern state, and there was a clearer conception of corruption at the end of the seventeenth century than there had been in the first decade of the century. The concept of corruption developed more slowly in France than in England, but French government showed a willingness to prosecute officials for corruption by the time of Colbert's ministry.[48]

Public interest was the standard for political propriety during the reign of Louis XIV as it is today, but it was defined differently. Public interest in the seventeenth century was defined as the crown's interests, and it was not always easy to distinguish between the crown's interests and the private interests of its officials. For this reason it was not always easy to determine when an individual's activities became corrupt and damaged the interests of the state. Nicolas Fouquet is an example. His case also demonstrates the primitive methods of administration in use at the time that helped to confuse public and private interests. The financial and accounting systems of the French state did not make it easy to distinguish between public and private monies, and it was often difficult to determine what was fraudulent accounting and what was not.

Conspicuously loyal to Mazarin during the early years of the Fronde, Fouquet as a reward had been allowed to purchase the office of procureur general in the Parlement of Paris. By 1652, he had acquired enough influence within the court to persuade the royalists to leave their Frondeur colleagues at Paris and to set up a parlement loyal to Mazarin at Pontoise. For his loyalty, he was rewarded by the Cardinal in 1653 with the office of minister of finance (*surintendant de finance*).[49] In this office he mobilized credit for the crown, using his own property as security for loans intended directly or indirectly for the crown and contracting loans on the security of state resources.[50] After 1655 he undertook to supply whatever sums Mazarin or the king required, subcontracting them to the financiers. Mazarin, too, advanced his own money to the crown and charged interest for his services, but—encouraged by Colbert—he sought to keep his commitments to a minimum while involving Fouquet as completely as possible.[51] During his finance ministry from 1653 to 1661, Fouquet borrowed about 30,000,000 livres for the state, much of it on his own credit. References to specific transactions involving his own resources are rare, but when Fouquet was seriously ill in June 1658, he drew up a statement mentioning that he had alienated 2,000,000 livres of his wife's property, which he used for loans to the king. He was too ill at this time to bargain with the financiers for money needed to supply the royal armies, so in desperation he raised the money by selling his wife's estate of Belle-Assize. When he was arrested on September 5, 1661, he had over 500 creditors, a number of whom had lent him money destined for the royal service. They included magistrates in the high courts of Paris, councillors of state and masters of requests, royal treasurers, members of his own immediate family and the families of his wife and mother, tax farmers, and munitioneers. Fouquet estimated that his total liabilities in September 1661 were 12,000,000 livres, of which 8,000,000 represented borrowing for loans to the state.[52]

Inspiring financial confidence, an atmosphere of credibility, was the main function of the minister of finance, and his participation in the day-to-day administration was limited. He did not supervise the practical details of securing advances on royal income from taxation, the other important means of securing loans. His clerks, especially his chief clerk, did this—they negotiated advances by financiers to the state with tax revenues as security. They had the trust and backing of the minister without having to endure his interference. The situation provided room for peculation, especially since the price demanded by financiers for credit (30 to 50 percent interest) was far above the fixed rate (5 to 6 or 16 to 17 percent) the king's servants could legally offer. In negotiating advances and loans the clerks took bribes, arranged deals on the side, and engaged in corruption to an extent far beyond what was needed to secure a reasonable rate of interest, and they were backed by Fouquet. The minister was forced to go along with his clerks in their illegal activities because he was responsible by law for what was done in his name, and if he had denounced them, he would have been considered more guilty than they. He must have known about the fraud that went on, even when he did not benefit personally from bribes such as those given to him regularly by tax farmers, but he had to cover for whatever his clerks did. There were no safeguards in the system against fraud.[53] It was a situation that encouraged the embezzlement of state funds.

Fouquet had the largest financial clientele in Paris government circles during the 1650s. He had 116 clients, followed closely by Cardinal Mazarin with a financial clientele of 114. Nicolas Monnerot, tax farmer, munitioneer, royal treasurer, and tax receiver, had the next largest financial clientele, 69 clients, while François Jacquier, munitioneer, had 56 clients. Colbert, Mazarin's intendant, had 55 clients. Monnerot was a client of Fouquet; Jacquier was in both Fouquet's and Mazarin's clienteles; Colbert was Mazarin's client, as was Fouquet himself. Abel de Servien, one of Mazarin's clients, and cominister of finance with Fouquet, had a much smaller clientele, only 17; and Gourville, another of Fouquet's clients, had a clientele of 15. The size of clienteles was not correlated to officeholding in the royal financial administration, and there was much overlapping in the fluid membership of these clienteles.[54]

Fouquet was arrested on September 5, 1661, on a variety of charges including treason and corruption and tried before a special *Chambre de justice* created in November. He was accused of financial misbehavior or malversations. It was claimed that he had made no distinction between his own and the king's money and that he had drawn up the royal accounts at his private residence. He was accused of participating himself in the revenue farms and tax contracts under assumed names and of taking bribes and pensions from tax farmers and munitioneers. And he was accused of profiting from the abuse of treasury bills. His entire nine-year financial administration was denounced as contrary to the king's interests and the interests of the state. In fact, it was the system that made no distinction between royal and private monies, as it made no distinction between public and private interests.

Fouquet had been made a scapegoat and was tried for political reasons: Colbert's desire to eliminate a political rival and to bury the evidence of Mazarin's corruption in which he had participated, and Louis XIV's desire to assume control himself of the royal financial administration. The charge of corruption was merely an excuse. In fact, Fouquet had been encouraged in his financial juggling by Mazarin, Colbert, and Louis XIV.[55] Much of what Fouquet had done, while technically illegal, was common practice among financial officials at all levels of the royal administration. The royal financial system operated only through illegal maneuverings, and the accounting system was incapable of preventing maladministration and fraud. It was difficult to condemn any but the most blatant cases of corruption because of the confusion within the system itself. There was an absence of inspections and systematic bookkeeping within the financial administration, and it was as difficult to separate royal and private interests as it was to separate royal and private monies. The demands of the patron-client system for services and rewards intensified this confusion between public and private. Charges of corruption became an excuse for political trials that had other purposes, and scapegoat trials for corruption in times of political crisis became common in eighteenth-century France.[56]

The chronic near-bankruptcy of the state and the inadequacies of the tax system meant that royal officials were paid low salaries during the Old Regime. Officials were expected to supplement their salaries by accepting gifts, favors, and perquisites. These payments were considered informal fees or tips not harmful to royal interests—in fact, they were beneficial because they supplemented the low salaries—unless they negatively influenced the judgment of royal officials. They were only considered bribes when they could be shown to have damaged or subverted the interests of the monarchy and the state and were substantial enough to have done so.

For example, most intendants made about 12,000 livres, which was not a large salary. They were not wealthy men.[57] For this reason, it was not unusual for an intendant to accept occasional small gifts in money or in kind. Gifts for intendants entering or leaving a province on tours of duty, or after long absences, were a common practice and included wine, jam, dried or fresh fruit, and game. The city of Nevers made a gift of twelve containers of jam to Jacques Le Vayer, the outgoing intendant in 1698, and a gift of twelve dozen bottles of wine, one pike, and one fat carp to Jean Bechameil de Nointel, the incoming intendant in 1699. In 1700 the city welcomed Bechameil de Nointel back from a trip to Paris with twelve boxes of dried fruit and four dozen oranges from Portugal. Etienne-Jean Bouchu was offered wine and fruit upon his arrival at Grenoble in 1686.[58] When intendant Dreux d'Aubray entered Aix-en-Provence for the first time in September 1630, the municipal consuls presented him with gifts of a tapestry, wine, jam, and torches.[59] The municipal government of a provincial capital sometimes contributed to the housekeeping expenses of an intendant, especially in frontier provinces, by offering free housing, a cash supplement for housing, or firewood. At Lyon the échevins offered Humbert de Chaponay free wine for his household and family. The intendant at Lyon in 1642 was allowed to bring wine into the city free of municipal taxes.[60] These gestures were considered gifts because they were not substantial in nature.

Gifts only became a problem when they were substantial in nature and influenced the intendants in such a way that they damaged royal interests. The intendants also accepted money gifts from the provincial Estates, and when these were substantial, they could be construed as bribes because they were meant to encourage the intendants to accept lower tax rates and more advantageous terms of payment. Intendant François Cazet de Vautorte was reprimanded by chancellor Séguier in 1643 for accepting money gifts from the General Assemblies of Provençal Communities.[61] Intendant Le Tonnelier de Breteuil, a client of the governor, the duc d'Orléans, was voted a gift of 7,000 livres in 1649 by the Languedoc Estates, "in consideration of his intercession with their master, His Royal Highness." The Estates of Languedoc had voted his predecessors, intendants Baltazar and Bosquet, gifts of 3,000 livres each in 1645.[62] The Estates of Brittany voted the intendant a total of 20,000 livres in the years from 1639 to 1647, and his clerk 3,500 livres from 1643 to 1647.[63] Although a common practice, money gifts from the provincial Estates were discouraged by the crown for fear they would negatively influence an intendant's judgment and damage royal interests.

In the years from 1630 to 1645, the Estates of Brittany voted a total of 1,238,000 livres in gifts or pensions to individuals, including 600,000 livres to Cardinal Richelieu as the governor; another 138,000 livres to his guards, secretary, and doctor; 342,000 livres to the duc de La Meilleraye, Richelieu's cousin, as the provincial lieutenant general; another 83,000 livres to his guards, secretary, and domestic servants; 56,000 livres to the two secretaries of state for Brittany who were Richelieu's clients, plus 19,000 livres to their clerk. In the same period, the Estates of Brittany voted an additional 367,626 livres to ten nobles, many of whom were royal officials connected to Richelieu.[64] These substantial gifts could be considered bribes only if they produced actions judged to damage royal interests, and since Richelieu was the king's chief minister, this judgment was unlikely to be made unless his enemies found a way to get rid of him. Then a charge of corruption might be leveled against Richelieu. The perception of corruption depended upon the individual, his activities, and the political situation at the time.

The gifts to various royal officials that the sieur de Gouberville made in attempting to keep a judicial office he had inherited from his father were not considered bribes because they did not endanger royal interests. The sieur de Gouberville was a country gentleman living in the Cotentin region of Normandy in the mid-sixteenth century. He kept a journal from 1553 to 1563 in which he made meticulous daily entries giving a surprisingly full view of his life in this decade. Gouberville had inherited the office of judge in the forestry court of the bailliage of Cotentin from his father. But a new royal edict decreed that in order to keep his office he had to take his commission to Bayeux. Uneasy about the situation, he decided to present a petition to Henri II asking to keep his office, making a trip to the royal court at the château of Blois necessary. He bought a new outfit for the trip and arrived at Blois on January 29, 1554.

Gouberville regularly attended mass with the king and the royal family, hoping for a chance encounter; he attended a royal ball and supper as a spectator; and he generally spent his time hanging around the château, especially when the quasi-public royal audiences were held in the main hall twice a week after dinner, hoping for an opportunity to speak to the king about his problem. In reality, there was little chance of that. Finally, he talked to a treasurer of the *Parties Casuelles* (a separate royal treasury dealing with offices) to whom he paid a fee of 1,300 écus (3,900 livres) plus a generous gift to have his name inscribed on the register of royal offices. He also paid fees to two royal secretaries to have a request presented at a meeting of the royal council and gave them generous gifts—in all likelihood, they never presented his request and justified their failure, if asked, by saying that the opportunity never arose. These payments were not considered bribes because they were paid to royal officials for services rendered, not to influence their judgment. In fact, these gifts were beneficial to the monarchy because they supplemented its low salaries.

Gouberville finally went home after six weeks at court. The whole trip had cost him about 5,000 livres. When the case was decided three years later, the office went to his neighbor and rival, sieur d'Arreville Hennot, who had gone to court at the same time—they had met at an inn on the way—and who evidently had more influential connections at court, had paid larger fees and gifts (bribes only by twentieth-century standards), or both, because he got the office.[65] In his journal Gouberville did not express anger at having to pay various officials for their services, at having to go to court which had been his own choice, or even at spending 5,000 livres and still losing the office: it was the way the system worked. He was not trying to subvert the system in making these payments.

If the monarchy's interests were not damaged by the payments of the sieur de Gouberville, they were harmed by the financial activities of Antoine de Valbelle, aptly described by René Pillorget as an *affairiste*, a politician who used his position and authority to feather his own nest: Valbelle had accumulated a large fortune in a short time by exploiting his royal judicial office of maritime admiralty lieutenant.[66] In January 1644 the consuls of Marseille, who had been named to office by his enemy, Governor Alais, sent a memoir to Mazarin titled, "The Malfeasance of the Admiralty Lieutenant." It ws a detailed list of the financial abuses of Valbelle. The consuls accused him of overcharging on fees for the tax forms he distributed, fees paid by litigants in his court, and ship registrations and inspections. They accused him of levying excessive fines, requiring extra passports and ship certificates for a fee, and taking advantage of the war to exact a fee from all ships that had previously docked in Spain. He had forced captains of outgoing merchant vessels to "borrow" sums of money from him payable upon their return, even if their cargoes were lost or seized, and for a fee he had permitted the export of prohibited merchandise such as wheat, even investing himself in the traffic in contraband.[67] The consuls complained that entry and exit fees for the port of Marseille were already too high, and that Valbelle was charging additional fees, pocketing the difference, and covering his tracks by refusing to give the ship captains receipts. His excessive demands were causing ships to avoid Marseille, thereby damaging its trade, lowering royal taxes, and damaging the crown's interests.[68]

On August 10, 1644, provincial intendant Champigny, a client of Alais, sent a report on Valbelle's corruption to Paris, ostensibly at the request of the consuls of Marseille. He repeated the charges of the January memoir, citing examples and adding verbatim accounts of his own interrogations of witnesses. Champigny estimated that Valbelle was making over 45,000 livres a year from his illegal activities at the expense of the crown, and wrote that "there is not in my opinion any official in France who has misused the authority of his office more nor exercised it more advantageously for those who are clients and business partners."[69] He declared that Valbelle's financial activities werre harming the interests of the crown.

The meticulous array of evidence is too overwhelming to deny the basic truth of these accusations: Valbelle was using his office of admiralty lieutenant for his personal profit and to reward his clients. He was able to purchase the fief of Montfuron, with annual revenues of 4,800 livres in the Basses-Alpes near Manosque, from the proceeds of his activities as admiralty lieutenant and his partnership in Marseille tax farming with Charles de Grimaldi, marquis de Régusse, and he was soon using the title of "sieur de Montfuron."[70] His gargantuan meals at the public trough had caused popular protest at Marseille in June 1644. Merchants and consumers widely detested the taxes he collected on merchandise. Angry citizens charged a conflict of interest when he ordered them to pay as admiralty lieutenant, with judicial appeal to the Parlement of Aix where his business partner, Régusse, sat as a president, and his brother Léon as a councillor. The Marseillais also charged his abuse of office in collecting excessive fees and fines.[71]

Valbelle's political enemies, governor Alais and intendant Champigny, sought to extract as much profit as possible from his embarrassment: they deluged the royal government at Paris with letters protesting his self-interest, unreliability, and unpopularity. They insisted that neither he nor his clients be allowed to hold office.[72] Valbelle retaliated in November 1644 when his young cousin, Jean-Philippe de Valbelle, Cosme's oldest son who was a galley captain, invaded the town hall of Marseille with fifty or sixty galley officers to stop the installation of Alais's appointees to municipal office.[73] Alais declared in a letter to Cardinal Mazarin on July 26, 1644, "I cannot be responsible for the future safety of Marseille, nor what may happen in the province, if these Valbelles in their insolence are protected at court, and if some example is not made to guarantee the service of the King."[74] Antoine de Valbelle demonstrates how easily a powerful provincial broker could become an overmighty subject.

The embezzlement of state funds, was considered corrupt then as now because it was a clear subversion of the public interest, an abuse of office for private gain by diverting royal funds into private hands, thereby damaging the interests of the crown. The same was true of forgery and fraudulent accounting.[75] Florent d'Argouges, marquis de Plessis, intendant in Burgundy from 1686 to 1694, was disgraced for misappropriating public funds, while intendant Michel Colbert at Alençon was imprisoned for fraudulent misrepresentation of mortgages on property. Charles Colbert de Saint Marc, intendant in Alsace, was recalled for financial mismanagement, while intendant de Demuin at La Rochelle was recalled for irregular accounts. Henri-Lambert, sieur d'Herbigny, marquis de Thibouville, intendant at Grenoble from 1679 to 1682, was recalled for irregularities in troop payment and troop billeting, including pocketing troop pay and threatening billeting to extort money from communities.[76] Graft and profiteering—taking advantage of the opportunities and resources of office to make money privately on the side by obtaining government supply contracts in partnership with someone else, taking kickbacks for awarding contracts, accepting pay-offs for appointments, investing in tax farming, lending money to the government or to tax farmers—was a shadowy area where it was difficult to draw the line between what was proper and improper. Many intendants engaged in these activities.[77] For example, Jacques Godard de Petit-Marais, intendant at Amiens in 1618 and in the army in Périgord in 1623, lent Antoine Feydeau, farmer general of the taxes of the *aides* and *gabelles*, the sum of 58,000 livres. Jean Baltazar and Le Picard de Perigny lent the royal government over 240,000 livres during their tenures in office as intendant and made a substantial profit.[78]

Jean Baltazar, a client of the governors of Languedoc, the Schombergs, was intendant in that province from 1643 to 1647. For a decade before he was officially appointed intendant, he acted as an agent for the Schombergs at Paris, and in this capacity became a major investor in a provincial tax farm, the *engagement* of the *equivalent*. He also lent money to the deputies of the Estates when they were in Paris during the 1630s, and was thus a creditor of the province for short-term loans. As intendant in Languedoc, Baltazar had ties with tax farmers and munitioneers. He became deeply involved in buying grain to send to the troops in Catalonia and was closely allied with local financiers who had purchased the office of treasurer of the Estates. He also had close ties with financiers at Montpellier, Béziers, and Narbonne. Baltazar had private interests in Languedoc even before he arrived in the province as intendant.[79]

Nicolas Arnoul is another example. Born into a family of Parisian royal secretaries, he was introduced into the service of Sublet de Noyers by his brother. He did so well that he attracted Richelieu's attention and was sent to Toulon to serve the Cardinal as a naval commissaire général. At Richelieu's death he refused to enter Mazarin's service, probably because he did not like him, and reentered the service of Sublet de Noyers, a mistake because Noyers was disgraced a few months later, forcing Arnoul into retirement. During the 1650s he mismanaged a modest family fortune. In debt for 100,000 livres by 1660, Arnoul saved something from the debacle by legally separating his wife's dowry of 90,000 livres from his own property six weeks before his creditors seized it to pay his debts. He was saved when he obtained the patronage of Colbert around 1664, probably through the good offices of a personal friend, François Berthelot, a cousin and client of the minister and an intendant of military supplies. Arnoul was named intendant of royal buildings at Fontainebleau, then sent to Marseille as intendant of the royal galleys in 1665. He served in this post with distinction. Eight years later he was sent to Toulon as naval intendant, but he soon had a stroke which left him paralyzed. He returned to Marseille to die.[80]

Arnoul was not a wealthy man, and his salary was modest. But on a salary of 12,000 livres a year with a large household to support, he paid off 32,000 livres to his Parisian creditors in three years and bought the fiefs of La Tour-Ronde and Vaucresson. He put most of his property in his wife's name to foil his creditors, and within ten years she had accumulated capital of 306,000 livres.[81] Where did Arnoul get this money? He supplemented his salary by taking advantage of his opportunities. He supplied saltpeter to the crown in partnership with an old friend from Paris, Jacques Lemasson, seigneur de La Fontaine, controller general of the salt tax for France.[82] His position as intendant of the royal galleys was useful in securing contracts. The intendants let contracts for public works projects—building canals, dredging rivers, enlarging ports, building or maintaining roads and royal fortifications—and they recommended and evaluated the contractors, a duty that provided financial and patronage opportunities.[83] Arnoul probably had a private arrangement with Henri Gérard de Bénat and the other contractors whom he recommended to Colbert to do the work of enlarging the port and city of Marseille.[84]

Arnoul had begun this project in 1666 at Colbert's request, and it took the rest of his tenure as intendant of the royal galleys at Marseille to complete it. His chief assistant was a Marseillais, Henri Gérard de Bénat. They met stubborn resistance from the city fathers. Members of the municipal council opposed razing the walls and enlarging the streets and harbor because the project involved demolishing the property of the wealthy merchants who controlled the city government. The engineering plans were contested and changed several times. There were charges that Arnoul and Bénat were taking kickbacks from construction, and relations with the consuls of Marseille became strained. However, Arnoul continued to work diligently with Colbert's full support, and when the improvements were finished they greatly improved life at Marseille.[85]

The accusations of the Marseillais had some foundation—Arnoul had purchased land in his wife's name bordering the harbor, and on this land he built private wharves and a waterfront complex known as the Domaine du Marquisat which was rented by his family to merchants and naval suppliers to the crown for decades after his death. Situated on the already pinched waterfront of France's largest port, such real estate was bound to have long-term commercial value. Thus, with Colbert's tacit permission, Arnoul lay the foundation of the family fortune. He had used his friend Henry de La Fond, war commissaire, to purchase part of the garden of the Benardines along the Marseille waterfront in 1669 to build a royal naval arsenal, then had La Fond buy him personally more of the garden for the ridiculously low sum of 15,600 livres. He built the waterfront complex on this land, which was valued at 143,500 livres in 1690.[86] Colbert, who was aware of Arnoul's activities, did not stop them, presumably because Arnoul was a competent intendant who had served the minister and the king well. His profits were discreet and moderate and did not endanger the crown's interests. But this was not always the case.

Jean-Baptiste de Brodart indulged his propensity for graft imaginatively in a variety of ways as intendant of the galleys at Marseille from 1674 to 1684 (he was Arnoul's successor), until he was dismissed by Colbert's son, the marquis de Seignelay, for corruption. For example, in 1675, Brodart was authorized to build two flûtes, military supply ships, at a cost of 20,000 to 25,000 livres each. After inordinate delay, Colbert discovered that Brodart had instead built two fighting ships of fifty and fifty-four guns each at a cost of 150,000 livres. Brodart spent over 60,000 livres in freight costs in the same year, although he was only authorized to spend 45,000 livres. In 1677, Colbert caught Brodart cheating the crown on freight services by submitting bills for the use of two flûtes of 500 tons each when he had actually shipped the supplies on less expensive ships of 200 and 400 tons each. In 1675 and 1676 Brodart emptied the galley stores at Marseille and shipped them to Messina in Sicily, sending far more than was needed, then refilled the stores in profitable collusion with the supplier, a man named Creissel, who was later shown to be Brodart's business partner and associate. Creissel, whose prices were higher than those of any other Marseille merchant, supplied a large percentage of the galleys' supplies, often using other names, and Brodart frequently accepted delivery of goods he jointly owned. A little later, he shipped large quantities of bad food and wine overseas. Colbert was constantly reprimanding him for his "inaccuracies."[87] Brodart retained his office for ten years, despite his indiscretions, because he was energetic, competent, and he did get things done, if in his own way at his own time. He had also been serving Colbert as a naval intendant since 1666, and the minister may have felt some obligation because of his long service.[88] Seignelay, Colbert's son, felt no such obligation. In a weak position at court, the object of rumors about corruption, Seignelay refused to be compromised: Brodart's profiteering had become blatant and he was dismissed in 1684, the year after Colbert's death. Brodart lacked influential connections at court—he did not have Seignelay's trust—and he lacked the rank and well-known family name that might have saved him. Moreover, his illicit activities were indiscreet and excessive.

In general, dismissal for corruption in the form of profiteering or graft depended on how greedy and notorious an official was. If he had made a large fortune in a short time and became known for his excesses, provoking public censure and protest, then he risked dismissal, even prosecution, depending on his political connections, especially if he was incompetent at his job. Intendant Jacques La Grange, for example, was recalled from Alsace in 1698, after serving there for twenty-five years, because he had made several million livres in partnership with army suppliers. His profiteering had become so notorious that it was impossible for the royal government to ignore.[89] Valbelle had the same problem, but his connections and the political situation in Provence permitted him to avoid dismissal or prosecution, although he came close to both.[90] Arnoul escaped censure because his profiteering was discreet and moderate, and because he was a competent intendant. Brodart was also competent at his job, which was why he lasted as long as he did, but his corruption became too blatant to ignore. Graft that was extensive enough to become well known was presumed to interfere with an official's duties and lessen royal revenues, thus damaging the crown's interests.

Palamède de Forbin was dismissed as governor of Provence by Louis XI in 1483 because of popular protest about his greed. First president of the Aix Chambre des Comptes and chief minister of René of Anjou, count of Provence, Palamède de Forbin had served as an envoy to the French king, Louis XI, in 1475 and had accompanied the count to Lyon for an interview with the king in 1476; it was probably then that he agreed to defend French interests. He convinced the count to leave Provence to an elderly, childless nephew, Charles, comte Du Maine, rather than to a young and vigorous grandson, because the nephew was disposed to leave the county at his death to the king of France, Louis XI, his cousin. When René of Anjou died in the summer of 1480, leaving the county to his nephew, Palamède de Forbin openly joined the French party and paid a visit to the French court.

Charles, comte Du Maine, made a tour of his new county and then died conveniently at Marseille in December 1481, leaving Provence to the French king as agreed. Having acted as a broker in securing the legacy, Palamède de Forbin was immediately rewarded. Royal letters were issued naming him governor of Provence, and he returned to Aix around Christmastime to convoke an Estates to sit the next month. He arrested the leader of the opposition, François de Luxembourg, a cousin of the late count, before the Estates sat, then convinced the deputies to ratify the treaty of annexation. When the Estates had gone home, Palamède toured the county to consolidate his position.

He also conducted extensive confiscations of the lands of his political opponents. He began with the county of Martigues belonging to François de Luxembourg, and distributed these lands among his family and clients to whom he also gave royal offices. He took the title of Grand Seneschal for himself. Provençal complaints about his greed became so vociferous, however, that Louis XI had to demand an accounting. High royal officials had heavy responsibilities, and fewer excesses were tolerated from them, especially those attracting notoriety. The king became convinced that Palamède was enriching himself and his dependents at the expense of the province, the royal domaine, and the royal treasury. Moreover, Louis XI did not want to lose his tenuous grip on a new province because of the excesses and unpopularity of a corrupt governor who was his agent, so he sacked him. Accusing Palamède of "malversations and particularism," the king revoked his governorship and sent him on a diplomatic mission to Florence. Jean, maréchal de Baudrincourt, governor of Burgundy, was sent to Provence to act as governor in his place.[91] Palamede de Forbin had performed a useful service for the French king in acting as a provincial broker to secure the annexation of Provence, but his greed, attracting public censure, lost him the king's favor and his office of governor.

Patronage was the standard form of recruitment to office until the nineteenth century.[92] The intendants, for example, promoted the careers of family members whenever they could. Nicolas Arnoul's son, Pierre, followed him as intendant of the royal galleys at Marseille and as naval intendant at Toulon. Pierre Cardin Lebret's son followed him as intendant in Provence and first president of the Parlement of Aix.[93] Claude Bouchu's son was named intendant in the Dauphiné through ministerial protection and his father's influence.[94] Twenty intendants serving Colbert were the sons and grandsons of intendants who had served Richelieu and Mazarin.[95] Army intendant Carlier had a brother, Pierre, who was a clerk in the war department, probably through his influence. Army intendant Jacques Charuel thanked Louvois in 1672 for the appointment of a nephew to the regiment of Picardy, and requested the office of *aide-major* for another relative, while Etienne Carlier asked that a Benedictine abbey in Roussillon be given to his brother, Dom Georges. In the same year, army intendant Michel Le Peletier asked Le Tellier's protection for the sieur de Courcelles, a relative who was a war commissaire, while intendant Louis Robert thanked Louvois for giving the abbey of Daimpon to his brother.[96]

Patronage as a means of recruitment and advancement was considered corrupt only when it resulted in the appointment of men of decidedly inferior ability because they were relatives, clients, or favorites. It was then known as the abuse of nepotism of favoritism, the excessive or improper use of influence for personal interest—patronage was considered corrupt when it saddled the state with obviously incompetent officials.[97] The abuses of nepotism and favoritism were not, however, consistently characteristic of patronage as a means of recruitment and advancement. Men of ability were recruited under this system. For instance, the faults of Richelieu's irresponsible nephew, Pont de Courlay, were balanced by the ability of his other nephew, Maillé-Brézé, a national hero who was as brilliant in naval administration as he was in warfare.[98] The faults of Mazarin's brother, Michel, archbishop of Aix, who was given to hasty words and fits of anger, were balanced by an old friend, Cardinal Bichi, bishop of Carpentras, a skillful diplomat whom Mazarin used frequently in negotiations.[99] Patronage as a means of recruitment and advancement allowed the entry and promotion of talented non-nobles, albeit not many, for instance, Claude Boisot, the chevalier Paul, Jean Hérauld de Gourville, and Abraham Du Quesne.[100] Richelieu, Mazarin, and Colbert were notorious for their nepotism, for promoting and enriching their relatives while in office, but they also dismissed relatives who were a public embarrassment and political liability because of their incompetence: Richelieu, for instance, dismissed Pont de Courlay as general of the galleys at Marseille, and recalled his brother, Alphonse, as ambassador at Rome.[101] More often, however, incompetent relatives were quietly transferred elsewhere in the government to posts that demanded less expertise.

To return to our original question, Did traditional political clientelism produce a high rate of political corruption? It would be more accurate to say that a failure to distinguish clearly between public and private interests—a confusion of public and private interests—intensified by primitive methods of administration and clientelism produced a high rate of corruption. Clientelism contributed to the problem of corruption, which had other causes. By early modern standards, many illegal practices were not considered corrupt. Some modern abuses—embezzlement of state funds, forgery, and fraudulent accounting at the expense of the state—were considered corrupt in the seventeenth century. But other practices fell into a gray area in which each case had to be decided on its merits, for instance, accepting gifts, taking advantage of financial opportunities while in office, and appointing dependents to office. These practices became the abuses of bribery, graft and profiteering, nepotism and favoritism, and they were considered corrupt when they subverted the interests of the crown. But it was not always easy to determine what damaged the interests of the crown. The definition of corruption varied over time and depended on the individual, the nature of his activities, and the problems and image of the government. Excesses that attracted public knowledge and censure often invited dismissal for corruption, although other considerations determined whether this actually occurred—family, rank, patronage connections, reputation for competence or incompetence, and the political situation at the time. Contemporaries almost certainly considered the political conflict produced by clientelism a more serious problem than its tendency toward corruption.

Critics of political clientelism have condemned its encouragement of short-term political goals, its channeling of state resources into the hands of special interest groups rather than into long-term projects for general growth and development, and its restriction of political participation to a narrow, self-serving elite pursuing its own goals at the expense of broader social and national interests. Critics charge that political clientelism produced political exclusivity and government unresponsiveness to the public welfare.

This book argues, however, that patron-broker-client ties and networks enabled the early modern French monarchy to integrate regional and national elites. It may have been selective integration, but in a traditional elitist society, it was integration of those who counted, the ruling elite. Moreover, traditional political clientelism was adaptable to social and political change. It easily accommodated itself to changing conditions and structures, for instance, to the development of a new form of political organization, an early modern bureaucracy. The early modern French state emerged from a clientelist system, aspects of which continued to survive and flourish within the new bureaucratic state. Political clientelism in early modern France created an environment in which constructive change could take place, and accommodated itself to that change. It may be argued that clientelism does not actually encourage or promote long-term growth or development because it has a tendency to encourage special interests and short-term gains, but it is going too far to say that clientelism is actually resistant to long-term growth, stifling political development and encouraging stagnation and immobility. This was not the case in early modern France where the flexibility of clientelism made it adaptable to political change, perhaps more so than government by formal political institutions. In fact, patron-broker-client ties and networks were often used as an alternative to ineffectual or uncooperative institutions.

While this book does not deny the flaws in clientelism as a political system, it emphasizes that clientelism also had positive, constructive aspects, encouraging political cohesion and contributing positively to the process of statebuilding. Traditional political clientelism was fluid and dynamic: new clients were easily attached, bringing with them new resources, and they were easily detached if the relationship was not a success; so were old clients who had become a political liability. The easy process of combination and recombination allowed the crown to accommodate to new alliances and power figures on the regional level, to seek the political advantage, to reconcile competing regional interests, and to buy off political enemies. Patron-broker-client ties and networks were used to achieve regional-national integration in states with weak central governments and strong regionalism such as early modern France. These ties and networks allowed the effective combination of personal loyalty and the material adhesive of royal patronage in an age when more impersonal or abstract attachments would have been difficult to maintain: they were a loose, flexible way of attaching powerful nobles and independent institutions and officials to a central government too weak to demand or enforce tighter attachments.

In surviving the feudal disintegration and political anarchy of the late Middle Ages, the French nobility had sharpened their political skills and developed historical experience in playing off one set of political forces against another. The result was a traditional ruling elite whose political sophistication qualified them for participation in the national arena, even if their home base was backward and primitive. Moreover, at a certain stage of political development reached by the mid-sixteenth century in France, provincial power figures had to find a Paris patron and access to royal patronage and the national political arena in order to continue exercising power at home. In this way members of the provincial ruling elite were integrated into the national political scene, and the national ruling elite was able to mobilize provincial resources. Provincial brokers thus became important political links and integrative agents.

Social science observers of clientelism, interested in its role in the political development of new states in the twentieth century, have tended to lack historical perspective or an understanding of clientelism as it existed in traditional historical societies. They have tended to use nineteenth- and twentieth-century models of traditional clientelism, that is, models extrapolated from modern societies with traditional characteristics.[102] These models have then been projected backward in time.[103] Critics who emphasize the flaws in clientelism often observe it from the vantage point of a more advanced political system with different values—a modern mass participation system—and apply these values to less advanced states. It is easy in this case to dismiss clientelism as backward or defective, and to ignore its positive aspects. Factionalism and corruption, the underside of clientele politics, were always a problem. In general, however, a system of reciprocal, unequal relationships as a method of government suited a traditional, hierarchical society such as early modern France very well.

Critics and advocates of clientelism as a political system may not be as irreconcilably opposed as they may first appear. This book suggests that the overall political effects of clientelism depend upon the level of the state's political development: the integrative aspects of clientelism encourage political cohesion and unity in less advanced states; the flaws of conflict, corruption, short-term goals, and exclusivity inhibit political functioning in more advanced states. Clientelism as a political system has both integrative and divisive effects, and is capable of producing both stability and instability—this duality is one of its basic characteristics. The overall effect of clientelism, whether cohesive or divisive, depends upon the state's political development, that is, the strength of its central government, the independence of its regional elites and institutions, and the extent of its political integration. In an unintegrated state with a weak central government and independent regional notables and institutions such as sixteenth-century France, the advantages of clientelism as a political system outweighed the disadvantages. But as the central government became stronger in the late seventeenth century and regionalism declined, the disadvantages became more serious. The political effects of clientelism were increasingly negative, causing more conflict than cohesion, and the inherently divisive aspects of clientelism began to outweigh its integrative aspects. The looseness and flexibility of personal attachments became less attractive because they generated a high rate of political conflict. Corruption was another inherent problem. As a result the state began to search for a more impersonal, professional basis for administrative relationships, and a new bureaucratic form of political organization began to emerge in seventeenth-century France.[104] Clientelism, however, had set the stage for the emergence of this new royal bureaucracy and produced the political stability that had helped make it possible.

Clientelism and Change

Observers of clientelism have remarked that it reflects the changing social and political structures in the society and state of which it is a part. Clientelism changes when the underlying structures of society change, although its basic corps of identifying characteristics remains the same.[105] Social science observers of clientelism, however, have made only sketchy attempts to describe the changes in clientelism over time, and these have been flawed by overgeneralization. Charles Tilly has noted that "the analysis of political development has had about the same relationship to historical experience as a dog on a long leash to the tree at the other end of the leash. The dog can roam in almost any direction. He can even get the illusion of rushing off on his own. But let him rush too far, too fast and his collar will jerk him back; it may even knock the wind out of him. Some political scientists want to break the leash or at least move the tree."[106]

Historians can make a valuable contribution to the interdisciplinary literature on political clientelism by investigating its changes over time. Is there a pattern to these changes? Is there an evolutionary pattern of development in clientelism? Does this pattern parallel the transition from traditional to modern societies? Few observers have tried to tackle the difficult problem of describing the stages in the evolution of clientelism, or its relation to the levels of development in the state and society of which it is a part.[107] Most studies are in their infancy for lack of evidence. Historical studies of clientelism may indicate if, indeed, a general evolutionary scheme is possible or at least clear up some of the confusion surrounding the nature of changes in clientelism over time.

Feudalism was transformed into clientelism, into what the English have called bastard feudalism, by the early fifteenth century.[108] Clientelism was a much blurred and bowdlerized form of feudalism: man-to-man personal ties of loyalty and mutual exchanges of service still existed, but they had changed.[109] Roland Mousnier and J. Russell Major have noted that the patron-client bond was not feudal, although it was a feudal legacy, because there was no oath of homage and no exchange of fiefs in the patron-client bond, choice of master was free, and services were not defined.[110] Sidney Tarrow has remarked that "observers often confuse the clientele relationship with feudalism; in reality, it is quite different. In a feudal society, social relations were formalized, hierarchical, and legally sanctioned. A logical pyramid of mutual obligations was built-up which was congruent with the requirements of the society for defense and solidarity ... *clientelismo*, however, is shifting and informal, and has no institutional recognition in concrete institutions."[111] Peter Lewis has noted that the functions of the two systems remain the same, that is, the acquisition of service in return for reward, but they differ in the form of reward and the means of ensuring that service is done in return for it. Land was replaced by money payments; tenure and neighborhood were mingled with more flexible loyalties engendered by power and ability; and the use of homage and fealty, the feudal contract, declined. He also notes that "while bastard feudalism has not been well-studied for late medieval France, it would appear to have been much the same as in England."[112]

There were important changes, however, in the size and composition of clienteles in the late sixteenth century during the Wars of Religion. Julian Dent has observed that "the history of France in the later sixteenth and earlier seventeenth centuries could be written, on one level at least, as a history of the changing phenomenon of the clientele."[113] Noble military clientage began to decline in these decades. Robert Harding has noted that the military clienteles of the provincial governors and lieutenants general, in particular their large gendarmes companies, began to decline in size during the late sixteenth century from lack of royal patronage and financial and political support from the Valois monarchy. The governors' clienteles deteriorated into regional religious parties, either Catholic or Calvinist, as France slipped into civil war. This trend was never reversed, and great noble clienteles after 1600 were less military and more political in composition and function. The decline of the gendarmerie had far-reaching consequences for French society because it meant the end of legitimate military clientage for the provincial nobility.[114] This trend is demonstrated by comparing the membership of great noble clienteles in the sixteenth century with those in the seventeenth century.

Clients of the ducs de La Trémoille, governors of Poitou in the sixteenth century, fit into four categories: household; estate and financial personnel; military; and local officials. Household clients included many of the gentleman officials who administered the family's lands and revenues and some domestic servants. Estate and financial clients included their estate administrators; seigneurial judges and officials; lawyers and accountants; financial agents and revenue collectors; tax farmers; supervisors of the family's seigneurial rights and governments; and their numerous assistants. Military clients of the La Trémoille included provincial nobles who were governors of the family's twenty-six castles and fortified châteaux; their gendarmes and guard companies; and the lieutenants and captains of various royal fortresses and fortified cities in Poitou and the west. Most of their military clients were either under their personal command or defended their life and châteaux. They had fewer political clients, who were usually local officials in the regions where the family owned land; the functions of these officials touched in some way upon the family property.[115] Centered on the family and its property, the La Trémoille clientele had many characteristics of a great noble household and was typical of great noble clienteles in the sixteenth century.

Military clients played an important role in sixteenth-century great noble clienteles, for example, that of Louis de Bourbon, prince de Condé. He was a Huguenot convert and governor of Picardy in the 1560s and 1570, who led his clients and supporters into revolt against the Catholic monarchy. Condé headed an extensive military clientele drawn from the provincial nobility, whose members included the lieutenant general of Picardy, various town governors and royal fortress commanders, members of his gendarmes and guard companies, members of his household, and some of the regional nobility who answered his call to fight against the crown. Needless to say, not all of Condé's supporters during the Wars of Religion were his clients—many followed him because they fought for his cause—and they were not always obedient; they often deserted his banner because of conflicting personal and regional interests.[116]

The membership of great noble clienteles changed during the Wars of Religion. The duc de Mayenne, for example, governor of Burgundy during these years, recruited numerous political clients—magistrates in the higher and lower provincial courts; mayors, municipal councillors and officials at Dijon, Mâcon, Autun, and other important towns; deputies and officers in the Burgundian Estates; tax farmers and officials.[117] We have already seen that in the early seventeenth century the governors of Provence, Guyenne, and Burgundy, the comte d'Alais, the ducs d'Epernon, and the princes de Condé maintained numerous political clients among whom were some intendants.[118]

The politicization of great noble clienteles accelerated in response to the statebuilding efforts of Richelieu, Mazarin, Colbert, and other royal ministers, who created and used extensive ministerial clienteles to help govern distant provinces. In response to the new ministerial administrative clienteles, great nobles recruited even more political clients. The rapid development of administrative clienteles and the growing politicization of great noble clienteles changed the nature of the patron-client bond in the seventeenth century. Clients were no longer asked by their patrons to provide primarily military service. They were increasingly expected to provide political and administrative services that promoted different values—they were expected to offer their patrons practical assistance in exercising power and governing in exchange for patronage. Political performance was emphasized in these exchanges, and clients were motivated to perform by promises of material rewards that had to be delivered for the relationship to continue. Widespread use of clients in this way helped to change the nature of the patron-client relationship by politicizing it, that is, by giving it a political tone or character. The general characteristics of these ties and networks remained the same, but within a basic corps of identifying characteristics the trend toward politicization produced a more impersonal, performance-oriented, less binding patron-client relationship. This was a general trend that began in the late sixteenth and continued into the eighteenth century, reflecting the impact of national statebuilding.

Patron-client relationships became more politicized as the early modern state developed. These changes in the nature of the patron-client bond were part of the process of political modernization that France underwent in the seventeenth century. Political scientists have noted that ties of solidarity and loyalty are weaker in modern political machines than in traditional clienteles, that materialistic rewards are more important in modern machines, that personal ties are more politicised, and that factionalism increases.[119] During the seventeenth century French patron-client relationships became more brittle, impersonal, materialistic, less durable and binding, more like modern machine relationships. This general change in the nature of the patron-client bond can be illustrated by comparing the patron-client relationships of fifteenth- and early sixteenth-century French seigneurs with those of the late seventeenth century. The earlier patron-client relationships had a more intimate, personal, extended household quality to them than the brisk, businesslike later relationships.

The entourage of Guillaume de Murol, a small seigneur in Auvergne at the beginning of the fifteenth century, was composed of his relatives, household servants, vassals, and clients.[120] Murol's relatives included a brother and the in-laws from two marriages. His household servants included a manager, several men and women domestic servants, and skilled workers who usually came from his fiefs.[121] Because of the plurality of homages, vassalage had already lost its vitality and Murol owed homage for his fief of Murol to Henri de Latour, bishop of Auvergne; homage for his fief of Chambon to the Dauphin of France; and homage for his fiefs of Saint Amant and Vialle to the seigneurs de Latour. In addition, he was closely attached to the comtes d'Auvergne, although he did not owe them homage.[122] He had originally been their client, but when the last comte had entered the service of the duc de Berry, he had entered the Latour clientele. Client ties were already replacing vassalage ties in the early fifteenth century.[123] Two families of noble vassals swore homage to Murol, the Bedos and the La Roche de Murol, who held land from him and were his clients; the latter family died out at the end of the century and willed their land to him. Murol had other vassals also, both noble and roturier, who held land from him or defended his château.[124]

Murol had a small circle of clients whom he trusted to perform various services such as buying livestock, initiating lawsuits, conducting negotiations, perhaps for a dowry, and going on missions, for instance, escorting family members. Murol's six most frequently mentioned clients were Guillaume Martin, his tenant at La Chassagne in the fief of Murol who was receiver and then procureur of this fief; Jean Chapus, the priest of Chambon who became receiver for the fief; Jean Chastres, a priest who was the vicar at Murol and went on occasional missions; Geraud Mesclart, doyen of the chapter of the church at Port à Clermont who lived in Murol's household, played an active role in administering his fief at Saint Amant, lent Murol money, and was his chief negotiator; Bernard Renoux from Clermont-Ferrand who was in the service of Madame de Murol; and Louis de Montvallat who was a noble from a seigneurial family in the Haute-Auvergne and may have been a relative or friend.[125] And there were his vassals, the Bedos and the La Roche de Murol, who were also his clients. Murol's clients, therefore, were either employees who had been given tasks in addition to their usual function as part of his entourage, household, or lands, or they were men who had other ties to him such as vassals, family, or friends. Murol's clients provided him with loyalty and service and received in return his protection and material assistance as the seigneur de Murol, including gifts in money and in kind and maintenance.[126] All of Guillaume de Murol's clients had a close, personal relationship with him.

The clients of Gilles de Gouberville, a petit seigneur of the Contentin peninsula in the mid-sixteenth century, enjoyed the same type of relationship. They included Lejaye, the maître d'hôtel of his household on his fief of Gouberville, who traveled with him and managed his nine men and nine women domestic servants, many of whom had also served his father; two personal companions, his half brother, Symmonet, and Langlois de Tréauville, known as Canteype, from an impoverished noble family; Cantepye's wife, Guillemette, Gouberville's illegitimate half sister who ran the household because he never married; two illegitimate half brothers, Noel and Jacques; messire Tronde, the vicar and later the curé of Gouberville; the vicar of Ménesqueville in Eure; and the curé of Russy in the Calvados.[127] These clients had a close, personal relationship with their patron as part of his household or lands.

Both Murol and Gouberville, however, were small rural seigneurs who headed farm households. Were the patron-client relationships of great seigneurs who had large households less personal and affectionate? Having one hundred clients in contrast to six or nine inevitably made many of these relationships less personal and more remote. But as we have seen, the patron-client relationships of the ducs de La Trémoille in sixteenth-century Poitou still had a personal, extended household quality much like those of Murol and Gouberville. They were not politicized, nor was the military clientele of the prince de Condé in Picardy. These clienteles can be compared with seventeenth-century administrative clienteles such as those of the Valbelles, Oppède, Bouchu, and the Boisots. These seventeenth-century clienteles were more politicized and functioned as political machines in helping their patrons to govern. They had a pragmatic, performance-oriented quality lacking in earlier noble clienteles, and they were more impersonal.

Colbert's relationship with his intendants in the late seventeenth century is another example. He corresponded with an extensive network of intendant-clients scattered throughout France, and his letters have a professional, politicized, businesslike tone absent from the letters of his administrative counterparts a century earlier. The minister was obsessed with promptness and efficiency, admonishing his clients to perform their administrative tasks with dispatch and care. He issued orders in the name of the king, and his clients wrote meticulous reports on their progress in executing his instructions, reaffirming their obedience to him and to the king. Their letters were brisk and to the point with little rhetoric and even less client language. Oppède's concern for detail and statistics in his letters to Colbert, for instance, recall the letters of Napoleonic prefects, and are very different from the casually disordered letters of his predecessors.

On December 25, 1671, Colbert wrote the comte de Grignan that "the aforementioned letters and orders will be sent to you by the first mail, and I think it superfluous to urge you to be punctual and exact in executing them, knowing with what zeal you apply yourself to the King's service."[128] Colbert on November 21 had written the comte de Grignan that "the King approves of the choice you have made of sieur Gerard to preside at the General

Assembly, and as success rests entirely on your efforts, His Majesty does not doubt that you will try to give Him greater proofs of your zeal. But I must say to you that His Majesty is beginning to remark that Provence is the only assembly which delays giving Him satisfaction. The examples of the assemblies last year should serve as a powerful reason to bring the deputies to do their duty."[129] A week later on November 27, Colbert wrote Grignan that "I don't doubt His Majesty appreciated learning that the deputies of the communities have all assured you of their zeal and obedience to His wishes. But it is necessary to oblige them to put their beautiful words into practice and vote what the King wants."[130] Colbert wrote a similar letter to intendant Rouillé at the General Assembly on November 17, 1682.[131] The tone of Louvois's administrative letters was the same.

Nicolas Arnoul assured Colbert on December 18, 1666, "I will do my best to accomplish what it pleases you to command me to do."[132] On August 7, he had written that "I pray God I shall cease to live if I fault Your service and the weight of my obligations."[133] Oppède wrote Colbert that "my first thought upon returning to this province was to swear to You a perfect attachment to the honor of Your protection by the punctual execution of Your orders."[134] The chevalier Paul wrote the minister that "I beg You very humbly to be persuaded that I have no wishes other than those of His Majesty and You, and I await the honor of Your orders, which I will always obey with great submission and respect."[135] Janson-Forbin assured Colbert that "I receive Your orders with submission, and I shall be all my life with dependence and respect."[136]

The brisk, businesslike tone of these letters of Colbert and his clients contrasts sharply with the personal, emotionally effusive tone of the client letters of Guillaume Du Vair and Louis de Bourbon, prince de Condé, a century earlier. On May 26, 1600, for example, Guillaume Du Vair, first president of the Parlement of Aix and provincial intendant, wrote his patron, Henri IV, to request royal letters for the son of president Coriolis to succeed him in office. He wrote that granting this request "is a thing worthy of a great King, especially characteristic of the singular goodness which is natural to Your Majesty, to recognize the service of the fathers in their children."[137] In a letter on April 12, 1605, Du Vair asked permission to come to court, "to humbly kiss the hands of Your Majesty."[138] In a letter to Henri IV on March 13, 1602, to request reversion letters for another president's son, Du Vair wrote that "Du Chaine has long and faithfully served You in an important post. Let him feel the effects of Your goodness ... I take this occasion to remind You of the faithful affection I have always employed in Your service."[139] Du Vair wrote on another occasion that "I very humbly kiss the hands of Your Majesty.... I am the least worthy of Your favor."[140]

Louis de Bourbon, prince de Condé and governor of Picardy, on June 26, 1558, wrote Madeleine de Savoie, duchesse de Montmorency and wife of the Old Constable to whom he was attached, "Madame, in addition to the infinite number of obligations through which I have been for so long tied to you, the benefit I have received from the augmentation of my health in this your house ... makes the duty and obedience which I want to show you all my life grown and be more deeply felt by me".[141] It was common in the sixteenth century to send gifts, for instance, swans, hunting birds, and rare foodstuffs, to patrons with florid letters of gratitude for their protection.[142]

These letters of Du Vair and Condé have a personal tone of affection, an abundance of flattery, and an emotional effusiveness lacking in the letters of Colbert and his clients. Taking into account the fact that Du Vair was writing to the king, not his minister, that Condé was writing to his patron's wife, even taking into account temperamental differences—Colbert was notorious for his coldness—it is still clear that there had been a change in the style and tone of patron-client letters by the late seventeenth century, and changes in style often reflect changes in values. Patron-client ties had become more politicized, impersonal, and pragmatic, less emotional and affectionate by the end of the seventeenth century.[143] Several causes of this change have already been discussed, such as the decline in military clientage and the rise of administrative clienteles. Other causes include the decrease in personal violence, the creation of Louis XIV's court at Versailles, and the decline in great noble households.

A decrease in violence in daily life in the seventeenth century encouraged a weakening in the bond of personal loyalty between patrons and clients. These relationships in the fifteenth and sixteenth centuries had exhibited more intense personal loyalty because the feudal legacy was stronger and physical force was still a primary means of achieving personal and political goals. A feudal vassal owed his lord military service and loyalty until death. Vassalage was disappearing in the fifteenth century, but loyalty until death remained a feudal ideal in clientelism, and conditions were turbulent enough that loyalty until death could be demanded from clients. However, there was a general decline in the use of physical force as a means of achieving goals in the seventeenth century—it was still a violent age but less so than in previous centuries—and the likelihood of a patron demanding loyalty until death from a client also declined.[144] By the late seventeenth century as the royal government became stronger, it was no longer necessary or even likely that a client would have to fight to the death for a patron. The decrease in violence in daily life permitted a general loosening in personal ties of loyalty between patron and client.

Louis XIV created an elaborate royal court at Versailles in the 1680s, revolving around him as the Sun King. He demanded permanent residence by the great nobles of France and their exclusive loyalty, which weakened other bonds between nobles. Roland Mousnier has noted that "the State of the Absolute Monarchy disrupted the seigneurial regime by constantly insinuating its justice, its laws, its fisc, its army between the nobles."[145] The Sun King as the embodiment of the French state became the primary focus of political loyalty. Roland Mousnier has elsewhere observed that "it was the State which became the master, and the subjects of the State the fidèles. Utilizing the tie of fidelity in this general and permanent fashion, Louis XIV, in effect, killed it, integrating it into another relationship that the emotion of fidelity had to nourish, the subject-state relationship."[146] Mousnier has also noted, "It seems that, little by little, these master-fidèle and protector-créature relationships, while still existing, declined after the Fronde. Louis XIV tried to be the only master and to tie himself directly to all his subjects as fidèles. To a large enough extent, it seems that he succeeded, and as he was the State-incarnate, his subjects began to acquire the habit of fidelity to the State, instrument of the national will. This change continued in the eighteenth century."[147] Personal loyalties tended to be transferred to Louis XIV as the embodiment of the French state, and a client served a patron who was a royal minister by serving the King, his master, as the personification of the state. Obedience to a ministerial patron became equated with obedience to the King. The letters of Colbert's Provençal clients, for instance, are filled with affirmations of their loyalty to the minister and the King, their obedience in executing the orders of the minister and the King, and their good intentions for the royal service rather than for Colbert's personal service. The use of the term créature, so prevalent under Richelieu, disappears from the letters of Colbert's clients: how could a client be Colbert's créature when their mutual task was to serve Louis XIV as the embodiment of the French state?

Patron-client ties, however, did not disappear from the political scene in the seventeenth century: these ties were not "killed" as they became increasingly politicized.[148] They were not consumed or absorbed by the demands of the developing early modern state and the demands of Louis XIV for exclusive loyalty. Noble clientage changed during the seventeenth century, but it did not disappear. Administrative clienteles, for example, flourished, although great noble clienteles began to decline in size and political importance: they became smaller and lost political influence during the reign of Louis XIV, as we shall see, although they did not disappear entirely. Patron-client ties and networks continued to exist in a looser form that was more pragmatic and political, less intensely personal and emotional. This change permitted the allegiance to the monarchy and dual loyalty evident in the letters of Colbert's clients: it allowed loyalty to the king as the embodiment of the French state to exist simultaneously with loyalty to an individual patron. Patron-client ties were transformed rather than weakened, adjusting to changes in French government and to the development of an absolute monarchy by assuming a less binding form compatible with other loyalties. It is a mistake to view this transformation negatively as a process of dilution or death—it was rather a constructive adaptation.

Medieval society of the upper ranks had centered on the great noble household, with its mob of servants and dependents. Clientelism in its language reflected the master-servant relationship of this patriarchical society in which the master or lord was responsible for the safety and welfare of his household, which in turn owed him loyalty, obedience, and service. The decrease in the size of great noble households during the reign of Louis XIV, however, sapped traditional values of loyalty, obedience, and service that were also client values. Young nobles were no longer sent as pages to great noble households. They were educated in schools where they learned other values, and those without prospects who wanted to advance in the world entered the service of a royal minister, that is, the royal bureaucracy, or the professions, rather than the domestic service of a great lord.[149] The result was a weakening of the patron-client bond.

The model for *grandes maisons*, large noble households, was the household of the king, the largest in France.[150] Henri III, for example, had a household of 1,064 persons between 1572 and 1574, and 1,096 in 1584, not including his guards who numbered 2,650 in 1579.[151] Henri IV was served by about 1,500 persons in his household not including his guards.[152] The households of close members of the royal family were nearly as large. The household of Henri III's brother, François, duc d'Anjou, was the second largest in France. In 1572, when he was seventeen, his household numbered 262. It increased to 415 in 1575, and in the next year when he received the duchies of Anjou, Touraine, and Berry, it numbered 942. In 1578, when he formally allied himself to William of Orange, it reached its greatest size—1,123—but had declined to 418 in 1584 with the decline in his political fortunes.[153] In 1606 Marie de Medici maintained a household of 464.[154] From 1622 to 1625, the household of Henriette-Marie, the unmarried daughter of Henri IV, numbered 192.[155]

The households of sixteenth-century great nobles were smaller copies of royal households.[156] The governors of major provinces, for example, could easily have 100 salaried individuals on their staff, the majority stationed at one or perhaps two provincial châteaux. The governor of Champagne had a staff of 113 on his account books in 1542. The governor of Dauphiné had 159 in 1556 and 164 in 1561. Another governor of Champagne had 96 in 1570.[157] The households of the ducs de La Trémoille increased from 45 in 1486 to over 90 in the 1530s.[158] The households of the Albrets, kings of Navarre, had 136 paid employees in 1529 and 138 in 1569.[159] The household of François Gouffier, seigneur de Crèvecoeur, a grand seigneur of Picardy who was governor of Compiègne, had 49 servants in 1593, which did not include his *maison militaire*, or guards and armed retainers.[160] The seigneur de Crévecoeur had a lower rank than the Albrets so his household was smaller: household size strictly followed rank in a status-conscious society.[161] Many sixteenth-century provincial governors and great nobles also kept a Paris townhouse where they deposited a skeleton staff and perhaps a few relatives and where they occasionally visited.[162]

Great nobles continued to maintain large households in the seventeenth century. For example, Bernard de La Valette, duc d'Epernon and governor of Guyenne in 1660, had 73 servants in his household, which did not include his guards.[163] Léonard-Philibert, vicomte de Pompadour and lieutenant general in the Limousin from 1621 to 1634, maintained a household of about 100 at his château of Pompadour, and Charles de Lorraine, duc de Guise and governor of Provence, kept a household of about 100 at his Marseille townhouse in 1631.[164] The household of Richelieu's nephew, the marquis de Pontcourlay, who was general of the royal galleys at Marseille, had 29 domestic servants in 1636, 44 when the 16 in his wife's service were included; this was after 15 servants had been dismissed to reduce expenses and did not include his guards.[165]

Great nobles and important officials such as provincial governors kept a company of guards, either mounted or on foot, usually about 40 men but often more, many of whom were noble. Governors also commanded provincial ordinance or gendarmes companies and often maintained their own regiment as well. These troops were drawn in part from the provincial nobility. Jean-Louis de La Valette, duc d'Epernon and governor of Guyenne, kept a company of 40 guards, about half of whom were noble.[166] The maison militaire of the duc de Gramont from 1650 to 1675 included 40 mounted guards, 1 mounted drummer, 2 mounted trumpeters, and several aides-de-camp.[167] Cardinal Richelieu maintained a household of 180 persons and 140 horses in 1639, which did not include a guard company of 150 footguards with muskets, or a guard company of 100 horseguards to whom 20 to 50 mounted gentlemen were added on special occasions.[168] Richelieu's household was nearly as large as households of members of the royal family: Gaston d'Orléans, for instance, had a household of about 400 in 1648, and Marie de Bourbon, duchesse de Montpensier, whom he married in 1626 and who died a year later in childbirth, had a household of 187.[169]

The princes de Condé, cousins of the king, had a domestic staff of 75 at their château of Chantilly in 1660 and 1675, and 83 in 1692, which did not include their maison militaire. The Grand Condé had been given a household of 13 when he left his mother at the age of seven, doubled to 26 when he went to Paris at the age of fourteen, and tripled when he became an adult.[170] The total household of the duc de Gramont, governor of Bayonne, Labourd, Basse-Navarre, and Béarn, numbered 106 in the years from 1650 to 1675. Ferdinand de La Baume, comte de Montrevel, royal lieutenant in Bresse and Charolais, had a household of about 60 domestic servants in 1653–54.[171] The comte de Grignan kept a household of 80 servants at his château of Grignan near Montélimar, which did not include his guard company or the staff at his Marseille townhouse.[172] Royal minister Pontchartrain kept a household of 113, and the duc de Nevers, although heavily in debt, kept a household of 146.[173] Audiger, a former steward at Versailles, in *La maison reglée*, published in 1692 but written earlier, declared that a married grand seigneur needed a household of at least 31 and preferably 36 to 38 servants, while his wife needed another 16 servants, and 6 to 7 more servants if there were children, for a bare minimum of 53 servants to staff a great noble household in the seventeenth century.[174]

Large entourages or retinues of nobles and armed men usually accompanied great nobles on their travels in the sixteenth century. For example, the governor of the Ile-de-France, entering the town hall of Paris in 1551, was accompanied by an entourage of 30 or 40 gentleman, and five years later his successor was followed into the same building by a retinue of 200 nobles. Fifty or sixty gentlemen accompanied the governor of Picardy, Charles de Cossé, to Rambouillet, and his successor, the prince de Condé, had a traveling retinue of 500 noblemen in 1560. In the same year, 500 nobles formed the retinue of the governor of Dauphiné; 65 nobles accompanied a royal lieutenant in Guyenne; and the governor of Languedoc appeared at Fontainebleau with 800 nobles in his train.[175] Henri de Montmorency-Damville, governor of Languedoc, met Henri de Navarre, the future Henri IV, at Castres in 1585 accompanied by 1,000 mounted noblemen.[176] When Montmorency's father, the Old Constable, returned from captivity in December 1558, he was met by 1,000 mounted gentlemen on the roads of the Vexin in the Ile-de-France; 800 gentlemen accompanied him to a meeting of the royal council at Fontainebleau in August 1560, and to the Estates General at Orléans a few months later.[177] The Albrets were accompanied in their wanderings by several hundred persons.[178] Henri, duc de Guise, was able to influence the Estates-General at Blois in 1588 because he could raise armed men from Paris and the provinces surrounding the capital, Brie, Picardy, Normandy, Soissons, Burgundy, and Orléans, although he did not do so.[179] It was noted that "he had the loyalty of the major cities, the high nobility and their clients, judges in most courts, the bishops and archbishops, and the lower clergy."[180]

Great nobles were still accompanied by large entourages or retinues in the seventeenth century, but these men were increasingly assembled for the occasion. The comte de Carcès appeared at an assembly of the Provençal nobility at Marseille in April 1649, accompanied by 300 of his noble clients and supporters.[181] Charles du Cambout, baron de Pontchâteau and client of Richelieu, arrived at Nantes in December 1636 to attend the Breton Estates, accompanied by 80 gentlemen loyal to him.[182] The maréchal de Maillé-Brézé, governor of Anjou and owner of extensive estates in that province, died suddenly in February 1650 while raising an army of several thousand from among his clients and tenants to fight for the prince de Condé.[183] In 1659, the duc de La Trémoille gathered 3,000 men in twenty four hours from among his family, household, friends, clients, and tenants to besiege the château of Bressuire to oust a criminal who had taken refuge there.[184]

By the early eighteenth-century, however, large noble households had become rarer, while large noble entourages had disappeared entirely.[185] For example, Henri-François de Foix-Candale, duc de Randan, according to legacies in his will in 1714, kept a staff of 12 to 15.[186] In 1786, Charles-François-Casimir de Saulx, comte de Tavannes, kept 15 servants in his Paris household plus an intendant.[187] The château de Menon in 1698 had a staff of 8 servants, plus local help hired from the village on a daily basis. The marquis's granddaughter, Marie-Louise, comtesse de Damas, lived in Paris or Versailles in the winter, spent summers at her château, and visited friends year-round. She kept a staff of 10 servants at her Paris townhouse in 1774. When she visited the château of Crux in the winter of 1776–77 she took 5 servants with her, and when she visited Langeron and Moulins in 1769, she took along 7 servants.[188] The twenty-year-old François-Louis de Bourbon, prince de La Roche-sur-Yon, had a household of 39 in 1684, increased by another 5 and possibly 10 servants by the time of his death in 1709; this was a small household for a royal prince.[189] The court nobility of late eighteenth-century Paris had households numbering in the 20s. The maréchal de Mirepoix employed 21 domestic servants, the prince de Lambesc 29, and the comte Dufort de Cheverny began married life with 15 servants.[190] Charles de Baschi, marquis d'Aubais (1686–1777), who lived year-round at his château of Aubais in Bas-Languedoc near Nîmes, kept a staff of 21 including 3 secretaries, and another skeleton staff of 9 at his Paris hôtel where he occasionally stayed.[191] At Bayeux in 1768, the largest household was that of the bishop who had a staff of seventeen.[192] The wealthiest nobles of Bayeux in the late eighteenth century, the marquis de Campigny, de Pierrepont, de La Rivière, the baron de La Tour du Pin, and the military governor of the town, Couvert de Coulons, kept about a dozen servants each.[193] These were much smaller households than the 53 servants declared a bare minimum for the household of a grand seigneur in the seventeenth century.

There were still some great nobles who maintained large households in the eighteenth century. The duc de Choiseul, for example, retired to his château of Chanteloup when he was banished from court by Louis XV in 1770; he maintained 54 liveried footmen and a staff of 300 to run the château. Known for his extravagance, Choiseul entertained constantly; he had 210 visitors at the château between 1770 and 1774, when Louis XV died and he could return to court.[194] In 1783, the cardinal de Rohan kept a large household at his château of Saverne in Alsace, including 14 maîtres d'hôtel, 25 valets, and 200 other servants.[195] But households of this size were rarer in the eighteenth century. They were usually maintained by very wealthy grands. Even in the seventeenth century, court nobles with limited incomes did not maintain large households. Madame de Sévigné, whose financial resources were limited, kept a household of about 30 at her château aux Rochers in Brittany.[196] The comtesse de Rochefort, living modestly in the country at the same time, employed about 30 servants.[197]

The households of provincial nobles in the eighteenth century were even smaller than those of court nobles, especially if they were nobles of moderate means. The marquis de Mirabeau noted that an eighteenth-century noble could live better and more cheaply in the country for 10,000 livres a year with 15 servants paid according to the wage scale of the region, than in Paris for 100,000 livres a year with ten servants paid according to the wage scale of the capital; living in Paris was always more expensive. An adequate income for an eighteenth-century provincial noble was 10,000 livres a year, which provided summer and winter residences, 4 to 6 servants, a coach, a complete pantry, wardrobe, and linen closet, a respectable library, and an occasional trip.[198] Michel de Roncherolles, marquis de Saint Pierre in Normandy where he lived year-round, had an annual income of 30,000 livres and a household of 10 servants. He was a prominent noble in the countryside around Rouen in 1703.[199] Increasingly in the eighteenth century, provincial nobles of moderate means lived in town during the winter. They had previously lived year-round in the countryside. But by 1700 they lived at their rural châteaux only in the summer and spent winter in a nearby town.[200] Maurice Agulhon, in studying 234 Var nobles in Provence in 1787–89, found that 118 lived inside the Var, on their lands with houses in nearby towns, while 58 lived outside the Var in towns: 33 in Aix-en-Provence, 6 in Marseille, 12 at Paris or Versailles, 4 in Nice, and 3 in other provinces; the residence of 26 was unknown.[201] Living full-time in towns tended to reduce the size of noble households.

By the eighteenth century, therefore, large noble households had become a thing of the past, and the number and variety of domestic servants had been reduced to those necessary to run an establishment. Nobles and gentlemen servants and pages had disappeared from households, and maisons militaires had been reduced to a doorguard, often Swiss because they were fashionable, and an occasional bodyguard. These changes can be demonstrated by comparing the staffs of noble households over a century. The household of Bernard de La Valette, duc d'Epernon in 1660, for example, had 73 servants including 16 noble and gentlemen servants, 8 pages, 2 maîtres d'hôtel, 1 doctor, 1 barber surgeon, 1 druggist, 5 secretaries, 2 messengers, 2 trumpeters, 1 doorguard, 3 chaplains, 2 butlers, 2 housekeepers, 1 household accountant, 5 valets, 8 footmen, 2 cooks, 1 baker, 2 greengrocers, 2 purveyors (to buy food), 1 gardener, 2 coachmen, 1 mastergroom, and 2 stablemen. In addition, as governor of Guyenne, he had a guard company of about 40 men.[202] From 1650 to 1675, the duc and duchesse de Gramont kept a household of 106, including several noble and gentlemen servants and pages, 1 intendant, 1 secretary, 1 maître d'hôtel, 5 valets, 1 wine steward, 1 chef, 1 fruit and vegetable cook, 1 spit boy, 1 kitchen boy with 2 assistants, 1 Swiss doorguard, 3 coachmen, 2 muledrivers, 1 postilion, 5 footmen, 1 carriage boy, 1 lackey, 2 lady's maids, 4 chambermaids, 1 governess, 1 wet nurse, and 2 female servants at their Paris townhouse, plus a skeleton staff at their rural château including 1 captain, 1 gamekeeper, 1 concierge, 1 tax receiver, 1 almoner, 1 gardener, and 1 *fontainier* in charge of the fountains, and a maison militaire of 40 horseguards, 1 mounted drummer and 2 trumpeters, and several aides-de-camp.[203]

These households can be compared to those of the comte de Saulx-Tavannes, the comtesse de Damas, and the marquis d'Aubais a century later. Nobles, whether officials, servants, pages, guards, gendarmes, or armed retainers, had disappeared from these households, and so had servants with specialized functions. In 1786, for example, the Paris townhouse of the comte de Saulx-Tavannes was staffed by 1 maître d'hôtel, 1 cook with 1 assistant, 2 coachmen, 1 Swiss doorguard, 2 footmen, 1 valet, and 6 male servants of unspecified duties. In 1774, the comtesse de Damas employed 1 coachman, 1 postilion, 1 cook, 1 lackey, 1 office boy, and 4 female servants of unspecified duties in her Paris townhouse. When she traveled she took along 1 chambermaid who probably doubled as a lady's maid, 2 lackeys, 1 cook, and 1 office boy. In 1698, her grandfather, the marquis de Menon, whose château she later inherited, had employed 1 governess, 1 coachman, 1 valet, 1 cook, 1 kitchen boy, 1 female servant, 1 gardener, and 1 housekeeper at the château, plus daily help from the village; she probably kept much the same staff.[204] In 1755 the marquis d'Aubais at his château in Languedoc employed 3 secretaries, 1 intendant (who was the wife of a secretary), 1 maître d'hôtel, 1 page (for his wife), 1 chambermaid, 1 cook, 1 coachman, 1 postilion, 2 game wardens, 1 lackey, 1 handyman (*serviteur à tout faire*), and 4 female servants. At his Paris house he kept a skeleton staff of 1 maître d'hôtel, 1 lady's maid, 1 cook, 1 coachman, 2 valets, 1 handyman, and 2 stable boys.[205]

The size of great noble households had declined by the early eighteenth century, and great noble entourages had disappeared entirely, because Louis XIV insisted upon the permanent residence of great nobles at court: Louis XIV moved his entire court to Versailles in May 1682 and lived there for the rest of his life. He domesticated the great nobles of France by bringing them to court to serve him in the royal household, replacing them as provincial governors and lieutenants general with the intendants and their subdélégués. Before the Fronde it had not been customary for the great nobles to live at court unless they had some reason for being there. But about 250 great nobles—there were 100,000 to 125,000 sword nobles in France, and about 250 of these were great nobles on terms of easy familiarity with the king—took up permanent residence at court and assumed positions in the royal household, which had grown to 4,000 persons by 1657 not including guards; this was triple the size of Henri III's household.[206] Courtiers acted out ceremonial roles in the royal household, competed for royal favor, and became preoccupied with questions of rank, status, and etiquette.[207] By staffing the royal household with great nobles, who were traditionally ambitious and unruly, the king put them where he could keep an eye on them and gave them something to do besides plot rebellion. He separated social prestige from political power and focused their attention on the former, and he divided the nobility into two groups, those at court and those in the country; henceforth there was little sympathy between the two.[208] The long-term goal of Louis XIV's strategy was to strengthen the monarchy and the royal government at the expense of the great nobles and their households, entourages, and clienteles.

Great nobles who lived permanently at court and served in the royal household did not maintain their own large households and entourages. Permanent residence at Versailles reduced the size of domestic staffs at seldom-visited country châteaux. Great nobles reversed the sixteenth-century pattern and kept a full staff at their Paris townhouses, where they stayed more often, and a skeleton staff at their rural châteaux. Maintaining a Paris residence was expensive and tended to reduce the size of great noble households. The old pattern prevailed, of course, if a noble lived full-time in the country from personal inclination, financial necessity, or because he was not received at court. Maintaining a large household at Versailles was out of the question because of the cramped living conditions—the palace was crowded, inadequate, and uncomfortable from the start. Nobles newly come to court without important connections had to take lodgings in the town and wait for years to be eligible even for an attic room. Most courtiers shared rooms; a suite of rooms for one was a rare privilege and a luxury. Many courtiers kept Paris townhouses, but they were seldom there because they were at Versailles dancing attendance on the king—not to be seen constantly at court was to condemn oneself to social obscurity and one's children to poverty. During the reign of Louis XIV, the court became the center of noble life, and banishment from the royal presence to a rural château was the most deadly penalty the king could inflict. As a result great noble households, whether in the country or in Paris, tended to decline in size after the 1680s. The funds for their upkeep were spent on other forms of status-seeking such as elegance in dress and livery, lavish entertaining, and high stakes at gambling.

Great noble entourages disappeared at the same time: there is no further mention of them in the documents. Louis XIV, the Sun King, did not like to be outshone—the fate of Nicolas Fouquet was a never-to-be-forgotten lesson in this respect. Fouquet had been disgraced because he made the mistake of eclipsing Louis XIV. The Sun King went everywhere surrounded by crowds of adoring courtiers, and he emphatically did not want his courtiers surrounded by their own adoring crowds. The formal entreé and the large entourage were symbols of power which the king took for himself alone.[209] A few domestic servants, therefore, took the place of the crowds of retainers and armed men that had surrounded great nobles in the sixteenth century. In any event, as the early modern state developed, there was greater physical security, and great nobles no longer needed to travel with 50 to 100 armed retainers for safety.[210]

The decline in great noble households during the last decades of the reign of Louis XIV, and the disappearance of great noble entourages, indicates that great noble clienteles probably declined in size, too, since their households and entourages provided many of their clients. Administrative clienteles continued to flourish in the eighteenth century, but great noble clienteles declined in size and political importance.[211] The reasons were the same as those for the weakening of the patron-client bond: the permanent residence of the great nobles at Versailles; the decline in noble military clientage; the loss of great noble control over the distribution of royal patronage; and the development of ministerial administrative clienteles. The basic cause, however, was the development of the early modern state.

When great nobles lived permanently at court, they no longer spent much time in the provinces where they owned estates or held office, and their absence weakened and impersonalized their ties of loyalty with the provincial nobility whom they no longer saw or knew, a trend intensified by the growing hostility between court and country. The decline in noble military clientage also caused great noble clienteles to shrink in size, a trend which had begun in the late sixteenth century and was speeded during Louis XIV's reign by the suppression of the *ban-et-arrière-ban*, the institutionalization of the *milice*, and the creation of a royal standing army. The ban-et-arrière-ban was the feudal military service that fiefholders owed the king as their lord. The ban was infrequently called in the seventeenth century, only four times in 1635, 1674, 1684, and 1695, and fell entirely into disuse after 1697; it was never called again.[212] It was replaced by the standing army of the king, created by Louvois after 1661, in which nobles bought commissions and served as officers. Noble military clientage was soon found only within the confines of the royal army.[213] The milice, originally a bourgeois municipal militia called during emergencies, was institutionalized by Louvois in 1688, levied by parish, and given a regular set of officers.[214] The result of these changes was to end independent noble military service during the reign of Louis XIV. Great nobles and their clients now served within the royal army under the direction of the monarchy.

A long-term effect of the great nobles' loss of control over the distribution of royal patronage and the reduction in their patronage power was to decrease the size of their clienteles, as we have already seen. Robe nobles, for instance, belonged to great noble clienteles in fewer numbers in the late seventeenth century than in the previous century because the edict of the Paulette in 1604 had made royal offices hereditary, removing them from the gift of the great nobles, and because Louis XIV at Mazarin's suggestion had issued a royal edict in October 1652, forbidding parlementaires to become clients of great nobles.[215] The development of ministerial administrative clienteles meant that great noble clients and potential clients such as robe nobles were gradually enticed away to serve in the new clienteles. As the crown had subverted great noble households by expanding the royal household and incorporating great nobles into it, thereby reducing the incentive for maintaining large noble households, so the crown subverted great noble clienteles by creating administrative clienteles of its own, diverting the flow of royal patronage to nourish these clienteles and enticing away great noble clients to serve in them. The result was a decline in the size and political importance of great noble clienteles. Administrative clienteles, in contrast, grew and flourished and were incorporated into the emerging new royal bureaucracy.[216]

A long-term effect of the decline in the size of great noble clienteles was a decline in great noble military and political power. When the clients of great nobles preferred to switch patrons than fight, or when their loyalty to the king was as strong as their loyalty to patrons, the great nobles lost the military capability to force the king to comply with their demands and thus lost political power. The civil war of the Fronde was the last time during the Old Regime that great levies of armed noblemen rode out, because it was the last time the great nobles were able to mobilize their clients in any numbers to fight; they were unable to do so after 1715. Noble military and political power was based on an informal patron-client system that the Bourbon monarchy attacked and weakened during the seventeenth century.

There was also the psychological impact of the grands' loss of power. The great nobles suffered a highly visible power loss in a short period of time in a status-conscious society preoccupied with public appearances. Symbols of power in this society were taken to indicate power itself, and appearing to lose power was considered the same as losing it. Within a generation large noble households dramatically decreased in size; great noble entourages disappeared; and the provincial clienteles of great nobles shrank in size. Provincial nobles were no longer called to fight by great nobles whom they seldom saw and by the end of the century provincial Estates, the formal political institution to which the largest number of sword nobles belonged, had disappeared in much of France that had enjoyed them earlier in the century, suppressed by the crown. This highly visible loss of power was psychologically devastating to what remained of great noble power, derived from an informal patron-client system in which a patron's ability to reward his clients was essential to securing their loyalty and service. It may have led to questions about the social identity and role of the great nobility as the traditional ruling elite.

In the seventeenth century, therefore, the ministers of a centralizing Bourbon monarchy created their own administrative clienteles in the provinces. These networks included brokers, who distributed royal patronage to secure provincial support for ministerial projects, and the intendants and their subdélégués, who were the new agents of the central government in the provinces. Only after the Fronde, when this alternative ministerial system was firmly in place, did the Bourbon monarchy dare to attack the clientage power base of the great nobles—their provincial clienteles that had proved so useful and dangerous in governing sixteenth-century France. In creating the early modern state, the Bourbon monarchy took control of the system of clientelism that had dominated the French nobility. The growth of strong royal government, therefore, was responsible for the reduction in size and political importance of great noble households and clienteles in seventeenth-century France and for the disappearance of great noble entourages.

Similar changes had occurred in England a century earlier under the Tudors. In response to royal demands for military service during the Hundred Years' War, the great lords of England had surrounded themselves with increasing numbers of armed retainers, mobilizing their tenants and exchanging oaths and formal indentures for service and loyalty with local knights and gentry who wore the lords' livery and badge as a sign of allegiance. During peace and the reigns of weak monarchs this system of maintenance was easily perverted, and indentured retainers became hired bullies causing turmoil and disorder. The first goal of the Tudors was not to destroy this system but to check its abuses. Only when they had erected an alternative power structure based on their own distribution of royal patronage to secure the loyalty and service of the magnates could they afford to knock away this dangerous but useful prop. For this reason the retaining system in England persisted until the end of the sixteenth century, although it was a shadow of its former self by 1600. This is demonstrated by the decline in numbers of liveried retainers and household servants. In the fifteenth and sixteenth centuries English magnate households had numbered in the hundreds, but this had changed by the mid-seventeenth century, when most large households employed 30 to 50 domestic servants. Liveried retainers and client gentry had disappeared, and there were fewer gentlemen among servants because livery had become a humiliating badge of servitude. For this reason magnates were no longer surrounded by crowds of gentlemen wherever they went, but were accompanied by a few footmen.[217]

Statebuilding in early modern France and England included the harnessing of the system of noble clientelism by the monarchy to use in creating a strong central government, and the emasculation of the system once it had served its purpose. It included the creation of ministerial administrative clienteles in the provinces to use as political machines in governing to replace great noble clienteles; the use of brokers to distribute royal patronage to secure the support of provincial nobles and institutions; the politicization of patron-client ties to permit dual loyalty to the king as the embodiment of the French state; and the monarchy's attack on the clientage base of great noble power. The monarchy's assumption of control over noble clientelism is a major achievement of early modern French statebuilding that has been overlooked by historians. Clientelism as a political system may have had its problems, but it served as a transitional bridge from a late medieval political structure in which there were diffuse power centers and strong regionalism to the absolute monarchy of Louis XIV with its strong central government and emerging royal buraucracy. The modern characteristics of Louis XIV's government should not be exaggerated—it was an early modern state that was only quasi-bureaucratic and, although formally centralized and hierarchical, it was also cumbersome, incoherent, and fragmented by special interest groups. But it provided stronger, more stable government than its predecessors had, and clientelism contributed to its development.

Epilogue Clientelism and Bureaucracy

What happened to patron-broker-client ties and networks as a royal bureaucracy emerged in France and the Revolution approached? What happened to provincial power brokers as the new intendants, quasi-bureaucrats, became dominant in provincial government? To discuss these problems, it is necessary to discuss the related questions: What is a bureacracy? When did it emerge in France? What was its relationship to clientelism?

A bureaucracy can be defined as a corps of specifically trained, examined, and appointed men who are fully salaried by the state, impartial in discharging their administrative duties, employed by the state in a hierarchy, and promoted according to seniority, merit, or a mixture of both. A shorter definition is a professional body of officials, permanent, paid, and skilled.[218] Historians and social scientists generally use the term bureaucracy in two ways.[219] The traditional political usage is government by bureaus: government by departments of the state staffed by appointed officials, organized hierarchically, and dependent on the sovereign authority of the state. Roland Mousnier has used the term in this way.[220]

Sociologist Max Weber has proposed the other widely used definition of a bureaucracy. He saw bureaucratization as the rationalization of political organization, the development of a system of impersonal rules, defined functions, and role specialization through which the officials of a bureaucratic state govern.[221] The ideal type of modern, rational bureaucracy according to Weber has six main characteristics: specialization, hierarchy, regulation, impersonality, performance, and efficiency. A bureaucracy has a clear-cut division of labor, hierarchy of office, and a chain of command. There are consistent rules applied to govern performance, and these rules are impersonal, rational standards regulating performance without personal considerations. Employment is based on performance, and on technical and professional qualifications, with protection against arbitrary dismissal. Maximum efficiency is a bureaucratic goal, and written records are kept to preserve details of official duties. These characteristics are the ideal, which has never been achieved by any state, but they exist as recognized goals in modern bureaucracies.[222]

The development of a bureaucracy was a prominent feature of European history. There has been much debate about when a bureacracy actually emerged in France, the first European state to develop this form of political organization. Opinions have ranged from the late sixteenth century through the First Empire because different definitions of bureaucracy have been used.[223] It has been widely accepted, however, that modern bureaucratic goals appeared for the first time in French government when Cardinal Richelieu established the intendants as permanent provincial administrators. The bureaucratization of the French state continued under Colbert, and by the end of Louis XIV's reign, French government showed some of the characteristics of an early modern bureaucracy. By the mid-eighteenth century bureaucratic goals were generally recognized as desirable in French government, if not always achieved in practice. If Weber's definition is used, there was some bureaucratization of French government in the seventeenth century and more in the eighteenth century, but the critical period for the emergence of a bureaucracy in France was the Revolution.[224]

The government of Old Regime France had many of the characteristics of the older clientelist system, which Weber has called "patrimonialism": the lack of separation between private and official, the treatment of political power as personal property and the foundation of the state as personal loyalty.[225] The patrimonial traits of Old Regime government included venality of officeholding and patronage as the chief mode of administrative recruitment and advancement. Patron-broker-client ties, however, existed inside and outside the emerging royal bureaucracy until the Revolution swept away the institutions of the Old Regime. Colbert's intendants, for example, were his own clients who owed him personal loyalty and service.[226] Brokers were still active in eighteenth-century politics.[227] During Colbert's ministry, brokers were slowly absorbed into the emerging royal bureaucracy, a trend that continued into the next century, and both intendants and brokers exhibited a blend of client and bureaucratic characteristics.

Roland Mousnier has observed that "the bureaucracy of late eighteenth-century France remains composed of clients devoted to their patrons, of créatures devoted to their protectors."[228] Mousnier has noted that the controllers general of finance gave Louis XIV a chain of clients and relatives who became secretaries to the royal council, tax receivers-general, treasurers of the provincial Estates (Languedoc and Dauphiné), and tax farmers.[229] Clientelist traits characterized the French ministeriat.[230] However, bureaucratic characteristics also began to appear in the French ministries around 1700, for instance, in the secretariat of foreign affairs.[231] The number of bureaucrats in French government gradually increased during the eighteenth century until a national administration emerged that remained much the same until the mid-nineteenth century.[232] The controller general of finance, for example, employed 360 bureaucrats in 38 offices in 1780, and the term bureaucracy came into use about this time, meaning government by *bureaux* or offices.[233]

The intendants were quasi-bureaucrats, a new breed of political animal. They displayed bureaucratic characteristics in their prior job training and experience, role specialization, administrative hierarchy and regulation, and specific patterns of career advancement based on performance and efficiency. Education and experience were important factors in their recruitment, while efficiency and performance were important in their advancement; incompetence or misconduct could lead to their recall or dismissal. They were members of an administrative hierarchy, and their authority came from written, revocable letters of commission. They could be recalled at any time, making them easier to regulate; their offices were not venal or hereditary. They were regularly rotated on tours of duty through the provinces to increase their reliability and impartiality, and they were usually strangers to the provinces when they arrived, resulting in fewer conflicts of interest, although conflicts did flourish when rotation was partially abandoned by Colbert. The intendants sent regular reports on provincial affairs to their administrative superiors, and government documentation gradually increased.[234]

Provincial brokers, in contrast, displayed clientelist characteristics. They were native-born or long-term provincial residents, patrons of provincial clienteles producing local interests and loyalties that often conflicted with their service to a patron. Brokers by function were not members of a formal administrative hierarchy, and their functions were not clearly defined—usually they were not even verbalized, much less described in written letters of commission. A broker wrote personal letters, not administrative reports, to his patron. Brokers were useful in attaching independent provincial nobles, institutions, and officials to the crown, but intendants made better royal administrators once they were attached. The intendants were more reliable and efficient, and easier to discipline when they were not.

The intendants, however, were not free of clientelist characteristics. They acted as brokers on behalf of their own interests and those of their patrons and clients. Besides subdélégués, the intendants' clients included royal magistrates, prévôt des maréchaux and their archers, royal prévôts or viguiers, public contractors, municipal and financial officials. For example, the intendants suggested reliable candidates to the crown for local judicial offices.[235] Intendant Pierre Cardin Lebret increased the number of archers at Marseille by eight, naming them himself. Antoine de Lauvens, prévôt des maréchaux at Aix, was one of Oppède's clients.[236] The royal prévôts, known as viguiers in Provence, were often suggested by the intendants.[237] In addition, there were the contracts awarded for public works projects and for naval and military supply. Arnoul took advantage of these contracts to name his own clients, and so did Ferrand de Villemain, intendant in Britany, who enlarged the postal routes and chose new postmasters in 1715.[238] The longer the intendants remained in a province, the more clients they acquired and the more intéressé they became. Their tours of duty were considerably longer under Colbert, who is usually credited with failing to establish permanently the tradition of rotation.[239]

The intendants did favors for friends and colleagues who were intendants and royal officials. These favors usually took the form of exempting their lands from troop billeting and reducing their tax assessments. For example, Chamillart, intendant at Caen, and Maupeou d'Ableiges, intendant at Poitou, did favors for other intendants as a professional courtesy.[240] François Laisnier asked Le Tellier to reduce taxes on Daumeray, a parish near Durtal in Anjou belonging to his brother. The intendants probably gave each other's lands preferential treatment when they carried out parish assessments. It was contended that the parishes in the *généralité* of Paris belonging to Favier Du Boullay, the intendant at Alençon in the years 1643–48 and 1653–66, had always been protected by his colleagues.[241]

The intendants were occasionally asked by their Paris patrons to provide favors for their relatives and dependents, and they usually obliged. For example, the lands of Colbert and his family, friends, and court protectors in Normandy were given preferential tax treatment, such as lower assessments, at his request. Colbert wrote the intendant at Rouen in 1679, thanking him for reducing the tax assessment of the lands of his son, Louis, and asking that this favor be extended to Louis's estate at Marais-Vernier.[242] At Colbert's request royal taxes on the lands of his brother, Colbert de Maulevrier, near Tours were reduced by 8,000 livres in 1670.[243] The minister had the parish of Pussort, in which his uncle held land, exempted from royal taxes.[244] He also had taxes reduced on his daughter's estates of Luynes and Fondettes near Tours.[245] Colbert did similar favors for court grands such as Madame de Montpensier for her village of Eu in 1682; the marquis de Piennes for her lands in Picardy; the duchy of Lavallière; and the lands of the marquis d'Antin, the son of Madame de Montespan.[246] Colbert protected the lands of his friend Turenne.[247] He was not the only minister to make such requests of the intendants. Chancellor Séguier's pressure on intendant Bernard de Fortia reduced by half the taxes on his parish of Sully from 1659 to 1661.[248] The correspondence of Le Tellier and Louvois are full of requests of this nature.[249]

The intendants of seventeenth-century France, therefore, were not always impartial, impersonal bureaucrats acting in the best interests of the monarchy and the state. They advanced their own financial and career interests, those of their families, clients, and professional colleagues, and those of their patron and his dependents. They were not chosen or promoted through a competitive examination or merit system; patronage was essential to their recruitment and advancement. They profited personally from their offices, although modestly in most cases. They built provincial clienteles of their own, composed of local officials and subdélégués whose members rapidly increased in the late seventeenth century, although their clienteles were smaller than those of provincial brokers and they occasionally acted as brokers for their clients. The intendants had fewer local and personal interests than provincial brokers, but they were not devoid of these interests: they were only less intéressé.

Provincial brokers did not disappear as an early modern bureaucracy emerged. They provided unofficial assistance to the intendants, acted as their subdélégués, and sometimes even became intendants themselves.[250] Former intendant Pierre de Marca and intendant Claude Bazin de Besons, for example, and Cardinal Bonzi and intendant Henri d'Aguesseau, governed Languedoc as administrative teams. Intendant Camus de Beaulieu and Claude Boisot worked together in the Franche-Comté. Boisot's brother-in-law, Nicolas-Louis Boudret, became the subdélégué of an intendant. Ulrich Obrecht was the subdélégué of intendant Jacques de La Grange in Alsace, while Jean Dietremann became the subdélégué of his successor. Oppède and his son, Jean-Baptiste, and Claude Bouchu and his son, Etienne-Jean, were intendants. Brokers continued to be used in governing peripheral provinces in the eighteenth century as demonstrated by the career of Cardinal de Boisgelin, archbishop of Aix from 1770 to 1804, who used his crédit at court on behalf of the Provençal General Assemblies which he regularly attended, and his crédit in Provence on behalf of the controller general and the royal ministers at Paris.[251] The careers of Provençal brokers Palamède de Forbin in the late fifteenth century, Henri de Forbin-Maynier d'Oppède in the mid-seventeenth century, and Cardinal de Boisgelin in the late eighteenth century demonstrate that the Paris government used brokers to secure the political integration of peripheral provinces throughout the Old Regime.

Anthropologist Sydel Silverman has suggested that brokers may represent a general form of community-nation relationship that disappears as the integration of the total society takes place.[252] Some anthropologists and political scientists have agreed that clientelist politics reflect a stage of political development. When a bureaucratic central government expands into the countryside, coming into direct contact with the regional elite and the masses, brokers become superfluous and play a minor role or disappear.[253] However, there has been disagreement with this view: Sidney Tarrow has found that brokers still play a role in the modern bureaucracies of France and Italy. He has studied the role of community mayors as center-periphery links in contemporary France and Italy, and found that mayors have transcended the historical role of local notables without reflecting the Weberian dream of the apolitical administrator.[254] Instead, they have become what he calls policy brokers. In a highly centralized, bureaucratic state such as modern France, the implementation of national policies toward local government requires initiative at the local level to direct goods toward particular communities and to capture resources from the state. In filling this function, the mayors act as policy brokers at the grass-roots level. They capture needed resources from the bureaucratic state for their region, and in the process they become important actors in the political adaptation of their communities to social and economic change. Tarrow conducted interviews with 248 mayors in four regions each of France and Italy. When the mayors were asked to discuss the most important aspect of their jobs, 54 percent in France and 34 percent in Italy said that it was seeking projects and program support that would bring about the community's modernization.[255]

Sociologist Michel Crozier believes that brokers continue to function in modern bureaucracies for a different reason. He has analyzed the problems existing in modern bureaucracies, specifically in the French bureaucracy of the 1960s.[256] He has found that modern bureaucracies are often inefficient and irrational, unable to solve problems or to respond constructively to change. Crozier believes that centralization and rigid, internal stratification become insurmountable barriers to communication within modern bureaucracies and with the outside world. Moden bureaucracies become inflexible, lose touch with reality, and cannot learn from mistakes.[257] Periodically, they become hopelessly dysfunctional and grind to a temporary halt, paralyzed, in what Crozier calls a social *blocage*.[258] The disparity between the impersonal rules and the variety of tasks the bureacracy has to perform become too great for it to function; the tensions between strata become too oppressive; the malaise of the lower echelons too overwhelming; the standardization and regulation too removed from reality.[259] However, personalism, informal understandings, and parallel power relationships such as patron-broker-client ties help to keep the wheels of the bureacracy turning. For example, a member of one strata utilizes his personal connections and telphones a friend in another strata, or in the outside world, to solve a problem, to obtain information, or to bypass a regulation. Brokers informally facilitate communication and exchanges of resources between bureaucratic layers and with the outside world. The lack of personalism within bureaucracies causes blockages.[260] Brokers help to restore personalism.[261]

Anthropologist Mart Bax has noted that brokers still play a role in twentieth-century Irish parliamentary politics as machine leaders. He has found that brokerage does not decrease as the authority of the central government expands into the countryside.[262] Increased centralization has resulted in the masses using a broker to communicate with the center. Particularism and parochialism have retarded communication, and brokers have resisted integration because it destroys their brokerage role.[263] It would seem, therefore, that brokers continue to play a role in modern bureaucracies by facilitating communication from the periphery to the center, within the bureaucracy and with the outside world, and that brokerage does not automatically disappear as integration and centralization take place. What are the political implications of the continued existence of brokers and brokerage in modern bureaucracies?

In studying modern government in Colombia, a state still undergoing political development in the twentieth century, Steffen Schmidt has observed that bureaucrats become brokers, and brokers become bureaucrats, which was also true in seventeenth-century French government. Schmidt has found that local patron-brokers or bosses in modern Colombia hold public appointed offices in the Colombian bureaucracy, and that bureaucrats act as political patron-brokers in defending their special interests for clients who are the recipients of public services. Schmidt has noted that "there has frequently been an explicit overlapping of political and bureaucratic patron or broker roles.... Modern bureaucrats can also be brokers."[264] Schmidt writes, "I shall argue, instead, that there is evidence to indicate that a technically better trained bureaucracy need not necessarily be (a) functionally specific in that the bureaucrat will follow orders from the top and not be willing to become politically active in defense of his own programs or (b) more impersonal."[265] This was also true of intendants during the Old Regime.

Weber's definition of a modern, impersonal, rational bureaucracy is widely recognized as being useful but problematic.[266] For example Weber has made progressive rationalization a distinctive feature of modern society, and he considers modern bureaucracy an ideal type of rationalization. This concept, however, does not explain geopolitical differences or widely varying historical and cultural backgrounds, for example, those of European, Soviet, and American bureaucracies. Weber explains bureaucratic differences as the result of evolution: different bureaucracies develop politically at different rates. Evolution explains the differences between early modern bureaucracies, modern Western bureaucracies, and Third World bureaucracies. In Weberian terms, the early modern French state was in transition from a traditional, patrimonial system to a modern, rational bureaucracy. Moden Colombia is in the same stage of political development. Weber's conceptualization implies that modern bureaucracies not attaining rational, impersonal characteristics are imperfect, defective, or incomplete.[267] In other words, bureaucracies containing traces of clientelism are less advanced bureaucracies in the process of development, the case for early modern France and modern Colombia.

But modern bureaucracies in Western advanced nations contain traces of clientelism, for instance, brokers and brokerage—none is an ideal, modern, rational, impersonal bureaucracy as Weber has described it. French bureaucracy is usually considered more permanent, professional, and freer from patronage abuses than its American counterpart, for instance.[268] Even modern French bureaucracy, however, long considered one of the most independent, cohesive bureaucracies in Europe, exhibits traces of clientelism. Modern French administration is not apolitical; it is frequently irrational and inefficient.[269] The patronage abuses that have characterized bureaucratic government in the big cities of America are notorious.[270] A patronage system exists side by side with a civil service or merit system in the American federal government.[271] Brokers operate within modern American bureaucracy.[272]

The question, then, is when does a bureaucracy reach maturity? When does a modern bureaucracy become rational and impersonal as Weber has described it? Increasingly, the answer appears to be "never" because Weber's ideal type of modern bureaucracy does not exist. Bureaucracy as a form of modern political organization may be more personal, informal, and irrational than Weber recognized. Modern bureaucracies may not be defective or incomplete if they retain some of the personal, irrational characteristics of political clientelism. Patronage, in fact, may provide a better motivation for political action than do bureaucratic salaries.[273] Weber may have exaggerated the impersonalism and rationality of bureaucracy as a form of political organization.

French government in the seventeenth century underwent the process of bureaucratization to combat some of the weaknesses in clientelism as a political system, the high rates of conflict and corruption. The problem of when a bureaucracy emerged in France, and what its nature was, might be better answered if clientelism was factored into the analysis: we need to ask when, or indeed if, clientelist traits disappeared. The answer may change our understanding of the development of early modern French bureaucracy. The continuing existence of brokers and brokerage within the French bureaucracy before and after the Revolution casts doubt upon the Weberian definition of bureaucracy, since clientelism continued to exist in a looser, more politicized form inside and outside the emerging French bureaucracy. Weber regards these two systems of political organization as separate by definition. But are they? In early modern France they overlapped to the extent that it is difficult to know where one stopped and the other began. What is their relationship in modern France?

The traditional view of Colbert's ministry is that he systematically organized and rationalized French administration, making it more bureaucratic.[274] French government under Colbert was certainly smoother-running, more efficient and stable than it had ever been, but it exhibited strong traces of clientelism. The modern observer should not exaggerate the rationality or impersonality of Colbert's administration. However, strong traces of clientelism do not make Louis XIV's government as patrimonial as Weber has described it.[275] After all Richelieu, Mazarin, and Colbert used clientelism to help create the early modern state and the new royal bureaucracy. The differences between clientelism and bureaucracy are not as distinct as Weber believed them, at least not in early modern France which originated the bureaucratic form of political organization.

CONCLUSION

Nobles, Brokers, and Statebuilding

Two fundamental obstacles stood in the way of strengthening the Paris government and extending its authority over the French countryside in the seventeenth century: the great nobles and their provincial clienteles, especially the provincial governors who acted as though their governments were private kingdoms; and the provincial Estates, sovereign courts, and municipal governments, independent regional institutions that staunchly resisted the expansion of the central government into their own spheres of power and influence.

In 1600, Henri IV needed to restore internal calm and stability to France after the Wars of Religion and the League. He had to cope with an uncooperative, quarrelsome nobility—Huguenots who were angry at his conversion and Catholics who were distrustful of his conversion. His successors became embroiled in the Habsburg War (1635–59) and had to seek higher taxes to support the troops needed to defeat the Spanish and the Austrians, a royal policy that provoked widespread popular revolt in the early seventeenth century culminating in the civil war of the Fronde at mid-century.[1] In order to collect taxes and obtain troops, the royal ministers had to extend the authority of the central government over the French countryside, especially over the quasi-independent frontier provinces and pays d'Etats which bore the brunt of the fighting and were the most disturbed and recalcitrant in paying taxes.

Henri IV had relied upon the traditional system of clientelism in governing the provinces: French monarchs for at least a century had used the great nobles and their clienteles in governing. Henri IV depended upon a few trustworthy clients who owed him personal loyalty to control the important provinces. They included Claude Groulard, Henri de Bourbon-Montpensier, Georges de Brancas, Aymar de Chaste, and Charles Timoléon de Beauxoncles in Normandy; René de Rieux, sieur de Sourdéac in Brittany; Guillaume Fouquet, sieur de La Varenne, Duplessis-Mornay, and Claude de La Châtre in the Loire valley; Sully and the sieurs de Lussan and Saint Luc in the west;

Alphonse d'Ornano in Guyenne; Jacques Nompar de Caumont de La Force in Béarn and Navarre; Montmorency-Damville in Languedoc; Du Vair and the duc de Guise in Provence; Lesdiguières in the Dauphiné; the duc de Nevers in Champagne; and Dominique de Vic, Charles de Rambures, and Eustache de Conflans in Picardy. It was not a large group of men, but they were reliable; the king wrote to them when he wanted information or needed something done.[2]

Henri IV's own view of the French power structure was somewhat different, of course. He needed to know who the unruly nobles were in order to curb them. He had to keep in touch with the moderate Huguenots to know what the radicals were doing. He had to keep informed about the towns. He needed to send reliable representatives to the Estates to coerce them into voting at least part of the tax monies he requested, and he sought to influence the debates of the parlements in order to have his legislation registered. As David Buisseret has observed, "In short, he had to be like a spider at the center of his web, constantly surveying the distant fringes, and ready if necessary to rush out in person to resolve a problem."[3]

Cardinal Richelieu was the first to recognize the administrative potential of using networks of ministerial clients as brokers of royal patronage in the provinces. He established these networks in provinces with unreliable governors, in distant frontier provinces suffering heavy troop movements and high taxes, in politically disturbed provinces, in provinces with Estates—often these were the same provinces. They included Provence, Languedoc, and Guyenne in the south, Burgundy, Alsace, and the Franche-Comté in the east, and Brittany in the west.[4] Instead of depending on a few reliable clients in each province to help him govern as Henri IV had done, Cardinal Richelieu created permanent networks of ministerial clients. He recruited local notables and officeholders who had influence and clienteles of their own—archbishops, bishops, and first presidents of high courts were favorite targets of recruitment—and placed them strategically as his clients within the provincial administration. He distributed royal patronage to secure their loyalty and support, which they in turn as brokers distributed to their own clients and supporters to widen the web of ministerial influence within the provinces. The new intendants were members of these networks. Ministerial administrative clienteles radiating outward from Paris with members acting as brokers of royal patronage helped Richelieu to secure provincial acceptance of higher taxes and more troops, to suppress popular protest, and to reconcile provincial institutions and nobles to greater control from Paris.

Cardinal Richelieu, therefore, was responsible for three administrative changes of lasting importance: the creation of permanent ministerial administrative clienteles in the provinces; the extensive brokerage of royal patronage through these networks to secure provincial loyalty and support for the policies and projects of the Paris government; and the establishment in the provinces of new agents of the central government, the intendants, who belonged to these networks and benefited from their help. Richelieu's successors, Mazarin and Colbert, preserved and developed these administrative networks and used them in governing. Mazarin allowed them to lapse temporarily in the decade before the Fronde but hurriedly restored them when the civil war broke out and he was forced to recall the intendants. Colbert used his own intendant-clients and his predecessors' provincial clients as administrative teams in managing the provincial Estates. His clients and their clients operated with the well-oiled precision of political machines set in motion from Paris.

Provincial brokers made a significant contribution to national statebuilding by helping to expand political integration and to strengthen the central government at Paris. As provincial notables who were clients of highly placed patrons in the Paris government, they helped to integrate the provincial and national ruling elites and, by using their provincial crédit and clients to help their Paris patrons achieve their political goals, they mobilized provincial resources for national purposes. Provincial brokers of royal patronage helped the Paris government to extend its control over independent provincial power structures, especially in peripheral provinces, and in this way contributed to the development of the early modern French state.

Provincial brokers helped to extend the control of the Paris government in several ways. They helped Paris patrons to secure the loyalty and support of provincial nobles and independent regional institutions such as the Estates, parlements, and municipal governments. French monarchs distributed royal patronage directly to the great nobles, especially those who had established themselves as provincial governors and lieutenants general—for example, the ducs de La Trémoille in the west, the Saulx-Tavannes in Burgundy, and the duc de Guise in Provence—to secure their loyalty and support and indirectly, through them, the loyalty and support of their large noble clienteles in the provinces, in this way attaching the provincial nobility to the throne.

But the great nobles were disobedient and politically unreliable, for example, the duc de Mayenne and the prince de Condé. As a result, Cardinal Richelieu began to channel royal patronage to more reliable clients of his own in the provinces, to lesser nobles and royal and provincial officials who helped him to secure the cooperation of independent regional institutions. Richelieu created networks of his own broker-clients in peripheral provinces and, by selectively distributing royal patronage to them and their clients, he was able to influence the political behavior of important regional institutions, a policy continued by his successors. For example archbishops Rébé and Marca helped their patrons, Richelieu and Mazarin, to control the Estates of Languedoc, while Oppède and his protégé, Janson-Forbin, helped their patrons, Mazarin and Colbert, to control the General Assemblies of Provençal Communities. Antoine d'Aguesseau and Claude Boisot managed the Parlements of Bordeaux and Besançon for Richelieu and Louvois. Cosme de Valbelle used his crédit and clients to keep the municipal government of Marseille loyal to Richelieu during the Cascaveoux Revolt, while Antoine de Valbelle used his influence and clients to hold Marseille for Mazarin during the Fronde.

Provincial brokers also helped the Paris government to extend its control over independent provincial power structures by acting as administrative troubleshooters in solving difficult problems. Not only did they act within formal political institutions to manipulate them and attach them to the throne, they also acted outside regular administrative channels as separate, informal structures to resolve unusual problems. For example, Cardinal Bichi negotiated with the rebellious parlementaires of Aix in 1649 on Cardinal Mazarin's behalf, while Archbishop Béthune mediated between the rebellious parlementaires of Bordeaux and Governor Epernon on the Cardinal's behalf. Boisot and Jobelot helped Louvois and Louis XIV to conquer the Franche-Comté.

Provincial brokers also collaborated with the new agents of the central government in the provinces, the intendants, and frequently helped them in performing their administrative duties. Cardinal Bonzi, for example, helped intendant Aguesseau to secure the cooperation of the Estates of Languedoc, while Claude Bouchu became intendant himself in Burgundy and used his father's clientele to help control the Estates. In Alsace and the Franche-Comté, brokers became subdélégués of the intendants. In these ways provincial brokers helped to strengthen the Paris government and extend its control over the French countryside. Early modern French statebuilding was, above all, the creation of a strong central government.

Provincial brokers of royal patronage who were members of ministerial clienteles helped to strengthen the central government in another way, by helping to undercut and destroy the power of the great nobles, the unreliable and traditional ruling elite of France. In the seventeenth century the crown increasingly used ministerial networks of broker-clients in governing the provinces in place of the great nobles and their clients. In fact, the crown used these networks to surround and contain unreliable great nobles and governors such as the comte d'Alais in Provence. By rechanneling the flow of royal patronage away from the provincial clienteles of the great nobles, ministerial networks simultaneously undermined their power based on large provincial clienteles that declined in size and strength as a result. The decrease in the flow of royal patronage through great noble hands was one reason for their participation in the civil war of the Fronde at mid-century. If the patronage policies of the royal ministers helped to cause the Fronde, however, they also helped the Bourbon monarchy to survive it and grow stronger by widening its base of support in the countryside, while simultaneously decreasing the power of the great nobles.

The rapid growth of administrative clienteles at the expense of great noble clienteles in the seventeenth century changed the nature of the patron-client bond, making it more impersonal, pragmatic, and utilitarian, less intensely emotional and personal. By the end of the century the patron-client bond had loosened enough to permit dual loyalty to the king as the embodiment of the French state, and clients became more likely to switch allegiance than to fight for a patron, especially if fighting meant rebelling against the crown. The result was a decrease in the military and political power of the great nobles based upon the willingness of their clients to fight for them.

Ministerial administrative networks increasingly dominated by the intendants were firmly anchored in place in the provinces as an alternative governing system to the great nobles and their clients after the Fronde. The Bourbon monarchy then escalated its attack upon great noble power by calling the grands to reside permanently at court and to serve in the royal household, thereby removing them from the provinces where they were replaced as royal administrators by the intendants and their subdélégués and reducing the size of their clienteles, households, and entourages.

The Bourbon monarchy's attack upon the clientage-based power of the great nobles in the seventeenth century, therefore, was a two-step process. Before the Fronde, the crown created its own administrative networks in the provinces and used the brokerage of royal patronage to obtain provincial loyalty and support, thereby reducing the flow of royal patronage through great noble hands, politicizing the patron-client bond, and reducing the size and strength of great noble clienteles. After the Fronde, which the Bourbon monarchy survived in part because of its provincial administrative networks, it recalled the great nobles from the provinces and replaced them with the intendants, thereby reducing even more the size and strength of their clienteles. In this way the Bourbon monarchy weakened the military and political power of the grands derived from their large provincial clienteles.

The Bourbon monarchy used the nobility of France, great and small, sword and robe, in constructing the early modern state, which rested on a broader base of noble support than has generally been recognized. The king and his ministers used royal patronage to reward the loyal service of great nobles and their clients, to recruit new noble supporters, to appease opponents, and to play off rivals for power, thereby strengthening the royal government and extending its control over France. Royal patronage was always a welcome addition to noble fortunes. But as royal government became stronger it reduced the flow of patronage to the great nobles and rechanneled it into other, more reliable noble hands, in this way reducing the power of the great nobles whom it no longer needed. The absolute monarchy of Louis XIV was thus able to weaken seriously, if not entirely destroy, the provincial power bases of its most formidable rivals, the great nobles. The Bourbon monarchy used the great nobles in statebuilding, and attacked their power when it was strong enough to do so.

Historians in recent years have emphasized the conflict in seventeenth-century French society, focusing in particular upon the role of alienated elite groups in the popular revolts leading to the civil war of the Fronde.[5] The number of such studies has perhaps given the impression there was greater discord in French society than there actually was. The popular revolts and the Fronde were a serious crisis, but what is more important is that the Bourbon monarchy survived this crisis to create Louis XIV's absolute state. This book has suggested a political technique or mechanism by which the Bourbon monarchy obtained elite support to survive the Fronde: it distributed royal patronage to a broad spectrum of provincial nobles to obtain their support—brokers, for example, were recruited from all ranks of the provincial nobility, and so were their clients—and it withheld the distribution of royal patronage to weaken its enemies.[6]

The Bourbon monarchy survived the Fronde to emerge stronger than ever before because it was able to harness the traditional system of clientelism on which great noble power was based and to use it in statebuilding. The monarchy gradually took control of noble clientelism in the sixteenth and seventeenth centuries, and used it to help construct the early modern state. As a political system, however, clientelism had inherent flaws of conflict and corruption, and these problems threatened the long-term stability and unity of the emerging absolute state. In a politically unintegrated state with a weak central government, such as sixteenth-century France, clientelism was a successful method of attaching regional elites and institutions to the throne. But in a more integrated state with a stronger central government, such as late seventeenth-century France, its problems of conflict and corruption appeared more serious and a new, more impersonal basis for administrative relationships had to be found. The result was an emerging corps of public officials, a new royal bureaucracy. The crown used clientelism in statebuilding, then developed a new bureaucratic system of political organization to replace it once the establishment of the absolute state was well under way.

Clientelism did not disappear, however. Administrative clienteles continued to flourish in the eighteenth century, after great noble clienteles had shrunk in size. Ministerial administrative clients and brokers were incorporated into the emerging royal bureaucracy while the intendants, new quasi-bureaucrats belonging to administrative clienteles, created their own clienteles in the provinces and occasionally acted as brokers. Clientelism continued to flourish inside and outside the new royal bureaucracy, demonstrating its flexibility by adjusting to new conditions.

Abbreviations

A.A.E.	Archives des Affaires Etrangères, Fonds France, Paris
ADBR, Aix, Marseille	Archives Départementales, Bouches-du-Rhône
A.C., Aix	Archives Communales, Aix
ANNALES: ESC	*Annales: Economies, Sociétés, Civilisations*, a Journal published quarterly by Librairie Armand Colin, Paris
A.P.	Archives du Palais, Monaco
B.M.	British Museum, London
B. Inguimbertine	Bibliothèque Inguimbertine, Carpentras
B. Marseille	Bibliothèque Municipale, Marseille
B. Méjanes	Bibliothèque Nationale, Paris
B.N., M.C.	Bibliothèque Nationale, Mélanges Colbert
B.N., Ms. fr. and Ms. fr. n. a.	Bibliothèque Nationale, Manuscrits français, and Manuscrits français nouvelles acquisitions
EDB	*Les Bouches-du-Rhône, encyclopédie départementale*, ed. Paul Masson, 17 vols. (Paris, 1913–17)
EDB, IV-2	*Dictionnaire biographique*
N.L.	Newberry Library, Chicago

Notes

Introduction

1. Lawrence Stone, *The Crisis of the Aristocracy, 1559–1641* (Oxford, 1965), p. 197; Alex Weingrod, "Power and Patronage," in *Patrons and Clients in Mediterranean Societies*, ed. Ernest Gellner and John Waterbury, (London, 1977), pp. 41–51; Robert Dahl, "The Concept of Power," *Behavorial Science* 2 (1952): 201–15.

2. Weingrod, "Power and Patronage," p. 42; Julian Dent, "The Role of Clientèles in the Financial Elite of France under Cardinal Mazarin," in *French Government and Society, 1500–1800: Essays in Memory of Alfred Cobban*, ed. John F. Bosher (London, 1973), p. 43; Alan Zuckerman, *The Politics of Faction: Christian Democratic Rule in Italy* (New Haven, 1979), p. 18.

3. Carl Landé, "The Dyadic Basis of Clientelism," in *Friends, Followers, and Factions: A Reader in Political Clientelism*, ed. Steffen Schmidt et al. (Berkeley, 1977), pp. xiii–xxvii.

4. James Scott, "Patron-Client Politics and Political Change in Southeast Asia," *American Political Science Review* 65 (March 1972): 91–114; also in Schmidt, *Friends, Followers, and Factions*, pp. 123–46.

5. Steffen Schmidt, "Patrons, Brokers, and Clients: Party Linkages in the Colombian System," in *Political Parties and Linkage: A Comparative Perspective*, ed. Kay Lawson (New Haven, 1980), pp. 266–88; idem, "The Transformation of Clientelism in Rural Colombia," in Schmidt, *Friends, Followers, and Factions*, pp. 305–22; Scott, "Patron-Client Politics and Political Change," pp. 126–28.

6. Dent, "The Role of Clientèles," pp. 43–44; Robert Harding, *Antomy of a Power Elite: The Provincial Governors of Early Modern France* (New Haven, 1978), pp. 21–23. Also see James Scott, "Corruption, Machine Politics, and Political Change," *American Political Science Review* 62 (1969): 1142–58; idem, "Patron-Client Politics and Political Change," pp. 123–44; Landé, "The Dyadic Basis of Clientelism," pp. *xix–xxv*.

7. Ernest Gellner, "Patrons and Clients," in *Patrons and Clients in Mediterranean Societies*, ed. Gellner and Waterbury, p. 1; Arnold Strickon and Sidney Greenfield, eds., *Structure and Process in Latin America: Patronage, Clientage, and Power Systems* (Albuquerque, 1972), p. 38; also see note 12 below.

8. See, for instance, René Pillorget, *Les Mouvements insurrectionnels de Provence entre 1596 et 1715* (Paris, 1975); Yves-Marie Bercé, *Histoire des Croquants: Etude des soulèvements populaires du XVIIe siècle dans le sud-ouest de la France*, 2 vols. (Paris, 1974), and *Croquants et Nu-pieds: Les Soulèvements paysans en France du XVIe au XIXe siècle* (Paris, 1974); John H. M. Salmon, "Peasant Revolt in Vivarais, 1575–1580," *French Historical Studies* 11 (1979): 1–28, and *Society in Crisis: France in the Sixteenth Century* (London, 1975).

9. Eric Wolf, "Kinship, Friendship, and Patron-Client Relations in Complex Societies," in

The Social Anthropology of Complex Societies, ed. Michael Banton (New York, 1966), pp. 1–22; also in Schmidt, *Friends, Followers, and Factions*, pp. 167–77.

10. Sydel Silverman, "Patronage and Community-Nation Relationships in Central Italy," *Ethnology* 4 (1965): 172–89, also in Schmidt, *Friends, Followers, and Factions*, pp. 293–304; John Powell, "Peasant Society and Clientelist Politics," *American Political Science Review* 64 (June 1970): 411–26, also in Schmidt, *Friends, Followers, and Factions*, pp. 147–61.

11. Schmidt, "Patrons, Brokers, and Clients," p. 267; Silverman, "Patronage and Community-Nation Relationships," p. 294.

12. John Morrill, "French Absolutism as Limited Monarchy," *Historical Journal* 21 (1978): 961–72; Denis Richet, *La France moderne: L'Esprit des institutions* (Paris, 1973), pp. 67–68; Pierre Goubert, *L'Ancien Régime*, vol. 2, *Les Pouvoirs* (Paris, 1973), pp. 15–19.

13. See Epilogue to chap. 6.

14. S.N. Eisenstadt and Louis Roniger, "Patron-Client Relations as a Model of Structuring Social Exchange," *Comparative Studies in Society and History* 22 (1980): 42.

15. Alex Weingrod, 'Patrons, Patronage, and Political Parties,' *Comparative Studies in Society and History* 10 (1969): 377–78; also in Schmidt, *Friends, Followers, and Factions*, pp. ix–x and 324–25.

16. Weingrod, "Patrons, Patronage, and Political Parties," "Power and Patronage," pp. 41–42, 48; Schmidt, *Friends, Followers, and Factions*, pp. ix–x. Steffen Schmidt has done extensive work on brokerage; see chap. 2, n. 3; so has Robert Kern; see *The Caciques: Oligarchical Politics and the Systems of Caciquismo in the Luso-Hispanic World* (Albuquerque, 1973), and *Liberals, Reformers and Caciques in Restoration Spain, 1875–1909* (Albuquerque, 1974).

17. Eisenstadt and Roniger, "Patron-Client Relations as a Mode," pp. 42–77; Alvin Gouldner, "The Norm of Reciprocity: A Preliminary Statement," *American Sociological Review* 25 (1960): 161–78, also in Schmidt, *Friends, Followers, and Factions*, pp. 28–43.

18. See, for example, Conrad Russell, *Parliaments and English Politics, 1621–1629* (Oxford, 1979), "Parliamentary History in Perspective, 1604–1629," *History* 61 (1976): 1–27, *The Origins of the English Civil War* (London, 1973); Paul Christianson, "The Peers, the People, and Parliamentary Management in the First Six Months of the Long Parliament," *Journal of Modern History* 49 (1977): 575–99, "The Causes of the English Revolution: A Reappraisal," *Journal of British Studies* 15 (1976): 40–75; Christopher Hill, "Parliament and People in Seventeenth-Century England," *Past and Present* 92 (1981): 100–24; Theodore Rabb and Derek Hirst, "Revisionism Revised: Early Stuart Parliamentary History," *Past and Present* 92 (1981): 55–99; Jack H. Hexter, "Power Struggle, Parliament, and Liberty in Early Stuart England," *Journal of Modern History* 50 (1978); 1–50, *The Reign of King Pym* (Cambridge, Mass., 1941); Derek Hirst, "Unanimity in the Commons: Aristocratic Intrigues and the Origins of the English Civil War," *Journal of Modern History* 50 (1978): 51–71.

19. Studies of Paris administrative client networks include Orest Ranum, *Richelieu and the Councillors of Louis XIII: A Study of the Secretaries of State and Superintendents of Finance in the Ministry of Richelieu, 1633–1642* (Oxford, 1963); Julian Dent, "The Role of Clientèles"; and Daniel Dessert and Jean-Louis Journet, "Le Lobby Colbert: Un royaume ou une affaire de famille," *Annales: ESC* 30 (1975): 1303–36. Studies of provincial clienteles include Yves Durand, ed., *Hommage à Roland Mousnier: Clientèles et fidélités en Europe à l'époque moderne* (Paris, 1981); and Robert Harding, *Anatomy of a Power Elite: The Provincial Governors of Early Modern France* (New Haven, 1978).

20. See chap. 1 for a discussion of the *fidélité* theory of Roland Mousnier.

21. See James Scott, "Political Clientelism: A Bibliographical Essay," in Schmidt, *Friends, Followers, and Factions*, p. 483.

22. As examples, see the articles in *Patrons and Clients in Mediterranean Societies*, Gellner and Waterbury, and *Structure and Process in Latin America*, ed. Strickon and Greenfield. France was not included in the study by Gellner and Waterbury.

23. See Sharon Kettering, *Judicial Politics and Urban Revolt in Seventeenth-Century France: The Parlement of Aix, 1629–1659* (Princeton, 1978).

24. See Edouard Baratier, ed., *Histoire de la Provence* (Toulouse, 1969); idem, *Documents de l'histoire de la Provence* (Toulouse, 1971).

25. One of the most noted of the older interpreters of the nobility's role as one of economic desperation and political parasitism was Lucien Romier, *Le Royaume de Catherine de Médicis*, 2 vols. (Paris, 1922), *Les Origines politiques des guerres de religion* (Paris, 1914), and *Catholiques et Huguenots à la cour de Charles IX* (Paris, 1924). A bibliographical introduction to the older interpretation is provided by Davis Bitton, *The French Nobility in Crisis, 1560–1640* (Stanford, 1969). The newer revisionist interpreters include J. Russell Major, "Crown and Aristocracy in Renaissance France," *American Historical Review* 69 (1964): 631–45, and "Noble Income, Inflation, and the Wars of Religion," *American Historical Review* 86 (1981): 21–48; Jonathan Dewald, *The Formation of a Provincial Nobility: The Magistrates of Rouen, 1499–1610* (Princeton, 1980); James Wood, *The Nobility of the "Election" of Bayeux, 1463–1666* (Princeton, 1980); and Harding, *Anatomy of a Power Elite*. Also see the essay by John H. M. Salmon, "Storm over the Noblesse," *Journal of Modern History* 53 (1981): 242–57.

26. For a clear statement reconciling the concepts of clientelism and horizontal classes, see Eric Wolf, *Peasants* (Englewood Cliffs, N.J., 1966), pp. 81–95. I am indebted to Charles Tilly for this reference. Patron-client ties were pervasive within the early modern French elite—they occurred in artistic and intellectual circles, in the church, in the army, and at court—but little is known about their nature and operation within the lower ranks of urban and rural society.

Chapter One

1. Molière, *Le Misanthrope ou l'atrabilaire amoureux*, Collection du repértoire Comédie-Française (Paris, 1977), pp. 7–19.

2. A.A.E., 1720, fols. 21–23, May 19, 1656.

3. Ibid., fol. 4, April 4, 1656.

4. B.N., M.C. 157, fol. 49, July 8, 1671.

5. Ibid. 114, fol. 777, February 27, 1663.

6. Roland Mousnier, *Les Institutions de la France sous la monarchie absolue*, vol 1, *Société et état* (Paris, 1974), p. 85.

7. Steffen Schmidt, "Patrons, Brokers, and Clients: Party Linkages in the Colombian System," in *Political Parties and Linkage: A Comparative Perspective*, ed. Kay Lawson (New Haven, 1980), pp. 266–88.

8. See the following articles in *Friends, Followers, and Factions: A Reader in Political Clientelism*, ed. Steffen Schmidt et al. (Berkeley, 1977): Carl Landé, "The Dyadic Basis of Clientelism," pp. xiii–xxvii and "Networks and Groups in Southeast Asia: Some Observations on the Group Theory of Politics," pp. 75–99; James Scott, "Patron-Client Politics and Political Change in Southeast Asia," pp. 123–46; John Powell, "Peasant Society and Clientelist Politics," pp. 147–61. See also Ernest Gellner, "Patrons and Clients," in *Patrons and Clients in Mediterranean Societies*, ed. Ernest Gellner and John Waterbury (London, 1977), pp. 1–6.

9. François de Bassompierre, *Journal de ma vie: Mémoires du maréchal de Bassompierre*, ed. M. de Chantérac, 4 vols. (Paris, 1870–1877), vol. 1, p. 69.

10. Ibid., 1, pp. ix, 41; ADBR, Aix, B 3339, fols. 84–92.

11. John Pearl, "Guise and Provence: Political Conflicts in the Epoch of Richelieu," (Ph.D. diss., Northwestern University, 1968), pp. 19–22.

12. Ibid., pp. 27–28.

13. Bassompierre, *Mémoires*, 1, pp. 196–98.

14. See Roland Mousnier, *The Assassination of Henry IV*, trans. Joan Spencer (New York, 1973).

15. Bassompierre, *Mémoires*, 1, p. 273.

16. Ibid., p. 276.

17. A.A.E., 1718, fol. 366, December 29, 1655, Mazarin to Governor Mercoeur.

18. Ibid., fol. 356, December 10, 1655, Mazarin to Valbelle's son.

19. A.A.E., 1719, fols. 381–82, December 11, 1654.

20. A.A.E., 1722, fols. 192–92v, August 10, 1658.

21. Ibid., fol. 210v, September 8, 1658.

22. A.A.E., 1725, fol. 84, September 16, 1659.

23. Eric Wolf, "Kinship, Friendship, and Patron-Client Relations in Complex Societies," in *The Social Anthropology of Complex Societies*, ed. Michael Banton (New York, 1966), pp. 1–22; also in Schmidt, *Friends, Followers, and Factions*, pp. 167–77. Wolf writes that "the relation between patron and client has been aptly described as a 'lop-sided friendship'" in Julian Pitt-Rivers, *The People of the Sierra* (New York, 1954), p. 140. Also see Michael Kenny, *A Spanish Tapestry: Town and Country in Castile* (Bloomington, Ind., 1962), p. 136.

24. Landé, "The Dyadic Basis of Clientelism," p. xx; Gellner, "Patrons and Clients," p. 4; Powell, "Peasant Society," p. 147; Sydel Silverman, "Patronage and Community-Nation Relationships in Central Italy," *Ethnology* 4 (1965): 175, also in Schmidt, *Friends, Followers, and Factions*, p. 296; Alex Weingrod, "Patrons, Patronage, and Political Parties," *Comparative Studies in Society and History* 10 (1969): 377, also in Schmidt, *Friends, Followers, and Factions*, p. 324; Scott, "Patron-Client Politics and Political Change," p. 125.

25. Sidney Mintz and Eric Wolf, "An Analysis of Ritual Co-Parenthood (Compadrazgo)," *Southeastern Journal of Anthropology* 6 (1950); 341–68; also in Schmidt, *Friends, Followers, and Factions*, pp. 1–15; Wolf, "Kinship, Friendship, and Patron-Client Relations," pp. 172–75; Arnold Strickon and Sidney Greenfield, eds., *Structure and Process in Latin America: Patronage, Clientage, and Power Systems* (Albuquerque, 1972), pp. 57–58; Ronald Weisman, "Patronage and Society: Social Relations in Renaissance Florence" (paper first presented at the Social Science Research Council conference on patronage in Southeast Asia, March 1978). For political friendship, see Matthias Gelzer, *The Roman Nobility*, trans. Robin Seager (New York, 1969), pp. 101–10.

26. B.N., M.C. 120, fol. 232, April 17, 1664.

27. A.A.E., 1725, fols. 461–64, October 5, 1660.

28. A.A.E., 1715, fol. 293, May 2, 1650; B.N., M.C. 141 bis, fol. 439, October 18, 1666.

29. A.A.E., 1716, fols. 461–62, February 20, 1652.

30. For the political uses of courtesy, see Orest Ranum, "Courtesy, Absolutism, and the Rise of the French State, 1630–1660," *Journal of Modern History* 52 (1980): 426–51.

31. Pierre de Lestoile, *Mémoires-journaux*, ed. Claude Petitot, 5 vols. (Paris, 1825), vol. 2, p. 215; vol. 3, p. 15; also cited by Mousnier in *Les Institutions de la France*, vol. 1, *Société et état*, p. 85. See chap. 5 on the duc de Mayenne.

32. A.A.E., 1706, fol. 291, October 18, 1639.

33. A.A.E., 1702, fols. 195–96, May 8, 1633.

34. B.N., Clairambault 392, fols. 90–94, Alais to the comte de Brienne, February 23, 1644. The bailli de Forbin, lieutenant general of the royal galleys at Marseille, asked the comte de Brienne "for the continuation of your good offices at court" in a letter on November 2, 1643; cf. A.A.E., 1719, fols. 381–82.

35. William Beik, "Client Systems and Provincial Government in Seventeenth-Century France: Search for a Method" (paper presented at the annual meeting of the American Historical Association at New York in December 1979). The expression "broken friendship" appears in a letter the comte d'Alais wrote to his friend Chavigny at court on January 9, 1646. Alais wrote that "the most substantial complaint I have against the abbé de La Victoire is his having broken by deceit the friendship with which you have honored me, and which has been very dear to me," cf. A.A.E., 1711, fols. 60–61.

36. B.N., Clairambault 397, fols. 382–83.

37. A.A.E., 1709, fols. 144–45.

38. A.A.E., 1723, fols. 360–61, February 20, 1659.

39. B.N., M.C. 157, fol. 49, June 12, 1671. Also see Landé, "The Dyadic Basis of Clientelism," p. xx; Scott, "Patron-Client Politics and Political Change," p. 125; Powell, "Peasant Society," pp. 147–48; Silverman, "Patronage and Community-Nation Relationships," p. 296; Weingrod, "Patrons, Patronage, and Political Parties," p. 324; Schmidt, "Patrons, Brokers, and Clients," p. 267.

40. E. de Juigné de Lassigny, *Histoire de la maison de Villeneuve en Provence*, 3 vols. (Lyon, 1900–1902), vol. 1, pp. 138, 232–33; EDB, IV–2, 497–502.

41. Orest Ranum, *Richelieu and the Councillors of Louis XIII: A Study of the Secretaries of State and Superintendants of Finance in the Ministry of Richelieu, 1633–1642* (Oxford, 1963), pp. 28–29.

42. Ibid., p. 8. Ranum wrote that "through the favor of the king, Richelieu and his créatures were able to dominate the government of France without opposition from factions for almost a decade"; cf. ibid., p. 9.

43. Ibid., pp. 37–38, 144.

44. Ibid., pp. 144–45.

45. Ibid., pp. 161, 165.

46. One of Bullion's contemporaries estimated his revenues to be 1,500,000 livres annually; see ibid., p. 164. Also see Jean-Pierre Labatut, "Aspects de la fortune de Bullion." *XVII*[e] *siècle* 60 (1963): 11–40.

47. Richard Bonney, *The King's Debts: Finance and Politics in France, 1589–1661* (Oxford, 1981), p. 181; Ranum, *Richelieu and the Councillors of Louis XIII*, pp. 152–53, 162–64.

48. Ranum, *Richelieu and the Councillors of Louis XIII*, pp. 77–78.

49. Georges Dethan, *Gaston d'Orléans, conspirateur et prince charmant* (Paris, 1959), pp. 159–65, 169, 172. Richelieu made a practice of putting his créatures into the households of important important political personages.

50. Ranum, *Richelieu and the Councillors of Louis XIII*, pp. 84–85.

51. Georges d'Avenel, ed., *Lettres, instructions diplomatiques et papiers d'état du Cardinal de Richelieu*, 8 vols. (Paris, 1853–1877), vol. 7, p. 946, vol. 4, pp. 117, 140.

52. Ibid., vol. 4, p. 170; A.A.E., 1702, fol. 56; ADBR, Aix, B 3348, fols. 856–64.

53. Avenel, *Lettres de Richelieu*, vol. 5, p. 927; vol. 7, pp. 758–60, 946, 1020, 1030.

54. Schmidt, "Patrons, Brokers, and Clients," p. 267; Weingrod, "Patrons, Patronage, and Political Parties," p. 324; Gellner, "Patrons and Clients," p. 4.

55. Roland Mousnier's description of fidelity first appeared in his classic 1945 study, *La Vénalité des offices sous Henri IV et Louis XIII*, 2d ed. (Paris, 1971), pp. 531–32, as follows:

> This society is still characterized by the uses of man-to-man personal ties of fidelity, by the establishment of great clienteles. A gentleman can only advance through the favor of a grand, a great noble.... He [the client] gives himself to him [a patron or protector], vows to him total allegiance, absolute devotion, consecrates to him his services, fights for him in duels, brawls, and pitched battles, speaks, writes, and intrigues for him, follows him in misfortune, even overseas, serves in prison for him, kills for him. In exchange, the master provides him with food and clothing, places trust and confidence in him, advances him in the world, obtains appointments for him, arranges his marriage, protects him, obtains his release from prison, makes stipulations in his favor in treaties with the king ending revolts. Although oaths of homage are rarely sworn except by fiefholders, a genuine tie of master to créature unites them, and their reciprocal duties are above all others, even obedience to the king, even service to the state.

Also see pp. 333–35, 576–78. This description has since been repeated by Mousnier many times. He has repeated it almost verbatim in *Social Hierarchies: 1450 to the Present*, trans. Peter Evans (New York, 1973), p. 87; *Peasant Uprisings in Seventeenth-Century France, Russia, and China*, trans. Brian Pearce (New York, 1970), pp. 24–25; *Les XVI*[e] *et XVII*[e] *siècles*, 4th ed. (Paris, 1965), pp. 177–78; "Les Concepts d' 'ordres,'' d' 'états,' de 'fidélité,' et 'de monarchie absolue' en France de la fin du XVe siècle à la fin du XVIIIe," *Revue historique* 502 (1972): 304; and in *Les Institutions de la France*, vol. 1, *Société et état*, pp. 86, 89.

56. Mousnier, *Société et état*, pp. 90–93; "Les Fidélités et les clientèles en France aux XVIe, XVIIe, et XVIIIe siècles," *Histoire sociale* 15 (1982); pp. 34, 44.

57. Mousnier, *Société et état*, pp. 86, 89, 93.

58. Ibid., pp. 89–90; "Les Fidélités et les clientèles," p. 42.

59. Ranum, *Richelieu and the Councillors of Louis XIII*, pp. 8–9; Mousnier, *Social Hierarchies*, p. 87, also *La Vénalité*, p. 532.

60. Denis Richet, *La France moderne: L'Esprit des institutions* (Paris, 1973), p. 80.

61. Mousnier, *Société et état*, p. 93.

62. Yves Durand, ed., *Hommage à Roland Mousnier: Clientèles et fidélités en Europe à l'époque moderne* (Paris, 1981); René Pillorget, *La Tige et le Rameau. Familles anglaises et françaises XVIe–XVIIIe siècles* (Paris, 1979), pp. 195–98. It has also been accepted by Pierre Lefebvre, see note 149, and by Michel Antoine, "L'Entourage des ministres aux XVIIe et XVIIIe siècles," in *Origines et histoire des cabinets des ministres en France* (Geneva, 1975), pp. 15–21.

63. See Robert Harding, *Anatomy of a Power Elite: The Provincial Governors of Early Modern France* (New Haven, 1978), pp. 36–37, 241, n. 70; Julian Dent, "The Role of Clientèles in the Financial Elite of France under Cardinal Mazarin," in *French Government and Society, 1500–1800: Essays in Memory of Alfred Cobban*, ed. J. F. Bosher (London, 1973), p. 55; William Beik, *Absolutism and Society in Seventeenth-Century France: State Power and Provincial Aristocracy in Languedoc* (Cambridge, 1985), pp. 15–17; Kristen Neuschel, "The Prince of Condé and the Nobility of Picardy: A Study of the Structure of Noble Relationships in Sixteenth-Century France" Ph.D. diss., Brown University, 1982), pp. 1–2; Mack Holt, "Patterns of *Clientèle* and Economic Opportunity at Court during the Wars of Religion: The Household of François, Duke of Anjou," *French Historical Studies* 13 (1984): 305–22.

64. Mousnier, "Les Fidélités et les clientèles," pp. 36, 44.

65. Ralph Giesey, "State-Building in Early Modern France: The Role of Royal Officialdom," *Journal of Modern History* 55 (1983): 194. A serious criticism of Mousnier's society of orders has been made by Armand Arriaza, "Mousnier and Barber: The Theoretical Underpinnings of the 'Society of Orders' in Early Modern Europe," *Past and Present* 89 (1980): 39–57. Also see John H. M. Salmon, "Storm over the Noblesse," *Journal of Modern History* 53 (1981): 242–57.

66. Mousnier, "Les Fidélités et les clientèles," pp. 37, 43–44. The exchange theory of social organization, which includes reciprocal gift-giving, supports my contention that the exchange of services was as important as the emotional bond in patron-client relationships. For bibliography see Schmidt, *Friends, Factions, and Followers*, pp. 456–88.

67. Michel Harsgor, "Fidélités et infidélités au sommet du pouvoir," in Durand, ed., *Hommage à Roland Mousnier*, p. 268.

68. Ibid., pp. 268–69, 270–73, 275–76.

69. Oppède and Gourville are discussed in this chapter; also see chap. 6 on Gourville.

70. Mousnier, *Société et état*, pp. 85–89. In his article, "Les Fidélités et les clientèles," Mousnier advises more research into the semantics of patronage, more textual studies, and the use of prosographical methods in studying clienteles; cf. pp. 36, 45–46.

71. Sydel Silverman, "Patronage as a Myth," in Gellner and Waterbury, *Patrons and Clients in Mediterranean Societies*, pp. 7–19. Mousnier warns in "Les Fidélités et les clientèles" that "the study of the bonds of loyalty in Old Regime France is hampered by semantics and the gap which possibly existed between actual practice and expressions used"; cf. p. 35.

72. Peter Laslett, *The World We Have Lost*, 2d ed. (London, 1971), pp. 150–55.

73. John Waterbury, "An Attempt to Put Patrons and Clients in Their Place," in *Patrons and Clients in Mediterranean Societies*, p. 329 and n. 1.

74. Emrys Lloyd Peters, "Patronage in Cyrenaica," ibid, pp. 275–76; Robert Kaufman, "The Patron-Client Concept and Macro-Politics: Prospects and Problems," *Comparative Studies in Society and History* 16 (1974); 285, n. 3, 305; Landé, "The Dyadic Basis of Clientelism," p. xxviii.

75. Scott, "Patron-Client Politics and Political Change," p. 130.

76. See chap. 2.

77. Gaston Rambert, *Nicolas Arnoul: Intendant des galères à Marseille, 1665–1674* (Marseille, 1931); Pierre Clément, ed., *Lettres, instructions et mémoires de Colbert, 1648–1683*, 10 vols. (Paris, 1861–1873), vol. 2, p. 467, n. 2; vol. 3, p. xxxvi; idem, ed., *L'Italie en 1671: Relation d'un voyage du marquis de Seignelay* (Paris, 1867); J. Balteau, ed., *Dictionnaire de biographie française*, in press, vol. 3 (Paris, 1939), p. 977.

78. Clément, *Lettres de Colbert*, vol. 3, p. 114.

79. Ibid., pp. 82–83.

80. Ibid., pp. 44–45.

81. Ibid., p. xxxviii.

82. René La Bruyère, *La Marine de Richelieu: Sourdis, archevêque et amiral* (*6 novembre*

1599–19 juin 1645) (Paris, 1948), pp. 44–45; Pierre-Joseph de Haitze, *Histoire de la ville d'Aix*, 6 vols. (Aix, 1880–1882), vol. 4, pp. 275–76; EDB, IV-2, 593. In March 1639, Richelieu wrote his nephew: "I have been asked from so many quarters to grant the requests you have made for extra money for the galleys that I am writing to say I cannot understand on what you base your demands. I don't doubt that the greatest reason is necessity, but that is caused by your own bad management, and I am not going to ask the King to remedy it," cf., Avenel, *Lettres de Richelieu*, vol. 7, pp. 798–800.

83. René La Bruyère, *La Marine de Richelieu: Maillé-Brézé, général des galères, grand amiral (1619–1646)* (Paris, 1945), pp. 46–47. Pont de Courlay defensively assured his uncle in a letter on December 31, 1636, that rumors of his debts were exaggerated and had been circulated by his enemies; cf. A.A.E., 1704, fols. 527–28. However, his household still had twenty nine members (forty four if sixteen in the service of his wife are counted) in 1636 after Richelieu had "reformed" it to reduce expenses; cf., Georges d'Avenel, *La Noblesse française sous Richelieu* (Paris, 1901), p. 184; Maximin Deloche, *La Maison du Cardinal de Richelieu* (Paris, 1912), pp. 53–54.

84. Avenel, *Lettres de Richelieu*, vol. 7, pp. 798–800, 798, n. 1; also see Richelieu's letter of August 26, 1636; cf. ibid., vol. 5, p. 569.

85. Avenel, *Lettres de Richelieu*, vol. 5, p. 481, June 6, 1636; p. 502, July 16, 1636; La Bruyère, *Maillé-Brézé*, p. 48; Maximin Deloche, *Un Frère de Richelieu inconnu: Chartreux, primat des Gaules, Cardinal, ambassadeur* (Paris, 1935), p. 215.

86. In August 1636, the galley captains complained of Pont de Courlay's ineptitude and mismanagement to Richelieu; cf., A.A.E., 1704, fol. 375; La Bruyère, *Maillé-Brézé*, pp. 45–47; Auguste Jal, *Abraham Du Quesne et la marine de son temps*, 2 vols. (Paris, 1873), vol. 1, pp. 72–73.

87. Avenel, *Lettres de Richelieu*, vol. 5, pp. 417–19; A.A.E., 1704, fols. 376, 419–22, 436–39, 444–45; 1706, fol. 29; 832, fols. 237–39; 829, fols. 210–13; Jal, *Du Quesne*, vol. 1, pp. 53, 72–73.

88. Avenel, *Lettres de Richelieu*, vol. 5, p. 569.

89. A.A.E., 1706, fols. 29, 34.

90. Ibid., fol. 12; A.A.E., 1704, fols. 458, 508–9; Jal, *Du Quesne*, vol. 1, p. 75.

91. Jal, *Du Quesne*, vol. 1, pp. 101–2; La Bruyère, *Maillé-Brézé*, pp. 47, 73, 89–90.

92. Sharon Kettering, *Judicial Politics and Urban Revolt: The Parlement of Aix, 1629–1659* (Princeton, 1978), pp. 126–27.

93. Waterbury, "An Attempt to Put Patrons and Clients in Their Place," pp. 329–30; Scott, "Patron-Client Politics and Political Change," p. 131.

94. Richard Bonney, "Cardinal Mazarin and the Great Nobility during the Fronde," *English Historical Review* 96 (1981): 823–24; see also chap. 5 herein.

95. A.A.E., 1715, fol. 293.

96. Jean-Pierre Labatut, *Les Ducs et pairs de France au XVIIe siècle* (Paris, 1972), pp. 260, 281, 288, 301.

97. Bonney, "Cardinal Mazarin and the Great Nobility," pp. 824–25; Ranum, *Richelieu and the Councillors of Louis XIII*, pp. 30–31, 81, 111 n. 6.

98. Kenneth Dunkley, "Richelieu and the Estates of Brittany, 1624–1640" (Ph.D. diss., Emory University, 1973), pp. 182–87.

99. Bonney, "Cardinal Mazarin and the Great Nobility," pp. 824–25; Georges Livet, *Le Duc de Mazarin, gouverneur d'Alsace* (Paris, 1954), pp. 18–21.

100. "Mémoires de Jacques de Parades de L'Estang, 1642–1674," *Le Musée; Revue Arlésienne* 13–35 (1875): 98–99.

101. Jal, *Du Quesne*, vol. 1, 516–18.

102. Jean-Pierre Labatut, "La Fidélité du duc de Navailles," in Durand, ed., *Hommage à Roland Mousnier*, pp. 187–88. Also see Marie-Louise Fracard, *Philippe de Montaut-Benac, duc de Navailles, maréchal de France (1619–1684)* (Niort, 1970).

103. Waterbury, "an Attempt to Put Patrons and Clients in Their Place," p. 331.

104. A.A.E., 1702, fols. 175–76.

105. Ibid., fol. 207.

106. A.A.E., 1703, fols. 99, 121, 350; 1704, fols. 23–24, 108–9. Commanding the galley, *La*

Séguirane, his brother, Gaspard, was killed during the recapture of the islands of Lérins, off the coast at Cannes, from the Spanish in 1637. Commanding the same galley, Henri's son, Reynaud, was seriously wounded in the famous naval battle off Genoa in September 1638; cf. Jean-Scholastique Pitton, *Histoire de la ville d'Aix* (Aix, 1666), p. 574; EDB, IV-2, 450–51.

107. Séguiran was named an honorary galley captain on June 16, 1635; cf., Charles de La Roncière, *Histoire de la marine française*, 6 vols. (Paris, 1899–1932), vol. 4, p. 576, n. 3.

108. A.A.E., 1704, fol. 521, December 22, 1636.

109. Ibid., fols. 108–9.

110. ADBR, Aix, B 3350, fol. 746, February 20, 1636; B.N., Dupuy 754, fols. 218–19; EDB, IV-2, 169; Haitze, *Histoire de la ville d'Aix*, vol. 4, pp. 277–78, idem, "Histoire de Provence sous le gouvernement du comte d'Alais," B. Méjanes 736, fols. 15–16, idem, *Portraits ou éloges historiques des présidents du Parlement de Provence* (Avignon, 1727), p. 113.

111. Jules de Cosnac, ed., *Mémoires de Daniel de Cosnac*, 2 vols., 2d ed. (New York, 1968), vol. 1, pp. xix, xxvi, xxviii, xxxiii, 2–5, 89–96, 191–225.

112. Ibid., p. 226.

113. Ibid., p. 228.

114. Ibid., p. 232.

115. Ibid., pp. 233–37.

116. Ibid., pp. 252–60, 270–71.

117. Scott, "Patron-Client Politics and Political Change," p. 131; Waterbury, "An Attempt to Put Patrons and Clients in Their Place," p. 330; Landé, "The Dyadic Basis of Clientelism," p. xxviii.

118. Holt, "*Clientèle* and Economic Opportunity"; Elie Barnavi, "Fidèles et partisans dans la ligue parisienne (1585–1594)," in Durand, ed., *Hommages à Roland Mousnier*, p. 144; F. Deshoulières, "Le Maréchal de La Châtre," *Mémoires de la Société des antiquaires du Centre*, 29: 167, 231–33; cited by Harding, *Anatomy of a Power Elite*, p. 36; "Lettres inédites de François de Noailles, évêque de Dax," ed. Philippe Tamizey de Larroque, *Revue de Gascogne* (1865), pp. 22–23; cited by Harding, p. 37.

119. Dent, "The Role of Clientèles," p. 56.

120. Ibid., p. 46.

121. Ibid.

122. See chap. 6.

123. A.A.E., 1720, fol. 55, September 12, 1656.

124. Ibid., fol. 207, August 2, 1633; A.A.E., 1705, fol. 158, October 22, 1636.

125. B.N., Clairambault 390, fol. 234, December 22, 1643.

126. A.A.E., 1725, fols. 461–64.

127. Ibid., fol. 483.

128. A.A.E., 1721, fols. 227–30, October 2, 1657.

129. Georges B. Depping, ed., *Correspondance administrative sous le règne de Louis XIV*, 4 vols. (Paris, 1850–1855), vol. 1, pp. 341–42, March 16, 1664.

130. B.N., M. C. 118, fol. 10. Colbert wrote intendant Rouillé on July 28, 1673, that "the deceased Monsieur d'Oppède was partial in all regarding this province"; cf. Clément, *Lettres de Colbert*, vol. 4, pp. 87–88.

131. B.N., M. C. 103, fols. 690–91, October 12, 1661.

132. A.A.E., 1722, fol. 126, May 7, 1658.

133. Haitze, *Histoire*, vol. 5, p. 418; A.A.E., 1720, fols. 14, 15, 28, 98, 359, 360–61. The tax was the *lods et ventes*.

134. Depping, ed., *Correspondance administrative*, vol. 2, pp. 111–14, 121–22.

135. John H. M. Salmon, "Rohan and Interest of State," in *Studien zur Geschichte eines politischen Begriffs*, ed. Roman Schnur (Berlin, 1975), pp. 134–39.

136. Ibid., p. 140. Also see J. A. Clarke, *Huguenot Warrior: The Life and Times of Henri de Rohan, 1579–1638* (The Hague, 1966).

137. Orest Ranum, *Artisans of Glory: Writers and Historical Thought in Seventeenth-Century France* (Chapel Hill, 1980), pp. 148–68.

138. Dent, "The Role of Clientèles," pp. 57–58.

139. Ibid., p. 43; Harding, *Anatomy of a Power Elite*, pp. 21–31; Nicolas Fessenden, "Epernon and Guyenne: Provincial Politics under Louis XIII" (Ph.D. diss., Columbia University, 1972), pp. 225–26; Jean-Pierre Gutton writes that "the fidèle, if he is lodged under the roof of his master, is his 'domestic' "; see *Domestiques et serviteurs dans la France de l'Ancien Régime* (Paris, 1981), p. 18.

140. Jeremy Boissevain, "Patronage in Sicily," *Man* 1 (March 1966): 18–33; reprinted in *Political Corruption: Readings in Comparative Analysis* (New York, 1970), ed. Arnold Heidenheimer, p. 142.

141. See Deloche, *Un Frère de Richelieu inconnu.* Carl Burckhardt asserts that Alphonse was mentally unstable and died mad, but gives no source for this; cf. *Richelieu and His Age*, vol. 2, *Assertion of Power and the Cold War*, trans. Bernard Hoy (London, 1970), p. 138.

142. Joseph H. Albanès, *Gallia Christiana Novissima*, 7 vols. (Valence, 1899–1920), vol. 1, pp. 140–41; Gabriel de Mun, "Un Frère de Mazarin: Le Cardinal de Sainte-Cécile, 1607–1648," *Revue d'histoire diplomatique* 18 (1904); 497–530; EDB, IV-2, 328; Georges Dethan, *Mazarin et ses amis* (Paris, 1968), pp. 39–45, 95, 344, n. 1; Haitze, *Histoire*, vol. 4, pp. 425–26, 450.

143. Albanès, *Gallia*, vol. 6, pp. 209–10; Dent, "The Role of Clientèles," p. 62; Pierre-Adolphe Chéruel and Georges d'Avenel, *Lettres du Cardinal Mazarin pendant son ministère*, 9 vols. (Paris, 1872–1907), vol. 4, p. 708, n. 1, p. 719, n. 2; vol. 7, pp. 666, 678; ADBR, Marseille, C 32, fols. 242v–43.

144. Albanès, *Gallia*, vol. 1, pp. 406–7; Dethan, *Mazarin et ses amis*, pp. 129–31; Pierre Goubert, *Louis XIV and Twenty Million Frenchmen*, trans. Anne Carter (New York, 1970), p. 19.

145. Dethan, *Mazarin et ses amis*, pp. 104–23; Pierre-Adolphe Chéruel, *Histoire de France pendant la minorité de Louis XIV*, 4 vols. (Paris, 1879–80), vol. 1, pp. 195, 233–37; vol. 2, p. 148. In a letter to his brother on November 25, 1644, Mazarin described Bichi as "the most devoted and loyal friend I have in the whole world"; see Chéruel, *Histoire de France*, vol. 2, p. 154; Philippe Tamizey de Larroque, "Les correspondants de Peiresc: Le Cardinal de Bichi, évêque de Carpentras," *Revue de Marseille et Provence* 30 (1884): 289–304; Chéruel and Avenel, *Lettres de Mazarin*, vols. 1 and 2, passim.

146. Charles de Grimaldi and Jacques Gaufridy, *Mémoires pour servir à l'histoire de la Fronde* (Aix, 1870), pp. 99–100; Albanès, *Gallia*, vol. 1, pp. 142–44; EDB, IV-2, 254; Jacques Billioud, *Le Livre en Provence du XVIe au XVIIIe siècle* (Marseille, 1962), pp. 135–36; René Pillorget, *Les Mouvements insurrectionnels en Provence de 1596 à 1715* (Paris, 1975), pp. 743–44.

147. Harding, *Anatomy of a Power Elite*, p. 27.

148. Yves-Marie Bercé, "Les Conduites de fidélité," in Durand, ed., *Hommage à Roland Mousnier*, p. 130.

149. Pierre Lefebvre, "Aspects de la 'fidélité' en France au XVIIe siècle: Le Cas des agents des princes de Condé," *Revue historique* 250 (1973): 63; Avenel, *La Noblesse française*, pp. 54, 448.

150. Cissie Fairchilds, *Domestic Enemies: Servants and Their Masters in old Regime France* (Baltimore, 1984), p. 12; Gutton, *Domestiques et serviteurs*, pp. 42–43.

151. Lefebvre, "Le Cas des agents des Condé," pp. 59–106; Fessenden, "Epernon and Guyenne," pp. 220–61; William Weary, "Royal Policy and Patronage in Renaissance France: The Monarchy and the House of La Trémoille (Ph.D. diss., Yale, 1972), pp. 88–116, 221–26.

152. Audiger, *La Maison reglée* (Paris, 1692), reprinted in Alfred Franklin, *La Vie Privéé d'autrefois. La vie de Paris sous Louis XIV. Tenue de maison et domesticité* (Paris, 1898), pp. 1–203.

153. See Gutton, *Domestiques et serviteurs*, p. 18; Sara Maza, *Masters and Servants in Eighteenth-Century France: The Uses of Loyalty* (Princeton, 1982), pp. 12–14.

154. See chap. 6.

155. Harding, *Anatomy of a Power Elite*, p. 21.

156. Dunkley, "Richelieu and the Estates of Brittany," p. 188.

157. Kettering, *Judicial Politics*, pp. 293–94.

158. Deloche, *La Maison du Cardinal de Richelieu*, pp. 181–83, 363–64, 484–85.

159. Félix Freudmann, *L'Etonnant Gourville (1625–1703)* (Paris and Geneva, 1960), pp. 10, 14, 21, 33. Also see chap. 6.

160. Lefebvre, "Le Cas des agents de Condé," p. 67.

161. See Georges Mongrédien, *Le Bourreau du Cardinal de Richelieu: Issac de Laffemas* (Paris, 1927); François Dornic, *Louis Berryer: Agent de Mazarin et Colbert* (Caen, 1968); Julian Dent, *Crisis in Finance: Crown, Financiers, and Society in Seventeenth-Century France* (London, 1973), pp. 121–22.

162. For an appreciation of the role of neighborhood in patron-client ties, I am indebted to Ronald Weissman, "Patronage and Society: Social Relations in Renaissance Florence."

163. A.A.E., 1710, fol. 261, October 29, 1645, Bichi to Mazarin. In a letter on December 23, 1645, Bichi described Oppède as "one of my best friends and one of the most faithful and zealous servants of Your Eminence"; see ibid., fol. 289; B. N., Ms. fr. 17390, fols. 79–82; A. D. Lublinskaya, ed. *Vnutrenniaia politika frantsuzskogo absoliutizma* (Leningrad, 1966), p. 352; A.A.E., 1714, fol. 273, Forbin de Saint Gilles to Mazarin, April 13, 1649.

164. Carcès was a kinsman through Oppède's maternal uncle, Castellane de La Verdière, who was Carcès's first cousin; cf., César Nostradamus, *L'Histoire et chronique de Provence* (Lyon, 1614), p. 849. The Castellanes were long-time clients and supporters of the Pontevès de Carcès; cf., A.A.E., 1719, fol. 157, August 12, 1656. The comte de Carcès at Aix sent the marquis de Castellane to Paris to speak to Cardinal Mazarin for him.

165. A.A.E., 1716, fol. 68, June 2, 1649. Carcès explained his support of the parlementaires by noting that "a quantity of my relatives and friends were fighting against the governor."

166. B.M., Harleian 4575, "Semestre de Provence par M. de Sève, conseiller d'état," fols. 77, 106v; B. Marseille 1792, *Relation véritable de ce qui s'est passé en la défaite des troupes de Provence (1649); Relation véritable de tout ce qui s'est passé en la bataille du Val en Provence (1649).*

167. On June 28, 1649, secretary of state Brienne wrote to Carcès that "it has been rumored at court that you appeared at the head of the parlementaire troops. That is exactly the opposite of what is good for the royal service"; see A.A.E., 1716, fol. 58. Carcès wrote to Mazarin on September 3, 1650, that he had received the letter from him ordering him to go to court. He had also learned of the summons from Bichi. He wrote that he was coming immediately; see ibid., fol. 351

168. Carcès had seen Bichi at Carpentras in August 1650; see A.A.E., 1716, fols. 337–337v.

169. Ibid., fol. 395, November 29, 1650, Oppède at Aix to Carcès at Paris. Oppède wrote that he was glad to hear of Carcès's safe arrival at Paris, and asked that he say a good word to Mazarin on his behalf.

170. B.M., Harleian 4490, fols. 2–3, August 15, 1656, Oppède to Mazarin.

171. Georges Cahen-Salvador, *Un Grand Humaniste: Peiresc, 1580–1637* (Paris, 1951), pp. 54–58, 77–79, 82–85, 91–93.

172. Landé, "The Dyadic Basis of Clientelism," p. xxvii. Landé notes that in horizontal alliances between equals or near equals, each was expected to give as much as he received. In vertical alliances between unequals, patrons gave more.

173. A.A.E., 1708, fol. 25, February 13, 1642. The relationship cooled in 1645; see 1711, fols. 60–61, January 9, 1646.

174. Gaspard de Séguiran was one of the best orators of his time, and published two volumes of sermons; cf. EDB, IV-2, 450–51. In a letter on March 22, 1635, Henri de Séguiran mentioned the continuing efforts of his uncle Gaspard at court on his behalf and that of their family; see A.A.E., 1703, fol. 99; also see Haitze, *Histoire*, vol. 4, pp. 114–15.

175. Henri de Séguiran, *L'Etat de l'armée navale commandée par Mgr. le duc de Guise, amiral et lieutenant général de la mer* (Bordeaux, 1622); ADBR, Aix, B 3349, fol. 230v; Marseille, IX B2, fols. 252, 267; Henri de Séguiran, "Procès-verbal contenant l'état véritable auquel sont les affaires de la côte maritime de Provence," B.N., Ms. fr. 24169, fols. 2–61; in Eugène Sue, ed., *Correspondance d'Henri d'Escoubleau de Sourdis, archevêque de Bordeaux, 1636–1642*, 3 vols. (Paris, 1836), vol. 3, pp. 221–319.

176. Through Colbert's patronage Du Quesne received the money to buy the fiefs of Le Bouchet, Val-Petit, and the barony of Valgrand; Le Bouchet and Valgrand were later made marquisats. Du Quesne also received 300,000 livres, and his son and nephew were each given a ship to command as captain; cf. Jal, *Abraham Du Quesne*, vol. 2, pp. 330–31, 403–5, 407.

Chapter Two

1. Pierre Clément, *La Provence et Colbert* (Toulon, 1862), p. 19, n. 1.

2. Henri de Séguiran, "L'Etat véritable de la côte maritime de Provence," in *Correspondance de Henri d'Escoubleau de Sourdis, archevêque de Bordeaux, 1636–1642*, ed. Eugène Sue, 3 vols. (Paris, 1839), vol. 3, pp. 257–62.

3. For the sovereign courts of Provence, see Louis Wolff, *Le Parlement de Provence au XVIIIe siècle* (Aix, 1920); EDB, III, 322–410, 424–48; Jean-Paul Charmeil, *Les Trésoriers de France à l'époque de la Fronde* (Paris, 1964). There is no study of the Aix Cour des Comptes. For the Estates of Provence, see Bernard Hildesheimer, *Les Assemblées générales des communautés de Provence* (Paris, 1935); EDB, III, 448–545, XIV, *Monographies communales: Marseille, Aix, Arles* (Paris and Marseille, 1935).

4. A.A.E., 1718, fol. 241, October 17, 1654.

5. Ibid., fols. 277–78, March 3, 1655.

6. A.A.E., 1719, fol. 419, March 31, 1655.

7. A.A.E., 1718, fol. 296, April 2, 1655.

8. Ibid., fol. 298, April 9, 1655.

9. A.A.E., 895, fol. 64.

10. For a definition of brokers and brokerage, I am especially indebted to Steffen Schmidt, "Patrons, Brokers, and Clients: Party Linkages in the Colombian System," in *Political Parties and Linkage: A Comparative Perspective*, ed. Kay Lawson (New Haven, 1980), pp. 266–88. Also see Schmidt, "The Transformation of Clientelism in Rural Colombia," in *Friends, Followers, and Factions: A Reader in Political Clientelism*, ed. Steffen Schmidt et al. (Berkeley, 1977), pp. 305–23; Sydel Silverman, "Patronage and Community-Nation Relationships in Central Italy," *Ethnology* 4 (1965): 172–89, reprinted in *Friends, Followers, and Factions*, pp. 293–304; Adrian Mayer, "Patrons and Brokers: Rural Leadership in Four Overseas Indian Communities," in *Social Organization: Essays Presented to Raymond Firth*, ed. Maurice Freedman (London, 1967), pp. 167–88; James Scott, "Patron-Client Politics and Political Change in Southeast Asia," *American Political Science Review* 65 (1972); 91–114, reprinted in Schmidt, *Friends, Followers, and Factions*, pp. 123–46; Jeremy Boissevain, *Friends of Friends: Networks, Manipulators and Coalitions* (Oxford, 1974), pp. 147–69; idem, "Patronage in Sicily," *Man* 1 (1966): 18–33, reprinted in *Political Corruption: Readings in Comparative Analysis*, ed. Arnold Heidenheimer (New York, 1970), pp. 138–52; John Powell, "Peasant Society and Clientelist Politics," in Schmidt, *Friends, Followers, and Factions*, pp. 147–61; Robert Paine, *Patrons and Brokers in the East Arctic*, Newfoundland Social and Economic Research Paper No. 2, Institute of Social and Economic Research (Memorial University of Newfoundland, 1966).

11. "Mémoires de Jacques de Parades de L'Estang, 1642–1674," *Le Musée: Revue Arlésienne*, 13–35 (1875): 236–62.

12. Ibid., p. 237. He also described Colbert as "a hard man, difficult to persuade," see ibid., p. 262.

13. Louis Monmerqué, ed., *Lettres de Madame de Sévigné*, 14 vols. (Paris, 1862–66), vol. 5, p. 143. Madame de Sévigné occasionally referred to Colbert as "Monsieur le Nord."

14. Ibid.

15. "Mémoires de Parades," p. 262. This was Jacques de Souvré, bailli in the Order of Malta, and its ambassador at Paris from 1649 until his death in 1670. See Claire-Eliane Engle, *Les Chevaliers de Malte* (Paris, 1972), pp. 125–26.

16. "Mémoires de Parades," p. 238.

17. Ibid., p. 247. He described their intrigues as "odious and ruinous to the public good," and their treatment of the Arles deputies as "shameful."

18. *Grand Larousse encyclopédique*, 10 vols. (Paris, 1960), vol. 3, p. 629.

19. B.M., Harleian manuscripts 4575, "Semestre de Provence par M. de Sève, conseiller d'Etat," fols. 128v–29; A.A.E., 1714, fols. 71–78, February 28, 1649; Charles de Grimaldi, marquis de Régusse, and Jacques Gaufridy, *Mémoires pour servir à l'histoire de la Fronde en Provence* (Aix, 1870), pp. 37–40; B.M., *Parlement de Bordeaux*, fol. 55; *Les Plaintes de la*

noblesse de Provence contre l'oppression du Parlement sur l'éloignement du comte d'Alais, leur governeur (1650), also conserved in B. Marseille, 1792.

20. A.A.E., 1713, fol. 233, August 14, 1648, Grimaldi to Mazarin from Rome.

21. Grimaldi and Gaufridy, *Mémoires*, p. 91; Pierre-Joseph de Haitze, *Histoire de la ville d'Aix*, 6 vols. (Aix, 1880–92), vol. 5, p. 54; A.A.E., 1723, fols. 550–51, June 17, 1659.

22. A.A.E., 1704, fols. 217–20, January 17, 1636.

23. Georges B. Depping ed., *Correspondance administrative sous le règne de Louis XIV*, 4 vols. (Paris, 1850–55), vol. 2, pp. 111–14.

24. Roland Mousnier, *Les Institutions de la France sous la monarchie absolue*, vol. 1, *Société et état* (Paris, 1974), p. 86, "Thus the fidèle belongs to his master body and soul"; p. 90, "The créature is really that from the point of view of his career, his protector has created him." I am suggesting that clients such as brokers, allies, professional colleagues, and neighbors were not totally dependent on their patron.

25. A.A.E., 1718, fol. 141; Grimaldi and Gaufridy, *Mémoires*, pp. 37, 43, 47, 58.

26. Grimaldi and Gaufridy, *Mémoires*, pp. 54, 57; Honoré Bouche, *La Chorographie ou description de Provence*, 2 vols. (Aix, 1664), vol. 2, p. 982.

27. Grimaldi and Gaufridy, *Mémoires*, p. 54.

28. Roland Mousnier, ed., *Lettres et mémoires adressés au chancelier Séguier, 1633–1649*, 2 vols. (Paris, 1964), vol. 2, p. 730, May 9, 1645.

29. Grimaldi and Gaufridy, *Mémoires*, p. 22.

30. Pierre-Adolphe Chéruel and Georges d'Avenel, *Lettres du Cardinal Mazarin pendant son ministère*, 9 vols. (Paris, 1872–1906), vol. 3, p. 1063.

31. A.A.E., 1714, fol. 268, April 13, 1649; also see 1716, fols. 246, 297–98, and B.N., Clairambault 427, fols. 223, 317.

32. ADBR, Aix, B 3357, fols. 8–11.

33. A.A.E., 1719, fols. 303–4, November 12, 1653; 1720, fol. 4, April 5, 1656; Haitze, *Histoire*, Vol. 5, p. 196; Grimaldi and Gaufridy, *Mémoires*, pp. 43–44, 47.

34. Grimaldi and Gaufridy, *Mémoires*, pp. 55–56; ADBR, Aix, B 3357; Marseille, C 988, February 25, 1653; "Abrégé des Etats de Provence, October 1652," B.N., Cinq Cents de Colbert 288, fols. 56–57.

35. Grimaldi and Gaufridy, *Mémoires*, p. 59.

36. Ibid.; Richard Holbrook, "Baron d'Oppède and Cardinal Mazarin: The Politics of Provence from 1640 to 1661" (Ph.D. diss., University of Illinois at Chicago Circle, 1976), pp. 38, 433. Holbrook did an extensive study of Oppède's fortune and consulted Oppède's *livre de raison* (account book) at the Château de Saint Marcel at Aubagne, near Marseille. The sum of 180,000 livres, which Oppéde paid for the office of first president, is confirmed by his livre de raison, fols. 122v–24. Also see ADBR, Aix, Fonds Lombard 309E, 1069, fol. 507 (1621); 1074, fol. 758 (1631); B. Inguimbertine, 1841, fol. 441v; Philippe de Commines, "Les Luttes du president de Forbin d'Oppède et du marquis de Grimaldi-Régusse pour la première présidence du Parlement de Provence" (paper presented at the Lourmarin Conference, 1972).

37. Grimaldi and Gaufridy, *Memoires*, p. 59.

38. Ibid., pp. 59–60; Haitze, *Histoire*, vol. 5, pp. 287–88.

39. Grimaldi and Gaufridy, *Mémoires*, p. 61.

40. B.M., Harleian 4575, fols. 128v–29.

41. Grimaldi and Gaufridy, *Mémoires*, pp. 42–44; Haitze, *Histoire*, vol. 5, pp. 195, 197; Jean-Scholastique Pitton, *Histoire de la ville d'Aix* (Aix, 1666), p. 454.

42. Grimaldi and Gaufridy, *Mémoires*, p. 61; ADBR, Marseille, C 988, September 25, 1653; A.A.E., 1718, fols. 174, 188–90.

43. A.A.E., 1719, fols. 307–8, December 7, 1653.

44. "Délibérations des Assemblées générales de Provence," ADBR, Marseille, C 32, fols. 169–220, 239–92; C 33, fol. 181; B.N., Ms. fr. 29655, fols. 79–84; Haitze, *Histoire*, vol. 5, pp. 244–45.

45. Haitze, *Histoire*, vol. 5, pp. 283–86; Grimaldi and Gaufridy, *Mémoires*, p. 62; B.N., *Catalogue des consuls et assesseurs de la ville d'Aix* (Aix, 1649). Melchior de Forbin de La Roque

married Aqua d'Oraison in 1647; see Scipion Du Roure, *Les Anciennes familles de Provence: Généalogie de la maison de Forbin* (Paris, 1906), p. 30.

46. B. Méjanes 608, "Administration du pays de Provence," fols. 94–122; A.C., Aix, BB 129, published as *Catalogue des consuls* (see note 45). Also see René Pillorget, *Les Mouvements insurrectionnels de Provence entre 1596 et 1715* (Paris, 1975), pp. 666–70, 747, 759–64; Grimaldi and Gaufridy, *Mémoires*, pp. 42–44; B. Marseille 1792, *Relation envoyée par un gentilhomme de Provence à un de ses amis de Paris* (Paris, 1651).

47. "Mémoires de Parades," p. 178.

48. A.A.E., 1719, fol. 431; ADBR, Aix, B 3358, fol. 528.

49. A.A.E., 1719, fol. 431.

50. The Parlement of Aix customarily reimbursed its deputies 1,000 to 2,000 livres for trips to Paris; see Prosper Cabasse, *Essais historiques sur le Parlement de Provence, 1501–1790*, 3 vols. (Paris, 1826), vol. 2, p. 254.

51. Sharon Kettering, *Judicial Politics and Urban Revolt: The Parlement of Aix, 1629–1659* (Princeton, 1978), pp. 193 n. 77, 198, 213; A.A.E., 1722, fols. 238–40, November 5, 1658; Grimaldi and Gaufridy, *Mémoires*, p. 87. Oppède wrote to Mazarin on December 9, 1659, inviting the Cardinal to stay at his town mansion when the court visited Aix. He remarked with pride that his house was so well exposed to the sun in winter that Mazarin would not need a fire either in the evening or morning; see A.A.E., 1725, fols. 175–78.

52. Grimaldi and Gaufridy, *Mémoires*, p. 91; B.N., Ms. fr. 17399, fols. 27–27v; 17407, fol. 124; B.N., M. C. 131, fols. 80–81, 531–32.

53. Pierre Clément, ed., *Lettres, instructions et mémoires de Colbert, 1648–1683*, 10 vols. (Paris, 1861–73), vol. 4, p. 55.

54. Holbrook, "Baron d'Oppède," p. 38; Alexksandra Dmitrievna Lublinskaya, *Vnutrenniaia politika frantsuzskogo absoliutizma, 1633–1649* (Leningrad, 1966), p. 268, Intendant Champigny to Chancellor Séguier, December 20, 1643.

55. Grimaldi and Gaufridy, *Mémoires*, p. 66.

56. Ibid., p. 65; ADBR, Aix, J. L. H. Hesmivy de Moissac, "Histoire du Parlement de Provence, 1501–1715," 2 vols., vol. 2, p. 185. Ondedei was described by Pierre-Joseph de Haitze as "a great friend of Oppède"; cf. Haitze, *Histoire*, vol. 6, p. 16. Ondedei himself mentioned his friendship with Oppède in writing to Mazarin on October 28, 1659; see A.A.E., 1725, fol. 147.

57. ADBR, Aix, Moissac, "Histoire du Parlement," vol. 2, p. 185; Haitze, *Histoire*, vol. 5, pp. 318, 328–32; Grimaldi and Gaufridy, *Mémoires*, pp. 36, 38, 60.

58. A.A.E., 1720, fol. 56. On September 16, 1656, Mazarin told Oppède to furnish 6,000 livres to naval officials "for the present necessity of the galleys" and "to reimburse [himself later] from a considerable fund which I will be sending." Oppède had no trouble in finding the money on this occasion; cf. A.A.E., 1721, fol. 33, Oppède to Mazarin, September 26, 1656. However, this was not always the case.

59. A.A.E., 1722, fol. 191v, August 10, 1658.

60. A.A.E., 1723, fol. 151, August 27, 1658.

61. A.A.E., 1725, fols. 79–79v, September 9, 1659.

62. Clément, *Lettres de Colbert*, vol. 1, p. 341, March 16, 1664.

63. Holbrook, "Baron d'Oppède," p. 35.

64. "Mémoires de Parades," pp. 269, 277; B. Apt, ms. 20, pièce 29; Pierre Daverdi, *Oraison funèbre de Henri de Forbin d'Oppède*, notes by A. J. Rance Bourrey (Marseille, 1889), p. 54.

65. René Pillorget, "Vente d'offices et journée des barricades du 20 janvier, 1649, à Aix-en-Provence," *Provence historique* 15 (1965): 45.

66. Grimaldi and Gaufridy, *Memoires*, pp. 20 (1643), 22 (1644), 164 (1646).

67. Ibid., pp. 92–95; A.A.E., 1722, fol. 139, June 19, 1658, Mazarin to Governor Mercoeur; 1725, fol. 148v, October 28, 1659, Oppède to Mazarin.

68. Grimaldi and Gaufridy, *Mémoires*, p. 36.

69. The sum of 50,379 livres as Régusse's minimum annual income is based on 16,086 livres in 1640 from interest on loans to communities and individuals; 4,500 livres from his Parlement office; 13,793 livres in 1638 from profits on investments in Marseille commerce; and 16,000 livres

from fiefs; see notes below. This total does not include revenues from his extensive investments in tax treaties or from his urban properties, so the real sum was undoubtedly higher. The figure of 1,000,000 livres for his total fortune is reached by multiplying 50,000 by 20, and is undoubtedly low, too.

70. Grimaldi and Gaufridy, *Mémoires*, pp. 4, 20.

71. A.P., Fonds 43-1, livre de raison or account book of Grimaldi-Régusse describing his commercial ventures. For example, his partnership with Marseille merchant Charles Mazenod, in which he received two-thirds of the profits, brought him 13,793 livres in 1638.

72. A.P., 43–2, 43–3 (not entirely paginated), livre de raison of Grimaldi-Régusse.

73. B.N., M. C. 7, fols. 49–55, in Depping, ed., *Correspondance administrative*, vol. 2, pp. 94–96. For an account of his tax farming, see Pillorget, *Les Mouvements*, pp. 553–61. His Marseille tax farm brought him 38,775 livres in 1643; see A. P., 43–1, fol. 22.

74. Grimaldi and Gaufridy, *Mémoires*, p. 3. See chap. 3.

75. Ibid., p. 65.

76. Ibid., pp. 7, 10–11; A. P., 43–4, fols. 11v–12, 14, 22–22v, 25v, 29; G. Lavergne, *Inventaire des archives de la famille Grimaldi-Régusse* (Monaco and Paris, 1911), pp. 20–22.

77. Lavergne, *Inventaire*, pp. 20, 23, 34, 35; Grimaldi and Gaufridy, *Mémoires*, pp. 10–11, 35, 65, 97; "Etat du florinage contenant le revenu noble de tous les fiefs et arrière-fiefs de Provence avec les noms des possesseurs fait par Maynier d'Oppède en 1668," B. Méjanes 630, fols. 22, 43, 44, 55, 93, 126; François-Paul Blanc, "Origines des familles provençales maintenues dans le second ordre sous le règne de Louis XIV: Dictionnaire généalogique" (Ph.D. diss., University of Aix-Marseille, 1971), pp. 679–82. Régusse owned extensive urban property at Marseille; see A.P., 43–1, fols. 31, 40, 41v, 44v. His fiefs provided an income of about 16,000 libres a year.

78. A.P., 43–1, fols. 14–16, 20; Grimaldi and Gaufridy, *Mémoires*, p. 87.

79. A. P., 43–1, fols. 10, 18, 19, 39; 43–2, fols. 1, 2, 4, 9v, 11, 18, 26v; Lavergne, *Inventaire*, p. 8. Régusse's account books for the 1640s show payments to a wet nurse and a tutor for his children, a lady's maid for his wife, and a valet for himself. His household probably included a chambermaid, cook, and coachman, too.

80. Grimaldi and Gaufridy, *Mémoires*, p. 11.

81. Holbrook, "Baron d'Oppède," pp. 34–39, 428–34.

82. Ibid. His lands in the Comtat Venaissin were valued at 36,000 livres, and his lands in Provence at 273,000 livres. He also had extensive urban property at Marseille.

83. A.A.E., 1725, fols. 79–79v, September 9, 1659.

84. Holbrook, "Baron d'Oppède," pp. 35, 46 n. 60.

85. Ibid.; Du Roure, *La Maison de Forbin*, p. 50; ADBR, Aix, Sénéchaussée, IV B/59, Insinuations 1637, fols. 699–705v.

86. A.A.E., 1725, fols. 79–79v; Holbrook, "Baron d'Oppède," p. 434. Oppède's regular income from his office of first president in 1671 was 7,450 livres, to which were added a special gift of 6,000 livres from the king and other royal pensions of 4,775 livres, for a grand total of 18,225 livres. Additional outside sources of judicial income, i.e., bribes and gifts, made this total higher.

87. Holbrook, "Baron d'Oppède," p. 22; Du Roure, *La Maison de Forbin*, p. 48; Blanc, "Origines des familles," pp. 672, 684–85; Fleury Vindry, *Les Parlementaires français au XVIe siècle*, 3 vols. (Paris, 1910), vol. 1, pp. 7, 8, 11, 19–20; EDB, IV–2, 209–14, 359–60; Balthasar de Clapiers-Collongues, *Chronologie des cours souveraines* (Aix, 1909–12), pp. 5, 6, 8, 9, 12, 17, 20, 75, 89; Roman d'Amat, ed., *Dictionnaire de biographie française*, tome 13, fasc. 80 (Paris, 1976), pp. 395–418; René Borricand, *Nobiliaire de Provence*: *Armorial général de la Provence, du Comtat Venaissin, de la principauté d'Orange*, 3 vols. (Aix, 1974–78), vol. 1, pp. 471–76.

88. Holbrook, "Baron d'Oppède," pp. 423–27, 430.

89. Jacqueline Carrière, *La Population d'Aix-en-Provence à la fin du XVIIe siècle* (Aix, 1958), p. 73; Jean-Paul Coste, *La Ville d'Aix en 1695: Structure urbaine et société*, 3 vols. (Aix, 1970), vol. 2, pp. 639, 641, 717, 960.

90. EDB, II, plate XIX; Jacques Cundier, *Portraits des premiers présidents du Parlement de Provence* (Aix, 1724), B. Méjanes 963, p. 51; Daverdi, *Oraison funèbre*, frontispiece.

91. Cundier, *Portraits*, p. 51: Haitze was the author of the text. Also see Pierre-Joseph

d'Haitze, *Portraits ou éloges historiques des premiers présidents du Parlement de Provence* (Avignon, 1727), p. 123.

92. "Mémoires de Parades," p. 277.

93. Grimaldi and Gaufridy, *Mémoires*, p. 54.

94. Anyone wanting to enter or leave Aix after January 20, 1649, needed a pass signed by Oppède; see "Deliberations du Parlement de Provence," B. Méjanes 953, fol. 209. In his memoirs, intendant Sève named Oppède as a leader of the 1649 revolt with Régusse, Forbin La Roque, and Decormis; see B.M., Harleian 4575, fol. 49v.

95. Grimaldi and Gaufridy, *Mémoires*, pp. 45–47.

96. ADBR, Aix, Moissac, "Histoire du Parlement," vol. 2, fol. 233; Adolphe Crémieux, *Marseille et la royauté pendant la minorité de Louis XIV*, 2 vols. (Paris, 1917), vol. 2, p. 683.

97. Clément, *Lettres de Colbert*, vol. 7, p. 20.

98. Grimaldi and Gaufridy, *Mémoires*, p. 6.

99. B.N., M. C. 7, fols. 49–53, in Depping, ed., *Correspondance administrative*, vol. 2, pp. 94–96.

100. Monmerqué, *Lettres de Sévigné*, vol. 6, pp. 423–24.

101. Maximin Deloche, *Un Frère de Richelieu inconnu: Chartreux, primat des Gaules, Cardinal, ambassadeur* (Paris, 1935), p. 37.

102. ADBR, Aix, Marseille, XXVII F 16, Timon-David, a biography of Oppède without title, p. 4; Daverdi, *Oraison funèbre*, p. 35.

103. B.M., Harleian 4575, fol. 49v; A.A.E., 1725, fol. 84, Mercoeur to Mazarin, September 16, 1659. See Table 3 for the membership of Régusse's clientele.

104. A.A.E., 1721, fols. 493–94, Coriolis to Mazarin, April 13, 1658.

105. Grimaldi and Gaufridy, *Mémoires*, p. vi.

106. Ibid., pp. 9, 35. She had eight children.

107. Ibid., pp. iii, 18. He used Grimaldi in signing letters to Paris, although he usually signed himself Régusse, and he used Grimaud in recording the births of his children; see A.P. 43–4, unpaginated at end.

108. Lavergne, *Inventaire*, pp. 2, 4, 15, 24.

109. B.M., Harleian 4575, fols. 128v–29.

110. A.A.E., 1716, fol. 423. See Table 2 for the membership of Oppède's clientele.

111. Carl Friedrich, *An Introduction to Political Theory* (New York, 1967), pp. 121–32; Neil McDonald, *Politics: A Study of Control Science* (New Brunswick, 1965); Robert Dahl, "The Concept of Power," *Behavioral Sciences* 2 (1952): 201–15.

112. B.N., Ms. fr. 18977, fols. 83–85, 87–99, 100–2; 17390, fols. 79–82; A.A.E., 1713, fols. 243–46.

113. B.N., Ms. fr. 17393, fols. 193–96; A.A.E., 1714, fols. 278, 309; Grimaldi and Gaufridy, *Mémoires*, pp. 39–40; B.M., Harleian 4575, fols. 121–22, 125v, 143v–44; Pillorget, *Les Mouvements*, pp. 591–96; idem, "Vente d'offices," p. 45.

114. A.A.E., 1717, fol. 317. The seigneur de La Verdière, Oppède's uncle, and the baron de Bormes, Oppède's brother-in-law, also raised troops in 1651; see B. Méjanes R.A. 3, "Mémoires de Messire Antoine de Valbelle," fols. 833–35v; Crémieux, *Marseille*, vol. 1, p. 399.

115. A.A.E., 1723, fols. 376–76v.

116. See chap. 1.

117. A.A.E., 1710, fols. 261, 289.

118. A.A.E., 1714, fols. 270–72, April 13, 1649, Forbin to Mazarin, noting that Oppède had visited Cardinal Bichi at Carpentras; ibid., fols. 291–92, April 27, 1649, Forbin to Mazarin, noting that he had visited Bichi and adding strong praise of Oppède.

119. A.A.E., 1721, fol. 35; "Mémoires de Parades," p. 114.

120. Boissevain, *Friends of Friends*, pp. 158–63.

121. Lavergne, *Inventaire*, p. viii; A.A.E., 1724, fol. 302, March 3, 1660.

122. A.A.E., 1727, fol. 40, January 2, 1663, letter from Mercoeur to Colbert expressing gratitude that Oppède's brother had been named bishop of Toulon.

123. In December 1657, Oppède had asked Mazarin for a priory for his younger brother, Louis, "who is looking for an opportunity to serve you," and thanked the Cardinal for granting

this request two months later; see A.A.E., 1721, fols. 289v–90, December 11, 1657; fol. 60, February 21, 1658. In August 1660, Oppède requested the abbey of Saint Floren in Auvergne for his brother, granted a month later; see A.A.E., 1725, fol. 408, August 7, 1660; fol. 429, September 14, 1660.

124. On June 20, 1651, Régusse's oldest son, Gaspard, was received as a lieutenant in the seneschal court at Brignoles, and on November 20, 1653, he was provided to his father's office of Parlement president *en survivance*, although he did not have the exercise of it for another thirty years; cf. Lavergne, *Inventaire*, p. viii.

125. Oppède had bought his office for 120,000 livres; see A.A.E., 1728, fols. 104–5, 255; ADBR, Aix, 3365, fols. 537–39v, 542–48; Clapiers-Collongues, *Chronologie*, p. 23.

126. A.A.E., 1718, fol. 422; 1720, fols. 121, 123, 149; 1722, fol. 72; 1724, fol. 84.

127. Ibid., March 21, 1659. Oppède also praised Forbin de La Roque's service in a letter to Mazarin on November 18, 1659; cf. A.A.E., 1725, fol. 166. Forbin de La Roque received a gift of 3,000 livres from the king in 1660 for his support of Oppède during the revolt at Aix in the previous year, Parlement president Foresta de La Roquette received 1,500 livres, and royal attorney Rabasse de Vergons 1,500 livres; see Holbrook, "Baron d'Oppède," pp. 37, 47.

128. Régusse's second son, Pierre, who became the baron de Moissac in 1685, received a commission as captain of an infantry regiment on June 8, 1652, and as captain of a light horse company on April 13, 1657; see Lavergne, *Inventaire*, p. 11; A.P., Fonds 7.

129. B.N., M. C. 139, fol. 139, fol. 108, August 7, 1666, Arnoul to Colbert.

130. Oppède's brothers, Vincent and Jean, both Knights of Malta, obtained suitable posts: Vincent became the commander of a galley squadron and Jean an officer in Mazarin's regiment; see Holbrook, "Baron d'Oppède," p. 29.

131. Schmidt, "Patrons, Brokers, and Clients," p. 267.

132. Scott, "Patron-Client Politics and Political Change," pp. 127–28.

133. B.N., Ms. fr. 17398, fol. 1, August 2, 1661.

134. Pillorget, *Les Mouvements*, p. 787.

135. B.N., M. C. 118 bis, fols. 531–32, 597, September and November 1663.

136. B.N., M. C. 127, fol. 136, January 12, 1665.

137. B.N., M. C. 122, fols. 202v–203.

138. In 1646, Valbelle was cleared of charges of misconduct by the Parlement of Toulouse where his case had been invoked; see Jean-Marc David, *L'Amirauté de Provence et des mers du Levant* (Marseille, 1942), pp. 188, 232; ADBR, Marseille, IX B2, fol. 696v, November 19, 1647. See chap. 3 on Antoine de Valbelle.

139. A.A.E., 1708, fol. 49, April 9, 1642; fol. 84, July 5, 1642; fol. 92, July 21, 1642; fol. 98, September 1, 1642; fol. 113, October 29, 1642; fol. 119, November 15, 1642.

140. B.N., Ms. fr. 17409, fol. 238, June 28, 1667; 17410, fol. 26, August 1667; fols. 78–79, September 1667; fol. 226, December 1667; 17411, fols. 380–380v, December 18, 1668.

141. Du Roure, *La Maison de Forbin*, p. 51; Pillorget, *Les Mouvements*, pp. 841–42.

142. Pillorget, *Les Mouvements*, pp. 803–7; also see pp. 681–84, 731, 841–47; Du Roure, *La Maison de Forbin*, p. 51; B.N., Ms. fr. 17404, fol. 13, January 21, 1664.

143. Pillorget, *Les Mouvements*, pp. 804–9.

144. A.A.E., 1725, fol. 149, October 28, 1659.

145. Julian Dent, "The Role of Clientèles in the Financial Elite of France under Cardinal Mazarin," in *French Government and Society, 1500–1800*, ed. John F. Bosher (London, 1973), pp. 46–47.

146. Depping, ed., *Correspondance administrative*, vol. 1, pp. 363–64. A scurrilous poster had appeared anonymously at Aix in October 1666 linking the names of Oppède and Guidy.

147. Clapiers-Collongues, *Chronologie*, pp. 104, 108; EDB IV–2, 259; ADBR, Marseille, C 2716 (December 31, 1669); Pillorget, *Les Mouvements*, pp. 935–36. Dominique Guidy wrote a history of the Parlement of Aix; cf. B. Méjanes R.A. 54, "Histoire du Parlement de Provence 1501–1671." Needless to say, Oppède is well treated in this history.

148. Depping, *Correspondance administrative*, vol. 1, p. 357, August 3, 1666.

149. Du Chaine and Grimaldi were involved in the 1659 revolt against Oppède at Aix; cf. Kettering, *Judicial Politics*, pp. 307–9, 317.

150. The office of governor of Antibes was customarily held by a member of the Forbin family.

151. Raymond Collier, *La Vie en Haute-Provence de 1600 à 1850* (Digne, 1973), p. 315; Pillorget, *Les Mouvements*, p. 611.

152. Pillorget, *Les Mouvements*, pp. 956–57.

153. He knew the king personally. He hoped to receive the office of Provençal lieutenant general to which Grignan was named in 1669.

154. Robert Paine, ed., *Patrons and Brokers in the East Arctic*, Newfoundland Social and Economic Papers No. 2, Institute of Social and Economic Research (Memorial University of Newfoundland, 1961), p. 6.

155. Paul Logié, *La Fronde en Normandie*, 3 vols. (Amiens, 1951), vol. 2, pp. 15 n. 29, 96–97, 99–101, 169–73.

156. Françoise de Bernardy, *Princes of Monaco: The Remarkable History of the Grimaldi Family*, trans. Len Ortzen (London, 1961), pp. 67–76.

157. Madeleine Foisil, *Mémoires du Président Alexandre Bigot de Monville: Le Parlement de Rouen, 1640–1643* (Paris, 1976), p. 39.

158. Ibid., p. 78.

159. Ibid., pp. 79–80.

160. Ibid., pp. 83–85.

161. Ibid., pp. 293–94.

162. William Beik, *Absolutism and Society in Seventeenth-Century France: State Power and Provincial Aristocracy in Languedoc* (Cambridge, 1985), pp. 224–28.

163. See chap. 1.

164. B.N., M.C. 103, fol. 708, October 20, 1661.

165. Ibid., 116 bis, fol. 572, August 8, 1663.

166. "Mémoires de Parades," p. 268.

167. Louis André, *Michel Le Tellier et Louvois* (Paris, 1942), pp. 283, 285, 286.

168. B. N., M.C. 128 bis, fol. 805, March 1665, Mérinville writing to Colbert from Narbonne in Languedoc as its governor.

169. Chéruel and Avenel, *Lettres de Mazarin*, vol. 2, p. 807, September 5, 1645, Mazarin to Clerville; A.A.E., 1726, fols. 16, 19, May 17 and 30, 1660, Mazarin to Clerville; B.N., M.C. 110, fol. 781, August 29, 1662, Clerville to Colbert; Depping, ed., *Correspondance administrative*, vol. 1, p. 648, October 9, 1661, Clerville to Colbert; Auguste Jal, *Abraham Du Quesne et le marine de son temps*, 2 vols. (Paris, 1873), vol. 1, p. 237; Clément, *Lettres de Colbert*, vol. 2, p. 435, n. 3.

170. Arnold Strickon and Sidney Greenfield, eds., *Structure and Process in Latin America: Patronage, Clientage, and Power Systems* (Albuquerque, 1972), pp. 179–80.

171. Grimaldi and Gaufridy, *Mémoires*, p. 41; A.A.E., 1716, fols. 297–98, 412–13; Haitze, *Histoire*, vol. 5, p. 194; B.M., Harleian 4575, fols. 127v–28.

172. Grimaldi and Gaufridy, *Mémoires*, pp. 45–47; A.A.E., 1717, fol. 317; A.C., Aix, BB 102, fol. 222v; Pillorget, *Les Mouvements*, pp. 665–71.

173. Kettering, *Judicial Politics*, pp. 291–94.

174. Grimaldi and Gaufridy, *Mémoires*, p. v.

175. Ibid., p. 67.

176. Kettering, *Judicial Politics*, pp. 307–9.

177. Grimaldi and Gaufridy, *Mémoires*, p. 63.

178. Kettering, *Judicial Politics*, pp. 302–15.

179. B.M., Harleian 4489, fols. 164–65, August 1656, Oppède to Séguier.

180. Pillorget, *Les Mouvements*, p. 731.

181. B.M., Harleian 4489, fols. 188–90, August 15, 1656, Oppède to Séguier.

182. A.A.E., 1721, fols. 324–29, 342–46, 348–51.

183. Kettering, *Judicial Politics*, pp. 305–7; Pillorget, *Les Mouvements*, pp. 759–61.

184. A.A.E., 1721, fols. 416–22, 425.

185. Ibid., fols. 441–44, 449–53.

186. Ibid., fols. 393–407, 431–34.

187. Ibid., fols. 493–94; B. Méjanes 954, "Délibérations du Parlement de Provence," fols. 158v–59; Haitze, *Histoire*, vol. 5, p. 415; Kettering, *Judicial Politics*, pp. 298–328.

188. A.A.E., 1722, fol. 126; in Chéruel and Avenel, *Lettres de Mazarin*, vol. 8, p. 708, May 7, 1658.

189. In January 1658, Grimaldi had opposed the levy of a new tax for military purposes, requested by Oppède and Mercoeur, and he had encouraged the other procureurs du pays to stand firm in their refusal to approve this tax; see A.A.E., 1721, fols. 167, 324–29, 330–35, 356, 371–73, 393–96. A steady stream of reprimands from Mazarin followed; see Chéruel and Avenel, *Lettres de Mazarin*, vol. 8, pp. 663, 675, 681, 703, 724; vol. 9, p. 717. Grimaldi, with precedence as Cardinal, was told not to be in Aix when Mazarin visited the city in January 1660. He retired to the Carthusians at Villeneuve-lès-Avignon, went to Rome as extraordinary ambassador, and did not return to Aix until 1662; see Commines, "Les Luttes," p. 18; EDB, IV–2, 254; Joseph H. Albanès, *Gallia Christiana Novissima*, 7 vols. (Valence, 1899–1920), vol. 1, p. 144.

190. Grimaldi and Gaufridy *Mémoires*, p. vi.

191. A.A.E., 1723, fols. 382–84v, February 27, 1659.

192. A.A.E., 1725, fol. 53, August 19, 1659.

193. Ibid., fol. 84, September 16, 1659.

194. Ibid., fol. 148v, October 28, 1659.

195. B.N., M.C. 118, fols. 324–25, November 13, 1663.

196. A.A.E., 1723, fols. 360–61.

197. Grimaldi and Gaufridy, *Mémoires*, pp. vii, 97–99; Commines, "Les Luttes," p. 20.

198. Grimaldi and Gaufridy, *Mémoires*, p. 97.

199. N.L., *Abrégés des délibérations des communautés de Provence* (Aix, 1612–89), 1661; ADBR, Marseille, C 39, fols. 297–319.

200. Grimaldi and Gaufridy, *Mémoires*, p. 92; A.A.E., 1726, fol. 200v, March 29, 1660, Oppède to the king.

201. Pillorget, *Les Mouvements*, p. 856.

202. Clément, *Lettres de Colbert*, vol. 4, p. 62; Depping, *Correspondance administrative*, vol. 1 p. 331.

203. AA.E., 1726, fols. 193–94, 195–96.

204. Grimaldi and Gaufridy, *Mémoires*, pp. 92–95.

205. Ibid. The comte de Brienne was secretary of state for Provence. Le Tellier, a royal minister, and Serroni, the bishop of Mende, had been clients of Mazarin, and were well known to Colbert. Colbert had begun his career as Le Tellier's secretary.

206. Régusse had written to Colbert from Aix on August 2, 1661, "to renew my avowal of obedience, and to ask that you grant me your favor and the honor of your protection"; see B.N., M. C. 103, fols. 298–99.

207. See chap. 4.

208. A.A.E., 1721, fol. 293v, December 18, 1657.

209. A.A.E., 1720, fols. 234, 240–43, 246–48, 285, 304–5, July through November 1657. Gravier was eventually dismissed for peculation.

210. Grimaldi and Gaufridy, *Mémoires*, p. 37; B.M., Harleian 4575, fols. 127v–131v. Régusse's attempt at mediation was unsuccessful.

211. Holbrook, "Baron d'Oppède," p. 37; A.A.E., 1726, fol. 154, royal letters of February 28, 1661.

212. B.N., M.C. 142 bis, fols. 488–89, December 8, 1666.

213. Ibid., 147, fols. 515–16, March 7, 1668.

214. A.A.E., 1727, fols. 210–12, June 12, 1660.

215. Pillorget, *Les Mouvements*, p. 787.

216. Silverman, "Patronage and Community-Nation Relationships," p. 300. Silverman proposes five different variations. The broker-client tie may also be kinship, employment, or political appointment, restricted to specific areas, sporadic, less emotionally intense, while mutual rights and obligations may vary. The types of brokers may also vary, that is, their background, customs, manners, and the ways in which they are recruited. Their functions may

vary. The size of clienteles may vary. And the degree or extent of their integration into the local system may vary.

217. See, for instance, letters of Régusse to Mazarin, A.A.E., 1713, fols. 36–37, January 28, 1648; 1714, fols. 138–41, February 25, 1649; 1714–1720, passim; Kettering, *Judicial Politics*, pp. 267, 271, 271–76; "Patronage and Politics during the Fronde," forthcoming in *French Historical Studies*.

218. Holbrook, "Baron d'Oppède," pp. 20–48; and chap. 4 herein.

219. A.A.E., 1700–1726, passim, especially 1720–1726; Pillorget, *Les Mouvements*, pp. 865–66.

220. A.A.E., 1726, fols. 234–35, October 25, 1658.

221. B.N., M. C. 114, fols. 189–90, January 9, 1663.

222. Depping, ed., *Correspondance administrative*, vol. 1, p. 179, January 15, 1667.

223. A.A.E., 1723, fol. 12; ADBR, Marseille, C 37, fols. 372v–75; ADBR, Aix, B 3368, May 31, June 1, 1658; A.C., Aix, AA 14, fol. 747.

224. A.A.E., 1723, fols. 376, 388v.

225. B.N., Ms. fr. 17390, fols. 79–82, August 11, 1648, Sève to Séguier; fols. 83–84, 87–88, 117–18, 171–72, August 12 and 18 and September 1, 1648, Oppède to Séguier protesting his innocence, supported by letters from opposition parlementaires Decormis and Forbin de La Roque; B.N., Ms. fr. 18977, fols. 83–85, 87–99, 100–2, August 6, 10, 11, 14, 1648, reports on parlementaires' activities by Sève; Lublinskaya, *Vnutrenniaia*, pp. 324–25, August 13, 1648, opposition parlementaires to Séguier maintaining their innocence.

226. A.A.E., 1713–1721, passim.

227. Grimaldi and Gaufridy, *Mémoires*, p. 87; Bouche, *La Chorographie*, vol. 2, pp. 1028–32; Haitze, *Histoire*, vol. 6, p. 1.

228. Grimaldi and Gaufridy, *Mémoires*, p. 89.

229. Ibid., p. 67; Bouche, *La Chorographie*, vol. 2, p. 1030; Edouard Baratier, ed., *Documents de l'histoire de la Provence* (Toulouse, 1971), pp. 216–17.

Chapter Three

1. *Félix et Thomas Platter à Montpellier, 1552–1559, 1595–1599: Notes de voyage de deux étudiants bâlois* (Montpellier, 1892), pp. 304–6; *Les Confessions de Jean-Jacques Bouchard, parisien, suivis de son voyage de Paris à Rome en 1630* (Paris, 1881), pp. 156–207; Charles de Brosses, *Lettres familières sur l'Italie*, 2d ed. (Paris, 1969), p. 37.

2. Henri de Séguiran, "Procès-verbal contentant l'état véritable auquel sont les affaires de la côte maritime de Provence," B.N., Ms. fr. 24169, fols. 2–61, Eugène Sue, ed., *Correspondance d'Henri d'Escoubleau de Sourdis, archevêque de Bordeaux, 1636–1642*, 3 vols. (Paris, 1836), vol. 3, pp. 221–319; R. Collier, J. Billioud, G. Rambert, L. Bergasse, R. Paris, *Histoire du commerce de Marseille, 1481–1789*, vols. 3–6 (Paris, 1951–57).

3. Gaston Rambert, *Nicolas Arnoul: Intendant des galères à Marseille, 1665–1674* (Marseille, 1931), p. 335, August 13, 1672.

4. Ibid., p. 300, March 26, 1670.

5. Ibid., pp. 106–87.

6. See Adolphe Crémieux, *Marseille et la royauté pendant la minorité de Louis XIV*, 2 vols. (Paris and Marseille, 1917); Mireille Zarb, *Les Privilèges de la ville de Marseille du Xe siècle à la Révolution* (Paris, 1961); René Pillorget, *Les Mouvements insurrectionnels de Provence entre 1596 et 1715* (Paris, 1975); Raoul Busquet, *Histoire de Marseille* (Paris, 1945); C. Carrière, M. Courdurie, F. Rebuffat, *Marseille, ville morte: La peste de 1720* (Marseille, 1968); Charles Carrière, *Négociants marseillais au XVIIIe siècle*, 2 vols. (Marseille, 1973).

7. James Scott, "Corruption, Machine Politics, and Political Change," *American Political Science Review* 62 (1969): 1142–58.

8. See Seymour Mandelbaum, *Boss Tweed's New York* (New York, 1965); William Riordan,

Plunkett of Tammany Hall (New York, 1963); Martin and Susan Tolchin, *To the Victor: Political Patronage from the Clubhouse to the White House* (New York, 1971); William Whyte, *Street Corner Society: The Social Structure of an Italian Slum* (Chicago, 1955); Harold Gosnell, *Machine Politics: Chicago Model*, 2d ed. (Chicago, 1968); Edward Banfield and James Wilson, *City Politics* (Cambridge, Mass., 1965); Edward Banfield, *Urban Government: A Reader on Administration and Politics* (New York, 1969).

9. Scott, "Patron-Client Politics and Political Change," p. 127. Also see Mart Bax, *Harpstrings and Confessions: Machine-Style Politics in the Irish Republic* (Amsterdam, 1976).

10. On Richelieu's scheme for naval reorganization, see Charles de La Roncière, *Histoire de la marine française*, 6 vols. (Paris, 1899–1932), vol. 4, pp. 567–77; René La Bruyère, *La Marine de Richelieu: Richelieu (9 sept, 1585–4 dec. 1642)* (Paris, 1958), pp. 37–47, 65–73; Henri Hauser, *La Pensée et l'action économique du Cardinal Richelieu* (Paris, 1944), pp. 24–26.

11. Kenneth Dunkley, "Richelieu and the Estates of Brittany, 1624–1640" (Ph.D. diss., Emory University, 1972), pp. 181–258; Arthur de La Borderie and Barthélemy Pocquet, *Histoire de Bretagne*, 6 vols. (Rennes, 1896–1904), vol. 5 (1515–1715), pp. 391–479.

12. Richelieu's nepotism was well known. See Carl Burckhardt, *Richelieu and His Age*, vol. 2, *Assertion of Power and the Cold War*, trans. Bernard Hoy (London, 1970), pp. 136–40.

13. Maximin Deloche, *La Maison du Cardinal Richelieu* (Paris, 1912), pp. 57–59, 71, 181–83.

14. See Orest Ranum, *Richelieu and the Councillors of Louis XIII* (Oxford, 1963).

15. William Weary, "Royal Policy and Patronage in Renaissance France: The Monarchy and the House of La Trémoille" (Ph.D. diss., Yale University, 1972), p. 111; Mack Holt, "Patterns of *Clientèle* and Economic Opportunity at Court during the Wars of Religion: The Household of François, Duke of Anjou," *French Historical Studies* 13 (1984): 305–22.

16. Julian Dent, "The Role of Clientèles in the Financial Elite of France under Cardinal Mazarin," in *French Government and Society, 1500–1800: Essays in Memory of Alfred Cobban*, ed. John F. Bosher (London, 1973), pp. 43–44; Robert Harding, *Anatomy of a Power Elite: The Provincial Governors of Early Modern France* (New Haven, 1978), pp. 21–23.

17. For instance, Madeleine Foisil writes in her introduction to the memoirs of Alexandre Bigot de Monville that "according to the rules of a society of clienteles and alliances, Bigot de Monville insists much on the relations and kinship ties between the numerous people mentioned in his memoirs." See Madeleine Foisil, ed., *Mémoires du Président Alexandre Bigot de Monville: Le Parlement de Rouen, 1640–1643* (Paris, 1976), p. 37.

18. Eric Wolf, "Kinship, Friendship, and Patron-Client Relations in Complex Societies," in Schmidt et al., eds., *Friends, Followers, and Factions: A Reader in Political Clientelism* (Berkeley, 1977), pp. 175–76; Carl Landé, "The Dyadic Basis of Clientelism," ibid., pp. xxxv–xxxvi; James Scott, "Patron-Client Politics and Political Change," ibid., p. 124.

19. Sharon Kettering, *Judicial Politics and Urban Revolt in Seventeenth-Century France: The Parlement of Aix, 1629–1659* (Princeton, 1978).

20. William Beik, *Absolutism and Society in Seventeenth-Century France: State Power and Provincial Aristocracy in Languedoc* (Cambridge, 1985), pp. 229–30; also see chap. 4 herein.

21. "Mémoires de Jacques de Parades de L'Estang, 1642–1674," *Le Musée: Revue Arlésienne*, 13–35 (1875): 113–15, 150, 278.

22. Ibid., p. 133.

23. Pillorget, *Les Mouvements*, pp. 604–6.

24. Nicolas Fessenden, "Epernon and Guyenne: Provincial Politics under Louis XIII" (Ph.D. diss., Columbia University, 1972), pp. 31–32, 238–44.

25. B.M., Harleian 4575, "Semestre de Provence par M. de Sève," fol. 96; Pillorget, *Les Mouvements*, p. 611. The crown made Montauroux a marquisat in favor of Lombard in 1671; see ibid., p. 876 n. 36.

26. Harding, *Anatomy of a Power Elite*, pp. 28–29, 31, 88–89, 97–98.

27. Kettering, *Judicial Politics*, pp. 118–22; A. D. Lublinskaya, ed., *Vnutrenniaia politika frantuzskogo absoliutizma, 1633–1649* (Leningrad, 1966), pp. 230–31, Intendant de La Potherie to Chancellor Séguier, April 4, 1633; J. L. H. Hesmivy de Moissac, "Difficultés entre le Parlement et les diverses autorités," B. Méjanes 936, fols. 377–80; "Délibérations du Parlement de Provence," B. Méjanes 952, fols. 117v–24.

28. Roland Mousnier, ed., *Lettres et mémoires adressés au chancelier Séguier (1633–1649)*, 2 vols. (Paris, 1964), vol. 2, pp. 559–60: Mousnier mistakenly gives the provenance of this letter as Aix, but it is Arles; Lublinskaya, *Vnutrenniaia*, pp. 271–72; B.N., Ms. fr. 18976, fols. 459–71; Pillorget, *Les Mouvements*, pp. 528–38 (Pillorget depends heavily for his account on the memoirs of Jacques de Parades de L'Estang); Kettering, *Judicial Politics*, pp. 131, 192–93.

29. Pillorget, *Les Mouvements*, p. 821 n. 655.

30. A.A.E., 1723, fols. 364–65, 366–67, February 21, 1659. Coriolis remained at Aix to keep an eye on events there; Coriolis was the brother-in-law of Forbin de La Roque, Oppède's cousin.

31. ADBR, Aix, 3351, fol. 284; Pierre-Joseph de Haitze, *Histoire de la ville d'Aix*, 6 vols. (Aix, 1880–92), vol. 4, pp. 295–96; A.A.E., 1706–1710, passim; Crémieux, *Marseille et la royauté*, vol. 1, pp. 168–73, 183–84, 302.

32. Landé, "The Dyadic Base of Clientelism," in Schmidt et al., eds., *Friends, Followers, and Factions*, p. xxxv; Alan Zuckerman, *The Politics of Faction: Christian Democratic Rule in Italy* (New Haven, 1979); see also chap. 6 herein.

33. Dr. Gabriel, "Origine de la maison de Valbelle," *Provence historique* 7 (1957): 22–23, 278–85; EDB, IV-2, 480–83; François-Paul Blanc, "L'Anoblissement par lettres en Provence à l'époque des réformations de Louis XIV, 1630–1730" (Ph.D. diss., University of Aix-Marseille, 1971), p. 569; Emmanuel Davin, "Une Grande famille provençale: Les Valbelle," *Bulletin de la société des amis du Vieux Toulon* 68 (1941): 89–112.

34. ADBR, Aix, B 3335, fol. 598, royal letters of July 25, 1586; "Mémoires de Messire Antoine de Valbelle," B. Méjanes R.A. 3, fol. 225v; Pillorget, *Les Mouvements*, pp. 218–23. The first president was Guillaume Du Vair, and the governor was Charles de Lorraine, duc de Guise.

35. Pillorget, *Les Mouvements*, pp. 220, 364; Crémieux, *Marseille et la royauté*, vol. 1, pp. 175–76; Busquet, *Histoire de Marseille*, p. 354; ADBR, Aix, B 3347, fol. 273v, royal letters of December 18, 1625. Also see Jean-Marc David, *L'Amirauté de Provence et des mers du Levant* (Marseille, 1942).

36. A.A.E., 1701, fols. 66–67, "Lettres du maréchal Vitry sur l'amirauté de Provence, 1628"; Jacques Gaufridy, "Histoire de Provence sous le règne de Louis XIII," B. Méjanes 790, fol. 5; John Pearl, "Guise and Provence: Political Conflicts in the Epoch of Richelieu" (Ph.D. diss., Northwestern University, 1968), pp. 76–79. It was estimated by Vitry in 1628 that annual fees at Marseille were 30,000 écus (90,000 livres), while fees of the other admiralty courts averaged 5,000 to 6,000 écus (15,000 to 18,000 livres) a year.

37. Pillorget, *Les Mouvements*, pp. 345, 365. Cosme de Valbelle's refusal to assist the Aix rebels was undoubtedly motivated as well by the fact that his brother-in-law, Louis de Paule, had been attacked and his house sacked by the rebels; see Gaufridy, "Histoire de Provence," B. Méjanes 790, fol. 71; Haitze, *Histoire*, vol. 4, pp. 182, 184–85; Jean-Scholastique Pitton, *Histoire de la ville d'Aix* (Aix, 1666), pp. 385–86; Honoré Bouche, *La Chorographie ou description de Provence*, 2 vols. (Aix, 1664), vol. 2, p. 882.

38. A.A.E., 1702, fols. 165–67.

39. Ibid., fols. 169–70. Richelieu also ignored a letter complaining about Valbelle from his nephew, Pont de Courlay, on May 25, 1637; A.A.E., 1706, fol. 25.

40. A.A.E., 1704, fol. 15, October 1, 1635.

41. Pierre-Joseph de Haitze, "Histoire de Provence sous le gouvernement du comte d'Alais," B. Méjanes 736, fol. 14; Crémieux, *Marseille et la royauté*, vol. 1, p. 175 n. 2; Charles de La Roncière, *Histoire de la marine française*, 6 vols. (Paris, 1899–1932), vol. 5, p. 37.

42. "Mémoires de Valbelle," B. Méjanes R.A. 3, fols. 5–16, 40; A.A.E., 1702, fol. 10; Crémieux, *Marseille et la royauté*, vol. 1, p. 176; Pillorget, *Les Mouvements*, pp. 542–43; David, *L'Amirauté*, p. 94. Léon de Valbelle, sieur de La Tour-Saint Symphorien, became friendly with Cardinal de La Rochefoucauld while serving as the deputy of the Provençal second estate to the Estates General of 1614; see "Mémoires de Valbelle," fol. 5; J. Michael Hayden, *France and the Estates General of 1614* (Cambridge, 1974), p. 262. The given name of a man's son, particularly his firstborn, the child's godparents, and the celebrants at his baptism often indicate patron-client ties.

43. Crémieux, *Marseille et la royauté*, vol. 1, pp. 186–265.

44. A.A.E., 1709, fol. 210, November 29, 1644.

45. A.A.E., 1710, fol. 39, February 21, 1645.

46. A.A.E., 1709, fols. 144–45, August 31, 1644.

47. B.N., Clairambault 408, fol. 121, November 20, 1646.

48. Crémieux, *Marseille et la royauté*, vol. 1, p. 177 and n. 2.

49. Sue, ed., *Correspondance d'Henri d'Escoubleau*, vol. 3, p. 25; René La Bruyère, *La Marine de Richelieu: Sourdis, archevêque et amiral (6 novembre 1594–18 juin 1645)* (Paris, 1948), pp. 217–18.

50. Zarb, *Les Privilèges de la ville de Marseille*.

51. Ibid., pp. 134–39, 144, 147, 210, 213.

52. Pillorget, *Les Mouvements*, pp. 364 n. 271, 365, 371, 372, 542, 543, 553, 645, 839; Crémieux, *Marseille et la royauté*, vol. 1, pp. 279, 281, 282; A.A.E., 1702, fol. 389.

53. B.N., Ms. fr. 18976, fols. 474–75; B. Méjanes R.A. 3, "Mémoires de Valbelle," fols. 97v–103v; Pillorget, *Les Mouvements*, pp. 562–64.

54. B.N., Clairambault 416, fol. 263.

55. B. Méjanes R.A. 3, "Mémoires d'Antoine de Valbelle," fol. 109.

56. A.A.E., 1710, fols. 223–24, August 1, 1645. Alais's coolness toward Chavigny may have partly been motivated by the latter's loss of influence at court.

57. B. Méjanes R.A. 3, "Mémoires d'Antoine de Valbelle," fol. 747; A.A.E, 1718, fol. 84, December 7, 1643; 1719, fol. 309, December 7, 1653; Crémieux, *Marseille et la royauté*, vol. 1, p. 181; Pillorget, *Les Mouvements*, p. 551.

58. A.A.E., 1711, fol. 141.

59. Charles de Grimaldi and Jacques Gaufridy, *Mémoires pour servir à l'histoire de la Fronde* (Aix, 1870), p. 22.

60. Pierre-Adolphe Chéruel and Georges d'Avenel, *Lettres du Cardinal Mazarin pendant son ministère*, 9 vols. (Paris, 1872–1906), vol. 2, p. 797, August 19, 1646; p. 812, September 27, 1646.

61. Pierre-Adolphe Chéruel, *Histoire de France pendant la minorité de Louis XIV, 1643–1653*, 4 vols. (Paris, 1879–80), vol. 2, pp. 413–14; Paul Logié, *La Fronde en Normandie*, 3 vols. (Amiens, 1951), vol. 2, p. 32.

62. Kettering, *Judicial Politics*, p. 259.

63. ADBR, Marseille, IX B2, fols. 590, 655, 785.

64. Ibid., fol. 696v; David, *L'Amirauté de Provence*, pp. 188, 232. The case was transferred to the Parlement of Toulouse.

65. A.A.E., 1711, fol. 283.

66. A.A.E., 1713, fol. 75.

67. Chéruel and Avenel, *Lettres de Mazarin*, vol. 2, p. 1,009.

68. Ibid., pp. 1,064, 1,073.

69. Ibid., p. 1,085.

70. Grimaldi and Gaufridy, *Mémoires*, p. 32; René Pillorget, "Vente d'offices et journée des barricades du 20 janvier, 1649, à Aix-en-Provence," *Provence historique* 15 (1965): 36. Léon de Valbelle visited Cardinal Bichi at Carpentras in the summer of 1649; cf. A.A.E., 1716, fol. 69, July 3, 1649; fols. 133–34, August 15, 1649.

71. A.A.E., 1714, fols. 67, 175, 229–30, 291–92, March 23, April 27, February 6, and March 8, 1649.

72. A.A.E., 1715, fols. 379–80.

73. Pillorget, *Les Mouvements*, pp. 637–74.

74. A.A.E., 1715, fol. 388.

75. A.A.E., 1716, fol. 36. Valbelle was also granted a pension and an office of councillor of state; see ADBR, Marseille, IX B2, fols. 785, 804.

76. Chéruel and Avenel, *Lettres de Mazarin*, vol. 5, pp. 664, 666, 669, 670, the Cardinal's letters of gratitude to his clients and supporters in Provence in March 1652; Georges d'Avenel, ed., *Lettres, instructions diplomatiques et papiers d'état du Cardinal de Richelieu*, 8 vols. (Paris, 1853–77), vol. 5, pp. 175–76 nn. 5 and 7; 262 n. 2. On December 13, 1650, the new acting governor, the marquis d'Aiguebonne, reported to Mazarin that Alais had finally left Toulon for court as ordered three months earlier; cf. A.A.E., 1716, fols. 407–8. Mazarin had recalled Alais on August 18, 1650; A.A.E., 1716, fols. 328, 332; Pillorget, *Les Mouvements*, p. 652.

77. A.A.E., 1718, fol. 84.

78. See chap. 6.

79. Pillorget, *Les Mouvements*, p. 714.

80. Crémieux, *Marseille et la royauté*, vol. 2, pp. 425–29; Busquet, *Histoire de Marseille*, pp. 258–59.

81. Charles de La Roncière, *Valbelle, le Tigre, marin sous Louis XIV* (Paris, 1935), pp. 32–34, 37; EDB, IV–2, 481. Jean-Philippe Valbelle (1615–1646), the oldest son of Cosme de Valbelle, a Knight of Malta and a distinguished galley captain who became vice-admiral, was seriously wounded at the battle of Barcelona in 1642 and died as a result of his wounds four years later.

82. Pillorget, *Les Mouvements*, pp. 767–77.

83. Ibid., pp. 777–83, 819–26.

84. EDB, XIV, *Monographies Communales: Marseille, Aix, Arles*, 219–27.

85. Roland Mousnier, *Les Institutions de la France sous la monarchie absolue*, vol. 1, *Société et état* (Paris, 1974), pp. 89–90; Dent, "The Role of Clientèles," in *French Government and Society*, ed. Bosher (London, 1973), pp. 44–45.

86. "Mémoires de Parades," pp. 107, 276–77.

87. A.A.E., 1714, fols. 127–34, February 25, 1649.

88. A.A.E., 1720, fol. 12, April 20, 1656.

89. Ibid., fols. 21–23, May 19, 1656.

90. Jean-Paul Coste, *Aix-en-Provence et le pays d'Aix* (Aix, 1964), pp. 49, 76; EDB, IV–2, 223.

91. ADBR, Aix, B 3356, fols. 691–92v; B 3358, fols. 1230v–32v; A.A.E., 1720, fol. 294v, August 30, 1657.

92. A.A.E., 1723, fols. 364–67; 1724, fol. 1725, fol. 200–1; Kettering, *Judicial Politics*, p. 286.

93. Scipion Du Roure, baron, *Les Anciennes familles de Provence: La Maison de Forbin* (Paris, 1906), pp. 48–50.

94. Georges B. Depping ed., *Correspondance administrative sous le règne de Louis XIV*, 4 vols. (Paris, 1850–55), vol. 1, pp. 363–64; EDB, IV–2, 259; ADBR, Marseille, C 2716 (December 31, 1669).

95. Pillorget, *Les Mouvements*, pp. 607, 681–84, 731, 841–42; Richard Holbrook, "Baron d'Oppède and Cardinal Mazarin: The Politics of Provence from 1641 to 1660" (Ph.D. diss., University of Illinois at Chicago Circle, 1976), pp. 7–8 and nn. 13, 27, 60, 63–64; A.A.E., 1716, fols. 423–24; 1720, fol. 35; Pierre Daverdi, *Oraison funebre de Henri de Forbin d'Oppède*, notes by A. J. Rance Bourrey (Marseille, 1889), p. 69 n. 1.

96. See chap. 4.

97. B. M., Harleian 4575, "Semestre de Provence par M. de Sève," fol. 49v; Grimaldi and Gaufridy, *Mémoires*, p. vi.

98. A.A.E., 1721, fols. 494–5, August 13, 1658.

99. A.A.E., 1725, fol. 84, September 16, 1659.

100. Balthasar Clapiers-Collongues, *Chronologie des officiers des Cours souveraines* (Aix, 1909–12), pp. 70, 80–81; EDB, IV–2, 299.

101. ADBR, Marseille, C 25, 26, 27, 29; B.M., Harleian 4468, fol. 142.

102. B.N., Dupuy 754, fols. 281v–82.

103. ADBR, Marseille, C 26, 27, 29; A.A.E., 1715, fols. 62–72; Chéruel and Avenel, *Lettres de Mazarin*, vol. 1, pp. 289–90, August 19, 1643, 582–83, February 10, 1643.

104. B.N., Clairambault 422, fols. 88–89, June 1649; A.A.E., 1716, fols. 22–24, June 15, 1649.

105. J. de Romefort, "Au temps de la Fronde: Lettres de guerre de Jacques de Cambis, baron d'Alès, maréchal du camp des armées du Roi (1645–1653)," *Mémoires de l'institut historique de Provence* 7 (1930): 83–89; B.N., Clairambault 422, fols. 122–23, June 22, 1649; B. Méjanes 853, "Délibérations du Parlement de Provence," fol. 239; B.N., Ms. fr. 18977, fols. 186–89; A.A.E., 1716, fols. 12–13, June 1, 1649, fol. 27, June 14, fol. 39, June 16, B.M., Harleian 4575, fols. 122v–23v, 126.

106. B.M., Harleian 4575, fols. 107–107v, 122; A.A.E., 1716, fols. 63–64, June 29, 1649.

107. A.A.E., 1708, fol. 49, April 8, 1642; 1715, fol. 88, February 1649.

108. B.M., Harleian 4575, fol. 127.

109. Harding, *Anatomy of a Power Elite* (New Haven, 1978), pp. 21–31.

110. Célestin Moreau, *Mémoires de Jacques de Saulx, comte de Tavannes* (Paris, 1858), pp. vii, xiii, 28 n. 3, 39–40, 103–5, 106 n. 1, 111.

111. Ibid., p. 70 n. 1.

112. Ibid., p. 65.

113. Richard Bonney, *Political Change in France under Richelieu and Mazarin, 1624–1661* (Oxford, 1978), p. 251. Le Goux de La Berchère was not accepted by the royal attorneys, who may have been Condé clients, and Condé intervened to replace him with his own client, Bouchu; see Elisabeth de La Cuisine, *Le Parlement de Bourgogne*, 3 vols. (Dijon, 1864), vol. 1, pp. 102–3.

114. Claude Arbassier, *L'Intendant Bouchu et son action financière (1667–1671)* (Paris, 1919), pp. 28–29.

115. Marc-Antoine Millotet, *Mémoire des choses qui se sont passées en Bourgogne depuis 1650 jusqu'à 1668* (Dijon, 1866), p. 13. I am indebted to James Collins for this reference. Also see La Cuisine, Le Parlement de Bourgogne, vol. 3, pp. 15, 37, 62.

116. La Cuisine, *Le Parlement de Bourgogne*, vol. 3, pp. 14, 62; Millotet, *Mémoire*, p. 11.

117. La Cuisine, *Le Parlement de Bourgogne*, vol. 3, pp. 8, 29; Depping, ed., *Correspondance administrative*, vol. 2, p. 75; J. F. Michaud and J. J. F. Poujoulat, eds., *Mémoires de Pierre Lenet* (Paris, 1838).

118. Millotet, *Mémoire*, pp. 3–4; also cited by Arthur Kleinclausz, *Histoire de Bourgogne* (Paris, 1924), p. 273; Alexandre Thomas, *Une Province sous Louis XIV: Situation politique et administrative de la Bourgogne, 1661–1715* (Dijon, 1844), p. 25.

119. La Cuisine, *La Parlement de Bourgogne*, vol. 3, pp. 15, 19; Bonney, *Political Change*, p. 362; Moreau, *Mémoires de Jacques de Saulx*, p. xiii.

120. Madeleine Foisil, "Parentèles et fidélités autour du duc de Longueville, gouverneur de Normandie pendant la Fronde," in *Hommage à Roland Mousnier: Clientèles et Fidélités en Europe à l'époque moderne*, ed. Yves Durand (Paris, 1981), pp. 156–57, 164.

121. Ibid., pp. 153–68; Paul Logié, *La Fronde en Normandie*, 3 vols. (Amiens, 1951), vol. 1, 64–65.

122. Fessenden, "Epernon and Guyenne," p. 222.

123. Ibid., pp. 205–15.

124. Jean Richard, ed., *Histoire de la Bourgogne* (Toulouse, 1978), p. 228.

125. Fessenden, "Epernon and Guyenne," pp. 223, 231, 247–51, 262. Also see Léo Mouton, *Un Demi-Roi, le duc d'Epernon* (Paris, 1922), and Yves Durand, *La Maison de Durfort à l'époque moderne* (Fontenay-le-Comte, 1975).

126. Fessenden, "Epernon and Guyenne," p. 256; also see chap. 1 herein on noble households.

127. A.A.E., 1707, fol. 226, September 15, 1640; 1709, fol. 68, April 8, 1644; 1710, fol. 162, June 27, 1645; fol. 178, July 11, 1645; fol. 230, August 22, 1645; 1711, fols. 60–60v, January 9, 1646.

128. Harding, *Anatomy of a Power Elite*, pp. 28–29.

129. Kettering, *Judicial Politics*, p. 131 and nn. 108, 109, 110.

130. Yves-Marie Bercé, *Histoire des Croquants; Etudes des soulèvements populaires au XVIIe siècle dans le sud-ouest de la France*, 2 vols. (Paris and Geneva, 1974), vol. 1, pp. 187, 306–15.

131. Bonney, *Political Change*, p. 300; Guillaume Girard, *Histoire de la vie du duc d'Epernon* (Paris, 1663), pp. 368, 449–50; Fessenden, "Epernon and Guyenne," p. 235.

132. Maximin Deloche, *La Maison du Cardinal de Richelieu* (Paris, 1912), p. 243; Mousnier, *Lettres*, vol. 1, p. 60 n. 60; Georges d'Avenel, *Richelieu et la monarchie absolue*, 4 vols. (Paris, 1895), vol. 4, p. 210.

133. C. E. J. Caldicott, "Le Gouvernement de Gaston d'Orléans en Languedoc (1644–1660) et la carrière de Molière," *XVIIe siècle* 16 (1979): 26.

134. Kettering, *Judicial Politics*, pp. 200–1; B.N., Clairambault 393, fols. 54–56, Alais to the comte de Brienne, April 15, 1644.

135. Sharon Kettering, "The King's Lieutenant General in Provence," *Canadian Journal of History* 13 (1978): 361–81.

Chapter Four

1. Adolphe Crémieux, *Marseille et la royauté pendant la minorité de Louis XIV*, 2 vols. (Paris and Marseille, 1917), vol. 2, p. 832.

2. Ibid., vol. 2, p. 837 n. 4, 848 n. 3; A.A.E., 1725, fol. 91, January 21, 1660.

3. César Nostradamus, *L'Histoire et chronique de Provence* (Lyon, 1614), pp. 1070–71; Honoré Bouché, *La Chorographie ou description de la Provence*, 2 vols. (Aix, 1664), vol. 2, p. 830; EDB, IV–2, 216; René Borricand, *Nobiliaire de Provence: Armorial général de la Provence, du Comtat Venaissin, de la principauté d'Orange*, 3 vols. (Aix, 1974–76), vol. 1 (A–G), pp. 480–85.

4. Fortia de Pilles wrote Mazarin several times in 1649, confirming the loyalty of Marseille; cf. A.A.E., 1714, fols. 159–60, 196–98, 270–72; 1715, fols. 89, 366–68. Mazarin trusted him because in a letter to his client Louis Le Roux d'Infreville at Toulon on February 15, 1649, the Cardinal told the naval intendant to send his papers secretly to Fortia de Pilles at Marseille for safekeeping; see A.A.E., 1714, fol. 103.

5. Crémieux, *Marseille et la royauté*, vol. 2, pp. 532–37, 554; René Pillorget, *Les Mouvements insurrectionnels en Provence entre 1596 et 1715* (Paris, 1975), pp. 771–81. Fortia de Pilles reaffirmed his loyalty to Mazarin in a letter on July 22, 1658; see A.A.E., 1723, fol. 59.

6. A.A.E., 1722, fols. 198, 200, August 19, 1658.

7. Ibid., fol. 230, October 4, 1658. Mazarin wrote to Fortia de Pilles on February 13, 1659, and again on May 1, expressing gratitude for his recent service at Marseille; see A.A.E., 1724, fols. 17v–18, 136–37.

8. A.A.E., 1715, fol. 293. Cardinal Bichi also recommended Fortia de Pilles to Mazarin in a letter on December 30, 1653; see A.A.E., 1719, fol 323.

9. The duc de Mercoeur shortly became viceroy in Catalonia, which the French had occupied in the 1640s.

10. A.A.E., 1720, fol. 88v. Mazarin had written to Pilles on October 14, 1654, expressing appreciation for his letters, declaring friendship, and promising to safeguard his interests; cf. A.A.E., 1718, fol. 240.

11. A.A.E., 1718, fol. 120, February 1657.

12. A.A.E., 1723, fols. 486–87, April 21, 1659. Fortia de Pilles had used the same term in a letter on August 6, 1658; see fols. 108–9.

13. Georges B. Depping, ed., *Correspondance administrative sous le régne de Louis XIV*, 4 vols. (Paris, 1850–55), vol. 1, p. 331.

14. ADBR, Marseille, C 41, fols. 193–209; N.L., *Abrégés des délibérations des communautés de Provence* (Aix, 1612–89), 1664; Bernard Hildesheimer, *Les Assemblées générales des communautés de Provence* (Paris, 1935), pp. 145–46, 148 n. 1.

15. See the red book listing the consuls of Aix, B. Méjanes 608, "Administration du pays de Provence," fols. 94–122; A.C., Aix, BB 129; B.N., *Catalogues des consuls et assesseurs de la ville d'Aix* (Aix, 1699). Also see Pillorget, *Les Mouvements*, pp. 666–70, 747, 757–64; Charles de Grimaldi and Jacques Gaufridy, *Mémoires pour servir à l'histoire de la Fronde en Provence* (Aix, 1870), pp. 42–44; B. Marseille 1792, *Relation envoyée par un gentilhomme de Provence à un de ses amis de Paris* (Paris, 1651).

16. Sévérin Icard, "Liste des syndics de la noblesse en Provence, 1548–1789," *Mémoires de l'Institut historique de Provence* 10 (1933): 65–86; EDB, IV–2, 210–11; Scipion Du Roure, baron, *Les Anciennes familles de Provence: Généalogie de la maison de Forbin* (Paris, 1908), pp. 37–38; J. Michael Hayden, *France and the Estates General of 1614* (Cambridge, 1974), p. 262.

17. Hildesheimer, *Les Assemblées générales*, pp. 93–94; B.N., M.C. 143, fol. 133v, March 23, 1667.

18. B.N., M.C. 128, fols. 338–39, March 13, 1665; Depping, ed., *Correspondance Administrative*, vol. 1, p. 357, August 3, 1666.

19. ADBR, Marseille, C 38, fols. 73–74, 103v, 106; C 2053, fol. 296, conciliar decree, December 7, 1658, authorizing the General Assembly to name the procureurs of the clergy; Hildesheimer, *Les Assemblees générales*, p. 91; A.A.E., 1723, fols. 234–35, October 30, 1658, 267, December 14, 273–76, December 19, 286, December 1658.

20. Hildesheimer, *Les Assemblées générales*, pp. 100, 120.

21. Ibid., pp. 111–15. The intendants attended the debates after 1688.
22. A.A.E., 1720, fol. 42, July 27, 1656.
23. B.N., M.C. 116, fol. 35, June 1, 1663.
24. N.L., *Abrégés*, 1671, pp. 9–10.
25. Ibid., pp. 18–19.
26. Ibid., 1673, pp. 3–10; 1674, pp. 4–11; 1675, pp. 4–14.
27. B.N., M.C. 156, fols. 246, 297, March 4 and 15, 1671.
28. B.N., *Catalogue*, p. 40; A. Edward Newton, ed., *The Letters of Madame de Sévigné*, 7 vols. (Philadephia, 1927), vol. 1, p. 213, November 24, 1673.
29. B.N., *Catalogue*, p. 41.
30. B.N., M.C. 158, fols. 74–76, 80–81, January 9, 1672; Depping, ed., *Correspondance administrative*, vol. 1, pp. 401–2, January 10, 1672.
31. B.N., M.C. 157 bis, fols. 782–83, November 29, 1671.
32. Depping, ed., *Correspondance administrative*, vol. 1, pp. 405–6.
33. Ibid., vol. 1, pp. 404–5, December 20, 1671; B.N., M.C. 157 bis, fol. 856, December 24, 1672.
34. Newton, *Letters of Madame de Sévigné*, vol. 1, p. 213, November 24, 1673.
35. Louis Monmerqué, ed., *Lettres de Madame de Sévigné*, 14 vols. (Paris, 1862–66), vol. 1, p. 213, November 13, 1673.
36. Ibid., vol. 2, p. 504, February 23, 1672; vol. 3, p. 83, May 23, 1672.
37. A.A.E., 1719, fols. 202–3, the marquis de Janson saw Ondedei, Mazarin's secretary, at Paris on his brother's behalf; Joseph H. Albanès, *Gallia Christiana Novissima*, 7 vols. (Valence, 1899–1920), vol. 2, p. 638; EDB, IV–2, 211–12; *Dictionaire de biographie française*, ed. Roman d'Amat, vol. 13, fasc. 80 (Paris, 1976), pp. 416–18; Grimaldi and Gaufridy, *Mémoires*, pp. 56–57; Du Roure, *La Maison de Forbin*, p. 20. Laurent de Forbin, marquis de Janson, had been Sabreur first consul of Aix in 1651. He was named viguier of Marseille in 1653 as a reward for switching his support to Marcoeur and Mazarin. He was camp master in the infantry regiment of Auvergne in 1655, and died in 1692 at Antibes where he was governor. He was a wealthy Provençal noble with annual revenues of at least 32,500 livres from land.
38. Pierre-Joseph de Haitze, *Histoire de la ville d'Aix*, 6 vols. (Aix, 1880–92), vol. 5, p. 195; B.N., M.C. 109 bis, fol. 957; 110, fol. 743; 128, fols. 338–39; 130, fol. 312; 140, fol. 212; Depping, ed., *Correspondance administrative*, vol. 1, p. 357; N.L., *Abrégés*, 1671, p. 5.
39. B.N., M.C. 148 bis, fols. 71–72.
40. Ibid., 128, fols. 338–39; 130 bis, fol. 943; 141 bis, fol. 672; 148 bis, fol. 375.
41. "Mémoires de Jacques de Parades de L'Estang, 1642–1674," *Le Musée: Revue Arlésienne* 13–35 (1875): 277.
42. Monmerqué, *Lettres de Sévigné*, vol. 2, p. 154, April 8, 1671.
43. B.N., M.C. 156, fol. 268, March 7, 1671.
44. Janson-Forbin served as ambassador again at Warsaw in 1680–1681, unofficial French envoy at Rome from 1690–1697, and as French ambassador from 1694 to 1696 and 1700 to 1706. Named to the Order of Saint Esprit in 1689, he became a cardinal in 1690. See Du Roure, *La Maison de Forbin*, p. 19; Jean-Pierre Labatut, *Les Ducs et pairs de France au XVIIe siècle* (Paris, 1972), p. 168; Arthur de Boislisle, ed., *Mémoires de Saint Simon*, 43 vols. (Paris, 1879–1928), vol. 4, pp. 73 n. 2, 276; vol. 23, pp. 366–73; B.N., M.C. 168, 169, 170, *passim*, Janson-Forbin's letters from Poland, Russia, 1674–75; B.N., Ms. fr. 10655–56, the same; private communication, Alexander Sedgwick, based on Arnauld correspondence, especially Pomponne's letters, Bibliothèque de l'Arsenal, mss. 6034–36. Also see M.J.C. Douais, *La Mission de M. de Forbin-Janson auprès du Grand Duc et la Grande Duchesse de Toscane, mars–mai 1673* (Paris, 1903); and abbé François Duffo, *Le Cardinal de Forbin-Janson. Ses négociations diplomatiques à Rome, 1691, 1692, 1693* (Paris, 1932).
45. Boislisle, *Saint Simon*, vol. 23, p. 369 n. 1, March 15, 1700.
46. Ibid., vol. 4, p. 275 n. 1.
47. Ibid., and vol. 20, p. 80; Albanès, *Gallia*, vol. 1, p. 996. Jacques II de Forbin-Janson, abbé de Saint Valéry, was archbishop of Arles from 1711 to 1714.

48. Boislisle, *Saint Simon*, vol. 23, p. 369. Saint Simon was a personal friend of Janson-Forbin.

49. Ibid., pp. 236 n. 4, 366–67.

50. Ibid., p. 367, and n. 21; vol. 1, p. 85 n. 6.

51. Ibid., vol. 17, p. 118 n. 3; B.N., M.C. 109 bis, fol. 957, July 24, 1662.

52. B.N., M.C. 158, fol. 74, January 9, 1672.

53. Haitze, *Histoire*, vol. 6, p. 75.

54. J. Russell Major, *Representative Government in Early Modern France* (New Haven, 1980), p. 630; Pierre Clément, *Lettres, instructions et mémoires de Colbert*, 10 vols. (Paris, 1861–73), vol. 1, p. 535.

55. Roger Duchêne, "Argent et famille au XVIIe siècle: Madame de Sévigné et les Grignans," *Provence historique* 15 (1965): 205–28; 16 (1966): 3–41, 587–620; Borricand, *Nobiliaire de Provence*, vol. 1, pp. 15–17, 297–99, 601–3; Janet Martindale Murbach, *Le Vrai visage de la comtesse de Grignan* (Toulouse, 1939), p. 86; Pierre Clément, *Portraits historiques* (Paris, 1855), "Le comtesse de Grignan, 1632–1715," pp. 146–74; Auguste Bailly, *Madame de Sévigné* (Paris, 1955); the marquis de Saporta, *La Famille de Madame de Sévigné en Provence d'après les documents inédits* (Paris, 1889). Grignan's titles included baron of Entrecasteaux and Vénéjean, seigneur of Saint Roman where he had a house, seigneur of Peyrolles, Mousteiret, and Mazargues, where he had a château. His favorite residences were his house at Marseille and his château at Mazargues near Marseille.

56. Boislisle, *Saint Simon*, vol. 12, p. 287 n. 6; *La Grande Encyclopédie*, 3 vols. (Paris 1866–1902), vol. 19, pp. 417–18; EDB, IV–2, 120; Clément, *Lettres de Colbert*, vol. 4, p. 103; Arthur de Boislisle, ed., *Correspondance des contrôleurs-généraux des finances avec les intendants, 1683–1715*, 3 vols. (Paris, 1874–97), vol. 2, pp. 109, 135–38, 141–42, 146; J. Marchand, *Un Intendant sous Louis XIV: Etude sur l'administration de Lebret en Provence (1687–1704)* (Paris, 1889), pp. 31–35, 293–98; Depping, ed., *Correspondance administrative*, vol. 4, pp. 381, 552.

57. Grignan hastily assembled 4,000 workers to erect fortifications in the army's path and earned the admiration of the duc de Savoie who wrote, "This old Grignan is quicker than we are." See Paul Masson, *La Provence au XVIIIe siècle*, 3 vols. (Paris, 1936), vol. 2, pp. 38–39; Pillorget, *Les Mouvements*, p. 880 and n. 49 for bibliographical references on the 1707 invasion; Edouard Baratier, ed., *Histoire de la Provence* (Toulouse, 1969), pp. 327–28; le duc de Savoie, *Histoire du siege de Toulon, 1707*, ed. Charles Laindent de La Donde (Toulon, 1834).

58. Du Chêne, "Argent et famille," p. 214; Monmerqué, *Lettres de Sévigné*, vol. 10, pp. 30–34, July 12, 1691; Marchand, *Un Intendant*, pp. 69–71; Madame Saint-René Taillandier, *Madame de Sévigné et sa fille* (Paris, 1938), pp. 153, 155, 156. The château was richly furnished with a large number of paintings and tapestries.

59. Taillandier, *Madame de Sévigné*, p. 153; Murbach, *Le Vrai visage*, p. 86; Boislisle, *Correspondance*, vol. 2, pp. 548, 560.

60. Monmerqué, *Lettres de Sévigné*, vol. 7, p. 124, November 6, 1680; Taillandier, *Madame de Sévigné*, pp. 155–56.

61. Masson, *La Provence au XVIIIe siècle*, p. 39.

62. Boislisle, *Saint Simon*, vol. 3, p. 393; also vol. 12, p. 59.

63. "Mémoires de Parades," p. 276.

64. Clément, *Lettres de Colbert*, vol. 4, p. 66, November 27, 1671.

65. Ibid., vol. 4, p. 105, December 29, 1673.

66. B.N., M.C. 157 bis, fol. 639, October 7, 1671; also see Depping, ed., *Correspondance administrative*, vol. 1, pp. 387–88; N.L., *Abrégés*, 1671; Hildesheimer, *Les Assembleés générales*, pp. 107–11, 147, 182–85; ADBR, Marseille, C 45; Marchand, *Un Intendant*, pp. 66–75.

67. B.N., M.C. 157 bis, fol. 639, October 7, 1671; also see Depping, ed., *Correspondance administrative*, vol. 1, pp. 387–88.

68. Depping, ed., *Correspondance administrative*, vol. 1, p. 387, September 25, 1671; also see Clément, *Lettres de Colbert*, vol. 4, pp. 62–63; Félix Tavernier, *Marseille et la Provence sous la royauté, 1481–1789* (Aix, n.d.), p. 116.

69. Depping, ed., *Correspondance administrative* , vol. 1, p. 387, October 9, 1671.

70. ADBR, Marseille, C 15, 16, 17, 19, 20, 22, 23, 24, 26 (1626–42).

71. Monmerqué, *Lettres de Sévigné*, vol. 9, p. 338, December 4, 1689; Hildesheimer, *Les Assembleés générales*, pp. 106–7.

72. Hildesheimer, *Les Assemblées générales*, p. 105; B.N., M.C. 157 bis, fol. 649, October 11, 1671; also see Depping, ed., *Correspondance administrative*, vol. 1, pp. 387–88.

73. B.N., M. C. 157 bis, fol. 693; October 25, 1671; fol. 700, October 28, 1671; Depping, ed., *Correspondance administrative*, vol. 1, pp. 390–91, October 25, 1671, p. 392, October 30.

74. Depping, ed., *Correspondance administrative*, vol. 1, p. 392, November 21, 1671; p. 393, November 18; p. 394, November 27; B.N., M.C. 157 bis, fol. 776, November 19; also see Clément, *Lettres de Colbert*, vol. 4, pp. 65–66. For Oppède's obituary, see *Gazette de France*, December 5, 1671.

75. Depping, ed., *Correspondance administrative*, vol. 1, p. 395, December 4, 1671, p. 396, December 13; also see Clément, *Lettres de Colbert*, vol. 4, pp. 66–67; B.N., M.C. 157 bis, fol. 838.

76. Depping, ed., *Correspondance administrative*, vol. 1, p. 398; also see Clément, *Lettres de Colbert*, vol. 4, p. 69.

77. Depping, ed., *Correspondance administrative*, vol. 1, p. 402; also see B.N., M.C. 158, fols. 156–57.

78. B.N., M.C. 157 bis, fol. 838; also see Depping, ed., *Correspondance administrative*, vol. 1, pp. 396–97.

79. Depping, ed., *Correspondance administrative*, p. 397; also see B.N., M.C. 157 bis, fol. 856.

80. Depping, ed., *Correspondance administrative*, vol. 1, p. 398, December 25, 1671; also see Clément, *Lettres de Colbert*, vol. 4, p. 68; N.L., *Abrégés*, 1671, pp. 41–44.

81. B.N., M.C. 158, fols. 70–71; also see Depping, ed., *Correspondance administrative*, vol. 1, pp. 400–1.

82. N.L., *Abrégés*, 1671, p. 42.

83. Clément, *Lettres de Colbert*, vol. 4, p. 69; also see Depping, ed., *Correspondance administrative*, vol. 1, p. 398.

84. B.N., M.C. 158, fols. 74–76, 167.

85. Du Chêne, "Argent et famille," pp. 221, 226. Grignan had a reputation for ostentatious, luxurious living—for living extravagantly and borrowing injudiciously—and Cardinal de Retz warned Madame de Sévigné to verify his fortune before marrying her daughter to him; cf. Murbach, *Le Vrai visage*, pp. 34, 56–57.

86. Arnaud Chaffanjon, *La Marquise de Sévigné et sa descendance* (Paris, 1962), p. 20.

87. Monmerqué, *Lettres de Sévigné*, vol. 1, pp. 69, 432 and n. 1; J. A. Aubenas, *Histoire de Madame de Sévigné* (Paris, 1842), p. 250. Also see Herbert Rowen, *The Ambassador Prepares for War: The Dutch Embassy of Arnauld de Pomponne, 1669–1671* (The Hague, 1957).

88. Monmerque, *Lettres de Sévigné*, vol. 5, p. 153.

89. Ibid., vol. 1, pp. 126–27; Aubenas, *Histoire de Madame de Sévigné*, pp. 244, 281. Madame de Sévigné's aunt was Henriette de Coulanges, marquise de La Trousse. Her cousin's wife was born Angélique Dugue-Bagnols, daughter of the intendant at Lyons, niece of Le Tellier, and first cousin of Louvois.

90. Monmerqué, *Lettres de Sévigné*, vol. 2, p. 498; vol. 3, p. 23; "Mémoires de Parades," pp. 113–14, 277; Depping, ed., *Correspondance administrative*, vol. 1, p. 189; B.N., M.C. 142, fols. 187–88, February 14, 1665; Albanès, *Gallia*, vol. 4, p. 597.

91. Monmerqué, *Lettres de Sévigné*, vol. 1, p. 105, app. 8, pp. 327–31, "List of persons named in the marriage contract of Madame de Grignan, January 27, 1669"; the original contract is conserved at the B.N., Suppléments français 2831. Edouard Baratier, Georges Duby, Edouard Hildesheimer, *Atlas historique, Provence, Comtat Venaissin, Principauté de Monaco, Principauté d'Orange, Comté de Nice* (Paris, 1969), pp. 139–40, "List of the great families of the Provençal Nobility."

92. Monmerqué, *Lettres de Sévigné*, vol. 1, pp. 125, 129; vol. 2, p. 326; Clément, *Lettres de Colbert*, vol. 4, p. 100 and n. 4, p. 101, and n. 1, pp. 102, 103; Depping, ed., *Correspondance administrative*, vol. 1, pp. 407–10, October and November 1673.

93. "Mémoires de Parades," p. 277.

94. Depping, ed., *Correspondance administrative*, vol. 1, pp. 409–10; Monmerqué, *Lettres de Sévigné*, vol. 3, p. 362 n. 5, December 1673.

95. Monmerqué, *Lettres de Sévigné*, vol. 2, p. 327; also see her letter of December 18, 1673; cf. Monmerqué, p. 319.

96. Depping, ed., *Correspondance administrative*, vol. 1, pp. 407–8; also see B.N., M.C. 166 bis, fols. 653–54.

97. B.N., M.C. 168, fol. 153; A.A.E., 1729, fol. 51.

98. Monmerqué, *Lettres de Sévigné*, vol. 4, p. 310.

99. Ibid., vol. 5, p. 122, December 6, 1679; Haitze, *Histoire*, vol. 6, pp. 90–91, 119, 129–30; B.N., M.C. 168, fol. 120, January 27, 1674; Albanès, *Gallia*, vol. 5, p. 665.

100. Boislisle, *Saint Simon*, vol. 23, p. 367, n. 1.

101. Monmerqué, *Lettres de Sévigné*, vol. 3, pp. 60–61, May 6, 1672.

102. Ibid., vol. 2, p. 236, June 7, 1671.

103. Ibid., vol. 2, p. 154, April 8, 1671.

104. Ibid., vol. 3, p. 75, May 16, 1672.

105. Ibid., vol. 2, p. 504, February 17, 1672; vol. 6, p. 450, June 12, 1680.

106. "Mémoires de Parades," p. 276.

107. Aubenas, *Histoire de Madame de Sévigné*, pp. 231, 248–49, 256–57, 371–72.

108. Haitze, *Histoire*, vol. 6, p. 91.

109. Monmerqué, *Lettres de Sévigné*, vol. 2, pp. 486–87, February 3, 1672.

110. "Mémoires de Parades," pp. 276–77.

111. Boislisle, *Saint Simon*, vol. 12, p. 59; Chaffanjon, *La Marquise de Sévigné*, p. 21.

112. Pierre Gachon, *Histoire de Languedoc* (Paris, 1921), pp. 162, 166; Jean-Baptiste Dubédat, *Histoire du Parlement de Toulouse*, 2 vols. (Paris, 1885), vol. 2, pp. 165–66; Claude de Vic and Joseph Vaissète, *Histoire génerale de Languedoc*, 15 vols. (Toulouse, 1893), vol. 12, pp. 1,031, 1,057.

113. Ibid., vol. 13, p. 328; Dubédat, *Parlement de Toulouse*, vol. 2, pp. 249–50.

114. Dubédat, *Parlement de Toulouse*, vol. 2, pp. 239–41.

115. François Gaquére, *Pierre de Marca (1594–1662): Sa Vie, ses oeuvres, son gallicanisme* (Paris, 1932), pp. 19–218; Pierre de Marca, *Histoire de Béarn, concernant l'origine des rois de Navarre* (Paris, 1640).

116. Gaquère, *Pierre de Marca*, pp. 241–52.

117. Ibid., pp. 219–21, 251–56; Vic and Vaissète, *Histoire générale de Languedoc*, vol. 13, pp. 297, 318, 363; Richard Bonney, *Political Change under Richelieu and Mazarin, 1624–1661* (Oxford, 1978), pp. 376–77, 404, 413–14; Francis Loirette, "L'Administration royal en Béarn de l'union à l'intendance (1620–1682): Essai sur le reattachment à la France d'une province frontière au XVIIe siècle," *XVIIe siècle* 65 (1964): 74; abbé Henry, *François Bosquet: Etude sur une administration civile et ecclésiastique au XVIIe siècle* (Paris, 1889).

118. The opposition in the Languedoc Estates included Nicolas Pavillon, bishop of Alet (1637–77); Gilbert de Choiseul, bishop of Comminges (1644–70); Louis Hercule de Lévis-Ventadour, bishop of Mirepoix (1655–79); Jean François de Percin de Montgaillard, bishop of Saint Pons (1644–49); Louis François de La Baume de Suze, bishop of Viviers (1621–90), and his nephew, Cambonas, bishop of Lodève (1671–90). See William Beik, *Absolutism and Society in Seventeenth-Century France: State Power and Provincial Aristocracy in Seventeenth-Century Languedoc*, (Cambridge 1985), pp. 121–24 University Press.

119. Ibid. Also see Xavier Azema, *Un Prélat janseniste: Louis Foucquet, évêque et comte d'Agde (1656–1702)* (Paris, 1962).

120. Gachon, *Histoire de Languedoc*, pp. 163–64; private communication from William Beik.

121. Private communication from William Beik.

122. See chap. 5.

123. See chap. 2.

124. ADBR, Aix, B 3359, fol. 464; Marseille, C 988, February 25, 1660.

125. B.N., M. C. 101–24, *passim*; N. L. *Abrégés*, 1661–1664.

126. N.L. *Abrégés*, 107, fol. 162, March 16, 1662; 141 bis, fol. 688, October 25, 1666; 157, fol. 294, September 1671.

127. Vicomte de Gérin, *Notice sur les sénéschaussées de Provence* (Avignon, 1889), p. 21.

128. Henri II de Bourbon, prince de Condé, was governor from 1631 to 1646, followed by Louis II, 1646–1651, 1660–76; Henri-Jules, 1676–1709; Louis III, 1709–10; Louis-Henri, 1710–40; and Louis-Joseph, 1740–89.

129. Marc-Antoine Millotet, *Mémoire des choses qui se sont passées en Bourgogne depuis 1650 jusqu'à 1668* (Dijon, 1864), pp. 11, 13; Alexandre Thomas, *une Province sous Louis XIV: Situation politique et administrative de la Bourgogne, 1661–1715* (Dijon, 1844), p. 25. Bouchu was reported variously to have died from plague, cholera, and peritonitis, cf. Jean Richard, *Histoire de Bourgogne* (Toulouse, 1978), pp. 217, 229; Gaston Roupnel, *La Ville et la campagne au XVIIe siècle: Etude sur la population du pays dijonnais* (Paris, 1955), p. 30 n. 82.

130. Bonney, *Political Change*, pp. 362–63; Charles Arbassier, *L'Intendant Bouchu et son action financière (1667–1671)* (Paris and Dijon, 1919), pp. 11–12, 18–21.

131. Arbassier, *L'Intendant Bouchu*, pp. 106, 164, 167–73.

132. Ibid., pp. 32–44; Henri Moreau, "Les Subdélégués dans la généralité de Bourgogne sous l'intendant Bouchu et ses premiers successeurs," *Annales de Bourgogne* 20 (1948): 165–89.

133. Bonney, *Political Change*, pp. 363–64; private communication from James Collins, who is finishing a study of taxation and finance in seventeenth-century France and to whom I am indebted for this material on Burgundy.

134. Henri Drouot and Jean Calmette, *Histoire de Bourgogne* (Paris, 1928), p. 284.

135. Arthur Kleinclausz, *Histoire de Bourgogne* (Paris, 1924), pp. 296–98; Arbassier, *L'Intendant Bouchu*, p. 13.

136. Edmond Esmonin, "Les Intendants du Dauphiné des origines à la Révolution," *Etudes sur la France des XVIIe et XVIIIe siècles*, ed. Edmond Esmonin (Paris, 1964), p. 99.

137. Thomas, *Une Province sous Louis XIV*, p. 348; Kleinclausz, *Histoire de Bourgogne*, p. 307.

138. Kleinclausz, *Histoire de Bourgogne*, plates facing pp. 298, 308; Bonney, *Political Change*, pp. 251–52; Thomas, *Une Province sous Louis XIV*, p. 384; Elisabeth de La Cuisine, *Le Parlement de Bourgogne*, 3 vols. (Dijon, 1864), vol. 1, pp. 102–3. In 1638 Condé forced the resignation of Le Goux de La Berchère as first president of the Parlement of Dijon, because he had not been accepted by the royal attorneys, in order to appoint his own client, Jean Bouchu, to the office. The Brûlarts were closely related by marriage to Le Goux, and this began a lengthy family feud.

139. Kleinclausz, *Histoire de Bourgogne*, p. 298. Brûlart's quarrelsomeness is apparent in his correspondance; see Elisabeth de La Cuisine, ed., *Choix de lettres inédites par Nicolas Brûlart*, 2 vols. (Dijon, 1859).

140. La Cuisine, *Lettres de Brûlart*, vol. 1, pp. 152, 158–60, 237–38, vol. 2, *passim*; Thomas, *Une Province sous Louis XIV*, pp. 408–18. Bouchu, writing to Colbert in 1663, described Brûlart as "mediocre in ability and presumptuous;" see Depping. ed., *Correspondance administrative*, vol. 2, p. 106.

141. Depping, ed., *Correspondance administrative*, vol. 2, pp. 105–10; Thomas, *Un Province sous Louis XIV*, pp. 355–58; Drouot and Calmette, *Histoire de Bourgogne*, p. 280; La Cuisine, *Lettres de Brûlart*, vol. 1, pp. 83–84, 121–24.

142. La Cuisine, Lettres de Brûlart, vols. 1 and 2, *passim*; Kleinclausz, *Histoire de Bourgogne*, p. 308.

143. La Cuisine, *Lettres de Brûlart*, vol. 1, pp. 12–13, Brûlart to Mazarin on behalf of Tavannes, June 24, 1657; pp. 121–24, the same, January 5, 1660; pp. 279–81, Brûlart to Le Tellier on behalf of Tavannes, April and May, 1663; pp. 72–73, Brûlart to La Vrillière on behalf of Harcourt, October 5, 1658; pp. 49–50, Brûlart to Mazarin on behalf of his brother, March 3, 1658; vol. 2, pp. 64–65, Brûlart to Grand Master of Malta, February 1667; vol. 1, pp. 124–45, January and February 1660, series of letters on disorders within the parlement and the conduct of advocate general Millotet; pp. 158–60, Brûlart to Mazarin on Millotet, April 20, 1660; p. 166, Brûlart to Fouquet on Millotet, May 26, 1660; pp. 155–56, Brûlart to Mazarin on councillors

Berbis, Legouz, and Malteste, March 9, 1660; p. 147, Brûlart to Fouquet on the conduct of president Des Barres, February 18, 1660; Thomas, *Une Province sous Louis XIV*, pp. 354, 361–63.

144. Maurice Gresset, *Le Rattachement de la Franche-Comté à la France, 1669–1678* (Besançon, 1978), p. 18; idem, "Un Fidèle de Louis XIV en Franche-Comté: Claude Boisot," in *Hommage à Roland Mousnier: Clientèles et fidélités en Europe à l'époque moderne*, ed. Yves Durand (Paris, 1981), pp. 169–82; Lucien Febvre, *Histoire de Franche-Comté* (Paris, 1922; Marseille, 1976). Also see André Corvisier, *Louvois* (Paris, 1984).

145. Maurice Gresset, *Gens de justice à Besançon de la conquête à la Révolution française (1674–1789)*, 2 vols. (Paris, 1978), vol. 1, pp. 150, 154 and n. 77, p. 165, n. 39, p. 186, and n. 36, pp. 215–16, vol. 2, 325, 474, 597.

146. Ibid., vol. 1, p. 217 n. 13.

147. Ibid., pp. 115, 118, 128, 165, 331–33, 632.

148. Ibid., p. 655.

149. Gresset, "Un Fidèle de Louis XIV," p. 181. Subdélégués are discussed in chap. 6.

150. Gresset, *Gens de justice*, pp. 333, 417.

151. Ibid., p. 218.

152. Ibid., p. 402.

153. Ibid., p. 333.

154. Ibid., pp. 192, 501, 566–67, 572.

155. Ibid., pp. 115, 117–18, 165 n. 39, 317, 473, 620, 638–39; Gresset, *Le Rattachement*, p. 32.

156. See chap. 3 on the Valbelles.

157. Pillorget, *Les Mouvements*, pp. 355–56; Bouche, *La Chorographie*, vol. 1, p. 17; vol. 2, pp. 873–74. Price increases occurred in 1603, 1608, 1622, and 1627. The salt tax jumped from two livres, fifteen sols a measure in 1598, to four livres, nine sols in 1622, to six livres, ten sols in 1627.

158. Alexksandra Dmitrievna Lublinskaya, ed., *Vnutrenniaia politika frantsuzskogo absoliutizma, 1633–1645* (Leningrad, 1966), p. 240; B.N., Cinq Cents de Colbert 288, fols. 22–22v; A.N., E 119A, fol. 32. In October 1634, the salt tax rose from six livres, ten sols a measure to twenty two livres, ten sols, and it was proposed that the measure be changed from the *emine*, the Provençal measure for salt and wheat valued at eight gallons, to the *minot*, the French measure used in Languedoc and valued at about two-thirds the emine.

159. Pillorget, *Les Mouvements*, pp. 364–72.

160. A.A.E., 1703, fols. 13–14.

161. Pillorget, *Les Mouvements*, pp. 373–74.

162. Paul Cousot, "Paul-Albert de Forbin, lieutenant général des galères, 1580–1661," *Provence historique* 19 (1969): 102; *Dictionnaire de biographie française*, p. 415; EDB, IV–2, 213–14.

163. Charles de La Roncière, *Histoire de la marine française*, 2 vols. (Paris, 1899–1932), vol. 4, p. 587 n. 3.; cites B.N., Dupuy 569, fol. 193, 1627 memoir.

164. A.A.E., 1703, fol. 122, April 12, 1635; 1704, fols. 436–39, October 6 and 7, 1636, fols. 444–45, October 14, 1636.

165. A.A.E., 1702, fol. 414, November 28, 1634.

166. A.A.E., 1706, fol. 59, June 6, 1637.

167. A.A.E., 1702–1709, *passim.*

168. A.A.E., 1704, fols. 423–24, September 29, 1636.

169. A.A.E., 1707, fols. 143–99, Forbin to Sublet de Noyers, 25 letters from January to October 1640; Cousot, "Forbin," 104–10; Eugène Sue, ed., *Correspondance d'Henri d'Escoubleau de Sourdis, archevêque de Bordeaux, 1636–1642,* 3 vols. (Paris, 1836), vol. 1, pp. lxxxviii–lxxxix; vol. 2, pp. 186–87; vol. 3, pp. 28–29, 82–83.

170. A.A.E., 1703–1708, letters of Forbin, Henri de Séguiran, sieur de Bouc, and Bernard de Besançon, seigneur Du Plessis, naval intendant in Provence from 1635 to 1637, mentioning their friendly relationship.

171. A.A.E., 1708, fol. 164, April 13, 1643; fol. 166, April 14, 1643; EDB, IV–2, 418.

172. Cousot, "Forbin," pp. 110, 116; Du Roure, *La Maison de Forbin*, pp. 105–7; Pierre-

Adolphe Chéruel and Georges d'Avenel, eds., *Lettres du Cardinal Mazarin pendant son ministère*, 9 vols. (Paris, 1872–1906), vol. 1, p. 849, April 13, 1643.

173. A.A.E., 895, fols. 50–51. On November 7, 1647, Mazarin asked Forbin to send him a memoir on the galleys; cf. fol. 99.

174. A.A.E., 1713, fols. 241–43, August 25, 1648; 1716, fol. 181, September 1649. Forbin "testified to a violent attachment to Your service," in writing to Mazarin on March 23, 1649; see A.A.E., 1714, fols. 227–28. In June 1659 and March 1660, Mazarin wrote Forbin that he had mentioned his "affair" to the Queen; see A.A.E., 1724, fols. 172, 177v, 280. Writing to Forbin on March 13, 1660, shortly before his death, Mazarin expressed concern for his health; see Chéruel and Avenel, *Lettres de Mazarin*, vol. 9, p. 931.

175. Grimaldi and Gaufridy, *Mémoires*, p. 30; Haitze, Histoire, vol. 5, pp. 79–80; A.A.E., 1714, fols. 227–28, March 23, 1649; fol. 273, April 13; fols. 291–92, April 27; fols. 336–37, May 25; 1716, fols. 12–13, 54, 60, June 1, 22, and 29; B.N., Ms. fr. 17393, fols. 203–4, May 29.

176. Pillorget, *Les Mouvements*, pp. 687–88; A.A.E., 1719, fols. 196–97, November 16, 1652; 1726, fol. 71, September 23, 1660.

177. René La Bruyère, *La Marine de Richelieu: Sourdis, archêveque et amiral (6 novembre 1594–18 juin 1645)* (Paris, 1945), pp. 27–33; Michel Perronet, *Les Evêques de l'ancienne France*, 2 vols. (Paris and Lille, 1977), vol. 1, p. 488; Louis Bertrand, *La Vie de Messire Henry de Béthune, archevêque de Bordeaux (1604–1680)*, 2 vols. (Paris and Bordeaux, 1902), vol. 1, p. 87; Nicolas Fessenden, "Epernon and Guyenne: Provincial Politics under Louis XIII" (Ph.D. diss. Columbia University, 1972), pp. 66, 69–74, 123 n. 1; Yves-Marie Bercé, *Histoire des Croquants: Etudes des soulèvements populaires au XVIIe siècle dans le sud-ouest de la France*, 2 vols. (Paris, 1974), vol. 1, p. 309.

178. La Bruyère, *Sourdis*, pp. 27–33; Fessenden, "Epernon and Guyenne," pp. 88–89; Georges d'Avenel, ed., *Lettres, instructions diplomatiques et papiers d'état du Cardinal de Richelieu*, 8 vols. (Paris, 1853–77), vol. 2, pp. 713–15, Richelieu to Sourdis, November 12, 1627; Franklin Palm, *The Economic Policies of Richelieu* (Urbana, Ill., 1920), pp. 53, 73–74.

179. La Bruyère, *Sourdis*, frontispiece.

180. Ibid., pp. 33–35; Fessenden, "Epernon and Guyenne," pp. 89–101, 116–19; Bertrand, *Henry de Béthune*, vol. 1, pp. 161–218.

181. Haitze, *Histoire*, vol. 4, p. 290.

182. Bercé, *Histoire des Croquants*, vol. 1, pp. 309–10; Fessenden, "Epernon and Guyenne," 116, 119, 124, 137–44. During the years from 1600 to 1620, Sourdis's brother put his clients into the municipal government of Bordeaux; cf. Fessenden, p. 32.

183. Fessenden, "Epernon and Guyenne," pp. 116, 137–44; Bercé, *Histoire des Croquants*, vol. 1, pp. 310–11. Jean de Briet was a senior councillor in the Grand'Chambre. He was originally appointed by the parlement to assist Sourdis, then became his client.

184. Bercé, *Histoire des Croquants*, vol. 1, pp. 58, 310.

185. A.A.E., 1706, fols. 76–77, 88.

186. La Bruyère, *Sourdis*, pp. 76, 135, 212–18; Sue, ed., *Correspondance de Sourdis*, vol. 1, pp. lxxxv–xcii, vol. 2, pp. 557–680, vol. 3, pp. 21–42, 57–63, 67, 69, 70, 84–86.

187. ADBR, Aix, B 3350, fol. 746; B.N., Dupuy 754, fols. 218–19; Haitze, *Histoire*, vol. 4, pp. 277–78; "Histoire de Provence sous le gouvernement du comte d'Alais," B. Méjanes 736, fols. 15–16. Dubernet was named first president by royal letters on February 20, 1636.

188. Albanès, *Gallia*, vol. 2, pp. 620–21.

189. La Bruyère, *Sourdis*, p. 45; René La Bruyère, *La Marine de Richelieu: Maillé-Brézé, général des galères, grand amiral, 1619–1646* (Paris, 1945), pp. 94, 179.

190. ADBR, Marseille, C 25, fols. 15, 19, 29–45, 72v–92v.

191. Ibid., fols. 54, 56, 58v–71. Earlier in the month, the procureurs du pays had sent deputies to the governor protesting the cost of maintaining these troops see fols. 52–53v.

192. Sue, ed., *Correspondance de Sourdis*, vol. 3, pp. 520–21; ADBR, Marseille, C 25, fol. 71; B.N., Dupuy 501, fols. 124–34; Haitze, *Histoire*, vol. 4, p. 296; Sharon Kettering, *Judicial Politics and Urban Revolt: The Parlement of Aix, 1629–1659* (Princeton, 1978), pp. 126–27. Vitry was ordered to the Bastille on September 18, 1636. Richelieu had informed Sourdis as early as April of his intention to replace Vitry; cf. La Bruyère, *Sourdis*, p. 64. Sourdis's rivals for the

appointment, the comte d'Harcourt and the archbishop of Lyon, were not strong possibilities; see Haitze, *Histoire*, vol. 4, p. 290.

193. ADBR, Marseille, C 25, fols. 58v–71.

194. Ibid.; Bouche, *La Chorographie*, vol. 2, pp. 911–12; A.C., Aix, BB 101, fols. 198v–200; B. Méjanes 608, fols. 94–122, published as *Catalogue des consuls et assesseurs de la ville d'Aix* (Aix, 1699).

195. Sue, ed., *Correspondance de Sourdis*, vol. 3, pp. 540–41, Sourdis to Sublet de Noyers, December 25, 1637, p. 529, the same, December 7, 1637.

196. ADBR, Aix, B 3351, fol. 284, October 29, 1637; Haitze, *Histoire*, vol. 4, pp. 295–96.

197. ADBR, Marseille, C 25, fol. 155.

198. Ibid., fols. 116, 157, 179v; A.C., Aix, BB 100, fols. 201v–202v; Sue, ed., *Correspondance de Sourdis*, vol. 1, pp. 536–38, December 15, 1637, Sourdis to Sublet de Noyers advising cancellation of the recent elections at Aix for *intrigues*, and the choice of individuals *mal intentionnés au service du Roi*. He thought elections should be permitted only when the tax was approved.

199. La Bruyère, *Sourdis*, p. 87.

200. ADBR, Marseille, C 23, fols. 250–92; B.N., Cinq Cents de Colbert 288, fols. 28–30v.

201. Pierre Blet, *Le Clergé de France et la monarchie*, 2 vols. (Rome, 1959), vol. 2, pp. 4–9. Also see his *Les Assemblées du clergé et Louis XIV de 1670 à 1693* (Rome, 1972).

202. Perronet, *Les Evêques*, vol. 1, pp. 482–83, 523; J. Michael Hayden, "The Social Origins of the French Episcopacy at the Beginning of the Seventeenth Century," *French Historical Studies* 10 (1977): 27–40.

203. Bertrand, *Henry de Béthune*, vol. 1, pp. 20–37, 69, 81–84, 88.

204. Ibid., pp. 94–139, 244, 246, 263.

205. Ibid., pp. 176–234, esp. 284–85, 285–86, 297, letters of Argenson, Béthune, and Du Plessis-Praslin; Charles Boscheron Des Portes, *Histoire du Parlement de Bordeaux depuis sa création jusqu'à sa suppression (1451–1790)*, 2 vols. (Bordeaux, 1878), vol. 2, pp. 37, 41–42.

206. Bertrand, *Henry de Béthune*, vol. 1, pp. 45–48, 249–50.

207. Albanès, *Gallia*, vol. 3, pp. 970–82.

208. A.A.E., 1711, fols. 289–90, November 23, 1646; B.N., Clairambault 397, fols. 397–98, February 23, 1645, fols. 311–12, December 23, 1646.

209. A.A.E., 1713, fols. 263–66.

210. B.N., Clairambault 397, fols. 325–26.

211. Ibid., fols. 303–4.

212. Ibid., fol. 306; B.N., Clairambault 419, fols. 73–74, January 19, 1649.

213. A.A.E., 1716, fols. 54, 60, June 22 and 29, 1649.

214. A.A.E., 1705, fols. 483, 485, February 24 and March 3, 1637.

215. Henri Gabriel O'Gilvy, *Nobiliaire de Guienne et de Gascogne*, 4 vols. (Paris, 1856–60, reissued 1973), vol. 3, pp. 345–50.

216. Haitze, *Histoire*, vol. 4, p. 278.

217. Ibid., p. 390; "Histoire de Provence," B. Méjanes 736, fols. 15–16; *Portraits ou éloges historiques des premiers présidents du Parlement de Provence* (Avignon, 1727), p. 113; EDB, IV–2, 169.

218. Alais protested to Richelieu that he was being attacked by Sourdis, whom he accused of *fourberies* of double dealing; see A.A.E., 1707, fols. 242, 297, January 22 and October 29, 1641.

219. See Sue, ed., *Correspondance de Sourdis*, vol. 3, on the archbishop's disgrace.

220. Jean-Scholastique Pitton, *Histoire de la ville d'Aix* (Aix, 1666), pp. 401–2; Haitze, *Histoire*, vol. 4, pp. 334–36; A.A.E., 1707, fols. 18–18v, Alais to Sublet de Noyers, February 21, 1640.

221. A.A.E., 1708, fols. 9–10, May 9, 1642.

222. Ibid., fols. 73–74, May 14, 1642.

223. Grimaldi and Gaufridy, *Mémoires*, p. 19. Alais's ties to Sublet de Noyers and to Chavigny helped him obtain the dismissal of Dubernet.

224. A.A.E., 1707, fol. 388, November 5, 1641.

225. Sue, ed., *Correspondance de Sourdis*, vol. 2, p. 203, July 1640.

226. B.N., Clairambault 388, fols. 18–21, September 1, 1643; Henri Thourel, *Jacques de Gaufridi et le Semestre de Provence* (Aix, 1880), p. 38; Haitze, *Histoire*, vol. 4, pp. 390–91. Dubernet's portrait is available in Jacques Cundier, *Portraits des premiers présidents du Parlement* de Provence (Aix, 1724), B. Méjanes 963.

227. O'Gilvy, *Nobiliaire*, vol. 3, pp. 351, 369, August 18, 1643.

228. Robert Boutruche, *Bordeaux de 1453 à 1715* (Bordeaux, 1966), p. 332.

229. Ibid.; Boscheron Des Portes, *Parlement de Bordeaux*, vol. 2, pp. 3, 7; Sal Westrich, *The Ormée of Bordeaux: A Revolution during the Fronde* (Baltimore, 1972), pp. 5–6.

230. Boscheron Des Portes, *Parlement de Bordeaux*, vol. 2, pp. 39–41, 134–35, 141–42.

231. O'Gilvy, *Nobiliaire*, vol. 3, p. 369.

232. Francis Monnier, *Le Chancelier d'Aguesseau: Sa conduite et ses idées politiques* (Paris, 1863, reprinted Geneva, 1975), pp. 30–31; A. Boullée, *Histoire de la vie et des ouvrages du Chancelier d'Aguesseau*, 2 vols. (Paris, 1835), vol. 1, p. 98; Bonney, *Political Change*, p. 79 n. 3.

233. Bonney, *Political Change*, p. 30 n. 3; Bercé, *Histoire des Croquants*, vol. 1, pp. 296, 305, 317.

234. Monnier, *Le Chancelier d'Aguesseau*, p. 446.

235. Camille Jullian, *Histoire de Bordeaux depuis les origines jusqu'en 1895* (Bordeaux, 1895, reissued Marseille, 1975), p. 478.

236. Boscheron Des Portes, *Parlement de Bordeaux*, vol. 2, pp. 453, 460, 466.

237. Boullée, *Aguesseau*, vol. 1, p. 100.

238. Bonney, *Political Change*, p. 251 n. 1; Pillorget, *Les Mouvements*, p. 127; Kettering, *Judicial Politics*, pp. 200–1; Jean-Claude Paulhet, "Les Parlementaires toulousains à la fin du dix-septième siècle," *Annales du Midi* 76 (1964): 193. Intendants who became first presidents included Faucon de Ris and Pellot at Rouen, Louis de Laisné at Dijon, Hélie de Laisné and Mesgrigny at Aix, and Morant at Toulouse.

239. Dubédat, *Parlement de Toulouse*, vol. 2, pp. 159–63.

240. Ibid., pp. 201–2.

241. William Beik, "Magistrates and Popular Uprisings in France before the Fronde: The Case of Toulouse," *Journal of Modern History* 46 (1974): 573–74.

242. Roland Mousnier, *Lettres et mémoires adressés au Chancelier Séguier (1633–1649)* 2 vols. (Paris, 1964), vol. 1, pp. 378–79, June 3, 1637.

243. Dubédat, *Parlement de Toulouse*, vol. 2, pp. 219, 221.

244. Lublinskaya, *Vnutrenniaia*, pp. 54–55.

245. Ibid., pp. 178–79.

246. Ibid., p. 182.

247. Ibid., pp. 186–87.

248. Beik, *Absolutism and Society*, pp. 229–30; Dubédat, *Parlement de Toulouse*, vol. 2, pp. 244, 247, 249–50.

249. Dubédat *Parlement de Toulouse* vol. 2, pp. 257, 259.

250. Ibid., p. 262. Also see Depping, ed., *Correspondance administrative*, vol. 2, pp. 111, 112–14. He was Gaspard de Fieubet, procureur general of the parlement.

251. Henri Oddo, *Le Chevalier Paul: Lieutenant général des armées du roi, 1598–1668* (Paris, 1896), pp. 3–70; Sue, ed., *Correspondance de Sourdis*, vol. 2, pp. 82–86. For the Knights of Malta, see Paul Bamford, "The Knights of Malta and the King of France, 1665–1770," *French Historical Studies* 3 (1964): 429–53; and Claire-Eliane Engel, *Histoire de l'Ordre de Malte* (Geneva, 1968). The Knights of Malta in principle required proof of sixteen quarters of nobility for admission, although in practice it was sufficient to be from a family that had been noble for a hundred years. See François Bluche, *Les Magistrats du Parlement de Paris au XVIIIe siècle (1715–1771)* (Paris, 1960), p. 332 n. 10; André Corvisier, "Les Généraux de Louis XIV et leur origine sociale," *XVIIe siècle* 42–43 (1959): 49. The chevalier Paul, therefore, was an exception to the usual admission policy of the Knights of Malta.

252. Oddo, *Le Chevalier Paul*, pp. 71–109; Pillorget, *Les Mouvements*, pp. 655, 678, 680, 687–90; EDB, IV-2, 503–4.

253. A.A.E., 1723, fols. 421–22, March 18, 1659. The chevalier Paul also affirmed his loyalty

to Mazarin in a letter on August 4, 1658; see fol. 96. Mazarin in a letter to the chevalier Paul mentioned their "particular friendship"; see A.A.E., 1718, fol. 49.

254. Oddo, *Le Chevalier Paul*, pp. 121–27; Crémieux, *Marseille et la royauté*, vol. 2, pp. 547, 550, 554, 564; Pillorget, *Les Mouvements*, pp. 775–76.

255. Oddo, *Le Chevalier Paul*, pp. 128–31.

256. Ibid., pp. 145–224. The duc de Beaufort had recommended the chevalier Paul for "a good benefice" in 1663 by describing him as "old and sick, having served the King well for many years without enriching himself"; see Auguste Jal, *Abraham Du Quesne et la marine de son temps*, 2 vols. (1873), vol. 1, pp. 301–2.

257. A.A.E., 1714–1717, *passim.*

258. A.A.E., 1716–1720, *passim.*

259. A.A.E., 1720–1726, *passim.*

260. Gresset, "Un Fidèle de Louis XIV," p. 176.

261. Gresset, *Le Rattachement*, doc. 28.

262. Gresset, "Un fidèle de Louis XIV," p. 176.

263. Ibid., pp. 176–78.

264. Ibid.

265. Ibid., p. 178.

266. Ibid., pp. 178–79; idem, *Gens de justice*, p. 215.

267. Gresset, "Un Fidèle de Louis XIV," p. 182.

268. EDB, IV–2, 49; A.A.E., 1720, fol. 225, July 5, 1657; 1722, fol. 34v, February 1, 1658. Mercoeur and La Penne had gone to court together in April 1655; see A.A.E., 1719, fol. 431.

269. Paul Gachon, *Les Etats de Languedoc et l'édit de Béziers (1632)* (Paris, 1887), pp. 87–89, 92–93; duc de Lévis-Mirepoix, *Aventures d'une famille française* (Paris, 1955).

270. Yves-Marie Bercé, "Les Conduites de fidélité: Exemples aquitains," in *Hommage à Roland Mousnier*, ed. Durand, p. 133.

271. Ibid., pp. 132–33; Georges d'Avenel, *La Noblesse française sous Richelieu* (Paris, 1901), p. 20; Yves-Marie Bercé, *Histoire des croquants: Etude des soulèvements populaires au XVIIe siècle dans le sud-ouest de la France*, 2 vols. (Paris, 1974), vol. 1, p. 120.

272. Julian Dent, "The Role of Clientèles in the Financial Elite of France under Cardinal Mazarin," in *French Government and Society, 1500–1800: Essays in Memory of Alfred Cobban*, ed. John F. Bosher (London, 1973), pp. 57–59.

273. Cousot, "Forbin," p. 115; A.A.E., 1703, fols. 297–99, July 10, 1635.

274. Boislisle, *Saint Simon*, vol. 3, p. 393; Chaffanjon, *La Marquise de Sévigné*, p. 20; Murbach, *Le Vrai visage*, pp. 34, 52–53. From a dowry of 200,000 livres, nearly 180,000 livres went to pay his debts.

275. Marchand, *Un Intendant*, p. 71 n. 1.

276. Boislisle, *Saint Simon*, vol. 4, p. 339; vol. 13, p. 288 n. 1, 428. In 1695, Grignan's son made a mésalliance and married the daughter of a wealthy tax farmer so that her dowry could be used to pay his father's debts. Grignan noted that "it is sometimes necessary to put manure on one's lands"; cf. Chaffanjon, *La Marquise de Sévigné*, p. 21; Bailly, *Madame de Sévigné*, p. 402.

277. A.A.E., 1722, fols. 53, 91, February 8 and March 7, 1658.

278. A.A.E., 1708, fol. 19, January 14, 1642; B.N., Ms. fr. 17404, fol. 21, January 15, 1664. His fief of Régusse at La Ciotat had a producing vineyard, and he proudly noted in his journal in October 1634 that "I sold my harvest, encasked my wine, bought some particulars, and had 189 livres left"; see A.P., 43–4, fol. 7v.

279. Chéruel and Avenel, *Lettres de Mazarin*, vol. 7, p. 670, October 12, 1656; vol. 3, p. 1,001, March 13, 1648.

280. A.A.E., 1703, fol. 68, February 24, 1635.

281. B.N., Ms. fr. 21313, fols. 16v, 90v, 216, 256, 307; 21314, fol. 163; 21315, fols. 72, 104.

282. This argument has been made most fully by Bonney in *Political Change*.

283. A.A.E., 1705, fol. 475, February 16, 1637; 1707, fols. 143–99, January to October 1640; Sue, ed., *Correspondance de Sourdis*, vol. 1, p. xc; vol. 2, p. 557; vol. 3, pp. 22, 28, 34–35, 62; Avenel, *Lettres de Richelieu*, vol. 6, pp. 878–79, October 1, 1641; Horric de Beaucaire, comte de,

Mémoires Du Plessis-Besançon (Paris, 1892); Gaston Rambert, *Nicolas Arnoul, Intendant des galères à Marseille, 1665–1674* (Marseille, 1931), p. 10.

284. See Daniel Dessert and Jean-Louis Journet, "Le Lobby Colbert: Un royaume ou une affaire de famille," *Annales: ESC* 30 (1975): 1303–36.

285. William Beik, *Absolutism and Society in Seventeenth-Century France*, pp. 112–113; Bonney, *Political Change*, pp. 71–72. 129–30, 376–77; Charles Godard, *Les Pouvoirs des intendants sous Louis XIV* (Paris, 1901), pp. 167–68.

286. Gresset, "Un Fidèle de Louis XIV," p. 176.

287. Kettering, *Judicial Politics*, pp. 105–8, 310–11.

288. N.L., *Abrégés*, 1661, p. 17; 1664, p. 11.

289. Rambert, *Nicolas Arnoul*, p. 249.

290. Depping, ed., *Correspondance administrative*, vol. 1, p. 787.

291. Ibid., p. 790; Rambert, *Nicolas Arnoul*, pp. 259–60.

292. Depping, ed., *Correspondance administrative*, vol. 1, p. 788.

293. Rambert, *Nicolas Arnoul*, pp. 226–28.

294. Ibid., p. 120.

295. Ibid., pp. 238–39, May 14, 1667.

296. Ibid., pp. 255–57, September 11, 1668.

297. Godard, *Les Pouvoirs*, p. 90. Saint Luc as lieutenant general in Guyenne had remained loyal to Mazarin, helped Harcourt to defeat Condé in 1652, and acted as governor after Condé went into exile.

298. Bonney, *Political Change*, pp. 89, 97, 130–31; Ernest O'Reilly, *Mémoires sur la vie privée et publique de Claude Pellot, 1619–1682*, 2 vols. (Paris, 1882).

299. Francis Loirette, "Un Intendant de Guyenne avant la Fronde: Jean de Lauson (1641–1648)," *Bulletin philologique et historique du Comité des Travaux Historiques et Scientifiques* (1957): 458–59.

300. See Franklin Ford, *Strasbourg in Transition, 1648–1789* (Cambridge, Mass., 1958).

301. Georges Livet, *L'Intendance en Alsace sous Louis XIV, 1648–1715* (Paris and Strasbourg, 1956), pp. 890–92.

302. Ibid., pp. 414, 457, 716–18.

303. Ibid., p. 456.

304. Jean Dietrich, who was influential in the Strasbourg municipal government, remained stubbornly Lutheran. He was a personal enemy of Obrecht because his father, Dominique, had been responsible for the execution of Obrecht's father; see ibid., pp. 417, 457, 533 n. 1, 651, 695, 795. Dietrich and Obrecht divided the municipal government into two camps after 1685. Their rivalry was used by the intendant for his own purposes; see ibid., pp. 744–45.

305. Ibid., pp. 719–20.

306. Ibid., pp. 520–21, 765. Obrecht used his authority to safeguard the rights of Catholics in order to irritate Dietrich; see ibid., pp. 457–58.

307. Ibid., p. 720, n. 1.

308. Ibid., pp. 722–23, 836.

309. Ibid., pp. 675, 866.

310. Ibid., p. 457, n. 1, 850–51, 875, n. 1, 878.

311. Ibid., pp. 722–23, 890.

312. For his letters see Jean Cordey, ed., *Correspondance du Maréchal de Vivonne relative à l'expédition de Messina, 1674–1767, 1767–1678*, 2 vols. (Paris, 1914), *passim*; B.N., M. C. 174 bis, fol. 421, July 11, 1677, the marquis d'Oppède at Messina to Colbert; Clément, *Lettres de Colbert*, vol. 4, pp. 59–61, July 30, 1677, Colbert to the marquis d'Oppède, intendant of the fleet at Messina.

313. Marie de Roux, marquis, *Louis XIV et les provinces conquises: Artois, Alsace, Flandre, Roussillon, Franche-Comté* (Paris, 1938), p. 135.

314. John H. M. Salmon, "Storm over the Noblesse," *Journal of Modern History* 53 (1981): 251.

315. Georges Avenel, *Richelieu et la monarchie absolue*, 4 vols., 2nd ed. (Paris, 1895), vol. 4, pp. 108–29; Bonney, *Political Change*, p. 299.

316. Roland Mousnier, "Notes sur les rapports entre les gouverneurs de provinces et les intendants dans la première moitié du XVIIe siècle," *Revue historique* 227 (1962): 339–51, reprinted in *La Plume, la faucille et le marteau* (Paris, 1970), pp. 201–13; Robert Harding, *Anatomy of a Power Elite: The Provincial Governors of Early Modern France* (New Haven, 1978), pp. 215–17.

317. Haitze, *Histoire*, vol. 4, pp. 295–96. Alais wrote regularly to Sublet de Noyers after 1640; cf. A.A.E., 1707 and 1708, *passim.*

318. Chéruel and Avenel, *Lettres de Mazarin*, vol. 2, p. 953, September 24, 1647; p. 959, October 11, 1647; Mousnier, *Lettres*, vol. 2, p. 1,080; Kettering, *Judicial Politics*, p. 140.

319. Kettering, *Judicial Politics*, p. 131; Mousnier, *Lettres*, vol. 1, pp. 155–61; A.A.E., 1707, May 22, 1650, Vautorte to Chavigny; fols. 392–93. November 1641, Alais to Sublet de Noyers.

320. Harding, *Anatomy of a Power Elite*, pp. 171–90. The governors were usually consulted about the choice of candidates for intendant and could veto the ministers' nominees; cf. Bonney, *Political Change*, p. 300.

321. William Beik, *Absolutism and Society in Seventeenth-Century France*, pp. 114–15. Beik emphasizes the importance of the intendants' local ties and clients and their Paris ties and clients; see ibid, pp. 98–103.

322. Henri Monin, *Essai su l'histoire administrative de Languedoc pendant l'intendance de Basville (1685–1719)* (Paris, 1884), pp. 2, 4.

323. Ibid., pp. 8–12; Ernest Sabatier, *Histoire de la ville et des évêques de Béziers* (Paris and Béziers, 1854, reprinted Marseille, 1977), pp. 340–73; private communication, William Beik.

324. See, for example, Bonney, *Political Change*. Also see Roland Mousnier, "Etat et commissaire: Recherches sur la création des intendants des provinces (1634–1648)," reprinted in *La Plume*, pp. 179–99; Esmonin, *Etudes sur la France*; Godard, *Les Pouvoirs*; Beik, *Absolutism and Society*, pp. 241–43.

Chapter Five

1. See Lucien Romier's description of the sixteenth-century nobility of provincial France, especially Picardy, in *Le Royaume de Catherine de Médicis: La France à la veille des guerres de religion*, 2 vols. (Paris, 1922), vol. 1, pp. 211–21. Jonathan Dewald has investigated kinship and client ties among the lesser Norman nobility in the late seventeenth and early eighteenth centuries; see "A Gentry Community in Early Modern France," paper presented at the annual meeting of the French Historical Society, New York University, March 1982.

2. Romier, *Le Royaume*, pp. 208–11; Robin Briggs, *Early Modern France, 1560–1715* (Oxford, 1977), pp. 2–7; Roland Mousnier, *Les Institutions de la France sous la monarchie absolue, 1598–1789*, vol. 2, *Les Organes de l'état et de la société* (Paris, 1980), pp. 65, 458; Peter Lewis, *Later Medieval France: The Polity* (New York, 1968), pp. 153–57, 225–26; Roger Doucet, *Les Institutions de la France au XVIe siècle*, 2 vols. (Paris, 1948), vol. 1, pp. 229–44; Guy Fourquin, *Lordship and Feudalism in the Middle Ages*, trans. Iris and A. L. Lytton Sells (London, 1976), pp. 230–31; Gaston Zeller, *Aspects de la politique française sous l'Ancien Régime* (Paris, 1964), pp. 207–39; J. Russell Major, "Crown and Aristocracy in Renaissance France," *American Historical Review* 69 (1964): 631–45.

3. David Buisseret, *Henry IV* (London, 1984), pp. 88–94.

4. Robert Harding, *Anatomy of a Power Elite: The Provincial Governors of Early Modern France* (New Haven, 1978), pp. 132–34.

5. Ibid., p. 135.

6. William Weary, "Royal Policy and Patronage in Renaissance France: The Monarchy and the House of La Trémoille" (Ph.D. diss., Yale University, 1972), pp. 121–23, 147–49.

7. Ibid., pp. 34, 40, 148–49, 201–3.

8. Romier, *Le Royaume*, vol. 1, p. 165.

9. Weary, "La Trémoille," p. 117.

10. Ibid., p. 88.

11. Ibid., pp. 43–49, 52.

12. Ibid., pp. 90–102.

13. Ibid., p. 93. On the governors' ordinance companies, see Harding, *Anatomy of a Power Elite*, pp. 21–27, 71–80.

14. Weary, "La Trémoille," pp. 41–42, 102, 203.

15. Ibid., p. 111.

16. Ibid., p. 114.

17. Ibid., p. 115.

18. Ibid., pp. 142, 145.

19. Ibid., pp. 34–35, 140–41.

20. Ibid., pp. 147–49.

21. Ibid., pp. 137–39.

22. Ibid., pp. 145–46.

23. Ibid., pp. 127–28.

24. "Mémoires de Jacques de Parades de L'Estang, 1642–1674," *Le Musée: Revue Arlésienne* 13–35 (1875): 236: Mercoeur acted on Oppède's behalf before he arrived at court in 1662; Jules de Cosnac, ed., *Mémoires de Daniel de Cosnac*, 2 vols. (Paris, 1852, New York, 1968), vol. 1, pp. 191–227; B.N., Ms. fr. 17407, fol. 188, October 27, 1666, Oppède to chancellor Séguier using Janson-Forbin as his messenger and agent; Pierre-Joseph de Haitze, *Histoire de la ville d'Aix*, 6 vols. (Aix, 1880–92), vol. 4, p. 335.

25. B.N., M. C. 130, fol. 250, August 8, 1665.

26. N. L., *Abrégés des communautés de Provence* (Aix, 1612–89), 1661, p. 14.

27. Claude-Bernard Petitot, ed., *Mémoires de Messire Claude Groulard (1588–1604)* in *Mémoires relatifs à l'histoire de France* (Paris, 1826), vol. 49, pp. 287–433; A. M. Floquet, *Histoire du Parlement de Normandie*, 7 vols. (Rouen, 1840–42), vol. 3, pp. 180–84, 234–73, 324–31, 449–55, 560–61, 572–73; Henri de Frondeville, *Les Présidents du Parlement de Normandie, 1499–1700* (Rouen and Paris, 1953), pp. 68–69; Buisseret, *Henry IV*, pp. 89–90.

28. Henri Drouot, *Mayenne et la Bourgogne, 1587–1596*, 2 vols. (Paris, 1937), vol. 1, pp. 103, 106–7, 112.

29. Ibid., p. 103.

30. Ibid., p. 97.

31. Ibid., pp. 93–94.

32. Ibid., pp. 97, 99.

33. Ibid., pp. 109–10. The duchy of Mayenne was in Maine, and most of his wife's lands were in Poitou and Guyenne.

34. Ibid., pp. 110–11.

35. Ibid., pp. 28–29, 96–97.

36. Ibid., pp. 98–115.

37. Ibid., pp. 74, 98.

38. Ibid.

39. Ibid., pp. 73 n. 1, 83 n. 2, 98.

40. Ibid., p. 99.

41. Ibid., pp. 100–1, 114.

42. Ibid., p. 97.

43. Ibid., pp. 76–77.

44. Ibid., p. 66.

45. Ibid., pp. 112–13.

46. Ibid., pp. 81–87, 116–17.

47. Ibid., p. 101.

48. Ibid., p. 145.

49. Ibid., pp. 77–78.

50. Ibid., pp. 87–88.

51. Ibid., p. 87 n. 1.

52. Ibid., p. 167.

53. Lawrence Stone, *The Crisis of the Aristocracy, 1588–1641* (Oxford, 1966), pp. 250–57; Wallace MacCaffrey, "Place and Patronage in Elizabethan Politics," in *Elizabethan Government and Society: Essays Presented to Sir John Neale*, ed. Stanley T. Bindoff (London, 1961), pp. 95–126; John Neale, "The Elizabethan Political Scene," in *Essays in Elizabethan History*, ed. John Neale (New York, 1958).

54. Georges d'Avenel, *La Noblesse française sous Richelieu* (Paris, 1901), p. 160; Richard Bonney, *The King's Debts: Finance and Politics in France, 1589–1661* (Oxford, 1981), pp. 24–26, 44, 72, 74, 76–77.

55. Léonce Pingaud, *Les Saulx-Tavannes* (Paris, 1876), pp. 4–16; idem, ed., *Correspondance des Saulx-Tavannes (1552–1573)* (Paris, 1877); Claude Petitot, ed., *La Vie de Gaspard de Saulx, seigneur de Tavannes*, 3 vols. (Paris, 1822) and *Mémoires de Messire Gaspard de Saulx, seigneur de Tavannes, 1522–1573*, 3 vols. (Paris, 1787), vol. 1, pp. v–xii, 2–3, 78–79, 155.

56. Pingaud, *Les Saulx-Tavannes*, p. 23; idem, *Mémoires*, vol. 2, pp. 65–66, 68–71, 73–75, 77.

57. Pingaud, *Mémoires*, pp. 107–8, 135, 182–83, 189–90.

58. Maurice Wilkinson, *The Last Phase of the League in Provence, 1588–1598* (London, 1909), pp. 8, 32, 40; Honoré Louis de Castellane, sieur Besaudun, *Mémoires pour servir à l'histoire de la Ligue en Provence, Besaudun, Bausset, Cassaignes* (Aix, 1866).

59. César Nostradamus, *L'Histoire et chronique de Provence* (Lyon, 1614), pp. 1,026–31, 1,070–71; Honoré Bouche, *La Chorographie ou description de Provence*, 2 vols. (Aix, 1664), vol. 1, pp. 809–19, 830, 850–51; Wilkinson, *The Last Phase*, pp. 49–50.

60. ADBR, Aix, B 339, fols. 84–92; John Pearl, "Guise and Provence: Political Conflicts in the Epoch of Richelieu" (Ph.D. diss., Northwestern University, 1968), p. 20. The royal gift of money may have been as large as 400,000 écus (1,200,000 livres), payable over four years.

61. H. Forneron, *Les Ducs de Guise et leur époque*, 2 vols. (Paris, 1877), vol. 1, p. 424; Bonney, *The King's Debts*, p. 76; Buisseret, *Henry IV*, pp. 48–49. Buisseret gives the sum as 629,500 livres.

62. Bonney, *The King's Debts*, p. 44; the duc de Sully, *Memoirs*, 2 vols. (London, 1877), vol. 2, p. 107.

63. Robert Harding, "Corruption and the Moral Boundaries of Patronage in the Renaissance," in *Patronage in the Renaissance*, eds. Guy Lytle and Stephen Orgel (Princeton, 1981), p. 60.

64. David Parker, *La Rochelle and the French Monarchy: Conflict and Order in Seventeenth-Century France* (London, 1980), p. 182.

65. Ibid., pp. 36–37.

66. Ibid., p. 182.

67. Ibid., pp. 182–83.

68. Romier, *Le Royaume*, vol. 1, pp. 223–39; Philip Knachel, *England and the Fronde: The Impact of the English Civil War and Revolution on France* (Ithaca, 1967), p. 143.

69. Franklin Charles Palm, *Politics and Religion in Sixteenth-Century France: A Study of the Career of Henry of Montmorency-Damville, Uncrowned King of the South* (Boston, 1927), pp. 106, 172; Arlette Jouanna, "Protection des fidèles et fidélité au roi: L'exemple de Henri Ier de Montmorency-Damville," in *Hommages à Roland Mousnier: Clientèles et fidélités en Europe à l'époque moderne*, ed. Yves Durand (Paris, 1981), pp. 282–86; Philippe Wolff, ed., *Histoire du Languedoc* (Toulouse, 1967), pp. 329–33.

70. Palm, *Politics and Religion*, pp. 108–9, 122–23, 150–56; Paul Gachon, *Histoire de Languedoc* (Paris, 1921), pp. 146–48. Also see Mark Greengrass, "The *Sainte Union* in the Provinces: The Case of Toulouse," *Sixteenth Century Journal* 14 (1983): 469–96; idem, "War, Politics, and Religion in Languedoc during the Government of Henri de Montmorency-Damville" (Ph.D. diss., Oxford, 1979); idem, *France in the Age of Henri IV: The Struggle for Stability* (London, 1984).

71. Palm, *Politics and Religion*, pp. 196–97, 207. For the Montmorency clientele of his son, Henri II, see Paul Gachon, *Les Etats de Languedoc et l'édit de Béziers (1632)* (Paris, 1887), pp. 84–92.

72. Harding, *Anatomy of a Power Elite*, pp. 154–57.

73. Ibid., pp. 143–49.

74. Jean-Pierre Labatut, *Les Ducs et pairs de France au XVIIe siècle* (Paris, 1972), p. 271.

Sully's fortune was estimated at 5,200,000 livres at the end of his life, and he was given a gift of 300,000 livres when he retired in 1610; see Bernard Barbiche, *Sully* (Paris, 1978), pp. 170–71, 179.

75. François Mougel, "La Fortune des princes de Bourbon-Conti, revenus et gestion (1655–1791)," *Revue d'histoire moderne et contemporaine*, 18 (1971): 33.

76. Daniel Roche, "Aperçus sur la fortune et les revenus des princes de Condé à l'aube du XVIIIe siècle," ibid., 14 (1967): 242.

77. Avenel, *La Noblesse*, p. 162.

78. Arthur de Boislisle, ed., *Mémoires de Saint Simon*, 43 vols. (Paris, 1879–1928), vol. 4 p. 339; vol. 12, p. 288 n. 1.

79. Avenel, *La Noblesse*, p. 162; Bonney, *The King's Debts*, p. 76.

80. Labatut, *Les Ducs et pairs*, pp. 250–52.

81. Avenel, *La Noblesse*, pp. 161–62.

82. Ibid., pp. 160–61.

83. Ibid., p. 178.

84. Harding, *Anatomy of a Power Elite*, p. 157; Joseph Revol, *Lesdiguières: Essai de psychologie militaire* (Paris, 1949), pp. 18, 22. Also see comte de Douglas and J. Roman, eds., *Actes et correspondance du connetable de Lesdiguières*, 3 vols. (Grenoble, 1878); Louis Videl, *L'Histoire de la vie du connetable de Lesdiguières* (Paris, 1638).

85. Georges d'Avenel, *Richelieu et la monarchie absolue*, 4 vols., 2nd ed. (Paris, 1895), vol. 2, p. 1; Bonney, *The King's Debts*, pp. 91–92.

86. Labatut, *Les Ducs et pairs*, p. 123.

87. Alphonse, baron de Ruble, ed., *Commentaires et lettres de Blaise de Monluc*, 5 vols. (Paris, 1864–72), vol. 1, p. 29; vol. 2, p. 332; cited by Harding, *Anatomy of a Power Elite*, pp. 148, 150; Blaise de Monluc, *Commentaires*, ed. Paul Courteault (Paris, 1964), pp. 767–68; cited by Arlette Jouanna, "Protection des fidèles et fidélité au roi," p. 280.

88. Harding, *Anatomy of a Power Elite*, pp. 149–54.

89. See chap. 1. Also see Orest Ranum, *Richelieu and the Councillors of Louis XIII: A Study of the Secretaries of State and Superintendents of Finance in the Ministry of Richelieu, 1633–1642* (Oxford, 1963); Mousnier, *Les Organes de l'état*, pp. 150–52; Georges Pagès, *La Monarchie d'Ancien Régime en France de Henri IV a Louis XIII* (Paris, 1928), p. 111; Denis Richet, *La France moderne: L'Esprit des institutions* (Paris, 1973), p. 80.

90. Richard Bonney, *Political Change in France under Richelieu and Mazarin, 1624–1661* (Oxford, 1978), pp. 76–89; Jean Bérenger, "Le Problème du ministériat au XVIIe siècle," *Annales: ESC* 29 (1974): 175; Pierre Goubert, *L'Ancien Régime*, vol. 1, *La Société* (Paris, 1969), pp. 153–54. Henri IV had begun this shift in reliance from the sword to the robe; see Roland Mousnier, *Le Conseil du Roi de Louis XII à la Revolution* (Paris, 1970), p. 10; cited by J. Russell Mayor, *Representative Government in Early Modern France* (New Haven, 1980), p. 388. For instance, the crown appointed eighty-eight members of the Parlement of Paris to high administrative positions between 1596 and 1633; see Mark Cummings, "The Long Robe and the Scepter: A Quantitative Study of the Parlement of Paris and the French Monarchy in the Early Seventeenth Century" (Ph.D. diss., University of Colorado, 1974), p. 166. Sully, Henri IV's finance minister, had his own clients within the royal administration in the provinces, particularly élus and commissaires; see Barbiche, *Sully*, pp. 55–58; also see J. Russell Major, "Henry IV and Guyenne: A Study Concerning the Origins of Royal Absolutism," *French Historical Studies* 4 (1966): 363–83; David Buisseret, "A Stage in the Development of the Intendants: The Reign of Henri IV," *The Historical Journal* 9 (1966): 27–38. However, Sully's clients were sent into the provinces from Paris and elsewhere. Sully did not deliberately recruit clients within the provincial elites as Richelieu did, and his clientele was much smaller than that of the Cardinal.

91. Carl Burckhardt, *Richelieu and His Age*, vol. 2, *Assertion of Power and the Cold War*, trans. Bernard Hoy (London, 1970), pp. 136–40.

92. William Beik notes that "in Languedoc the existence of two widely separated capital cities, Toulouse and Montpellier, each with it own sovereign court, led to a polarization of social circles which kept any one family or group from dominating the province. I suspect that 'concentrated' provinces like Provence, Guyenne, or Normandy were different from 'split'

provinces like Languedoc, Brittany or Dauphiné in this respect"; see his "Client Systems and Provincial Government in Seventeenth-Century France: Search for a Method," paper presented at the annual meeting of the American Historical Association, New York, December 1979. For a contemporary example of the use of clientelism in governing, see John Waterbury, *The Commander of the Faithful. The Moroccan Political Elite—A study in Segmented Politics* (London, 1970).

93. Sharon Kettering, *Judicial Politics and Urban Revolt in Seventeenth-Century France: The Parlement of Aix, 1629–1659* (Princeton, 1978), pp. 111–28.

94. Joseph H. Albanès, *Gallia Christiana Novissima*, 7 vols. (Valence, 1899–1920), vol. 1, pp. 137–38; EDB, IV–2, 415; Maximin Deloche, *Un Frère de Richelieu inconnu: Chartreux, primat des Gaules, cardinal ambassadeur* (Paris, 1935).

95. ADBR, Aix, B 3348, fols. 856–64, April 1632, royal letters of provision as lieutenant general; Georges d'Avenel, ed., *Lettres, instructions diplomatiques et papiers d'état du Cardinal Richelieu*, 8 vols. (Paris, 1853–77), vol. 4, p. 170, April 1631. Saint Chamond declared himself Richelieu's créature in a letter from Sisteron on May 30, 1632; see A.A.E., 1702, fol. 56. Also see Sharon Kettering, "The King's Lieutenant General in Provence," *Canadian Journal of History* 13 (1978): 366–68.

96. Bouche, *La Chorographie*, vol. 2, pp. 911–12; A.C., Aix, BB 101, fols. 198v–200; B. Méjanes 608, fols. 94–122; B. Méjanes 736, "Histoire de Provence sous le gouvernment du comte d'Alais," fols. 15–16; B.N., Dupuy 754, fols. 218–19; A.A.E., 1705, fols. 483, 485, 1717, fol. 390; Albanès, *Gallia*, vol. 2, pp. 620–21; René La Bruyère, *La Marine de Richelieu: Maillé-Brézé, général des galères, grand amiral (1619–1646)* (Paris, 1945), pp. 94, 179; idem, *La Marine de Richelieu: Sourdis, archevêque et amiral (6 novembre 1594–18 juin 1645)* (Pais, 1948), p. 45; Charles de La Roncière, *Histoire de la marine française*, 6 vols. (Paris, 1899–1932), vol. 4, p. 618; vol. 5, pp. 12 n. 3, 64, 70, 106, 119; Auguste Jal, *Abraham Du Quesne et la marine de son temps*, 2 vols. (Paris, 1873), vol. 1, pp. 63, 65–66, 105. Also see Eugène Sue, ed., *Correspondance d'Henri d'Escoubleau de Sourdis, archevêque de Bordeaux, 1636–1642*, 3 vols. (Paris, 1836).

97. The eight intendants in Provence who were Richelieu's clients included Nicolas Arnoul, naval intendant at Toulon, 1640–42; Dreux d'Aubray, provincial intendant, 1630–31; Charles de Besançon de Bazoches, temporary naval commissioner, 1640–41; Bernard de Besançon, seigneur Du Plessis, naval intendant at Toulon, 1635–37; François de Bochart, seigneur de Champigny-Saron, provincial intendant, 1636–40, 1643–47; Jean Lequeux, naval intendant at Toulon, 1641; Charles de Machault, temporary army commissioner, 1636; Michel Particelli, sieur d'Hémery, temporary naval commissioner, 1635–36. The other seven intendants in Provence who were not Richelieu's clients included Charles de Brûlart de Léon, temporary royal commissioner to Estates, 1632; Noel Brûlart, baron de La Borde, temporary royal commissioner, 1633; Jacques Talon, temporary royal commissioner, 1634; Gaspard Du Gué, temporary army commissioner, 1636; Charles Le Roy de La Potherie, provincial intendant, 1630–33; Jean de Lauzon, sieur de Liré, provincial intendant, 1636–38; François Cazet, seigneur de Vautorte, provincial intendant, 1640–43.

98. Roland Mousnier, ed., *Lettres et mémoires adressés au Chancelier Séguier (1633–1649)*, 2 vols. (Paris, 1964), vol. 2, pp. 1,204–5.

99. René Pillorget, "Les Cascaveoux: L'Insurrection aixoise de l'automne 1630," *XVIIe siècle* 64 (1964): 8.

100. B.N., Ms. fr. 24169, fols. 2–61, Henri de Séguiran, "Procès-verbal contenant l'état véritable auquel sont les affaires de la côte maritime de Provence," in Sue, ed., *Correspondance de Sourdis*, vol. 3, pp. 221–319.

101. B. Méjanes 736, "Histoire de Provence," fol. 14; La Roncière, *Histoire de la marine*, vol. 4, p. 576 n. 3; vol. 5, p. 37; EDB, IV–2, 450–51; Jean-Scholastique Pitton, *Histoire de la ville d'Aix* (Aix, 1666), p. 574. Their galleys were named *La Valbelle* and *La Séguirane*.

102. See chaps. 3 and 4.

103. A.A.E., 1725, fols. 420, 429–29v, 478, 483, 492–492v, 497–497v.

104. B.N., M. C. 157 bis, fols. 782–83, November 19, 1671.

105. Haitze, *Histoire*, vol. 6, p. 75, in the year 1669.

106. A.A.E., 1725, fols. 179–80, December 13, 1659.

107. William Beik, *Absolutism and Society in Seventeenth-Century France; State Power and Provincial Aristocracy in Seventeenth-Century Languedoc.* (Cambridge, 1985), p. 236–37. Also see Gachon, *Les Etats*, pp. 84–92; idem, *Histoire de Languedoc*, pp. 160–63; Charles Montchal, *Mémoires de M. de Montchal, Archevêque de Toulouse* (Rotterdam, 1718); R. Monlaur, *La Duchesse de Montmorency (1600–1666)* (Paris, 1898).

108. Julian Dent, "The Role of Clientèles in the Financial Elite of France under Cardinal Mazarin," in *French Government and Society, 1500–1850: Essays in Memory of Alfred Cobban*, ed. John F. Bosher (London, 1973), pp. 41–69; idem, *Crisis in Finance: Crown, Financiers, and Society in Seventeenth-Century France* (London, 1973); Daniel Dessert and Jean-Louis Journet, "Le Lobby Colbert: Un royaume ou une affaire de famille," *Annales: ESC* 30 (1975): 1303–36; Daniel Dessert, "Finances et société au XVIIe siècle, à propos de la Chambre de Justice de 1661," *Annales: ESC* 29 (1974): 847–81; Jean-Claude Dubé, "Clients des Colbert et des Pontchartrain à l'intendance de Québec," in *Hommages à Roland Mousnier*, ed. Durand, pp. 199–212; Douglas Baxter, *Servants of the Sword: French Intendants of the Army, 1630–1670* (Urbana, Ill., 1976), pp. 53–59; André Corvisier, "Clientèles et fidélités dans l'armée française aux XVIIe siècles," in *Hommages à Roland Mousnier*, ed., Durand, pp. 213–36; Mousnier, *Les Organes de l'état*, pp. 71–78, 179; Yvonne Bézard, *Fonctionnaires maritimes et coloniaux sous Louis XIV: Les Bégon* (Paris, 1932); Jean-Louis Bourgeon, "Balthazar Phélypeaux, marquis de Châteaunuef, secretaire d'Etat de Louis XIV (1638–1700)," in *Le Conseil du Roi de Louis XII à la Révolution*, ed. Roland Mousnier (Paris, 1970) pp. 131–52; Jean Bérenger, "Charles Colbert, marquis de Croissy," ibid., pp. 153–74; William Roth, "Jean-Baptiste de Colbert, marquis de Torcy," ibid., pp. 175–203; L. Boisnard, *Une Famille de ministres aux XVIIe et XVIIIe siècles: Les Phélypeaux*, 2 vols. (Paris, 1975).

109. On Michel Mazarin, see chap. 1; Georges Dethan, *Mazarin et ses amis* (Paris, 1968), pp. 39–45, 95, 344 n. 1; Haitze, *Histoire*, vol. 4, pp. 425–26, 450; Albanès, *Gallia*; EDB, IV–2, 328. On Infreville, see Jacques d'Infreville, *Le Chevalier d'Infreville et les marquis de la mer* (Grenoble, 1973).

110. Albanès, *Gallia*, vol. 1, pp. 142–44; EDB, IV–2, 254; Charles de Grimaldi and Jacques Gaufridy, *Mémoires pour servir à l'histoire de la Fronde* (Aix, 1870), p. 67.

111. Mousnier, ed., *Lettres au Chancelier Séguier*, vol. 1, pp. 121–28; Pierre-Adolphe Chéruel and Georges d'Avenel, *Lettres du Cardinal Mazarin pendant son ministère*, 9 vols. (Paris, 1872–1906), vol. 2, p. 954, September 24, 1647; vol. 3, p. 333; Dent, "The Role of Clientèles," p. 54; A.A.E., 1712, fols. 264–67, October 29, 1647, Sève's letters of commission as intendant in Provence.

112. Hyacinthe Serroni was named bishop of Orange in the Comtat Venaissin in 1647, and Joseph Zongo Ondedei was named bishop of Fréjus along the Provençal coast in 1654. See chap. 1; Albanes, *Gallia*, vol. 1, pp. 406–7; vol. 6, pp. 209–10; Dethan, *Mazarin*, pp. 129–31; Chéruel and Avenel, *Lettres de Mazarin*, vol. 4, pp. 700 n. 1, 719 n. 2; vol. 7, pp. 666, 678; ADBR, Marseille, C 32, fols. 242v–43. Serroni was a temporary royal commissioner for naval and financial affairs in Provence from 1654 to 1656.

113. The six intendants in Provence who were Mazarin's clients were the chevalier Louis-Nicolas de Clerville, temporary royal commissioner for fortifications, 1660–61; Aymar de Chouppes, marquis de Chouppes, temporary army commissioner at Aix, 1658; Jean-Baptiste de Colbert, temporary naval commissioner at Toulon, 1654; Louis Le Roux d'Infreville, naval intendant at Toulon, 1646–49; Alexandre de Sève, provincial intendant, 1646–49; Louis Testard de La Guette, naval intendant at Toulon, 1660–61. Chouppes, Infreville, and Sève had previously served Richelieu. See *Mémoires du marquis de Chouppes* (Paris, 1861), pp. 3–5, 9, 11–39, 41–61, 204, 206–8, 220, 238–55. Sève was serving Richelieu in August 1637; see Avenel, *Lettres de Richelieu*, vol. 5, p. 1,052. Infreville was serving Richelieu in 1629; *Mémoires de Chouppes*, vol. 7, p. 977, May 31, 1629. The other five intendants in Provence who were not Mazarin's clients were Jacques de Chaulnes, 1650; Jacques Dyel de Miromesnil, 1651; Jean d'Estampes de Valençay, 1649; Geoffroy Luillier d'Orgeval, 1656; and Habert de Montmort, 1644. All were temporary royal commissioners who stayed in Provence less than a year.

114. Henri de Séguiran, sieur de Bouc, first president of the Cour des Comptes at Aix, is not

included in this group because he had ceased to serve Richelieu after 1636. He was loyal to Mazarin during the Fronde but politically inactive.

115. Jerôme de Grimaldi, Mazarin's old friend, is not included because he became estranged from the Cardinal shortly after his arrival at Aix; see Kettering, *Judicial Politics*, pp. 307–9, 326. Laurens d'Urre, marquis d'Aiguebonne, a client of Mazarin and acting governor of Provence from 1650 to 1652, is not included for the same reason. He became estranged from the Cardinal in the winter of 1651–52, and was recalled; see ibid., pp. 291–95.

116. The marquis d'Aiguebonne was given the power to command in Provence in the absence of Alais by royal letters of September 21, 1650, published by the Parlement of Aix on December 19 after Alais's departure; cf. Grimaldi and Gaufridy, *Mémoires*, pp. 45–47; A.C., Aix, BB 102, fol. 222v; A.A.E., 1717, fol. 317. Aiguebonne was a trusted client of Mazarin, which is indicated by the nature of their correspondence in 1650–51; cf. A.A.E., 1716, 1717, passim.

117. Beik, pp. 238–39. *Absolutism and Society*, also see Georges Dethan, *Gaston d'Orléans, conspirateur et prince charmant* (Paris, 1959), pp. 37, 108–9, 113, 116–17, 128.

118. Dethan, *Gaston d'Orléans*, pp. 157–58; C. E. J. Caldicott, "Le Gouvernment de Gaston d'Orléans en Languedoc (1644–1660) et la carrière de Molière," *XVII siècle* 116 (1979): 21.

119. Caldicott, "Le Gouvernement," pp. 17–42; Beik, *Absolutism and Society*, pp. 238–39.

120. Beik, *Absolutism and society*, pp. 240–41; *Mémoires de Chouppes*; on Mérinville, see Kettering, "The King's Lieutenant-General in Provence," pp. 374–75.

121. Robert Boutruche, *Bordeaux de 1453 à 1715* (Bordeaux, 1966), p. 321.

122. Nicolas Fessenden, "Epernon and Guyenne: Provincial Politics under Louis XIII" (Ph.D. diss., Columbia University, 1972), pp. 66–86.

123. Charles Boscheron Des Portes, *Histoire du Parlement de Bordeaux depuis sa création jusqu'à sa suppression (1451–1790)*, 2 vols. (Bordeaux, 1878), vol. 2, p. 443; Francis Loirette, "Un Intendant de Guyenne avant la Fronde: Jean de Lauson (1641–1648)," *Bulletin philologique et historique du Comité des Travaux Historiques et Scientifiques* (1957): 442; Paul Courteault, *Histoire de Gascogne et de Béarn* (Paris, 1938), p. 259.

124. Fessenden, "Epernon and Guyenne," pp. 235–37.

125. Yves-Marie Bercé, *Histoire des Croquants: Etude sur les soulèvements populaires au XVIIe siècle dans le sud-ouest de la France*, 2 vols. (Paris, 1974), pp. 667–68.

126. Loirette, "Un Intendant de Guyenne," pp. 433–61.

127. La Bruyère, *Maillé-Brézé*, pp. 89–90.

128. Courteault, *Histoire de Gascogne*, p. 262; Sal Westrich, *The Ormée of Bordeaux: A Revolution during the Fronde* (Baltimore, 1972), pp. 1–20.

129. Ibid., pp. 73, 83.

130. Arthur Kleinclausz, *Histoire de Bourgogne* (Paris, 1924), p. 275; Gaston Roupnel, *La Ville et la campagne au XVIIe siècle: Etude sur les populations du pays dijonnais* (Paris, 1955), pp. 191 n. 55, 213, 223.

131. Roupnel, *La Ville et la campagne*, pp. 176, 225; Kleinclausz, *Histoire de Bourgogne*, pp. 274–75.

132. Ernst Kossmann, *La Fronde* (Leiden, 1954), p. 159; Roupnel, *La Ville et la campagne*, p. 35 n. 101; Kleinclausz, *Histoire de Bourgogne*, pp. 275–77; Henri Drouot and Jean Calmette, *Histoire de Bourgogne* (Paris, 1928), pp. 261–65. Also see Marc-Antoine Millotet, *Mémoire des choses qui se sont passés en Bourgogne depuis 1650 jusqu'à 1668* (Dijon, 1866). Millotet is an essential source on the Burgundian Fronde.

133. Bonney, *Political Change*, pp. 61 n. 2, 275 n. 1. Louis de Laisné, sieur de La Marguerie, was intendant in Burgundy from 1650 to 1654, and first president of the Parlement of Dijon from 1654 to 1657.

134. Jean Richard, ed., *Histoire de la Bourgogne* (Toulouse, 1978), p. 256.

135. J. Russell Major argues that Marillac had attempted to suppress the Estates, especially in provinces without *élections*, and to establish *élus* in their place. His policy was reversed by Richelieu because of the dissatisfaction it provoked. Richelieu allowed the Estates to exist but he sought to weaken their authority and to control their decision making, and his strategy was

continued by Colbert and Louis XIV; see Major, *Representative Government in Early Modern France* (New Haven, 1980), pp. 524, 581–99, 664.

136. Ibid., pp. 519–621, 660–64.

137. Ibid., pp. 634–36.

138. Ibid., pp. 600, 640–41.

139. Ibid., pp. 663–64.

140. Charles Godard, *Les Pouvoirs des intendants sous Louis XIV* (Paris, 1901), pp. 158–72; Bernard Hildesheimer, *Les Assemblées générales des communautés de Provence* (Paris, 1935).

141. Major, *Representative Government*, p. 664.

142. Dessert and Journet, "Le Lobby de Colbert," pp. 1,303–36.

143. Colbert's clients in Provence included Nicolas Arnoul, intendant of the galleys, 1665–74; Pierre Arnoul, naval intendant, 1674–79; Claude Bazin, royal commissioner, 1664–65; Alexandre de Belleguise, royal commissioner, 1666–69; Jean-Baptiste de Brodart, intendant of the galleys, 1674–84; Louis-Nicolas de Clerville, commissioner for naval fortifications, 1661–64; Louis Le Roux d'Infreville, naval intendant, 1665–70; Louis de Machault, army commissioner, 1661; Louis Matharel, naval intendant 1670–73; Thomas-Alexandre Morant, provincial intendant, 1680–87; Jean-Baptiste de Rouillé, provincial intendant, 1672–80; Louis Testard de La Guette, naval intendant, 1661–65. Arnould, Clerville, Infreville, Rouillé, and La Guette had also served Colbert's predecessors.

144. Colbert used thirteen Provençal brokers, nine of whom had previously served Mazarin. Eight of these belonged to the Forbin or Grignan clans, and one was a Forbin client. The remaining Provençal brokers included Fortia de Pilles, the chevalier Paul, Jean-Baptiste de Valbelle, and Mercoeur. Of Colbert's twenty-six clients in Provence, fifteen had previously served Richelieu or Mazarin, about 55 percent. They included five intendants, nine Provençal brokers, and the comte de Mérinville.

145. Rouillé was followed as intendant in Provence in 1680 by Thomas-Alexandre Morant, seigneur de Soulles, formerly intendant in the Bourbonnais, who served until 1687 when he became first president of the Parlement of Toulouse. He was replaced by Pierre Cardin Lebret, another client of Colbert.

146. See chaps. 3 and 4; and Alexandre Thomas, *Une Province sous Louis XIV: Situation politique et administrative de la Bourgogne, 1661–1715* (Dijon, 1844).

147. Godard, *Les Pouvoirs*, pp. 161, 171–72.

148. Major, *Representative Government*, p. 640.

149. Colbert inherited and used Mazarin's clients in Languedoc including Pierre de Bonzi, the bishops of Lavaur, Montpellier, Saint Papoul, and Saint Pons, Gaspard de Fieubet, first president in the Parlement of Toulouse, and his clients. See Beik, *Absolutism and Society*, pp. 241–34.

150. Georges B. Depping, ed., *Correspondance administrative sous le règne de Louis XIV*, 4 vols. (Paris 1850–55), vol. 1, pp. 64–75.

151. Ibid., p. 67.

152. Ibid., pp. 51–75.

153. Major, *Representative Government*, pp. 642–43. Also see Beik, *Absolutism and Society*, pp. 124–29.

154. Depping, ed., *Correspondance administrative*, vol. 1, pp. 68, 284; Pierre Clément, *Lettres, instructions et mémoires de Colbert*, 10 vols. (Paris, 1861–73), vol. 7, p. 445; J. Adher, "La Préparation des séances des Etats de Languedoc d'après des documents inédits," *Annales du Midi* 25 (1913): 467.

155. Major, *Representative Government*, p. 645; Godard, *Les pouvoirs*, pp. 168–70.

156. Godard, *Les pouvoirs* pp. 168–170; Clément, *Lettres de Colbert*, vol. 4, p. 49; Depping, ed., *Correspondance administrative*, vol. 1, pp. 333–34, Mérinville to Colbert, March 2, 1664.

157. Depping, ed., *Correspondance administrative*, p. 376.

158. Major, *Representative Government*, pp. 636, 647–48, 664. Also see Armand Rebillon, *Les Etats de Bretagne de 1661 à 1789* (Paris and Rouen, 1932).

159. See chap. 2 on the motivation of brokers. Also see Sharon Kettering, "Patronage and

Politics during the Fronde," forthcoming in *French Historical Studies*. Parlementaires displayed a similar blend of motives; see Kettering, *Judicial Politics*, pp. 249–50.

160. Kettering, *Judicial Politics*, pp. 187, 206, 209–10, 213–15, 265–66; ADBR, Marseille, C 15, fol. 131.

161. Kettering, *Judicial Politics*, p. 87; idem, "The King's Lieutenant General in Provence," p. 379.

162. James Collins, paper on the Estates of Brittany presented at the annual conference of the American Historical Association, Chicago, December 1984.

163. See chaps. 3 and 6 on the Estates' attempts to influence intendants and other royal officials through gifts of money.

164. Godard, *Les Pouvoirs*, p. 17 n. 2; Douglas Baxter, *Servants of the Sword: French Intendants of the Army, 1630–1670* (Urbana, Ill., 1976), pp. 47–59; André Corvisier, "Clientèles et fidélités dans l'armée française aux XVIIe et XVIIIe siècles," in Durand, ed., *Hommages à Roland Mousnier*, pp. 213–36; Bonney, *Political Change*, pp. 401–18; Louis André, *Michel Le Tellier et Louvois* (Paris, 1942); idem, Louvois (Paris, 1984); Georges Livet, *L'Intendance d'Alsace sous Louis XIV, 1648–1715* (Strasbourg, 1956); Maurice Gresset, *Le Rattachement de la Franche-Comté à la France, 1668–1678* (Besançon, 1978); idem, *Gens de justice à Besançon de la conquête à la Révolution (1674–1789)*, 2 vols. (Paris, 1978).

165. Major, *Representative Government*, pp. 643–44.

166. See epilogue.

167. See chap. 2.

168. Vendôme was born in 1654, and became governor *en survivance* with his father four years later. He never resided in Provence and visited only briefly. He spent eighteen years in the army in Flanders and commanded the French army during the War of the Spanish Succession, capturing Madrid and ending Habsburg hopes of regaining the Spanish throne at the battle of Villaviciosa in 1710. He was buried in the Escorial in 1712.

169. B.N., M. C. 170, fol. 235.

170. Ibid., 174 bis, fol. 421, July 11, 1677; Clément, *Lettres de Colbert*, vol. 4, pp. 59–61, July 30, 1677; Jal, *Du Quesne*, vol. 2, p. 210; Balthasar Clapiers-Collongues, *Chronologie des officiers des cours souveraines* (Aix, 1909–12), p. 23; Scipion Du Roure, baron, *Généalogie de la maison de Forbin* (Paris, 1906), p. 53. Jean-Baptiste did not permanently pursue a career outside Provence. Once the Forbin problem was solved, he received no more appointments from Colbert and returned to Provence to serve quietly as parlement president, an office his father had purchased for him, until his death in 1701.

171. Du Roure, *Généalogie*, p. 53; A.A.E., 1728, fols. 191–92.

172. B.N., M. C. 166 bis, fol. 153, May 18, 1674, Janson-Forbin to Colbert from Warsaw as the new French ambassador. In a letter in October 1675, Janson-Forbin thanked Colbert for recognizing his service as Polish ambassador by making one of his nephews a marquis; see A.A.E., 1729. fol. 51.

173. B.N., M. C. 170, fols. 235, 318; 170 bis, fol. 581.

174. Louis Monmerqué, ed., *Lettres de Madame de Sévigné*, 14 vols. (Paris, 1862–66), vol. 5, pp. 184–85, 210.

175. Ibid., vol. 4, p. 524.

176. Charles de La Roncière, *Valbelle, le Tigre, marin de Louis XIV, 1637–1681* (Paris, 1935), pp. 47–52. Based upon manuscript 1194 (R.A. 4) at the Bibliothéque Méjanes of Aix, "La Vie de Monsieur le bailli de Valbelle, chef d'escadre des armées navales de France par M. Desprès, capitaine de Brûlot, 1684."

177. Ibid., pp. 66–67; Pillorget, *Les Mouvements*, pp. 838, 840.

178. A.A.E., 1725, fols. 302–3, 350–53.

179. La Roncière, *Valbelle, le Tigre*, pp. 75–80.

180. Ibid., pp. 95–233. Naval intendant Testard de La Guette wrote to Colbert on Valbelle's behalf in 1663, and his name appeared on a list of qualified ship captains in 1664. He was given a ship two years later, and embarked upon a distinguished career in the royal navy.

181. B.N., M. C. 145, fols. 389–90, September 27, 167.

182. Ibid., 170 bis, fol. 731, February 23, 1675.

183. Jal, *Du Quesne*, vol. 2, pp. 131, 133–35.

184. La Roncière, *Valbelle, le Tigre*, pp. 231–34; Paul Bamford, *Fighting Ships and Prisons: The Mediterranean Galleys of France in the Age of Louis XIV* (Minneapolis, 1973), pp. 101–2, 127.

185. Bonney, *Political Change*, pp. 290–92.

186. Ibid., p. 287; Georges Pagès, "Autour du Grand Orage: Richelieu et Marillac, deux politiques," *Revue historique* 179 (1937): 63–97; Georges Mongrédien, *La Journée des dupes: 10 novembre 1630* (Paris, 1961); Pierre de Vaissière, *L'Affaire du maréchal de Marillac* (Paris, 1924); Philippe Erlanger, *Richelieu and the Affair of Cinq-Mars*, trans. Gilles and Heather Cremonesi (London, 1971); Jame Kitchens, "Judicial *Commissaires* and the Parlement of Paris: The Case of the Chambre de l'Arsenal," *French Historical Studies* 12 (1982): 323–50.

187. Orest Ranum, "Richelieu and the Great Nobility: Some Aspects of Early Modern Political Motives," *French Historical Studies* 3 (1963): 184–204; Bonney, *Political Change*, p. 290.

188. Pagès, *La Monarchie d'Ancien Régime*, p. 111.

189. Harding, *Anatomy of a Power Elite*, pp. 21–107, 138–42; also see Romier, *Le Royaume*, vol. 1, pp. 188–210.

190. Harding, *Anatomy of a Power Elite*, p. 190, also see pp. 171–217.

191. Richard Bonney, "Cardinal Mazarin and the Great Nobility during the Fronde," *English Historical Review* 46 (1981): 827–28.

192. Célestin Moreau, ed., *Mémoires de Jacques de Saulx, comte de Tavannes* (Paris, 1858), pp. xvi, 67, 70.

193. Harding, *Anatomy of a Power Elite*, pp. 46–107.

194. Ibid., pp. 136–38; Romier, *Le Royaume*, vol. 1, pp. 160–64.

195. Romier, *Le Royaume*, vol. 1, pp. 214–30; Harding, *Anatomy of a Power Elite*, pp. 46–47; Bonney, *The King's Debts*, pp. 24–29.

196. Bonney, *The King's Debts*, pp. 71–72.

197. Ibid., pp. 77–78, 85, 87, 92–93.

198. Ibid., pp. 126–27, 140, 170–172, 175, 177, 197–98; Roland Mousnier, *La Vénalité des offices sous Henri IV et Louis XIII*, 2d ed. (Paris, 1971), pp. 529–665; idem, "The Fronde," in *Preconditions of Revolution in Early Modern Europe*, ed. Robert Forster and Jack Greene (Baltimore, 1970), pp. 131–59; Kettering, *Judicial Politics*, pp. 182–285. Mallet's figures on certain expenses paid by the French treasury show an increase in the amounts spent on pensions and gifts from 1605 to 1630, and a decrease after 1630 until the end of the Fronde; cf. Bonney, *The King's Debts*, pp. 306–7.

199. Mousnier, *La Vénalité*, pp. 222–48; Harding, "The Moral Boundaries," pp. 50–53; Bonney, *The King's Debts*, pp. 61–62; Kettering, *Judicial Politics*, pp. 216–50; François Bluche and Pierre Durye, *L'Anoblissement par charges avant 1789*, 2 vols. (Paris, 1962).

200. Lewis, *Later Medieval France*, pp. 153–56; Jonathan Dewald, *The Formation of a Provincial Nobility: The Magistrates of the Parlement of Rouen* (Princeton, 1980), pp. 88–89; Elie Barnavi, "Fidèles et partisans dans la Ligue parisienne (1585–1594)," *Hommages à Roland Mousnier*, ed. Durand, pp. 139–52.

201. Mousnier, *La Vénalité*, pp. 594–606; idem, "Sully et le conseil d'état et des finances," *Revue historique* 192 (1941): 72–80; Raymond Kierstead, *Pomponne de Bellièvre* (Evanston, Ill., 1968), pp. 130–34; J. Russell Major, "Bellièvre, Sully, and the Assembly of Notables of 1596," *Transactions of the American Philosophical Society*, N.S. 64 (1974), pt. 2, 29–30; idem, "Henry IV and Guyenne: A Study Concerning the Origins of Royal Absolutism," *French Historical Studies* 4 (1966): 363–83.

202. Mousnier, *Le Conseil du Roi*, pp. 17–20. Between 1515 and 1665, the number of royal offices in France increased from 4,041 to 46,047. This was an increase from about one official for every 4,700 inhabitants in 1515 to about one official for every 380 inhabitants in 1665; see Harding, "Corruption and the Moral Boundaries," p. 50 n. 9. Also see John H. M. Salmon, "Venality of Office and Popular Sedition in Seventeenth-Century France," *Past and Present* 37 (1967): 26–47.

203. Labatut, *Les Ducs et pairs*, p. 262; Bonney, *The King's Debts*, p. 157.

204. Maximin Deloche, *La Maison du Cardinal de Richelieu* (Paris, 1912), p. 485.

205. Labatut, *Les Ducs et pairs*, p. 148.

206. Ranum, *Richelieu and the Councillors*, pp. 30–32; La Bruyère, *Maillé-Brézé*; Deloche, *Un Frère de Richelieu.*

207. Séguier left a fortune of 4,000,000 livres; see Mousnier, *Lettres*, vol. 1, p. 34. Bullion's annual revenues were estimated by contemporaries at 1,500,000 livres; see Ranum, *Richelieu and the Councillors*, p. 164. Bullion's total fortune at his death was 7,826,864 livres; see Jean-Pierre Labatut, "Aspects de la fortune de Bullion," *XVIIe siècle* 60 (1963): 11–40. Chavigny's fortune was considerable; see Ranum, *Richelieu and the Councillors*, pp. 84–85.

208. Bonney, *The King's Debts*, pp. 260–61; Daniel Dessert, "Pouvoir et finance au XVIIe siècle: La Fortune du Cardinal Mazarin," *Revue d'histoire moderne et contemporaine* 32 (1976): 164.

209. Dessert, "Pouvoir et finance," pp. 161–63.

210. Ibid., p. 177; Bonney, *The King's Debts*, pp. 260–61; Julian Dent, *Crisis in Finance: Crown, Financiers, and Society in Seventeenth-Century France* (London, 1973), p. 178.

211. Dessert, "Pouvoir et finance," pp. 178–79.

212. Daniel Dessert, "L'Affaire Fouquet," *L'Histoire* 32 (1981): 39–47; Bonney, *The King's Debts*, pp. 248–71, esp. 264 n. 1; Georges Mongrédian, *L'Affaire Foucquet* (Paris, 1973), pp. 20, 30, 48; Dent, *Crisis in Finance*, p. 178.

213. Bonney, *Political Change*, p. 297.

214. Dessert, "Pouvoir et finance," pp. 178–80; "Finances et société au XVIIe siècle: À propos de la Chambre de Justice de 1661," *Annales: ESC* 29 (1974): 864–65.

215. Labatut, *Les Ducs et pairs*, pp. 257–70.

216. Bonney, *The King's Debts*, pp. 127–30, 155–56; idem, *Political Change*, pp. 288–89.

217. Bonney, *Political Change*, pp. 292–97.

218. Célestin Moreau, ed., *Choix des Mazarinades*, 2 vols. (Paris, 1853). Also see Bonney, "Cardinal Mazarin and the Great Nobility," pp. 818–33, and "Cardinal Mazarin and His Critics: The Remonstrances of 1652," *Journal of European Studies* 10 (1980): 15–31.

219. Bonney, "The Remonstrances of 1652," 15–31, and *Political Change*, pp. 294–96. Also see *Demandes des princes et des seigneurs qui ont pris des armes avec le parlement et people de Paris*, in *Choix des mazarinades*, vol. 1, 431–37.

220. *Mémoires de Jacques de Saulx*, pp. 10–11. In 1651, Condé demanded the government of Provence for his brother Conti; cf. pp. 68–69.

221. Chéruel and Avenel, *Lettres de Mazarin*, vol. 2, p. 797, August 19, 1646; p. 814, September 27, 1646.

222. Bonney, "Cardinal Mazarin and the Great Nobility," pp. 827–28.

223. Knachel, *England and the Fronde*, pp. 195–96.

224. This is also the opinion of Harding, *Anatomy of a Power Elite*, p. 34. For the role of secretaries of state as court brokers, see pp. 32–36.

225. Notable exceptions are Robert Harding and Richard Bonney.

226. Neale, "The Elizabethan Political Scene"; Linda Levy Peck, "Court Patronage and Government Policy: The Jacobean Dilemma," in *Patronage in the Renaissance*, pp. 27–46; Conrad Russell, ed., *The Origins of the English Civil War* (London, 1973); Menna Prestwich, *Politics and Profit under the Early Stuarts: The Career of Lionel Cranfield* (Oxford, 1966); John Morrill, *The Revolt of the Provinces* (London, 1976).

Chapter Six

1. John H. Plumb, *The Growth of Political Stability in England, 1675–1725* (London, 1967), pp. xvi–xviii.

2. Charles Tilly, "Reflections on the History of European State-Making," *The Formation of National States in Western Europe*, ed. Charles Tilly (Princeton, 1975), pp. 25–46.

3. Max Weber, *Economy and Society: An Outline of Interpretive Sociology*, ed. Guenter Roth and Claus Wittich, trans. Ephraim Fischoff, 3 vols. (New York, 1968), vol. 3, pp. 1,028–55, 1,393–1,401.

4. Luigi Graziano, "Patron-Client Relationships in Southern Italy," *European Journal of Political Research* 1 (1973): 3–5, also in *Friends, Followers, and Factions: A Reader in Political Clientelism*, ed. Steffen Schmidt et al. (Berkeley, 1977), p. 361; idem, "A Conceptual Framework for the Study of Clientelism," Western Societies Program Occasional Paper No. 2, Cornell University, April 1975; idem, "Center-Periphery Relations and the Italian Crisis: The Problem of Clientelism," in *Territorial Politics in Industrial Nations*, ed. Sidney Tarrow (New York, 1978), p. 293; Sidney Tarrow, *Peasant Communism in Southern Italy* (New Haven, 1967), pp. 68–69, 74; Peter Lange and Sidney Tarrow, eds. *Italy in Transition* (London, 1980), pp. 149–50.

5. Robert Kaufman, "The Patron-Client Concept and Macro-Politics: Prospects and Problems," *Comparative Studies in Society and History* 16 (1974): 302–5; Alex Weingrod, "Patrons, Patronage, and Political Parties," *Comparative Studies in Society and History* 10 (June 1969): 398.

6. Sydel Silverman, "Patronage and Community-Nation Relations in Central Italy," in Schmidt, *Friends, Followers, and Factions*, pp. 293–300; also see Anton Blok, *The Mafia of a Sicilian Village, 1860–1960: A Study of Violent Peasant Entrepreneurs* (Oxford, 1974).

7. René Lemarchand, "Political Clientelism and Ethnicity in Tropical Africa: Competing Solidarities in Nation-Building," in Schmidt, *Friends, Followers, and Factions*, pp. 115–18.

8. See chap. 3. John H. M. Salmon has emphasized the problem of conflict in a society dominated by patron-client ties in *Society in Crisis: France in the Sixteenth Century* (London, 1975).

9. Samuel N. Eisenstadt and Louis Roniger, "Patron-Client Relations as a Model of Structuring Social Exchanges," *Comparative Studies in Society and History* 22 (January 1980): 46, 72.

10. For a discussion of this problem, see Wallace MacCaffrey, "Place and Patronage in Elizabethan Politics," in *Elizabethan Government and Society: Essays Presented to Sir John Neale*, ed. Stanley T. Bindoff (London, 1961), pp. 95–126.

11. Sharon Kettering, *Judicial Politics and Urban Revolt in Seventeenth-Century France: The Parlement of Aix, 1629–1659* (Princeton, 1978), pp. 274, 281, 286.

12. A.A.E., 1721, fols. 232–35.

13. Kettering, *Judicial Politics*, pp. 105–8.

14. Ibid., pp. 74–75, 305.

15. A.C., Aix, BB 103, fol. 59; A.A.E., 1721, fols. 274–75, 426.

16. A.A.E., 1721, fols. 435–36; 1722, fol. 139; 1723, fols. 87, 179, 384v, 399v.

17. B.N., M. C. 140, fol. 135, September 4, 1666, Janson-Forbin to Colbert; 141 bis, fol. 672, October 24, 1666, Oppède to Colbert.

18. Joseph Marchand, *Un Intendant sous Louis XIV: Etude sur l'administration de Lebret en Provence, 1687–1704* (Paris, 1889), pp. 213–19, 222.

19. Ibid., pp. 219–22.

20. Julian Ricommard, "Les Subdélégués des intendants aux XVIIe et XVIIIe siècles," *L'Information historique* 24 (1962–63): 146–47.

21. Marchand, *Un Intendant*, pp. 55–60; Julien Ricommard, "Les Subdélégués en titre d'office en Provence, 1704–1715," *Provence historique* 14 (1964): 243–71, 336–78; Henri Fréville, *L'Intendance de Bretagne (1689–1790)*, 3 vols. (Rennes, 1953), vol. 1, pp. 82–84.

22. Roland Mousnier, *Les Institutions de la France sous la monarchie absolue, 1598–1789*, vol. 2, *Les Organes de l'état et la société* (Paris, 1980), pp. 510–11; Charles Godard, *Les Pouvoirs des intendants sous Louis XIV* (Paris, 1901), pp. 23–33; Julien Ricommard, "Les Subdélégués des intendants jusqu'à leur érection en titre d'office," *Revue d'histoire moderne* 12 (1937): 353; Fréville, *L'Intendance de Bretagne*, vol. 1, pp. 112–13; idem, "Notes sur les subdélégués généraux et subdélégués de l'intendance de Bretagne aux XVIIIe siècle," *Revue d'histoire moderne* 12 (1937): 409; Raoul Busquet, "Les Subdélégués de Provence," *Etudes sur l'ancienne Provence*, ed. Raoul Busquet (Paris, 1930), pp. 303–9. Colbert sent a circular letter to the provincial intendants in 1674, 1680, and 1683, ordering the suppression of superfluous subdélégués, without much

effect; see Mousnier, *Les Organes de l'état*, pp. 505–7; Ricommard, "Les Subdélégués aux XVIIe et XVIIIe siècles," pp. 143–45.

23. Ricommard, "Les Subdélégués aux XVIIe et XVIIIe siècles," p. 146; idem, "Les Subdélégués jusqu'à leur érection," p. 384; Godard, *Les Pouvoirs*, pp. 23, 25–26.

24. Ricommard, "Les Subdélégués jusqu'à leur érection," p. 385; idem, "Les Subdélégués aux XVIIe et XVIIIe siècles," p. 146.

25. The intendants' written authority also became more comprehensive as time went on. See the commissions of Dreux d'Aubray, seigneur d'Offemont, intendant in Provence from 1630 to 1631, and Pierre Cardin Lebret, intendant in Provence from 1687 to 1704; Gabriel Hanotaux, *Origines de l'institution des intendants des provinces (1550–1631)* (Paris, 1884), pp. 295–302; Marchand, *Un Intendant*, pp. 361–64.

26. Richard Holbrook, "Baron d'Oppède and Cardinal Mazarin: The Politics of Provence from 1640 to 1661" (Ph.D. diss., University of Illinois at Chicago Circle, 1976), pp. 35, 63–64.

27. Kettering, *Judicial Politics*, pp. 101–2, 234.

28. Ibid., Holbrook, "Baron d'Oppède," pp. 429–30.

29. Ibid., Holbrook, "Baron d'Oppède," pp. 429–30.

30. René Pillorget, *Les Mouvements insurrectionnels en Provence entre 1596 et 1715* (Paris, 1975), pp. 731, 804, 842.

31. B.N., M. C. 137 bis, fols. 667–69.

32. Ibid., 143, fol. 330v, March 1667.

33. Félix Freudmann, *L'Etonnant Gourville (1625–1703)* (Paris, 1960), pp. 10, 21, 26–27, 34–35, 38–39, 63–65. Also see J. F. Michaud and J. J. F. Poujoulat, ed., *Mémoires de Pierre de Lenet*, 2 vols. (Paris, 1838); Léon Lecestre, ed., *Mémoires de Gourville (1646–1701)*, 2 vols. (Paris, 1894).

34. Freudmann, *L'Etonnant Gourville*, pp. 68, 79–85, 90–94.

35. See chap. 1. Cosnac was a rival of Gourville for the favors of the prince de Conti and Cardinal Mazarin, and he was responsible for Gourville's stay in the Bastille from November 1656 to April 1675, at Mazarin's orders, supposedly for indiscreet words about the Cardinal to Conti, which were reported by Cosnac; see Freudmann, *L'Etonnant Gourville*, pp. 69–70.

36. Pierre-Joseph de Haitze, *Histoire de la ville d'Aix*, 6 vols. (1880–92), vol. 4, pp. 93–94; B.N., Dupuy 754, *Remontrance au peuple de Provence (1649)*, fol. 218; Jacques Gaufridy, "Histoire de Provence sous le règne de Louis XIII," B. Méjanes 790, fol. 7.

37. Philippe Tamizey de Larroque, ed., *Lettres de Peiresc aux frères Dupuy*, 7 vols. (Paris, 1888–98), vol. 6, pp. 337–38, letter in December 1625.

38. A.A.E., 1701, fol. 12, Oppède to Richelieu, May 12, 1627; Georges d'Avenel, ed., *Lettres, instructions diplomatiques et papiers d'état du Cardinal de Richelieu*, 8 vols. (Paris, 1853–57), vol. 2, p. 474, Richelieu to Oppède, June 20, 1627, vol. 3, pp. 566–68, the same, March 7, 1630.

39. ADBR, Marseille, IX B2, fol. 160, Parlement's remonstrance of May 20, 1626, on Guise; Tamizey de Larroque, ed., *Lettres de Peiresc*, vol. 6, pp. 346–52, letter in January 1626; "Délibérations du Parlement de Provence," B. Méjanes 951, fols. 385–86, 388–92, August 29 and 31, 1629, fols. 519–21v, November and December 1630. Also see Kettering, *Judicial Politics*, pp. 114–15.

40. Pierre Deyon, *Amiens, capitale provinciale: Etude sur la société urbaine au XVIIe siècle* (Paris, 1967), pp. 452–60.

41. Amable Floquet, *Histoire du Parlement de Normandie*, 7 vols. (Paris, 1840–42), vol. 5, p. 88; Madeleine Foisil, *La Révolte des Nu-Pieds et les révoltes normandes de 1639* (Paris, 1970), p. 260.

42. See Kettering, *Judicial Politics*, "The Causes of the Judicial Frondes," *Canadian Journal of History* 17 (August 1982): 275–306, and "Patronage and Politics during the Fronde," forthcoming in *French Historical Studies*.

43. Robert Harding, "Corruption and the Moral Boundaries of Patronage in the Renaissance," in *Patronage in the Renaissance*, ed. Guy Lytle and Stephen Orgel (Princeton, 1981), pp. 47–48; Arnold Heidenheimer, ed., *Political Corruption* (New York, 1970); G. E. Aylmer, *The State's Servants: The Civil Service of the English Republic, 1649–1660* (London, 1973), p. 183.

44. James Scott, *Comparative Political Corruption* (Englewood Cliffs, N.J., 1972), p. 4.

45. Ibid., p. 5; John F. Bosher, "The French Government's Motives in the Affaire du Canada, 1761–1763," *English Historical Review* 47 (January 1981): 62–63.

46. Bosher, "Affaire du Canada," pp. 66–68; Scott, *Comparative Political Corruption*, pp. 3–4.

47. Nannerl Keohane, *Philosophy and the State in France: The Renaissance to the Enlightenment* (Princeton, 1980), pp. 151–82.

48. Harding, "Corruption," pp. 63–64; Menna Prestwich, *Politics and Profit under the Early Stuarts: The Career of Lionel Cranfield* (Oxford, 1966), pp. 223–26. On England also see Joel Hurstfield, *Freedom, Corruption, and Government in Elizabethan England* (Cambridge, Mass., 1973); John A. W. Gunn, *Politics and the Public Interest in the Seventeenth Century* (London, 1969).

49. Julian Dent, *Crisis in Finance: Crown, Financiers and Society in Seventeenth-Century France* (London, 1973), pp. 67–68.

50. Ibid., p. 68.

51. Richard Bonney, *The King's Debts: Finance and Politics in France, 1589–1661* (Oxford, 1981), pp. 252–53.

52. Ibid., pp. 253–55; Dent, *Crisis in Finance*, pp. 68–70.

53. Dent, *Crisis in Finance*, pp. 72–77.

54. Julian Dent, "The Role of Clientèles in the Financial Elite of France under Cardinal Mazarin," in *French Government and Society, 1500–1800: Essays in Memory of Alfred Cobban*, ed. John F. Bosher (London, 1973), pp. 49–53, 55–57.

55. Bonney, *The King's Debts*, pp. 265–71; Daniel Dessert, "Pouvoir et finance au XVIIe siècle: La fortune du Cardinal Mazarin," *Revue d'histoire moderne et contemporaine* 23 (1976): 161–81.

56. For instance, see Guy Frégault, *François Bigot: Administrateur français*, 2 vols. (Ottawa, 1948); Bosher, "Affaire du Canada," pp. 59–78;" Jean de Maupassant, *Un Grand armateur de Bordeaux: Abraham Gradis (1699?–1780)* (Bordeaux, 1917). For another famous eighteenth-century corruption trial, see Claude Sturgill, *Claude Le Blanc: Civil Servant of the King* (Gainesville, 1975), pp. 167–74.

57. Richard Bonney, *Political Change in France under Richelieu and Mazarin, 1624–1661* (Oxford, 1978), pp. 212–13; Godard, *Les Pouvoirs*, p. 19.

58. Godard, *Les Pouvoirs*, pp. 21–22.

59. Kettering, *Judicial Politics*, p. 157.

60. Godard, *Les Pouvoirs*, p. 21; Bonney, *Political Change*, p. 211.

61. B.N., Ms. fr. 17376, fol. 42.

62. C. E. J. Caldicott, "Le Gouvernment de Gaston d'Orléans en Languedoc (1644–1660) et la carrière de Molière," *XVIIe siècle* 16 (1979): 26. The provincial Estates of Burgundy, Artois, Bresse, and the Mâconnais also frequently added gifts of 1,000 to 16,000 livres to the intendant's salary; see Godard, *Les Pouvoirs*, pp. 20–21.

63. From a paper on the Estates of Brittany in the early seventeenth century, presented by James Collins at the annual conference of the American Historical Association, Chicago, 1984, including a table titled, "Pensions of the Estates of Brittany, 1631–1648." Also see his "Taxation in Bretagne, 1598–1648" (Ph.D. diss., Columbia University, 1978).

64. Ibid. Also see chap. 3.

65. Claude Blangueron, *Gilles de Gouberville: Gentilhomme du Cotentin, 1522–1578* (Coutances, 1969), pp. 61–67. Also see abbé A. Tollemer, ed., *Un Sire de Gouberville: Gentilhomme campagnard au Cotentin de 1553 à 1562* (Paris, 1873, 1972); Madeleine Foisil, *Le Sire de Gouberville. Un Gentilhomme normand au XVIe siècle* (Paris, 1981).

66. Pillorget, *Les Mouvements*, p. 714; B. Méjanes, "Mémoires de Messire Antoine de Valbelle," fols. 63v, 205.

67. B.N., Ms. fr. 18593, "Sur les malversations commis par le lieutenant de l'amirauté du Levant, janvier 1644," fols. 244–47, 258–305.

68. Ibid., fols. 238–43.

69. Ibid., fols. 297–300; Jean-Marc David, *L'Amirauté de Provence et des mers du Levant* (Marseille, 1942), p. 187.

70. Ivan Rampal, *Un Vieux domaine provençale: Cadarache* (Marseille, 1945), pp. 121, 125; B. Méjanes 630, "Etat du florinage contenant le revenu noble de tous les fiefs et arrière-fiefs de Provence avec les noms des possesseurs fait par Maynier d'Oppède en 1668," fol. 76; René Pillorget, "Destin de la ville d'Ancien Régime," in *Histoire de Marseille*, ed. Edouard Baratier (Toulouse, 1973), pp. 178–79.

71. B.N., Ms. fr. 18976, "Mémoire touchant l'émotion populaire arrivée à Marseille le 28 juin," fol. 475; Pillorget, *Les Mouvements*, pp. 544–45, 553–64; Adolphe Crémieux, *Marseille et la royauté pendant la minorité de Louis XIV*, 2 vols. (Paris, 1917), vol. 1, p. 190.

72. Alexksandra Dmitrievna Lublinskaya, *Vnutrenniaia politika frantsuzskogo absoliutizma, 1633–1649* (Leningrad, 1966), pp. 316–17; A.A.E., 1709, fols. 126–27, 144–45, 209–12, 1710, fol. 39.

73. B.N., Ms. fr. 18976, fols. 474–75; B. Méjanes R.A. 3, "Mémoires de Valbelle," fols. 97v–103v; Pillorget, *Les Mouvements*, pp. 562–64. Jean-Philippe de Valbelle (1615–46), the oldest son of Cosme de Valbelle, a Knight of Malta, and a distinguished galley captain who became vice admiral, was seriously wounded at the battle of Barcelona in 1642, and died four years later from his wounds; see Charles de La Roncière, *Valbelle, le Tigre, marin de Louis XIV, 1627–1681* (Paris, 1935), pp. 32–34, 37; EDB, IV–2, 481.

74. A.A.E., 1709, fols. 126–27.

75. Aylmer, *The State's Servants*, p. 140.

76. Godard, *Les Pouvoirs*, pp. 433–34.

77. Georges Livet, *L'Intendance d'Alsace sous Louis XIV 1648–1715* (Paris, 1956), p. 836. Professor Livet calls seventeenth-century royal administrators who confused public authority and private interests "administrators-entrepreneurs."

78. Bonney, *Political Change*, p. 210.

79. William Beik, *Absolutism and Power in Seventeenth-Century France: State Power and Provincial Aristocracy in Seventeenth-Century Languedoc*, (Cambridge, 1985), pp. 109–11. Also see his article, "Two Intendants Face a Popular Revolt: Social Unrest and the Structure of Absolutism in 1645," *Canadian Journal of History* 9 (1974): 243–62.

80. Gaston Rambert, *Nicolas Arnoul: Intendant des galères à Marseille, 1666–1674* (Marseille, 1931), pp. 9–46, 155, 202–3; Daniel Dessert and Jean-Louis Journet, "Le Lobby Colbert: Un royaume ou une affaire de famille," *Annales: ESC* 30 (1975): 1,320–22, 1333 n. 12.

81. Rambert, *Nicolas Arnoul*, pp. 33, 40, 44.

82. Ibid., pp. 23, 41 n. 37.

83. Godard, *Les Pouvoirs*, pp. 332–56.

84. Rambert, *Nicolas Arnoul*, pp. 35–37.

85. Ibid., pp. 53–87.

86. Ibid., pp. 40–46, 96–99; Paul Bamford, *Fighting Ships and Prisons: The Mediterranean Galleys of France in the Age of Louis XIV* (Minneapolis, 1973), p. 59.

87. Bamford, *Fighting Ships and Prisons*, pp. 90–93.

88. M. Prevost and Roman d'Amat, eds., *Dictionnaire de biographie française*, (Paris, 1956), vol. 7, p. 393. Brodart had served under Arnoul at Marseille in 1665; see B.N., M. C. 130, fol. 95, June 6, 1665.

89. Godard, *Les Pouvoirs*, p. 433.

90. Legal proceedings against Valbelle, stemming from the 1644 popular protest against him at Marseille, were transferred to the Parlement of Toulouse, which cleared him of all charges in 1646; see David, *L'Amirauté*, pp. 188, 232; ADBR, Marseille IX B2, fol. 696v, November 19, 1647.

91. EDB, III, 204–7, 219–21, 284–85; Prevost and d'Amat, eds., *Dictionnaire de biographie française* (Paris, 1976) vol. 8, p. 412; Scipion Du Roure, *Genéalogie de la maison de Forbin* (Paris, 1906), pp. 9–11, 72–73; Edouard Baratier, ed., *Histoire de la Provence* (Toulouse, 1969), pp. 219–22; Gustave Arnaud d'Agnel, *Politique des rois de France en Provence*, 2 vols. (Paris, 1914).

92. See, for example, Clive Church, *Revolution and Red Tape: The French Ministerial Bureaucracy, 1770–1850* (Oxford, 1981).

93. Marchand, *Un Intendant*, p. 40.

94. Edmond Esmonin, "Les Intendants du Dauphiné des origines à la Révolution,"in *Etudes sur la France des XVIIe et XVIIIe siècles*, ed. Edmond Esmonin (Paris, 1964), p. 99.

95. Bonney, *Political Change*, p. 439.

96. Douglas Baxter, *Servants of the Sword: French Intendants of the Army, 1630–1670* (Urbana, Ill., 1976), pp. 53–59.

97. Harding, "Corruption," pp. 48–50; Hurstfield, *Freedom, Corruption and Government*, pp. 149–50.

98. See René La Bruyère, *La Marine de Richelieu: Maillé-Brézé, général des galères, grand amiral, 1619–1646* (Paris, 1945).

99. Georges Dethan, *Mazarin et ses amis* (Paris, 1968), pp. 104–23; Pierre-Adolphe Chéruel, *Histoire de France pendant la minorité de Louis XIV, 1643–1653*, 4 vols. (Paris, 1879–80), vol. 8, pp. 195, 233–37; vol. 2, pp. 148, 154; Philippe Tamizey de Larroque, "Les Correspondants de Peiresc: Le Cardinal Bichi, évêque de Carpentras," *Revue de Marseille et Provence* 30 (1884): 289–304.

100. Auguste Jal, *Abraham Du Quesne et lamarine de son temps*, 2 vols. (Paris, 1873), vol. 1, pp. 6–7.

101. Maximin Deloche, *Un Frère de Richelieu inconnu: Chartreux, primat des Gaules, cardinal, ambassadeur* (Paris, 1935), pp. 227–369.

102. Both Silverman and Lemarchand use models of traditional clientelism based on nineteenth- and twentieth-century societies with traditional characteristics. See notes 6 and 7 above.

103. René Lemarchand does this in his article with Keith Legg, "Political Clientelism and Development: A Preliminary Analysis," *Comparative Politics* 4 (1972): 149–78.

104. See epilogue to chap. 6.

105. Eisenstadt and Roniger, "Patron-Client Relations as a Mode of Structuring Social Exchanges," pp. 46, 72; Carl Landé, "The Dyadic Basis of Clientelism," in Schmidt, *Friends, Followers, and Factions*, p. xxviii; Kenneth Brown, "Changing Forms of Patronage in a Moroccan City," in *Patrons and Clients in Mediterranean Societies*, ed. Ernest Gellner and John Waterbury (London, 1977), p. 310; Emrys Lloyd Peters, "Patronage in Cyrenaica," in Gellner and Waterbury, eds., *Patrons and Clients*, p. 275; Steffen Schmidt, "Bureaucrats as Modernizing Brokers," *Comparative Politics* 6 (1974): 449. Roland Mousnier has noted that the nature of the patron-client bond in France varies with the period; see "Les Fidélités et les clientèles en France aux XVIe, XVIIe, et XVIIIe siècles," *Histoire sociale* 15 (1982): 46.

106. Charles Tilly, "Reflections on the History of European State-Making," Introduction to *The Formation of National States in Western Europe*, ed. Charles Tilly (Princeton, 1975), p. 3.

107. Among the best-known attempts are those by James Scott, "Corruption, Machine Politics, and Political Change," *American Political Science Review* 62 (1969): 1,142–58, and "Patron-Client Politics and Political Change in Southeast Asia," in Schmidt, *Friends, Followers, and Factions*, pp. 123–46; Lemarchand and Legg, "Political Clientelism and Development;" pp. 149–78; Lemarchand, "Political Clientelism and Ethnicity," in Schmidt, *Friends, Followers, and Factions*, pp. 100–22; Lemarchand acknowledges the influence of Jean Maquet, "Institutionalisation féodale des relations de dépendence dans quatre cultures interlacustres," *Cahiers d'Etudes Africaines* (1969): 402–14, and Luigi Graziano, "Patron-Client Relationships in Southern Italy," in Schmidt, *Friends, Followers, and Factions*, pp. 360–77.

108. On bastard feudalism, see K. B. McFarlane, "Bastard Feudalism," *Bulletin Institute Historical Research* 20 (1943–45): 161–80, and "Parliament and Bastard Feudalism," *Transactions Royal Historical Society* 4 ser. 26 (1944): 53–79; Helen Cam, "The Decline and Fall of English Feudalism," *History* 25 (1940): 216–33; N. B. Lewis, "The Organisation of Indentured Retinues in Fourteenth-Century England," *Transactions Royal Historical Society* 4 ser. 27 (1945): 29–39; William Dunham, *Lord Hastings' Indentured Retainers, 1461–1485* (New Haven, 1955); Bryce Lyon, *From Fief to Indentures: The Transition from Feudal to Non-Feudal Contract in Western Europe* (Cambridge, Mass., 1957).

109. On feudalism, see Marc Bloch, *French Rural History*, trans. Janet Sondheimer (Berkeley, 1966), and *Feudal Society*, trans. L. A. Manyon (Chicago, 1961); Georges Duby, *La Société aux XIe et XIIe siècles dans la région mâconnaise* (Paris, 1953), *Rural Economy and Country Life in the Medieval West*, trans. Cynthia Postan (Columbia, S.C., 1968), and *The Early Growth of European Society*, trans. Howard Clarke (Ithaca, 1974); Carl Stephenson, *Medieval Feudalism* (Ithaca, 1942); F. L. Ganshof, *Feudalism*, trans. Philip Grierson (London, 1944).

110. Mousnier, *Les Institutions*, vol. 1, *Société et état* (Paris, 1974), pp. 90–93, "Les Fidélités et les clientèles," p. 44; J. Russell Major, "The Crown and the Aristocracy in Renaissance France," *American Historical Review* 69 (1964): 635.

111. Tarrow, *Peasant Communism in Italy*, p. 69.

112. Peter Lewis, "Decayed and Non-Feudalism in Later Medieval France," *Bulletin Institute Historical Research* 37 (1964): 157–84. Michel Gilsenan notes that Marc Bloch, the French historian who wrote several classic studies of feudalism, did not discuss patron-client relationships because he did not see them "as either descriptively or analytically primary for understanding feudal society"; "Against Patron-Client Relations," in Gellner and Waterbury, eds., *Patrons and Clients*, p. 182.

113. Dent, "The Role of Clientèles," p. 44.

114. Robert Harding, *The Anatomy of a Power Elite: The Provincial Governors of Early Modern France* (New Haven, 1978), pp. 74–75, 97–99; Jack H. Hexter, "Storm over the Gentry," *Reappraisals in History* (Evanston, Ill., 1961), pp. 144–48.

115. See chap. 5. Also see William Weary, "Royal Policy and Patronage in Renaissance France: The Monarchy and the House of La Trémoille" (Ph.D. diss., Yale University, 1972).

116. Kristen Neuschel, "The Prince of Condé and the Nobility of Picardy: A Study of the Structure of Noble Relationships in Sixteenth-Century France" (Ph.D. diss., Brown University, 1982).

117. See chap. 5. Also see Henri Drouot, *Mayenne et la Bourgogne, 1587–1596*, 2 vols. (Paris, 1937).

118. See chaps. 3 and 4. Also see Nicolas Fessenden, "Epernon and Guyenne: Provincial Politics under Louis XIII" (Ph.D. diss., Columbia University, 1972), pp. 220–62.

119. Scott, "Corruption, Machine Politics, and Political Change," pp. 1,144, 1,147–48; "Patron-Client Politics and Political Change in Southeast Asia," in Schmidt, *Friends, Followers, and Factions*, pp. 140–44. Patron-client ties in early modern society were also more pervasive and formal than in modern society.

120. Pierre Charbonnier, *Guillaume de Murol: Un Petit seigneur auvergnat au début du XVe siècle* (Clermont-Ferrand, 1973), p. 81.

121. Ibid., pp. 81–94.

122. Ibid., pp. 68–69.

123. Ibid., pp. 70, 97.

124. Ibid., pp. 94–97.

125. Ibid., pp. 111–18.

126. Ibid., pp. 118–21.

127. Blanguernon, *Gilles de Gouberville*, pp. 77–79, 133, 139–41, 175.

128. Pierre Clément, ed., *Lettres, instructions et mémoires de Colbert, 1648–1683*, 10 vols. (Paris, 1861–73), vol. 4, p. 68.

129. Clément, ed., *Lettres de Colbert*, vol. 4, p. 65.

130. Ibid., p. 66; Georges B. Depping, ed., *Correspondance administrative sous le règne de Louis XIV*, 4 vols. (Paris, 1850–55), vol. 1, pp. 394–95.

131. Depping, ed., *Correspondance administrative*, vol. 1, pp. 410–11.

132. Ibid., pp. 793–94; also B.N., M. C. 149, fol. 700.

133. B.N., M. C. 139, fols. 107–12.

134. Ibid., 110, fol. 327, August 6, 1662.

135. Ibid., 141 bis, fol. 439, October 18, 1666.

136. Ibid., 130, fol. 312, June 21, 1665.

137. B.N., Dupuy 64, fol. 127.

138. Ibid., fol. 149.

139. Ibid., fol. 137.

140. Ibid., fol. 111, June 22, 1597.

141. Neuschel, "The Prince of Condé and the Nobility of Picardy," p. 64 and note 4.

142. Ibid., p. 65 and note 5.

143. The change in the style of administrative correspondence has been noted by René Pillorget; see *Les Mouvements*, pp. 865–66. Colbert's businesslike inclinations have also been noted by Daniel Dessert and Jean-Louis Journet; see "Le Lobby Colbert," pp. 1,333–36.

144. See Lawrence Stone, "Interpersonal Violence in English Society, 1300–1980," *Past and Present* 101 (1983): 22–33.

145. Roland Mousnier, "Recherches sur les soulèvements populaires en France avant la Fronde," *Revue d'histoire moderne et contemporaine* 5 (1958), 81–113, reprinted in *France in Crisis, 1620–1670*, ed. Peter J. Coveney (London, 1973), p. 162.

146. Mousnier, *Les Institutions*, vol. 1, *Société et état*, pp. 91–92.

147. Mousnier, "Les Fidélités et les clientèles," p. 43.

148. This view is shared by René Pillorget, *La Tige et le rameau: Familles anglaises et françaises XVIe–XVIIIe siècles* (Paris, 1979), p. 210.

149. Cissie Fairchilds, *Domestic Enemies: Servants and Their Masters in Old Regime France* (Baltimore, 1984), p. 4; Mervyn James, *Family, Lineage, and Civil Society: A Study of Society, Politics, and Mentality in the Durham Region, 1500–1640* (Oxford, 1974), pp. 177–98; Jack H. Hexter, "The Education of the Aristocracy in the Renaissance," *Reappraisals in History* (New York, 1961), pp. 45–75.

150. Jean-Pierre Gutton, *Domestiques et serviteurs dans la France de l'Ancien Régime* (Paris, 1981), p. 21.

151. Ibid., p. 29.

152. David Buisseret, *Henry IV* (London, 1984), p. 94.

153. Mack Holt, "Patterns of *Clientèle* and Economic Opportunities at Court during the Wars of Religion: The Household of Francois, Duke of Anjou," *French Historical Studies* 13 (1984): 308.

154. Louis Batiffol, *La Vie intime d'une reine de France aux XVIIe siècle. Marie de Médicis*, 2 vols. (Paris, 1908), vol. 1, p. 138.

155. Eugène Griselle, *Etat de la maison du roi Louis XIII* (Paris, 1912), pp. 83–88.

156. For descriptions of the royal household, see Roger Doucet, *Les Institutions de la France au XVIe siècle*, 2 vols. (Paris, 1948), vol. 1, pp. 102–30; Mousnier, *Les Institutions*, vol. 2, *Les Organes de l'Etat*, pp. 115–31; Jacqueline Boucher, "L'Evolution de la maison du roi des derniers Valois aux premiers Bourbons," *XVIIe siècle* 34 (1982): 359–79; Buisseret, *Henry IV*, pp. 94–106.

157. Harding, *Anatomy of a Power Elite*, p. 27.

158. Weary, "Royal Policy and Patronage in Renaissance France," p. 88 n. 1.

159. J. Russell Major, "Noble Income, Inflation, and the Wars of Religion in France," *American Historical Review* 86 (1981): 38–39. Also see Nancy Roelker, *Queen of Navarre, Jeanne d'Albret, 1528–1572* (Cambridge, Mass., 1968).

160. Gutton, *Domestiques et serviteurs*, pp. 40–41.

161. Fairchilds, *Domestic Enemies*, p. 11.

162. Harding, *Anatomy of a Power Elite*, p. 27; Georges d'Avenel, *La Noblesse française sous Richelieu* (Paris, 1901), p. 55.

163. Fessenden, "Epernon and Guyenne," p. 255.

164. Yves-Marie Bercé, "Les Conduites de fidélité: Des Exemples aquitains," in *Hommage à Roland Mousnier: Clientèles et fidélités en Europe à l'époque moderne*, ed. Yves Durand (Paris, 1981), p. 130; A.A.E., 1701, fol. 228, Guise to Richelieu, March 12, 1631.

165. Avenel, *La Noblesse française*, pp. 53–54, 184.

166. Fessenden, "Epernon and Guyenne," p. 255.

167. Gutton, *Domestiques et serviteurs*, pp. 41–42.

168. Avenel, *La Noblesse française*, p. 485; Maximin Deloche, *La Maison du Cardinal Richelieu* (Paris, 1912), pp. 363–64.

169. Georges Dethan, *Gaston d'Orléans, conspirateur et prince charmant* (Paris, 1959), pp.

351–52; Griselle, *Etat de la maison du roi*, pp. 160–65. Richelieu's household expenditures of 400,000 to 500,000 livres a year were comparable to those of Gaston d'Orléans and the Queen Mother, Marie de Médicis; cf. Avenel, *La Noblesse française*, pp. 484–85.

170. Avenel, *La Noblesse française*, pp. 54, 448; Pierre Lefebvre, "Aspects de la 'fidélité' en France au XVIIe siècle: Le Cas des agents des princes de Condé," *Revue historique* 250 (1973): 62.

171. Gutton, *Domestiques et serviteurs*, pp. 41–43.

172. Madame Saint-René Taillandier, *Madame de Sévigné et sa fille* (Paris, 1938), pp. 153–56.

173. Pillorget, *La Tige et le rameau*, pp. 183–84; Fairchilds, *Domestic enemies*, p. 12.

174. Alfred Franklin, *La Vie privée d'autrefois. La Vie de Paris sous Louis XIV. Tenue de maison et domesticité* (Paris, 1898), pp. 1–203; Avenel, *La Noblesse française*, pp. 51–53, 485.

175. Harding, *Anatomy of a Power Elite*, p. 21.

176. Franklin Charles Palm, *Politics and Religion in Sixteenth-Century France: A Study of the Career of Henry of Montmorency-Damville, Uncrowned King of the South* (Boston, 1927), p. 172; also see Arlette Jouanna, "Protection des fidélités et fidélité au roi: L'exemple de Henri Ier de Montmorency-Damville, in *Hommage à Roland Mousnier*, ed. Durand, pp. 279–96; Mark Greengrass, "The *Sainte Union* in the Provinces: The Case of Toulouse," *Sixteenth Century Journal* 14 (1983): 469–96, and "War, Politics, and Religion in Languedoc during the Government of Henri de Montmorency-Damville" (Ph.D. diss., Oxford University, 1979).

177. Lucien Romier, *Le Royaume de Catherine de Médicis: La France à la veille des guerres de religion*, 2 vols. (Paris, 1922), vol. 1, p. 214.

178. Major, "Noble Income, Inflation, and the Wars of Religion," p. 37.

179. Elie Barnavi, "Fidèles et partisans dans la Ligue parisienne (1585–1594)," in *Hommages à Roland Mousnier*, ed. Durand, p. 140.

180. Ibid.

181. Kettering, *Judicial Politics*, pp. 293–94.

182. Kenneth Dunkley, "Richelieu and the Estates of Brittany, 1624–1640" (Ph.D., diss., Emory University, 1972), pp. 187–88.

183. Antonin Débidour, *La Fronde angevine: Tableau de la vie municipale au XVIIe siècle* (Paris, 1877), pp. 117–18, 133.

184. Yves-Marie Bercé, *Histoire des croquants: Etude des soulèvements populaires au XVIIe siècle dans le sud-ouest de la France*, 2 vols. (Paris, 1974), vol. 1, p. 120.

185. The decline in the number of large noble households in the eighteenth century has also been noted by Gutton, *Domestiques et serviteurs*, p. 46; Pillorget, *La tige et le rameau*, pp. 198–99; Fairchilds, *Domestic Enemies*, p. 15; and Sarah Maza, *Servants and Masters in Eighteenth-Century France: The Uses of Loyalty* (Princeton, 1983), pp. 208–9.

186. Jean-Pierre Labatut, *Les Ducs et pairs de France au XVIIe siècle* (Paris, 1972), p. 315.

187. Robert Forster, *The House of Saulx-Tavanes: Versailles and Burgundy, 1700–1830* (Baltimore, 1971), pp. 122–23.

188. Jacques Jarriot, "Une Famille de 'bons ménagers': La branche nivernaise Des Menon de Charnizay aux XVIIe et XVIIIe siècles," *Revue d'histoire moderne et contemporaine* 23 (1976): 80–101.

189. Auguste de Caumont, duc de La Force, *Le Grand Conti* (Paris, 1922), pp. 43, 45–46, 283. There was a substantial reduction in the number of offices in the household of the princes de Condé from 1644 to 1709; cf. Lefebvre, "Aspects de la fidélité," p. 61.

190. Fairchilds, *Domestic Enemies*, p. 15; comte Dufort de Cheverny, *Mémoires*, ed. Robert de Crêvecoeur, 2 vols. (Paris, 1909), vol. 1, p. 164.

191. Emile Léonard, *Mon village sous Louis XIV d'après les mémoires d'un paysan* (Paris, 1941), pp. 58–69.

192. Maza, *Servants and Masters*, p. 205.

193. Olwen Hufton, *Bayeux in the Late Eighteenth Century: A Social Study* (Oxford, 1967), pp. 41, 43.

194. Gaston Maugras, *La Disgrâce du duc et de la duchesse de Choiseul* (Paris, 1903), pp. 121, 124, 178–79, 208, 321–23.

195. Pillorget, *La Tige et le rameau*, p. 184.

196. Albert Babeau, *La Vie rurale dans l'ancienne France* (Paris, 1883), pp. 173–74, cites letter of July 22, 1671; Léonard, *Mon village*, p. 58; Gutton, *Domestiques et serviteurs*, p. 65.

197. Fairchilds, *Domestic Enemies*, p. 12; Charles de Ribbe, *Une Grande dame dans son ménage au temps de Louis XIV d'après le journal de la comtesse de Rochefort (1689)* (Paris, 1889), p. 137.

198. Léonard, *Mon village*, p. 58; Robert Forster, "The Provincial Noble: A Reappraisal," *American Historical Review* 68 (1962–63), p. 691.

199. Jonathan Dewald, "A Gentry Community in Early Modern France," paper presented at the annual meeting of the French Historical Society, New York University, March 1982.

200. Timothy J. A. Le Goff, *Vannes and Its Region: A Study of Town and Country in Eighteenth-Century France* (Oxford, 1981), pp. 273–74.

201. Maurice Agulhon, *La Vie sociale en Provence intérieure au lendemain de la Révolution* (Paris, 1970), p. 90.

202. Fessenden, "Epernon and Guyenne." pp. 255, 257.

203. Gutton, *Domestiques et serviteurs*, pp. 42–43.

204. Jarriot, "Une Famille de bons ménagers," pp. 94, 97.

205. Léonard, *Mon village*, pp. 58–69.

206. John B. Wolf, *Louis XIV* (New York, 1968), pp. 270, 272, 363–64; Gutton, *Domestiques et serviteurs*, p. 32.

207. Wolf, *Louis XIV*, pp. 269–85; Warren H. Lewis, *The Splendid Century* (New York, 1953), pp. 1–61; Jacques Leuvron, *Daily Life at Versailles in the Seventeenth and Eighteenth Century*, trans. Claire Eliane Engle (London, 1968), and *Les Courtisans* (Paris, 1960); duc de La Force, *Louis XIV et sa cour* (Paris, 1956); William L. Wiley, *The Formal French* (Cambridge, Mass., 1967), pp. 133–88.

208. Wolf, *Louis XIV*, pp. 363–66; Lewis, *The Splendid Century*, pp. 144–59.

209. Wiley, *The Formal French*, pp. 164–88; Orest Ranum, "Courtesy, Absolutism, and the Rise of the French State, 1630–1660," *Journal of Modern History* 52 (1980): 426–51.

210. Pillorget, *La Tige et le rameau*, pp. 198–99.

211. Mousnier, *Les Organes de l'Etat*, pp. 71–78, 149, 159, 170–79, 211–12, 410–11, 439–40, 443. See epilogue to chap. 6.

212. Marcel Marion, *Dictionnaire des institutions de la France aux XVIIe et XVIIIe siècles* (Paris, 1968), p. 34; Pierre Goubert, *L'Ancien Régime*, 2 vols. (Paris, 1973), vol. 2, *Les pouvoirs*, p. 115.

213. Louis André, *Michel Le Tellier et l'organisation de l'armée monarchique* (Paris, 1906), and *Le Tellier et Louvois* (Paris, 1943); André Corvisier, *L'Armée française de la fin du XVIIe siècle au ministère de Choiseul*, 2 vols. (Paris, 1964), and "Clientèles et fidélités dans l'armée française aux XVIIe et XVIIIe siècles," *Hommages à Roland Mousnier*, ed. Durand, pp. 213–36; Baxter, *Servants of the Sword*, pp. 54–59; Emile Léonard, *L'Armée et ses problèmes au XVIIIe siècles* (Paris, 1958).

214. Marion, *Dictionnaire*, pp. 376–77; Georges Girard, *Racolage et milice (1701–1715): Le Service militaire en France à la fin du règne de Louis XIV* (Paris, 1922), pp. 163–65.

215. Private communication from Richard Bonney. See H. Mailfait, *Un Magistrat de l'ancien régime: Omer Talon, sa vie et ses oeuvres* (Paris, 1902), pp. 41–42.

216. See epilogue to chap. 6.

217. Lawrence Stone, *The Crisis of the Aristocracy, 1558–1641* (Oxford, 1965), pp. 201–17; Hexter, "Storm over the Gentry," pp. 144–48.

218. Wolfram Fischer and Peter Lundgreen, "The Recruitment and Training of Administrative and Technical Personnel," in *The Formation of National States in Western Europe*, ed. Charles Tilly (Princeton, 1975), p. 459.

219. Michel Crozier, *The Bureaucratic Phenomenon*, trans. by author (Chicago, 1964), p. 3.

220. According to Roland Mousnier, the characteristics of the new national bureaucracy in France included competitive recruitment of members to assure their competence and honesty; ranking in an administrative hierarchy; definition of duties and responsibilities by law; loyalty and obedience to the good of the state; salaried, permanent employment for life by the state with a pension at retirement; and public honor and respect for serving the state. See *Les Institutions de*

la France sous la monarchie absolue, 2 vols. (Paris, 1980), vol. 2, *Les Organes de l'Etat et la Société*, pp. 79–80.

221. Max Weber wrote that a bureaucratic state adjudicates and administers "according to rationally established law and regulation, a legal and administrative system whose functioning can be rationally predicted," *Economy and Society: An Outline of Interpretive Sociology*, ed. Guenter Roth and Claus Wittich, trans. Ephraim Fischoff, 3 vols. (New York, 1968), vol. 3, p. 1,394. Weber also wrote that a bureaucratic state is characterized by "formal employment, salary, pension, promotion, rational specialization and training, functional division of labor, well-defined areas of jurisdiction, documentary procedures, hierarchical sub- and superordination," p. 1,393. Also see pp. 956–58; Max Weber, *The Theory of Social and Economic Organization*, ed. Talcott Parsons, trans. A. M. Henderson and Talcott Parsons (New York, 1947), p. 331.

222. Weber, *Theory of Social and Economic Organization*, and see Peter Blau and Marshall Meyer, *Bureaucracy in Modern Society* (New York, 1956), pp. 18–21; Michael Dalby and Michael Werthmann, *Bureaucracy in Historical Perspective* (Glencoe, Ill.), pp. 3–21; Robert Merton, ed., *Reader in Bureaucracy* (Glencoe, Ill.), pp. 27–32, 48–52.

223. Clive Church, *Revolution and Red Tape: The French Ministerial Bureaucracy, 1770–1850* (Oxford, 1981), p. 320 n. 23.

224. Ibid., pp. 11–12, 307.

225. In comparing a modern, rational bureaucracy with its predecessor, a patrimonial state, Weber observed that "the patrimonial office lacks above all the bureaucratic separation of the 'private' and the 'official' sphere.... Political administration and political power are treated as a purely personal affair, and decisions are based on personal discretion. Essentially it [the patrimonial state] is based not on the official's commitment to an impersonal purpose and not on obedience to abstract norms, but on strict personal loyalty," in *Economy and Society*, vol. 3, p. 1,029.

226. See Yvonne Bézard, *Fonctionnaires maritimes et coloniaux sous Louis XIV: Les Bégon* (Paris, 1932); Jean-Claude Dubé, "Clients des Colbert et des Pontchartrain à l'intendance de Québec," in *Hommage à Roland Mousnier: Clientèles et fidélités en Europe à l'époque moderne*, ed. Yves Durand (Paris, 1981), pp. 199–212.

227. Charles Tilly, in studying the Vendée, the great uprising in the west of France in 1793, noted that peasant brokers were the elite of the community who mediated between it and the national structure intersecting it. He wrote that peasant brokers "gain power through their extraordinary access to information and to powerful individuals on the outside, and frequently have a good deal of influence over the contacts of other community members with outsiders'; see Charles Tilly, *The Vendée: A Sociological Analysis of the Counterrevolution of 1793* (Cambridge, Mass., 1964), p. 80.

228. Mousnier, *Les Organes de l'Etat*, pp. 211–12. Julian Dent has noted that "under the renewed monarchy [Louis XIV's government after 1661] the clientèle system simply shrank. The role that it had played under Mazarin was essentially an abnormal one which had evolved to fill the gap left by the eclipse of full authority on the death of Louis XIII. Under the restored monarchy, the clientèle system became merely a way of doing business, of carrying out plans decided in the *conseil du roi* [royal council] with the king presiding over the taking of important decisions"; see Julian Dent, "The Role of Clientèles in the Financial Elite of France under Cardinal Mazarin," *French Government and Society, 1500–1800*, ed. John F. Bosher (London, 1973) p. 68.

229. Mousnier, *Les Organes de l'Etat*, pp. 71–78, 159, 410–11, 439–40, 443. Also see Yves Durand, *Les Fermiers généraux au XVIII*[e] *siècle* (Paris, 1971); Guy Chaussinand-Nogaret, *Les Financiers de Languedoc au XVIII*[e] *siècle* (Paris, 1970); Daniel Dessert, "Finances et société au XVIIe siècle: À propos de la Chambre de justice de 1661," *Annales: ESC* 29 (1974): 847–81, and "Le 'Laquais-Financier' au Grand Siècle: Mythe ou réalité," *XVII*[e] *siècle* 122 (1979): 21–36; Julian Dent, *Crisis in Finance: Crown, Financiers and Society in Seventeenth-Century France* (London, 1973); Andrée Chauleur, "Le Rôle des traitants dans l'administration financière de la France de 1643 à 1653," *XVII*[e] *siècle* 65 (1964): 16–49.

230. Mousnier, *Les Organes de l'Etat*, pp. 149, 170–79.

231. John Rule, "Colbert de Torcy, and Emergent Bureaucracy, and the Formation of French Foreign Policy, 1698–1715," in *Louis XIV and Europe*, ed. Ragnhild Hatton (Columbus, Ohio, 1976), pp. 261–88.

232. Mousnier, *Les Organes de l'Etat*, p. 79. See Church, *Revolution and Red Tape*, and Theodore Zeldin, *The Political System of Napoleon III* (London, 1958).

233. Mousnier, *Les Organes de l'Etat*, p. 202; Church, *Revolution and Red Tape*, p. 320 n. 26.

234. This analysis was influenced by John Armstrong, "Old Regime Governors: Bureaucratic and Patrimonial Attributes," *Comparative Studies in Society and History* 14 (1972): 2–29; also see idem, "Old Regime Administrative Elites: Prelude to Modernization in France, Prussia, and Russia," *International Review of Administrative Sciences* 38 (1972): 21–40.

235. Pierre Dubuc, *L'Intendance de Soissons sous Louis XIV* (Paris, 1902), pp. 155–56.

236. Charles Godard, *Les Pouvoirs des intendants sous Louis XIV* (Paris, 1901), p. 101; B.N., Ms. fr. 17404, fol. 13, January 21, 1664, Oppède to Séguier.

237. Dubuc, *L'Intendance de Soissons*, pp. 35–38; M. J. Bry, *Les Vigeuries en Provence* (Paris, 1910).

238. Henri Fréville, *L'Intendance de Bretagne (1689–1790)*, 3 vols. (Rennes, 1953), vol. 1, pp. 130–32.

239. The turnover of intendants in the northern pays d'élections averaged every three years between 1653 and 1666, and every five years between 1666 and 1763; see Richard Bonney, *Political Change in France under Richelieu and Mazarin, 1624–1661* (Oxford, 1978), p. 204. Another historian fixes the average tenure of intendants in the twenty two *généralités* of the pays d'élections at four years, six months, from 1661 to 1688; six years, nine months, in the newly conquered frontier provinces; and nine years, five months, in the *pays d'états*, of which Provence was one; see Mousnier, *Les Organes de l'Etat*, p. 505.

240. Edmond Esmonin, *La Taille en Normandie au temps de Colbert (1661–1683)* (Paris, 1913), pp. 159–60.

241. Bonney, *Political Change*, pp. 206–7.

242. Esmonin, *La Taille en Normandie*, pp. 153–54.

243. Ibid., p. 155.

244. Ibid., p. 158.

245. Ibid., p. 156.

246. Ibid.

247. Ibid., p. 159.

248. Bonney, *Political Change*, p. 206 n. 3.

249. Esmonin, *La Taille en Normandie*, pp. 157–58.

250. For the vital role of local subdélégués in the permanent establishment of the intendants in the provinces, see Peter J. Coveney, *France in Crisis 1620–1675* (London, 1977), pp. 56–57; John H. M. Salmon, "Venality of Office and Popular Sedition in Seventeenth-Century France," *Past and Present* 37 (1967): 33; Georges Pagès, *Les Origines du XVIII*[e] *siècle au temps de Louis XIV (1680–1715)* (Paris, 1961), p. 23.

251. Abbé E. Lavaquery, *Le Cardinal de Boisgelin (1732–1804)*, 2 vols. (Paris, 1920).

252. Sydel Silverman writes, "It may be that the mediator represents a general form of community-nation relationship characteristic of a form which regularly gives way as the process of integration of the total society advances," "Patronage and Community-Nation Relations in Central Italy," in *Friends, Followers, and Factions: A Reader in Political Clientelism*, ed. Steffen Schmidt et al. (Berkeley, 1977), pp. 303–4.

253. Anton Blok, "Variations in Patronage," *Sociologische Gids* 16 (1969): 365–86; Alex Weingrod, "Patrons, Patronage, and Political Parties," *Comparative Studies of Society and History* 10 (June 1969): 377–400; James Scott, "Corruption, Machine Politics, and Political Change," *American Political Science Review* 62 (1969): 1,142–58.

254. Sidney Tarrow, *Between Center and Periphery: Grassroots Politicians in Italy and France* (New Haven, 1977), p. 138.

255. Ibid., pp. 1–11, 128–33.

256. Michel Crozier, *The Bureaucratic Phenomenon* (Chicago, 1964), *The Stalled Society* (New York, 1973), *The World of the Office Worker*, trans. David Landau (Chicago, 1965). Also

see *Ou va l'administration française*? (Paris, 1974), *Décentraliser les responsabilités: Pourquoi? Comment?* (Paris, 1976).

257. Crozier, *The Bureaucratic Phenomenon*, pp. 187–95, *The Stalled Society*, pp. 78–95.

258. This term was first used by Stanley Hoffman to describe French society at the end of the Third Republic, see *In Search of France* (Cambridge, Mass., 1963).

259. Crozier, *The Bureaucratic Phenomenon*, pp. 195–98. For a criticism of Crozier's thesis, see François Bourricaud, "Michel Crozier et le syndrome de blocage," *Critique* 26 (1970): 960–78.

260. Tarrow, *Between Center and Periphery*, pp. 27–31.

261. See note 272 below.

262. Mart Bax, *Harpstrings and Confessions: Machine-Style Politics in the Irish Republic* (Amsterdam, 1976), p. 52. He writes that "the odd thing is that despite interference of the center into the citizens' lives, brokerage does not disappear from the Irish scene. Indeed, as the center's services increase, the Irish politician appears to become busier playing his brokerage role," p. 52.

263. Ibid., pp. 193–94.

264. Steffen Schmidt, "Bureaucrats as Modernizing Brokers," *Comparative Politics* 6 (1974): 426.

265. Ibid.

266. Alvin Gouldner, "On Weber's Analysis of Bureaucratic Rules," in *Reader in Bureaucracy*, ed. Robert Merton (Glencoe, Ill., 1952), pp. 48, 52; Carl Friedrich, "Some Observations," ibid., pp. 27–32. The pioneer in the attacks upon Weber's concept of bureaucracy was Robert Merton, "The Unanticipated Consequences of Purposive Social Action," *American Sociological Review* 1 (1936): 894–904, "Bureaucratic Structure and Personality," *Social Forces* 18 (1940): 560–68. The first to work out the logical implications of Merton's analysis were James March and Herbert Simon, *Organizations* (New York, 1958). A series of American commentators followed in Merton's footsteps: Reinhard Bendix, *Max Weber: An Intellectual Portrait* (New York, 1960); Alvin Gouldner, *Patterns of Industrial Bureaucracy* (Glencoe, Ill., 1954); Philip Selznick, *TVA and the Grass Roots* (Berkeley, 1949); Peter Blau and W. Richard Scott, *Formal Organizations* (San Francisco, 1961).

267. Ernest Gellner and John Waterbury, eds., *Patrons and Clients in Mediterranean Societies* (London, 1977), p. 4. This assumption is also made by Armstrong, "Old Regime Governors."

268. Ezra Suleiman, *Politics, Power and Bureaucracy in France: The Administrative Elite* (Princeton, 1974), pp. 3–10; Sidney Tarrow, *Between Center and Periphery*, p. 2; Walter Sharp, *The French Civil Service: Bureaucracy in Transition* (New York, 1931), pp. 84–90; Jolyon Howarth and Philip Cerny, *Elites in France: Origins, Reproduction and Power* (New York, 1982). Also see Grant McConnell, *Private Power and American Democracy* (New York, 1970); Martin and Susan Tolchin, *To the Victor: Political Patronage from the Club House to the White House* (New York, 1971); Peter Richards, *Patronage in British Government* (London, 1963).

269. Suleiman, *Politics, Power, and Bureaucracy*, pp. 35–36, 239–81, 316–51; and see note 39 above. Also see Terry Clark, *Prophets and Patrons: The French University and the Emergence of the Social Sciences* (Cambridge, Mass., 1973), pp. 66–92.

270. Seymour Mandelbaum, *Boss Tweed's New York* (New York, 1965); Edward Banfield and James Wilson, *City Politics* (Cambridge, Mass., 1965); Charles Merriam, *A More Intimate View of Urban Politics* (New York, 1929).

271. See Martin and Susan Tolchin, *To the Victor*.

272. See, for instance, Michael Isikoff, "Power Brokers: Veteran Alexandria Lobbyist has the Ear of Virginia Governor," *The Washington Post*, March 13, 1982, A1, 19; "The Newest Power Brokers," ibid., July 11, 1983, C1, C9; Steven Roberts, "Reagan's First Friend" (Senator Paul Laxalt), *The New York Times Magazine*, March 21, 1982, pp. 26–27, 32–39, 70–71; John Jenkins, "The Law Choreographers: Tips from the Top," *District Lawyer* 5 (1981): 23–30; Robert Caro, *Power Broker* (New York, 1974) (a biography of Robert Moses), and *The Years of Lyndon Johnson: The Path to Power* (New York, 1982).

273. Tolchin, *To the Victor*, p. 304. For a good presentation of the arguments for and against civil service versus patronage, see Paul David and Ross Pollock, *Executives for Government: Central Issues of Federal Personnel Administration* (Brookings Institute, 1957), pp. 115–48.

274. See, for instance, Ernest Lavisse, ed., *Histoire de France*, vol. 7, pt. 1 (Paris, 1911), pp. 186–89; Pierre Clément, *Histoire de Colbert et de son administration*, 2 vols., 3rd ed. (Paris, 1892); James King, *Science and Rationalism in the Government of Louis XIV, 1661–1685* (Baltimore, 1949).

275. Weber, *Economy and Society*, vol. 3, p. 1,033.

Conclusion

1. The bibliography on popular revolts in early seventeenth-century France and the Fronde at mid-century is immense. For a brief introduction, see Peter J. Coveney, *France in Crisis, 1620–1675* (London, 1977), including selected bibliography.

2. David Buisseret, *Henry IV* (London, 1984), pp. 88–94. Also see Mark Greengrass, *France in the Age of Henri IV: The Struggle for Stability* (London, 1984).

3. Buisseret, *Henri IV*, p. 94.

4. See Kenneth Dunkley, "Richelieu and the Estates of Brittany, 1624–1640" (Ph.D. diss., Emory University, 1972), pp. 181–258; Arthur de La Borderie and Barthélemy Pocquet, *Histoire de Bretagne*, 6 vols. (Rennes, 1896–1904), vol. 5 (1515–1715), pp. 391–479.

5. See, for example, Roland Mousnier, "The Fronde," *Preconditions of Revolution in Early Modern Europe*, eds. Robert Forster and Jack Greene (Baltimore, 1970), pp. 131–159; John H. M. Salmon, "Venality of Office and Popular Sedition in Seventeenth Century France," *Past and Present*, 37 (1967), 26–47.

6. William Beik has noted that "Louis XIV's great 'contagion' of obedience was the result, not of repression, but of a more sucessful defense of ruling class interests, through collaboration and improved direction": see *Absolutism and Society in Seventeenth-Century France: State Power and Provincial Aristocracy in Languedoc* (Cambridge, 1985), p. 31. Beik has also noted that "Louis XIV's success in Languedoc stemmed from his almost instinctive ability to reinforce class rule. . . under Louis XIV it was perfectly clear that hierarchy would be reinforced, the claim of the privileged to their share of society's resources would be guaranteed, and collaboration would be properly rewarded"; see ibid., pp. 333–34. I share the view that the success of absolutism was directly related to the monarchy's ability to secure elite collaboration, but I differ from Beik on how this was achieved and on its broad theoretical implications.

Bibliography

Primary Sources

Manuscripts

Archives du Ministère des Affaires Etrangères, Paris, Fonds France
Affaires intérieures, Provence, 794, 795, bis, 796, 797, 800, 809, 817, 823, 824, 829, 858, 890, 895, 903, 906, 911, 925.
Provence, XVIIe siècle (1590–1703), 1700–1730.

Archives départementales des Bouches-du-Rhône, Marseille
Délibérations des Etats et des Assemblées générales des communautés (1616–1687), C 15–51.
Amirauté de Marseille, IX B2, IX B3.
Correspondance royale, C 986, 987, 988.
Manuscript biography of Oppède, untitled, by Timon-David, 81 pp., XXVII F 16.

Archives départmentales des Bouches-du-Rhône, Aix-en-Provence
Fonds des notaires, Berlie, 217, 227E, 228, 232, 234, 235, 301E; Lombard, 309E, 1067, 1070, 1071, 1072, 1074, 1077.
Lettres royaux (1625–1680), B 3347–B 3368.
Jean-Louis Hyacinthe Hesmivy de Moissac, "Histoire du Parlement de Provence, 1501–1715," 2 vols.

Archives communales, Aix-en-Provence, Fonds anciens
Actes constitutifs et politiques, AA 1, AA 5, AA 6, AA 14, AA21.
Délibérations des assembleés de la maison commune, BB 99, 100, 101, 102, 103, 103, 104, 105.

British Museum, London, Harleian manuscripts
4442, "Lettres de divers officiers au chancelier Séguier, 1659–1661."
4468, "Relation de toutes les choses se sont passées dans l'armée commandée par Monsieur le comte d'Harcourt et Monsieur le maréchal de Vitry, 1636."
4489, "Copies des lettres écrites par Mgr. le chancelier et lettres originales audit seigneur, 1656."
4493, "Lettres des officiers des provinces à Mgr., 1658–1662."
4575, "Semestre de Provence par M. de Sève, conseiller d'Etat."

Bibliothèque Inguimbertine, Carpentras
1841, "Actes et mémoires pour l'histoire de Provence depuis l'an 1590 jusqu'à 1637."
L. 482, "Correspondance du premier président d'Oppède chargé par interim du gouvernement de la Provence en l'absence de Louis de Vendôme (1656–1658)."
L. 492, "Copie des lettres de Messrs. de Lionne et de Colbert et des lettres qui leur sont addressées par le duc de Mercoeur et le président d'Oppède du 8 janvier 1664 au 27 août 1665."

Bibliothèque municipale, Marseille

1792, "Recueil de divers pièces (mazarinades) sur les troubles de Provence."

Bibliothèque Méjanes, Aix-en-Provence

The first number is the item number in the *Catalogue général des manuscrits des bibliothèques publiques de France*, vol. 15 (Paris, 1894), by the abbé Albanès, for which there are two supplements, and the second number in parentheses is the call number at the Méjanes. Short titles have been used.

714 (792) "Mémoires du pays de Provence par Le Bret, intendant."

715 (259) "Mémoires concernants la Provence redigés par M. Le Bret, intendant."

777 (R.a. 9), "Recueil de mémoires et pièces sur la Provence et la ville d'Aix," fol. 116, "Les grandes mémoirs de Jacques de Gaufridi, 1622–1666."

790 (625), "Histoire de Provence sous le règne de Louis XIII, par Jacques Gaufridy."

793 (R.A. 26), "Mémoires de Jacques de Gaufridy."

794 (R.A. 39), also 795 (736) and 796 (R.A. 39), "Histoire de Provence sous le fameux gouvernement du comte d'Alais par le sieur Pierre-Joseph de Haitze."

798 (R.A. 73), "Mémoires de Charles de Grimaldi, marquis de Régusse."

800 (389), "Mémoires de Jean Robert de Brianson aixois (1633–1696)."

812 (836), "Histoire des troubles de Marseille sous la Fronde," appearing in "Recueil A, Provence," secs. 2 and 3.

927 (R.A. 3), "Mémoires de M. Antoine de Valbelle, dressées en 1682 par maître Jean Russel, avocat en la cour."

929 (R.A. 25), "Mémoires d'Antoine de Félix, mort en 1675."

938 (R.A. 54), also 939 (904), 940 (905), 941 (1113), and 942 (944), "Histoire du Parlement de Provence (1501–1671) par Dominique Guidy."

947 (902), also 948–949 (R.A. 43), "Histoire du Parlement de Provence (1501–1715) par Jean-Louis Hyacinthe Hesmivy de Moissac," 2 vols.

968–982 (947–961), "Délibérations du Parlement de Provence," 15 vols.

1142 (R.A. 47), "Abrégé des délibérations du corps de la noblesse de Provence."

1143 (630), "Etat du florinage contenant le revenu noble de tous les fiefs et arrière-fiefs de Provence avec les noms des possesseurs fait par Maynier d'Oppède en 1668."

1182 (377), "Mémoire abrégé sur la vie de Magdeleine de Gaillard-Longjumeau."

1184 (632), also 1185 (802) and 1186 (R.A. 6), "Vie de seigneurs Jean et Gaspard de Pontevès comtes de Carcès."

1194 (R.A. 4), "La Vie de Monsieur le bailli de Valbelle, chef d'escadre des armées navales de France par M. Desprès, capitaine de brûlot."

1421 (1286), "Recueil d'actes notariés et pièce diverses relatives à l'histoire de Provence et du comté de Nice."

Archives du Palais, Monaco

Fonds 43, "Livres de raison de Charles de Grimaldi-Régusse, 1619–1654."

A good printed inventory to the extensive collection of Grimaldi-Régusse family papers, conserved in the Palace Archives, has been done by G. Lavergne, *Archives de la famille de Grimaldi-Régusse*, Monaco and Paris, 1911.

Bibliothèque Nationale, Paris

Fonds Clairambault 387–430, Correspondance du comte de Brienne, secrétaire d'état, 1643–1650.

Cinq Cents de Colbert 204, "Registre des dépêches et correspondance de Colbert concernant le commerce extérieur et intérieur (1669)"; 288, "Précis ou abrégés des Etats de Provence, 1620–1664."

Fonds Dupuy 64, 154, 155, 194, 498, 659, 672, 754, miscellaneous.

Manuscrits français 6880–6900, Correspondance de Michel le Tellier (1640–1678); 10655–10656, "Correspondance diplomatique relative aux affaires de Pologne, Turkie et Transylvanie (1671–1679)," letters of Toussaint de Janson-Forbin; 12769, "Recueil des lettres," letters of Toussaint de Janson-Forbin; 16518, "Parlement et Etats de Provence, remontrances"; 17367–17412,

Correspondance du chancelier Pierre Séguier, 1633–1669; 18593, "Sur les malversations du lieutenant de l'amirauté"; 18975–18977, "Recueil de pièces et manuscrits concernant la Provence"; 24166, "Mémoire touchant le Parlement de Provence"; 24169, "Procès-verbal contenant l'état véritable de la côte maritime de Provence par Henri Séguiran de Bouc"; 20655–20656, "Papiers de Henri-Auguste de Loménie, comte de Brienne, 1640–1644."
Manuscrits français nouvelles acquisitions 21306–21327, Correspondance de Nicolas et Pierre Arnoul (1665–1680).
Mélanges de Colbert 7, fols. 49–53, "Mémoire sur le Parlement de Provence, 1663"; 26, vols. 1 and 2, Correspondance de Henri-Louis de Loménie, comte de Brienne (1661); 101–176 bis, Correspondance de Colbert, 1649, 1656–1660, 1661–1674.

Newberry Library, Chicago
K 1392. 716, *Abrégés des délibérations de l'Assemblée générale des communautés de Provence*, 2 vols. Aix, 1612–1689, 1710–1785.
A 54. 35, *Gazette de France*, 82 vols., Paris, 1631–1678, 1683–1709, 1721–1756, 1761–1785.

Published

Arnuald, Simon de, marquis de Pomponne. *Mémoires*, ed. J. Mavidal. 2 vols. Paris, 1860.
Arnoul, Nicolas. Excerpts from correspondence with Colbert published by Gaston Rambert, *Nicolas Arnoul: Intendant des galères à Marseille, 1666–1674*. Marseille, 1931, pp. 211–341, letters from 1666–1673.
Baratier, Edouard, ed. *Documents de l'histoire de la Provence*. Toulouse, 1971.
Barbiche, Bernard, and Buisseret, David. *Les Oéconomies royales de Sully*. Paris, 1970.
Bassompierre, François, maréchal de. *Journal de ma vie: Mémoires du maréchal de Bassompierre*. 4 vols. Paris, 1870–1877.
Béthune, Maximilien de, duc de Sully. *Mémoires*, eds. J. F. Michaud and J. J. F. Poujoulat. Paris, 1881.
Bigot de Monville, Alexandre de. *Mémoires du Président Alexandre Bigot de Monville: Le Parlement de Rouen, 1640–1643*. Paris, 1976.
Berger de Xivrey, M., and Gaudet, J., eds. *Recueil des lettres missives de Henri IV*. 9 vols. Paris, 1843–76.
Boislisle, Arthur de, ed. *Correspondance des contrôleurs-généraux avec les intendants des provinces, 1683–1715*. 3 vols. Paris, 1874–79.
Bouchard, Jean-Jacques. *Les Confessions de Jean-Jacques Bouchard, parisien, suivies de son voyage de Paris à Rome en 1630, publiées pour la première fois sur les manuscrits de l'auteur*. Paris, 1881.
Bouche, Honoré. *La Chorographie ou description de Provence et l'histoire chronologique du même pays depuis l'établissement de son comté jusques aujourd'hui*. 2 vols. Aix, 1664.
Brosses, Charles de. *Catalogue des consuls et assesseurs de la ville d'Aix*. Aix, 1699.
——. *Lettres familières sur l'Italie*, Paris, 1869.
Brûlart, Nicolas de. *Choix de lettres inédites*, ed. Elizabeth de La Cuisine. 2 vols. Dijon, 1859.
Castellane, Honoré Louis de, sieur de Besaudun. *Mémoires pour servir à l'histoire de la Ligue en Provence. Besaudun, Bausset, Cassaignes*. Aix, 1866.
Chouppes, Aymar de, marquis. *Mémoires du marquis de Chouppes (1612–1673), lieutenant général des armées du roi*, ed. Célestin Moreau. Paris, 1861.
Clapiers-Collongues, Balthasar de. *Chronologie des officiers des cours souveraines, publiée, annotée et augmentée par le marquis de Boisgelin*. Aix, 1909–12.
Colbert, Jean-Baptiste. *Lettres, instructions et mémoires, 1648–1683*, ed. Pierre Clément. 10 vols. Paris, 1861–73.
Cosnac, Daniel de. *Mémoires*, ed. Jules de Cosnac, comte. 2 vols. Paris, 1852. Reprint. New York, 1968.
Cundier, Jacques. *Portraits des premiers présidents du Parlement de Provence*. Aix, 1724.
Depping, Georges B., ed. *Correspondance administrative sous le règne de Louis XIV*. 4 vols. Paris, 1850–55.

Douglas, comte de, and Roman, J., eds. *Actes et correspondance du connétable de Lesdiguières*. 3 vols. Grenoble, 1878.

Du Plessis-Besançon, Bernard. *Mémoires*, ed. Horric de Beaucaire, comte. Paris, 1892.

Girard, Guillaume. *Histoire de la vie du duc d'Epernon*. Paris, 1663.

Gourville, Jean Hérault de. *Mémoires de Gourville (1646–1702)*, ed. Léon Lecestre. 2 vols. Paris, 1894.

Grillon, Pierre. *Les Papiers de Richelieu. Section politique intérieure. Correspondance et papiers d'état, 1624–1629*. 4 vols. Paris, 1975–80. In progress.

Grimaldi, Charles de, marquis de Régusse, and Gaufridy, Jacques. *Mémoires pour servir à l'histoire de la Fronde en Provence*. Aix, 1870.

Haitze, Pierre-Joseph de. *Portraits ou éloges historiques des premiers présidents du Parlement de Provence*. Avignon, 1727.

———. *Histoire de la ville d'Aix, capitale de la Provence*. 6 vols. Aix, 1880–92.

Lenet, Pierre de. *Mémoires*, ed. J. F. Michaud and J. J. F. Poujoulat. Paris, 1838.

Lestoile, Pierre de. *Mémoires-journaux*, ed. J. F. Michaud and J. J. F. Poujoulat. 10 vols. Paris, 1875–83.

Loménie, Louis-Henri, comte de Brienne. *Memoires de Louis-Henri de Loménie, Comte de Brienne, secrétaire d'état sous Louis XIV*, ed. F. Barrière. 2 vols. Paris, 1828.

Lublinskaya, Alexksandra Dmitrievna, ed., *Vnutrenniaia politika frantsuzskogo absoliutizma, 1633–1649* (The Internal Politics of French Absolutism). Leningrad, 1966.

Mazarin, Jules. *Lettres du Cardinal Mazarin pendant son ministère*, ed. Pierre-Adolphe Chéruel and Georges d'Avenel. 9 vols. Paris, 1872–1906.

Méry, L., and Guidon, F. *Histoire analytique et chronologique des actes et délibérations du corps et conseil de la municipalité de Marseille depuis le Xe siècle jusqu'à nos jours*. 2 vols. Marseille, 1841–43.

Millotet, Marc-Antoine *Mémoire des choses qui se sont passées en Bourgogne depuis 1650 jusqu'à 1668*. Dijon, 1866.

Monluc, Blaise de. *Commentaires et Lettres*, ed. Alphonse, baron de Ruble. 5 vols. Paris, 1864–72.

———. *Commentaires*, ed. Paul Courteault. Paris, 1964.

Monmerqué, L., and Paulin, J., eds. *Les Historiettes de Tallemant de Réaux: Mémoires pour servir à l'histoire du XVIIe siècle*. 9 vols. Paris, 1834.

Moreau, Célestin, ed. *Choix de Mazarinades*. 2 vols. Paris, 1853.

Mousnier, Roland, ed. *Lettres et mémoires adressés au Chancelier Séguier, 1633–1649*. 2 vols. Paris, 1964.

Nostradamus, César de. *L'Histoire et chronique de Provence*. Lyon, 1624.

Oddo, Henri. *Le Chevalier Paul: Lieutenant général des armées du roi, 1598–1668*. Paris, 1896. Letters of the chevalier Paul, pp. 227–71.

Parades de L'Estang, Jacques de. "Mémoires, 1642–1674," *Le Musée: Revue Arlésienne, historique et littéraire*. 2nd ser. 13–35 (1875–76): 97–281.

Peiresc, Nicolas Claude Fabri de. *Lettres aux frères Dupuy*, ed. Philippe Tamizey de Larroque. 7 vols. Paris, 1888–98.

Pingaud, Léonce, ed. *Correspondance des Saulx-Tavannes (1552–1573)*. Paris, 1877.

Pitton, Jean-Scholastique. *Histoire de la ville d'Aix, capitale de la Provence, contenante toute de qui s'est passée de memorable dans son état politique jusqu'à l'année 1665*. Aix, 1666.

Platter, Félix and Thomas. *Félix et Thomas Platter à Montpellier, 1552–1559, 1595–1596. Notes de voyage de deux étudiants bâlois*. Montpellier, 1882.

Richelieu, Armand Jean de Plessis, cardinal, duc de. *Lettres, instructions diplomatiques et papiers d'état du Cardinal de Richelieu*, ed. Georges d'Avenel. 8 vols. Paris, 1853–77.

———. *Mémoires du Cardinal de Richelieu*, ed. Horric de Beaucaire, comte. 10 vols. Paris, 1907–31.

Rochechouart, Louis-Victor, comte de Vivonne. *Correspondance du maréchal de Vivonne relative à l'expédition de Candie, 1669*, ed. Jean Cordey. Paris, 1910.

———. *Correspondance du comte de Vivonne, général des galères, pour l'année 1671*, ed. Jean Cordey. Paris, 1910.

———. *Correspondance du maréchal de Vivonne relative à l'expédition de Messine, 1674–1676, 1676–1678*, ed. Jean Cordey. 2 vols. Paris, 1914.

Ruffi, Antoine de. *Histoire de la ville de Marseille*. Marseille, 1696.

Saint Simon, Louis de Rouvray, duc de. *Mémoires*, ed. Arthur de Bouislisle. 43 vols. Paris, 1879–1930.

Sapey, Charles-Alexandre. *Etudes biographiques pour servir à l'histoire de l'ancienne magistrature françcaise: Guillaume Du Vair, Antoine le Maistre*. Paris, 1858, pp. 337–488, letters of Du Vair to Henri IV, 1597 to 1608.

Saulx, Gaspard de, seigneur de Tavannes. *Mémoires*. 3 vols. Paris, 1787.

———. *La Vie de Gaspard de Saulx, seigneur de Tavannes (1509–1573)*, ed. Claude Petitot. 3 vols. Paris, 1822.

Saulx, Jacques de, comte de Tavannes. *Mémoires*, ed. Célestin Moreau. Paris, 1858.

Seignelay, Jean-Baptiste Colbert, marquis de. *L'Italie en 1671: Relation d'un voyage du marquis de Seignelay*, ed. Pierre Clément. Paris, 1867.

Séguiran, Henri, sieur de Bouc. *L'Etat de l'armée commandée par Mgr. le duc de Guise, amiral et lieutenant général de la mer*. Bordeaux, 1622.

Sévigné, Marie de Rabutin-Chantal, marquise de. *Lettres*, ed. Louis Monmerqué. 14 vols. Paris, 1862–66.

Sourdis, Henri d'Escoubleau de, archbishop of Bordeaux. *Correspondance, 1636–1642*, ed. Eugène Sue. 3 vols. Paris, 1839.

Tavernier, Félix. *Marseille et la Provence sous la royauté, 1481–1789: Textes pour l'enseignement de l'histoire*. Marseille, n.d.

Tollemer, abbé de. *Un Sire de Gouberville: Gentilhomme compagnard au Cotentin de 1553 à 1562*. Paris, 1873, reissued 1972.

Videl, Louis. *L'Histoire de la vie du connétable de Lesdiguières*. Paris, 1638.

Villeroy, Nicolas de Neufville de. *Mémoires d'Estat par Monsieur de Villeroy*, ed. J. F. Michaud and J. J. F. Poujoulat. Paris, 1838.

Secondary Sources

Aboucaya, Claude. *Les Intendants de la marine sous l'ancien régime*. Paris, 1958.

Agulhon, Maurice. *La Vie sociale en Provence intérieure au lendemain de la Révolution*. Paris, 1970.

Albanès, Joseph H. *Gallia Christiana Novissima: Histoire des archevêchés, evêchés et abbayes de France*. 7 vols. Valence, 1899–1920.

André, Louis. *Michel Le Tellier et Louvois*. Paris, 1942.

Arbassier, Charles. *L'Intendant Bouchu et son action financière (1667–1671)*. Paris and Dijon, 1919.

Arriazi, Armand. "Mousnier and Barber: The Theoretical Underpinnings of the 'Society of Orders' in Early Modern Europe." *Past and Present* 88 (1980): 39–57.

Avenel, George d'. *Richelieu et la monarchie absolue*. 4 vols. Paris, 1895.

———. *La Noblesse française sous Richelieu*. Paris, 1901.

Aylmer, G. E. *The King's Servants: The Civil Service of Charles I, 1625–1642*. London, 1961.

———. *The State's Servants: The Civil Service of the English Republic, 1649–1660*. London, 1973.

Baehrel, René. *Une Croissance: La Basse-Provence rurale (fin XVIe siècle à 1789)*. Paris, 1961.

Bamford, Paul. *Fighting Ships and Prisons: The Mediterranean Galleys of France in the Age of Louis XIV*. Minneapolis, 1973.

———. "The Knights of Malta and the King of France, 1665–1700." *French Historical Studies* 3 (1964): 429–53.

Baratier, Edouard, ed. *Histoire de la Provence*. Toulouse, 1969.

———, ed. *Histoire de Marseille*. Toulouse, 1973.

———, Duby, Georges, Hildesheimer, Edouard. *Atlas historique, Provence, Comtat Venaissin, Principauté de Monaco, Principauté d'Orange, Comté de Nice*. Paris, 1969.

Barbiche, Bernard. *Sully*. Paris, 1978.

Barnavi, Elie. *Le Parti de Dieu. Etude sociale et politique des chefs de la Ligue parisienne, 1585–1594*. Louvain, 1980.

———. "La Ligue Parisienne (1585–1594); Ancêtre des partis totalitaires modernes?" *French Historical Studies* 11 (1974): 29–57.

Bax, Mart. *Harpstrings and Confessions: Machine-Style Politics in the Irish Republic*. Amsterdam, 1976.

———. "Patronage Irish Style: Irish Politicians and Brokers." *Sociologische Gids* 17 (1971): 179–91.

Baxter, Douglas. *Servants of the Sword: French Intendants of the Army, 1630–1670*. Urbana, Ill., 1976.

Beik, William. "Magistrates and Popular Uprisings in France before the Fronde: The Case of Toulouse." *Journal of Modern History* 46 (1974): 585–608.

———. "Two Intendants Face a Popular Revolt: Social Unrest and the Structure of Absolutism in 1645." *Canadian Journal of History* 9 (1974): 243–62.

———. *Absolutism and Society in Seventeenth-Century France: State Power and Provincial Aristocracy in Languedoc*. Cambridge, 1985.

Bercé, Yves-Marie. *Histoire des Croquants. Etudes des soulèvements populaires au XVIIe siècle dans le sud-ouest de la France*. 2 vols. Paris and Geneva, 1974.

Bertrand, Louis. *La Vie de Messire Henry de Béthune, archevêque de Bordeaux, 1604–1680*. 2 vols. Paris and Bordeaux, 1902.

Bézard, Yvonne. *Fonctionnaires maritimes et coloniaux sous Louis XIV: Les Bégon*. Paris, 1932.

Bitton, Davis. *The French Nobility in Crisis, 1560–1640*. Stanford, 1969.

Blanc, François-Paul. "L'Anoblissement par lettres de Provence à l'époque des reformations de Louis XIV, 1630–1730"; and "Origines des familles provençales maintenues dans le second ordre sous le règne de Louis XIV: Dictionnaire généalogique." Ph.D. diss., University of Aix-Marseille, 1971.

Blangueron, Claude. *Gilles de Gouberville: Gentilhomme du Cotentin, 1522–1578*. Coutances, 1969.

Blet, Pierre. *Le Clergé de France et la monarchie*. 2 vols. Rome, 1959.

———. *Les Assemblées du clergé et Louis XIV de 1670 à 1693*. Rome, 1972.

Bloch, Jean-Richard. *L'Anoblissement en France au temps de François I*. Paris, 1934.

Blok, Anton. *The Mafia of a Sicilian Village, 1860–1960: A Study of Violent Peasant Entrepreneurs*. Oxford, 1974.

———. "Patrons as Brokers." *Sociologische Gids* 16 (1964): 379–86.

Bluche, J. François. *Les Magistrats du Parlement de Paris au XVIIIe siècle (1715–1771)*. Paris, 1960.

———. "L'Origine des sécrétaires d'état de Louis XIV, 1661–1715." *XVIIe Siècle* 42–43 (1959): 8–22.

Bluche, J. François, and Durye, Pierre. *L'Anoblissement par charges avant 1789*. 2 vols. La Roche-sur-Yon, 1962.

Boissevain, Jeremy. *Friends of Friends: Networks, Manipulators, and Coalitions*. Oxford, 1974.

———. "Patrons as Brokers." *Sociologische Gids* 16 (1969): 379–86.

Bonney, Richard. *Political Change in France under Richelieu and Mazarin, 1624–1661*. Oxford, 1978.

———. *The King's Debts: Finance and Politics in France, 1589–1661*. Oxford, 1981.

———. "The French Civil War, 1649–1653." *European Studies Review* 8 (1978): 71–100.

———. "Cardinal Mazarin and His Critics: The Remonstrance of 1652." *Journal of European Studies* 10 (1980): 15–31.

———. "Cardinal Mazarin and the Great Nobility during the Fronde." *English Historical Review* 46 (1981): 818–33.

Borricand, René. *Nobiliaire de Provence: Armorial général de la Provence, du Comtat Venaissin, de la principauté d'Orange*. 3 vols. Aix, 1974–76.

Boscheron Des Portes, Charles. *Histoire du Parlement de Bordeaux depuis sa création jusqu'à sa suppression (1451–1790)*. 2 vols. Bordeaux, 1878.

Bosher, John F. "The French Government's Motives in the Affaire du Canada, 1761–1763." *English Historical Review* 47 (1981): 59–78.

Boullée, A. *Histoire de la vie et des ouvrages du chancelier d'Aguesseau*. 2 vols. Paris, 1835.

Bourgeron, Jean-Louis. *Les Colbert avant Colbet*. Paris, 1973.

Boutruche, Robert. *Bordeaux de 1453 à 1715*. Bordeaux, 1966.

Briggs, Robin. *Early Modern France, 1560–1715*. Oxford, 1977.

Buisseret, David. *Sully and the Growth of Centralized Government in France, 1598–1610*. London, 1968.

———. *Henry IV*. London, 1984.

Burckhardt, Carl. *Richelieu and His Age*. Vol. 2, *Assertion of Power and Cold War*, trans. Bernard Hoy. New York, 1970.

Busquet, Raoul. *Etudes sur l'ancienne Provence*. Paris, 1930.

———. *Histoire de Marseille*. Paris, 1945.

Cahen-Salvador, Georges. *Un Grand Humaniste: Peiresc, 1580–1637*. Paris, 1951.

Caldicott, C. E. J. "Le Gouvernment de Gaston d'Orléans en Languedoc (1644–1660) et la carrière de Molière." *XVIIe siècle* 116 (1979): 17–42.

Charbonnier, Pierre. *Guillaume de Murol: Un Petit seigneur auvergnat au début du XVe siècle*. Clermont-Ferrand, 1975.

Chaussinand-Nogaret, Guy. *La Noblesse au XVIIIe siècle, de la féodalité aux lumières*. Paris, 1976.

Chéruel, Pierre-Adolphe. *Histoire de France pendant la minorité de Louis XIV*. 4 vols. Paris, 1879–80.

———. *Histoire de France sous le ministère de Mazarin*. 3 vols. Paris, 1882.

Church, Clive. *Revolution and Red Tape: The French Ministerial Bureaucracy, 1770–1850*. Oxford, 1981.

Clément, Pierre. *Histoire de la vie et de l'administration de Colbert*. 2 vols. Paris, 1873.

Coste, Jean-Paul. *Aix-en-Provence et le pays d'Aix*. Aix, 1964.

———. *La Ville d'Aix en 1695. Structure urbaine et société*. 3 vols. Aix, 1970.

Courteault, Paul. *Histoire de Gascogne et de Béarn*. Paris, 1938.

Cousot, Paul. "Paul-Albert de Forbin, lieutenant général des galères, 1580–1661." *Provence historique* 19 (1969): 101–17.

Coveney, Peter J. *France in Crisis, 1620–1675*. London, 1977.

Crémieux, Adolphe. *Marseille et la royauté pendant la minorité de Louis XIV*. 2 vols. Paris and Marseille, 1917.

Cubells, Monique. *La Provence des Lumières: Les Parlementaires d'Aix au XVIIIe siècle*. Paris, 1984.

Daverdi, Pierre. *Oraison funèbre de Henri de Forbin d'Oppède*, notes by A. J. Rance-Bourrey. Marseille, 1889.

David, Jean-Marc. *L'Amirauté de Provence et des mers du Levant*. Marseille, 1942.

Davis, Natalie. *Society and Culture in Early Modern France: Eight Essays*. Stanford, 1975.

Deloche, Maximin. *La Maison du Cardinal de Richelieu*. Paris, 1912.

———. *Un Frère de Richelieu inconnu: Chartreux, primat des Gaules, cardinal, ambassadeur*. Paris, 1935.

Dent, Julian. *Crisis in Finance: Crown, Financiers and Society in Seventeenth-Century France*. London, 1973.

———. "The Role of Clientèles in the Financial Elite of France under Cardinal Mazarin." In *French Government and Society, 1500–1800: Essays in Memory of Alfred Cobban*, ed. John F. Bosher. London, 1973, pp. 41–69.

Dessert, Daniel. "Finances et société au XVIIe siècle: À propos de la Chambre de Justice de 1661." *Annales: ESC* 29 (1974): 847–81.

———. "Pouvoir et finance au XVIIe siècle: La Fortune du Cardinal Mazarin." *Revue d'histoire moderne et contemporaine* 32 (1976): 161–81.

———. "Le 'Laquais-Financier' au Grand Siècle: Mythe ou réalité." *XVIIe siècle* 122 (1979): 21–36.

———. "L'Affaire Fouquet." *L'histoire* 32 (1981): 39–47.

Dessert, Daniel, and Journet, Jean-Louis. "Le Lobby Colbert: Un royaume ou une affaire de famille." *Annales: ESC* 30 (1975): 1,303–36.

Dethan, Georges. *Gaston d'Orléans, conspirateur et prince charmant*. Paris, 1959.

———. *Mazarin et ses amis*. Paris, 1968.

Devienne, Dom. *Histoire de la ville de Bordeaux*. Bordeaux, 1771.

Dewald, Jonathan. *The Formation of a Provincial Nobility: The Magistrates of the Parlement of Rouen*. Princeton, 1980.

Deyon, Pierre. *Amiens, capitale provinciale: Etude sur la société urbaine au XVIIe siec le*. Paris, 1967.

———. "A propos des rapports entre la noblesse française et la monarchie absolue pendant la première moitié du XVIIe siècle." *Revue historique* 221 (1964): 341–56.

Dickerman, Edmund. *Bellièvre and Villeroy: Power in France under Henry III and Henry IV*. Providence, R. I., 1971.

———. *Dictionnaire de biographie française*, ed. J. Balteau, M. Prevost, R. d'Amat. 13 vols to date. Paris, 1933.

Diefendorf, Barbara. *Paris City Councillors in the Sixteenth Century. The Politics of Patrimony*. Princeton, 1983.

Dornic, François. *Louis Berryer: Agent de Mazarin et Colbert*. Caen, 1968.

Doucet, Roger. *Les Institutions de la France au XVIe siècle*. 2 vols. Paris, 1948.

Drouot, Henri, *Mayenne et la Bourgogne, 1587–1596*. 2 vols. Paris, 1937.

Drouot, Henri, and Calmette, Jean. *Histoire de Bourgogne*. Paris, 1928.

Dubé, Jean-Claude. *Claude-Thomas Dupuy: Intendant de la Nouvelle France (1678–1738)*. Montréal and Paris, 1969.

Dubédat, Jean-Baptiste. *Histoire du Parlement de Toulouse*. 2 vols. Paris, 1885.

Dubuc, Pierre. *L'Intendance de Soissons sous Louis XIV*. Paris, 1902.

Duchêne, Roger. "Argent et famille au XVIIe siècle: Madame de Sévigné et les Grignans." *Provence historique* 15 (1965): 205–228; 16 (1966): 3–41, 587–620.

Durand, Yves. *La Maison de Durfort à l'époque moderne*. Fontenay-le-Comte, 1975.

———, ed. *Hommage à Roland Mousnier: Clientèles et fidélités en Europe à l'époque moderne*. Paris, 1981.

Du Roure, Scipion. *Les Anciennes familles de Provence: Généalogie de la maison de Benault de Lubières*. Paris. 1906.

———. *Les Anciennes familles de Provence: Généalogie de la maison de Forbin*. Paris, 1906.

Eisenstadt, Samuel N., and Roniger, Louis. "Patron-Client Relations as a Mode of Structuring Social Exchange." *Comparative Studies in Society and History* 22 (1980): 42–77.

Elias, Norbert. *The Civilizing Process*, trans. Edmund Jephcott, two volumes. New York, 1978 and 1982.

———. *Court Society*, trans. Edmund Jephcott. New York, 1983.

Esmonin, Edmond. *La taille en Normandie au temps de Colbert (1661–1683)*. Paris, 1913.

———. *Etudes sur la France des XVIIe et XVIIIe siècles*. Paris, 1964.

Everitt, Alan. *Change in the Provinces: The Seventeenth Century*. Leicester, 1969.

———. *The Local Community and the Great Rebellion*. London, 1969.

Fairchilds, Cissie. *Domestic Enemies: Servants and Their Masters in Old Regime France*. Baltimore, 1984.

Febre, Lucien. *Histoire de la Franche-Comté*. Paris, 1922. Reprint. Marseille, 1976.

Fessenden, Nicolas. "Epernon and Guyenne: Provincial Politics under Louis XIII." Ph.D. diss., Columbia University, 1972.

Floquet, Amable. *Histoire du Parlement de Normandie*. 7 vols. Paris, 1840–42.

Foisil, Madeleine. *La Revolte des Nu-Pieds et les révoltes normandes de 1639*. Paris, 1970.

———. *Le Sire de Gouberville. Un gentilhomme normand au XVIe siècle*. Paris, 1981.

Forster, Robert. *The Nobility of Toulouse in the Eighteenth Century*. Baltimore, 1960.

———. *The House of Saulx-Tavannes: Versailles and Burgundy, 1700–1830*. Baltimore, 1971.

———. *Merchants, Landlords, Magistrates. The Depont Family in Eighteenth-Century France*. Baltimore, 1980.

Forster, Robert, and Ranum, Orest, eds. *Family and Society: Selections from the Annales.* Baltimore, 1976.

Fourquin, Guy. *Lordship and Feudalism in the Middle Ages*, trans. Iris and A. L. Lytton Sells. London, 1976.

Fracard, Marie-Louise *Philippe de Montaut-Benac, duc de Navailles, maréchal de France (1619–1684)*. Niort, 1970.

Frégault, Guy. *François Bigot: administrateur français.* 2 vols. Ottowa, 1948.

Freudmann, Félix. *L'Etonnant Gourville (1625–1703)*. Paris, 1960.

Fréville, Henri. *L'Intendance en Bretagne (1689–1790)*. 3 vols. Rennes, 1953.

———. "Notes sur les subdélégués généraux et subdélégués de l'intendance de Bretagne aux XVIIIe siècle." *Revue d'histoire modern* 12 (1937): 408–48.

Frondeville, Henri. *Les Présidents du Parlement de Normandie, 1499–1700.* Paris and Rouen, 1953.

———. *Les Conseillers du Parlement de Normandie au XVIe siècle (1499–1594)*, Paris and Rouen, 1960.

———. *Les Conseillers du Parlement de Normandie sous Henri IV et sous Louis XII (1594–1640)*. Paris and Rouen, 1964.

Gachon, Paul. *Les Etats de Languedoc et l'édit de Béziers (1632)*. Paris, 1887.

———. *Histoire de Languedoc.* Paris, 1921.

Gellner, Ernest, and Waterbury, John, eds. *Patrons and Clients in Mediterranean Societies.* London, 1977.

Godard, Charles. *Les Pouvoirs des intendants sous Louis XIV.* Paris, 1901.

Goubert, Pierre. *L'Ancien Régime.* Vol. 1, *La Societé.* Paris, 1969. Vol. 2, *Les Pouvoirs.* Paris, 1973.

———. *Beauvais et le Beauvaisis de 1600 à 1730.* Paris, 1960.

———. *Clio parmi les hommes.* Paris, 1976.

Gresset, Maurice. *Gens de justice à Besançon de la conquête à la Révolution françcaise (1674–1789)* 2 vols. Paris, 1978.

———. *Le Rattachement de la Franche-Comté à la France, 1668–1678.* Besançcon, 1978.

Gruder, Vivian. *The Royal Provincial Intendants: A Governing Elite in Eighteenth-Century France.* Ithaca, N.Y., 1968.

Gutton, Jean-Pierre. *Domestiques et serviteurs dans la France de L'Ancien Régime.* Paris, 1981.

Hanley, Sarah. *The Lit de Justice of the Kings of France.* Princeton, 1983.

Harding, Robert. *Anatomy of a Power Elite*: The Provincial Governors of Early Modern France. New Haven, 1978.

———. "Corruption and the Moral Boundaries of Patronage." In *Patronage in the Renaissance*, ed. Guy Lytle and Stephen Orgel, pp. 47–64. Princeton, 1981.

Hatton, Ragnhild, ed. *Louis XIV and Absolutism.* Columbus, Ohio, 1976.

———, ed. *Louis XIV and Europe.* Columbus, Ohio, 1976.

Hayden, J. Michael. *France and the Estates General of 1614.* Cambridge, 1974.

———. "Deputies and Qualities: The Estates General of 1614." *French Historical Studies* 3 (1964): 507–24.

———. "The Social Origins of the French Episcopacy at the Beginning of the Seventeenth Century." *French Historical Studies* 10 (1977): 27–40.

Heidenheimer, Arnold, ed. *Political Corruption: Readings in Comparative Analysis.* New York, 1970.

Henry, abbé. *François Bosquet: Etude sur une administration civile et ecclésiastique au XVIIe siècle.* Paris, 1889.

Herr, Richard. "Honor versus Absolutism: Richelieu's fight against duelling." *Journal of Modern History* 27 (1955): 281–88.

Hexter, Jack H. *The Reign of King Pym.* Cambridge, Mass., 1940.

———. "Power Struggle, Parliament, and Liberty in Early Stuart England." *Journal of Modern History* 50 (1978): 1–50.

Hildesheimer, Bernard. *Les Assemblées génerales des communautés de Provence.* Paris, 1935.

Hill, Christopher. "Parliament and People in Seventeenth-Century England." *Past and Present* 92 (1981): 100–24.

Hirst, Derek. *The Representatives of the People? Voters and Voting in England under the Early Stuarts*. Cambridge, 1975.

———. "Unanimity in the Commons: Aristocratic Intrigue and the Origins of the English Civil War." *Journal of Modern History* 50 (1978): 51–71.

Holbrook, Richard. "Baron d'Oppède and Cardinal Mazarin: The Politics of Provence from 1640 to 1661." Ph.D. diss., University of Illinois at Chicago Circle, 1976.

Holt, Mack. "Patterns of *Clientèle* and Economic Opportunity at Court during the Wars of Religion: The Household of François, Duke of Anjou." *French Historical Studies* 13 (1984): 305–22.

Huppert, George. *Les Bourgeois Gentilshommes: An Essay on the Definition of Elites in Renaissance France*. Chicago, 1977.

Hurstfield, Joel. *Freedom, Corruption and Government in Elizabethan England.* Cambridge, Mass., 1973.

Infreville, Jacques d'. *Le Chevalier d'Infreville et les marquis de la mer*. Grenoble, 1973.

Jal, Auguste. *Abraham Du Quesne et la marine de son temps*. 2 vols. Paris, 1873.

James, Mervyn. *Family, Lineage, and Civil Society: A Study of Society, Politics, and Mentality in the Durham Region, 1500–1640*. Oxford, 1974.

———. *English Politics and the Concept of Honour, 1485–1642*. Supplement No. 3 *Past and Present*. Oxford, 1978.

Jullian, Camille. *Histoire de Bordeaux*. Bordeaux, 1895.

Kaufman, Robert. "The Patron-Client Concept and Macro-Politics: Prospects and Problems." *Comparative Studies in Society and History* 16 (1974): 284–308.

Kent, Francis William. *Household and Lineage in Renaissance Florence. The Family Life of the Capponi, Ginori, and Rucellai*. Princeton, 1977.

Keohane, Nannerl. *Philosophy and the State in France: The Renaissance to the Englightenment*. Princeton, 1980.

Kern, Robert, ed. *The Caciques: Oligarchical Politics and the System of Caciquismo in the Luso-Hispanic World*. Albuquerque, 1973.

———. *Liberals, Reformers, and Caciques in Restoration Spain, 1875–1900*. Albuquerque, 1974.

Kettering, Sharon. *Judicial Politics and Urban Revolt: The Parlement of Aix, 1629–1659*. Princeton, 1978.

———. "The King's Lieutenant General in Provence." *Canadian Journal of History* 13 (1978): 361–81.

———. "A Provincial Parlement during the Fronde: The Reform Proposals of the Aix Magistrates." *European Studies Review* 11 (1981): 151–69.

———. "The Causes of the Judicial Frondes." *Canadian Journal of History* 17 (1982), 275–306.

———. "Patronage and Politics during the Fronde," Forthcoming in *French Historical Studies*.

———. "The Historical Development of Political Clientelism," Forthcoming in *Journal of Interdisciplinary History*.

Kierstead, Raymond. *Pomponne de Bellièvre: A Study of the King's Men in the Age of Henri IV*. Evanston, Ill., 1968.

———, ed. *State and Society in Seventeenth-Century France*. New York, 1975.

Kitchens, James. "Judicial *Commissaires* and the Parlement of Paris: The Case of the Chambre de l'Arsenal." *French Historical Studies* 12 (1982): 323–50.

Kleinclausz, Arthur *Histoire de Bourgogne*. Paris, 1924.

Kossmann, Ernst. *La Fronde*. Leiden, 1954.

Labatut, Jean-Pierre. *Les Ducs et pairs de France au XVII*[e] *siècle*. Paris, 1972.

———. "Aspects de la fortune de Bullion." *XVII*[e] *siècle* 60 (1963): 11–40.

La Bruyère, René. *La Marine de Richelieu: Maillé-Brézé, général des galères, grand amiral, 1619–1646*. Paris, 1945.

———. *La Marine de Richelieu: Sourdis, archevêque et amiral (6 novembre 1594–18 juin 1645)*. Paris, 1948.

———. *La Marine de Richelieu: Richelieu (9 sept. 1585–4 dec. 1642)*. Paris, 1958.

Lansky, David. "Paternal Rule and Provincial Revolt in Seventeenth-Century France: The Social Basis of the Fronde in Rouen." Ph.D. diss., University of California, Berkeley, 1982.

La Roncière, Charles de. *Histoire de la marine française*. 6 vols. Paris, 1899–1932.

———. *Valbelle, le Tigre, marine de Louis XIV, 1627–1681*. Paris, 1935.

Laslett, Peter. *The World We Have Lost*, 2d ed. London, 1971.

———. "La Famille et le ménage: Approches historiques." *Annales: ESC* 27 (1972): 847–72.

Laslett, Peter, and Wall, Richard, eds. *Household and Family in Past Time*. Cambridge, 1972.

Lavaquery, abbé E. *Le Cardinal de Boisgelin (1732–1804)*. 2 vols. Paris, 1920.

Lefebvre, Pierre. "Aspects de la 'fidélité' en France au XVIIe siècle: Le Cas des agents des princes de Condé." *Revue historique* 250 (1973): 59–106.

Lemarchand, René, and Legg, Keith. "Political Clientelism and Development: A Preliminary Analysis." *Comparative Politics* 4 (1972): 149–78.

Lewis, Peter. *Later Medieval France: The Polity*. New York, 1968.

———. "Decayed and Non-Feudalism in Later Medieval France." *Bulletin Institute Historical Research* 37 (1964): 157–84.

Livet, Georges. *L'Intendance en Alsace sous Louis XIV, 1648–1715*. Paris and Strasbourg, 1956.

Logié, Paul. *La Fronde en Normandie*. 3 vols. Amiens, 1951.

Loirette, Francis. "Un Intendant de Guyenne avant la Fronde: Jean de Lauson (1641–1648)." *Bulletin philologique et historique du Comité des Travaux historiques et scientifiques* (1957): 433–61.

———. "L'Administration royale en Béarn de l'union à l'intendance, 1620–1682: Essai sur le reattachement à la France d'une province frontière au XVIIe siècle." *XVIIe siècle* 65 (1964): 66–108.

———. "La Sédition bordelaise de 1675, dernière grande révolte urbaine de l'Ancien Régime." *Actes du 102e Congrès national des Sociétés Savantes, Section d'histoire moderne et contemporaine*, t. 11. Paris, 1978.

Lublinskaya, Alexksandra Dmitrievna. *French Absolutism: The Crucial Phase, 1620–1629*, trans. Brian Pearce, Cambridge, 1968.

Lyon, Bryce. *From Fief to Indenture: The Transition from Feudal to Non-Feudal Contract in Western Europe*. Cambridge, Mass., 1957. Reprint New York, 1972.

MacCaffrey, Wallace. "Place and Patronage in Elizabethan Politics." In *Elizabethan Government and Society: Essays Presented to Sir John Neale*, ed. Stanley T. Bindoff, pp. 95–126. London, 1961.

McFarlane, K. B. "Bastard Feudalism." *Bulletin Institute Historical Research* 20 (1943–45): 161–80.

Major, J. Russell. *The Estates General of 1560*. Princeton, 1951.

———. *The Deputies to the Estates General in Renaissance France*. Madison, Wis., 1960.

———. *Representative Institutions in Renaissance France, 1421–1559*. Madison, Wis., 1960.

———. "The Crown and the Aristocracy in Renaissance France." *American Historical Review* 69 (1964): 631–45.

———. "Henry IV and Guyenne: A Study concerning the Origins of Royal Absolutism." *French Historical Studies* 4 (1966): 363–85.

———. "Bellièvre, Sully, and the Assembly of Notables of 1596." *Transactions of the American Philosophical Society*, n. 3. 64 (1974): 3–34.

———. "Noble Income, Inflation, and the Wars of Religion in France." *American Historical Review* 86 (1981): 21–48.

———. *Representative Government in Early Modern France*. New Haven, 1980.

Marchand, Joseph *Un Intendant sous Louis XIV: Etude sur l'administration de Lebret en Provence, 1687–1704*. Paris, 1889.

Marion, Marcel. *Dictionnaire des institutions de la France aux XVIIe et XVIIIe siècles*. Paris, 1923. Reissued 1972.

Masson, Paul. *La Provence au XVIIIe siècle*. 3 vols. Paris, 1936.

———, ed. *Les Bouches-du-Rhône, encyclopédie déparementale*. 17 vols. Paris, 1913–37.

Maza, Sarah. *Servants and Masters in Eighteenth-Century France: The Uses of Loyalty.* Princeton, 1983.

Meyer, Jean. *La Noblesse bretonne au XVIII*[e] *siècle.* 2 vols. Paris, 1966.

———. *Noblesse et pouvoir dans l'Europe de l'ancien regime.* Paris, 1973.

———. "Un Probleme mal posé: La noblesse pauvre. L'exemple breton au XVIIIe siècle." *Revue d'histoire moderne et contemporaine* 18 (1971): 151–88.

Mongrédien, Georges. *Le Bourreau du Cardinal de Richelieu: Isaac de Laffemas.* Paris, 1927.

———. *La Journée des dupes, 10 november 1930.* Paris, 1961.

———. *Colbert.* Paris, 1963.

———. *L'Affaire Fouquet.* Paris, 1973.

Monin, Henri. *Essai sur l'histoire administrative de Languedoc pendant l'intendance de Basville (1685–1719).* Paris, 1884.

Monnier, Francis. *Le Chancelier d'Aguesseau: Sa conduite et ses idées politiques.* Paris, 1863. Reissued Geneva, 1975.

Moreau, Henri. "Les Subdélégués dans la généralité de Bourgogne sous l'intendant Bouchu et ses premiers successeurs." *Annales de Bourgogne* 20 (1948): 165–89.

Morrill, John. *The Revolt of the Provinces: Conservatives and Radicals during the English Civil War, 1630–1650.* London, 1976.

———. *Seventeenth-Century Britain, 1603–1714.* Folkestone, 1981.

———. "French Absolutism as Limited Monarchy." *Historical Journal* 21 (1978): 961–72.

Mougel, François. "La Fortune des princes de Bourbon-Conti, revenus et gestion (1655–1791)." *Revue d'histoire moderne et contemporaine* 18 (1971): 30–49.

Roland Mousnier. *La Vénalité des offices sous Henri IV et Louis XIII.* Rouen, 1945. Reissued Paris, 1971.

———. *L'Assassinat d'Henri IV: 4 mai 1610.* Paris, 1964.

———. *Les XVI*[e] *et XVII*[e] *siècles.* Vol. 4 in *Histoire générale des civilisations*, 4th ed. Paris, 1965.

———. *Le Conseil du roi de Louis XII à la Révolution.* Paris, 1970.

———. *Pesant Uprisings in Seventeenth-Century France, Russia, and China*, trans. Brian Pearce. New York, 1970.

———. *La Plume, la faucille et le marteau: Institutions et société en France du moyen age à la Révolution.* Paris, 1970.

———. *Social Hierarchies: 1450 to the Present*, trans. Peter Evans. New York, 1973.

———. *Les Institutions de la France sous la monarchie absolue.* Vol. 1, *Société et état.* Paris, 1974. Vol. 2, *Les Organes de l'état et de la société.* Paris, 1980.

———. *La Stratification sociale à Paris aux XVII*[e] *et XVIII*[e] *siècles: L'échantillon de 1634, 1635, 1636.* Paris, 1976.

———. *Paris, capitale au temps de Richelieu et de Mazarin.* Paris, 1978.

———. "The Fronde." In *Preconditions of Revolution in Early Modern Europe*, ed. Robert Forster and Jack Greene. Baltimore, 1970, pp. 131–59.

———. "Recherches sur les soulèvements populaires en France avant la Fronde." *Revue d'histoire moderne et contemporaine* 5 (1958): 81–113.

———. "Notes sur les rapports entre les gouverneurs de provinces et les intendants dans la première moitié du XVIIe siècle." *Revue historique* 227 (1962): 339–50.

———. "L'Evolution des institutions monarchiques en France et ses relations avec l'état social." *XVII*[e] *siècle* 58–59 (1963): 57–72.

———. "Le Concept de classe sociale et l'histoire." *Revue d'histoire économique et sociale* 48 (1970): 449–59.

———. "D'Aguesseau et le tournant des ordres aux classes sociales." *Revue d'histoire économique et sociale* 49 (1971): 449–64.

———. "Les Concepts de'ordres,' d' 'états,' de 'fidélité' et de 'monarchie absolue' en France de la fin du XVe siècle à la fin du XVIIIe." *Revue historique* 502 (1972): 289–312.

———. "Les Fidélités et les clientèles en France aux XVIe, XVIIe, et XVIIIe, siècles." *Histoire sociale* 15 (1982): 35–46.

Mousnier, Roland; Labatut, Jean-Pierre; and Durand, Yves. *Problèmes de stratification sociale. Deux cahiers de la noblesse pour les Etats Généraux de 1649–1651.* Paris, 1965.

Namier, Lewis. *The Structure of Politics at the Accession of George III*. 2d ed. London, 1957.

Neale, John. *The Elizabethan House of Commons*. London, 1949.

———. "The Elizabethan Political Scene." *Essays in Elizabethan History*, pp. 59–84. New York, 1958.

Neuschel, Kristen. "The Prince of Condé and the Nobility of Picardy: A Study of the Structure of Noble Relationships in Sixteenth-Century France." Ph.D. diss., Brown University, 1982.

Nouillac, Joseph. *Villeroy: Secrétaire d'Etat et ministre de Charles IX, Henri III, et Henri IV (1543–1610)*. Paris, 1909.

Oddo, Henri. *Le Chevalier Paul: Lieutenant général des armeés du Levant, 1598–1668*. Paris, 1896.

O'Gilvy, Henri. *Nobiliaire de Guienne et Gascogne*. 4 vols. Paris, 1856–60. Reissued 1973.

Orléans, H. de, duc d'Aumale. *Histoire des princes de Condé pendant les XVIe et XVIIe siècles*. 8 vols. Paris, 1863–96.

Pagès, Georges. *La monarchie d'Ancien Régime en France de Henri IV à Louis XIII*. Paris, 1928.

———. *Les Institutions monarchiques sous Louis XIII et Louis XIV*. Paris, 1933. Reissued 1962.

———. *Les Origines du XVIIIe siècle au temps de Louis XIV (1680–1715)*. Paris, 1961.

———. "Autour du 'grand orage': Richelieu et Marillac, deux politiques." *Revue historique* 169 (1932): 477–95.

Paine, Robert, ed. *Patrons and Brokers in the East Arctic*. Newfoundland Social and Economic Papers No. 2, Institute of social and Economic Research, Memorial University of Newfoundland, 1961.

Palm, Charles Franklin. *Politics and Religion in Sixteenth-Century France: A Study of the Career of Henry of Montmorency-Damville, Uncrowned King of the South*. Boston, 1927.

Parker, David. *La Rochelle and the French Monarchy: Conflict and Order in Seventeenth-Century France*. London, 1980.

———. "The Social Foundation of French Absolutism, 1610–1630." *Past and Present* 53 (1971): 67–89.

Pearl, John. "Guise and Provence: Political Conflicts in the Epoch of Richelieu." Ph.D. diss., Northwestern University, 1968.

Peck, Linda Levy. "Court Patronage and Government Policy: The Jacobean Dilemma." In *Patronage in the Renaissance*, ed. Guy Lytle and Stephen Orgel, pp. 27–46. Princeton, 1981.

Perroy, Edouard. "Feudalism or Principalities in Fifteenth-Century France." *Bulletin Institute Historical Research* 20 (1943–45): 181–86.

———. "Social Mobility among the French noblesse in the Later Middle Ages." *Past and Present* 21 (1962): 25–38.

Pillorget, René. *Les Mouvements insurrectionnels de Provence entre 1596 et 1715*. Paris, 1975.

———. "Destin de la ville d'Ancien Régime." In *Histoire de Marseille*, ed. Edouard Baratier, pp. 163–99. Toulouse, 1973.

———. "Les Casaveoux: L'insurrection aixoise de l'automne 1630." *XVIIe siècle* 64 (1964): 3–30.

———. "Vente d'offices et journées des barricade du 20 janvier, 1649, à Aix-en-Provence." *Provence historique* 15 (1965): 25–63.

———. "Luttes de factions et intérêts économiques à Maseille de 1598 à 1618." *Annales: ESC* 27 (1972): 705–30.

Pingaud, Léonce. *Les Saulx-Tavannes*. Paris, 1876.

Plumb, John H. *Sir Robert Walpole*. Vol. 1, *The Making of a Statesman*. Boston, 1956. Vol. 2, *The King's Minister*. Boston, 1961.

———. *The Growth of Political Stability in England*. London, 1967.

Porchnev, Boris. *Les Soulèvements populaires en France de 1623 à 1648*. Paris, 1963.

Prestwich, Menna. *Politic and Profit under the Early Stuarts: The Career of Lionel Cranfield, Earl of Middlesex*. Oxford, 1966.

Rabb, Theodore, and Hirst, Derek. "Revisionism Revised: Early Stuart Parliamentary History." *Past and Present* 92 (1981): 55–99.

Rabb, Theodore, and Rotberg, Robert, eds. *The Family in History: Interdisciplinary Essays.* New York, 1973.

Radouant, René. *Guillaume Du Vair, l'homme et l'orateur jusqu'à la fin des troubles de la Ligue (1556–96).* Paris, 1907.

Rambert, Gaston. *Nicolas Arnoul: Intendant des galères à Marseille, 1664–1674.* Marseille, 1931.

Ranum, Orest. *Richelieu and the Councillors of Louis XIII: A Study of the Secretaries of State and Superintendents of Finance in the Ministry of Richelieu, 1633–1642.* Oxford, 1963.

———. *Paris in the Age of Absolutism.* New York, 1968.

———. *Artisans of Glory: Writers and Historical Thought in Seventeenth-Century France.* Chapel Hill. N.C., 1980.

———. "Richelieu and the Great Nobility: Some Aspects of Early Modern Political Motives." *French Historical Studies* 3 (1963): 184–204.

———. "Courtesy, Absolutism, and the Rise of the French State." *Journal of Modern History* 52 (1980); 426–51.

Ricommard, Julian. "Les Subdélégués des intendants jusqu'à leur érection en titre d'office." *Revue d'histoire moderne* 12 (1937): 338–407.

———. "Les Subdélégués des intendants aux XVIIe et XVIIIe siècles." *L'information historique* 24 (1962–63): 139–48.

———. "Les Subdélégués en titre d'office en Provence, 1704–1715." *Provence historique* 14 (1964): 243–71, 336–78.

Richard, Jean, ed. *Histoire de la Bourgogne.* Toulouse, 1978.

Richet, Denis. *La France moderne: L'Esprit des institutions.* Paris, 1973.

———. "La Formation des grands serviteurs de l'état (fin XVIe–debut XVIIe siècle)." *L'arc* 65 (1976): 54–61.

———. "Aspects socio-culturels des conflits religieux à Paris dans la seconde moitié du XVIIe siècle." *Annales: ESC* 32 (1977): 764–89.

Roche, Daniel. "Aperçus sur la fortune et les revenus des princes de Condé à l'aube du XVIIIe siècle." *Revue d'histoire moderne et contemporaine* 14 (1967): 216–43.

Romier, Lucien. *La Carrière d'un favori. Jacqus d'Albon de Saint André.* Paris, 1909.

———. *Le Royaume de Catherine de Médicis: La France à la veille des gueres de religion.* 2 vols. Paris, 1922.

Rosenberg, Charles, ed. *The Family in History.* Philadelphia, 1975.

Rothrock, George. "Officials and King's Men: A Note on the Possibility of Royal Control of the Estates General." *French Historical Studies* 2 (1962): 504–10.

Roupnel, Gaston. *La Ville et la campagne au XVIIe siècle: Etude sur les populations du pays dijonnais.* Paris, 1922. Reissued 1955.

Rowen, Herbert. *The Ambassador Prepares for War: The Dutch Embassy of Arnauld de Pomponne, 1669–1671.* The Hague, 1957.

Rule, John, ed. *Louis XIV and the Craft of Kingship.* Columbus, Ohio, 1969.

———. "Colbert de Torcy, and Emergent Bureaucracy, and the Formation of French Foreign Policy, 1698–1715." In *Louis XIV and Europe*, ed. Ragnhild Hatton, pp. 261–88. Columbus, Ohio, 1976.

Russell, Conrad. *Parliaments and English Politics, 1621–1629.* Oxford, 1979.

———. "Parliamentary History in Perspective, 1604–1629." *History* 61 (1976): 1–27.

———, ed. *The Origins of the English Civil War.* London, 1973.

Sabatier, Ernet. *Histoire de la ville et des évêques de Béziers.* Paris and Béziers, 1854. Reissued Marseille, 1977.

Salmon, John H. M. *Society in Crisis: France in the Sixteenth Century.* London, 1975.

———. "Rohan and Interest of State." In *Studien sur Geschichte einer politischen Begriffs*, ed. Roman Schnur, pp. 132–42. Berlin, 1975.

———. "Venal Office and Popular Sedition in Seventeenth-Century France." *Past and Present* 37 (1967): 21–43.

———. "The Paris Sixteen, 1584–1594: The Social Analysis of a Revolutionary Movement." *Journal of Modern History* 44 (1972): 540–76.

———. "Peasant Revolt in Vivarais, 1575–1580." *French Historical Studies* 11 (1979): 1–28.

———. "Storm over the Noblesse." *Journal of Modern History* 53 (1981): 242–57.

Schmidt, Steffen. "Bureaucrats as Modernizing Brokers." *Comparative Politics* 6 (1974): 425–50.

Schmidt, Steffen, et al., eds., *Friends, Followers, and Factions: A Reader in Political Clientelism.* Berkeley, 1977.

Schmidt, Steffen. "Patrons, Brokers, and Clients: Party Linkages in the Colombian System." In *Political Parties and Linkage: A Comparative Perspective*, ed. Kay Lawson, pp. 266–88. New Haven, 1980.

Scott, James. *Comparative Political Corruption*. Englewood Cliffs, N.J., 1972.

———. "Corruption, Machine Politics, and Political Change." *American Political Science Review* 62 (1969): 1,142–58.

Sharpe, Kevin, ed. *Factions and Parliament: Essays on Early Stuart History*. Oxford, 1979.

Stone, Lawrence. *The Crisis of the Aristocracy, 1559–1641*. Oxford, 1965.

———. *The Family, Sex and Marriage in England, 1500–1800*. New York, 1977.

———. "The Rise of the Nuclear Family in Early Modern England: The Patriarchal Stage." In *The Family in History*, ed. Charles Rosenberg, pp. 13–57. Philadelphia, 1974.

———. "Interpersonal Violence in English Society, 1300–1980." *Past and Present* 101 (1983): 22–33.

Strickon, Arnold, and Greenfield, Sidney. *Structure and Process in Latin America: Patronage, Clientage, and Power Systems*. Albuquerque, 1972.

Sturgill, Claude. *Claude Le Blanc: Civil Servant of the King*. Gainesville, Fla., 1975.

Sutherland, Nicola M. *Catherine de Medici and the Ancien Régime*. London, 1966.

———. *The French Secretaries of State in the Age of Catherine de Medici*. London, 1967.

Tarrow, Sidney, ed. *Territorial Politics in Industrial Nations*. New York, 1978.

Tarrow, Sidney. *Between Center and Periphery: Grassroots Politicians in Italy and France*. New Haven, 1977.

Tarrow, Sidney, and Lange, Peter, eds., *Italy in Transition*. London, 1980.

———. *Partisanship and Political Exchange in French and Italian Local Politics: A Contribution to the Typology of Party Systems*. London, 1974.

Teal, Elizabeth Salmon. "The Renaissance Seigneur: Advocate or Oppressor?" *Journal of Modern History* 37 (1965): 131–50.

Temple, Nora. "The Control and Exploitation of French Towns during the Ancien Régime." *History* 51 (1966): 16–34.

Thomas, Alexandre. *Une Province sous Louis XIV: Situation politique et administrative de la Bourgogne, 1661–1715*. Dijon. 1844.

Tilly, Charles, ed. *The Formation of National States in Western Europe*. Princeton, 1975.

Tolchin, Martin and Susan. *To the Victor: Political Patronage from the Club House to the White House*. New York, 1971.

Vaissière, Pierre de. *Gentilshommes campagnards de l'ancienne France*. Paris, 1903.

Van Doren, L. Scott. "Revolt and Reaction in the City of Romans, Dauphiné, 1579–1580." *The Sixteenth Century Journal* 5 (1974): 71–99.

Walcott, Robert. *English Politics in the Early Eighteenth Century*. Cambridge, Mass. 1956.

Weary, William. "Royal Policy and Patronage in Renaissance France: The Monarchy and the House of La Trémoille." Ph.D. diss., Yale University, 1972.

Weber, Max. *The Theory of Social and Economic Organization*, ed. Talcott Parsons, trans. A. M. Henderson and Talcott Parsons. New York, 1956.

———. *Economy and Society: An Outline of Interpretative Sociology*, ed. Guenter Roth and Claus Wittich, trans. Ephraim Fischoff, 3 vols. New York, 1968.

Weingrod, Alex. "Patrons, Patronage, and Political Parties." *Comparative Studies in Society and History* 10 (1969): 377–85.

Westrich, Sal. *The Ormée of Bordeaux: A Revolution during the Fronde*. Baltimore, 1972.

Wilkinson, Maurice. *The Last Phase of the League in Provence, 1588–1598*. London, 1909.

Wolff, Philippe, ed. *Histoire de Languedoc*. Toulouse, 1967.

Wood, James. *The Nobility of the Election of Bayeux, 1463–1666. Continuity through Change*. Princeton, 1980.

———. "The Decline of the Nobility in Sixteenth and Early Seventeenth Century France: Myth or Reality? *Journal of Modern History* 48 (1976): on demand.

———. "Demographic Pressure and Social Mobility among the Nobility of Early Modern France." *Sixteenth Century Journal* 8 (1977): 3–16.

———. "Endogamy and *Mésalliance*, the Marriage Patterns of the Nobility of the *Élection* of Bayeux, 1430–1669." *French Historical Studies* 10 (1978): 375–92.

Zarb, Mireille. *Les Privileges de la ville de Marseille du Xᵉ siècle à la Révolution*. Paris, 1961.

Zeller, Gaston. *Les Institutions de la France au XVIᵉ siècle*. Paris, 1948.

———. *Aspects de la politique française sous l'Ancien Régime*. Paris, 1964.

———. "L'Administration monarchique avant les intendants, parlements et gouverneurs." *Revue historique* 197 (1947): 180–215.

Zuckerman, Alan. *The Politics of Faction: Christian Democratic Rule in Italy*. New Haven, 1979.

Index